The Great Ideas

Martha Graham (1894–1991) in *American Document*.

The
Great Ideas
Today

1991

Encyclopædia Britannica, Inc.

CHICAGO
AUCKLAND • GENEVA • LONDON • MADRID • MANILA • PARIS
ROME • SEOUL • SYDNEY • TOKYO • TORONTO

Figure 7 in "The New Pythagoreans III" is reproduced from
"The Vestibular System and the General Motor System," by H. H. Kornhuber,
in *Handbook of Sensory Physiology,* edited by H. H. Kornhuber, p. 601.
Copyright © 1974 by Springer-Verlag, Berlin.
Reprinted with permission of Springer-Verlag.

Library of Congress Number: 61-65561
International Standard Book Number: 0-85229-550-2
International Standard Serial Number: 0072-7288

A NOTE ON REFERENCE STYLE

In the following pages, passages in *Great Books of the Western World* are referred to by the initials *"GBWW,"* followed by a roman numeral (indicating the first edition of 1952 [I] or the second edition of 1990 [II]) with volume and page number. Thus, *"GBWW* I: 5, 100; II: 4, 112" refers to a passage from Sophocles' *Oedipus the King,* which is on page 100 in Volume 5 of the first edition, and on page 112 in Volume 4 of the second edition. Sometimes only one reference will be given, since the contents of the first and second editions differ. Also note that passages quoted in an article may differ from the translation of that passage in either the first or second edition, since newer translations of some works are included in the second edition.

Gateway to the Great Books is referred to by the initials *"GGB,"* followed by volume and page number. Thus, *"GGB* 10, 39–57" refers to pages 39 through 57 of Volume 10 of *Gateway to the Great Books,* which is James's essay, "The Will to Believe."

The Great Ideas Today is referred to by the initials *"GIT,"* followed by the year and page number. Thus, *"GIT* 1968, 210" refers to page 210 of the 1968 edition of *The Great Ideas Today.*

Contents

Preface

As readers of this annual know, Encyclopædia Britannica's *Great Books of the Western World* was first published in 1952. It contained fifty-one volumes of writings from Homer to Freud and two volumes of index called *The Syntopicon*. Most readers of *The Great Ideas Today* are owners of that set, the contents of which, properly indexed, remain as important and as relevant as they were at that time.

That original set has, however, been superseded, as of the end of 1990, by a new, second edition of *Great Books of the Western World*—a set containing sixty volumes including a revised *Syntopicon* which also indexes the authors who have been added, some from former times and some from the twentieth century. Of the older authors, a number appear in new and better translations than those that were available in 1952 or than those for which permission was available at that time. The authors newly translated are Homer, the Greek tragedians and Aristophanes, Lucretius, Virgil, Saint Augustine (*The Confessions*), Dante, Chaucer, Montaigne, Cervantes, and Goethe. It will be noted that they are for the most part poets, and it will be realized that translations of poetry tend to be good only for the time in which they are written. It may be pointed out as well that the last half of the century is one in which advances in translation have been achieved that appear to be absolute, and that of those translations which are included in the new set, some at least are likely to prove permanent, or at least to be satisfactory for a long time.

Let it be emphasized that the new *Great Books of the Western World* is, with the difference just noted, very largely the old one reissued, because most of the works originally chosen still seem the right ones to include. Four authors have for various reasons been dropped, however—Apollonius, Sterne, Fielding, and Fourier—and no fewer than fifteen have been added to the list of writings from before, or just after, 1900. In addition, forty-four new authors from the first half of the twentieth century appear in the added volumes (55–60), some of them represented by relatively brief works. The principles of selection are explained in a companion volume to the new set called *The Great Conversation*, which is not strictly part of it, as was the case with the original set, but which reprints much of the essay by Robert M. Hutchins that constituted the first volume of that set.

As a result of this change, all the volumes in the new set have different numbers from those they bore in the old one—and as a consequence of that, references to both sets will be found in this volume of *The Great Ideas Today,* as well as in all subsequent ones. The translations will not always match, but readers who want to look things up can find their way. Of course, some citations will be to authors who appear only in the new set.

As for the contents of this year's *The Great Ideas Today,* there is room for at least a brief review. In Part One, devoted to "Current Developments in the Arts and Sciences," will be found an essay by Professor Michael Edidin, of Johns Hopkins University, on the interesting and important subject of immunology—a discussion the editors have long wanted to have and now are able to provide. The workings of the immune system in humans, certainly, is a very complicated affair, but Professor Edidin manages to indicate what the basic processes are in language that a layman can follow.

This is followed by another new subject for our annual, contemporary dance, of which this year we publish an almost encyclopedic account by Sally Banes of Cornell University. Our age has been a great one for this art, as those who follow it are aware—great in classic ballet as well as in the modern works of Merce Cunningham and Martha Graham, to name no others—and Professor Banes furnishes a survey that will interest even those who know nothing of the matter, while those who are already informed will value its generosity and justice.

Part Two of the volume is devoted, as usual, to "Reconsiderations of Great Books and Ideas." Here will be found yet another essay by Thomas K. Simpson, the last in his series devoted to the idea of science but not the last on other subjects that we hope to get from him, who is so able to connect the Great Books and contemporary scientific matters and is, as such, a valuable resource. This article by him concludes the discussion of consciousness which he began last year. At the end of it he arrives at a striking vision of the right place for science in our time and in our human lives.

Otto Bird reappears also with an account of the liberal arts—an ancient and later a medieval concept nowadays known only for its mostly meaningless application to undergraduate education—which he recalls and then convincingly translates into modern terms. Anyone who wonders what the liberal arts really are, and what has happened to them, and whether they correspond to anything we have in contemporary life, will find this article instructive.

And in this same section is a brief essay by Mortimer J. Adler, our editor, on basic education at the present time—in particular, the topic of multiculturalism, which he considers in both its proper, and what he regards as its improper, application to the question of what children should be learning in school these days.

Part Three, "Special Features," offers an account of mostly academic theology as we have it nowadays in the United States, by Professor William J. Abraham of Southern Methodist University. The theology with which Professor Abraham is concerned is Christian only, and his remarks on at least the Protestant part of the subject reach to an area we have not previously tried to cover in *The Great Ideas Today*.

In Part Three we also publish the first of two articles by Bruce Venable, a tutor at St. John's College, Santa Fe, New Mexico, on music as a liberal art—how it was one, and whether it is one still. Mr. Venable is learned in early church music as in many other areas of the subject, which he is able to contrast with the secular music we are more likely to recognize these days, and which he does not think inferior.

As for "Additions to the Great Books Library" (Part Four), we provide in the first place a selection of documents relating to the American Bill of Rights, of which this year marks the bicentennial. The selection has been put together by our frequent contributor George Anastaplo, a noted authority on constitutional questions, indeed the author of a recent commentary on the Constitution of the United States. The documents, beginning with Magna Carta, clearly show the provenance of the salient phases in the Bill of Rights, none of which had to be invented, though all were carefully considered in some of the first business the federal government embarked on after it was authorized. Professor Anastaplo has kindly provided the introduction, in which the various documents are discussed.

Still another discussion of the liberal arts follows—this time a reprint from William Whewell's account of them, and of their proper place in education, which was written first in 1845. Whewell was the head of Trinity College, Cambridge, at the time, and an influential figure in the topics to which he applied himself there. His distinction between what he calls the permanent and the progressive studies is often recalled.

Finally, we offer one of Anton Chekhov's best short stories, called "Ward Number Six," in which a doctor in charge of an insane asylum in turn-of-the-century Russia appears as both a master and a victim of the system of treatment prevailing there, as do certain of the inmates and the friends and associates of the doctor. It is a painful story—as so many of Chekhov's writings are—that no one ever forgets.

PART ONE

Current Developments in the Arts and Sciences

The Biology of Immune Responses

Michael Edidin

Michael Edidin was educated at the University of Chicago and earned a
doctorate in zoology with Sir Peter Medawar at University College, London
(1963). He was subsequently a postdoctoral fellow at the Weizmann
Institute, Israel, and a research fellow in the department of bacteriology
and immunology at the Harvard Medical School. In 1966 he went to teach
at Johns Hopkins University in Baltimore, where since 1975 he has been
professor of biology. In addition, he is adjunct professor of biophysics in the
School of the Arts and Sciences and adjunct professor also of immunology
in the department of molecular biology and genetics at the Hopkins
Medical School.

Professor Edidin has written over 120 papers on the subject of immunology and cell biology and was editor with M. H. Johnson of *Immunobiology
of Gametes,* published by the Cambridge University Press (1977).

Introduction

Immune responses against microbes are crucial for our survival. In the past three decades we have come to understand a good deal about the logic of immune responses and about the cellular and molecular basis of this logic. The results of experimental immunology have not yielded a full and consistent theory, but they do allow informed intervention and modification of human immune responses. Our need for a practical immunology has grown enormously. There is a need to reduce or suppress immune responses in allergy treatment and during transplantation. There is a very great and pressing need to prevent the loss of immune responsiveness caused by infection with human immunodeficiency viruses (HIVs).

I will devote most of this essay to a discussion of immune mechanisms developed in response to fundamental evolutionary problems, and the ways in which these problems were solved on both the cellular and the molecular level. The latter part of the essay will summarize the current approaches to, and the state of, certain problems in applied immunology.

The fortress of Acre ('Akko) rises out of the Mediterranean Sea on the coast of Israel. It is an elaborate and beautiful structure; its great stone seawalls are topped with towers, and its courts connect by arched tunnels. The fortress is a history of the region. Its oldest parts, now half-hidden by sea or earth, were built by the Crusaders, and it was elaborated, extended, and modernized by the Turks. Its structure and complexity remind the immunologist of another great complex that protects against invasion—the complex of organs, cells, and molecules that functions as our immune system. The oldest parts of the complex are sometimes hard to see, but they still support the rest of the elaborate structure, which would not work without them.

Besides supplying a metaphor, the fortress of Acre provokes the immunologist to think about medieval history and the flow of trade between Europe and the East. Spice was an important part of this trade because it could hide the flavor of spoiled meat. Dead flesh is invaded by all sorts of parasites. It becomes a home for the many microorganisms that abound in air, water, and soil. Live flesh is not usually invaded, but not for want of trying. Any living creature is a valuable source of food and shelter for other creatures, and so is constantly assaulted by

3

them. Immunity to these assaults is an important part of the physiology of any organism.

The problems of immunology

Immune responses are elaborations of solutions to three connected and ancient problems: the problem of defining "self," the problem of distinguishing "self" from "foreign," and the problem of preserving "self" by preventing "foreign" from settling down and taking over.

Two sets of solutions to these problems have evolved. The older, so-called *innate immunity,* is like the rough stone courses of the Crusader walls—it is basic and fundamental, but it is not complete or subtle and does not anticipate changes well. Innate immune responses alone are not enough to protect the body, even though we need them. A second solution, *adaptive immunity,* is thus added to the first. It is very different from innate immunity in origin and in its modes of recognition of "foreign." Adaptive immunity is efficient, flexible, and subtle; yet, it protects only if it can connect with the older, innate immune response. The younger, adaptive immune response is very good at recognizing "foreign," but the older is the one that actually stops and destroys the invaders.

We first meet the problem of distinguishing "self" and dealing with "foreign" in protozoa, which are single-celled animals that feed on particles of organic matter and on cells smaller than themselves. The abundance of protozoa suggests that the advantages of a life spent capturing debris and smaller prey outweigh the dangers. Though the greatest of these dangers is that of being eaten by something larger, there is also a real chance that a given single cell will be invaded by a smaller cell instead of capturing it. The integrity of the cell is violated and "self" subverted, as it becomes shelter and food source for its invader.

"Self" has two senses when applied to a single-cell organism, for example the amoeba, which usually reproduces asexually by dividing. One sense of "self" is genetic. A colony of amoebae that has arisen as a clone—with all its cells descended through cell division from a single ancestor—is a single "self," since all members of the clone are genetically identical. They have all descended from their ancestor without any changes in the genetic material, such changes generally being wrought through sexual reproduction. Death of one or more of the cells in the clone does not mean an end to a particular set of genes. "Self" in this sense still requires that each cell have some protection against invasion by "foreign," since without such protection the entire colony is likely to be destroyed once one of its members is invaded by another organism. For example, a bacterium can invade one member, then reproduce itself and go on to invade other members of the clone.

A second sense of "self" might be termed geometric or physical. This is the sense in which the single amoeba functions. "Self" begins at its surface, and anything outside of that surface is "foreign." For the amoeba in the first instance, "foreign" is food; so, food-processing and destruction of harmful foreign molecules and cells are the same. The ways in which amoebae seek, capture, and digest "foreign" are not unique to them and their kin. They are also used by amoeba-like cells that destroy invading bacteria and damaged cells in multicellular animals.

An amoeba wandering along a surface may meet "foreign" by chance, blundering into a bacterium or a food particle that is directly in its path, or by following a trail of chemicals that has spread out in the water surrounding such particles like an oil slick. However the amoeba manages to meet the foreign particle, the particle can stick to its surface because the amoeba is covered by branched molecules that form a sort of Velcro, entangling whatever it touches. The particle and the piece of the amoeba's surface to which it is stuck are then pulled into a disassembly line that breaks down large foreign bodies, molecules, and even whole cells, into their component small molecules.

This disassembly line is formed by a series of closed sacs made of the same fatty material as the cell surface. The fatty membranes surrounding each sac keep its contents from leaking into the cell at large and also ensure a thorough digestion of the sac's contents. A foreign particle gets into one of these sacs when the bit of the surface to which it is stuck pinches off and seals up. The process of trapping a particle and delivering it to the interior is called *phagocytosis* and is central to immunity in all animals.

Once inside a cell, the sac is passed along a series of stations. At each station, acid and enzymes which can break chemical bonds are pumped into the sac, making it progressively more hostile to its contents. The trapped foreign material gradually vanishes like the Cheshire Cat. Structure, proteins, and genetic information (DNA) vanish. They are turned into a solution of small molecules that supports growth of the cell.

At the end of the digestion the foreign material has been broken down into its component parts. Its functional proteins have been broken down into amino acids, its genetic material into sugars and phosphates. These component parts may be burned by the amoeba as fuel, or they may be assembled into the amoeba's own proteins. The molecules of the foreign material have been destroyed and have no chance of subverting or damaging the host cell.

If harmful invaders of the amoeba reproduced as slowly as the amoeba itself, the disassembly line and the amoeba's surface coat would be very good protection indeed. In this case, even if a population of harmful foreign organisms could evolve in ways that aided them in getting around the disassembly line, the invaders' tricks could be coun-

5

tered by evolutionary changes in the amoeba population so they could resist the new forms of invaders, since evolution is limited by the rate of reproduction. But the most dangerous invaders of a single cell like an amoeba are bacteria and viruses. Both these life-forms reproduce much faster than amoebae. This means that they can evolve variants that subvert or avoid the disassembly line in a much shorter time than the amoebae can evolve to counter them.

It is an important general rule that threats due to the diversity and heterogeneity of invading organisms are countered and anticipated by diversity and heterogeneity in the immune response. This is even true for the very basic innate immunity at work in protozoa. The disassembly line for destroying foreign materials is manned by many different families of enzyme molecules, each capable of breaking a different kind of chemical bond. These enzymes are helped in their work by the acid in the sacs, which distorts and disrupts almost every kind of large molecule that is important for life. Many changes would have to occur and accumulate before a bacterium or a virus could avoid destruction by the enzymes and acids of the disassembly line, and the chances of this happening are small.

There are some ways in which a few mutations in a bacterium help it to evade destruction. Some mutations are trivial. One such mutation results in the loss of surface molecules, which then keeps the bacterium from sticking to the amoeba surface and protects it from digestion. But this loss also prevents the bacterium from invading the amoeba and benefiting from the larger cell's stores of food material. A second kind of mutation produces a toxin that kills the amoeba. The mutant bacterium can feed on the wreckage but cannot shelter there.

A third change, more complicated than the other two, results in the secretion of a thick, waxy, acid-resistant coat that blocks its digestion. The bacillus causing tuberculosis is an example of a wax-covered bacterium that enters the cell's digestive sacs and resists the attack by acid and enzymes. The bacillus takes up residence in the sacs, feeds on their contents, and reproduces there. The invaded cell is not killed at once but lingers on, providing food and shelter to the invader.

Unlike a bacterium that has to keep its proteins about it, a virus only needs its proteins to protect its genetic instruction set, DNA or RNA, until it is delivered to a cell. A virus avoids destruction of its genetic material if it manages to stick to the outside of a cell and inject its nucleic acid directly into the cell cytoplasm, instead of being carried into the cytoplasm in a membrane sac. This threat is countered in part by the properties of the surface of the attacked cell. The surface coat of sticky material used to pick up particles from the surroundings is much thicker than a virus. The fatty membrane surface must be penetrated if a viral attack is to succeed, and it remains out of the reach of a virus stuck in the surface coat.

Sensors and specificity

My description of feeding and immunity in an amoeba was explicit about the importance of the categories "self" and "foreign," but it did not divide these categories further. A response that treats all particles and cells outside the responder as "foreign," rather than distinguishing between different forms of "foreign," has very little specificity. In fact the amoeba can tell different kinds of "foreign" apart. It can sense the kind of chemicals leaking from a bacterium or another cell and move toward or away from the source of these chemicals, depending upon what it senses. It can also feel the extent to which a foreign particle sticks to its surface and can respond to this by phagocytosis and the formation of digestive sacs. Its responses to the outside world make finer distinctions than those subsumed under "self" and "foreign." Senses and responses are specific for different parts of the outside world.

All of the elaboration of the immune systems in multicellular animals, and even the formation of multicellular animals, is ultimately an elaboration of specificity. Single cells gain the ability to make fine distinctions between molecules in their environment, especially between molecules on neighboring cells. These distinctions are made through changes in the shape and stickiness of cell surface proteins. Before continuing with the description of immune responses, I want to describe briefly the molecular basis for, and the meaning of, "specificity," the way in which protein molecules are constructed, and the way in which their structures can distinguish features on other molecules.

All proteins are constructed from mixtures of some twenty different amino acids. Part of each amino acid can form a chemical, covalent bond with any other amino acid, and these yield a long chain of amino acids. This chain folds on itself to form sheets or helices, and these in turn can fold into rods or spheres.

The folding of a protein and the shape that it takes once it is folded depend upon the forces between groups of atoms in the different amino acids. Some of these atoms attract like atoms in other parts of the chain or in the water surrounding it. Other atoms, for example those that bear electric charges, attract their opposites. Still other atoms repel one another. The force between any two groups of atoms is much weaker than the force that holds together the chemical bond, but collectively the forces between all of the interacting atoms can flex the chemical bonds of the protein backbone and shape the once linear protein into a complicated folded structure.

Because the forces between the atoms are weak, a folded protein constantly flexes, changing its shape slightly, "breathing." Limits to this flexing are set by the flexibility of the backbone and by chemical bonds between rare, sulfur-containing amino acids that are positioned along the backbone in such a way that they face one another when the protein

7

is folded. Even though they are stabilized by the extra chemical bonds between sulfur atoms, the structures of most proteins can be distorted or even broken up by external forces.

We see one example of the way in which external forces distort protein structure when we cook one of the great egg-based sauces, béarnaise or hollandaise. These are prepared by disrupting the shape of egg proteins with gentle heat. The misshapen proteins stick to one another, thickening the sauce. More subtle changes of shape than those caused by heat often occur when one protein binds to another. Such subtle changes are important in immune recognition and in the action of some molecules of immunity.

Protein specificity

The sheets and globes of a folded protein are not smooth. They are broken by peaks and cavities and crossed by ridges. A properly folded protein molecule binds to another molecule in a manner, and to an extent, that depends upon the precise arrangement of the peaks, valleys, and ridges, and on the parts of the amino acids that cover or line each one. For example, a peak on the surface of a protein that contains many positively charged atoms will repel another molecule with a ridge of the same charge but will attract and bind a molecule with a valley full of negatively charged atoms.

There are many peaks, ridges, and valleys on a single protein, and together they largely fix the ways in which a protein can fit with other molecules. Some combinations of surface features will accommodate the shapes of many other molecules, especially if the protein that bears them is flexible and can change its shape slightly to accommodate the captured molecule. However, such accommodating proteins may not bind molecules very tightly. Other combinations of surface features will only accommodate a very few molecular shapes and ignore or repel all other molecules. This greatly restricts the kinds of molecules that can be bound, but it results in very tight binding of the few shapes that do fit.

The complementary fit of one molecule with another is recognition at the molecular level. The specificity of recognition lies in the details of the molecular fit and in the strength of the bonds between the molecules—the tightness of their fit. Cellular recognition and specificity depend upon molecular recognition but can be extended and refined because one cell carries many different recognition molecules on its surface. A large palette of such recognition molecules was required for the evolution of multicellular animals. Most of these molecules were required for the proper association of cells in tissues—organization of "self"—but others evolved for recognition of "foreign."

Animals made up of many cells could only arise when recognition molecules proliferated. The simplest form of recognition must have come about as a result of the binding of like molecules on neighboring cells. This level of molecular recognition is enough to keep cells adhering to and in contact with one another. The genetic and physical definitions of "self" then converge, since the clone of cells that defines genetic "self" now consists of a single mass of cells stuck to one another. The cells are held together by forces that are stronger than the forces attracting them away from each other and back to the single life.

Life in a mass of cells offers two great advantages over life as a single cell. A multicellular organism because of its large size is less likely to be prey to organisms larger than itself. Multiplication of cells also allows development of specializations; different cells perform different functions. The cells are linked together, and their functions coordinated, by cellular, chemical, or electrical communication systems.

Both increased size and cell specialization complicate the task of the immune system—the defense of the animal against invasion. Larger size means that there are now many smaller organisms that can profit from invading. Cell specialization means that not all cells are good at trapping, phagocytosis, and the destruction of foreign invaders. These are now functions of different groups of cells and evolve independently.

As cells specialize, they segregate from the mass of tissue cells in the body, associating selectively with their own kind—liver with liver, brain with brain, and so forth. This adds new meaning to "self." All the cells in a single animal may be a genetic "self" because they are all descended by division from a single fertilized egg, and they may all be a physical "self" because they are all part of the same mass of cells, the same organism, but they are divided by their appearance and function. The surfaces of cells with different functions display different collections of recognition molecules, so they meet with, and are met by, the outside world in different ways. Each different surface is nevertheless part of "self," and immune mechanisms must be able to read and spare all of the forms of "self" while acting to stop "foreign" from taking over.

Surfaces and barriers

Immunity begins at the surface of a multicellular animal just as it begins at the surface of a single-celled animal. Therefore we will leave issues of specificity for a while and turn to the ways in which surfaces are organized to function as defenses.

Though a single cell presents only one surface to the world, multicellular animals are all constructed as tubes inside tubes and so present two big surfaces to the outside world: the outer surface of the outermost tube and the inner surface of the innermost tube. In humans these are the skin, on the one hand, and the inner surface of the long digestive

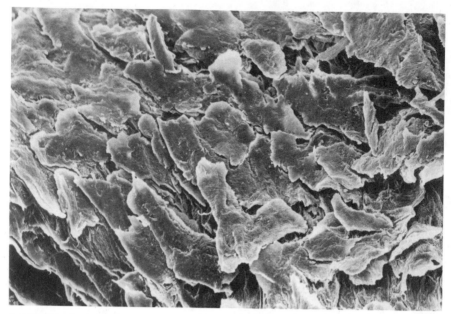

A splinter's-eye view of the surface of human skin, magnified a thousandfold. Large flat cells stuffed with protein are loosely stacked on the skin surface. They form a dead, disposable, outer shield for the body. Beneath these cells are still larger cells, sticking close to one another. This living shield is carefully stitched together to block all but the most violent intrusions.

and respiratory tube that runs from the mouth to the intestines by way of the stomach, on the other.

The strategy of protection is the same for both surfaces, though its execution is slightly different on the outside surface than it is on the inside surface. This strategy has three elements—to keep possible invaders from sticking to the surface, to keep the surface free of cracks and holes that can be penetrated, and to coat the surface with chemicals which prevent anything that does stick from growing.

In the case of the skin, the outermost layer of our defenses, invaders adhere to a layer of dead cells that constantly flakes off the underlying living cells. Any microorganisms that do stick to this layer must penetrate it and reach the living flesh beneath, or be cast off. If the attackers reach the living surface of the skin they find a continuous layer of cells attached to one another by especially strong connections. Bands of molecules girdle each cell and adhere to one another so tightly and so completely that attacking cells, molecules, and even tiny salt ions cannot pass through to the interior. The chances of a successful invasion by microbes that are stuck to the skin are lowered even more by the acidity of the skin surface. This slows the microbes' growth and so reduces the chance that they can proliferate and persist until they find an opening in the skin.

The surface of the digestive and respiratory tubes is more exposed and at hazard of invasion than the skin. Unlike the skin, this surface is wet and dark, and in its function it is constantly taking in masses of viruses, bacteria, and fungi. The digestive part of the tube also meets protozoa and even small multicellular worms. Sticking of the invaders is discouraged by the great quantities of mucus that coat the tube. This material is similar in composition and in effect to the coating on an amoeba's surface. It sticks to newly arrived particles and bundles them up. These bundles are moved through the digestive tube and either digested or excreted. In our respiratory tube, the bundles are swept off the surface by the beating of rodlike structures, called cilia, on some of the cells lining the tube. These sweepings usually end up in the stomach, where enzymes and acid bath destroy them.

Particles that are not trapped and swept away in mucus find a tight surface sealed against them by cellular structures that function like those in the skin. If they can stick, they may meet hostile enzymes and detergents, especially in the long reaches of the intestinal tract. The bacteria that do manage to invade this tract are usually those able to poison its cells, gaining entry to the body when a dying cell dissolves and leaves a gap in the lining of the tube.

The road to the lungs is paved with mucus and swept by powerful brooms. Two kinds of cells are evident in this surface view of the trachea. The cells with smooth domed surfaces, broken only by small bumps, secrete mucus. The mucus itself is not seen here because it has been washed away during preparation of the tissues. Normally the mucus is stirred and moved along by a second kind of cell whose long, slender cilia are apparent in the picture. The cells are magnified about three thousandfold.

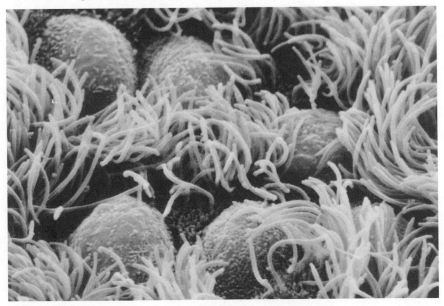

Defenses beneath the surface

B.B. Nature has provided, in the white corpuscles as you call them—in the phagocytes as we call them—a natural means of devouring and destroying all disease germs. There is at bottom only one genuinely scientific treatment for all disease, and that is to stimulate the phagocytes. [1]

Sir Ralph Bloomfield Bonington here exaggerates his medical science, but he is certainly right about the importance of phagocytic cells in defending the body.

Despite all its complexity, the first line of defense is often breached. Anyone who has ever run a splinter into a finger knows this and knows something of the consequences. If the splinter is not removed, the flesh around it becomes red and swollen. After a few days the splinter is forced out, and the flesh quiets and heals. The cells that surround the splinter and the chemical signals they bring to it are parts of the second line of defenses of the innate immune response.

Cells like the ones that surround the splinter are at work and on patrol in all multicellular animals. They specialize in and exaggerate the feeding and sensing traits of an amoeba and use these traits exclusively to detect and destroy intruders.

The exaggeration, or rather the changes, of the amoeba's disassembly line to improve its destructiveness takes several forms. One is an ability to increase greatly the amount and activity of the destructive enzymes in the digestive sacs when certain signals are received from the outside world. The signals usually come in the form of molecules commonly shed by bacteria. They put the phagocytic cell on alert, ready to engulf and digest any bacterium it touches.

Some cells make another change, adding an additional method of destruction—the burning of bacteria by especially active forms of oxygen. These especially active oxygen molecules are produced by the cell after it swallows a foreign organism. Their production is so great that the cell sucks in large amounts of the starting material for the especially destructive form, which is ordinary oxygen, like a runner in the middle of a race. The active oxygen molecules that are formed damage and destroy foreign matter so efficiently that it cannot even be used for food. Cell function here is purely destructive.

The third extension of the mixed digestive and protective functions of a single cell is the creation of a new form of packaging for digestive enzymes and defensive chemicals. Very large numbers of these molecules are packaged together in a granule, packed so tight that there is no room to receive anything to digest. Packages of enzymes can be dumped into a digestive sac or may be dumped outside the cell to attack a bacterium or other invader. The packages also contain molecules that bind vitamins and metals required for cell growth.

Other granules contain detergent-like proteins. These proteins can disrupt all kinds of cells by disturbing their cell membranes. The proteins appear to be a useful defense against infections by protozoa and by large parasites like worms. The larger invaders can throw off or repair most other attacks, and they are bigger than many phagocytes, but the detergent seems to damage them enough to slow their spread, if not to kill all of the infestation.

Concentrated enzymes dumped outside a cell can also chop up "self" cells. This is useful in cleaning up a spot damaged by infection, but it may harm healthy cells and produce more damage than an invader. The chemical inhibitors of cell growth also can inhibit growth of host cells, and detergents destroy all membranes indiscriminately. The power of the immune system is felt when it is misdirected as well as when it hits its mark. This may be one of the selective pressures driving the evolution of specificity in immune responses. The greater the specificity, the less likely a response is to damage "self" as well as "foreign."

Wandering cells and signals

Wandering phagocytic cells are relatively few and must patrol enormous tracts of tissue, leaving much of the body unguarded at any moment. Animals with efficient circulations filter the circulating fluids by sending them past groups of phagocytic cells that are fixed in one place, for example the spleen or the liver. This is good for catching invaders in the blood, but it does not solve the problem of defending the tissues. Phagocytes are carried around in the blood, but they are separated from tissues by the thickness of the cells of the blood vessels. Their view of the parts of the body outside of the blood and lymph is about as good as a view of the woods from a car moving on a highway.

Phagocytes, like drivers on a highway, respond to advertising. Indeed, they are tuned to molecules that advertise invasion of, and damage to, tissues off their road. These chemical advertisements send three messages whose meaning can be very narrow or very broad. The meaning of each class of message depends upon the specificity of the *receptor* proteins that bind them at the surface of a phagocyte.

The three broad messages are: "infection here," "damaged cells here," and "other phagocytes here." Examples of narrower messages are "bacteria are synthesizing protein and multiplying here—follow this chemical trail to find them," or "your fellow cells have met bacteria and are gearing up to destroy them by producing large amounts of enzymes—join us."

Circulating phagocytes respond to any of these signals by getting off the highway and following the signal, a trail of chemicals, to its source. There, depending upon what is found, phagocytic cells activate

13

their enzymes, prepare for cell division, or signal for other cells to join them. The pus and swelling around a splinter wound is the debris of the local battle mounted against the intruder by cells that have left the circulation in response to signals from the bacteria coating the splinter and from the cells damaged by it.

In animals without circulatory systems, wandering cells can only walk, not drive. Even in animals with circulatory systems, a significant fraction of the wandering cells also choose to walk instead of driving. They crawl through normal tissue, covering the territory at a slow rate. They can detect all of the chemical signals that reach their cousins in circulation, and they respond to these signals by speeding up their rate of crawl and directing it to the source of the signal.

Besides detecting the signals released from damaged cells and from invaders, cells crawling over other cells can also read their surfaces for signs of change. Not all cell damage releases chemicals from the damaged cell. Often, the proteins displayed at its surface are changed—they have new bits of protein spliced to them—but they are not released from the surface. These changes in protein shape mark the damaged cell for removal. They are only sensed when a wandering cell actually crawls over the damaged cell and feels its surface. The fit of the cell's proteins to the proteins of the wandering cell sends a very localized message about the state of the cell whose surface is being felt.

Damage to a cell is not the only thing that changes its surface. Viruses infecting cells often leave bits of their proteins behind on the cell surface. Other traces of infection appear on the cell surface as the virus replicates and sets the cell's synthetic machinery to making virus proteins. Because these changes are local, much damage may be done before the changes are visible from the highway of the circulation.

Local surveillance also prevents the growth of cells that have dropped out of their society and transformed to cancer cells. The multiplication of these cells is unchecked by their neighbors. This loss of control is usually accompanied by changes at the surface of the tumor cells, and these changes are even harder to detect at a distance than are the surface changes following infection by viruses.

Specificity and the cell surface

Molecular recognition by cells takes us back to the problem of recognizing and distinguishing "self" and "foreign." We know that some "self" molecules, for example those that signal "follow me to the infection," are directly recognized by receptors of great specificity and sensitivity. The important signals that coordinate cellular attacks on "foreign" are read even when they are weak and there are very few signaling molecules about. High specificity also reduces "cross-talk" between signals in the innate immune system and chemical signals between cells in other parts of the body—for example, the nervous system.

We are less clear about the mechanism for recognition of "foreign" or "altered self." Does this recognition use receptors for "foreign," or does it test for "self"? Such a test could be made by comparing the molecules encountered by a cell with some standard set of molecules on its own surface. Mismatches would be the signal for a destructive response by the phagocyte against the cell being investigated. Presumably a test by matching would require each wandering cell to feel the surface of other cells it encountered, searching for molecules that fit well together. This search and fit could proceed so that molecule A on the surface of cell 1 would find molecule A on the surface of cell 2 and bind to it. In this case, like recognizes like. Another way of checking for "self" could require that molecule A on cell 1 bind molecule Z on cell 2, while molecule Z on cell 2 binds molecule A on cell 1. The rule for this search is that one kind of "self" molecule must bind to a complementary "self" molecule.

Positive tests for "self" seem to have the advantage of setting a strict standard of recognition, not requiring a cell to anticipate the kinds of "foreign" molecules it might encounter. However, such positive tests are not a good way to differentiate "self" from "foreign" in immune responses. There are two reasons for this. For one thing, "foreign" is defined as a negative or the absence of a "self" marker. This could set off unwanted and inappropriate immune responses when "self" is misread for some reason.

A second reason for not using positive recognition of "self" to define "foreign" is even more compelling than the first. Using only a few molecules as standards opens the way for foreign organisms to masquerade as "self" by displaying molecules that can bind to the receptors for "self." We can conceive of very complicated arrays of receptor proteins that read a whole set of signal-flag proteins that together code for "self," but even the whole set of flags could be imitated by rapidly mutating and evolving bacteria or viruses. A complicated signal would also invite a high level of misreading and inappropriate responses by phagocytes and other protective cells.

An alternative way of sensing and weighing the outside is to ignore "self" and carry a set of receptor molecules that are specific for the most common foreign molecules of invaders. This is the case for the most common changes in the surface of renegade "self"; namely, cells transformed to cancer cells. A cell bearing receptors for "foreign" or "changed" can anticipate some part of the universe of invaders.

There is a real risk that such a population of cells will fail to recognize some parts of the universe of "foreign," and that the organism owning these cells will be invaded and overrun. This risk can be greatly reduced if the cells of an individual have different receptors for "foreign."

The risk can be reduced further if every individual in a population of relatives has some receptors for "foreign" that are different from the receptors found in any other member of the population.

Despite the risks of missing some invaders, protecting cells of all animals appear to detect markers of "foreign" rather than markers of "self." The receptor proteins on their surfaces have broad specificity for the most common molecules of bacteria, fungi, and some viruses— molecules that cannot be changed without killing the microorganism. The binding of a bit of one of these bacterial or fungal molecules to one or more of the receptor proteins is what sends the signals for a cell to migrate from the blood or to increase the amount of destructive enzymes within its digestive sacs.

Molecules of a bacteria's coating, its cell wall, and fragments of bacterial proteins are examples of molecules that are recognized as "foreign" by animals.

All bacteria are surrounded by some sort of porous but strong cell wall; they exert considerable pressure on this wall, and the wall must resist this pressure so that the bacterium does not burst like a balloon. At the same time, the wall structure must be open enough to allow gases, food, and wastes to pass to and from the bacterium. This combination of properties required for life as a bacterium limits the molecules used to construct the cell wall to certain mixtures of lipids, proteins, and sugars. (Of course, we can look at this from another way and suggest that the evolutionary invention of a particular kind of cell wall polymer set limits to the way in which bacteria could evolve. The point is that bacteria cannot build working cell walls in any other way than they do now.)

Even though the details of the mixtures are different from one kind of bacterium to another, the shapes and sticking forces of many of the cell wall molecules do not vary much. These shapes can be detected by receptors on the surfaces of phagocytes and other wandering cells. The receptor molecules do not stick equally well to all kinds of cell wall molecules, so they may not signal until a fairly large number of molecules have accumulated around them. They usually do signal in time to bring phagocytes down on the invaders to destroy them.

Receptors for fragments of bacterial cell walls are found on the cells of many different kinds of animals, ranging from horseshoe crabs to humans. Clearly, the fight between bacterial invaders and their targets has been going on for hundreds of millions of years.

While bacteria make many different kinds of proteins whose shapes and characteristics vary enormously, all of the proteins begin with the same amino acid, n-formylmethionine. This amino acid and its use are peculiar to bacteria. Any protein shed from the bacterium, or even a fragment of this protein that contains its starting sequence, discloses the bacterium's hiding place to any cell with surface receptors that can bind n-formylmethionine. Wandering cells have evolved very specific and sensitive receptors for this special amino acid. These act as chemical direction finders, leading the cell toward the bacteria. As it closes in, less sensitive receptors for cell wall molecules come into play and activate enzymes and other machinery of destruction.

Signals, amplifiers, and responses

Is sensitivity specific always? No. Not every encounter between a receptor and a molecule that fits to its surface is successful. There is a chance that everything will go just right, resulting in the two molecules snuggling together, and a chance that some thing or things will disturb the pair as they attempt a fit and keep them apart. The stronger the affinity of the receptor for its bound molecule is, the better the odds are of making a fit. Higher affinity usually goes along with greater specificity; very specific receptors have a better chance of trapping rare molecules than do less specific receptors.

The receptors for n-formylmethionine peptides are high-affinity, highly specific, and sensitive to a very few molecules. Because they direct a wandering cell toward the source of the proteins, the infecting bacteria, the sensitive receptors also amplify the signal to the lower affinity, less specific receptors that detect bacterial cell wall products. Receptors for cell wall materials, which have little chance of capturing a molecule from a dilute solution, are dragged by their cell into a region rich in cell walls, and thus the receptors' chances of successfully engaging a molecule go up enormously.

The directed walk of a cell toward a source of threat is a primitive way of amplifying signals from the source. It is equivalent to improving radio reception by moving closer to the station. Reception could be more easily improved either by building a better, more sensitive radio receiver, or by increasing the station's power (amount of signal broadcast).

Responses need to be amplified as well as signals. Cells, whether circulating in the blood and lymph, or walking through the tissues, are outnumbered by invading microbes. They cannot increase their response by increasing in numbers, because they grow more slowly than the invaders. Instead, they increase their rate of phagocytosis and also make more chemicals to destroy bacteria that they have swallowed.

Chemical defenses against bacteria

Chemicals dissolved in body fluids can circulate through an animal more quickly and penetrate tissues more thoroughly than cells. Chemicals serve two functions of immune protection. One function is to signal between cells of the body. The other aims directly at destruction of microbes. Chemical mediators, particularly proteins, serve to amplify both signals and destructive responses.

I earlier made a brief mention of signals between phagocytic cells that tell them to join a contest between "self" and "foreign." This is an example of signal amplification. A few molecules of chemical "broadcast" by one phagocyte stimulate other phagocytes to produce and release more of the same signal, recruiting still more phagocytes to the hunt.

Some of the same chemical signals that bring phagocytes into action are also used to activate cells of other sorts and to coordinate their responses. A good example of this is a protein called interleukin 1, or IL-1, produced by phagocytes. IL-1 is made when phagocytes are irritated by foreign materials as diverse as mineral crystals, viruses, or bacteria. (This protein was named *interleukin* because it was discovered from its effects on the behavior and growth of the white cells of blood, the leukocytes. This group of cells includes the scavengers and phagocytes whose behavior I have been describing in a general way.)

IL-1 is not only a growth factor for phagocytic cells. It has broad physiological effects, many of which are anti-infective and others of which help in healing and recuperation. These effects include raising body temperature to fever heat, inducing sleep, changing rates of production of corticosteroid and protein hormones, and increasing the rate of production of new red blood cells. The production of IL-1 and its circulation enhance and integrate the body's responses to an invasion by foreign organisms.

The scope of action and importance of IL-1 are probably even greater than the last paragraph suggests, since it is produced and released by skin cells, connective tissue cells, and several other types of cells, as well as by phagocytes.

IL-1, in some form, is a very old molecule. The wandering phagocytic cells of starfish produce a molecule like IL-1 and respond to it. This molecule of starfish is recognized by human cells, and so some portion of it must have remained constant in structure during the time since starfish and vertebrate ancestors diverged in evolution.

IL-1 rouses cells in the body to appropriate responses. It defends by signaling. Other chemical defenses attack bacteria and viruses directly. They may do this passively, by binding to trace elements like iron that the bacteria need to grow, or actively, by breaking chemical bonds in bacterial cell walls, or even by actively punching holes in a bacterium, allowing water to enter and burst open the bacterial cell.

The collection of proteins that, working together, punches holes in bacteria is known as the *complement*. There are more than a dozen kinds of molecules in the whole collection. About nine of these kinds, working in sequence, are needed to punch holes in a bacterium, but smaller numbers of complement proteins can attack bacteria and fungi in other ways that lead to their destruction.

The specificity of the key complement components for microbes is very broad. In fact, they form chemical, covalent bonds with the microbial surface, instead of relying on a receptor-like fit between the protein molecule and the bacterium. A complement protein covalently linked to a surface turns into an enzyme that modifies molecules still in solution so that they too react with the bacterial surface. Thus the reaction amplifies itself locally by generating more and more actively destructive molecules.

The complexes of complement and bacteria, as well as fragments chopped from complement proteins as they act on each other, can attract phagocytic cells. Many kinds of phagocytes have receptors for complement proteins on their surfaces. Some of these receptors detect complement fragments and direct cell locomotion toward their source. Other receptors can distinguish between the shape of complement proteins free in solution and the shape of complement proteins that have bound to bacteria. Complement proteins fixed to bacterial cells then act as connectors, making a bacterial cell surface a good fit for receptors on the surface of a phagocyte. Once bound to these receptors, the complement-decorated bacterium is efficiently and rapidly ingested by phagocytosis and destroyed, thus amplifying the response to microbes.

Complement molecules, and other active defensive molecules of innate immunity (as opposed to molecules that purely signal), are constantly made and secreted by many different kinds of cells. For example, in mammals, much of the complement is made by cells of the liver, cells that are not specialized for immune defenses. Production of most of these defensive molecules is constant. With few exceptions, the amounts of these molecules in the body fluids do not change much in response to infection.

The multiple functions of complement molecules—binding different surfaces at different parts of the same protein cluster—anticipate important functions of the other great part of immune responses, adaptive immunity. The most abundant molecules of adaptive immunity, antibodies, are also soluble proteins with different functions in different parts of each molecule. Some of the functions of antibody molecules, particularly that of binding to receptors on the surfaces of phagocytes, are the same as functions of complement proteins, but they are performed by very different molecular structures.

We have now sketched out a view of the foundation stones of all immune responses: the barriers, cells, and chemicals that together constitute our innate immunity to invasion. This system blocks and recognizes "foreign," anticipating very broad categories of attacks, and responds in a rough and ready way to such attacks. Some of these responses are so rough that they damage "self" as well as "foreign."

I will leave our description of innate immunity here and turn to consider the general features of adaptive immunity, the physiological responses to "foreign" that most of us know as immune responses. I will describe the molecules and cells that are important in adaptive immunity and trace their evolution from cell receptors of "self" to soluble proteins detecting "foreign." We will see how the evolution of a new group of molecules and the cells to use them leads to an immune response that is more discriminating, subtle, flexible, and finely finished than the innate immune response, and how the two ways of responding, innate and adaptive, converge and mingle to constitute an integrated physiological whole.

The origins and qualities of adaptive immunity

A new form of immunity seems to have arisen with the evolution of vertebrates. The solution to the problem of recognizing "foreign" has been so elaborated that the specificity and fitness of vertebrate responses seems qualitatively different from responses of invertebrates. In fact, just as innate immune mechanisms may be seen as an extension and elaboration of certain functions of protozoa, so adaptive immunity may be seen as an extension, though a very large extension, of the immune functions of innate immunity.

Adaptive immunity is so called because an animal seems to adapt its response to be highly specific for the invading organism. This adaptation in response to an environmental change thus appears Lamarckian. Cells and molecules specific to the invader seem to arise only after invasion. But appearances deceive; the adaptation is actually Darwinian. The appropriateness and specificity of the response are due to selective stimulation and clonal growth of single cells in a large and diverse population of potential immune cells. Cells of this population realize their potential when they meet "foreign" of the appropriate sort and meet it in the appropriate way. The proper meeting of cell and "foreign" stimulates the cells to produce large amounts of anti-"foreign" proteins. These antibodies are found in the blood and other body fluids after infection or deliberate immunization.

The functions required for innate immunity—namely, signaling, amplification, and recognition—are also functions of adaptive immunity. But as we have noted, these functions are performed by molecules that are different in structure and sharper in specificity than cognate molecules of innate immunity.

There are also several important innovations in amplification of the immune response. The growth of antibody-producing cells amplifies production of antibodies at a rate commensurate with the rate of replication of microbes. The persistence of some of the cells that are stimulated to multiply after infection ensures that the adaptive immune system has a memory. Its response to a second infection by a given kind of microbe is faster and larger than its first response.

The specificity and memory of immune responses have been known for thousands of years:

> Yet it was with those who had recovered from the disease that the sick and the dying found most compassion. These knew what it was from experience, and had now no fear for themselves; for the same man was never attacked twice—never at least fatally. And such persons not only received the congratulations of others, but themselves also, in the elation of the moment, half entertained the vain hope that they were for the future safe from any disease whatsoever. (Thucydides, *The History of the Peloponnesian War,* bk. 2, chap. 7; *GBWW* I: 6, 400; II: 5, 400.)

Though we have been spared the terror of the plague, our experience with common childhood diseases—measles, mumps, chicken pox—has given all of us some sense of the properties of an adaptive immune response. We know that exposure to mumps, or vaccination by injection of modified mumps virus, protects us or our children from ever again being infected by mumps. One exposure to the virus has prepared our adaptive immune response so that it responds rapidly to later infections and crushes the infection before the virus can spread through the body. We also know that recovery from mumps confers no protection from measles, and vice versa. Our immune memory is specific for mumps, and memory and rapid responses to measles can come only after the body is challenged by the measles virus.

Molecular evolution and comparative molecular anatomy

Molecules and cells that make up the specific, adaptive immune responses to a virus or bacterium are specialized, and they divide the functions of response to "foreign," control of the response, and targeting of the response. Though there are differences in cell and molecular function required by this division of labor, all of the elements of specific immune responses—cells and molecules—are related to each other by evolutionary descent from some few common ancestors. The line of descent can be traced through the structures of present-day protein molecules.

Classical studies of the evolution of structure in organisms analyzed evolutionary lineages by means of three biological disciplines: paleontology, comparative embryology, and comparative anatomy. Only paleontology gave a truly historical view of the way in which evolution had proceeded. The other two disciplines dealt with living organisms and so had no explicit historical component; time relationships could

21

only be inferred with the help of the fossil record. There were always dangers in this approach of mistaking secondary and late-evolved characteristics of embryo or adult animals for persistent primitive and early-evolved features.

These dangers of the comparative method present themselves anew in modern studies of the comparative anatomy of molecules. I will sketch a plausible outline of the way in which a large family of related molecules evolved; but this sketch is based on the protein sequences of, and genetic codes for, a collection of molecules that exist today. We cannot sequence fossil proteins or DNA; that is, we do not know the order of their development. Instead we compare and arrange sequences and relate them to what we know of the evolution of whole animals. This gives a plausible and self-consistent picture of the evolution of molecular evolution. It is probably correct in most of its parts, but it omits a good deal and may need to be taken with a grain of salt from the Precambrian ocean.

The study of the comparative anatomy of protein molecules depends upon our knowledge of protein shape and structure. As we have seen earlier, a protein that is a linear string of amino acids is folded and given shape by the forces between atoms of each amino acid. To learn the shape of a particular protein we must first read its amino acid sequence and then, somehow, construct a three-dimensional image of linear sequence.

We can read the linear form of a protein either by directly reading the sequence of its amino acids or by reading the linear nucleic acid code for the protein and using well-understood rules for translating the code from nucleic acids into amino acids. Today this sort of reading is relatively easy, straightforward, and highly automated.

Readings of many proteins and comparison of their sequences tell us about their degree of relatedness—their homology. Here, as in comparative anatomy, homology is taken to imply descent from a common ancestor. Two proteins may be homologous over their entire length, or they may be related only in some patches and not others. This patchy homology reflects the origin of all large genes and proteins from a few thousand small ancestral genes that, over time, have duplicated and joined together.

Learning the shape of a protein is much more difficult than learning its linear form, which is the sequence of its amino acids. Theory allows some prediction of the shape taken by linear sequences of amino acids, but this theory is not enough to re-create the three-dimensional form of a molecule from its amino acid sequence. Instead, we must make an image of the actual structure of the protein, an image whose details are as small as atoms.

The details in any image depend upon the color of the light or, more precisely, on the wavelength of the radiation used to make the image.

The shorter the wavelength of light, the finer the detail that is resolved. An intricate object or complicated scene yields more of its detail to our eyes in blue light than in red because the wavelength of blue light is shorter than the wavelength of red light. Atoms of a protein molecule are much smaller than the wavelength of any light that we can see. Instead of visible light, very short wavelength radiation or X ray is used to make an image of the atoms. The X-ray pictures of a crystal composed of many molecules of the same protein can be transformed, using a considerable amount of computation, to a pattern of shapes in space, a pattern of the atoms in the protein.

Once the transformation is done, the linear sequence of amino acids in the protein can be mapped onto its three-dimensional pattern. Now the anonymous blobs of atoms in space take on names and chemistries; we can associate particular amino acids with particular features of protein folding and form. For example, we find that amino acids that are not very soluble in water are folded into the interior of the protein and kept away from its surface, which is bathed in water. We also find that amino acids that are widely separated in the linear sequence are brought closer together when the protein is folded and that, so folded, they exert forces on one another, or even react chemically.

Once we have mapped one kind of linear sequence onto a three-dimensional structure, we can predict the form of homologous sequences with some confidence. It is now fairly easy to map many new amino sequences onto one known three-dimensional image of a protein. Doing this, we can compare the three-dimensional structure of many homologous proteins or of homologous patches in proteins, even if a structure has only been formally determined for one member of the homology.

The use of sequence to predict structure by generalizing from one known structure is invaluable in the comparative anatomy of molecules. It lets us construct evolutionary relationships between fully formed and therefore functional molecules, rather than merely comparing the backbones or codes of these molecules. The history and the ancestry of the molecules of adaptive immunity has been written using the principles sketched here.

"Self"-recognition molecules

Though wandering cells seem to detect "foreign" rather than "self," positive recognition of "self" by "self" is used by cells to stick together and position themselves in tissues during the development of an organism. It appears that the first molecules used for cell positioning in early multicellular animals recognized and stuck to like molecules on neighboring cells. Other recognition molecules evolved from this starting point. These molecules recognize complementary, rather than identical, molecules.

From comparison of protein sequences, we learn that several groups of "self"-recognition molecules and the proteins of adaptive immunity form a single "nation" of molecules. Members of each tribe of the nation are related in form and function, and the three tribes are related by descent from a common ancestor. The form of this ancestral protein is preserved and repeated in a tribe of proteins used to stick cells of the central nervous system to one another and to position them. It is also found and elaborated in another tribe of proteins that stick leukocytes of different sorts to one another, allowing them to communicate information about, and participate in, immune responses.

The two tribes of "self"-recognition molecules are related to a third tribe whose member proteins bind "foreign" as well as "self." The exquisite specificity of adaptive immunity inheres in these proteins. The proteins of the third tribe have evolved acute specificity for "foreign" from an ancestral structure that originally functioned to recognize "self."

The tribe of "self"-recognition molecules that function in the nervous system is probably the oldest of the three. Members of this tribe are known to be required for the organization of nervous systems in both invertebrates and vertebrates. Members of the other two tribes only function in vertebrates. They seem to be one of the evolutionary "inventions" that contribute to the origin of the vertebrate subphylum.

With this historical perspective we will now look at the structure of some of the proteins of the *immunoglobulin* (Ig) nation.

"Our Founder," the sticky lump of protein that began the immunoglobulin nation, was a small molecule made up of eighty to one hundred amino acids. The forces between groups of atoms on the particular amino acids of its sequence molded the linear form of the protein into a series of zigzag sheets. The sheets alone were too rigid to fold, but they were connected by other amino acids that form flexible links. These allowed the whole structure to form a barrel shape. Two sulfur-containing amino acids were brought into proximity by the folding, and the chemical bond between the two sulfur atoms stabilized the barrel.

The structure of a modern-day protein quite similar to "Our Founder" is shown in figure 1. This protein is slightly larger than its hypothetical ancestor; it is made of 110 amino acids. The extra thirty amino acids do not change its shape and arrangement of sheets but rather follow the ancestral pattern. The lines of figure 1 follow the linear sequence, the backbone, of the protein and so emphasize the way in which it folds. The zigzag sheets are seen as seven horizontal lines, roughly parallel to one another. Though it is not clear in the figure, one set of three sheets lies above the other set of four sheets.

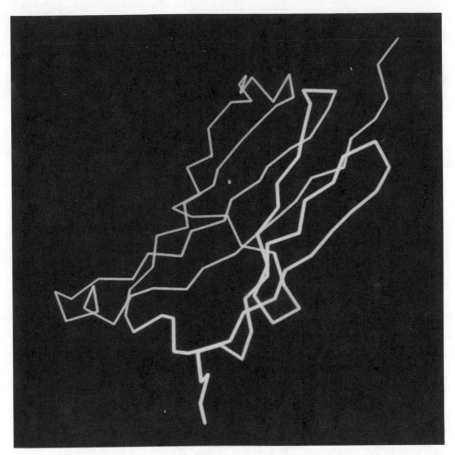

Figure 1. The bright lines trace the linear form of an immunoglobulin domain. This compact barrel-shaped structure is the building block from which many important molecules of the immune system are constructed.

The more or less vertical lines that connect the sheets are loops. The amino acids of the loops are much more variable than those of the sheets, and the loop structures are much more flexible than the sheets. We might think of the loop regions as the protein frontier. Here, things are less organized than in other regions. There is a good deal of open space—water around the loop—and so there is great freedom to move and change. In contrast, the sheets seem like an old established neighborhood or city. Most of their surfaces feel the forces of neighboring sheets and all are crowded together. There is little room to move, and a change in any one amino acid must be accommodated by changes in all of its many neighbors.

The lines and curves of figure 1 emphasize the flexibility and interior arrangement of an immunoglobulin domain. Figure 2 emphasizes the

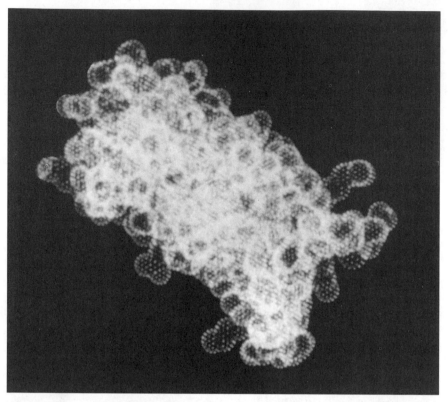

Figure 2. This image of an immunoglobulin domain shows its bulk. The image was made by a computer program that first strings together the linear sequence of amino acids making up the protein, and then assigns and displays a volume for each atom of each amino acid. Though most of the atoms cannot be seen in this image, a few of the outlying ones appear as dotted spheres.

bulk of the molecule. It literally fills in the image in figure 1 by adding the atoms that project from the amino acids of the backbone and by showing all the atoms as spheres. We have less sense here of a molecule that can flex to accommodate the binding of another molecule, but a better sense of the broad surfaces that can stick to complementary surfaces on other molecules.

The unit of protein shown in the two figures is called an *immunoglobulin domain.* It takes this name because it was first identified as a region or domain of the structure of antibody proteins. These proteins are members of a larger group of proteins called *globulins.* They are *immune globulins,* a phrase that has been modified to *immunoglobulins.*

Immunoglobulins are made of a string of immunoglobulin domains, each somewhat different from the others. Some of these domains bind "self," and others bind "foreign." "Self"-binding depends upon the surfaces of the domains; "foreign"-binding uses the flexible loops.

Immunoglobulins

Immunoglobulins are the largest, the most varied, and the most abundant of all the molecules that are built from immunoglobulin domains. For all their variation, their construction never hides its origins. This is clear in the image of the most abundant immunoglobulin, immunoglobulin G, or IgG, shown in figure 3. The Y-shaped molecule is a string of immunoglobulin domains. Each arm of the Y is made of four immunoglobulin domains. The eight domains at the top of the molecule are connected to another four domains, forming the stem of the Y.

A total of twelve immunoglobulin domains are arranged as four linear amino acid chains. Two identical small chains are called *light chains,* and two identical larger chains are called *heavy chains*. One light chain pairs with and sticks to one end of each heavy chain. The opposite ends of the two heavy chains pair with each other. Each half of an IgG molecule, one light chain plus one heavy chain, is a mirror image of the

Figure 3. A complete immunoglobulin molecule. The arms that bind "foreign" are at the top of the picture. Each arm is formed by a light chain made of two immunoglobulin domains wrapped around a portion of the heavy chain made of two immunoglobulin domains. The molecule is represented here by sticks, rather than balls, so its twelve domains each look less bulky than the domain that is shown in figure 2. The light chains are brighter domains that appear to be in the foreground of the picture.

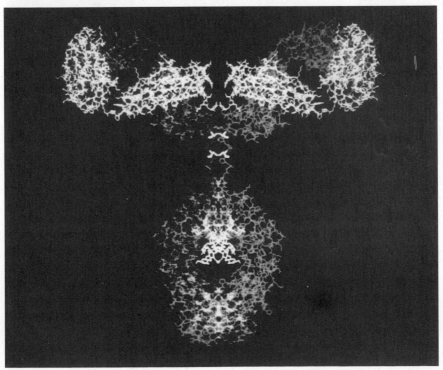

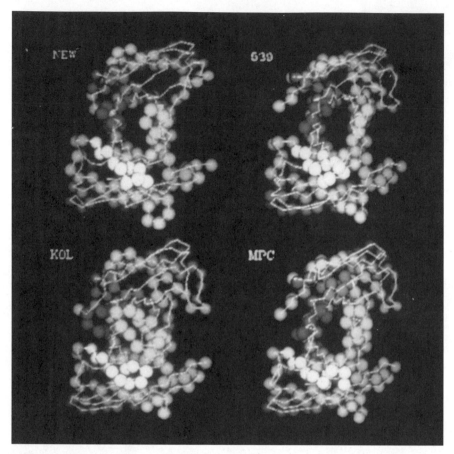

Figure 4. A "foreign" molecule's views of IgG. End-on views of the binding sites of four different IgG molecules. Atoms are represented as spheres. Three of the four binding sites are cavities, of different sizes and shapes. The fourth binding site, at the lower left, extends toward the viewer as a kind of knob.

other. This doubling means that there are two sites to bind "foreign" on each immunoglobulin molecule—two chances to capture an invader before it can proliferate.

As has been said, the binding sites for "foreign" are modified loops of the amino acids connecting the zigzag sheets that are characteristic of an immunoglobulin domain. End-on views of four different binding sites, as each would be seen by "foreign," are shown in figure 4. Three of the four are holes in the protein surface; the fourth is a knob. Each of the three holes fits a protrusion on some foreign protein; the knob fits into a corresponding hole on yet another protein.

The loops in the binding region are properly positioned because the surfaces of immunoglobulin domains attract and stick to one another. They keep the old "self"-recognition properties of their ancestors. This sticking of like to like patches gives the whole immunoglobulin molecule its form and mirror-image symmetry.

If you think that the stem of the immunoglobulin molecule in figure 3 is too far from the binding site to have anything to do with binding "foreign," you are correct. The stem region is entirely devoted to "self"-recognition. Domains of the stem bind to other "self" molecules in solution and to receptors on cells, including phagocytic cells. Like the complement molecules of innate immunity, immunoglobulin molecules function as adapters, bringing invaders into specific, high-affinity association with the cells and chemicals that can destroy them.

One adapter molecule with four or five functions in its stem and perhaps a few hundred variations that recognize "foreign" seems like a very great advance over the cell-surface receptors for "foreign" and the complement molecules of innate immunity. It by no means exhausts the varieties of immunoglobulin. The stem region alone comes in half a dozen or more varieties within a single species. The details of each variety of stem determine just how it binds to other "self" and how it functions.

The IgG molecule that we have diagramed is the "journeyman" immunoglobulin. It is produced in greatest abundance after infection, and it can bind to a great variety of cell receptors. There are three other varieties of immunoglobulin whose stem regions have become specialized for binding to just a few kinds of chemicals and receptors.

Good toothbrushing helps to reduce cavities, but we also depend on a variety of antibodies in saliva to keep down the number of cavity-forming bacteria in the mouth. This specialist immunoglobulin is called IgA. It is built from two molecules, each similar to IgG in size and structure. The half-molecules of IgA differ from IgG because their stems are specialized for joining to stems of like molecules. Other parts of the stems bind to receptors on the bottom surface of the cells that line respiratory and food tubes, among them the cells of the salivary glands. The receptors bring IgA molecules into the cell but keep them away from the disassembly line. Instead, they deliver the IgA molecules intact to the top surface of the cell, which is the surface of the tube. There, the IgA molecules are released into the fluid in the tube where they can bind to foreign organisms and kill them before they can colonize the surface.

Because it is made of two molecules similar to IgG, IgA has four sites for binding "foreign," but these seem almost an accident of its construction. The receptors that transport IgA across cells recognize its many stems. This multiplicity, and not the multiple binding sites for "foreign," is required for proper function.

There is no doubt about the importance of multiplicity in the jumbo antibody called *macroglobulin,* or IgM. IgM is constructed of five IgG-sized units and so has ten identical binding sites for "foreign." IgM is the best adaptive defense to bacteria whose cell walls are made of repeated units. The multiple sites of IgM can find multiple targets, and so the chances of the antibody molecule successfully locking onto a bacterium are very high.

A very few molecules of IgM can serve as a trip wire for invasion. Once the antibody is locked on its target, its multiple stems come into play. They very effectively bind one of the complement proteins, and this directs an attack that ends with the disintegration of the bacterium. The chemical mess made in the attack also attracts phagocytic and other cells that can respond to the infection.

An IgM molecule is about ten times more efficient at directing lysis of a bacterium than are IgG molecules, but it is only the size of five IgG molecules. Specialized "self"-recognition by IgM subunits results in an efficient packaging of destructive power, as well as a good signal for other cells.

The third example of specialized "self"-recognition in an immunoglobulin stem is a molecule called IgE. Many of us know the effect of this specialized Ig molecule, even if we do not know its name. IgE is the immunoglobulin of allergic reactions. It is the culprit behind the wheezes and sniffles of hay fever as well as more threatening allergic reactions such as those against penicillin. IgE seems to turn us against ourselves and to have no redeeming quality of protection against "foreign." However, it is likely that the muscle contractions and mucus secretion triggered when IgE binds to a specialized leukocyte are beneficial in expelling parasites, especially worms that live in the gut. We must presume that on an evolutionary scale of time and suffering, the long-term benefits of this expulsion outweigh the disadvantages of most allergic reactions.

The variation and the range in function of the stem of an immunoglobulin Y is slight compared with the variation in the single function of binding "foreign" by the arms of the Y. The sequence of each of the two chains in an arm, the light chain and the heavy chain, can be drawn at random from a family of hundreds of possible sequences. Since the binding site for "foreign" is constructed from light and heavy chains together, this means that tens of thousands of different binding sites can be created by random combination of light and heavy chains.

Forty thousand different sites seem not to be nearly enough to give the required subtlety and specificity to adaptive immune recognition of these chains. Moreover, genetic mechanisms have evolved in mammalian cells to increase the variety of immunoglobulin binding sites for "foreign." All of these genetic mechanisms also work to introduce random variation into the linear sequence of an immunoglobulin binding region. They increase the possible varieties of "foreign"-binding sites to around 100,000,000. This much potential variation cannot be realized in the lifetime of any one individual.

The potential for diversity of binding regions in mammalian immunoglobulins is the height of immunoglobulin rococo. Other vertebrates use much less elaborate genetic mechanisms to diversify the binding sites of their immunoglobulins. Animals, birds, frogs, and fish seem to get along well with a more restricted, though still large, anticipation of "foreign."

Immunoglobulins and the body's response to "foreign"

Serum from a patient who has recovered from an infection of diphtheria or pneumonia can protect another individual from infection and can even arrest the progress of disease in another patient. This observation, made at the end of the nineteenth century, is one of the cornerstones of the modern study of immunology. It shows that the response of "self" to "foreign" can be localized to some chemical principle in the blood. The patient, immunized in the course of the disease, or by deliberate inoculation with a harmless form of a microbe, has responded to the foreign features of the microbe, its antigens, with serum antibodies that specifically block infection.

Once antibodies were purified from blood, they could be used as chemicals that could be studied to understand what features of "foreign" they recognize. Studies show that antibodies detect shapes of molecules and cells. They bind to corners, bumps, and loops that protrude from proteins, viruses, and bacteria in their native state. It is as if the binding site cannot be bothered with the details of linear sequence but looks instead at the results of that sequence.

There seems to be no limit to the forms that can be recognized by antibodies. Antibodies are even produced against antigens that do not exist in nature, such as chemicals that are called into existence in the laboratory. If antibody binding sites were constructed to rules that insisted on the fussy details of just which amino acid followed another, then it would be improbable for an antibody to be contrived that would bind to the chemist's latest invention.

The emphasis on recognizing shape, regardless of everything but the most basic chemistry (charge and water solubility), greatly increases the chances of an antibody being ready to bind to any "foreign" novelty that comes along. Given this facility, it is surprising that antibodies do not regularly turn up forms that bind quite well to "self." Anti-"self" antibodies are found, but they rarely increase to levels that damage or even threaten "self." We will find reasons for this in the regulation of immune responses, but before we can look at the physiology of immune responses we need to know something about the structure and habits of two other members of the immunoglobulin tribe, each of which recognizes "foreign" in its own way.

31

Transplantation antigens

Though it would seem that the transplantation of tissues and organs is a modern technique, successful tissue transplants have been made for over a thousand years. These grafts were made to reconstruct noses, lips, and ears that had been lost to the edged weapons of war, or in India to the judgment of a court.

In all successful cases, the graft donor and the recipient were the same person. It has long been known that grafts donated by one person to the body of another always fail, though the reasons have not been understood. Saints Cosmas and Damian performed a miracle by successfully grafting the leg of a Moor to a European. In other cases the recipient was less fortunate and there was no miracle to save the graft:

> A certain inhabitant of Bruxels, in a combat, had his nose mowed off, and addressed himself to Tagliacozzus, a famous Chiurgeon, living at Bononia, that he might procure a new one; and when he feared the incision of his own arme, he hired a Porter to admit it, out of whose arme, having first given the reward agreed upon, at length he digged a new nose. About thirteen moneths after his returne to his owne country, on a suddaine, the ingrafted nose grew cold, putrified, and within a few days dropt off. . . . [2]

It was thought that the death of the donor caused the death of the separated part or, as Samuel Butler told the story:

> So learned *Taliacotius* from / The brawny part of Porter's Bum, / Cut supplemental Noses, which / Would last as long as Parent breech: / But when the date of *Nock* was out, / Off dropt the Sympathetick Snout. [3]

Both versions claimed to show that there was a sympathy between the donated tissue and its donor, surely an excellent example of "self"-recognition.

Though the survival time of thirteen months is exceptional, everything else about the first story rings true. Absent special treatment, skin donated by anyone except an identical twin is rejected as foreign to the body. The rejection is an adaptive immune response. It is specific for the tissue of a particular donor and it has memory for the donor, rejecting a second donation more vigorously than it did the first.

Graft rejection is a serious clinical problem, and until recently it was also an utterly vexing and disturbing immunological problem. There seemed to be no reason why a large part of the immune system anticipated foreign tissue grafts. The best guess was that some other examples of "foreign," perhaps bacteria or viruses, resembled structures on normal cells, and so, immune responses meant for microbes were turned against grafts of normal cells. This is not a very strong argument, since

A seventeenth-century view of graft rejection. The living
recipient of a new nose mourns the death of the
nose and of its donor.

it leads immediately to the question of why one person's cells have a set
of graft antigens that differs from almost everyone else's antigens. We
are left with the feeling that graft rejection is important but that we do
not know why it is important.

We learn part of the context from the structure of graft rejection
antigens, today burdened by history with the clumsy name *major histocompatibility complex molecules,* or MHC molecules. These prove to
recognize and bind "foreign" in a form that is quite different from the
form recognized by antibodies. MHC molecules are followers of the
rules, sticklers for linear codes. They do not detect shape and form;
rather, they bind small pieces of the linear sequence of a protein.

MHC molecules cannot bind to whole protein molecules, let alone
whole viruses or bacteria. Choice bits of linear sequence must be carved
from the protein and fed to the molecule. This means that MHC

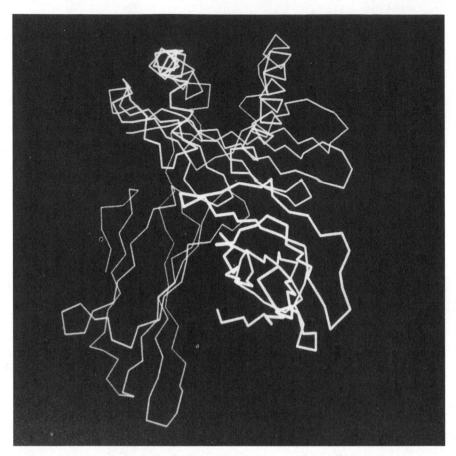

Figure 5. The bright lines trace the form of an MHC molecule. One of its immunoglobulin domains is at the lower left. The second domain is at the lower right. The rest of the molecule contains sheets and coils of amino acids forming a groove at the top. Compare figure 1.

molecules never meet "foreign" until some part of "foreign" has got inside a cell and has been at least partly taken to pieces by the cell's digestive and destructive enzymes.

"Foreign" will be consigned for carving and sampling by MHC molecules if it has been taken up by a phagocyte. Bits of "foreign" will also be created in cells that are infected with a virus. Replication and assembly of the viral proteins is by no means perfect, and defective molecules are scrapped on the spot. Whichever way the pieces are made, MHC molecules can only bind the "foreign" that is inside a cell. If they do not have "foreign" to bind, they will bind "self" peptides, scraps of the failures of normal protein synthesis.

A picture of an MHC molecule shows a structure looking like a pair of immunoglobulin domains wearing a very large hat (fig. 5). The hat

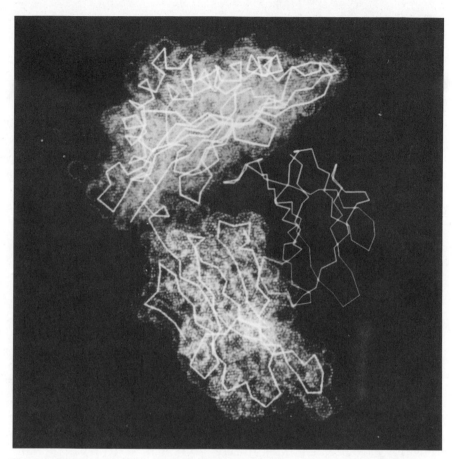

Figure 6. Side view of an MHC molecule. The shape suggests that the small immunoglobulin domain (shown only in linear form) to the right acts to keep the rest of the MHC molecule closed around a fragment of "foreign" bound to a groove near the top of the molecule.

contains a groove that can be filled with a fragment of foreign antigen. This groove appears open and empty; it ought to hold quite a large piece of protein or other antigen, but it cannot. It is not clear why only small fragments can be bound by the structure shown in figure 5.

Another view of the MHC molecule suggests a way it can open and close. In this view (fig. 6), the top of the molecule looks like a bent spring. It seems that it would fly up from its base were it not for a small protein, a single immunoglobulin domain, that is attached to its undersurface. This small protein latch keeps the MHC molecule in form. Antigen fragments are bound before it is latched. Once the latch is closed, fragments can no longer enter or leave the binding site.

There are many different forms of the binding site for "foreign" peptides, though not as many, by a factor of a million or more, as there are different forms of antibody-binding sites. MHC molecules get by with this limited variation because each variety of binding site can bind many different "foreign" peptides. The binding of any one peptide is a thousand times weaker than the binding of antigen by antibody, but once the groove snaps shut, the peptide is trapped and held in place.

Decorating the cell surface

Though most immunoglobulin molecules are dissolved in the blood and body fluids, some of them decorate cell surfaces. One form of decoration consists of molecules bound by their stems to "self" receptors on phagocytic cells. The empty molecules are brandished at passersby until they find and bind to "foreign." Then the complex of antigen and antibody is dragged into the cell and broken into peptides that can be loaded into MHC molecules and again displayed at the surface.

Other antibody molecules reflect their ancestry and never leave the surface of specialized white cells called *B lymphocytes,* or *B cells.* The antibody molecules are anchored to the surface by a region that is missing from the antibody molecules in blood. When an anchored molecule binds antigen, it also is dragged inside and chopped to bits. But, before this happens, the surface Ig starts a series of messages to the cell that culminate in cell division.

MHC molecules are not shed by the cells in which they are made, and most remain at the surface of the cells that made them. Here they advertise the state of the cell that they adorn. If all is well, the MHC molecules bear "self" peptides, not "foreign." These are ignored by cells that have been educated to respond only to MHC plus "foreign" peptide, but to ignore MHC plus "self."

If a cell has swallowed "foreign," or been infected by it, then this state is advertised by MHC molecules stuffed with "foreign." Specialized cells respond to the advertisement in ways that, directly or indirectly, further an immune response. These cells are a different sort of white blood cell called *T lymphocytes,* or *T cells.* Such lymphocytes carry what may be the oldest, and is certainly the strangest, of all of the tribe of molecules that recognize "foreign."

In most cases when immunity cannot be transferred by injecting serum antibodies from one individual into another, it can be transferred by injecting lymphocytes. The lymphocytes do not produce antibodies but are the cells that effect immunity. These are T lymphocytes, and they bear receptors for "foreign" that are similar in overall structure and in location of the binding site to one arm of an antibody Y.

Though the shape of the T lymphocyte receptors resembles that of an antibody, their behavior toward "foreign" is about as far from that of an antibody as one can get. T lymphocytes recognize neither the shape nor the peptides of "foreign." They can only sense "foreign" peptides cradled in a "self" MHC molecule. The T lymphocyte receptor recognizes the shape of a "self" MHC molecule that has been altered by the binding of a short sequence of amino acids from a "foreign" protein.

There are a limited number of ways that an MHC molecule can be distorted by a peptide. This is probably the reason why we reject grafts from just about all donors. Our T lymphocytes cannot distinguish the shapes of the graft's MHC molecules from the shape of "self" MHC molecules that have bound fragments of "foreign."

The cellular and molecular basis of an immune response

The intricacies of molecular recognition all have their place in the dance of immune cells. The dance begins when a microbe enters the body; it grows to a frenzy and then subsides. The sections that follow give an account of the way in which antibodies, cells, and receptors interact to check the spread of an infection.

The immune response to one kind of microbe may appear to produce mostly antibody, while the response to a different microbe may appear to produce mostly immune T lymphocytes and little or no antibody. This is deceptive, since both immune cells and antibodies are usually made against any infecting microbe. Rather than describing responses of one sort or another, I shall narrate the course of a rather generalized response to a microbe, bacterium, or virus multiplying in the body.

Imagine, then, that a microbe has broken through the mechanical barriers of the innate immune system and lodged in the tissues. Here it begins to reproduce itself. If it is a virus, it will first penetrate a host cell and take over the cell's synthetic machinery. If it is a bacterium, the microbe will reproduce outside of host cells.

The microbe and tissue damage that it causes will evoke innate immune responses by phagocytes. These responses may not be enough to destroy the microbe. They will damage some of the microbes, and fragments of damaged microbes will be carried away from the site of infection. Whole molecules, even whole microbes, as well as small fragments of molecules, will be carried away in the fluid percolating between the cells, the lymph. Phagocytic cells will also carry away their burden of partly digested microbes and microbial peptides.

The intact microbes and their more or less intact proteins soon meet collections of B lymphocytes. The antibody (immunoglobulin) genes of each B lymphocyte have a unique configuration. To a good approximation, no two B lymphocytes can make identical antibodies.

The surface of each B lymphocyte is decorated by antibody molecules whose binding sites for "foreign" are coded by uniquely configured genes of the cell. The chances are high that surface antibodies on some of the B lymphocytes can bind one of the many different bumps and shapes of the microbe's proteins and sugar molecules.

A B lymphocyte is stimulated to divide when enough of its surface antibodies bind a "foreign" antigen. Thus an antigen selects clones of B lymphocytes for growth and expansion. The population of B lymphocytes evolves to contain many cells that produce antibodies to the "foreign" antigen and secrete these antibodies into the blood and lymph. In a few days the proportion of all B lymphocytes able to respond to the infection has increased considerably.

As antigen-specific B lymphocytes proliferate, antibodies appear in serum that react with the infecting microbe. No such antibodies could be found before infection. At the level of the whole animal and the blood, this response appears to be an adaptive response to the infection, a Lamarckian response. But the response is made by the selective stimulation of cells that have the genetic potential for proliferating and producing antibody. Hence the cell population evolves in a classical Darwinian fashion through selective growth of individual cells in a pool of genetically variable cells.

The earliest part of the adaptive immune response only requires that B lymphocytes meet moderately high concentrations of intact "foreign." The antibody produced in this part of the response is mainly IgM, the large, effective, multivalent antibody that is very good at tying up many antigens and delivering them to phagocytes. This limited response alone may be enough to stop the infection. If it is, IgM antibodies will appear in the blood and lymph and then quickly disappear as the cells making them die. The rise and fall of blood antibody levels takes about a week.

Help

Early in the course of an infection, B lymphocytes need no help from other cells. There is lots of "foreign" around, and much of this is in the form of big pieces of material that can bind to surface antibodies on B lymphocytes. Most bacteria also release clouds of cell wall molecules which help to stimulate B lymphocytes to divide.

After a few more days, when the immune response has progressed further, there is lots of "foreign" debris in the body, but fewer whole microbes. At this point B lymphocytes need help to carry the immune response further. Alone they cannot proliferate and express their full genetic potential for antibody structure. T lymphocytes, themselves alerted to "foreign" and activated, bring help and control to the B lymphocytes.

Cellular "help," a very sophisticated mechanism for stimulating and controlling B lymphocytes, depends upon the oldest of cellular immune mechanisms, phagocytosis. The helper T lymphocytes are alerted to "foreign" by fragments of antigen displayed in the MHC molecules of macrophages, one of the phagocytes.

Resting T lymphocytes dock at a phagocyte through their receptors for "self" MHC and "foreign" peptide. Though the first step in the docking is antigen-specific, all subsequent steps are quite general.

The adhesion between the T lymphocyte and the phagocyte is strengthened by adhesions between other molecules on the cells' surfaces. Some of these adhesion molecules are also members of the immunoglobulin nation. They carry on the oldest business of the nation, adhering like to like on the surface of the opposing cell.

Activation of a T lymphocyte, like its adhesion, is mediated by very general stimuli. One of the most important of these is the growth factor IL-1, the factor that we first meet in innate immunity as a very general growth factor and signal. When delivered to a T lymphocyte, IL-1 pushes the cell to further growth and differentiation. Some of the differentiated cells will spend their lives as helpers of B lymphocytes.

Alerted and activated T lymphocytes find B lymphocytes engaged with antigen but unable to proliferate without a second signal. B lymphocytes and T lymphocytes adhere to one another, first using antigen-specific receptors and MHC molecules, and then using general adhesion receptors, mainly molecules of the immunoglobulin nation. Once in good contact with the B lymphocyte, the helper T lymphocyte delivers chemical signals that are enough to push the B lymphocyte to multiplication, maturation, and production of more antibody.

Though B lymphocytes are not professional phagocytes like macrophages, they do ingest, digest, and display fragments of the antigen bound by their surface antibody. This allows T lymphocytes to engage them through the receptor for "self" MHC plus "foreign" peptide, the same receptor that is used to engage macrophages.

The immune response to infection grows as the first antibodies to be released bind antigen and fix complement. Phagocytic cells have surface receptors for antibody and complement molecules. Their phagocytosis of antibody-coated antigen is much more efficient than phagocytosis of naked antigen. Therefore, the more antibody binds antigen, the more efficiently it is taken up by phagocytes and the more phagocytes display complexes of MHC and "foreign."

The increased display of MHC plus "foreign" in turn increases the number of T lymphocytes that are activated, and the increase in T lymphocytes increases the number of B lymphocytes driven to continue antibody production. The immune response feeds on itself and grows.

Phagocytosis leads to more antibody production. More antibodies lead to more phagocytosis. But the B lymphocyte population does not expand forever. B lymphocytes need antigen and help to continue their proliferation, and as the levels of antibody increase, the amount of remaining "foreign" decreases. Clones of B lymphocytes whose antibody binds weakly to the antigen are no longer stimulated and die out. Clones that make high-affinity antibody that binds well take advantage of the situation and expand even more.

The types, as well as the affinities, of antibodies change with time. As the response progresses, IgM disappears; it has served its function of making lots of complexes with antigen and delivering these to phagocytes. High concentrations of IgG and IgA appear and persist in the blood and tissue fluids for long periods.

The genetics of an antibody response

Like the early rise in response to infection, the maturation of the immune response in affinity and diversity of antibodies appears to be a Lamarckian adaptation of an individual to a changed environment. The maturation is actually due to Darwinian selection of cells in a population.

The two sorts of evolutionary responses, Lamarckian and Darwinian, imply two different sorts of genetic material—"soft," or influenced by environment, and "hard." It is the triumph of Darwinism to show how selection of existing variations in a "hard" heredity leads to changes that adapt a population to change in its environment. These changes come about at a cost to the population of the loss of some genes, in that individuals carrying them die before reproducing. The growth of antibody-producing cells depends upon the selection of some cells for growth. Antigen that binds to their surface Ig is the selective agent.

The selection and changes in the population are unlike Darwinian selection in three important ways. First, no one clone grows to take over the entire population. Second, the cells not selected for growth do not die. They persist for weeks, if not months, ready to divide if a new challenge appears. Third, the immunoglobulin genes of stimulated cells are in a sense "soft." Immunoglobulin genes in a growing, dividing B lymphocyte are rearranged and mutated in response to signals from antigen and from T lymphocyte helper cells.

Complete genes for immunoglobulin chains are constructed from a series of small genes. One of these small genes, itself assembled from a few even smaller genes, codes for the manufacture of just the binding site of the antibody. The first complete immunoglobulin heavy chain made in a B lymphocyte is spliced together from the small gene for the binding region and an adjacent small gene that codes for the stem region of an IgM.

The assembled IgM gene codes for the antibody displayed on the surface of the B lymphocyte. It is the only gene assembled until that surface antibody binds antigen and the B lymphocyte is signaled to grow and multiply. Once the cell is stimulated, it rearranges its genes again, cutting the gene for the binding site away from the small gene for IgM and joining it to one of the other genes for an antibody stem—IgG, IgA, or IgE. When a particular stem gene is chosen, all the others that lie between it and the gene for the binding site are cut away and destroyed. The B lymphocyte differentiates by devouring parts of its own chromosome.

The cutting and pasting to make genes for new kinds of antibody is directed both by the presence of antigen at the cell's surface and by growth factors emitted from T lymphocytes as part of their help to B lymphocytes. In a way that is not yet understood, these growth factors not only signal the B lymphocyte to grow, they also direct it to cut away a certain amount of the genome so that it produces just one IgG or IgA. At this level of resolution, it does appear that genes of a growing, dividing B lymphocyte are modified by its environment.

A second "softness" in immunoglobulin heredity shows up in the small gene for its binding site. Unlike almost all other genes in a somatic cell, this gene mutates in the course of cell division. Though some of the mutations wreck the immunoglobulin gene, others change the binding site so that it binds better to the antigen that originally stimulated the B lymphocyte. The tendency to mutations (though not the mutations themselves) is a direct response by a B lymphocyte to a changed environment.

The end of the response and its aftermath

The dance of the lymphocytes subsides as the microbe that provoked the dance is dealt with by antibodies, phagocytes, granulocytes, and complement. The dance leaves the body with memories of the infecting microbe. These memories are more concrete and substantial than most. They take the form of cells that have been changed from their primitive state to a state of readiness to respond to subsequent infections.

Most B lymphocytes, when stimulated by antigen and helper signals, rush through their life's course of rearranging and mutating the genes that code for their antibodies. At their peak, such cells commit all of their resources and energies to pouring antibodies into the blood and lymph. They become plasma cells swollen with the machinery of protein synthesis and with stores of antibody about to be released. After a few days to a week in this state, they die.

Not all cells in a single clone of B lymphocytes follow the route to plasma cellhood. If they did, B lymphocytes would be ignorant of history and their immune response would have no memory. Each new generation of B lymphocytes would respond and adapt to every microbe in the same way. Immune responses to repeated infections by the same kind of microbe would be no different from the response to the first infection by that microbe.

41

B lymphocytes do preserve their history and keep their memory of earlier infections. A clone of antibody-producing cells is founded by a single B lymphocyte making antibody with one particular kind of binding site for "foreign." Many descendants of this cell, each making the same antibody as the founder (though perhaps with slight improvements introduced by mutation), stop in the course of their development and maturation. They remain committed to responding to antigens of the microbe that stimulated their fellow cells, but they do not respond again until a fresh infection occurs.

The response that follows reinfection is faster and larger than the first response, because there are more cells ready to respond than there were before the initial infection. This is why one exposure to a disease, or a deliberate immunization against it, protects an individual from later reinfection. The first exposure to the disease primes the immune system and raises it to a state of readiness that can be maintained for years. This heightened readiness effectively stops infections before they can take hold.

How to deal with viruses

Viruses reproduce inside of host cells and may even spread from cell to cell without ever getting out into the body fluids. Once a virus is inside a cell, it cannot be killed by antibodies.

Though the viruses inside a cell are safe from antibodies and phagocytes, they cannot hide from T lymphocytes. Inevitably some fragments of viral proteins are wrapped up in "self" MHC molecules and brought to the surface of an infected cell. These hints of "foreign" within are detected by the receptors on cousins of helper T lymphocytes. These sinister cousins, *effector T lymphocytes,* may be better termed killer T lymphocytes. They read the surfaces of infected or foreign cells directly and respond to the readings by killing the foreigner.

Effector T lymphocytes dock with their targets by fixing their antigen-specific receptors to the complexes of "self" MHC and "foreign" on the surface of the infected cell. Adhesion by the receptors is just enough to hold the cells together, but not enough to keep them together for the final attack. Other surface molecules on the effector cell also bind to the surface of the cell, and this strengthens the hold of the effector on its target.

The adhesion receptors are themselves members of the immunoglobulin nation. They bind to the outside of an MHC molecule at a place on its immunoglobulin-like region. Thus in this most sophisticated cell interaction, they function in the ancient manner of the immunoglobulin nation by sticking like to like, immunoglobulin domain to immunoglobulin domain.

Once an effector cell is firmly anchored to its target, it rearranges its cytoplasm so that any protein secreted by it is poured directly onto the surface of the target instead of being secreted at the side of the cell opposite the target and so wasted. This intimacy is similar to the intimacy achieved in T lymphocyte help of B lymphocytes, but here it is fatal rather than helpful.

Adherent effector cells use both direct attack and propaganda to kill. Some effectors punch holes in the membranes of target cells. These holes are made by packets of complement-like proteins stored in granules in the cytoplasm of the attacking cell. Other effectors seem to persuade the target cell to commit suicide, apparently by turning on enzymes that destroy the target's DNA.

However the trick is done, the lethal attack by an effector cell on a target is not specific. Both complement-like proteins and propaganda can destroy any cell to which they are turned. The specificity of cell killing is achieved by the targeting of the effector cell through its receptors for "self" MHC plus peptide.

Though they never make or release antibody, effector T lymphocytes follow the same sort of dance as B lymphocytes. An effector needs to be helped by its cousin, a helper T lymphocyte. The helper delivers signals of lymphokines and other stimuli to move immature killer cells to maturity and full function.

Helper and effector T lymphocyte clones spawn long-lived memory cells as well as short-lived killers. Though we know little about the states and lifetimes of the memory T lymphocytes, we do know that they lie dormant for long periods and come awake to dance again when an infection returns. The dancers may join and help memory B lymphocytes to higher levels of antibody production, or they may act on their own to eliminate the infection.

Why not attack "self"?

The molecules binding and damaging "foreign" antibodies and T lymphocyte receptors are coded for and made independently of "foreign." The exuberant variation of their binding regions is created by random and imprecise couplings of small genes, and by mutations in these genes. These genetic mechanisms can create more than ten million different bindings for antibodies or T lymphocyte receptors. The probability is high that some of these variations will yield antibodies and receptors that bind to "self" instead of to "foreign." This is particularly likely for T lymphocyte receptors, since these detect subtle changes in the shape of a "self" molecule.

Antibodies and receptors against "self" could subvert and destroy their begetter from within instead of defending it from attacks from without. Though a rare mistake is made, for the most part anti-"self" is rigorously removed from lymphocyte populations by a process that is termed "education" but is more like combat training with live ammunition.

The training of both T and B lymphocytes is possible because these cells, like people, begin life as immature, undeveloped individuals that only gradually express their potential. The developing cells are tested by "self" antigens at different stages of their lives, and in slightly different ways. If a cell expresses a receptor for "foreign" antigen, it passes the test and continues to mature and prepare for its next test. If a cell expresses a receptor that can bind "self," it fails the test and is consigned either to death or to life as a hermit.

The frequency of lymphocytes that can react with "self," and the stringency of selection against them, is suggested from the observation that 90% of all developing T or B lymphocytes die before they are mature enough to leave the tissues in which they develop and enter the general circulation. Some of these cells die because they fail to arrange their collections of small, incomplete genes into anything that looks like a complete immunoglobulin gene or a T lymphocyte receptor gene; but many other cells die because they have successfully constructed a complete gene, and that gene codes for a cell surface protein that reacts against "self."

Some growing cells, the clever but thuggish teenagers of the population, manage to smuggle anti-"self" receptors out of their school and into circulation. Like some teenagers, they have not thought about the future and do not quite know what faces them. They find that even in circulation, anti-"self" cannot be turned against cells of the body. Instead, contact with the antigens of "self" at an almost-mature stage paralyzes a T or B lymphocyte so that it can never again respond to antigen. The mature paralyzed cell may live for many years. (We know this because such cells can be evoked experimentally.) Thus, a cell that has escaped the first test of its schooling condemns itself to life in solitude when it fails its second test against "self." Failure of this test locks the genes of the cell so that it can never again divide and found a clone of immune cells.

Other T lymphocytes that have slipped past the first test for reaction with "self" find themselves changing sides when tested a second time. Instead of turning off and becoming solitary, these T lymphocytes become policemen for anti-"self." They thwart and suppress the responses of other cells that recognize and could respond to "self." We do not know how the policing T lymphocytes act to prevent an anti-"self" response, but we do know that violent bouts of "self"-destructive immunity break out if the T lymphocyte police let down their guard.

The adaptive immune response that we have described is the response of populations of lymphocytes to stimulation by "foreign." The response is adaptive and specific for a particular foreign invader. Adaptation and specificity are achieved, not by molding molecules or cells to a pattern dictated by "foreign," but by selecting cells that can bind "foreign" from a large population of variants and then stimulating these cells to multiply and reproduce their kind.

Though there is enormous variety and abundance of antigen-specific T and B lymphocytes, surface receptors, and serum antibodies, these rarely react against "self." The price of this internal peace is a very high rate of cell death during the development and maturation of the populations of lymphocytes that respond to "foreign."

All adaptive and specific immune response depends heavily upon nonadaptive, very general, and nonspecific cell functions for its workings. The two most important functions are cell-to-cell adhesion, and phagocytosis. The first of these is as old as multicellular animals. The second is even older, for it is the feeding mechanism of single-celled organisms like amoebae.

Cell adhesion dominates the transactions between cells, whether they be antigen presentation, stimulation of B lymphocytes by helper T lymphocytes, or killing of infected "self" by effector T lymphocytes. Phagocytosis looms even larger than cell adhesion. The cellular intake and degradation of "foreign" first helps to clear it from the body, then advertises its presence to T lymphocytes and, as an antibody response mounts, again works to clear "foreign." The oldest, broad, cellular response to "foreign" is central to the newest, sharp response. Evolution has not discarded the responses of innate immunity but instead has built specific responses on its rough-hewn foundation.

So far, we have looked at immune responses from the point of view of "self." "Foreign" is an invader, something to be rejected and pushed out or destroyed before it can take hold and usurp resources of food and cells. However, it is good to look at infection from the point of view of "foreign" as well as from that of "self." The altered perspective sharpens our sense of the biology of invasion and might even gain some sympathy for the problems of being "foreign."

A microbe and its host are like two people pushing against opposite sides of a half-open door. The two can remain in more or less stable equilibrium for a long time. If one overpowers the other, the door swings fully open or fully shut, and there can be serious consequences for one or both of those pushing.

The protective immune responses of "self" usually shut the door quite effectively. There are many microbes that never get any foothold in "self," but not for want of trying. Rare and strange microbes infect people and animals whose "self"-protection is damaged by drugs or ir-radiation, or because of rare genetic conditions that destroy all of the T or B lymphocytes. When these microbes do take hold, they often grow exuberantly and kill their host. They have pushed the door wide open.

An infecting microbe that can push open the door to "self" goes tumbling through to oblivion. Exuberant growth kills the host, and the microbe is left without food, shelter, or means of transmission of its progeny to fresh fields. The microbes that usually infect us push the door partway open, interfering with or outmaneuvering immune responses, but never quite overwhelming "self."

Rapid growth is the first line of attack on the immune responses of "self." Viruses and bacteria can multiply much faster than can cells of the immune system. Thousands of bacteria and tens of thousands of viruses can be reproduced in the time that it takes for one lymphocyte to produce two daughter cells. Up to a point, an infection can outrun a specific response. A newly landed microbe is only contained by the diligence of phagocytes working unaided by antibody.

The advantages of rapid reproduction are lost when a microbe makes a second try at infecting an individual. The memory in the immune system quickly brings out abundant lymphocytes and antibodies. These add their weight to that of the phagocytes and the door slams shut.

Memories can be cheated by changes in the appearance of a microbe. Viruses are particularly good at this. As they spread through a population they alter their genes so that their population gradually acquires different antigens from its ancestors. This allows a virus to reinfect a previously infected host several times without provoking memories of earlier infections. Each wave of virus appears new and different to the immune system, and only a primary response is mounted. That is at least one of the reasons why colds drag on for weeks and weeks, beyond all reasonable limits.

If an immune response is slow off the starting mark, or if it cannot quickly eliminate a microbe, the invader may change its surface in a single host. Viruses can do this because their population always contains some accidental genetic variants that can resist host immunity. These variants grow until they too are recognized as "foreign" and destroyed. Meanwhile, another generation of variants may appear, and these in turn must be dealt with by the cadres of lymphocytes.

Much larger invaders, even those that grow as slowly as their hosts' cells, also evade or blunt immune responses by changing their antigens and forcing the host to start all over again with a primary immune response.

Populations of trypanosomes—protozoan parasites—are genetically programmed to change their surface antigens. After infection, host antibodies select against trypanosomes with standard surface antigens, say antigens one and two. A few of the trypanosomes in the body have already gone on to make antigens three and four, losing antigens one and two in the process. The variant antigens are rare, and so they have not stimulated many cells of the immune system. This allows the variant cells to build a new population of invaders. By the time the host is immune to antigens three and four, variants arise expressing antigens five and six. This progression goes on as long as the infection goes on. The trypanosomes have some genetic tricks for never going back to the antigens they have expressed earlier.

Other protozoa use sex and genetic recombination to multiply the variants of their surface proteins. Though slower than the antigenic changes of trypanosomes and certainly slower than those of viruses, changes in the course of sexual reproduction increase the chances of the parasite successfully infecting a host that has not encountered these antigens.

Bacteria often do not use sex and genetics to defeat or depress the immune system. They use poison instead. Many bacteria secrete chemicals that poison cells, interfere with cell signaling, or block the production of some molecule specifically required for an immune response. Some viruses also take this tack.

One group of viruses has the skill to shut off just the production of MHC molecules. Cells without surface MHC molecules cannot alert lymphocytes to their infection. Larger microbes, for example the protozoa that cause malaria, play a variation on this theme. They spend part of their lives in erythrocytes, which are poor in MHC molecules and so provide a quiet, unadvertised, and unnoticed retreat for the malaria parasite.

A look at practice

Practical, applied immunology has a far older history than does basic, experimental immunology. Just as steam engines were built before there ever was a science of thermodynamics, so immunization prevented disease long before antibodies were ever imagined.

The earliest branch of practical immunology was deliberate inoculation with infectious matter, which caused a mild disease that left the patient immune to further attacks. The most celebrated inoculation was for smallpox. Crusts and scabs from the pocks were inhaled or scratched into the skin. Infection in this way usually caused a mild disease that immunized against smallpox for life.

A happy accident mimics some antigens of smallpox in the surface proteins of a related pox virus that infects and pockmarks cows. Though he knew nothing of viruses or lymphocytes, Edward Jenner realized that humans infected by touching the blistered pocks of infected cows were never seriously ill with cowpox and were ever after immune to smallpox. His insight led to the inoculation of cowpox instead of small-pox and gave a name to all such methods, *vaccination* (from the Latin, *vaca,* meaning "cow").

Today vaccination, the oldest form of practical immunology, has been joined by many other applications. Organ and tissue transplantation, immune attacks on cancer, and the treatment of depressed immune responses are all practical, though sometimes fledgling, branches of immunology. Though progress in these areas has been uneven, there would be little progress in any of them without our knowledge of basic immunology. I will conclude this essay with some brief comments about applied immunology and something about the way it promises to develop.

All vaccines are meant to achieve the same goal, protection from disease, by stimulating an immune response to some part of the microbe or other agent that causes the disease. There are many more problems in the way of achieving the goal. These problems are social and political as well as scientific and technical. The problems, like the goal, are common to all vaccines.

The scientific and technical problems of vaccine production involve identifying the disease-causing microbe, making biologically harmless antigens from it, and packaging these antigens in a form that will stimulate the immune systems of most or all people vaccinated.

The cowpox vaccine against smallpox is an instance in which nature has packaged the antigens into an especially good form, a whole virus. Cowpox is not harmful to humans and grows for a time after injection of live virus. This multiplies the amount of antigen that is delivered to the immune system. The increase in antigen ensures a thorough activation of the lymphocytes and production of lots of memory cells as well. One cowpox vaccination protects against smallpox for a lifetime.

Though no other virus is as convenient as cowpox, other viruses can be trained to replicate without causing disease. The virus used in the Sabin polio vaccine is one such trained virus. It replicates itself in humans but does not invade the nervous system. There are antigens shared by all polio viruses, so the immune response against the tamed virus also protects against infection and damage by wild viruses.

Many viruses and all bacteria are untamable. No living form of these microbes can be given as a vaccine without running real risks of disease. Instead, the microbes are killed by one means or another, and the killed microbes or molecules separated from them are used to vaccinate. The immune system deals more efficiently with killed microbes than with live, but immunization with this form of vaccine may be less profound and long-lasting than immunization with a live, replicating organism.

Sometimes having antibodies against only one bacterial protein is enough to stop disease. Bacteria that poison the cells surrounding them release free poison molecules. Vaccines against diphtheria and tetanus are made from harmless forms of the poisons secreted by the diseased bacteria. The antibodies against the poisons are enough to prevent clinical illness.

The technical problems with all of the microbial vaccines are problems of growing enough microbes or cells, purifying the needed molecules or microbes, and preparing a vaccine that immunizes efficiently. Even though they are difficult, these problems all have rational solutions.

Some of the social and political problems of vaccination are soluble by reason and technique. It is possible to make vaccines sturdy enough to be carried and stored without refrigeration. It has been possible to make a vaccination gun that is easier to use and less frightening than a needle and syringe. Once a vaccine for a disease has been devised and tested, it requires only national will and proper organization to vaccinate all those who are at risk for a disease.

Will, planning, and reason accomplish much, but there are other social problems that feed on unreason, rumor, fear, and selfishness. These problems are harder to solve and require more effort than the solution of the problems of vaccine construction and delivery. There are two main social problems of vaccination, which are problems in different parts of society.

The first problem is rejection or neglect of people who most need the vaccination. This is a problem of perception and sympathy, but it ought to have a rational solution. The more individuals that are healthy in a society, the less the society will be burdened by the costs of health care and the disruption of otherwise productive lives. Though neglect may not be benign, it can be confronted. Changes in government policy can greatly extend vaccination programs and protect all citizens.

The second social and political problem of vaccination is the misperception of the dangers of vaccines, and the inflation of these dangers so that they appear to outweigh the benefits of protection from disease. This is very much a matter of individual people making decisions with little information and a lot of fear.

Vaccination always carries a slight risk, because there are always unknown factors in the process. Though the vaccine is thoroughly tested and as pure as possible, the people who are to be vaccinated are an uncontrolled lot, varying in their genetic makeup, their health, and the quality of their immune systems. This means that every so often vaccination brings on an unpleasant reaction. The reaction may be as mild as an itchy rash that goes away in a short time, or as severe as a high fever, or even convulsions.

The acceptance of a vaccine can turn on just how often side effects seem to occur and how threatening they seem to be. If reactions are thought to be common or serious, then people who should be vaccinated, or whose children should be vaccinated, ignore the benefits of protection from infection. Instead of worrying about a disease itself, they concentrate their worries on the possible bad effects of the vaccine.

The use, protective effects, and side effects of two different vaccines point up the differences in public acceptance of vaccination. One vaccine, smallpox, rarely causes unexpected reactions in injected people. In one series of 1.5 million vaccinations, there were fourteen severe reactions to the vaccine and there was one death that might have been due to vaccination.

The 1.5 million vaccinated people were protected from a disease that kills 10–30% of all infected people and leaves the rest scarred for life. This is probably the best ratio of benefit to risk of any vaccine. This high ratio of benefit certainly helped the acceptance of smallpox vaccination in this country. Acceptance was also helped by attitudes toward medicine and science in the period when smallpox vaccination was almost universal in the United States, the 1950s and 1960s. Today, views of self and of medicine and science have changed. Medicine is expected to deliver perfect care, and natural science is feared as an agent of change and the unnatural. In this climate, there is a continuing discussion about the risks of using cowpox virus in the construction of other vaccines.

Another vaccine, which protects against whooping cough, is not well accepted today. The vaccine is made from whole killed pertussis bacteria. This crude vaccine immunizes effectively, but about half the infants given the vaccine have some kind of reaction to it. The reaction is usually a rash or a mild fever, lasting about a day. However, there are rare serious complications that follow pertussis vaccination. One child per hundred thousand may have convulsions or other serious illness, and one or two children have died after whooping cough vaccination.

The side effects of pertussis vaccine have been widely publicized in the press and on television. The emphasis of all the publicity has been on anecdotal and emotional responses. It would seem from the stories told that careful, loving parents ought not to have their infants vaccinated against whooping cough, at least not using the present vaccine. These parents look to present danger and not to the future.

Clearly a better whooping cough vaccine is needed, one that is made from purified bacterial proteins, and not from whole bacteria. However, we can learn from epidemics in other countries that many more children die of whooping cough than are ever threatened by reactions to the vaccine.

Two countries, Great Britain and Japan, had epidemics of whooping cough after parents stopped having their children vaccinated against it. By 1973, 80% of British infants were vaccinated shortly after birth and there were at most a few thousand cases of whooping cough reported each year. Because of scare stories, by 1978 only 30% of infants were immunized to whooping cough. A few years later these unvaccinated children began going to day-care centers and kindergarten, sharing and swapping microbes with all of their playmates. Epidemic whooping cough returned to Britain. There were 30,000 cases and twelve deaths in a year.

Japan had the same experience. Parents stopped having their children vaccinated after publicity about the deaths of two infants; these were supposedly due to the vaccine. By 1975 less than 25% of infants were vaccinated. Four years later, when the unvaccinated children began going to school, there were 13,000 cases of whooping cough in a year and 41 deaths. It took several years to stop the epidemic.

To me, both sets of numbers from these two countries say "Yes, vaccinate," even though the heart may say "No."

The future of vaccines

There are many vaccines to come. Some are nearly with us, some are just ideas. Wide use of any of them will depend upon planning and policy as much as on the science that goes into them. This essay is not the place, nor am I the person, to talk about public health policies, but I would like to give you some idea about the problems that have to be solved and that limit the creation of any new vaccine.

There is an old recipe for turtle soup that begins "First, catch a turtle and lead it home." This is also the way to begin construction of a new vaccine—first, identify a molecule of the microbe or parasite of interest that is so efficiently recognized as "foreign" that an immune response to it alone can stop an infection.

Finding the right molecule is harder than we would like because of the abundant varieties of structures, especially in viruses and protozoan parasites. Recall that structural variants—mutants—are common in all populations of viruses, and that immunity against one just gives a different one the chance to take over. There are virus molecules whose structure never varies; for example, the molecules that the viruses use to attach their receptor proteins to cells. Even these molecules may not be useful for vaccine production. The invariant protein used by one cold virus to bind to cells is hidden in pits on the virus surface. The diameter of a pit is so small that an antibody molecule cannot reach inside to bind the receptor protein. This arrangement is probably used by many other viruses. They keep their most sensitive spots well hidden.

The search for suitable vaccine molecules of protozoa and multicellular parasites is even more difficult than the search for these molecules in viruses. Most of the parasites have complicated life cycles during which the invaders take on different forms, live in different cells of the body, or even in different hosts. The molecules that could be targets for immunity change at each step of the parasite life cycle, and it is not at all clear which one should be used for vaccination.

51

Once a good antigen has been found, it must be packaged so that it will stimulate a strong immune response, production of lots of antibody, and many immune cells. Strong responses require T lymphocyte help for B lymphocytes producing antibody and for effector T lymphocytes responding to virus infection. One bacterial vaccine has been greatly improved by attaching molecules of the complex sugars in the bacterial cell wall to molecules of proteins from other bacteria. The cell wall sugars alone do not stimulate T lymphocytes, and infants do not make much antibody when they are only immunized with the sugars. The protein from the other bacterium does stimulate T lymphocytes. Joined together, the two molecules provoke a strong and thorough response to the sugars and so protect from infection by a microbe that is the leading cause of meningitis in children under five.

Another approach to packaging vaccine antigens goes back to Jenner's virus, vaccinia. The DNA of this virus can be engineered to include a gene for a protein from a different virus. The altered virus bears the protein coded by the foreign gene and so delivers a new foreign antigen to the person or animal vaccinated. This packaging has even been used to vaccinate wild foxes against rabies. A vaccinia virus with one harmless protein of rabies virus on its surface can spread through a whole group of foxes and immunize them against the whole, harmful rabies virus.

This sketch should show that there are problems in developing and testing new vaccines, problems that start in the laboratory but lead to much larger problems in society and politics. There are likely to be many new vaccines brought out through testing in the next few years. It remains to be seen how many of them will actually be used. Successful use of any one of the vaccines under development against infectious bacteria, malaria parasites, rabies, or human immunodeficiency virus will change the lives of millions of people for the better.

Tissue and organ grafts

Failed grafts and even successful grafts plagued seventeenth-century medicine. Besides the account of the Tagliacotian nose and its rejection, we have stories of early blood transfusions that promised a good deal:

> Here Dr. Croone told me, that, at the meeting at Gresham College
> to-night . . . there was a pretty experiment of the blood of one dogg let
> out, till he died, into the body of another. . . . This did give occasion
> to many pretty wishes, as of the blood of a Quaker to be let into an
> Archbishop, and such like; but, as Dr. Croone says, may, if it takes,
> be of mighty use to man's health, for the ammending of bad blood by
> borrowing from a better body. [4]

As it turns out, transfusion proved dangerous if not fatal. Blood transfusion was formally banned in France and does not seem to have been much practiced elsewhere.

In another case in the seventeenth century, a graft of calf bone was used to repair the hole in the head of a wounded soldier. The bone itself was not rejected and the wound was repaired. Unfortunately for the soldier, the Church objected to this unnatural graft and ordered the bone removed. It was replaced with a silver plate.

Despite the setbacks and difficulties of transplantation, the technique was used in the eighteenth century in an attempt to replace lost teeth with the real thing instead of with painful artificial teeth. These grafts were no more successful than earlier tissue grafts. Though one of the experimenters, John Hunter, managed to graft the spur of a cock to its comb, he did nothing to help the progress of transplantation or dentistry.

Tissue grafting and blood transfusion have revived and flourished in this century. Once the genetics and immunology of red blood cell antigens were understood, in the 1920s and 1930s, blood became safe and was commonly used.

Tissue transplantation between individuals, especially skin transplantation, revived without the benefit of any knowledge of the genetics or the immunology of graft rejection. Though they were always rejected, skin grafts proved to be useful in treating burned patients whose own skin could not be used to cover the burns.

Experiments with mice showed that genetics was important to the fate of a tissue graft but did not identify an MHC. The genetics of human tissue and organ grafting were not worked out until the 1960s and 1970s. Surgeons forced the pace of this work, transplanting kidneys to unrelated recipients whose immune responses were depressed by irradiation or by treatment with drugs.

Once the human MHC was defined, donor organs could be typed and matched with the most nearly identical recipient. Matching MHC of kidney donor and recipient prevents the recipient's T lymphocytes from destroying the graft. They see its surface molecules as "self," not as "foreign."

Some graft antigens are hard to detect and match, and though these are not major histocompatibility complex factors, they do provoke slow and steady host immune responses that lead to the destruction of the grafted kidney. Slow rejections can be prevented by using drugs that act like radiation and block the multiplication of immune cells, together with steroids that inhibit the activity of immune lymphocytes.

The better the match of donor and recipient MHC, the lower the dose of drugs needed to prevent rejection, and the better the chances of graft function and long-term survival. At present, 95% of all grafts matched to their recipients for all eight MHC antigens survive indefinitely with little or no need for drug treatment, and even 75% of grafts that are mismatched to the recipient in two of the eight antigens survive and function for a long term.

Even modestly imperfect matches of graft and donor MHC are uncommon. Very often a surgeon had to make do by transplanting an MHC-incompatible organ that would ordinarily be rejected. Rejection was only prevented by large doses of drugs or radiation. This treatment interfered with all of the immune system and with other dividing cells as well. It made patients very ill and threatened them with death from bacterial infection.

In the late 1970s a new drug was found, a small peptide isolated from a fungus, that is specific for T lymphocytes and has little effect on other dividing cells. This peptide called *cyclosporin A* appears to interfere with signaling between activated T lymphocytes after they meet antigens for the first time. With their signals confused or blocked, the T lymphocytes reacting against the foreign organ graft fail to divide and do not attack the graft.

Cyclosporin A has little effect on memory T lymphocytes. It does not interfere much with protection against bacterial or viral infection, since most of the microbes that infect transplant patients are common organisms that are known to the immune system. There are some side effects of cyclosporin A. One important one, ironically, is kidney damage.

The benefits of cyclosporin A have been far greater than the damage due to its side effects. The drug has opened a whole new world of possibilities for successful organ transplantation. The problems in this world go beyond science and medicine to problems of society's choices about medical treatment and the use of scarce resources, problems that are part of a larger set of questions about modern health care, problems beyond the scope of this essay.

Cancer immunology—"self" gone wrong

Cancer cells are "self" in rebellion. We can only expect to create a useful cancer immunology if the rebels fly their own special flag— antigens that are recognizable in cancer cells but not in normal tissue.

The difficulties of discovering the cancer flag, and of devising ways to immunize against it, are even greater than the difficulties of finding antigens for vaccines against parasites. At least it is known that infected people make immune responses to parasites. It is clear that lymphocytes respond to tumor cells in laboratory culture dishes. On the other hand, the evidence that people mount immune responses against their own cancers is often subjective or very general. Because of this, the field of cancer immunology has had a slow growth, with as many troughs of confusion and despair as peaks of insight.

Two very general pieces of evidence that cancers provoke immune responses came from clinical observations. The first is that cancers are more common in people whose immune responses are damaged and depressed than in people whose immune responses are functioning well.

One group of people with depressed immune systems are transplant patients who have been treated in the old way with drugs that interfere with the immune system generally. The other large group are people infected with HIV who have AIDS. People in both groups seem to have more of certain cancers than people whose immune responses have not been depressed, but no clear cause-and-effect relationship has been shown.

Other evidence of immune responses to common human cancers is the observation that the cells of many cancers—of bowel, breast, or lung—are surrounded by collections of lymphocytes that look like activated cells of the immune system. This (like the statistics on cancer frequency in certain patients) gives only a correlation between immune activity and cancer.

The way to an immunological treatment of cancer passes from observations and statistics to the laboratory bench and then back to the patient. It can be shown that lymphocytes taken from a patient's own tumor, or from nearby lymph nodes, can kill the patient's cancer cells when mixed with these cells in a dish. The killing is specific, a hallmark of an immune response, and is mounted by T lymphocytes.

Killing of tumor cells in the culture dish is not complete, and cancer-killing lymphocytes cannot be found in every patient. Still, the experiments show that immune cells are responding to a tumor, recognizing cancer cells as "changed" or not-"self." The problem is to learn why these cells do not manage to kill all of the cancer cells in a patient.

One reason why killer cells cannot dispose of cancer cells may be simply that many cancers are treated by radiation or by drugs that block cell division. The drugs slow or stop the growth of the cancer cells, but they also interfere with immune cells. There may not be enough immune effector cells to deal with all of the cancer cells in a cancer patient.

Though tumors do not always yield killer T lymphocytes, they do yield homing lymphocytes that can find their way back to the cancer cells from wherever they are injected. The homing lymphocytes are now being used in several novel immunological treatments of cancer.

One use of the homing cells assumes that some of them can kill cancer cells, but that more killers are needed to destroy the tumor completely. These additional cells are obtained by removing lymphocytes from a piece of the tumor and growing the lymphocytes in a culture dish loaded with chemical signals for cell division and activation. After weeks of aggressive growth, the cells, greatly increased in number, are injected back into the patient. Many of them return to the place of their ancestors, in and around the mass of cancer cells. The descendants of the first cells to infiltrate the tumor go to work on the cancer cells, and reduction or disappearance of the cancer has been seen in a number of patients.

A second treatment has been devised that only requires that the lymphocytes recognize the cancer cells. The lymphocytes are multiplied outside the body as in the other treatment. A gene for a tumor toxin is also installed in the cells, so they produce this toxin.

We can expect that the toxin-producing cells will use immune receptors to find their way back to the tumor. Once they find the tumor, the toxins produced by the lymphocytes will kill the tumor cells, even if the lymphocytes are not able to kill with their own native toxins. Genetic engineering and immunology have combined to reproduce one of nature's oldest immune effectors, a cell that binds its target through specific receptors for antigen and then delivers an unspecific signal directly to the surface of the target cell.

Immune failure—human immunodeficiency virus and AIDS

Most viruses dodge and kick their way through the immune response. The viruses are out to gain time to reproduce and spread. Their dodges and kicks make a little room and help them to gain a little more time, without overwhelming or destroying immune responses.

One group of closely-related viruses does destroy immune responses. These human immunodeficiency viruses (HIVs) find homes in immune cells, and their housekeeping cripples immune responses to a whole world of "foreign" and "changed."

HIV settles in the oldest parts of the immune response, macrophages and other phagocytic cells, and in one of the newest parts, helper T lymphocytes. Once established, the virus replicates and slowly spreads from cell to cell. After a time, adventurous variants of HIV often appear, and these spread out to settle in the brain, the colon, and other tissues.

The virus, from its point of view, has found the ideal home and an ideal way of life. It has plenty of living space; its host lives for many years after infection, giving the virus a chance to spread itself more; and it avoids immune destruction.

Antibodies are made after HIV infection. (The presence of these antibodies in the blood is used as a first test for infection.) Unfortunately, HIV is not destroyed by the antibodies, probably because once it is established it never leaves the shelter of a cell and so is never caught by antibodies in the blood.

Macrophages seem to manage well even though they are infected, but helper T lymphocytes gradually disappear in the months and years after infection. It is not known if infected T lymphocytes are destroyed by the virus itself, or if the infected cells look like "foreign" and are destroyed by their own cousins, the effector (killer) T lymphocytes.

However it happens, the number of helper T lymphocytes grows smaller and smaller. By the time that it is down to about one-sixth of the normal number, perhaps years after infection, the immune system is in a bad way. Without help from T lymphocytes the body can no longer protect itself from invasion by bacteria, common viruses, fungi, and protozoa. One or more of these can take hold, spread fiercely, and threaten life.

Loss of T lymphocyte help also allows some "self" cells to go out of control. Rare tumors appear that are seldom seen except in people with AIDS. T lymphocytes policing "change" evidently can no longer do their work. B lymphocytes also go out of control. Some shirk any response. Others produce lots of antibodies against "self" instead of "foreign." Both of these odd and "self"-damaging responses reflect the failure of the supervision of B lymphocytes by T lymphocytes.

AIDS, once established, is fatal. It can be slowed but not stopped. Though drugs and other treatments conceivably may be found that can stop established disease, it would be better by far to protect against HIV, instead of trying to root it out after it has become established.

Immunology now shows some promise both in treatment of AIDS and in prevention. Treatment would be helped if we knew why helper T lymphocytes disappear. If this were understood, it might be possible to treat people in the early stages of infection so that their immune responses are reestablished.

Prevention of AIDS could come by way of an effective vaccine. Devising and testing a workable vaccine is difficult for at least three reasons. First, HIV can take many different antigenic forms. Further, we do not know which sort of immune response, that of antibodies or of T lymphocytes, is the best at blocking invasion by HIV. Lastly, HIV is a virus of humans, and it takes some care to devise ethical tests of possible vaccines.

None of these three problems is unique to AIDS. They arise in the development and testing of any vaccine. Many different approaches are being taken to vaccination against AIDS. Some of these involve application of novel genetic engineering to vaccine construction; others use more conventional approaches to the preparation of viral antigens. I expect, and certainly hope, that one or more successful vaccines will appear.

Vaccines take time to test and develop, and more time to apply. Even with great success and luck, it will be years, perhaps a decade, before a safe and effective anti-HIV vaccine can be given to all. The production and distribution of that vaccine will have all of the social and political problems that attend the use of any vaccine.

We have used the image of two contestants pushing on either side of a door to sum up the balance between invading pathogens and the resisting immune system. HIV seems, in this image, to cheat by tripping up its opponent. In fact, HIV has established itself following all of the rules for successful life as a parasite. Though it suppresses resistance to itself by infecting cells of the adaptive immune system, it does not kill its hosts quickly or destroy their populations completely.

The virus is not exceptionally strong. It is mainly transmitted by sexual intercourse, probably through the lymphocytes that are always present in semen, and by blood. Both ways of transmission protect the virus from extremes of temperature or dryness that could destroy it.

It is easy to block transmission of HIV, and we need to think more about new ways to do this. For example, the same detergents that are used in spermicidal contraceptives kill HIV and infected calls very effectively. This way of stopping HIV might be used by many people who avoid using the most widely known anti-HIV devices, condoms. It would be appropriate if immunology could succeed in stopping this disease of the immune system, but meanwhile let us stop the disease by any methods that work.

Like other epidemic microbes, HIV takes hold first and spreads fastest in people who are at the margin of national or world society. The sudden appearance and rapid spread of HIV has followed the course of many earlier disease epidemics. HIV infection and its epidemic spread can be controlled by public health measures that have been used to control other epidemics throughout history.

Resistance to intelligent control comes mainly from the mainstream where the groups most often infected at present are viewed as deviant or outside of society. The statistics of the AIDS epidemic, as well as the histories of earlier epidemics, show that the disease is spreading and will continue to spread to the mainstream. Its slow manifestation masks this spread, so that it is not as evident as the spread of influenza or plague, but its spread is as certain. Unless the public health dimensions of AIDS are recognized politically and acted upon, any and all of the possible vaccines to HIV that may be developed will be ineffective.

Conclusion

Immunology has its origins in medical practice, physiology, and pathology. It began as a science of protection from disease and of the protective activities of serum. Immunology has evolved to a point where we know much of the genetics and cell biology that underlie the protection from disease. We know the molecules that are important, the cells that produce these molecules, and the ways in which these cells dance together to produce a response to "foreign."

We certainly do not know enough. The frustrations in the treatment of AIDS alone show this. The next steps in the development of immunology ought to be those that bring it back from cells and molecules to physiology. These steps are being taken today. They begin to fulfill the reductionist promise that we can not only dissect but can also synthesize anew from the parts. Once again, "activities" are sought in blood and cell culture. Now they can be chemically characterized, engineered, and used to change the physiology of organisms. This promises both a more useful clinical immunology and a more thorough understanding of the basic phenomena of immune responses.

1. G. B. Shaw, *The Doctor's Dilemma*, Act 1 (New York: Brentano's, 1911), p. 28.
2. J. B. van Helmont, *A Ternary of Paradoxes, Of the Magnetic Cure of Wounds . . .* , trans. Walter Charleton (London: J. Flesher for W. Lee, 1650).
3. "Hudibras," Part I, Canto I, lines 279–84 (Oxford: Clarendon Press, 1967).
4. *The Diary of Samuel Pepys*, ed. Henry B. Wheatley (New York: Harcourt, Brace and Co., 1924), pp. 60–61.

Twentieth-Century Dance

Sally Banes

Sally Banes, who received master's and doctorate degrees from New York University, is associate professor of dance and theater history at Cornell University. The author of *Terpsichore in Sneakers: Post-Modern Dance* (1987) and *Democracy's Body: Judson Dance Theater 1962–1964* (1983), she was, from 1980 to 1986, the Performance Art critic for the *Village Voice*, and, from 1982 to 1988, the editor of *Dance Research Journal*. She has written on dance, theater, and performance art for numerous publications, including *Ballet Review, Connoisseur, Dance Chronicle, Dance Magazine, The Drama Review, Performing Arts Journal,* and *Soho Weekly News*.

Professor Banes edited *Footnote to History,* by Si-lan Chen Leyda (1984), and *Soviet Choreographers in the 1920s,* by Elizabeth Souritz (1990), and contributed the chapter on break dancing to *Fresh: Hip Hop Don't Stop* (1985). At present she is writing *Amazing Grace,* a cultural history of 1963, avant-garde performance, and the body.

A recipient of grants from the John Simon Guggenheim Foundation and the American Council of Learned Societies, Professor Banes is also a past president of the Dance Critics Association and currently serves on the National Endowment for the Arts Dance and Interarts panels, the New York State Council on the Arts Dance panel, and the Fulbright Fellowship Dance panel.

In twentieth-century theatrical dancing, certain regularities appear that are quite distinctive. One is the quest for cultural identity through nation and ethnicity. Another is the pursuit of individual identity through inner searches. And a third is the succession of artistic generations through conflict, resulting in a series of artistic revolutions.

Modern theatrical dancing encompasses not only the history of contacts, clashes, and synthesis of various cultures in the New World with the cultural appropriation that is the heritage of nineteenth-century colonialism, but also the expression of particular national identities—what it meant, at a given historical moment, to be "truly" American, Russian, or German. The symbolic use of the body, fundamental to dance, has been a potent means for expressing cultural anxiety and encoding cultural identity. Bodies, borders, and identities seem to have a semiotic link. Moreover, the union of the various arts on the dance stage enhances body symbolism with the meanings lent by music, costume, and decor. That is, in dance there are multiple channels along which the specifics of cultural identity may be expressed.

In their aspiration to break with the academic art of the past, early twentieth-century dance artists, like visual artists and composers, often borrowed forms from folk art, non-Western tribal art, and other traditions outside the academic canon. For visual artists, like Pablo Picasso in his African-inspired works, this often meant eschewing pictorial representation and its associated conventions, like perspective. For composers, like Claude Debussy in his Indonesian-inspired works, this often meant de-emphasizing melody and variation, flattening dynamics, and stressing the percussion and repetition so central to non-Western music.

Contemporary dance, whether on the ballet stage or in the "art dance" of the modern dance stage, made use of successive shifts in the other arts, with newly non-illusionistic sets and musical discoveries; to these it added movements that challenged the Western *danse d'école* with sinuous Oriental lines, folkish angles and energies, and the use of the floor and of unexpected parts of the body. Often what seemed startlingly innovative, unprecedented, and singularly modern in its abstraction to European and American eyes was simply the dislocating introduction of conventions from a different tradition, either from a distant culture or from premodern folk practices in one's own culture.

61

This practice has continued in various ways, ranging from the primitivist nostalgia of the early decades of the century to the stridency of the interwar years, and then to the ironies of postmodernism. The desire to break with one's own academic tradition has often been rhetorically linked with finding a still truer national identity than artists had expressed in the past. But the means to attaining that cultural expression often, paradoxically, has been a search for models and techniques outside of one's own culture. That is, the formation of one's own cultural particularity often has been effected in contrast to the other, and sometimes it is actually framed by appropriating the other.

Much of the earliest twentieth-century modern dance and ballet came out of a drive toward primitivism—an urge that we now see as an essentialist, nostalgic desire to regain a mythical, archaic, communal cohesion. To artists and intellectuals of the time, that prelapsarian state seemed to have been eroding gradually since the rise of capitalism in the Renaissance, and much more violently since the Industrial Revolution. But surely this urge to return to the imagined simplicity of the past was not merely an isolated impulse to retreat from the shocks of modern life. It was partly produced by the economics of a colonial world politics in which the exotic cultures of the non-Western world had themselves become an available modern commodity. The early modern choreographers sought dances that—like the tribal dances they read about or saw imported to Western capitals—were indivisible from music and from social meaning. They yearned for dances that were part of the fabric of spiritual and community life. They sought, in one way or another, to redeem dance: to erase the gap between spectator and performer created by secular theater and to reunite theatrical dancing with vernacular dancing. This was a paradox of modern culture, for it was only by theatrical means that this antitheatrical desire could be expressed.

Fertile experimentation and prodigious activity in modern choreography around the turn of the century reflected the enormous economic expansion in Europe and America during the period 1870–1913. Technological advances and the unprecedented concentration of urban populations created new social forms as well as massive dislocations. In America, increased immigration and urbanization, the settling of the West, and the colonization of Latin America had similar effects. Contacts with colonized cultures revitalized European and American culture even as they undermined the colonized cultures. Those contacts exposed Westerners to different ideas about beauty and art, to different forms of music and dance, and to different ways of viewing and using the human body. In the United States, the conglomeration of different ethnic groups in urban centers brought different bodily practices into conflict but also inspired the synthesis of new dance forms, such as the tap dance that fused African syncopation with Irish step dancing.

The Loïe Fuller Theater at the Paris Universal Exposition of 1900.

The Western view of a civilization becoming prosperous, efficient, and cultivated was dramatized in the series of Great Industrial Exhibitions of the late nineteenth century. They purveyed the latest achievements of a world moving with increasing speed—a world in which divisions of time and space were shrinking—in pavilions organized by nationality or product. Contrasted to the swiftly changing West were the ostensibly static "backward" parts of the world—what we now would call the Third World—represented by picturesque pavilions showing "native pastimes." And the exhibitions also included palaces of fine arts and industry and amusement parks. Thus every aspect of modern culture—including the underbelly of colonized cultures and the split between high and low arts—was represented in the exhibition's miniature model of the contemporary world.

The Paris Universal Exposition of 1900 was not only an important example of such exhibitions. It had a direct effect on the modern arts, for its pavilions—with their visions and sounds of electricity, of democratization, of Russian folk art, of Japanese theater, and in general of foreign music, dance, and crafts of all kinds—stirred the imaginations of artists, composers, poets, and choreographers. Among those who visited the Paris Exposition were the American dancers Isadora Duncan and Ruth St. Denis, the Russian intellectual (and impresario-to-be) Sergey Diaghilev, the French composer Debussy, and the Spanish painter Picasso. The American dancer Loïe Fuller had her own theater at the Exposition, where she performed her phantasmagoric transformation spectacles with silk and colored lights; Fuller also presented other performers, including the Japanese dancer Sada Yacco. Moreover, a political alliance between France and Russia had recently been made; it was cemented by the enthusiastic reception of the Russian pavilion by the French, and the ground was laid for the even more passionate welcome the Ballets Russes would shortly be shown in Paris. [1]

The forerunners of American modern dance

In America at the turn of the century, dancing on stage was not identified with "high art" but with popular entertainments. Although ballet was produced in the United States, both by touring companies and by native dancers, there was no American academy of European classic dancing comparable to that at La Scala in Milan, the Paris Opéra, or the Russian Imperial School of Ballet in St. Petersburg. The three American forerunners of modern dance—Fuller, Duncan, and St. Denis—all began their careers dancing in vaudeville. However, performances in Europe allowed these artists to synthesize the idea of serious dancing with the popular and ethnic dance forms they borrowed and modified. They also flouted European dance traditions in what was seen as a peculiarly American way, in order to effect a break with ballet and to found a new genre of theatrical art dancing.

Although at least Duncan and St. Denis had studied ballet, this generation of innovators was more powerfully influenced by other forms of bodily training. One of these was the American physical culture movement, a juncture of health advocacy, social reform, and feminist body liberation. This initiative created physical education programs in public schools and physical culture clubs, and it inspired many middle-class women to perform free-form movement, both indoors and out.

A second major influence was the teaching of François Delsarte, a French theorist of the body who analyzed movement, posture, and gesture and wrote manuals for actors. Delsarte's teachings involved exercises for the improvement of posture and for relaxation, and middle-class women began to study with Delsarte teachers, not for the purpose of professional actor's training, but in order to enhance their amateur dramatic readings and to improve their bodies. Delsarte also theorized about the meaning of specific gestures, charting zones of expression in the body and proposing that every gesture corresponds to a specific emotional state; he further maintained that formalized gestures communicate better than natural ones. Not only did these aspects of American turn-of-the-century movement culture inspire an emerging generation of choreographers to put their faith in the body as a medium of expression; they also created a receptive audience for experiments in new movement styles. [2]

Loïe Fuller (1862–1928), born in Illinois, was a child performer who sang, acted, and gave temperance lectures. At fifteen she joined a stock theater company, where she played soubrettes and learned about the technical stagecraft required for the spectacular transformations of the popular theater of the day: dioramas, steam curtains, and magic-lantern projections. She also learned to do skirt dancing, a typical genre of vaudeville entertainment, related to cancan, that featured the manipulation of the costume to music. An inventor, dress reformer, and enterprising businesswoman as well as an artist, by the early 1890s she had appeared on stage without a corset, produced a play in London, and created a new form of dancing that won her international acclaim.

Simplifying, abstracting, and systematically organizing the skirt dancer's techniques, Fuller sculpted fantastic shapes out of the diaphanous fabrics of her greatly exaggerated costumes, sometimes using wands to extend the image even further. She was, perhaps, influenced by the Japanese theater troupes she at times produced in Europe; she wrote that she was always fascinated with Japanese culture. [3] With lighting designs of her own invention, involving carbon arc lights, gels painted with hand-mixed colors, and underlighting, and using black curtains and rugs to isolate and seemingly suspend herself in space, she turned her own body into a proto-cinematic screen for the projection of light and color transformations. Celebrated by the Symbolists as the "visual embodiment of the idea," she was a kind of living Art Nouveau object, with her use of iridescent colors and organic, sinuous, vegetative forms—as in *Le Lys du Nile* (1895), in which she coiled masses of fabric into the changing forms of a lily and lit herself from under the stage through a glass trapdoor. The poet Stéphane Mallarmé saw her as "at once an artistic intoxication and an industrial achievement." Fuller was, for a fin de siècle imagination inflamed with Japanism, both utterly modern and yet as stylized as a Hokusai print. [4]

Isadora Duncan (1877–1927), born in San Francisco, also performed in the popular theater as a young woman. By 1900, after early work in New York City, she had moved with her family to Europe, where she viewed classical sculpture, at first in the museums of western Europe and then on a trip to Greece in 1904. That year she also met Edward Gordon Craig, the avant-garde theater director and designer; opened her first school (in Grünewald, Germany); and toured Russia. Duncan's slogan for her child pupils, who studied at the school (and her later schools in Paris and the Soviet Union) year-round and tuition-free, was "Beauty, Freedom, and Health." Being part of the European theater community—meeting people like Craig and Konstantin Stanislavsky, seeing Eleonora Duse perform—was crucial to Duncan's development as a dramatic dancer.

This link to the progressive theater of her day was part of Duncan's effort to raise the values of dancing to a serious art. She applied

"[Loïe] Fuller sculpted fantastic shapes out of the diaphanous fabrics of her greatly exaggerated costumes."

the reforms of stage decor advocated by Craig and Adolphe Appia in the plain blue curtains she used, and she freed the dancer's body by dispensing with a corset and shoes and wearing a simple Greek tunic. As well, she broke with the standard musical practice of the time. Rather than dancing to second-rate music by hack composers, she dared to interpret great symphonic music through dance. Like Fuller—who turned skirt dancing, a popular entertainment form, into high art— Duncan saw new potentials in a dance form that already existed. She transformed "revived Greek dancing," the cavorting in tunics fashionable as a leisure activity among bourgeois housewives in the prewar years, into a unique artistic expression. Although she was inspired by the idea of the Greek chorus, by the shapes of classical sculpture and architecture—and equally by the bacchic frenzy she saw in the dances of possession depicted on Greek vases—Duncan did not pretend to reconstruct ancient dances. Rather, she combined what she saw as the spirit

Isadora Duncan dancing in an amphitheater in Athens, Greece, 1903.

"[Ruth] St. Denis's unique contribution to the new genre of art dancing was her adaptation of Indian, Japanese, and Egyptian lore and dancing."

and function of ancient dance with a Californian's love of movements culled from nature, in particular the ebb and flow of wave formations. Duncan's search for what she called "first movements" (the physical source of human motion in the solar plexus), as well as her stress on simple movements like running, skipping, and jumping for what she felt were their universal legibility, seem part and parcel of the utopian primitivism that led, in other ways, to both ancient Greece and nature.

After the accidental death of her two children, Duncan's dancing became less buoyant and more monumentally somber. When World War I broke out, she offered her school in Paris as a hospital for wounded soldiers, and she danced the *Marseillaise* and the *Marche Slave*. In 1920, viewing her own revolutionary art as an appropriate expression of the October Revolution, she accepted an invitation from the new Soviet government to open a school in Moscow. There she married the Russian poet Sergey Yesenin. Touring America with her husband and preaching bolshevism—as well as baring her breast—in the anti-Communist early 1920s, Duncan was roundly repudiated. She died in 1927, strangled when her scarf caught in the wheel of a car at Nice.

Although Duncan left no institutional legacy—the schools were short-lived, and her own participation in them was dilatory—her teaching was carried on by a small group of disciples and their pupils. But her indirect legacy includes Soviet modern dance and gymnastics, the reforms in Russian ballet by Michel Fokine, Aleksandr Gorsky, and others, and the work of British choreographers Marie Rambert and Frederick Ashton. [5]

If Duncan looked to an earlier era of Western culture in order to cleanse modern life of what she saw as its industrial soot and psychic mechanization (she hated jazz music), Ruth St. Denis (1877–1968) looked to Asia for a spiritual anodyne. Born Ruth Dennis in rural New Jersey, St. Denis grew up meeting artists and intellectuals in the bohemian boarding house her mother ran. Her mother, who had graduated from medical school and was an ardent dress reformer, feminist, and Christian Scientist, trained her in Delsarte methods. Family friends introduced her to Hindu thought through theosophy. Like Duncan and Fuller, St. Denis too did her apprenticeship on the popular stage, doing acrobatic and skirt dancing at dime museums, roof garden theaters, in the stock theater company of Augustin Daly, and in David Belasco's historically meticulous extravaganzas. However, seeing Genevieve Stebbins turn Delsarte exercises into expressive concert dances powerfully moved her to search for a more serious form of art dancing. Eventually, like the Duncans, the entire Dennis family moved to New York City to support the daughter's performing career, and, like Fuller and Duncan, St. Denis (as Belasco renamed her) found in Europe the first sympathetic milieu for her experiments in concert dancing. Unlike the other two, however, St. Denis returned to the United States in 1909, where her career blossomed both on the vaudeville stage and in art theaters.

St. Denis's unique contribution to the new genre of art dancing was her adaptation of Indian, Japanese, and Egyptian lore and dancing, which profited from the current vogue for Orientalism in both intellectual circles and popular culture. Americans were particularly attracted to the simultaneous sensualism and moralism of her works. For instance, in *Radha* (1906), with movement material borrowed from

Ted Shawn

a Coney Island sideshow, and performed to music from Léo Delibes's opera *Lakmé,* a temple goddess voluptuously celebrated the five senses, ultimately renouncing them all to achieve self-realization.

With the rise of ballroom dancing and "Castlemania," St. Denis looked for a way to expand her repertory. She took a partner, Ted Shawn (1891–1972), a former divinity student and at this time a ballroom and interpretive dancer. They married and set up a school in Los Angeles, called Denishawn, where students learned Delsarte and Jaques-Dalcroze eurythmics (a system of visualizing music through the body), as well as ballet, various forms of Asian dance, and dance history. Hollywood studios sent actresses there, and Denishawn dancers not only put on enormous pageants (e.g., *A Dance Pageant of Egypt, Greece, and India* [1916]) but also appeared in D. W. Griffith's epic film *Intolerance.* Shawn complemented St. Denis's Orientalism with other "exotic" dances—Spanish, North African, Native American—and also made comic dances on themes of everyday modern American life. Influenced by the teaching of eurythmics and perhaps by Duncan's lyrical dances, St. Denis further experimented with "music visualizations" that had neither narrative nor sumptuous decor but found expressive links with symphonic music.

The school closed, then moved to New York; the company toured the United States, Europe, and Asia; and the couple separated and formed separate dance troupes. But in one form or another, Denishawn lasted until the 1930s. It trained the next generation of American modern dancers; three of its lead dancers, Martha Graham, Doris Humphrey, and Charles Weidman, would be the leaders of the American modern dance movement of the 1930s onward. Its musical director, Louis Horst, went on to work with Graham and to put his stamp on the relations between music and dance as well as on choreography for nearly half a century: in his dance composition classes and in his books Horst stressed the emotional content of musical form, which he taught should dictate the form of the dance. [6] And, as important, Denishawn created large popular audiences for the emerging genre of modern dance.

After St. Denis and Shawn split up, she advocated religious dancing and established a Society of Spiritual Arts, which eventually became the Church of the Divine Dance. Shawn organized an all-male dance company and built a dance studio and school in the Berkshires. By the 1940s this had grown into the eclectic Jacob's Pillow Dance Festival, which Shawn directed until his death. With his muscular choreography for his company and his indefatigable producing activity, Shawn was instrumental in shifting American attitudes toward dancing men, setting the stage for such athletic male dancers as Gene Kelly. [7]

It would seem paradoxical that these artists tried to make a uniquely American dance form by borrowing wholesale from other cultures. The material was based on foreign cultures, though it was not authentic by any means. But somehow the appropriation of otherness was transformed, in the rhetoric of the times, as constituting a quintessentially American quality. A critic wrote that St. Denis had "an originality and a spirit that is entirely of this country," and St. Denis herself wrote that Denishawn was "representative of the spirit of America." Duncan looked to the past to create "the dancer of the future" and envisioned America dancing her Greek dances of freedom. [8]

But the polyglot nature of the early modern dance in America is really not so surprising, given the urban culture of the turn of the century, in which both an influx of recent immigrants and southern blacks moving northward tried to assimilate themselves into the American melting pot. America had long lived under the shadow of western European culture. To try on the trappings of different non-European cultures was itself a way of breaking with European art and forging a new, distinctly American culture. That is, American cultural identity was asserted not by contrasting with, but by absorbing, otherness.

Central European modern dance

Europe itself, however, and especially Germany, was receptive to the new American modern dance because it, too, was undergoing the throes of industrial modernization and throwing off the shackles of imperial society. And it had its own burgeoning physical culture movement. For German artists as well, part of the strategy of modernization—in both aesthetic and political terms—was to embrace the vitality of "primitive" art. Not only were artifacts from tribal cultures available for view in ethnographic museums; various artists, like Emil Nolde, even undertook travel to Asia and the South Pacific. The German Expressionist artists were also connoisseurs of German medieval folk art. As Nolde put it, "There are enough overrefined, pallid, decadent works of art and perhaps that is why artists who are vital and developing seek guidance from vigorous primitives. . . . Exotic arts—just like the earliest primitive European folk art, masks, and ornaments—all of it seemed very close to me. . . . The primeval power of all primitive people is germinal." [9]

The study of non-Western music and dance was a powerful stimulus for various strands of central European modern dance. Émile Jaques-Dalcroze (1865–1950), a Swiss music teacher, had studied Arabic music in Algeria. He created his system of "rhythmic gymnastics" (called eurythmics in England and the United States) to train students in musical perception—in particular, the rhythmic patterns so key to much non-Western music. Students practiced complex rhythmic structures by translating them into bodily movements. In 1910 Dalcroze established his Institute for Applied Rhythm in Hellerau, near Dresden, Germany. There he worked with Appia, the visionary stage designer, on demonstrations in which the very shape of the stage—its irregular stairsteps—dictated the rhythms of the performers' movements. His students included Mary Wigman and Marie Rambert. In 1920 the school moved to Vienna (it was closed by the Nazis in 1938), and Dalcroze returned to Geneva to teach. Though Dalcroze was neither a dancer nor a dance teacher, his system was influential in shaping modern dance and modern ballet in the United States, Europe, and the Soviet Union.

Rudolf von Laban (1879–1958), born in Bratislava, studied art, theater, and dancing in Paris in 1900. Touring North Africa as a revue dancer, he was inspired by Arabic and African dances and began introducing new dance ideas when he returned to Germany in 1907. In 1910 he opened a school in Munich, and during World War I he worked in Zürich and Ascona. He often used improvisation for freedom in movement exploration. His dancers contributed to several Dada events in Zürich. Laban organized "movement choirs," festive communal dances for amateurs, which became popular in Germany in the 1920s and the 1930s. He organized the dance contributions to the 1936 Olympics but then fled the Nazis, eventually settling in England in 1938. A theoretician as well as a practical man of the theater, Laban devised a system of dance notation and analyzed movement style in both dance and everyday activity along formal and expressive axes. There was, he believed, a system of harmonics in the human use of space that could provide the basis for healthier, more efficient movement. Although his own choreography has not survived, his notation system has proved a flexible, comprehensive system for documenting dance and is used worldwide to preserve dances of various styles and genres.

71

"Mary Wigman . . . became the most important exponent of the central European style of modern dance, which came to be known in Germany as Ausdruckstanz (expressive dance)."

Mary Wigman (1886–1973), a student of both Dalcroze and Laban, began dancing late—at the age of twenty-seven. Yet she became the most important exponent of the central European style of modern dance, which came to be known in Germany as *Ausdruckstanz* (expressive dance). Wigman's first solo, *Witch Dance* (1914; second version 1926), initially performed while she was still Laban's assistant, seems to owe something of its eerie, powerfully contorted beauty to the ghosts and witches of nō dramas and other non-Western dance forms. Wigman performed most of the dance seated on the floor; her costume was a drape of silk brocade and a mask of her own face, which, modeled after nō masks, gave her a remote, Asian look; the music was naked percussion. Wigman described this dance as "a rhythmic intoxication." [10]

Wigman was fascinated by non-Western instrumentation—flutes, bells, gongs, and drums from India, Thailand, Africa, China. Often the musical accompaniment for her dances was primarily percussion, and some dances were performed in silence. Other masks, like that for Moloch in *Totenmal* (1930), seem to have been influenced by tribal art. And both the ecstatic spinning and the languid passivity that sometimes structured her dances have non-Western roots as well.

Like St. Denis, Wigman was preoccupied with a mystical quest for spiritual transcendence. She wrote that as a young woman, she "look[ed] even toward the Orient for a mystic answer to a wordless riddle." [11] But her dances emphasized a different aspect of that quest— the struggle with evil and the acceptance of death. Her movements— crouching, crawling, or simply lying—clung close to the earth. Or she whirled until she fell. The American critic Margaret Lloyd wrote that "Wigman's was largely an ecstasy of gloom, stressing the demonic and macabre, as if to exorcise through movement the secret evils in man's nature." [12] Wigman's style—related to the intense style of acting developed in the "shriek-plays" of German Expressionist theater, the telegraphic, percussive poems and dialogue of Expressionist writers, and the angular, distorted shapes of Expressionist painting and film—reflected the sense of apocalyptic despair and revolutionary zeal unleashed in a Germany suffering from war and its aftermath and felt by its younger generation to be rapidly disintegrating. She believed that dance could express not only emotions but the entire inner life of humankind. Like other artists of her generation, she was not only fascinated with the pressure and threat of implosion in current society but also expressed hope for a regeneration of humanity. She made dances of death—like *Dance Macabre* (1923), *Dance of Death* (1926), *Totenmal* (1930), *Sacrifice* (1931), and *Lament for the Dead* (1936)—but she also made dances of life: *Festive Prelude* (1926), *Celebration* (1928), *Maternal Dance* (1934), and *Rejoice, My Heart* (1942).

In 1920 Wigman opened a school in Dresden, which became a center for German modern dance. The most important German dancers and choreographers of the period studied and performed with her— including Hanya Holm, Gret Palucca, Yvonne Georgi, Max Terpis, Margarethe Wallmann, and Harald Kreutzberg. For a generation these and other choreographers replaced opera house ballet dancing with *Ausdruckstanz*. Horst saw Wigman perform in Europe and returned to the United States with new ideas for modern dance. In 1931 Wigman toured America and, on the suggestion of Sol Hurok, the impresario,

Kurt Jooss in *The Green Table*.

that she open a branch of her school there, she immediately sent Holm to New York to establish one. The Dresden school was closed in 1943, then reopened when Wigman moved to Leipzig in 1945. Finally, after settling in West Berlin in 1950, Wigman continued to train dancers into the 1960s. But after World War II, *Ausdruckstanz* was no longer a vital movement in West Germany. Ballet returned to dominate the opera house stages, until a new generation, searching once again in the 1960s for its cultural identity, built on its dance heritage of the Weimar years in creating a new genre of dramatic dance, known as *Tanztheater*.

Kurt Jooss (1901–79), another student of Laban's, combined *Ausdruckstanz* with ballet. In 1927 he became director of the dance department at the Essen Folkwang School and the following year founded the Folkwang Tanztheater. He choreographed steadily from 1924, offering political and social comment in his works. Jooss's most well-known dance is *The Green Table* (1932), a stark antiwar ballet featuring a tragicomic peace conference and a terrifying medieval figure of death. Leaving

Germany in 1933, Jooss and his company, by now called the Ballets Jooss, settled in Devon, England, where Laban later came to work with them. After the war the company disbanded, and Jooss worked briefly in Chile before returning in 1949 to Essen and the Folkwang School, where he taught until his retirement in 1968.

A different school of German dance developed, independently from *Ausdruckstanz*, at the Bauhaus (in Weimar and Dessau) in the 1920s. Like Russian Constructivism, the Bauhaus aesthetic was an analytic, even mathematical, one, emerging from the philosophy of the *Neue Sachlichkeit* (New Objectivity). However, its utopian, streamlined abstractionism was Janus-faced, for it emerged from an educational program based on the medieval guild system. Like the earlier efforts of William Morris in England, the Bauhaus intended to link art and industry through the vision of the artist as an unalienated craftsman whose designs could offer a different kind of mass production.

The Bauhaus *Abstrakter Tanz*, developed by Oskar Schlemmer, came out of his studies of the visual representation of the human figure and its potential for abstraction. As in Laban's studies of human movement, the space around the human figure was analyzed geometrically, and often the figure itself, altered by padded costumes or phosphorescent sticks, was seen as a reductive system of interacting lines and shapes. Since the motions were based on work movements, the performers did not have to be trained dancers. These dances were not meant to be expressive of anything outside of the concrete forms, colors, and patterns of bodily mechanics they revealed. Still, Schlemmer's description of the three sections of *Triadisches Ballett* (1922) included emotional qualities: "a gay burlesque . . . ceremonious and solemn . . . a mystical fantasy." [13] Besides their theatrical experiments, the Bauhaus artists carried out paratheatrical activities as part of daily life, in the manner of preindustrial folk culture: kite festivals, dances, lantern parades.

In their disparate ways, both *Ausdruckstanz*, inspired by primitivist notions of Oriental frenzy and abandon, and *Abstrakter Tanz*, inspired by medievalist notions of unalienated labor and free play, reflected and contributed to a German culture struggling to find its identity in a time of political and economic crisis. Unity and authenticity of experience, above all, was the rallying cry; dance seemed to provide or at least point to these. But as in early American modern dance, often it was dance that had its roots in a distant place that was most influential in pointing toward a dance of the future. [14]

The Ballets Russes

At the turn of the century, the Russian ballet was the finest in the world, having consolidated the best of the French and Italian schools and married that virtuosic technique to symphonic music, especially that of Peter Ilich Tchaikovsky. However, after the golden decade of the classic ballets of the 1890s—including *The Sleeping Beauty* (1890) and *Swan Lake* (1895)—the ballet was growing stale artistically. Marius Petipa, the transplanted French choreographer who produced the Russian school of the late nineteenth century, had been choreographing in St. Petersburg for nearly fifty years when in 1903 he made his last ballet. Like Russian artists and intellectuals in other fields, the younger generation of ballet dancers felt restive and sought change. The revolutionary events of 1905 fanned the flames of their artistic revolt.

This generation produced two important ballet reformers: Gorsky and Fokine. Unlike the American forerunners of modern dance, they stayed within the confines of ballet discourse—having grown up in the one culture in the world where ballet still commanded aesthetic power—but, like Fuller, Duncan, and St. Denis, they were inspired by archaic and exotic ideals.

Aleksandr Gorsky (1871–1924) joined the Bolshoi Ballet in Moscow in 1900, where he initiated a program of dramatic action ballets, the antithesis of Petipa's glittering formal structures. After Duncan's visit to Russia, Gorsky experimented not only with Greek themes (as in *Eunice and Petronius* [1915], to music of Frédéric Chopin) but also with a freer use of the arms and torso, and with a substitution of tunics for tutus.

Michel Fokine (1880–1942) was a soloist at the Mariinsky Theater. He explored Greek themes in his own earliest works (such as *Acis et Galatée* [1905]). Fokine led the younger generation at Petipa's own theater in urging institutional and aesthetic reform. He called for greater dramatic and stylistic unity among the various theatrical elements of the ballet spectacle, and, like Gorsky, he pioneered in freeing the arms and torso for greater expressive power. His *Chopiniana* (1908; later known as *Les Sylphides*) was both a tribute to the Romantic ballet of the early nineteenth century and a loosening of dance from the demands of plot and character.

Soon Fokine became acquainted with Sergey Diaghilev (1872–1929), who had been the editor of *World of Art (Mir Iskusstva)* magazine. Diaghilev was an ardent Wagnerite and one of a circle of musicians, artists, and writers who championed both the European avant-garde and Russian neonationalist composers and visual artists. He organized exhibitions of Russian art in St. Petersburg and began bringing Russian art to Paris in 1906, in the form of a visual art exhibition. In 1907 he returned to Paris to organize concerts of Russian music; in 1908 he presented Modest Mussorgsky's opera *Boris Godunov*, featuring Fyodor Chaliapin.

In 1909 Diaghilev brought a company of dancers and singers from the Russian Imperial Theater. They dazzled Paris with Fokine's ballets and scenes from Russian operas. Ballet dancing of that caliber had

Sergey Diaghilev

not been seen regularly in Paris for over fifty years. The seasons of Russian ballet continued for the next twenty years, soon crystallizing into an independent company—Les Ballets Russes. Its tours expanded to London, Monte Carlo, the rest of Europe (though never Russia), and the Americas. Diaghilev engaged the finest dancers and choreographers, including Adolph Bolm, Vaslav Nijinsky, Anna Pavlova, Tamara Karsavina, Lydia Lopokova, Léonide Massine, Bronislava Nijinska, Serge Lifar, and George Balanchine. He also commissioned work from Europe's finest visual artists and composers, including Picasso, Henri Matisse, Georges Rouault, Natalya Goncharova, Mikhail Larionov, Erik Satie, Debussy, and Igor Stravinsky. Diaghilev's potent blend of artistic innovation and virtuosic classical dance technique indelibly altered the shape of ballet for the present century.

Important to the early seasons of the Ballets Russes was a sumptuous fin de siècle Orientalism, featuring sado-erotic scenes in vibrant colors with languishing *femmes fatales* and vigorous male dancing of the sort that had not been seen on Paris stages for several generations. Two exemplars of this genre were *Cléopâtre* (1908), in which the Egyptian queen, played by the elegant actress Ida Rubenstein, is taken from a mummy case and unwrapped in a kind of dance of the veils, seduces a young man, then forces him to drink poison; and *Schéhérazade* (1910), a tale from *The Thousand and One Nights,* in which the sultan's fa-

Vaslav Nijinsky in *Le Spectre de la rose.*

vorite concubine instigates an orgy in the harem while her husband is
away, makes love to the Golden Slave (danced lustily by Nijinsky), and
unwittingly sets the scene for a massacre when the sultan interrupts
them. Léon Bakst's extravagant decors and costumes for these ballets
and for *Le Dieu Bleu* and *Thamar,* with their brilliant clashing colors
and their sinuous lines, inspired new fashions in haute couture and
interior design.

But what was even more impressive to Parisian audiences, and what
became the most characteristic feature of the prewar Ballets Russes,
was the representation of "Russianness" that Diaghilev purveyed in
his Slavophile ballets, with their aural and visual images of pagan bar-
barism. The music of neonationalist composers such as Nikolay Rimsky-
Korsakov, Aleksandr Borodine, Mussorgsky, and the young Stravinsky

Anna Pavlova in *The Dying Swan.*

set the tone with their borrowings from Slavic folk melodies and their unfamiliar harmonies and rhythms. As well, the sets, by neonationalist painters like Nicholas Roerich and Alexander Golovine, created a landscape of exotic Russian folk decoration. Finally, the shapes and rhythms of Russian folk dancing and the vigorous performance by the ensemble broadened the expressive capabilities of the ballet technique. The *Polovetsian Dances* from the opera *Prince Igor,* for instance, presented during the Ballets Russes's first season, with a chorus of male opera singers, featured swooning captive women and savage warriors, led by the ebulliently virile Bolm. *L'Oiseau de feu (The Firebird;* 1910), an amalgam of traditional Russian fairy tales with overtones of *Swan Lake,* told the story of Ivan Tsarevich, who captures the Firebird and, on freeing her, is given a magic feather with which to call on her in time of need. This he does in order to free the beautiful Tsarevna from the monster Kostchei and his grotesque retinue, and the ballet concludes with a wedding procession.

These Russian spectacles were crowned by Nijinsky's *Le Sacre du printemps* (*The Rite of Spring;* 1913), subtitled "Pictures from Pagan Russia," in which a maiden is sacrificed by dancing herself to death in a terrifying, frenzied fertility ritual, to the throbbing sounds of Stravinsky's dissonant polyrhythms. The awkward, huddled poses of the dancers (with their laced leggings and clumsy peasant shoes emphasizing their turned-in legs), their ecstatic jumps and rhythmic pounding of the earth, and the vivid, mystical rocky hillside of Roerich's sets jarred the senses as much as the music did. [15]

After 1914, cut off from Russia by the war and then the Russian Revolution, and bereft of both Fokine and Nijinsky as choreographers, Diaghilev shifted his artistic policy. He no longer exported Russian theatrical dancing to the West. Although all his choreographers and many of the dancers remained Russian, Diaghilev now became primarily the purveyor of European artists to European audiences, making use of painters of the École de Paris and modern composers like Les Six, as well as writers like Jean Cocteau. Picasso designed *Parade* (1917), *Le Tricorne* (1919), *Pulcinella* (1920), and *Cuadro Flamenco* (1921), and the curtain for *Le Train Bleu* (1924). Other artist-designers included Gia-

Scene from *Le Sacre du printemps*, choreography by Vaslav Nijinsky.

como Balla, Matisse, Juan Gris, Georges Braque, André Derain, Max Ernst, Joan Miró, Rouault, and Giorgio de Chirico.

During this period, scores were commissioned from Satie, Francis Poulenc, Georges Auric, Darius Milhaud, Vittorio Rieti, Stravinsky, and others. *Parade,* the product of a collaboration among Massine, Satie, Picasso, and Cocteau, was seen as the triumph of modernism, with its cubist decor and costumes, its imagery from popular culture (including American silent film), and its "noise music," with sirens, gunshots, and typewriters. The title referred to the practice of performing outside a circus sideshow to attract audience members indoors; the string of performers included two managers, a dancing horse, a Little American Girl, a Chinese conjurer, and two acrobats.

At the same time, Diaghilev introduced a new primitivist exoticism by means of a number of Spanish ballets, inspired during the company's tour in Spain. *Las Meninas* (1916), with choreography by Massine, music by Gabriel Fauré, sets by Carlo Socrate, and costumes designed by the Spanish painter José-María Sert, was named for the painting by Diego Velázquez. It evoked courtly elegance with its pavane for two couples. However, *Le Tricorne,* choreographed by Massine, to music by Manuel de Falla, used authentic Spanish folk dances in its retelling of the novel about the miller's wife, her jealous husband, and her attempted seduction by the old governor. *Cuadro Flamenco* actually featured a group of Spanish dancers performing traditional dances to gypsy music, as part of the Ballets Russes program.

Almost as "ethnographic," but with an unexpectedly non-exotic subject matter, were the portrayals of contemporary life in France in two Nijinska ballets. *Les Biches* (1924; music by Poulenc, decor by Marie Laurencin) showed a fashionable house party with its eccentric characters and multiple flirtations. *Le Train Bleu* (libretto by Cocteau, music by Milhaud, decor by Henri Laurens, costumes by Coco Chanel, and curtain by Picasso) showed an afternoon at the beach in Deauville, with flappers, a woman tennis player, and an athlete.

Despite his constant search for the new, Diaghilev also fostered classicism in his repertory. *The Sleeping Princess* (1921), a London revival of Petipa's *Sleeping Beauty,* with additional choreography by Nijinska, was initially conceived as a way to subsidize the more avant-garde productions. But it was also a salute to the earliest days of the *Mir Iskusstva* circle and the masterpiece of classical ballet so beloved by Diaghilev's first collaborators. Bakst designed the production. The original Aurora, Carlotta Brianza, danced the role of Carabosse (the Wicked Fairy), and during the course of the season three superlative Mariinsky-trained ballerinas danced Aurora: Olga Spessivtzeva, Vera Trefilova, and Lubov Egorova.

Apollon Musagète (1928), choreographed by Balanchine to music by Stravinsky, with decor by André Bauchant, told the story of the birth of

Apollo, his discovery of his own powers, his instruction by the Muses, and his ascent to Mount Parnassus. Balanchine, Diaghilev's last choreographer, had cut his teeth on the avant-garde both in Russia and in Paris—with productions like the Constructivist *La Chatte* (1927; music by Henri Sauguet, costumes and decor by Naum Gabo and Antoine Pevsner). But for him, *Apollo* (as it later was called) was a revelation that led to the road to neoclassicism. The ballet celebrates classical values; as Edwin Denby wrote, *Apollo* created an "impression of the grandness of man's creative genius, depicting it concretely in its grace, its sweet wit, its force and boldness, and with the constant warmth of its sensuous complicity with physical beauty. . . . [I]t is an homage to classicism's sensuous loveliness as well as to its brilliant exactitude and its science of dance effect." [16] Balanchine attributed his own abiding interest in choreographic clarity to the discovery, in Stravinsky's score, of distilled family relationships between tones, which the choreographer analogized to gestures, and the possibility of clarifying through reduction. [17]

Though the Ballets Russes experimented in many new directions, the thread of Russian spectacle in Diaghilev's repertory continued—albeit with a new generation of modernist Russian designers, who also found sources in peasant art—in productions like *Le Soleil de nuit* (1915), based on folktale motifs, with choreography by Massine, decor by Larionov, and music by Rimsky-Korsakov, and *Contes Russes* (1917), an episodic ballet that was also based on Russian folktales, with choreography by Massine, decor by Larionov, and music by Anatoly Lyadov. There was a new production of *Sacre* (1920), with choreography by Massine. *Chout* (1921), a tale about a Russian buffoon, was choreographed by the cubo-futurist painter Larionov in collaboration with a company dancer, Thadée Slavinsky, to music by Sergey Prokofiev. And Nijinska choreographed *Les Noces* (1923), a stark picture of a peasant wedding that shows marriage as an economic alliance that rips young women from their friends and family. It was danced to songs by Stravinsky that featured traditional Russian wedding songs and laments.

Both *Les Noces* and Nijinska's *Night on Bald Mountain* (1924; set to music by Mussorgsky), had designs by Goncharova. Massine's *Le Pas d'Acier* (1927), to Prokofiev's music, and with a Constructivist set by Georgi Yakulov, was a tribute to the new Russian art of the Soviet dispensation, with its machine dances and evocation of factory sights and sounds. *Ode* (1928) mixed an eighteenth-century poem by the Russian poet and scientist M. V. Lomonosov with state-of-the-art film and slide projections. [18]

The Diaghilev company created a worldwide passion for dance that sent aspiring young girls to ever-increasing numbers of ballet schools and also produced rival companies. One of these was organized by Anna Pavlova (1881–1931), the lyrical ballerina who had danced in the first several seasons of the Ballets Russes but who, after 1911, regularly

Alexandra Danilova and Anton Dolin in *Le Bal*, choreography by George Balanchine, 1929; designs by Giorgio de Chirico.

toured the world with her more conservative repertory, building broad audiences for classical ballet. Her repertory included Fokine's *Dying Swan*—her signature piece—and such ballets as *The Fairy Doll* and *Gavotte* (both choreographed by Ivan Clustine).

More akin to Diaghilev's company was Les Ballets Suédois (1920–25), organized by a Swedish businessman, Rolf de Maré, which mixed its own native folklore (as in *Dansgille* [1921]) with Spanish themes (as in *Ibéria* and *El Greco* [1920]) and collaborations with avant-garde artists and composers. Its entire repertory was choreographed by a Swedish choreographer, Jean Börlin. *Les Mariés de la Tour Eiffel* (1921), conceived by Cocteau, with music by five members of Les Six (Auric, Arthur Honegger, Milhaud, Poulenc, and Germaine Tailleferre), was a surrealistic satire of a bourgeois wedding party. Masks and exaggerated costumes created a cartoon effect in this fast-paced farce. Various characters emerged from the photographer's camera, including a bathing beauty, a lion, and the wedding couple's future child, who massacres the wedding party.

La Création du monde (1923), with libretto by Blaise Cendrars, jazz-inspired music by Milhaud, and designs by Fernand Léger, was based on an African creation myth. Animals designed like African masks peopled the stage, born of a tree created by the gods. A primordial couple was born, then mated as the animals, shamans, and sorcerers joined in a frenzied dance. *Relâche* (1924; music by Satie, libretto and decor by Francis Picabia, and film by René Clair) was an apotheosis of Dada performance. Its title means "no performance," and its attack on the audience continued with Satie's scandalous music, banks of reflectors shining lights in the spectators' eyes, a smoking fireman, a farcical cinematic entr'acte, dancing without music, and a group of dancers stripping from evening clothes to long underwear. *Relâche* went farther than Diaghilev ever would in embracing the Parisian avant-garde's gesture of utter contempt for bourgeois taste. [19]

The Diaghilev company (and its rivals and imitators) brought ballet into the modern world, not only with its contemporary themes, but also by associating it with modern art and modern music. Ballet became an art form worthy of serious consideration by other artists and intellectuals. As well, Diaghilev—though himself an impresario, not a dancer—was instrumental in creating the century's most important ballet choreographers, especially Balanchine, who became the most prolific and influential ballet choreographer of the twentieth century. The Diaghilev company also supplied key personnel to many of the international and national ballet companies that blossomed in 1930–50. The pattern of artistic collaboration among equals that Diaghilev pioneered would supply both ballet troupes and modern dance companies, like that of Merce Cunningham, with a model to emulate throughout the rest of the century.

American modern dance

A new generation of modern dancers emerged in the United States in the 1920s; several of them came from the Denishawn school and company. There was a feeling, in the postwar years, that the decorative exoticism of the Denishawn era was exhausted. Graham later wrote, "a dance form, whether it be Spanish, Russian, Oriental, or even modern European, when transplanted or grafted on a completely alien culture loses its creative energy and becomes decadent or, at best, merely decorative." [20]

The new American modern dancers knew about the stark, percussive German *Ausdruckstanz,* and they felt that the new postwar age demanded a parallel new movement in American dance that was also more vital, more austere, and more authentic than the impressionistic aesthetic dancing of the early years of the century. Still, while eschewing the ornamentalism and foreign sources of the previous generation, the historical modern dancers also turned to primitivism, albeit in a new, starker, and indigenous mode. They linked talk of finding their own true ways of moving with finding an American cultural style. In seeking to find the "essence" of American dancing, they turned to American Indian ceremonies, to the ecstatic frenzies of the Shaker religious sect, and to traditional folk dancing and popular entertainments.

Graham, her music director and companion Horst, and Humphrey and Weidman left the Denishawn company to pursue their new courses. Their searches were framed by the rhetoric of both national and generational identity. As well, the discovery of the self through the body's expressive powers was an oft-stated goal.

Martha Graham (1894–1991) grew up in California, the daughter of a psychiatrist. An avid athlete, she began studying dance late, at the Cumnock School junior college in Los Angeles. She joined Denishawn in 1916, taking classes and then performing with the company. As a favorite of Shawn's, she was featured in several roles, including *Malagueña,* a Spanish-flavored duet with Shawn. After leaving Denishawn in 1923, Graham danced with the sophisticated Greenwich Village Follies revue for two years and then, in 1925, hired by the young director Rouben Mamoulian, she began to teach modern dance at the Eastman School of Music in Rochester, New York. There she formed her first company. In 1926 Graham gave her first independent New York concert of her own choreography—still heavily influenced by Denishawn.

But by 1927–28, when she had already started teaching in her own New York studio, Graham began to show works with a more sober mien, like *Revolt, Immigrant,* and *Poems of 1917.* She developed her technique, emphasizing forceful movements of the torso, lower back, and pelvis in spirals and in contraction and release. Sitting on, lying on, and falling to the floor allowed for gravity to exert its pull. The use of parallel positions of the legs and feet, angular positions of the limbs and torso, and massed powerful figures in groups added to the severity of her style.

In 1930 Graham and Horst traveled through New Mexico. Impressed by the rituals of the Native American Penitente cult, a synthesis of Catholic ceremony with native practices, Graham returned to New

Martha Graham (center) and twelve
women perform in *Primitive Mysteries*.

York to invent a new primitivism. In *Primitive Mysteries* (1931; music by Horst), choreographed for Graham and twelve women, Graham performed the role of a ritual figure that condensed the aspects of initiate, virgin, and crucified. For Graham, Indian ritual was both exotic and quintessentially American. Like the Greek dance for Duncan, Russian spectacles for Diaghilev's audiences, and Oriental theater for Wigman, this ritual promised spiritual wholeness. Its purpose, she wrote, was "awareness of life, complete relationship with that world in which [the Indian] finds himself; it is a dance for power, a rhythm of integration."

Moreover, the traditional dances of American Indians and blacks for Graham were, paradoxically, both indigenous and alien, both ancient and the stuff of the new American modern dance:

> These are primitive sources which, though they may be basically foreign
> to us, are, nevertheless, akin to the forces which are at work in our life.
> For we, as a nation, are primitive also—primitive in the sense that we
> are forming a new culture. We are weaving a new fabric, and while it is
> true that we are weaving it from the threads of many old cultures, the
> whole cloth will be entirely indigenous. The dancers of America may
> be Jewish and Spanish and Russian and Oriental, as well as Indian and
> Negro. Their dancing will contain a heritage from all other nations, but
> it will be transfigured by the rhythm, and dominated by the psyche of
> this new land. [21]

The stylization of movement and exploration of myth would continue throughout Graham's work, not only in further dances based on Indian themes (like *Ceremonials* [1932] and *El Penitente* [1940]), and on Greek themes (which began to appear, with *Dithyrambic*, in 1931), but also in her dances about the mainstream American heritage (such as *American Provincials* [1934], *Frontier* [1935], and *Appalachian Spring* [1944]). *American Document* (1938) took the form of a minstrel show to enact emblematic episodes from American history. The mythic quality of Graham's dance-dramas was enhanced by symbolic props (often by Isamu Noguchi) and costumes, as well as by her use of split characters and fragmented, episodic narrative lines that, by scrambling events chronologically, seemed to create a quality of timelessness.

Graham was celebrated even by Lincoln Kirstein, the champion of ballet, for creating dances that expressed a national identity. "Martha Graham has a specifically American quality which cannot be ignored and which must be apparent to everyone," Kirstein wrote.

> It is not a red, white and blue patriotic exuberance, nor even the naive
> free-blown boundlessly hopeful openness of the young continent which
> Europeans always professed to see in Isadora. . . . She has created a kind
> of candid, sweeping and wind-worn liberty for her individual expression
> at once beautiful and useful, like a piece of exquisitely realized Shaker
> furniture or homespun clothing. [22]

But Greek myth proved more and more fertile for Graham's choreography. In particular, in dances like *Cave of the Heart* (1946) about Medea, and *Night Journey* (1947) on the Oedipus legend, she narrated events from the female protagonist's point of view.

Graham was the most persistent and prolific choreographer of her generation, a generation that redefined modern dance for a new era. She outlived most of her peers and continued to direct her company and to choreograph for it until her death. She developed a distinctive style of dance based on using physical metaphors for psychological conflicts. Moreover, as a powerful leader of modern dance running an influential school, she became a sounding board for generations of dancers who trained with her, sometimes imitated her, and broke away from her; among them were Erick Hawkins, Cunningham, and Paul Taylor. From the 1920s to the present, dancers have regularly made pilgrimages to New York to study Graham's technique at her studio. To many, modern dance means Martha Graham. [23]

Doris Humphrey (1895–1958) grew up in Chicago, where she studied folk dance, tap, clog, and ballet. She was already teaching ballroom and aesthetic dancing in her own studio in Oak Park when she joined Denishawn in 1917. When she left in 1928, she was a lead dancer, teacher, and choreographic collaborator on St. Denis's music visualizations. But she and her dance partner, Charles Weidman (1901–75), like Graham, sought a more serious artistic and intellectual role for dance. Also like Graham, they sought an authentic mode of American dance, especially when, on Denishawn's tour of the Orient, Humphrey saw the disparities between St. Denis's impressions of Asian dance and the real thing. Humphrey later wrote, about her years of Denishawn Orientalia, "I felt as if I were dancing as everyone but myself. I knew something about how the Japanese moved, how the Chinese or Spanish moved, but I didn't know how I moved or what the American heritage should be. . . . It was imperative to find out what we were as Americans and as contemporary dancers." [24]

Weidman, who had grown up in Nebraska and studied ballet with Theodore Koslov, had a flair for social satire and often was inspired by American popular culture, as in *American Saga* (1936), based on the life of Paul Bunyan; *Flickers* (1941), with its silent-film characters gone awry; and two autobiographical salutes to nineteenth-century Americana, *On My Mother's Side* (1940) and the cartoonlike *And Daddy Was a Fireman* (1943). At times, however, as in *Lynchtown* (part of *Atavisms;* 1936), a chilling portrayal of mass hysteria, and *A House Divided* (1945), about the violence of the Civil War, the tone was sober and critical— an attempt to remind his compatriots, even in wartime, of the dark underbelly of American society.

Humphrey, too, looked to American themes in such works as *American Holiday* (1938), *Square Dances* (1939), and *Song of the West* (1940–

Doris Humphrey (center) and members
of the Humphrey-Weidman Company in
The Shakers.

42). With *The Shakers* (1931), like Graham in *Primitive Mysteries,* she
found a source for ritual dancing in an American sect. This celibate
cult attempted to shake off sin through dancing; Humphrey's piece
showed a Shaker meeting where men on one side and women on the
other joined in an ecstatic dance of transcendence, evoked in repetitive
heavenward leaps. In *Dionysiaques* (1932), Humphrey even invoked the

ancient Cretan bull cult in a dance about a ritual fertility sacrifice. However, though her dances were almost always concerned with social relations, usually they took a more abstract form than Graham's.

Some of Humphrey's dances, like *Passacaglia* (1938), seemed almost so abstract as to be music visualizations. But in this dance the sharing of roles between the two genders, the democratic relations between leaders and followers in the ensemble, and, of course, the exalted grandeur of the music itself created an image of social harmony. *New Dance* (1935) was a utopian vision of cooperative work and pleasure in which individuality was valued even as the group cohered in rhythmic counterpoint.

Like many of her peers, Humphrey referred to her quest as a physical expression of the self. In searching for a unique way of dancing, she spoke of "moving from the inside out." [25] The technique Humphrey developed was based on her idea that all movement takes place in the dynamic "arc between two deaths"—the static positions of lying prone and standing erect. Based on the alternation of the breath cycle, the constant veering from and regaining of equilibrium—fall and recovery—created drama on both a purely physical and a symbolic level. Not as stylized as Graham's technique, Humphrey's vocabulary built on daily gestures. She was especially interested in the architectonics of dance and sometimes used a series of gray boxes to alter the levels of the stage space. After the Humphrey-Weidman Company disbanded in the mid-1940s, Humphrey choreographed for the company of her student José Limón and continued to teach at the Juilliard School as well as at the summer American Dance Festival at Connecticut College. Humphrey was a theorist as well as an artist. In her book *The Art of Making Dances* (1959), she set out her ideas about the craft of choreography. Though her choreography remains in the repertory of many companies and is often reconstructed, in many ways it is Humphrey's book that has had the most powerful impact on succeeding generations. [26]

In 1931 Hanya Holm (c. 1893–   ) opened the Mary Wigman School of Dance in New York City, but by 1936, as a result of anti-Nazi sentiment, Wigman gave Holm permission to change the name of the school to the Hanya Holm Studio. It was one of the leading modern dance studios in New York until its closing in 1967. Holm had studied with Dalcroze and Wigman, taught at Wigman's studio, and toured the United States with Wigman's company in 1930–31. Her students included Valerie Bettis, Don Redlich, Glen Tetley, and Alwin Nikolais. With Graham, Humphrey, and Weidman, Holm was part of Bennington College's summer dance festival and school from 1934 to 1941. Holm was renowned as a choreographer of social conscience. Her dance *Trend* (1937), for instance, showed an apocalyptic, redemptive vision of society's decline and destruction. Her *Metropolitan Daily* (1938) satirized urban newspapers. *Tragic Exodus* (1939) mourned the persecution and forced exile of Jews. In *They Too Are Exiles* (1940), an outcry against Nazi despotism, the juncture of dance and ethnicity was the symbol for political repression. In one section, various groups performed their ethnic dances of identity—but a dictator-figure, The Possessor, violently stopped them.

Holm was also interested in exploring the American side of her national affiliation, in such works based on American folk material as

Hanya Holm performing in *Work and Play*.

Namesake (1942), based on Edgar Lee Masters's *Spoon River Anthology;* *Ozark Suite* (1957); *Walt Whitman Suite* (1945); *What So Proudly We Hail* (1942); and *Sousa March* (1955). Besides her work for the concert stage, in the forties Holm began choreographing for Broadway musicals. *Kiss Me, Kate* (1948), *My Fair Lady* (1956), and *Camelot* (1960) are perhaps her best-known works. [27]

Another important politically committed choreographer was Tamiris (née Helen Becker, 1905–66). Unlike most of the modern dance choreographers of her generation, Tamiris was trained as a ballet dancer, studying with Fokine and Rosina Galli. She even performed with the Metropolitan Opera Ballet before embarking on a career in modern dance in 1927. Modern dance, she felt, provided an appropriate form for her chosen themes. Like Holm, she made Americana dances, such as her own *Walt Whitman Suite* (1934) and the dances for *Stovepipe Hat* (1944), a folk play about Abraham Lincoln. And, like Holm, her dances did not merely celebrate American culture; they asked profound questions about social crises like unemployment and lynch mobs (*Momentum* [1936]) and the prospects of war (*Harvest 1935* [1935]). Tamiris was concerned with racial oppression, and she was interested in black culture, a political commitment that shaped two important works: the suite *Negro Spirituals* (1928–42) and *How Long Brethren?* (1937), a call for racial justice choreographed to African-American protest songs. In 1944 she participated in an interracial revue that toured the country to barnstorm for President Roosevelt's reelection. Also recalling Holm, Tamiris's sympathy for the workingman led her to choreograph for the popular Broadway stage; her musicals included *Up in Central Park* (1945), with a skating ballet straight out of Currier and Ives; a revival of *Show Boat* (1946), with Pearl Primus as the lead dancer in the African dances; and *Annie Get Your Gun* (1946), which included an Indian ballet taken from her earlier *Stovepipe Hat*. Tamiris was involved in organizing dancers for better working conditions and for political expression in the thirties and from 1936 to 1939 was a staff choreographer for the WPA Federal Theatre Dance Project in New York. With her husband, Daniel Nagrin, she directed the Tamiris-Nagrin Dance Company in 1960–63. [28]

These choreographers offered left-wing criticisms of American capitalist culture in the 1930s. In this they were joined by many younger dancers, some of them members of Graham's and Humphrey's companies, who, often allied with the nascent labor union movement and with Communist Party cultural organizations, formed political dance troupes like the Red Dancers, New Duncan Dancers, Modern Negro Dance Group, New Dance Group, and Theater Union Dance Group. Their umbrella organization was the Workers' Dance League, which— like the Workers' Theatre League and the Film and Photo League— fostered social agitprop through art. The dancers' themes included celebrations of the Soviet Union (as in Sophie Maslow's *Two Songs About Lenin* [1934]), support for the Loyalists during the Spanish Civil War, the dangers of German Fascism (as in the Nature Friends Dance Group's *Kinder, Kueche und Kirche* [1934]), and American racism (as in the Modern Negro Dance Group's *Black Hands, Black Feet* [1934] and the Red Dancers' *Scottsboro* [1934]).

During the Popular Front period, the Workers' Dance League softened their class conflict rhetoric and renamed themselves the New Dance League, often turning to the celebration of American folk themes in their dances, and inviting the more "establishment" modern dancers and dancers of other genres to join their concert programs. Out of this political dance effort, only the New Dance Group, with its studio offering training in a variety of dance techniques, survives. [29]

Meanwhile, on the West Coast, Lester Horton (1906–53) was devising dances based on Indian lore. As a young man in Chicago, Horton had studied with Bolm and had worked with the Japanese modern dancer Michio Ito. He also studied Native American dancing. Horton went to Los Angeles in 1928 with his pageant *The Song of Hiawatha* and remained there for the rest of his life. His Indian dances included *Takwish, the Star Maker* (1932), *Aztec Ballet* (1934), *Sun Ritual* (1935), *Rain Quest* (1935), and *Totem Incantation* (1948). In his 1929 article "American Indian Dancing," written the year before Graham was inspired by Native American ceremonies, Horton wrote, "A dance can be built upon these art forms that would be truly representative of this great country, something new and fundamental." [30]

Horton also choreographed political works, including the antifascist *Dictator* (1935); *The Mine* (1935), about a strike after a mine disaster; the epic *Chronicle* (1937), a critical narrative of American history; *Tierra y Libertad!* (1939), about the Mexican revolution; and *The Park* (1949), about the Los Angeles Police Department's brutality toward Chicanos. The technique that Horton developed incorporated various kinds of world dance, and, although he was white, his group was racially integrated from the beginning, with American Indian, Mexican-American, African-American, and Euro-American members. His dancers included Bella Lewitzky, Carmen de Lavallade, Joyce Trisler, James Truitte, the future fashion designer Rudi Gernreich, and Alvin Ailey, whose own technique, when he came to form his company in New York, was firmly based on Horton's teachings. [31]

Thus on both coasts the formative period now known as historical modern dance set up, in the interwar years, a model of an expressive art built on a curious mix of self-exploration, exotic appropriation, nationalist celebration, and socially conscious criticism. If the dancers of this generation shared self-exploration and a taste for the exotic with the forerunners of modern dance who produced them, it was their sense of national identity and social conscience that not only distinguished their dancing from what came before but also from what followed, the second-generation modern dancers who turned toward abstraction.

African-American concert dancing

In the twenties and thirties another genre emerged on the dance concert stage: African-American concert dancing. African-Americans had contributed to American popular dance culture since its beginnings— informally in dance halls and, by the end of the nineteenth century, in theaters, with black minstrel shows and the black vaudeville circuit. Some African-American entertainers, such as Bert Williams, even appeared in white vaudeville shows. But the African-American entry into concert dancing began in the 1920s, during the Harlem Renaissance, when for the first time blacks were able to gain access to theater spaces, financing, and jobs as dancers, composers, musicians, and writers for the stage. Although nightclubs like the Cotton Club in New York City featured African-American entertainers, both owners and audiences were white. However, also during this time, a spate of all-black musicals, beginning with *Shuffle Along* (1921; Flournoy Miller and Aubrey Lyles, choreographers; Noble Sissle, lyricist, and Eubie Blake, composer)— written by blacks originally for black audiences—moved from Harlem to Broadway. These black musicals entertained both races and provided jobs for a generation of artists—some of whom (such as Josephine Baker and Bill Robinson) became international stars. The musicals also introduced jazz music to the Broadway stage, as well as black dances like the Charleston and tap, which would become an indelible part of white American musical comedy.

Some black performers gained fame and fortune through the black musicals of the twenties—shows like *Plantation Revue, Dixie to Broadway, Runnin' Wild,* and *Chocolate Dandies*—and the social and popular dance repertoire of white America was powerfully influenced by the African heritage filtered through the revue dances. Still, as the names of these shows suggest, the image of African-Americans purveyed by the black musicals often perpetuated the racial stereotypes of the minstrel show. In this context of widening possibilities for black dancers, however, there was another kind of dance that emerged from the Harlem Renaissance—the aspiration to high art, rather than entertainment, in the form of concert dancing. And African-American artists looked for ways to create high art that would be uniquely theirs, not an imitation of Euro-American culture.

Paralleling the literature, music, and theater of the period, African-American artists sought both forms and content shaped by their history and heritage. In this regard, like their white peers in concert dancing, they too trafficked in primitivism. But their use of the exotic was a search for their own cultural links to Africa, a coding of their own cultural identity not in terms of the Other, but in terms of the history of the self. Hemsley Winfield (1907?–34), whose mother was a playwright, was an actor who became a dancer after filling in for the role of Salomé in Oscar Wilde's play. He founded the Negro Art Theater Dance Group in Harlem in 1931. The group's first concert, proudly billed as the "First Negro Concert in America," included dances based on African themes. It also included dances by Denishawn graduate Edna Guy, which were set to black spirituals, as well as two Orientalist dances, also by Guy, in the manner of St. Denis. Dancing the Witch Doctor in the voodoo ballet for *The Emperor Jones,* which he choreographed in 1933, Winfield became the first African-American to dance at the Metropolitan Opera. The same year, his group performed in Hall Johnson's play *Run, Little Chillun!,* choreographed by Humphrey.

Winfield's group may have offered the first *professional* concert of black dancing in the United States. But in 1925 the first documented concert was given by students in the Creative Dance Group at Hampton Institute, a black college in Virginia. Their aesthetic program was three-pronged, involving reconstructions of actual African dances, such as *Wyomamie,* based on marriage rituals; modern dances based on black American folk material like the juba and the cakewalk; and dramatic dances, like *Middle Passage,* about the transatlantic slave trade. The Hampton example set a model for other black colleges in the South, which also formed dance companies, and many of the members of its dance group, on graduating, became teachers who passed on these ideas about African-American dance to their students. Just as white modern dance was being spread through college dance clubs and physical education departments, whose faculty attended the Bennington summer sessions, black concert dancing was proliferating through black colleges as succeeding generations carried on the tradition of presenting African-American cultural history in dance form. This tradition continues to the present day.

Another important pioneer of African-American concert dance was Asadata Dafora, an African born in Sierra Leone, who studied music in Europe. He came to New York in 1929 and in 1934 produced *Kykunkor: The Witch Woman,* a full-length pageant of sumptuously theatricalized African dance and music. The cast included both native Africans and African-Americans, and the successful format and use of African material set a rich precedent. With the neo-African cultural revival following the Black Power movement of the late sixties, a number of dance groups devoted themselves to presenting African ritual dance on Dafora's model. Charles Moore, one of Dafora's students, was instrumental in carrying on this strand of African-American concert dancing.

In 1937 a German, Eugene Von Grona, organized the American Negro Ballet, a modern dance troupe, which made its debut at the Lafayette Theater in Harlem. Also by 1937, the white world of modern dance had been opened to black choreographers. That year, a Negro Dance Evening at the 92nd Street YMHA, a central venue for modern dance, featured Guy, Dafora, and the younger dancers Katherine Dunham and Talley Beatty. Various modern dance groups, including Graham's, also included black dancers.

Katherine Dunham (1910–   ) trained as an anthropologist at the University of Chicago and with Melville Herskovits while also studying dance. She combined her two professions doing field research in the Caribbean. She then began to present her company in spectacular shows that featured theatricalized Caribbean folk dances, such as *Tropics* (1937), and *Le Jazz Hot* (1938), *Tropical Revue* (1943), and *Bal Nègre* (1946).

Recalling Diaghilev's presentations of Russian pageantry to European audiences, but from a trained anthropological perspective, Dunham created ethnographic spectacles with claims to authenticity that also electrified her audiences. She ferreted out "pure" African-American dances outside of the United States, where she felt that Africanisms persisted more strongly. And, consistent with so many other modern dancers, she had come to the paradoxical conclusion that the truly American dance could only be found, in its essence, outside of mainstream United States culture. She wrote, in 1938:

Katherine Dunham drew from her combined training in anthropology as well as dance to create "ethnographic spectacles."

Realizing that the amalgamation of the Negro into white America has in a large measure brought about a complete lack of contact with those things which were racially his, I have recently begun an intensive study of the Negro under other less absorbing cultural contacts; in the West Indies the French, Spanish and English influence have been of far less importance than that of the American in this country. In the recreational and ceremonial dances of the island peasantry are preserved the dance forms which are truly Negro. [32]

In the 1940s and 1950s, Dunham worked in Broadway musicals. She and her company appeared in *Cabin in the Sky* (1940; choreographed by

Balanchine), and in *Carib Song* (1945), which Dunham choreographed. In Hollywood she worked on *Star Spangled Rhythm* (1941), *Stormy Weather* (1943), and other films and made a short color film of her own, *Carnival of Rhythm* (1941). She also continued to present revues with her own company through the 1960s. During 1945–55 she ran the Dunham School of Dance in New York, which, under the direction of former company member Syvilla Fort, taught the technique Dunham had synthesized from Caribbean, African, and European styles. In 1963 Dunham choreographed the dances for *Aida* at the Met. A number of important African-American dancers and choreographers— including Beatty, Janet Collins, Lavinia Williams, Jean-Léon Destiné, and Moore—came from Dunham's company and school, while her indirect influence has strongly shaped African-American concert dance for half a century.

Pearl Primus (1919–   ), also an anthropologist, came to specialize in African dances. Born in Trinidad, she moved to New York as a child. She became a premed student at Hunter College. But at the same time, she studied dance at the New Dance Group and in 1943 made her debut with *African Ceremonial*. After choreographing dances like *Strange Fruit,* about a lynching, and *Hard Time Blues,* about sharecropping (both 1943), she made a research trip to the South in 1944, where she visited black churches, prayer meetings, and sharecroppers. In 1948 she made her first of many trips to Africa, finding source material that was to inspire her choreography thereafter.

These were the pioneers of African-American concert dancing. [33] Dunham and Primus, in particular, consolidated an African-American modern dance style, building on formats and themes used by earlier black dancers, and inspired by the ritual dances of African cultures and the legacy of those dance traditions in the Americas. They celebrated the values and practices of African-American culture, they criticized American racism, and they served as role models in the black community. When in the sixties African-Americans once again put their political struggle in the center stage of American life, a new generation of black dancers, formed by these earlier pioneers, already possessed a dance idiom to affirm their cultural identity.

In the sixties a new, post-civil-rights movement of black dance emerged. If Dunham's and Primus's works celebrated African-American culture by theatricalizing its rituals and folkways, the next wave of young black choreographers, inspired by the Black Power movement, had more militant ways of coding black culture. This was a new twist on the enduring question of how American dance could most faithfully convey, or represent, American experience. In this case, the content was overtly oppositional. Rod Rodgers (1939–   ), who had grown up near Detroit, Michigan, and danced with Hawkins before forming his own company, wrote, in 1968:

Katherine Dunham and Pearl Primus (above) *"consolidated an African-American modern dance style, building on formats and themes used by earlier black dancers."*

> The dance that I do is Afro-American, simply because I am Afro-American. My blackness is part of my identity as a human being, and my dance exploration is evolving in relation to my total experience as a man. . . . Each dance I create has grown out of my personal experience as a black American. [34]

Rodgers presented his dances, both those based on African-American folk themes and abstract studies, to inner-city audiences, like children in Harlem, Brooklyn, and the Bronx, in the late sixties. By the eighties, the playwright Ntozake Shange was still describing him as an artist "free in movement and committed, through dance, to the end of racism, nuclear war, and hunger." [35]

Eleo Pomare (1937–   ), born in Colombia, grew up in Panama and Harlem. He attended the School of Performing Arts in New York and studied with Kurt Jooss in West Germany in the fifties; he formed a company and began showing work in the mid-sixties. *Blues for the Jungle*

(1965) is a paradigmatic work by Pomare, with vignettes showing street people in Harlem from a shopping-bag lady to a junkie to a street-corner preacher. The confrontational politics of the late sixties were reflected as the dancers jumped off the stage and into the aisles of the theater. Pomare spoke of this period of his work as formed by the Black Power movement:

> I used to think constantly of pleasing white audiences. I used to
> see through blue eyes. Now, the new black consciousness, the black
> revolution in the streets and in the arts supports and sustains me. [36]

Moreover, what it meant to be black at that moment in American history was the message of his dances, and he very consciously departed from the ethnographic folk style of earlier black choreographers in order to convey it.

> I don't create works to amuse white crowds, nor do I wish to show
> them how charming, strong, and folksy Negro people are. . . . Instead
> I'm showing them the Negro experience from inside: what it's like
> to live in Harlem, to be hung-up and uptight and black and wanting
> to get out. And I'm saying it in a dance language that originates in
> Harlem itself. [37]

Other choreographers such as Arthur Hall in Philadelphia, Chuck Davis (now in Durham, N.C.), and Moore in New York responded to the Black Power movement of the late sixties by researching and re-creating West African dances to acknowledge the strong ties between African and African-American culture. Shange describes Hall's *Fat Tuesday,* a re-creation of African dance transplanted to New Orleans:

> A high ceremony of candles, sequins, and drums, with a deity draped
> in yellow and black, undulating under marvels of feathers, takes us
> back once again to some form of parity. A movement not defiled—or
> at least not violated. . . . Double-dutch to sand-dancing, roller-disco to
> Lucumbe, alive and well in Cuba. There is always a continuity to our
> movement. [38]

Yet another movement in African-American dance grew out of the Black Power movement of the 1960s. In 1968, after Martin Luther King's assassination, Arthur Mitchell, then a soloist with the New York City Ballet, decided to teach ballet in Harlem to African-Americans and to build an all-black classical ballet company. To run the school he hired Karel Shook, a white dancer who had taught ballet at Dunham's school in the fifties. The school has groomed a generation of black dancers who have joined Mitchell's company and other ballet companies in the United States and Europe.

Mitchell's ballet company, Dance Theatre of Harlem, had its debut in 1970, sparking surprising controversy about the suitability of black

Marie Rambert

bodies for performing classical ballet. Time has largely settled the question. Although its dancers are all black, the repertory includes ballets by white choreographers such as Balanchine, Nijinska, Fokine, Jerome Robbins, John Taras, Ruth Page, and William Dollar. And the company performs classics like *Swan Lake* and *Giselle* (which in 1984 it performed with a Louisiana bayou-country setting). But Dance Theatre of Harlem is also a showcase for African-American choreographers, including Mitchell, Louis Johnson, and William Scott. Johnson's *Forces of Rhythm* (1971) is a paradigmatic work for the Dance Theatre of Harlem, creating a spectacular, dynamic competition between African dance and classical ballet. Mitchell's company has shown that black dancers can do both with equal virtuosity, transcending the tension between their African and the European dance legacies.

Post-Diaghilev European ballet

In an atmosphere of rising nationalism in Europe in the 1930s, many of the British dancers left jobless after the deaths of Diaghilev and Pavlova returned home to try to build a national ballet. Two major companies were established in the 1930s: what would eventually be called the Royal Ballet (since 1946 the resident company at Covent Garden) and Ballet Rambert.

The Royal Ballet, known first as the Vic–Wells Ballet, then from 1940–56 as the Sadler's Wells Ballet, was directed from its inception in 1931 by Ninette de Valois (1898–   ; born Edris Stannus in Ireland), who danced with Diaghilev 1923–25. De Valois and Ashton, who began with Rambert, were the chief choreographers for de Valois's company until after World War II, when it became a repertory company with a broad roster of new works, revivals, and classics, and a star ballerina in Margot Fonteyn.

Marie Rambert (1888–1982; born Cyvia Rambam in Warsaw) studied Duncan-style dancing, and studied and taught with Dalcroze. Diaghilev hired her to be Nijinsky's rhythmic adviser for *Sacre* and to dance in his company. Moving to London when World War I broke out, she formed a company, at first known as the Marie Rambert Dancers, then the Ballet Club (at the Mercury Theater), and after 1935, the Ballet Rambert. Although Rambert occasionally produced classic ballets, her company was first and foremost a progressive one. Under the directorship since 1986 of Richard Alston (1948–   ; a British modern dance choreographer who studied with Cunningham and in the seventies had his own troupe, Strider), the Ballet Rambert continues to present and commission experimental ballets.

Frederick Ashton (1904–88), born in Ecuador of English parents, was encouraged to choreograph by Rambert, and from 1926 onward, he did so prolifically, at first for Rambert's company. Then in 1935 he became the chief choreographer of de Valois's Vic–Wells company, and eventually succeeded de Valois (in 1963) as the director of the Royal Ballet. Ashton was the prime exemplar of the English style: purity of line, pristine simplicity, and an overall feeling of serenity, as shown in a work like *Symphonic Variations* (1946; music by César Franck), a plotless ballet for six dancers. [39]

Two other choreographers shaped the post-Diaghilev English ballet. Antony Tudor (1908–87), who studied with Rambert, choreographed several signature works for her company. Among these was *Jardin aux Lilas* (1936; music by Ernest Chausson), a psychological drama about a woman entering into a loveless marriage. In 1939 Tudor moved to the United States to work with American Ballet Theatre, where he continued to develop his distinctive style of dramatic choreography that plumbs the depths of human emotion. Andrée Howard (1910–68) was an original member of Rambert's company. With Tudor, she went to the United States to work with American Ballet Theatre in 1939. Howard soon returned to England, where she continued to choreograph on a free-lance basis.

The English ballet as it was formed in the thirties was in many respects a descendant of the Russian ballet. Its audiences were trained by the London seasons of the Diaghilev Ballets Russes, its dancers came from his company, and its major producers, also from his company, emulated his practices. Yet, in an assertion of national identity, the new generation of British ballet dancers created a style distinguished by its clarity, graciousness, restraint, and gentle wit.

Even post-Diaghilev French ballet was at first ruled by a Russian, Serge Lifar (1905–86), who had been Diaghilev's lead male dancer in the second half of the 1920s. In 1929 Lifar became the head of the Paris Opéra Ballet, which had languished since the late nineteenth century and now, inspired by the Ballets Russes's example and overhauled by Lifar, once again became a flourishing company.

However, in France, as in England, a sense of national affiliation eventually led French dancers to break from the Paris Opéra and its Russian-born leadership, although it was only after World War II that several members of the younger generation emerged, working with various small, short-lived companies. These included Les Ballets des Champs-Élysées, which lasted from 1945 to 1950, with Roland Petit (1924–) and Jeanine Charrat (1924–) as chief choreographers, and Petit's Ballets de Paris, founded in 1948 and starring his wife, Renée "Zizi" Jeanmaire. Maurice Béjart (1927–) is the most well-known post-World War II French choreographer. He formed his first company in 1953. In 1960, invited to the Théâtre Royal de la Monnaie

Frederick Ashton (left) and Robert Helpmann (for years the partner of Margot Fonteyn) rehearsing their roles as the Ugly Sisters in *Cinderella*.

in Brussels, he formed the Ballet du XXe Siècle. Béjart's choreography, like Petit's, is dramatically erotic and had a special appeal to the youth counterculture of the sixties.

Meanwhile in the 1930s, two rival, at times interlocking, successors to Diaghilev's company appeared: the Ballet Russe de Monte Carlo (produced at first by Colonel W. de Basil and then by Sergei Denham) and the Original Ballet Russe (de Basil's second company). The de Basil Ballet Russe de Monte Carlo hired dancers from the Diaghilev company and offered ballets from the Diaghilev repertory as well as new works by Balanchine, Nijinska, and Massine. Balanchine left the de Basil company in 1933 to work for the short-lived company Les Ballets 1933, which produced several of his ballets and *The Seven Deadly Sins,* a collaboration with Kurt Weill and Bertolt Brecht. Massine succeeded Balanchine as ballet master of the Ballet Russe. In 1938, with Denham as its new impresario, the Massine company toured London and the United States. The Ballet Russe took up residence in New York during World War II and became the most popular touring ballet company in America during the war and postwar years. At times it vied for audiences with the second de Basil company, which took up residence in London as the Covent Garden Russian Ballet (it would change its name several more times), toured North and South America and Australia during the war, returned to London in 1946, and disbanded the following year.

Thus the Diaghilev legacy was decentralized in the thirties. The company's repertory was spread to various new troupes, serving as a firm basis for additions by Diaghilev's former choreographers and by new choreographers groomed by Diaghilev's former dancers. The Diaghilev internationalism continued in the various Ballet Russe companies, while simultaneously various efforts were made to use the Diaghilev model to build specifically national ballets.

Soviet ballet

The values of the nineteenth-century Russian ballet were epitomized by the emulation of Louis XIV's court in the glittering, imperial *Sleeping Beauty* (1890). After the October Revolution, even on the ballet stage choreographers experimented with new social formations, often featuring Russian folk dances. For example, Kasian Goleizovsky (1892–1970) with *The Whirlwind* (1927) and Fyodor Lupukhov (1886–1973) with *Red Whirlwind* (1924) both allegorized the fall of the Romanov empire and the coming of a new political order. Both choreographers expanded the ballet vocabulary with movements taken from popular entertainments, from acrobatics to jazz dancing. Also in the twenties, modern dance studios, including that of Duncan and her imitators, as

Maya Plisetskaya (right) and Vladimir Levashev perform in *The Stone Flower*.

well as studios influenced by Dalcroze and Wigman, mushroomed in an era of political and artistic experimentation. The studios of Nikolai Foregger and Vera Maya specialized in machine dances, and in the dramatic theater, biomechanics, revue dancing, and circus tricks made actors into dancers. [40]

However, the relative political and economic freedom afforded by Lenin's New Economic Policy, which in turn gave rise to experimentation in the arts, began to be curtailed by the late twenties. In ballet the turning point toward conservatism was *The Red Poppy* (1927), choreographed by Lev Lashchilin and Vassily Tikhomirov, which had a revolutionary theme—the liberation of China—but took a standard nineteenth-century approach to the story ballet, complete with an opium-dream fantasy scene. *The Red Poppy* created socialist realist heroes in the Soviet naval captain and the exploited dancer who dies to save him and world communism. Indeed, part of its great appeal was the spirited Yablochko, a Russian folk dance performed by the Soviet sailors.

After 1932, when Socialist Realism became the official Soviet style, such heroes were requisite in new ballets, such as Rostislav Zakharov's *The Fountain of Bakhchisarai* (1934) and Leonid Lavrovsky's *Prisoner of the Caucasus* (1938) and *The Stone Flower* (1952). However, the nineteenth-century classics remained in the repertory of the two great Russian ballet institutions, the Kirov and the Bolshoi ballets. After the era of choreographic experimentation in the twenties, the Soviet ballet was known primarily for the virtuosic technical training of its dancers, especially under the leadership of Agrippina Vaganova. But the stream of Russian dancers to the West that had supplied Diaghilev with his finest performers continued. When Rudolf Nureyev defected in 1961, eventually joining the Royal Ballet and dancing with many other companies, he brought with him a new standard of male dancing, as well as many classic works from the Russian repertory, which he mounted for various European companies. In the seventies two more famous defectors, Natalya Makarova and Mikhail Baryshnikov, settled in the United States. Meanwhile, in the Soviet Union in the eighties, *glasnost* opened up new directions, ranging from the reconstruction of *The Golden Age* (1930), an experimental ballet by Vassily Vainonen, Leonid Yacobson, and Vladimir Chesnakov that featured acrobatic football players and jazz dancers with the Kirov Ballet, to the setting of Balanchine's *Scotch Symphony*.

American ballet

Before the 1930s, ballet in America had largely consisted of touring European companies. Starting in the thirties, the American ballet began to define itself in opposition to the Russian dominance (meaning that of the Ballets Russes and its successor companies) in ballet in the Western world.

As in Europe, this initiative was framed in terms of national identity. Kirstein, one of the founders of the New York City Ballet, wrote in 1937 that "we may have to pay for an aggressively nationalistic period at present to offset the recent drag of Russian blackmail, but if so, it will be only a transient and healthy reaction." [41] For Kirstein the way to a "native" American ballet was three-pronged: first, American folklore and history should be plumbed for subject matter; second, new ballets should be choreographed to classical music; and third, choreographers must tap American vernacular forms of dance: the two-step, the lindy hop, the Susy-Q, the big apple, and other forms of jazz dancing, as well as square dancing and vaudeville. Kirstein labeled these forms "American character dancing—our parallel to the national dances of Spain, Italy or Russia." [42]

But it was Kirstein, ironically, who helped create the American ballet by another method altogether—importing to the United States the greatest Russian-trained choreographer of this century, George Balanchine (1904–83). Balanchine, who had choreographed in Petrograd before leaving the Soviet Union in 1924, worked for Diaghilev from 1925 to 1929. After Diaghilev's death, Balanchine enlisted in a rapid succession of companies: the Paris Opéra, the Royal Danish Ballet, the Ballet Russe de Monte Carlo, and Les Ballets 1933. Then, on Kirstein's invitation, he arrived in New York to organize a classical academy, the School of American Ballet, founded in 1934. From this school Balanchine selected the students who formed his first American company, the American Ballet, which had its first New York season at the Adelphi Theater in 1935. The seven ballets, all by Balanchine, given during that season included a new ballet, *Serenade,* to the music of Tchaikovsky, a classical meditation on ballet technique; there were also ballets to the music of Franz Schubert and Franz Liszt made for Les Ballets 1933; and there was a salute to Balanchine's new adopted country: *Alma Mater,* a ballet about American college football rituals, set to music by Kay Swift.

The American Ballet was invited to be the resident company at the Metropolitan Opera in 1935. There it remained for three controversial years; Balanchine was unhappy about his lack of artistic freedom, and the management was dissatisfied with the modernist opera ballets he devised. The company disbanded after Balanchine left the Met in 1938. It was then revived briefly in 1941 to tour South America. Reorganized in 1946 as Ballet Society, with a subscription audience, this company produced new works by Balanchine (including Paul Hindemith's *Four Temperaments* [1946] and Stravinsky's *Orpheus* [1948]) and by Taras, Todd Bolender, and Lew Christensen. In 1948 the company joined the New York City Center and was renamed the New York City Ballet; in

George Balanchine assists Allegra Kent during a rehearsal.

1964 it took up residence in the New York State Theater at Lincoln Center. Although it continued to present ballets by choreographers in the company—including Robbins (after 1949) and Peter Martins (after 1978)—it was Balanchine as artistic director (right up to his death) who put his stamp on the repertory and company style. [43]

This Russian choreographer was the one who truly Americanized ballet, not so much by adopting American themes for subject matter, along Kirstein's suggested lines, as by reworking the classical technique to suit American long-limbed bodies and the brisk American tempo. It was Balanchine's school that became the fundamental American ballet institution, setting standards of technical prowess, recruiting students from the provinces, producing many of the greatest American dancers,

Arthur Mitchell and Diana Adams in *Agon*.

and, funded by the Ford Foundation, training teachers who disseminated that technique nationwide.

Balanchine did, of course, regularly dabble in Americana. For instance, besides *Alma Mater,* there was *Jones Beach* (with Robbins, 1950; music by Jurriaan Andriessen and bathing suits by Jantzen) and *Bayou* (1952; music by Virgil Thomson), based on Acadian folklore. Both *Western Symphony* (1954; music by Hershy Kay), a plotless ballet with elegant academic steps that managed at the same time to evoke barroom dancing in the American West, and *Square Dance* (1957), which juxtaposed the strict forms of American folk dancing with those of classical music by Antonio Vivaldi and Arcangelo Corelli, were typically Balanchinian mixtures of classical ballet moves and vernacular dance forms. While working on *Stars and Stripes* (1958), a splashy spectacle replete with baton-twirling majorettes and a giant flag, done to marching music by John Philip Sousa, Balanchine was asked whether his new ballet had a story. He replied that it did—"the United States." [44]

There are many Balanchine ballets influenced by or about jazz, from *Jazz Concert: Ragtime* (1960; music by Stravinsky), a short duet that suggested European "jazz age" adaptations of the American vernacular, to *Who Cares?* (1970), a series of Gershwin songs with a kaleidoscope of moods mirrored in solo, duet, and ensemble episodes. Perhaps his best-known jazz ballet is *Slaughter on Tenth Avenue* (1936; music by Richard Rodgers), a miniature satire of a hard-boiled detective story, originally choreographed as part of the musical comedy *On Your Toes* but in 1968 reworked for the New York City Ballet.

Balanchine's work in the 1930s for the Broadway stage and the Hollywood screen often dealt with American themes—such as *Louisiana Purchase* (1940); the all-black musical *Cabin in the Sky* (1940), featuring Dunham's dancers; and the movie *Star-Spangled Rhythm* (Paramount, 1942). While his speed, his syncopated rhythms, and his ballerinas' thrust-forward hips and angled wrists have all been in some measure influenced by American culture (jazz and black dance), his choreography also ranges over the romantic (as in *La Source* [1968; music by Delibes]) and traditional (he did a *Swan Lake* and a *Nutcracker*). But the bulk of his ballet repertory is neoclassical and abstract.

Apollo (1928), the ballet created for Diaghilev's company that set Balanchine on the road to neoclassicism, has remained in the repertory. It was not only an affirmation, through the symbolism of Greek mythology, of that sense of classical values—a world with the human body and its artistic and physical powers joined at the center—it was also a ratification of the so-called classical ballet technique of the nineteenth century, with its five positions, balances on pointe, leg extensions, jumps, and intricate footwork. When practice clothes were substituted for the original tunics, the classicism of the steps emerged even more clearly. Yet this familiar technique was expanded in surprising ways: for instance, Apollo walks on his knees, and the Muses shuffle on their heels. The young god balances all three Muses, their extended legs forming the spokes of a wheel, on his back, then harnesses them like a troika-drawn chariot. Apollo's duet with Terpsichore, the Muse of dance, seems to contain within it a meditation on the art form's unique potential for the poetry of physical expression.

Concerto barocco (1941; music by J. S. Bach) is one of Balanchine's most rigorous and well-known pure-dance works. It is a dazzling example of Balanchine's ability to make the dance a visual embodiment of the musical score, so closely do the actions correspond to the voices, rhythms, and shapes of the music. The intricate, rapid counterpoint of the music finds its translation into dance in the precise, constantly interweaving patterns of the group, the "pretzeled" positions of the partnering, and the statement-response mirroring of the two women soloists. And this approach was perfected in *Agon* (1957; music by Stravinsky), a ballet in twelve parts for twelve dancers that, although based on Renaissance dance forms, is utterly modern in its thrust and energy. Kirstein wrote of its complexity, precision, and intensity:

> No dance work has been more highly organized or is so dense in
> movement in its bare twenty minutes. . . . The choreography projects a

111

steel skeleton clad in tightly knit action, lacing a membrane of movement over a transparent net of contrapuntal design, which in shifting concentration on separate dancers gives an impression of intense drama. . . . Group numbers assume the well-oiled synchronism of electrical timekeepers. . . . Dancers are manipulated as irreplaceable spare parts, substituting or alternating on strict beats. . . . Yet the aura is not mechanistic but musical, disciplined, witty. [45]

The other first-rank, long-lasting American ballet institution founded during the time of rising nationalism between the two world wars, eventually known as American Ballet Theatre, also had its origins in the Russian ballet. Mikhail Mordkin (1881–1944), who had danced with the Bolshoi Ballet and Diaghilev's first Paris season, toured the United States with Pavlova and then with his own company before returning to the Bolshoi in 1912. However, like Balanchine he left the Soviet Union in the early 1920s. Mordkin came to the United States in 1924. Out of the company and school he formed in New York came the nucleus of a new company, Ballet Theatre, in 1939.

That ballet was categorized along national lines in the thirties is clear not only from Kirstein's "Blast at Ballet," which practically sets up a pre-World War II cold war between Russia and the United States, but also from the separate wings Ballet Theatre established in its early years. These were: the Russian wing, the English wing, and the American wing. Headed by Anton Dolin, the Russian wing served as a museum of the classical ballet with productions such as *Giselle, Swan Lake,* and with several newer ballets by Russian-born choreographers like Fokine, Bolm, Mordkin, and Nijinska. The English wing, headed by Tudor, gave works by Tudor and Howard. The American wing, headed by Eugene Loring, in its first season (1940) presented Loring's *The Great American Goof* and Agnes de Mille's *Black Ritual.* This ballet, set to Milhaud's *La Création du monde,* featured an all-black cast, including some of Dunham's dancers. New ballets by Balanchine and Massine were soon added to Ballet Theatre's repertory, and new dancers were recruited from the various Ballet Russe companies, including Alicia Markova and Igor Youskevitch. The company produced its own choreographer, Robbins, with *Fancy Free* (music by Leonard Bernstein) in 1944. A contemporary ballet about three sailors on leave having a fling in New York, it served as the basis for the Betty Comden and Adolph Green musical *On the Town* (1944) and also set a precedent for an American vernacular character dance style that culminated in the Robbins-Bernstein musical *West Side Story.*

Tudor and Robbins trained a new generation of American dancers like Nora Kaye, Harold Lang, Michael Kidd, the Cuban dancer Alicia Alonso, and the British dancer Hugh Laing. Herbert Ross, who later worked as a film director (*Play It Again Sam* and *The Turning Point*), also choreographed for the company. By 1950 both Robbins and Tu-

Jerome Robbins in *Fancy Free.*

dor had left Ballet Theatre (Tudor was to return in 1974). Thereafter, Lucia Chase and the designer Oliver Smith, codirectors from 1945, followed a conservative policy of maintaining some ballets from the early repertory, acquiring new versions of classical full-length ballets (and occasionally commissioning new ballets) and recruiting stars from the United States and abroad. It was primarily as a ballet museum and star vehicle that American Ballet Theatre was known up through the seventies. [46]

On Chase's resignation in 1980, Soviet-trained Baryshnikov was appointed director. He inaugurated a new regime, once again grooming dancers within the company and strengthening the ensemble to create a coherent company style, simultaneously classical and adventurous, and commissioning "crossover" ballets by modern and postmodern choreographers like David Gordon, Mark Morris, Karole Armitage, and Twyla Tharp (who Baryshnikov appointed to the artistic staff in 1988). Once again, it was a transplanted Russian who put his unique stamp on the shape of American dance. After Baryshnikov's resignation in 1989, Jane Hermann (the former presentations director of the Met) and Smith took over as codirectors in early 1990. It seemed that after a decade of renovation and experimentation, American Ballet Theatre would return to ballet conservation. Baryshnikov, however, had fostered the most innovative ballet choreography of the post-Balanchine era, in particular with his collaborations with Tharp and his contribution to the crossover ballet. Baryshnikov has an unusually progressive vision of restructuring the ballet dancer's performing experience. Typically, after his departure from the American Ballet Theatre he formed a small touring modern dance company that featured himself and dancers from leading modern dance troupes performing choreography by Morris.

In 1936 Kirstein organized another ballet company, Ballet Caravan, with many of the same dancers as Balanchine's American Ballet, in order to build his dream of a specifically all-American repertory. [47] Ballet Caravan's productions included Christensen's *Pocahontas* (1936) and *Filling Station* (1937), and Loring's *Billy the Kid* (1938). Ballet Caravan merged with the American Ballet for the 1941 South American tour, but this company, called American Ballet Caravan, disbanded on its return. America, it seemed, was not interested enough in ballet to support either Balanchine's or Kirstein's company. Kirstein, holding up as examples the Littlefield Ballet in Philadelphia and the Ruth Page ballets in Chicago, called for a broad network of regional American ballet companies, a circuit for touring, cooperating with local symphony orchestras, and commissioning works from contemporary American composers. [48] His vision of a truly American decentralized ballet institution only began to be realized during the dance boom of the seventies. And although in the eighties some of those regional companies succumbed to financial woes, others, including the Boston Ballet, the Miami City Ballet, the Chicago Ballet, and the Pacific Northwest Ballet, all directed by former members of the American Ballet Theatre or the New York City Ballet, began to rival even the major New York companies.

In the 1940s even the Ballet Russe began Americanizing its repertory. The company produced its first work by an American choreographer in de Mille's *Rodeo* (1942). Set to music by Aaron Copland, this was a folk drama about a tomboy cowgirl and her blossoming romance that incorporated American vernacular movements into the ballet vocabulary; it was the nucleus of the choreography she did for the musical *Oklahoma!* Between 1944 and 1946, without any company of his own, Balanchine joined the Ballet Russe and produced several ballets. Then in 1947 Bettis staged *Virginia Sampler,* and Page restaged *Frankie and Johnny* (1938; co-choreographed with Bentley Stone). The Ballet Russe's roster of stars from 1938 to the end of its regular New York seasons in 1950 and its demise in 1962 included Alexandra Danilova, Markova, Mia Slavenska, Youskevitch, Mary Ellen Moylan, Leon Danielian, and Maria Tallchief. Its personnel peopled both New York and regional ballet companies as well as the ballet schools that would produce the next several generations of American ballet dancers.

By the time of John F. Kennedy's election to the presidency in 1960, the cold war was at its height. Not only were Americans conscious of the "missile gap" in the arms and science race with the Soviet Union; many believed that there was also an arts gap. Thus state sponsorship of dance tours abroad became part of a multipronged international political competition that also included the eventual establishment of the National Endowment for the Arts, in the public sector, and the underwriting of a major grant to the School of American Ballet, in the private sector. If dance had been a "weapon" for communist agitation in the 1930s, in the late fifties and sixties it became a tool for spreading the values of democracy abroad. For instance, Robbins organized the short-lived Ballets: U.S.A., which was formed in 1958 to show European audiences America's contribution to ballet. Its final performance was at the White House in 1962. Robbins tried to clarify the particular brand of nationalism that led to the founding of this company:

> The name of the company was chosen, not in any way to represent
> all of dance in the United States. . . . Nor was it meant to suggest
> "Americans" in terms of folklore or that it employs only native talent.
> I feel and believe very strongly that ballet dancing in America, [a]
> regional and imported product (much as were the forefathers of the
> people who now dance it), has been completely influenced and drastically
> changed by this nation and the culture in which it has grown up. We
> in America dress, eat, think, talk, and walk differently from any other
> people. We also dance differently, and this brilliant art of our dancers—
> unmistakably from the U.S.A.—has gained more friends and greater
> respect abroad than many people realize. [49]

Moreover, Robbins pointed out that the dancers in his company "represented almost every national trait, strain, and background," and that, while not encyclopedic, their repertory ranged widely, "from the classic ballet danced in tights, tutus, [and] toe shoes to our own current jazz style, most often performed in sneakers and knee guards." [50]

Modern dance companies like those of Ailey, Taylor, and Graham also toured Europe, South America, the Middle East, North Africa, and Asia, sponsored by the State Department. But the height of cold war competition came in the exchange visits of the Bolshoi Ballet (in 1959 and 1963) and the Kirov Ballet to the United States (in 1961) and the New York City Ballet's visit to the Soviet Union (in 1962). When Balanchine was greeted in Moscow with the words "Welcome to Moscow, home of the classic ballet," the choreographer replied: "I beg your pardon. Russia is the home of romantic ballet. The home of classic ballet is now America." [51]

Post-World-War II modern dance

It was partly the traditional tie between modern dance and politics that made several members of the second generation of modern dancers shy away from literal content. In the late forties and fifties, McCarthyism put a damper on radical political expression in art in the United States. Abstraction became a way out (even if an unconscious one to many artists) and, in its own way, another kind of political expression—one that spoke metaphorically of artistic freedom. But also, there were new, immediate models for abstraction. Modernist European artists had arrived during the war; they brought with them fresh winds of avant-garde formal theatrical experiment.

José Limón (1908–72) stands somewhere between the first and second generations of modern dancers. A younger contemporary and student of Humphrey, he danced with the Humphrey-Weidman company in the 1930s and began to choreograph his own works in 1931. But it was not until 1947 that Limón formed his own company, inviting Humphrey to serve as artistic codirector. Her works for the company complemented his own broad humanistic vision, as in his *Missa Brevis* (1958), to Zoltán Kodály's music, a paean of faith in face of war, showing people in a bombed-out city rebuilding their lives; or *Legend* (1968), about the history of black slavery in the United States. These were dances that showed a "universal" concern with people's fates.

However, many of Limón's dances were more narrowly shaped by his Mexican heritage. For instance, *La Malinche* (1949) was a retelling, in the framework of a peasant fiesta, of the legend of the native Mexican Indian woman who became Cortés's mistress, was repudiated as a traitor by her own people, but returned from the dead to help fight a revolution.

In an essay entitled "An American Accent," Limón distinguished American modern dance both from the frivolity of European ballet and from the gothic visions of German modern dance. He wrote:

> I was by origin a Mexican, reared in the United States. [When I began dancing I knew] I must find the dance to say what I had to say about what I was. . . . I view myself as a disciple and follower of Isadora Duncan and of the American impetus. . . . I try to compose works that are involved with man's basic tragedy and the grandeur of his spirit. [52]

However, others were drawn to formal experiment. Alwin Nikolais (1912–   ) studied with Holm and also with Graham, Humphrey, Weidman, and Horst. As a young man, he had worked in the theater as a technician, a puppeteer, and an accompanist for silent films. The brand of dance-theater he devised was related to the experiments of the Bauhaus, in which the human body was abstracted and sometimes extended into space. For instance, in the "Noumenon" section of *Masks, Props, and Mobiles* (1953), the dancers moved inside stretch jersey bags, which they manipulated into different shapes as they tilted, sat, stretched their arms, and so on. These creatures, who moved almost like humans but whose bodies were unrecognizable as members of our species, had a science-fiction quality analogous to the popular film genre of the fifties.

Essential to Nikolais's theater of forms is the use of his own lighting designs, projections, and other effects to create illusions. He also composes his own electronic music. Objecting to the obsession with the expressive subjectivity he sees in so much modern dance, he has devoted himself to abstraction and pointed out that this itself constituted a new freedom—"freedom from the domination of the concrete . . . freedom from the literal and peripheral self of man . . . [freedom from] the subject-vehicle demanded by fixation and reference to the literal scene." [53]

Paul Taylor (1930–) experimented in the 1950s with dances that had almost no movement, like *Epic* (1957), in which he stood still, gestured, and slowly advanced across the stage to a score by John Cage in which a recording of the current time ticked off the seconds. Taylor, who danced with Cunningham and then Graham while choreographing his own work, moved from these austere Cageian explorations of movement to the opposite extreme: pure, rapid, dense motion which he called "dance scribbling," assimilating this style of choreographing to the action painting of the Abstract Expressionists. *Junction* (1961) was the first of these essays. With *Aureole* (1962; music by G. F. Handel), he began making more lyrical dances to classical music. Taylor's repertory is broad in style, reflecting his own sense of ambivalence about the human condition. On the one hand, there are deliberately ugly dances in the "coarse vernacular," like *Scudodrama* (1963); on the other, dances that underscore human nobility, like *Esplanade* (1975). Taylor's company seems to be a metaphor for democracy in action; not only his choreographic style, but also the body types, sizes, and personalities of his dancers vary widely.

Alvin Ailey (1931–89) danced in Los Angeles with Horton and formed his own company in New York in 1958. Emerging in the context of the civil rights movement, Ailey's company presented his dances, often on African-American themes, to African-American music. For instance, *Revelations* (1960), his best-known work, is a dance in several episodes and varying moods set to spirituals. In it, Ailey captures the importance of the church in the life of the black community, showing sinners repenting ("Sinner Man"), a couple reaching out in hope ("Fix Me Jesus"), a rousing baptism ("Wading in the Water"), and a climactic finale that sets the whole church community testifying ("Rocka My Soul in the Bosom of Abraham"). As a repertory company, the Alvin Ailey American Dance Theater performs works by an eclectic roster of choreographers, from Shawn, Horton, Dunham, Primus, and Donald McKayle to Rudy Perez and Bill T. Jones. About his decision to integrate his then all-black company in 1962, Ailey said, "I wanted my dancers to feel that they were not just 'black dancers,' that they were

Paul Taylor and Bettie de Jong in *Scudodrama*.

a part of society. . . . An integrated company enlarges the statement
I've been trying to make." [54] After Ailey's death, Judith Jamison, a
former soloist in the company, became its head.

Perhaps it goes without saying that the most important modern dance
choreographer in post-World War II America was Merce Cunningham (1919–   ). Like Nikolais and like Taylor in his dance scribbling,
Cunningham seems to make dances that are metaphors for freedom.

Judith Jamison performing in the solo *Cry*, choreographed for her by Alvin Ailey.

Cunningham is well known for his laissez-faire collaborations with contemporary composers—especially Cage—and visual artists—especially Robert Rauschenberg and Jasper Johns—and for his use of chance techniques in choreographing his dances, beginning with *Sixteen Dances for Soloist and Company of Three* (1951). The independence of the dance from the music has been key to Cunningham's way of working. That is, the music and dancing are created independently and are meant simply to coexist in time and space. This mutual autonomy is one symbol for freedom, though Cunningham has explained it as reflecting the arbitrary correspondences of sight and sound experiences in daily life.

Cunningham's use of chance fomented a democratic revolution on the dance stage: it decentralized the space and undercut traditional hierarchies of body parts. Democratic, too, is his interest in the diversity of human movement. Everyone walks differently, Cunningham has pointed out; a walk is as individual as a fingerprint. Thus, he believes, everyone also dances differently. This marvelous capacity humans have for individual expressivity in such simple acts of locomotion creates sufficient expression in dancing, in his view; there is no need for external literary meanings. His dances are not meant to represent anything outside the dance but have an inborn expressiveness that often seems to signify values like freedom, flexibility, and plenitude. For instance, in *Channels/Inserts* (1981), originally choreographed for the film camera, the action takes place in different rooms (including the hallway) of the Cunningham studio in New York. As the dancers run from space to space, coalesce in groups, and change partners, they seem to be exercising complete individual choice. In one section of the dance, the men perform a series of solo virtuosic jumps on a short staircase. Not only are their bodies amazingly limber and inventive, but also they seem to keep coming in endless supply.

Cunningham was born in Centralia, Washington; he performed social and tap dancing as a boy and began his formal study of dance at the Cornish School in Seattle. After studying with Graham in 1939 at the Bennington School of Dance, held that summer at Mills College, he was invited to join her company. While still dancing with Graham in the early forties, Cunningham began to show his own solo work to Cage's music, such as *Root of an Unfocus* (1944). He also choreographed *The Seasons* (1947) for Ballet Society and taught at the School of American Ballet in 1948–51. In 1953 he formed the Merce Cunningham Dance Company, which first performed during a summer residency at Black Mountain College, and in 1959 he opened his studio in New York.

As virtuosic and technically precise as pure ballet, Cunningham's technique makes use of the contracting spine inherited from Graham, together with the vertical bodily orientation, elegant line, and articulate footwork stressed by classical technique. A prolific worker, he has choreographed over one hundred dances and also regularly creates events in which parts of his dances are spliced together anew, with different music and costumes. In many ways, Cunningham is a classicist; yet he welcomes the use of high technology and has designed several dances specifically for film and video.

Cunningham's approach to dance has been profoundly influenced

Photomontage of Merce Cunningham in *Root of an Unfocus*.

by non-Western thought, though his dance technique is purely Euro-American. The very notion of using chance was inspired by the *I Ching*, which he often uses to structure dances. In *Sixteen Dances,* his first piece structured by chance operations, Cunningham used the nine permanent emotions of Indian classical theater as a conceptual basis for the movements. Cunningham's biographer, David Vaughan, has pointed out the importance of Zen thought to Cunningham's aesthetic—especially in his use of stillness—and the enduring impact on him of his native Pacific Northwest, with its Asian-influenced culture. [55] Yet there is much about Cunningham's work that looks to his dance roots in American popular culture, from *Rag-Time Parade* (1950) to *Grange Eve* (1986) and *Carousal* (1987), and in the strong percussive rhythms, sometimes reminiscent of tap dancing, in his dances generally.

Not only has Cunningham changed the way we see dance in terms of its structure, its space, its relationship to music, and its meaning; he has also, like Graham, been a powerful teacher and dance master whose work has both influenced much of the choreography that followed him and served as a challenge to younger dancers to experiment even more radically. The Judson Dance Theater of the sixties and the postmodern dance movement it seeded was an extension and a response to Cunningham's rethinking of dance discourse. [56]

Postmodern dance

In dance, the term *postmodern* came into use in the early 1960s, when Yvonne Rainer and other emerging choreographers used it to differentiate their work from that of the preceding generation—modern dance. Many of the new generation had studied new methods of dance composition at the Cunningham studio with Robert Dunn, a musician who had studied with Cage. Several of Dunn's students organized a concert at the Judson Memorial Church in Greenwich Village in 1962, and out of this group grew the Judson Dance Theater, a loosely organized cooperative choreography collective that lasted for two years and spawned most of the innovative dance artists of the next two decades. [57]

The postmodern choreographers were not necessarily united stylistically. Their methods ranged from chance procedures to improvisation to picture-scores to rule-games and tasks, and from a minimalist interest in sustaining "one thing" to a welter of multimedia. Their vocabulary, too, partook of a uniquely early sixties spirit of democratic pluralism, radically extending the previous generation's metaphors for equality. Choreographers such as Rainer, Gordon, Simone Forti, Steve Paxton, Deborah Hay, Trisha Brown, Lucinda Childs, Judith Dunn, and Elaine Summers embraced unstylized ordinary activities—child's play, social dancing, daily tasks—as well as the more specialized actions of athletics, ballet, and modern dance techniques. In their work lay the seeds of both the analytic, reductive work of the seventies and a baroque, theatrical style that reemerged in the eighties.

Although these choreographers in no way represented stylistic homogeneity, they were united in their anti-modern project—that is, their desire to make dances that departed from the values and practices of the modern dance of Wigman, Graham, Humphrey, Limón, and followers. They also wanted to go even further than Cunningham did, making freedom more than just a metaphor—for example, by using improvisation in performance.

The postmodern dancers of the sixties transmuted Cunningham's (and others') abstraction into reflexivity—a meditation on how the dance was made, what it meant, and its role in dance history. This was accomplished through a variety of means—including manifestos, the insertion of verbal material in the dance itself, nudity, and ordinary movements. Their dances were often abstract and reflexive, but just as often ironic, dealing in everyday materials and inspecting historical and vernacular conventions. Perhaps because the body is so drenched with social and political symbolism, it was possible to create such symbolic meanings even in ostensibly nonrepresentational dance.

For instance, in Rainer's *We Shall Run* (1963), the dance consisted, on one level, of people running at a steady pace in different floor patterns, grouping and regrouping. But a number of factors—the grandiose music by Hector Berlioz, the serious calm of the dancers' demeanor, the variety of their body types, the very steadiness of their pace, and the way the paths allowed neither any one person nor any one gender to take a leader's role (while they did allow for individual forays from the group)—made this dance seem to be as much about a vision of a utopian, democratic community as it was a dance "about" a particular kind of movement or choreographic structure. It was light-years away from the distant nobility of Humphrey's *New Dance*. Its down-to-earth simplicity expressed the informality of a new generation. [58]

Other cultural themes of the early sixties pervaded these dances, not only reflecting many of the issues of post-World-War-II American society, but at times contesting and even, at times, creating them. In this time of a "troubled feast"—where, despite a cornucopia of goods and an economy more and more geared toward pure consumption, there were pockets of poverty and overarching racist inequities—these dances spoke of freedom and democracy, embracing improvisational and collective methods. The superabundance of objects was satirized in such dances as Childs's *Carnation* (1964)—where, under attack from household items like sponges, a colander, and a plastic garbage bag, a young woman remade her body into a surrealist object. Another such object-dance was Kenneth King's *cup/saucer/two dancers/radio* (1964), in which all the items in the title were leveled into a frighteningly de-humanized homogeneity. But also, in this pre-feminist moment, dance performance was a venue where the woman artist was fully empowered, carving out a zone for women's work and a status for the woman artist that foreshadowed feminist demands of the seventies.

These dances redefined the body, releasing it from what the post-modern generation saw as the heroic, symbolically overinflated images of historical modern dance (for instance, Graham's Greek mythological heroines or the distillation of Shakespearean passion in Limón's *Moor's Pavane*). Instead, the dancer became what the Russian literary critic Mikhail Bakhtin had earlier called "the grotesque body": festive, exor-bitant, confusing inside and outside, focusing on the "lower" processes of sex, ingestion, and digestion, and all the orifices that lead into and out of the body. [59] Appropriate to the expansive sixties, the grotesque body is itself a figure of abundance. Forti's playful *Huddle* (1961) was a cross between a football formation and a jungle gym to climb on. Carolee Schneemann's orgiastic *Meat Joy* (1964) was a revel of human and animal flesh. In Paxton's *Physical Things* (1966), the audience passed through a one-hundred-foot plastic tunnel, reminiscent of a digestive tract, decorated with trees and fake grass. In the "love" section of Rainer's *Terrain* (1963), she and William Davis assumed a sequence of erotic poses based on Indian temple sculpture. Robert Morris appropriated the nude tableau of Édouard Manet's nineteenth-century painting *Olympia* in his own *Site* (1964). These dances aggres-

Carolee Schneemann's *Meat Joy* being performed at the Judson Memorial Church in Greenwich Village. Photograph © 1964 by Peter Moore.

sively asserted the facts of the body, expressing a cultural moment of confidence, economic expansion, and teeming creativity.

By the early seventies, a new phase of consolidation and analysis had begun in postmodern dance, as many choreographers pursued specific projects unearthed by the wide-ranging experiments of the sixties. This research aspect of the avant-garde laboratory superseded the playfulness of the earlier decade, as a serious work ethic emerged in both the rhetoric and the methods of the postmodern choreographers. The "work" was factual, down-to-earth, objective—a style often arrived at through task activities that, as Morris noted as early as 1965, served as a useful strategy for producing concentrated, unself-conscious, "real" movement. [60] Scores, verbal commentary, and ordinary movements and postures also contributed to the search for movement detached from personal expression. The absence of music and special lighting, scenery, or costumes increased the movement's importance—since the movement became all there was to concentrate on. The anti-illusionist approach demanded close viewing and clarified the smallest unit of dance, shifting the emphasis from the phrase to the step or gesture, inviting the spectator to concentrate, in an almost scientific way, on the choreographic structure and the movement per se.

Rainer's *Trio A* (1966), also known as *The Mind is a Muscle, Part I*, was a harbinger of this trend. A single phrase, four and one-half minutes long, it dispensed with phrasing, development, climax, the virtuosic feat, and the fully extended body of modern dance—substituting energy equality, equality of parts, found movement, and human scale—as Rainer herself explained. [61] The movements were all abstract, yet they were performed with a tasklike energy and concentration. Various strategies for short-circuiting the performer's gaze added to the neutral, objective performance demeanor. The choreographic structure was that of a list; one movement followed another without any particular dancerly logic, underscoring Rainer's observation that "Dance is hard to see. It must either be made less fancy, or the fact of that intrinsic difficulty must be emphasized to the point where it becomes almost impossible to see." [62]

Similarly, Brown's accumulation pieces and structured pieces and various dances by Childs used structural devices such as repetition and reversal, mathematical systems, geometric forms, and comparison and contrast to encourage the perusal of pure, often simple movement. For instance, in *Accumulation* (1972), Brown strung together a series of hand gestures and other small-scale movements according to a mathematical progression for fifty-five minutes. In Childs's *Calico Mingling* (1973), four dancers traced similar, but not identical, paths that consisted only of circles, semicircles, and straight lines. A steady, brisk walk either forward or backward, with arms swinging freely, was the extent of their movement vocabulary. Although much of the dance seemed to consist of repetition, it was the low-contrast interweaving of the slight variations on the pattern that supplied the dance's interest. [63]

Austere in form, and concerned with ideas rather than craft or virtuosic performance, analytic postmodern dance was consistent with—and consciously aligned itself with—the practice of minimalist sculpture. It was also a fitting art for a post-Watergate, post-oil-crisis America—sober, factual, conservationist in terms of energy and theatrical means. Very often, non-Western movement disciplines served as alternative techniques to challenge modern dance traditions and provided new means for focusing on small-scale aspects of the choreographic process. The interest in these forms showed the results of two aspects of the American sixties: the formation of new cultural contacts between East and West and an increasing skepticism toward American and Western values among the younger generation. Paxton borrowed aspects of the Japanese martial art aikido as training for the Contact Improvisation "art-sport" he initiated. In this way he followed the forerunners of modern dance, who had also borrowed from aspects of popular culture to make their high art. But Paxton's Contact Improvisation, in its turn, became part of its practitioners' daily lives. Hay and Forti based their fluid, meditative phrasing on the Chinese martial art t'ai chi ch'uan.

In Steve Paxton's *Physical Things* (1966), the audience participated by passing through a
one-hundred-foot plastic tunnel. Photograph © 1966 by Peter Moore.

Rainer's late dance pieces reflect her interest in narrative, sparked by a trip to India where she observed classical theater forms like kathakali.

Thus during the late sixties and seventies both the white and the black avant-garde looked away from the West for inspiration, but with aims and from motives unlike those which had driven the forerunners of modern dance.

By the eighties, a second generation of American postmodern chore-ographers—many of them students and followers of the first genera-tion—had emerged, and many of them, in turn, had already begun to rebel on their own against the previous generation's formalism. Once again, as in the sixties, stylistic diversity prevailed, though certain traits recurred—notably, an alliance with the avant/pop music world (and its logical outcome: increased popularity) and an interest in expression, narrative, and the traditions of dance history. [64] This was true, to varying degrees, not only of the upcoming generation of younger choreographers but of those who had come of age in the sixties, at the beginning of the postmodern dance movement, as well. In this respect, recent work by the avant-gardists of the sixties and seventies and their progeny joined forces with the historically dissimilar projects of chore-ographers such as Tharp and Mark Morris. Its references to classicism and to other dance cultures, its plenitude of theatrical means, and its in-creased accessibility made this latest chapter of postmodern dance more like postmodernism as described by Charles Jencks in architecture—with its blend of popular accessibility and esoteric historical references—than the analytic postmodern dance of the seventies had been.

The work of Tharp, which had its roots in the analytic phase of postmodern dance, seemed by the mid-seventies to diverge from these structuralist, minimalist—and, admittedly, specialized—concerns. As Tharp began to explore popular music and dancing, at times going so far as to insert the vernacular into the ballet tradition—in works like *Eight Jelly Rolls* (1971) and *Deuce Coupe* (for the Joffrey Ballet, 1973)—she became a practitioner of postmodernist dance in Jencks's sense. The rigor of her choreographic structures persisted, while the musicality of her phrasing and her catholic taste in musical accompaniment gained her wider, more popular audiences.

Tharp's moves prefigured and meshed with several key directions of the eighties. For a number of reasons—ranging from the aesthetic to the economic—the interests of the first generation of postmodern choreographers shifted to large-scale, spectacular, multimedia collabo-rations (often under the auspices either of the Brooklyn Academy of Music's Next Wave Festival, or of progressive ballet companies). These collaborations allowed for interactions between the art forms but also created broader-based audiences drawn equally from the music, dance, and visual art communities. Childs's *Dance* (1979), a collaboration with the visual artist Sol LeWitt and the composer Philip Glass, is paradigmatic of this shift, as is Brown's *Set and Reset* (1983), a collaboration with Robert Rauschenberg and composer Laurie Anderson (who attracted an entirely new, pop music audience). If the minimalist seventies reflected the austerity of the decade, the new collaborative dance spectacles of the eighties were partly the product of expansionist Reaganomics.

At the same time, a younger generation emerged in the 1979–80 season—including Jones and Arnie Zane, Jim Self, Johanna Boyce, Molissa Fenley, and Armitage—who, themselves impatient with the seemingly puritanical seriousness and dry asceticism of the analytic approach, independently found various means to reinstate theatricality while remaining committed to the avant-garde venue. Further, a post-Tharp generation—whether directly descended from her company, like Sara Rudner and Nina Wiener, or inspired by her example (one with wider circulation and impact than that of her analytic colleagues)—began to appear as well. Both these groups nudged avant-garde dance in the eighties away from the visual art world and into the music world.

Besides the desire for political representation, there was an aesthetic cultural pluralism at work in the eighties that broadened both the pool of participants and the audience appeal. A number of Japanese dancers, including Eiko and Koma, Yoshiko Chuma, and Min Tanaka, introduced techniques from *butoh* and Japanese avant-garde theater; the alternative techniques plundered by various choreographers and producers—from *capoeira,* salsa, and break dancing to tap dancing and juggling—showed the postmodern proclivity not only for traditions from other cultures but also for those despised or overlooked from American subcultures and popular culture.

A number of factors contributed to the move into the ballet arena of a number of postmodern choreographers, including Gordon, Childs, Laura Dean, Armitage, Morris, Fenley, Self, and Ralph Lemon. Among these factors were the Joffrey Ballet's success with Tharp's ballets in the seventies, leading to commissions by such producers as the Jacob's Pillow Dance Festival, Bruce Marks (first at Ballet West and then at the Boston Ballet), and Baryshnikov (at American Ballet Theatre). The death of Balanchine in 1983 pointed up the need for younger choreographic talent in the ballet world, and the growing regional ballet movement created a constant demand for new works. As well, the postmodernists themselves were newly interested in history and tradition. [65] Armitage, formerly a Cunningham dancer, has often collaborated with the painter David Salle. Not only has she made a piece for American Ballet Theatre (*The Mollino Room* [1986]), she also began hiring ballet dancers for her own company, which presented her own blend of ballet and its deconstruction.

The eighties produced a major choreographer in Mark Morris (1956–   ). Born and raised in Seattle, Morris studied folk dancing, ballet, flamenco, and modern dance and performed briefly with Dean.

Mikhail Baryshnikov (right) with Leslie Brown and Ricardo Bustamante in *The Mollino Room*, written for the American Ballet Theatre by Karole Armitage.

The director since 1980 of the Mark Morris Dance Group, he continued regularly to give seasons in New York when his group was in residency at the Théâtre Royal de la Monnaie, Brussels, in 1988–91. Morris's work ranges broadly but is always informed by his strong sense of musicality. Although *Mythologies* (1987), his interpretations of Roland Barthes's theoretical writings on popular culture, was inspired by written texts ("The World of Wrestling," "Soap-Powders and Detergents," and "Striptease"), more often his dances are formed by musical genre and style. He is particularly attracted to vocal music and has choreographed Yoko Ono's rock songs, Henry Purcell, country and western, and Indian film scores.

Morris is also notable for his ungendered or cross-gendered casting. His eclectic movement style—as often grotesque or banal as it is lyrical—and his sense of irony not only fit comfortably but actually seem to produce his equally strong sense of spirituality. In 1990 Morris teamed up with Baryshnikov, who had just left the American Ballet Theatre, on a modern dance collaboration. The White Oak Project, which Baryshnikov organized as a touring company, involved eight dancers—a mix of ballet and modern dancers—and a repertory entirely choreographed by Morris. [66]

Finally, in the eighties and into the nineties a new multiculturalism pervaded postmodern dance. Issues of identity—race, ethnicity, gender, and sexuality—became paramount. While some of these issues of political identity were explored and celebrated in dance previously by such groups as the Alvin Ailey American Dance Theater, Dance Theatre of Harlem, and Ballet Hispanico, in the eighties for the first time various groups of young choreographers identified themselves as bicultural in a specifically avant-garde mode: African-American *and* postmodern; Latino *and* postmodern; feminist *and* postmodern; gay *and* postmodern. Their work is equally informed by their postmodern dance heritage and their political identities. They see their affiliation with political groups as a radical engagement that impinges on and disrupts their art form's discursive practices.

For instance, several festivals of new Latino dance, performance art, and film—such as La Misma Onda, Tour de Fuerza, and ¡Muévete!—presented dances by Puerto Rican, Cuban, and other Latino artists that specifically dealt with such issues as bilingualism, cultural displacement, and even the image of Latin dance in mainstream American popular culture. *No Regrets* (1988), a collaborative work by choreographer Merián Soto and visual artist Pepón Osorio, both Puerto Ricans, takes the form of a specifically Spanish popular genre—the *fotonovela*, a cross between a comic book and a romance novel, with photographs. In *Candela* (1988), Cuban-born performance artist Carmelita Tropicana satirizes the forties Carmen Miranda film genre—and Dunham-style revues, as well. The dance critic Joan Acocella wrote, about Viveca

Keith Sabado (foreground) and Donald Mouton perform in the "Striptease" portion of *Mythologies,* by Mark Morris, interpreting popular culture.

Vázquez's *Mascando Ingles* (1984): "Her dancers do bizarre things—pummeling their chests, tripping themselves, crawling backward—as if these actions denoted something quite ordinary. . . . Forced to speak a new language, Vazquez forces the body to do the same." [67]

As well, a number of young black choreographers have set out to explore issues of race and African-American culture, but in a postmodern vein. Jawole Willa Jo Zollar and the Urban Bushwomen, in works like *Praise House* (1990), about the religious experiences of Southern black women, and *Shelter* (1988), about life in the urban streets, explore themes not only of race but also of gender and class. Zollar incorporates African and African-American performance traditions in her work; *I*

Don't Know, But I've Been Told If You Keep Dancin' You'll Never Grow Old (1989) was a celebration of black vernacular kids' dance forms like drill teams and stepping. Ishmael Houston-Jones, whose dance roots are partly in the predominantly white Contact Improvisation network, takes up themes not only of racial identity but also of gay identity. Bill T. Jones, in *Last Supper at Uncle Tom's Cabin / The Promised Land* (1990), used texts ranging from rap to prayer to *Uncle Tom's Cabin* to LeRoi Jones's *Dutchman* to fit questions about racial oppression (and a vision of a multicultural utopia) together with questions of feminism and sexual preference.

Feminism and sexual preference, in fact, inform the work of various choreographers in the eighties and the early nineties. The collective Wallflower Order, as its name suggests, was created to question women's traditional roles in dance. Senta Driver and Fenley, among others, purveyed an image of women as powerful and athletic. Jane Comfort, Boyce, and others have made dances about mothering. An entire festival, Men Together (1980), featured dances on gay themes. And in Self's dance *Jim Self and Julio Torres Getting Married: A Wedding for the 90s* (1990), the choreographer and his real-life male lover celebrated their gay, multicultural union in terms that at times alluded to other marriages not sanctioned by the state; e.g., "jumping the broomstick" at slave weddings.

Thus the question of cultural identity, which shaped the quest for modern dance at the turn of the twentieth century, once again animates choreographers at the turn of the twenty-first century.

International avant-garde dance

If the analytic American postmodern dance of the seventies reflected a new American sobriety, two important developments in recent dance internationally, developing in Japan and West Germany in the sixties and seventies, mirrored those countries' rising fortunes by posing artistic challenges to the United States' previous dominance.

In Japan, the choreographer Tatsumi Hijikata (1929–86) began in 1963 to use the term *anokoku butoh* ("dance of darkness") to describe his work and that of his peers, like Kazuo Ohno. *Butoh* stands in a dialectical relationship to the classical dance-theater forms of Japan: for instance, it uses traditional conventions like white body makeup, slow motion, and female impersonation. However, much of *butoh* is meant to be a revolutionary volley of protest against Japanese culture—not only its traditional arts, but also its social values—by a young, alienated postwar generation. Its dance movements are often colored more by the dancers' study of German modern dance than of classical theater. Perhaps, too, *butoh* was partly galvanized by Cage's 1962 visit to

Tokyo. American Happenings—which were themselves influenced by a Japanese avant-garde visual arts movement, the Gutai group—were an influence. So was Fluxus, an American neo-Dada performance group that had a Japanese wing, Hi-Red Center, as well as several Japanese members, including Ono, in New York. But above all, this generation wanted to create a form of dance not only specific to its view of Japanese culture but also specific to Japanese bodies. [68]

As "dance of darkness" implies, *butoh*'s themes are cosmic: death, birth, and spiritual transformation. They are also social in their depiction of the dark side of life: violence, insanity, deformation. Often the stretched time of the *butoh* performance allows for multiple images—from the grotesque to the lyric, from the tragic to the comic—to blossom slowly and fade away.

Bonnie Sue Stein has described *butoh* performances of various sorts in the following terms:

> The spotlight settles on a flamboyant figure perched on the edge of an
> orchestra seat. A 79-year-old man—face and hands painted white, lips
> bright red—wears an old-fashioned black velvet dress, a crumpled pink
> hat, and high-heeled shoes. He adjusts his hat, dabs his face, lowers
> his eyes and flutters his eyelids. With mincing arms, he becomes the
> grotesque shadow of a young coquette. He drapes himself across the
> edge of the stage in the serpentine curves of traditional femininity,
> then kicks his foot high like a carefree young lover. To the slow
> koto music, he skips, flutters, and poses. Finally he smiles, drops one
> shoulder and tilts his chin like a scared and puzzled child, curtseys, and
> tiptoes away. [Ohno in *Admiring La Argentina* (1977), a tribute to the
> Spanish dancer]. . . .
> With arms outstretched, 15 to 20 men and women walk across the
> large proscenium stage, their muscles tensed and vibrating as if carrying
> a heavy load. Their semi-nude, white-painted bodies are partially
> covered by open kimonos worn backward. A stocky man with a heavy
> wooden armoire strapped to his back runs huffing and grunting around
> the stage, searching for a place to rest his burden. He is a cross between
> a Keystone cop and a Shakespearean fool. [Dai Rakuda-kan in *Sea
> Dappled Horse* (1980)]. . . .
> A young woman is barely visible in the back corner of the dimly lit
> stage. . . . She sways gently backward before taking each small, brave
> step. She advances, imperceptibly, until she reaches center stage and is
> encircled in a pool of light. The tall sheaf of wheat she carries vibrates
> with her body. Natsu Nakajima of Muteki-sha is delicately, silently
> inching her way through *Niwa* (1982), her "garden." [69]

Taking a variety of forms, *butoh* attempts to reach primordial states of life and death, showing human existence as fleeting and constantly changing—one small part of nature in general. The intensity of *butoh*, the way it views every passing moment as a crisis of the body, was in part a reaction to what was seen as the overly abstract Western modern dance of Cunningham and his followers. But of course, as Western dance itself became more theatrical and emotional in the eighties, *butoh* emerged as an influential form, reaching appreciative Western audiences. A number of *butoh* artists, including Eiko and Koma, Tanaka, and Poppo Shiraeshi, work in New York.

Hijikata wrote to a fellow *butoh* performer:

> In our body, history is hidden . . . and will appear in each detail of our expressions. In *butoh* we can find, touch, our hidden reality—something can be born, can appear, living and dying at the same moment. The character and basis of *butoh* is a hidden violence. It is a filthy child who has the special ability for *butoh*—because he knows how to create beautiful patterns. *Butoh* should be viewed as enigmatic as life itself. I am not sure in the end whether it is a trap or a secret correspondence with something. [70]

Eiko (left) and Koma, *butoh* artists, perform in *Grain*.

The postwar generation of West German choreographers had turned to ballet as their chosen medium after the leaders of *Ausdruckstanz* either fled the country or became associated with the Nazi regime during World War II. However, by the sixties, a younger generation, which had been exposed to both the student revolution in West Germany and the techniques of American modern dance (which they knew had been influenced, in its turn, by the German dance of the twenties) was once more moved to discover a "truly German" form of dance. Choreographers like Johann Kresnik, Pina Bausch, and Gerhard Bohner began experimenting with nonballet forms that were more theatrical and expressive in order to make political and emotional statements. In 1973 two events consolidated the power of this new movement, called *Tanztheater* (to distinguish it from *opernballett*). One was the death of John Cranko, the South African-born choreographer who had directed the Stuttgart Ballet since 1961 and, as well, served for several years as chief choreographer at the Munich Opera. Cranko's death left an enormous gap in the leadership of West German ballet. That same year, Pina Bausch (1940–   ), who had studied with Jooss at the Essen Folkwang and briefly danced with Paul Taylor in America, was appointed director of the Wuppertal Ballet. [73]

The dances by Bausch, and by younger *Tanztheater* choreographers such as Reinhild Hoffmann, Susanne Linke, and Mechthild Grossmann, have dealt with feminist themes, especially in their concern with violence against women, by men in particular and by society in general. Often these issues of sexual and political power are expressed by exaggerating them and repeating them to the boiling point. Bausch's images of alienation and angst are underscored by her loose collage structures that seem to imply an ultimate state of disconnectedness even among the most intensely lived moments of individual and social life.

In the seventies, *Tanztheater* gained more and more of a foothold in various West German state dance companies and was welcomed all over Europe as both a challenge to what had been felt as American dominance in modern dance and an alternative to what was seen (in the 1970s, at least) as an overly formalist American postmodern dance. As the West German dance critic Jochen Schmidt wrote:

> Pina Bausch . . . has expressly determined that she is less interested
> in how people move as in what moves them. . . . Whereas the
> young Americans—inasmuch as they are descendants of the
> Cunningham-Nikolais generation which defined dance as "motion,
> not emotion"—are fascinated by dance itself, their German dance
> colleagues want to learn something and transmit something about their
> surroundings, about people's daily lives, their cares, fears, problems
> and joys. Dance serves them as a means for release and humanizing.
> They therefore have a more realistic, earthy and heavy—but also more
> concrete, social and political effect than their American counterparts.

Mikhail Baryshnikov and Natalya Makarova rehearse *Other Dances*, which was created for them by Jerome Robbins in 1976.

Is the "German nature" in dance again to be described as primarily "deep"? Without a doubt, but for once that is no drawback. . . . This "depth" and "gravity" are . . . a necessary corrective to the American art of lightness, which all too quickly becomes an art of insignificance. [72]

Conclusion

The fortunes of twentieth-century dance have been inextricably linked to the political vicissitudes of the countries that produced it. America reached its adulthood at the turn of the century and contributed to world culture by inventing a new genre—modern dance. Similarly, when the Weimar Republic promised a renaissance of German culture, German modern dance flourished. Dance played an important part in the convulsions of the Soviet revolution, and by mid-century the competition between the Soviet Union and the United States—and their joint dominance of world power—was often expressed in the exchange of and contest between dance companies. When Soviet ballet dancers, acknowledged as the greatest technicians in the world, defected to the West—Nureyev in 1961, Makarova in 1970, and Baryshnikov in 1974—the West claimed to offer greater creative potential. With *glasnost,* the competition turned temporarily into a generous sharing of artists and resources. A bilateral *Swan Lake,* produced by the Boston Ballet in 1990, starred several Soviet dancers without the need for defections. And yet, as the United States' world hegemony weakened in the 1970s and 1980s, the rising fortunes of Japan and West Germany, the world's richest nations, gave them a new lease on the dance vanguard. As the European community anticipated its 1992 unity, it rejected any artistic dependence on the United States.

By 1991, as this article was being written, *glasnost* was closing down, war raged in the Middle East, and recession had hit worldwide. These factors, added to the persistent searches for national, ethnic, generational, and self identity, will undoubtedly shape yet a new direction in dance in the last decade of the twentieth century.

1. Philippe Jullian, *The Triumph of Art Nouveau: Paris Exhibition 1900,* trans. Stephen Hardman (London: Phaidon Press, 1974).

2. Elizabeth Kendall, *Where She Danced* (New York: Knopf, 1979); Nancy Lee Chalfa Ruyter, *Reformers and Visionaries: The Americanization of the Art of Dance* (New York: Dance Horizons, 1979); Suzanne Shelton, *Divine Dancer: A Biography of Ruth St. Denis* (Garden City, N.Y.: Doubleday, 1981).

3. *Fifteen Years of a Dancer's Life* (1913; reprint ed. New York: Dance Horizons, n.d. [1978?]).

4. Sally Sommer, "Loïe Fuller," *The Drama Review,* vol. 19, no. 1 (T65) (March 1975), pp. 53–67; Frank Kermode, "Poet and Dancer Before Diaghilev," *Puzzles and Epiphanies* (New York: Chilmark Press, 1962), pp. 1–28.

5. On Duncan, *see* Kendall, and Deborah Jowitt, *Time and the Dancing Image* (New York: William Morrow, 1988), pp. 67–102.

6. See *Pre-Classic Dance Forms* (New York: Dance Observer, 1937; reprint ed. New York: Dance Horizons, 1968), and, with Carroll Russell, *Modern Dance Forms in Relation to the Other Modern Arts* (San Francisco: Impulse Publications, 1961).

7. On St. Denis's and Shawn's careers, *see* Shelton.

8. Henry C. Warnack, "Catches Mood of Great Sea," Los Angeles *Daily Times* clipping in Denishawn Scrapbooks, vol. 2, The Dance Collection, New York Public Library; St. Denis, "The Education of the Dancer," *Vogue*, 1 April 1917 (both are quoted in Shelton, p. 132); Isadora Duncan, *The Art of the Dance*, ed. Sheldon Cheney (New York: Theatre Arts, Inc., 1928).

9. *Jahre der Kämpfe, 1902–14* (Years of Struggle, 1902–14) (Berlin, 1934), quoted in Victor H. Meisel, ed., *Voices of German Expressionism* (Englewood Cliffs, N.J.: Prentice-Hall, 1970), pp. 35–36.

10. *The Language of Dance*, trans. Walter Sorrell (Middletown, Conn.: Wesleyan University Press, 1966), p. 40.

11. Walter Sorrell, ed., *The Mary Wigman Book* (Middletown, Conn.: Wesleyan University Press, 1975), p. 28.

12. *The Borzoi Book of Modern Dance* (New York: Alfred A. Knopf, 1949; reprint ed. New York: Dance Horizons, 1974), p. 12.

13. "Man and Art Figure," in Walter Gropius, ed., *The Theater of the Bauhaus*, trans. Arthur S. Wensinger (Middletown, Conn.: Wesleyan University Press, 1961), p. 34.

14. On German modern dance, *see* Susan Allene Manning and Melissa Benson, "Interrupted Continuities: Modern Dance in Germany," *The Drama Review*, vol. 30, no. 2 (T110) (Summer 1986), pp. 30–45.

15. On the prewar Diaghilev company and its iconography and reception, *see* Joan Acocella, "The Reception of Diaghilev's Ballets Russes by Artists and Intellectuals in Paris and London, 1909–1914," diss., Rutgers University, 1984.

16. "The Power of Poetry," *New York Herald Tribune*, 23 Oct. 1945, reprinted in *Looking at the Dance* (New York: Horizon Press, 1968), pp. 132–33.

17. Bernard Taper, *Balanchine: A Biography* (New York: Times Books, 1984), pp. 99–100.

18. On Diaghilev's company and in particular on the way his thoroughly European modernism was based on exotic folklore, *see* Lynn Garafola, *Diaghilev's Ballets Russes* (New York and Oxford: Oxford University Press, 1989).

19. Sally Banes, "An Introduction to the Ballets Suédois," *Ballet Review*, vol. 7, nos. 2 and 3 (1978–79), pp. 28–59. On the film *Entr'acte* from *Relâche*, see Noël Carroll, "Entr'acte, Paris and Dada," *Millennium Film Journal*, no. 1 (Winter 1977–78).

20. 1932; reprinted in Merle Armitage, ed., *Martha Graham: The Early Years* (Los Angeles: 1937; reprint ed. New York: Da Capo Press, 1978), p. 99.

21. 1932; reprinted in Armitage, p. 100.

22. In Armitage, p. 32.

23. *See* Don McDonagh, *Martha Graham* (New York: Praeger, 1973); Martha Graham, *The Notebooks of Martha Graham* (New York: Harcourt, Brace, Jovanovich, 1973). Also, *see* Jowitt for studies not only of Duncan, Graham, and other modern dancers but also of ballet and postmodern dance.

24. *Dance Observer*, March 1962; reprinted in Selma Jeanne Cohen, *Doris Humphrey: An Artist First* (Middletown, Conn.: Wesleyan University Press, 1972), p. 266.

25. Letter to her parents, 8 Aug. 1927, quoted in Jowitt, p. 164.

26. On Humphrey, *see* Marcia B. Siegel, *Days on Earth: The Dance of Doris Humphrey* (New Haven, Conn.: Yale University Press, 1987), and Cohen.

27. *See* Lloyd, pp. 155–72, and Walter Sorell, *Hanya Holm: The Biography of an Artist* (Middletown, Conn.: Wesleyan University Press, 1969).

28. *See* Lloyd, pp. 132–55, and Christena L. Schlundt, *Tamiris: A Chronicle of Her Dance Career 1927–1955* (New York: New York Public Library, 1972).

29. *See* Lloyd, pp. 173–97, and the periodicals *Workers' Theater* and *New Theater*.

30. In *American Dancer* (June 1929); quoted in Larry Warren, *Lester Horton: Modern Dance Pioneer* (New York: M. Dekker, 1977), p. 29.

31. On Horton's career, *see* Warren.

32. "The Future of the Negro in Dance," *Dance Herald,* March 1938, p. 5, quoted in Lynn Fauley Emery, *Black Dance in the United States from 1619 to 1970* (New York: Dance Horizons, 1980), p. 253.

33. On African-American dance generally, *see* Emery.

34. "A Black Dancer's Credo: Don't Tell Me Who I Am," *Negro Digest* (July 1968), pp. 16–17, quoted in Emery, pp. 304, 306.

35. "Who Says Black Folks Could Sing and Dance?" *Dance Magazine,* vol. 57 (August 1983), p. 79.

36. Thomas A. Johnson, "I Must Be Black and Do Black Things," *New York Times,* 7 Sept. 1969, sec. II, p. 31, quoted in Emery, p. 310.

37. Ric Estrada, "Three Leading Negro Artists and How They Feel About Dance in the Community: Eleo Pomare, Arthur Mitchell, Pearl Primus," *Dance Magazine,* vol. 42 (November 1968), p. 46.

38. Shange, p. 80.

39. David Vaughan, *Frederick Ashton and His Ballets* (New York: Knopf, 1977).

40. Elizabeth Souritz, *Soviet Choreographers in the 1920s,* trans. Lynn Visson, edited and with an introduction and additional translation by Sally Banes (Duke University Press, 1990). On the modern dance studios, *see* Mary Grace Swift, *The Art of the Dance in the U.S.S.R.* (Notre Dame, Ind.: University of Notre Dame Press, 1968). Also, *see* Natalia Roslavleva, *Era of the Russian Ballet* (London: Gollancz, 1966).

41. "Blast at Ballet" (1937), reprinted in Kirstein, *Three Pamphlets Collected* (Brooklyn: Dance Horizons, 1967), p. 87.

42. Ibid., p. 90.

43. On New York City Ballet, *see* Lincoln Kirstein, *The New York City Ballet* (New York: Knopf, 1973).

44. Nancy Reynolds, *Repertory in Review: 40 Years of the New York City Ballet* (New York: Dial Press, 1977), p. 187.

45. *Movement and Metaphor: Four Centuries of Ballet* (New York: Praeger, 1970), pp. 242–43.

46. *See* Charles Payne, *American Ballet Theater* (New York: Knopf, 1978).

47. On the Americanization of ballet, and modern dance as well, *see* Lynn Garafola, "Toward an American Dance: Dance in the City," in Leonard Wallock, ed., *New York: Culture Capital of the World, 1940–1965* (New York: Rizzoli, 1988), pp. 157–87.

48. Kirstein, "Blast at Ballet."

49. Program note, quoted in Anatole Chujoy and P. W. Manchester, eds., *The Dance Encyclopedia* (New York: Simon and Schuster, 1967; revised and enlarged edition), s.v. "Ballets: U.S.A.," p. 111.

50. Ibid.

51. Taper, p. 278.

52. "An American Accent," in Selma Jeanne Cohen, ed., *The Modern Dance: Seven Statements of Belief* (Middletown, Conn.: Wesleyan University Press, 1969), p. 23.

53. "No Man From Mars," in Cohen, ed., *The Modern Dance,* pp. 63–64.

54. Joseph Mazo, *The Alvin Ailey American Dance Theater* (New York: Morrow, 1978), p. 13.

55. "Merce Cunningham and the Northwest," Proceedings of the Twelfth Annual Conference of the Society of Dance History Scholars Conference (Riverside, Calif.: Society of Dance History Scholars, 1989).

56. On Cunningham's work, *see* Merce Cunningham, *Changes: Notes on Choreography,* ed. Frances Starr (New York: Something Else Press, 1969); James Klosty, ed., *Merce Cunningham* (New York: Saturday Review Press, 1975); David Vaughan, "Locale: The Collaboration of Merce Cunningham and Charles Atlas," *Millennium Film Journal,* nos. 10/11 (1981), pp. 18–22; Roger Copeland, "The Politics of Perception," *The New Republic* (17 Nov. 1979), pp. 25–30; Noël Carroll and Sally Banes, "Cunningham and Duchamp," *Ballet Review,* vol. 11 (Summer 1983), pp. 73–79; and Merce Cunningham in conversation with Jacqueline Lesschaeve, *The Dancer and the Dance* (New York: M. Boyars, 1985).

57. *See* Sally Banes, *Democracy's Body: Judson Dance Theater 1962–1964* (Ann Arbor, Mich.: UMI Research Press, 1983).

58. I saw a reconstruction of this dance, directed by Rainer, at Bennington College, Bennington, Vermont, 18 April 1980.

59. *Rabelais and His World,* trans. Helene Iswolsky (Cambridge, Mass.: MIT Press, 1968; reprint ed. Bloomington, Ind.: Indiana University Press, 1984).

60. *See* "Notes on Dance," *Tulane Drama Review,* vol. 10, no. 2 (Winter 1965, T30), pp. 170–86.

61. "A Quasi Survey of Some 'Minimalist' Tendencies in the Quantitatively Minimal Dance Activity Midst the Plethora, or an Analysis of *Trio A,*" first published in Gregory Battcock, ed., *Minimal Art* (New York: E. P. Dutton, 1968), pp. 263–73. It also appears in Yvonne Rainer, *Work 1961–73* (Halifax, Nova Scotia: The Press of The Nova Scotia College of Art and Design; New York: New York University Press, 1974), pp. 63–69.

62. Ibid., p. 68.

63. *See* Sally Banes, *Terpsichore in Sneakers: Post-Modern Dance* (Boston: Houghton Mifflin, 1980; 2d ed., Middletown, Conn.: Wesleyan University Press, 1987), for descriptions of dances by Brown, Childs, and other postmodern choreographers.

64. On expression and meaning in postmodern dance, *see* Noël Carroll and Sally Banes, "Working and Dancing: A Response to Monroe Beardsley's 'What Is Going On in a Dance?' " *Dance Research Journal,* vol. 15 (Fall 1982), pp. 37–41, and Noël Carroll, "Post-Modern Dance and Expression," *Philosophical Essays in Dance,* ed. Gordon Fancher and Gerald Myers (New York: Dance Horizons, 1981), pp. 95–104. Also, *see* Noël Carroll, "The Return of the Repressed: The Re-Emergence of Expression in Contemporary American Dance," *Dance Theatre Journal,* vol. 2, no. 1 (1984), pp. 16–19, 27, and Deborah Jowitt, "The Return of Drama," *Dance Theatre Journal,* vol. 2, no. 2 (1984), pp. 28–31.

65. Sally Banes, "Pointe of Departure," *Boston Review* (October 1986), pp. 12–13.

66. On Morris, *see* Joan Acocella, "Morris Dances," *Art in America,* vol. 76 (October 1988), pp. 178–82; Joan Acocella, "Mark Morris and the Classical Vision," *Art in America,* vol. 79 (January 1991), pp. 51–55. On the White Oak Project, *see* Joan Acocella, "Baryshnikov Goes Modern," *Connoisseur* (November 1990), pp. 118–19.

67. "Loisaida Story," *7 Days,* 9 Nov. 1988, p. 62.

68. *See* Bonnie Sue Stein, "Butoh: 'Twenty Years Ago We Were Crazy, Dirty, and Mad,' " *The Drama Review,* vol. 30, no. 2 (T110) (Summer 1986), pp. 107–25. *See also* the other articles on *butoh* in this issue of *TDR,* and Susan B. Klein, "Ankoku Buto: The Premodern and Postmodern Influences on the Dance of Utter Darkness," Master's thesis, Cornell University, 1987.

69. Stein, pp. 107, 110.

70. "To My Comrade," note to Natsu Nakajima, reprinted in program notes for Nakajima's *Niwa* and quoted in Stein, p. 125.

71. *See* Manning and Benson; Ann Daly, ed., "Tanztheater: The Thrill of the Lynch Mob or the Rage of a Woman?" pp. 46–56; and the other articles about *Tanztheater* in *The Drama Review,* vol. 30, no. 2 (T110) (Summer 1986).

72. *Ballett International* (June/July 1982), p. 13, quoted by Anna Kisselgoff in the symposium "German and American Dance: Yesterday and Today," transcribed in Daly, ed., "Tanztheater," p. 47.

Reconsiderations of Great Books and Ideas

The New Pythagoreans III:
The Scientists of the Mind (Part Two)

Thomas K. Simpson

Thomas K. Simpson is a frequent contributor to *The Great Ideas Today*. Until 1990, when he retired, he was a tutor at St. John's College in Annapolis, Maryland, and Santa Fe, New Mexico. Under a grant from the National Endowment for the Humanities, he worked recently on an edition of papers on the electromagnetic field by James Clerk Maxwell, designed to make Maxwell's text accessible to readers without special training in mathematics and sciences. He has served over the years as a consultant to museums and is currently working with the Science Museum of Minnesota on the development of exhibits which would make it possible for museum visitors to participate in serious experimentation in the fundamental principles of physics. Other projects include a study of Leon Trotsky's *History of the Russian Revolution* and a computer investigation of a claim by Henri Poincaré that nothing in principle prevents consistent intuitions of non-Euclidean geometry, including those with dimensionality greater than three.

    Mr. Simpson's education was at the Virginia Polytechnic Institute, at St. John's, at Wesleyan University, and at Johns Hopkins University, where he earned a doctorate in the history of science and technology.

I. Introduction: The story thus far

This is the fourth, and last, of a series of articles whose purpose has been to take the measure of the idea of science in our time. Its premise has been, not only that the way of doing science and its relation to the public weal have changed dramatically in the years since the beginning of World War II and the inception of the Manhattan Project, but that the very idea of science itself has been undergoing fundamental change. This has been explored systematically through the series, beginning with the physicists, then turning to the biologists, and finally in the most recent article to the scientists of the mind, who are our present concern as well. It has been necessary to divide the topic of the psychologists; the installment last year dealt primarily with the question of perception and left to be dealt with in this final article what might be the ultimate concern in any study of mind, the question of knowledge. Since this is a question which strikes us as being philosophical before it is scientific, we will have to begin by examining carefully the scientific ground on which we now find ourselves standing. The "idea of science" will be put to the test in its effort to speak to a question many may feel is essentially beyond its competence. We may be testing in effect the question, "What are the limits of the competence of the sciences?"

Thus in order, as the lawyers say, to "lay a foundation" for the inquiry we are about to make, it will be necessary at the outset to stake out some rather high ground for the sciences. My own sense is that the previous segments of this long essay have opened the prospect of a concept of science far broader and more inclusive than the limited image which was conventional fifty years ago. It used to be thought that "science" could confine itself to empirical fact and testable theory in such a way that its outcome was assuredly valid within stated limits: it was said to be "objective," and its special merit was as an oasis of confidence in a world otherwise torn by conflict over questions of belief and value which escaped such rational resolution. There were conventional formulations of something called "scientific method," which by a discipline of stages was thought to insure that scientific truth could be held to its objective track.

After the experience of the sciences over the past fifty years, that view if urged today would seem naive. It assumed that the foundations were secure: that a fact was a fact, that laws were laws, and that a natural course of scientific investigation unfolded in a fairly obvious fashion as opportunities for new learning opened before our inquiring eyes. The essence of the idea of science was then "objectivity" and the fruits of objectivity, a limited but wondrous realm of "scientific truth." In a way, it was a divine comedy, a cosmos secure within a crystal sphere, at the center of which the scientist knew his commanding place. If it had a hell, that had not yet become manifest. But from the larger point of view of the inquiring mind, it was a straitjacket. This essay has made bold to call that long period of confidence in the sciences the Deep Freeze and has seen the liberation from it over these recent decades as a melting of unwarranted constraints. Things have become much more complicated, but the prospects for human reason are far more promising.

To gain perspective for this radical review—that is, a review which presumed to question science at its foundations—the first essay of the series turned to Plato, whose stock-in-trade is the doubting of what seems to normal people obvious. That essay looked first at Plato's *Timaeus* (*GBWW* I: 7, 442–77; II: 6, 442–77), a Pythagorean origin myth which derives the world from beginnings which have their home only in the intellect, and then turned to our contemporary physicists. The likeness was striking: our physicists are thinking like Pythagoreans! What that means is that "matter" is no longer the terra firma on which a reductive "materialism" might rest. We are certainly not left with idealism in any comfortable sense: far from it, the experience of the Trinity site made sure that science would be identified with the harshest of realities and could no longer be taken as benign. That very contradiction, between the release from "materialism" on the one hand and the confrontation with a harsh and destructive reality on the other, is very close to an inner contradiction which runs throughout the Platonic dialogues between the primacy of intellect and the works of necessity. This contradiction is at the foundation of what was known to the Greeks as "tragedy," and it may be as much a mystery to us today as it was to the Pythagoreans and to Plato as well, for whom it was the central, generative insight. We see how complicated the problem of the sciences has become: even those born long since the event remain witnesses to the awe which gripped observers at the Trinity site, the mystery for our time beyond which science in its old manifestation could not pass. An experience such as that is deeply thought-provocative; the Greeks had a phrase for it— *pathei mathein,* "to learn through suffering." The strange suggestion is that serious thought works in just this way. We do not really learn at the highest level without suffering serious contention between what we intend and what we produce, without the dismay which is perhaps what Aristotle means by "wonder" as the beginning of philosophy.

If science is not objective and contained, then what is it? These essays have been urging a reconsideration of Plato's ancient answer: knowledge, if it is anything, is *dialectical*. Not much is gained by reiterating a word like this, so let me try to say as exactly as possible what it appears to mean in the present context.

We normally think of secure knowledge as founded on principles, from which we reason, as we say, "logically." It is hard, and unnecessary, to avoid a spatial metaphor: let us think of the principles as at the top and imagine that we reason logically "down" from them, toward particular conclusions. Euclid's geometry has been the classic model of this, from Plato's time to our own; let us hope that it is still taught and learned in some recognizable form in our schools today. It has to be revised only slightly to give us the classic model of the "objective" sciences. The conclusions, in the Baconian model, bring us to confrontation with empirical fact and thereby put the premises to the test. If conclusions from them agree with fact, the premises are to that extent confirmed; the more they fit, the surer we get. If they fail to fit, we rework the premises in appropriate ways, and a process of refinement begins which will tend to converge on correct principles, in the sciences in this tradition called "laws." The facts are apparent to anyone who repeats the experiment, and public scrutiny of the whole process insures the objectivity of the result.

I realize that this is something of a caricature, for many subtle refinements had been made before a new era turned our thinking around; but it catches the essence of the idea of science as objective.

If science is dialectical, however, the first principles are in play in a more serious sense, and for all the experimenting, mind cannot rest with them. The principles come from somewhere else, and they are tested in realms other than those of the laboratory. The operative clash is not so much between principle and laboratory fact but between principle and principle, or between principle and some larger human context. Indeed, it becomes evident that a "fact" is a datum only in context: it is an answer to a question which first had to be asked. The principles, often more covertly than overtly, set the agenda for the investigation and hence, in some fundamental way, dictate the possible facts. If science is dialectical, we cannot rely on the laboratory alone to put the principles to the test, but we must look instead to their other, larger sources.

Whether philosophically or politically, our assumptions set the agenda for the sciences, and in very fundamental ways they direct the course of their developing truth. What recent decades have shown unmistakably is that this is not a minor or easy corrective to our account of the idea of science but entails anguish and makes all the difference in the world. It is not in itself bad news, nor does it justify a skeptical stance. It only makes manifest that the scientific questions are larger, and in a sense more interesting and important, than we had thought. Science must be recognized as of a piece with human inquiry on the largest scale;

whatever we conclude in other realms will bear on the sciences, and vice versa. The outcomes of the sciences will yield possibilities which are immediate challenges to our thinking in all domains. In short, there is no longer ground for imagining a separation of the sciences or "scientific truth" from the general human inquiry; both science and all other realms are immensely enriched by this new inclusion. It is true, and we should be happy it is true, that scientific truth is revealed as fragile, even precarious, in ways we had not anticipated. It is indeed exactly as fragile and precarious as all other human truth, from which we can no longer imagine it is isolated.

Some disclaimers are in order, lest such a bold proposition seem unacceptable on its face. Of course, brilliant work is being done daily in conventional terms in the scientific laboratories, far more so perhaps in this new era I am calling "dialectical" than ever before. Firm stones are being added to an edifice at a breathtaking rate. Each is indeed a solid addition to a structure of some sort, but what is that edifice? We can certainly do wondrous things today that we could not do yesterday, but which of all these latent possibilities shall we set out to pursue, and how shall we frame the questions we pose ourselves? To vary the metaphor, which way is "forward" in the progress of the sciences? That is no longer a second, separate question: it dictates what we do in the laboratories, it dictates what the facts will be, for facts are now in every sense extremely expensive and are fraught, as we know, with social consequence.

It is evident that science, once it is seen in this light, becomes dubious, and we might tend to turn from it in despair or well-justified fear, even a certain understandable sense of revulsion. But that would be a great mistake, exactly the wrong conclusion. For the sciences, though they cannot be taken as separable or autonomously true, are of a piece with our total human enterprise insofar as it has any claim to rationality. The sciences remain, with a new intensity as they become increasingly aware of their critical role in society, perhaps the best rational forum our world knows. Scientists, like the rest of us, are probably only very partially aware of the larger significance of what they are doing—if they kept that in mind, they could never get anything done. But in truth they are exercising disciplines of unrelenting reason which are very possibly mankind's best hope for a future better than the morass in which we currently find ourselves. The "facts" will not dictate such directions, but minds committed to the practice of reason cannot be contained in the old, narrow bounds. We have much to learn from the scientists of the world, and perhaps not primarily about new tricks with molecules. We need to think about what this entails. At least, it will not be inappropriate now to turn to the scientists for their guidance in thinking about thinking—in attempting to give new consideration to the question of the nature of human knowledge.

II. The pharmacopoeia of the psyche

We began an inquiry into the scientists' perspectives on human knowledge in last year's essay by turning to a second Platonic dialogue, the *Theaetetus* (*GBWW* I: 7, 512–50; II: 6, 512–50), in which the question is asked, "What is knowledge?" [1] Borrowing this question from the dialogue, we felt assured that it would be posed with full earnestness, and that the suggestions we then got from the scientists might be treated as philosophical rather than merely as "scientific." If we are right about the dialectical character of science, of course, the scientific and philosophical questions are not ultimately distinct but ought to tend to converge in the present discussion.

Last year, the first phase of this discussion of the psyche dealt with the simpler systems which were Theaetetus's initial attempts at the definition of "knowledge"—namely, that "knowledge is perception." Our modes of perceiving, discussed in that essay, or even those of speaking, all seemed naturally to invite laboratory investigation and yielded the easier answers—but the underlying search must go on now for knowledge itself. In that discussion, we saw how the dialogue's question became, not merely formal—that is, a matter of finding a definition in words, all efforts toward which fail within the dialogue—but much more substantive. In the manner characteristic of the Socratic dialogues the question returned to the questioner, and we saw that it is not a verbal answer we need—not "knowledge" in that formal sense—but much more substantively, the effort to *know Theaetetus,* and to be assured of the reality and continuity of his being. The question of knowledge proceeded by way of geometry but ended by centering on the geometer. The dialogue wondered at his integrity: how the youth and the dying man joined in the singleness of the one self, to whose character he had been unwaveringly true. We thought that in this, Theaetetus prefigured ourselves, and the mystery of the unity of our own Being. This is surely the Being it is most important for any one of us to know! To know him would be to know ourselves. What trace might such a profound search leave in the modern sciences? What account can the sciences give of us, and, especially, of us as knowers?

One approach in the modern world has taken the form of a long and often rewarding effort to conceive the psyche as a *system,* a connected machine or network of sorts. There has for a long while now been an understandable preoccupation with the guiding thought of an electrical system, which might process information in the manner of the computer. Much has been learned—more, one suspects, for the art of the computer than for the understanding of the mind—and the prospects are excellent that important insights are now brewing. This is especially true as the computer, our new form of "animal model," approaches success in modeling the processes of development and learning. How-

147

ever successful, though, this line of investigation is inherently limited by its concern with the *outsides,* rather than the *insides,* of the mental process. The question of "artificial intelligence" is in itself not idle, but arguments built on it which attempt to question seriously whether that is "all there is" fall quickly into vacuity. [2]

Those who conceive the psyche on the model of the computer think in terms of functional elements around which one can somehow draw boxes, which process something which is dubiously called "information." These are then joined by lines which represent paths of connection which are at least temporarily definite. Along those paths, "electrical" impulses are understood to flow in such a way as to convey some time-coded message. The complex of these messages, acted upon in regular ways by the boxes which received and decoded them, then generate new signals to be sent on along further, distinct routes. There results in this overall signal-patterning an image—some may claim, the essence—of the life of the psyche. Because the number of pathways is so great, with immensely ramifying connections—while the functions specified for the boxes permit every sort of combination and interaction—it may seem to such designers that this image is endlessly resourceful and hence in some sense "doomed to success."

In saying that we are dealing here with a system which is throughout *electrical,* we seem to be making, then, a very special sort of claim. What do we have in mind, in speaking here of "electricity"? Evidently, a subtle, undifferentiated substance, without qualities and thus varying in magnitude alone, common coin of the system: very nearly the material of mathematics itself. It becomes a kind of pure, Cartesian magnitude, capable of taking on as rapidly as we might wish virtually any form in time and space we conceive for it. [3] How convenient for us that it is so easily tracked! Tapping the neural net wherever we please, we can present it to our most sophisticated laboratory instrumentation, capture its measures in the form of graphs, write if we wish its configurations as mathematical equations, and operate upon it—summing, averaging, analyzing, and transforming, performing cross correlations or statistical gymnastics of every sort. Finally, we can intervene arbitrarily, by introducing and tracking "electrical" impulses at will throughout the system. It makes for clean experimenting, articulates smoothly with the computer, and, with the development of microelectrodes to probe individual neurons, has encouraged the very elegant techniques of modern neurophysiology.

Essentially, the analysis of the system into these finite elements seems to assure that we are working within the generic computer concept which has become known, after its author, Alan Turing, as the "Turing Machine." [4] Despite the radical simplicity of the elements assigned it, Turing's conceptual model reproduces in principle the function of any classic computer, however advanced, proceeding step-by-step and at each step performing strictly in accordance with a rule or "algorithm," which tells it how to act on an input to produce an output. The question becomes, can we imagine that any complication of such algorithmic devices, proceeding however rapidly and in whatever numbers, could reproduce the phenomena of the human mind? The human cortex includes some ten billion nerve cells, each of which we might think of as acting algorithmically in this manner. We know what fabulous results emerge from the operations of supercomputers, each element of which is as simple as Turing's paradigm. What more could we ask? Yet—carried to completion, what psyche would this Cartesian comedy endow us with?

Not quite the psyche we live with, one suspects. Two reasons, a lesser and a greater, underlie this reservation: (1) The Turing machine operates by steps which are sequential in time, while the cells of the brain fire in a massively parallel system, widely interconnected. What arises is a time pattern consisting in the greater or lesser synchronicity of the firings of any number of cells in any parts of the cortex; it has even been seriously proposed that this time pattern may be what we mean by an "idea," and its correlate may be consciousness. [5] I believe this is not analyzable in Turing form.

(2) There is a greater reason, however: the principle that the simple aggregation of any number of elements cannot yield a *whole,* while in the matter of knowing and Being, our present concern, wholeness is essential. As was stated last year in Part One of this discussion of the mind, the problem of the whole, the *holon,* becomes an absolutely essential component of the reasoning of the *Theaetetus,* where the problem is posed by Socrates as the question of "Hesiod's wagon." [6] All the parts together do not of themselves make a "wagon"! Lucretius, in *De rerum natura* (*On the Nature of Things*), paints the severest picture of what we might call this algorithmic problem (*GBWW* I: 12, 1–97; II: 11, 1–91). The utter, seemingly indissoluble gloom which hangs over Lucretius's poem belongs intrinsically to all atomism: no collection of atoms can constitute more than they are, an aggregate. [7] Hooking them together with artful devices accomplishes nothing in this matter, as Lucretius well knows. Anything that makes them more than that heap must come from somewhere else. Atomisms secretly borrow from other sources: Lucretius confronts his fate by weaving most beautiful hexameters, but in so doing, he subtly subverts his own thesis and appeals to a higher source. For we grant the beauty of the verse, not by virtue of the hookings-together of nouns and verbs or the placing of sounds, but by tacit appeal to something prior in our minds which knows and recognizes those patterns he has woven and takes delight in the recognition. Similarly, if it is patterns among parallel or synchronous firings of myriad cells which we recognize and by which we know, we still meet the question, whence do we recognize those patterns? As in

the case of Lucretius's verse, a whole must preexist, and until that is identified, the puzzle of our "knowing" has not been solved.

To this point, however, we have been telling only half the story. It is true that brain research, and discussions of the brain, have tended to be preoccupied since the quiverings of Luigi Galvani's first frog with these mythic charms of the electric pulse, and with some sense that we are dealing with a "wiring" problem of great complexity—essentially, an analyzable machine. But there exists another story, far more curious in the telling and less amenable to summary, which approaches the same brain as "chemical." The possible meanings of that term are even harder to determine than are the meanings of "electric." We have no notion really of what we signify by "electricity," but we seem to be able to get away with conceptual surrogates—subtle little fluids flowing in tiny little pipes! With "chemistry," however, this is harder. What shall we imagine when we speak of a "chemical reaction"? Images out of elementary laboratories, of pouring one thing into another to observe lively consequences, seem to be of no help. So at least we found in the earlier essay in this series, devoted to the sciences of life, where we saw how tricky the "chemical" question became as we tried to follow the course of metabolic processes through the body. We were dealing with molecules which were spatial structures with something like lock-and-key relations between enzymes and their substrates. [8] We were forced to leave behind stereotypes of the "chemical" and to think in terms instead of intricate matchings of information structures suggesting the reading and writing of intricate texts.

It is as if the syntactic bond had taken on dynamic power in a grammar of the molecules. When we propose that the brain may be seen as a "chemical" system, we are suggesting that when thought occurs, or the psyche senses or wills, such richly configured, dynamic molecular texts are actively publishing and seeking interpretation. If so, the unity which makes up the Being preceding that recognition we call "knowing" may quite plausibly be recorded in molecular libraries. The fact that such texts are at once significant and dynamic—guiding the flow of the streams of energy which we know as purpose and drive—would comport well with the recognition that there is no human knowing without caring: our reason never acts except to an end.

The brain's chemical system is not only complex in conception but by the same token experimentally intractable. Perhaps this is reason enough for its neglect in most accounts, which traditionally emphasize the neater electrical system. In place of the convenience of the quick, stable, and ubiquitous electron, caught neatly by electrodes and run expeditiously through meters—a matter of mere quantity, of amplitudes and times—brain chemicals are of vastly different sorts, their qualitative differences are of great importance, and they come and go in time and space in ways which, though ultimately not undisciplined, are certainly far more difficult to trace or summarize. But their very intractability is becoming the key to the enormous promise of this alternative, chemical myth of the mind. [9]

Here in any case are new orders of interest and possibility: we begin to perceive the prospect of a more promising likeness to the moody, mercurial psyche of lights and shadows we know on a daily basis. If the psyche of electrical mythology seemed almost too perfectly adapted to analysis and calculation to serve as model for our chaotic selves, the story we tell now in chemical terms will tend to be one of more global relations such as mood, state, or purpose, and of successions which, though they do not calculate so well, presage greater richness. Here we have psyche suggesting Goethe rather than Descartes. [10]

It has long been known that beside the electrical system there was the endocrinal one, in which signals were encoded in molecules we call *hormones;* transmission was by way primarily of the bloodstream, and the introduction of these generalized signals, carried throughout the body, seemed most like an act of publication. The bloodstream itself, richly endowed with such messenger molecules, becomes a kind of bulletin board or current gazette. Receptor sites which recognize the hormonal signal molecules bind them out of the general circulation, whereupon a great variety of events transpire according to the nature of the hormone and its target cell.

This picture remains valid, though it simply does not go far enough, since it does not speak of the virtually universal interweaving of the chemical and the electrical modes, which now makes the combined picture far more interesting than the sum of the two alone. A well-known example of a potent hormonal substance—one among a great number operative in the body—is adrenaline, which when published throughout the system sets the entire body and mind into a state of emergency and alert, focusing organs throughout the body to the coordinated state of readiness for "fight or flight." [11] Hormones in general have the effect of integrating many organs in this manner on a broad scale, and though they may thus initiate sudden action, they tend rather to act on time scales far slower than those of the neural pulses. Reflecting on the hormonal system in its distinction from the electrical, we will speak later in this essay of its origin in roots deeper in evolutionary time and its direction to broad vital activities of nutrition, reproduction, and defense shared widely through the kingdoms of life. As it ultimately makes connection with the neural system, the hormonal system appears to act on complexes closer to the brain stem—that is, to the "old brain" belonging to evolutionary phases of the reptile and the first mammals: phases incorporated, still, "deepest" and, it is important to recognize, continuously at work in our modern selves.

We see a revealing pattern here: the old mode is slow, widespread, and hence integrative of the whole organism; it bears in its qualitatively

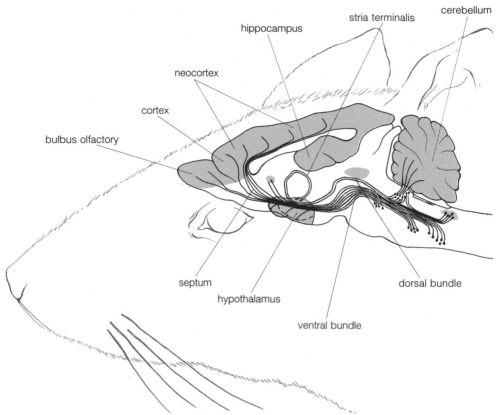

Figure 1. Neurons sensitive to common chemical neurotransmitters group as coherent systems; this figure depicts the noradrenaline system of the rat. Pathways run here from centers of taste, close to the brain stem at the right of the figure, forward to invoke the hypothalamus and widespread areas of the neocortex and hippocampus in the phenomenon of appetite. The hypothalamus in turn releases hormones which are "published" widely throughout the body, as shown in figure 3.

rich molecular structures both the primary patterns and the deeper dynamic of the mind. The new mode, the domain of the neuron, is quick and complex. It seems likely that the old mode is not just the source of drives, and hence the initiator of all our striving, but also the seat of the patterns, and hence of all knowing as well. It is the unconscious, chthonic foundation; the electrons by contrast course in the quick, conscious mind, but is this not in response to a deeper bidding, and do not the patterns, sources of knowing and recognition, lie first in the domain of the old?

How do these two modes interrelate? The first clue to the interweaving of the "electric" and the "chemical" systems lies in an elementary correction to the "electrical" account. Seen as a wiring diagram, the neural net assumes firm connections between the axon of one cell and the dendrite or cell body of the next. In fact, however, where the simple story wants a junction, there is actually a highly significant interval called the *synaptic cleft*. By common measures it is extremely small, but in terms of process it is absolutely decisive. We should remember, first, that the "electrical" pulse in the nerve fiber, though provable as such by galvanometric measures, is actually the consequence of a propagating physiochemical process involving a lively action on the part of ions passing transversely through the cell membrane. The electrical pulse transmitted longitudinally is in fact the consequence of a lateral pulse of charged potassium and sodium ions, through the membrane which bounds the nerve fiber. (Ions are atoms which have acquired an electric charge; it is important to note here that though they thus convey charge, as electrons do, they are far heavier and hence engage in motions which are relatively sluggish.) This differential opening and closing of that membrane is a rapid chemical switch in the cell wall, but since the atoms involved are, as ions, charged, the chemical switch is at the same time electrical.

What arrives, then, at the terminal of the axon at which it is to communicate with the succeeding dendrite is actually an ionic pulse, duly registering as "electrical" because the ions are electrically charged (fig. 2). This pulse initiates an intricate sequence of chemical events which results in the emission of a neurotransmitter, another wordlike molecule which will have the effect of conveying the pulse across the synaptic cleft to a selected receptor site on the far side. It is thereupon incorporated into the receiving neuron, and following the intervention of a "second messenger," a new "electrical" pulse is sent on its way.

Why such a complication of the otherwise conceptually simple "electrical" system? It is hazardous to announce reasons for biological events, yet it is clear that this synaptic intervention in the conduction process introduces a rich domain of new possibilities. Once the strict channel of the conduction path has been broached, substances will be able to flow in and out of the gap. If these new molecules are structurally related to the neurotransmitter or its receptor, they can intervene to *modulate* the conduction process, augmenting or inhibiting it—typically, for example, occupying the reception site so as to block transmission, or blocking the cleanup of the neurotransmitter so that the junction in effect remains activated. Stimulant and depressive drugs, for example, act in this way. [12] Through the device of the synaptic cleft, then, the "electrical" and "chemical" systems meld ubiquitously—and while we may still think of them in separation as the neural and the hormonal, with their broad functions categorically distinct, we can also see that they are ultimately one truly organic system, little analogous to that envisioned by the computer programmer. The "electrical" is now actually only an incident of the ionic play of the "chemical"—the hormonal effects of mood, desire, or arousal can everywhere be expected to

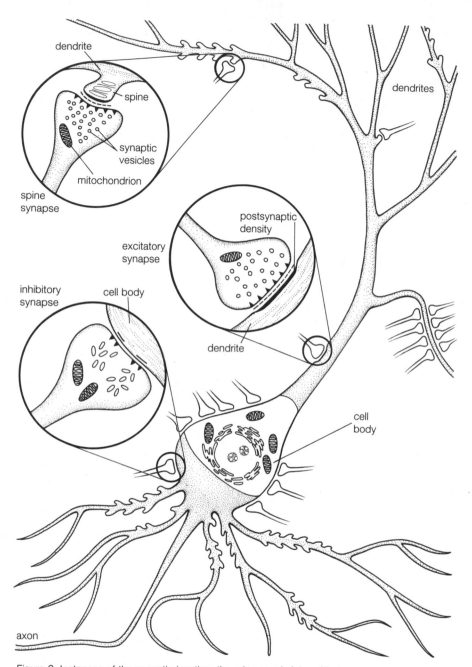

dendrite

spine

synaptic
vesicles

mitochondrion

spine
synapse

dendrites

excitatory
synapse

postsynaptic
density

inhibitory
synapse

cell body

dendrite

cell
body

axon

Figure 2. Instances of the synaptic junction, the microscopic interval between
external nerve endings and the wall of a neuron, through which the nerve signal is
communicated. In this gap, distinct chemicals may intervene to modulate nerve action,
acting either to excite or to inhibit transmission.

infuse as instigator or moderator that which we might otherwise have thought of as simply "mental." Here is the elixir which would cause the computer to spring to life.

We see how much more interesting the neurophysiological picture is becoming and, as we leave behind the more simplistic Cartesian notions, how much more nearly it is beginning to model what we can recognize as familiar human experience—in which "thought" fades in the absence of the colorations of interest and concern which are of its essence. How boring and unnatural it is to be given an unmotivated, "purely mental" task! We may see here the opening in the physiological model to the intuitive function of mind, not explicated in conventional accounts of *logos,* but related to Being in ways the *Theaetetus* suggested. [13] The new sense of organization to a controlling end fits, too, what we have seen earlier concerning the selectivity of the perceptual "searchlight," which revealed our visual system as quite unlike a camera in that we are able to see only what we have earnestly set out to find. [14] If we were to read back the implications of this woven system into the domain of information processing, we might see some uncomfortable vision arising of the endocrinal computer: a computer which was not only purposeful, moody, and emotional, but which incorporated some counterpart of the intellectual intuition of *nous!* The implication seems to be that the endocrinal computer would become knowing if it held within it the molecular patterns. Perhaps if the design were carried to completion, it would turn out to be us.

In the instance of adrenaline, the hormonal system rouses us to aversive behaviors of pain, fear, anxiety, stress—thoroughly familiar colorations, surely, of the life of the psyche, as familiar in the classroom or office, or when reading the daily paper or the mail, as ever on the battlefield or hunt. What about those other ways, however, which seek affirmative goals? They, too, are the work in the psyche of hormones, and if anywhere we are to find the structures of final cause and the good, of desire, caring, and purpose, it must be in those hormones which activate what the psychologists tend, with an eye rather perhaps to mice than to men, to call the "reward system."

Let us turn, then, (*see* fig. 3) to the principal center of endocrinal action, a closely coupled system consisting of the hypothalamus, thought of as an organ of the "brain," and the pituitary, thought of as a gland, and thus an organ of the "body." Since it has become clear, however, that the hypothalamus is itself indeed a gland, sending to the pituitary master hormones which are among the most powerful of biological substances, the distinction between "body" and "brain" would seem at this point deeply, and indeed appropriately, confused. It is in any case the pituitary which addresses the system as a whole, releasing hormones which travel with the blood throughout the body and, as they do so, summon to action either agent organs of the body directly, or other

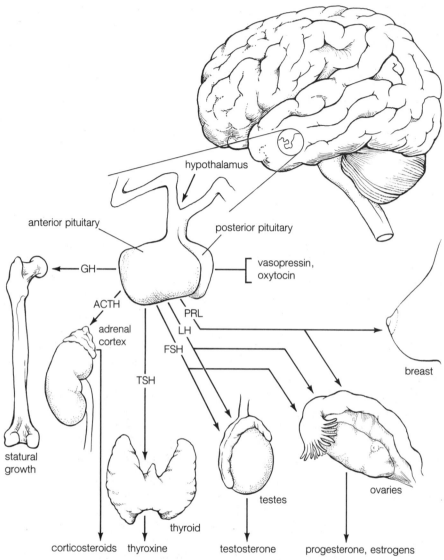

hypothalamus

anterior pituitary

posterior pituitary

GH

vasopressin,
oxytocin

ACTH

PRL

adrenal
cortex

LH

FSH

breast

TSH

statural
growth

testes

ovaries

corticosteroids   thyroxine

thyroid

testosterone

progesterone, estrogens

Figure 3. Chemical signals of the endocrine system originating in the hypothalamus are dispersed, sometimes in relays, throughout the body. The symbols in the figure denote hormones, each of which affects specific receptor sites. Thus ACTH (adenocorticotropic hormone) addresses the adrenal cortex, which in turn releases a wide range of corticosteroids. (Note that it is the inner adrenal medulla, directly connected to the nervous system and thus not shown here, which releases adrenaline into the general blood circulation, in very large quantities and in very short times.) Other hormones denoted on the diagram are growth hormone (GH), thyroid-stimulating hormone (TSH), follicle-stimulating hormone (FSH), luteinizing hormone (LH), and prolactin (PRL).

glands which in turn issue further hormones in a system of intricate ramification and subtlety.

Perhaps the fundamental principle to be recognized is that for the psyche, pleasure is a real and positive experience: it is not, as Sigmund Freud tends to suggest, merely the release from pain or excessive stress. The evidence for this is, as it turns out, simple and decisive. Experiments can be devised in which an animal has the option of stimulating an area of its own brain in which electrodes have been implanted, through actuation of a lever. Very specific loci in the hypothalamus have been identified which the animal will choose to stimulate repeatedly in this way, even to the exclusion of food or drink—and even, it is reported, to the point of death by starvation. [15] These show all the signs, then, of being "pleasure centers," and though they are close to the vital centers for thirst and hunger, they are physically distinct. Room for ambiguity might remain, since the laboratory animal cannot report its point of view; but as it happens, opportunistic experiments have been done with human patients during neural surgery, and it has been found that electric stimulation of the corresponding centers indeed does give rise to intense sensations of pleasure in the human psyche as well. [16]

It is important not to misunderstand the significance of discoveries of this kind: they do not reduce to trivial conclusions that pleasure might become the goal of a society designed by animal psychologists. Rather, we see that our account of the psyche is licensed to include as one component, and evidently a central one, the positive experience of delight. How we weigh that fact is a real question, but it is evident that a psyche which for any reason failed to participate in that experience would confront a life abnormally gone blank. The larger significance of the fact of pleasure becomes manifest when we realize that this is not a question of one isolated tile in the mosaic of the psyche: speaking as we are now of the hormonal system, in which global ramification is the rule, we recognize that modulations of this pleasure, in every degree from the least glow of satisfaction through the highest intensity of joy, will constitute a coloration through its presence or absence in virtually all of the psyche's activities.

It is interesting that science, by its own machinations, has at last caught up with our humanity. The chemical system is seen to enlist the entire brain, and the body as well, into a single, deeply moved and moving affective system; it is even far less clear than it once was where the boundaries of "brain" and "body" might lie, or how significant they are proving to be. We cannot attempt here to trace the paths by which this occurs—they are far too intricate and still only partially known. The hypothalamus, guardian of our lives, is guardian of life in permanence as well; it summons the pituitary to release hormones activating the gonadal organs, ovaries or testes, to shift the delicate,

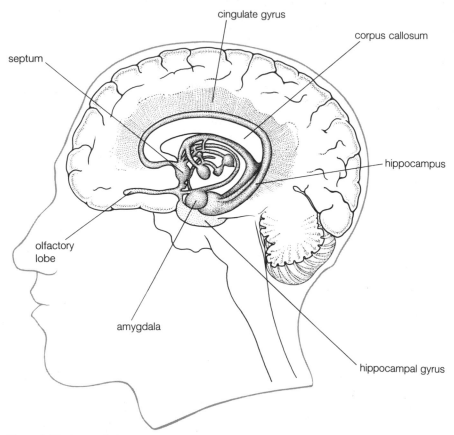

Figure 4. The human limbic system, inherited from primitive mammals, which organizes widespread areas of the brain into coherent emotional states. Its amplifying power may be likened to the operation of a "neural laser."

ever-changing balance of male and female hormones in the body system as a whole (we are all, always, responding to both). In this mode, there is ground for the deep distinction of *anima* and *animus* of Carl Jung. [17] The consequences are myriad and adapted in every instance to what we are seeing, hearing, saying, or touching. The limbic system, center of what is called "emotion," processes these matters in the first instance at the portal of the brain, on behalf of mind and body. The amygdala in particular has an amazing grip upon the mind, for its few cells in their processes ramify to send signals to perhaps billions of cells throughout the brain (fig. 4).

Not only do a few cells in this way govern the reactions of a vast number widely distributed in many areas of the brain; it is a very important principle in addition that they do this in time coordination, so that there is not only a high order of amplification of effect but a coherence which locks the reacting areas in a common time phase. The analogy to laser action, in which many atoms are triggered to release light in a common time phase, is striking: perhaps we should suggest the term *neural laser*. [18]

With this principle of coherent amplification of neural effect, we are seeing one seemingly very promising approach to the problem which we have brought with us from the *Theaetetus*, that of the unity of the person. We recall that earlier we referred to brain-stem functions as providing coherent timing signals which appeared to be giving rise to the pacing of the act of thought, yielding the poetic line or the musical phrase. If we ask about unity of the person over time, the function of memory, we meet a third instance of the same general principle. It was once thought necessary to locate specific "memory areas" in the brain, but one more recent suggestion is that even a single memory trace may be distributed over broad areas in the manner of the optical hologram. [19] In the hologram, each part of the image exists in distribution over the whole film; use of a small portion of the film will give not just one part of the image but the whole image at a low level of resolution. The entire film contributes to the reconstruction of the entire image at full resolution. In order that this occur, however, the illumination is best provided by a laser, since the light reaching each portion must be in full time coherence with that striking all other portions. On the holographic principle, then, memory must be invoked from all contributing portions of the cortex in strict time coherence, and there must be a timing pulse of a sort to provide such coherent activation. Again, the "laser" action of brain-stem centers seems suited to this function.

All aspects of our mental life are illuminated by affective governance such as that originating with the amygdala and published through the body by way of the hypothalamus and pituitary; it includes what we know as Eros, and in its gains and losses it lights and shadows our thinking, planning, and dreaming in every aspect of our lives. What it means is that all motion—as much that of a mathematical or political argument, as a romance or a family crisis—is moved by the sense of goal.

This is what Aristotle called *telos*, the goal, called by Latin tradition the "final cause." [20] He says in effect that there can be no motion without it, since motion by definition is toward something and thus *begins* with the end: only so does it have the structure of beginning, middle, and end which makes it whole or distinguishes it from unmemorable flux. Aristotle's cosmos is assembled on this basis, for if all things did not move toward the first motion as their end, being would not cohere. So with the *Theaetetus*, which as we have seen is housed in an act of devotion, without which the conversation would have never occurred, or been imagined, or had it occurred, been remembered.

It is good, indeed, to see that neurophysiology has brought us to the point of recognizing that it is by no means foreign to our sciences to escape the bounds of the "information" concept and the computer model, and to see that the mental system can be truly such only to the extent that it too coheres in motion toward an end. Some of us may remember, from the first of this series of essays, that a quantum mechanical system (that is, a fundamental account of what is called "matter") cannot be grasped unless the whole is placed first in our thinking. What we ordinarily call "causality"—that of the time sequence—is derivative from final cause, for material particles as it is for a mind constituted of them. [21]

"Programming" in a narrow sense of a predetermined, calculative ordering is not, evidently, the logic appropriate to theories of the mind: we know well enough that our mental experience is not of that sort, and we would certainly not wish it so. The endocrinal model of the mind, which rings so much more convincingly of our experience, implies a logic of another sort. There is yet another "logic" which has recently gained attention, and which seems to suggest an important third way for the mind. This is the mode addressed in "chaos theory." [22] The most accessible model of this kind may be the weather pattern shaping to a storm: would the advent of the storm have been predictable if sufficient data had been gathered in advance? The classical answer would have argued that problems of predictability lie in the paucity of information: the outcome is in principle determinate; the problem is only that the information grid must be tightened. With more data, more frequently gathered from closer spaced weather stations, the weather would ultimately be predictable. This seems, indeed, to make good sense. But chaos theory has decided otherwise: major outcomes are so sensitive to small events—the leverage of the tiniest event on the outcome is so great—that predictability is unthinkable; the phenomenon is appropriately referred to as the "butterfly effect," since the claim is that the flick of an insect's wing can swing the ultimate outcome.

The paradigm for the weather system is formally defined as "chaos," but this in turn becomes the name for a new form of order. Surprisingly, indeed, it develops that from situations of chaos there regularly emerges a common pattern, which in turn entails a new sort of orderliness, in the form, for example, of emergent periodicities with successive ranges of doubling or tripling of their periodicities. The same phenomena can be demonstrated with problems over a wide range, from population dynamics to coupled pendulums. It is not the substance, but the formal structure, which is in question.

Returning to the example of the weather system, we can see that the analogy to the human psyche is almost inescapable. The brain has at least the complexity of the atmosphere, with connectivities which insure that there could not be simple prediction. We know well in our own experience that phenomena pass over it like summer clouds or weather fronts; there are depressions and elevations, turbulence. For King Lear, the outer storm is no merely arbitrary symbolic correlate of the inner. It seems evident: the logic of highly connected, nonlinear chaotic systems as the theory develops will be a revealing third paradigm for the mind. [23] The "fractal" patterns which are becoming so familiar arise from the same logic. The sense of emergent orders which shape themselves from what would have seemed drifting or chaotic randomness fits much of our inner experience; the interplay of chance and order has much to do with artistic creation, the unfolding events of a novel, or the emergence of a new phrase in a sonata. As we muse, searching our thoughts or awaiting inspiration, are we not treading fractal paths?

One thing is clear: if we are to pay attention now to the new sciences of the mind, to open the way to serious investigation of the richness and possibility of our human psyche, very new tasks lie ahead. If we are ready to begin the work of shaking off the limiting postures of a narrow objectivity and the pretensions of a causality of mindless "law," with all the limitations of vision which go with these old points of view, then the sciences of the mind indeed hold great promise. We will be opening new ways, and no one can say at this moment where they might take us.

III. The divided self

Normally, as we have often seen in the course of this odyssey, the animal psyche must stand as surrogate for our own: we can invade the brain of a lower animal, or subject it to tests, using procedures we would never apply to human subjects. Only in the case of the highest, language functions, for which there is little help to be sought from an animal model, has this been impossible—and just there we have had to leave many experimental points untested and many immediate questions unresolved. Only chance injuries, leading for example to the crucial aphasias, have played the role of fortuitous, random experiments.

Since the 1950s, however, there has been one breathtaking exception to this stricture on human experimentation. As is now well known, extreme cases of otherwise uncontrollable epilepsy have been treated by the most drastic of surgeries: severing of the corpus callosum, an immense cable of nerve fibers joining point-for-point the two hemispheres of the human brain (fig. 5). In normal function, some fifty million axons running in both directions keep the left and right hemispheres in the most immediate and detailed communication with each other, and one would have supposed that removal of this fundamental cable would bring mental function to a standstill. [24] The striking result of these surgeries, of which there have now been many, has been, on the contrary, that while the epilepsy is normally controlled, the daily functioning of these patients is to outward appearances very little altered.

161

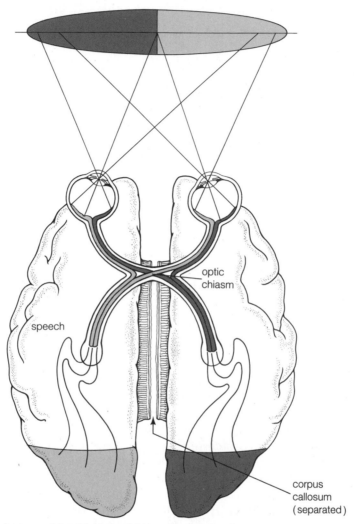

Figure 5. Anatomy of the "divided self." Here the corpus callosum, which normally binds the left and right hemispheres of the brain into close collaboration, has been surgically divided, leaving each hemisphere to regard its own half of the world. The optic chiasm has been so crafted by evolution that the left optic field of both eyes is connected to the right hemisphere, and the right optic field of both eyes is connected to the left hemisphere.

After the passage of a long period of recovery from the neural trauma following such surgery, patients are able to assume undemanding roles in society; few people would notice anything unusual in their daily behavior; and it has been said that one could easily pass a routine physical examination without a physician noticing anything awry.

Fortunately, it occurred to certain neurophysiologists that these procedures constituted an opportunistic experiment of the first order of importance—for with this, in some cases, near-total disconnection, it would be possible for the first time to make contact with the two hemispheres directly, and in unprecedented separation from one another. Since as we have seen our speech centers are most often found in the left hemisphere, the right brain is in itself largely or totally mute. Addressing it directly, it is very much as if we were able to bypass the exclusive claim of speech to monitor the gates of consciousness and, by this unexpected backdoor, bring the mind of the investigator into direct and extensive relation to one major domain of the Unconscious.

Many patients have cooperated in detailed investigations of this new-found world within the psyche: what has emerged has been the uncanny sense that once the central cable is cut, we are dealing with two strikingly independent minds, one articulate and thus formally the home of the "person"—the other, though for the most part utterly mute, giving abundant, unmistakable signs of a hidden human intelligence, vigorously and autonomously at work. Behind that veil of silence, who could be certain there was not a second *person* present in the experiments? Many sober neurophysiologists have disclaimed such dramatic formulations of the question, though the original investigator, Roger Sperry, has come to see it in very nearly these terms:

> Everything we have observed in many kinds of task performances over
> many years of testing reinforces the conclusion that the mute hemisphere
> has an inner experience of much the same order as that of the speaking
> hemisphere though differing in quality and cognitive faculties. . . .
> Clearly the right hemisphere perceives, thinks, learns, and remembers,
> all at a very human level. . . . [25]

However this phenomenon is best formulated, it presents us in a disturbingly new way with the old question: where is to be found that single self, which, if it is anything, must be unified, an unbroken whole? It is surely misleading to put the question in such impersonal, neutral terms: for it is we, whose cables are intact but whose hemispheres are now revealed—our own veils implicitly lifted—as in some sense intrinsically dual, who must ask the question, each one in the voice of the dominant hemisphere: "Who in this *am I?*" Freud put the same question otherwise when he invoked what the analytic literature in English calls the ego, but which he called in German simply, *the I: das Ich*. All our modern insights seem to converge to threaten the personal Being this question puts on the line, and the neurophysiologists, not least, have pressed their science to come up with something more promising than the conventional reductionist, "materialist" answer. It is easiest to say, and disconcertingly easy to maintain, that the self is a forgivable illusion: in the terms we met first in the *Theaetetus*, there is no entity that must be an intrinsically unbroken *whole*, but only an *aggregation*, a functioning assemblage held together by fifty million strings. No wagon for Hesiod;

only a temporarily bound-up heap of so many assorted parts. Yet the utter conviction of the dialogue was that in looking at Theaetetus, we were seeing a person, seeing through the flux of perception to the firm ground of one Being, through a lifetime.

Let us consider the typical experience of a split-brain patient. Because as we have seen the right-hand field of vision is presented entirely to the left brain, and the left to the right, it is possible by way of the eye to address each hemisphere in separation from the other—*aisthesis* in the plural! Furthermore, the right hemisphere governs the left hand, the left the right, so each hemisphere can be given its own tactile task. The right brain, it is important to add, although it is normally largely or entirely mute, will to some extent understand spoken instructions. Michael Gazzaniga, at once a pioneering investigator and a bold interpreter of these phenomena, describes the following experiment:

Pictures are shown separately to the two hemispheres; in the case described, a chicken claw is shown to the left brain (by being placed in the right visual field), and a snow scene, to the right brain. Each brain remembers its picture, and then the patient (or should we say, "the patients"?) is (are) shown a set of other pictures in full view: i.e., both brains now see the whole set of pictures. Each is to choose a picture which is appropriate to the one just presented; among the set are a shovel (to go with the snow scene) and a chicken (to go with the chicken claw). Each brain's own hand reaches forward to select its own picture: the right brain's left hand rightly chooses a shovel to go with the snow scene it is holding in memory, while the left brain (which of course has no notion of snow scenes) properly uses its (right) hand to pick the chicken to go with the claw it has in its mind. The next step particularly interests Gazzaniga: the right brain cannot of course be asked to give *reasons,* but the left can. When asked then why the shovel was chosen, it (arrogating to itself the representation of a whole person) *makes up an excuse.* Utterly ignorant of the real reason the shovel was chosen, it explains that the shovel was needed to shovel out the chicken shed! [26]

One would like to be able to characterize the lurking, silent "right hemisphere person"—surely we could learn something new and important about ourselves if we could enter this previously undisclosed realm of our psyche. These researches are, however, endlessly complex, and it is easy to misrepresent the results: romantic characterizations of the two hemispheres following too closely upon the first research results have been a source of exasperation to disciplined scientists. Yet some broad generalizations remain valid, and they ring true to some already long-familiar distinctions.

The right brain is sensitive to emotional tone and character in a voice, or in music; it picks up the semantics of sounds in the environment, and the immediate meanings of words, especially concrete words. It is true in general that its perceptions are holistic, immediate, and supersede the temporal: when a task becomes analytic, demands logical analysis or attention to sequence in time, it becomes a left-brain task. In general, in the connected brain, tasks shift hemispheres from right to left as they become verbal, and certainly when they become syntactic. It is possible to watch the development of right-brain skills in the developing child, and to track their decline, correspondingly, in the aging. Older people tend to compensate for such losses in facial recognition or spatial orientation by, for example, the use of alternative "cognitive strategies"—using verbal labels, benchmarks, and route sequences, where overall orientations and immediate grasp are imperfect. The fact that the right brain/left brain asymmetry, or *lateralization,* is on the average less marked in female than in male brains gives some physiological foundation to the sense that the feminine mode is more intuitive, less word-dominated, than the masculine. [27]

Reliance on split-brain surgery and opportunistic observations based on pathologies have marked what is evidently a relatively crude and early era of human neurophysiology—as indeed has dependence with respect to other questions on animal models, where translation from the animal to the human psyche is always uncertain. We seem now to be on the threshold of an entirely new domain of investigation. New instruments are transforming the neurophysiological laboratory; at long last, the surgeon is beginning to put aside his dreadful knife! The reader will no doubt be well aware of these new methods, "tomographies" in which the cuts are made by particle- or photon-beams. Not only are they noninvasive, but they are verging on living, real-time investigations which will let us watch the physiological progress of our own, ongoing thought.

One example, often cited, will serve to suggest the possibilities which lie ahead. The "PET scan," *positron emission tomography,* is achieved by introducing a radioactively labeled sugar-surrogate into the blood-stream to the brain; it is taken up with glucose in proportion to a cell's metabolic rate, but accumulates to yield a detectable radioactive output. It is thus possible to use arrayed gamma-ray detectors to identify and locate the brain cells active at any moment. In this way, the distribution of the brain's activity can be monitored; the result, a computer construction, is presented in the color-pattern mode which inevitably suggests a thermal interpretation, as if the active areas were "hot" spots—as indeed, metaphorically, they are. By such means it is possible (*see* fig. 6) to monitor a shift of thought over the terrain of the cortex.

Here is a telling example. A PET scan will confirm that in listening to music most of us who are not musicians will function in the domain of the right brain: our listening will be intuitive, immediate in the literal sense of "unmediated" or direct, and we will be tracking the experience emotionally—in fact, as has been shown in extensive studies,

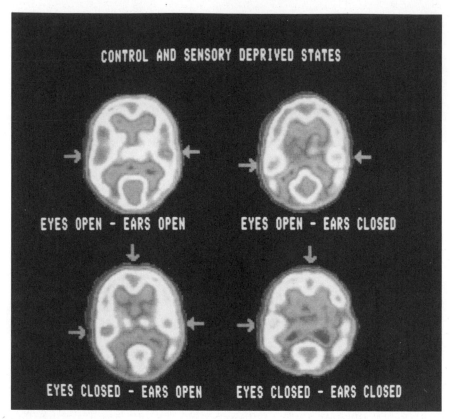

Figure 6. PET scan images under a variety of conditions; the brain is viewed from above, and the person is facing forward. The distinction between activity of the visual and auditory areas of the cortex is very clear.

with overt or covert incipient kinesthetic motions as well. [28] This experience, though strongly kinetic, is not "temporal"—we are making no reflective measurement of the time, establishing none of the forward or backward counts or comparisons which constitute an awareness or concept of time: our experience thus in the manner we have ascribed to the right brain "supersedes" time. It is in a certain sense *simple,* perhaps "primitive": it is innocent of analysis, of conceptual reflection, or verbal or symbolic categorization. But if now we are asked to attend to the tempo, key, or instrumentation—to make a judgment of this sort about the music—the PET scan will swing to reveal that we bring into play the analytic powers of the left brain. Musicians tend to listen with the left brain, evidently aware as most of us are not of formal structures and developments. If one who is listening thus with the left brain is asked instead to attend to the emotional quality of the music, the brain pattern will swing back, through the cable of the corpus callosum, to the right.

What we are saying of music has its counterpart in speech. A right-brain-damaged patient may speak accurately with the full powers of the Wernicke's and Broca's areas and yet be unable to convey or grasp emotional tone in speech: which must mean in turn that an essential dimension of meaning is lost. If we think on the other hand in terms of a sentinel's function, listening for an untoward sound, this will on the whole be right-brain work. If it is an open question what this sound might be, the last and highest pitched portions will be caught first; then, there will be an alertness and expectation of some semantically significant sound—an engine's sound, or a splash of water. This is still the right brain, drawing upon its vast lexicon of significant noises of the environment. But if we recognize and name it, and go on to tell ourselves to listen acutely for the sound of a marine engine of this or that sort, for example, we have shifted. The crux seems to be *language:* if a name springs to mind or a thought forms up, we have shifted to the domain of *onoma* and *logos,* and that seems to be the left brain. In practice, of course, the two richly coupled hemispheres must work in tandem, with quick and subtle tilts, divisions, and combinations of the mind's complex activity. Much of the effect of the right brain must take the form of some diffuse modulation or coloring of the whole, invoking the rich hormonal processes which we have discussed.

With all respect to the cautions on which the researchers rightly insist, we must at this point permit ourselves to draw an inescapable conclusion. Here, in demonstrable phenomena of the physiology of the brain, we are surely meeting again, in the mode of a new form of oracle, that distinction which was so fundamental for us in the *Theaetetus:* between the semantic power of single image, standing alone and inviting intuitive grasp, which we called *paratactic,* and the connected power of the predicated word to form thought, we called *syntactic.* In the connected reasoning of linked predications is what we call the power of logic, but in the singleness and intensity of the image looms that other mode of meaning (by contrast, grammatical, and thus in some sense poetic) which we saw preceded and, in a way, encompassed the reasoning of the Socratic argument. We see now that it is the primary channel to emotion.

Let us say this: the cortex's gateway to the drives or instincts—the moving powers of the soul—seems to lie through this immediacy of the right brain. By contrast, conscious awareness worked out in the connectedness of outer or inner discourse belongs to the left brain. The union of these two is the living experience of the whole person which is surging continuously through the vital threads of the corpus callosum. The right brain deals most with what is single, and whole; the left, with analysis and articulations. In the right brain we recognize the figure of Parmenides, silent spokesman for the One; and in the left, the Ionian motions which keep our thoughts circling. Nothing is solved by way of this recognition: but perhaps, seeing the old question in a new light, we will see in it as well some new significance, the prospect of some new order of understanding.

IV. Consciousness as a fact of science [29]

It was once common wisdom that strictures of objectivity demanded the exclusion of subjective data from a truly scientific psychology. The result was a behavioral science which necessarily omitted what must always most interest us in psychology, our personal inner experience. If science has indeed taken the fundamental turn we have claimed for it, and has left the criterion of simple objectivity behind, then that old stricture is no longer binding. Phenomena of consciousness may now be recognized as facts, as worthy as any others of inclusion in the scientific study of the mind, and with this admission, the science has enormously expanded its boundaries and its interest for us. Sperry, whom we quoted earlier, has written in this connection:

> Once science thus modifies its traditional materialist-behaviorist stance and begins to accept in theory, and to encompass in principle, within its causal domain the whole world of inner, conscious, subjective experience (the world of the humanities), then the very nature of science itself is changed. The change is not in the basic methodology or procedures, of course, but in the scope of science and in its limitations, in its relation to the humanities and to values and in its role as a cultural, intellectual, and moral force. [30]

With the doors and windows thus thrown open to the rich world of mental experience, the questions become those of a new empiricism: what will be the observational and experimental procedures of this new psychology, which is at last genuinely a science of the mind, and what will the new empiricism, which includes subjectivity, reveal? These are new seas and new shores, but already results are reported which suggest the continents that lie ahead.

To see how an experiment incorporates subjective data in a central way, let us look at the demonstration and strict measurement of something called the *readiness potential*. [31] The experiment is really quite simple. Electroencephalography measurements are taken covering several areas of the brain as well as the activating potential for some muscle, for example, the right index finger. Great care is taken to assure that there is *no* "stimulus"—that this is a genuinely spontaneous act. The person is thus asked to make the ultimate act of pure subjectivity: by free will, to move that finger. The electroencephalograph of course jumps into action, as do the activating potential and the finger.

In what way does this become a crucial experiment? The record is in effect taken *in reverse:* the whole being recorded, that portion is analyzed which immediately *preceded* having been the action potential and the finger motion. When this experiment is repeated many times, and the results averaged, a striking pattern emerges (fig. 7). During a period of some eight-tenths of a second preceding the action potential, a strong and regular potential appears in the electroencephalogram (EEG). This evidently corresponds to the conscious act of deciding to move the finger, and extending over this time (which is very long by neural standards) prepares the entire system to carry out the act. It is therefore known as the preparatory potential: the "trace" of a conscious act. Of course it does not prove anything about free will or the independent existence of mind; it serves merely to illustrate one way in which the conscious act may enter the experimental scene and bring with it a theoretical concept which thereupon becomes grist for the mills of theory. It is permissible but not necessary to hypothesize, as John Eccles does, that during that period, mind acts on matter.

Various forms of experiments have been done with subjective mental objects. In one famous series of investigations it was shown that when mental images are moved about in the imagination on command, they take longer to traverse greater distances. Proportionately greater times were required to travel greater distances on an introspective map, in obedience to Galileo's laws of uniform motion! [32] Other experiments have worked with "competition" between a sensory image and an object visualized in the imagination. It is also possible in the case of certain lesions to observe the decoupling of sensation and perception, so that sense, not naming what it sees, entails the experience of the "blank look" of nonrecognition. Jean-Pierre Changeux himself speaks of distinct types of mental objects and prefers to formulate these results by asserting that there is a material correlate for the mental object. [33] One striking suggestion is the one Changeux makes in a passing reference to Bertrand Russell: the bonding of mental objects may be like the chemical bond, a *sharing*, as of electrons. Since the junction of neurons is electrochemical in nature, Russell's analogy begins to look more like a bridge you could walk across! Thoughts may bond, by way of their neurons, on quantum principles.

All we need to conclude from these experiments at the moment is that consciousness need no longer be excluded from the experimental sciences. To put it more positively: mental objects enter science now with essentially the same status as material objects; consciousness has the status of mass or energy. What relations consciousness, thus acknowledged, will have to neurophysiological phenomena is now a question of experimental investigation and theoretical speculation. There would seem to be no reason *in principle* to exclude the possibility that events of consciousness (such as the act of will in our first experiment) will have a causal effect on physiological events, or, on the other hand, that events

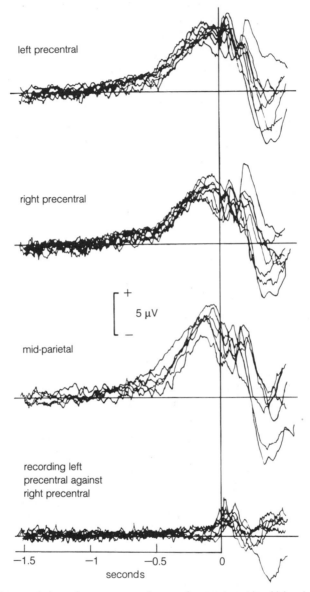

left precentral

right precentral

┌ +
│   5 μV
└ −

mid-parietal

recording left
precentral against
right precentral

−1.5   −1   −0.5   0

seconds

Figure 7. Electroencephalography measurements spanning a moment in which voluntary motion of the right index finger takes place. The recording, or electroencephalogram (EEG), is made continuously, and then analyzed *ex post facto,* since the experimenter cannot know when the subject's act of free will is to occur. Working backwards in the record, it is found that on the temporal scale of neural events, a potential in fact occurs long before the physical act is initiated. This is believed to be the physical record of an act of will. The fourth graph is recorded differently, in such a way as to show only the motor event itself.

will occur in one domain which have no counterpart at all in the other. The important point is that at this amazing stage of the sciences of the mind—evidently at the threshold of major developments—"anything" is quite possible.

V. The human genome as the "Book of Life"

At a crucial point in an earlier segment of this essay, on the "sciences of life," attention turned to the genetic foundation of our life processes. [34] A reader with sufficient stamina might want to turn back to that section at this point; at any rate, I have just done so and am prepared to report briefly. It was observed that according to some deep plan for the architecture of living things, organisms are in general designed on a double scheme: one way to put this was in terms of "governance" and "process"—governance or control on the part of the enduring genetic material, execution in the transience of the actual life of an individual being at a place and a time in the world. Correspondingly, two characteristic branches of the domain of organic molecules are involved. On the side of execution, the processes of life are actually carried out by way of molecules called proteins; these are complications of elemental units called amino acids, of which there are, interestingly, about as many as there are letters in the alphabet. The amino acids combine in sometimes huge, textlike structures, which carry out the processes of life on the time scales of our lives and lifetimes, year-by-year, day-by-day, second-by-second. Though the materials of the body, its cells and its fabrics, are not necessarily themselves proteins, whatever their actual constitution they tend to be managed, built, and unbuilt by way of the operations of the proteins, which take their own shape and instructions from the genetic material.

The ultimate function of governance is invested in a material of a different kind, the DNA (deoxyribonucleic acid). The DNA is in some sense primary: here resides the genetic record of who and what we are and the plan of the life strategy we call human—the phases of development, maturation, and decline. To speak again very schematically, the DNA seals the text it bears with a constancy greater than that of diamond: its memory spans the millennial scales of evolutionary time. As we "humans" evolved, in a process culminating some hundred thousand years ago, it was the idea of man which was being inscribed in the DNA, which has preserved that essential form to this day. In this sense it is under its deepest direction that I write these very words. Like the proteins, the DNA must be understood as in some very real sense a *text;* here, the letters are just four, the nucleic acids. Schematically, it is transcribed first into related RNA, which in turn governs the assemblage of the proteins and sets them going.

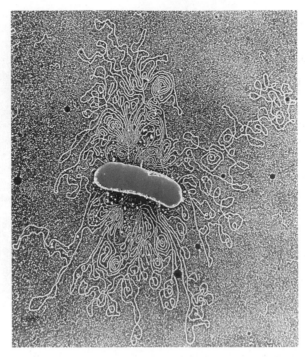

Figure 8. Electron micrograph of the DNA of a single cell of the bacterium *Escherichia coli*. Though it has been released here from the cell by experimental methods, the single molecule remains intact and supercoiled. This "Book of Life" must indeed be extremely tightly coiled, as the length of the full "text," consisting of some four million base cells, is seven hundred times the length of the cell into which it is packed. The human DNA is more than one thousand times as long as that of the bacterium.

There is one respect, however, in which it may be misleading to think of these molecular forms simply in terms of "texts." While they do encode both the broadest plans and subtlest details of life and its infinite activities, this coding is not only in the linear sequences, which remind us of the stream of discourse or the line of printed type, but also in crucial spatial configurations in which these concatenate. Thus the spiral form of the "double helix" of the DNA and RNA is essential to their mutual function: by virtue of this crafty shape, DNA is able to retain the stability of the ages while spinning open and closing again to replicate its forms in the RNA at what are for most of us simply unthinkable speeds. Only in this way can the timeless plan be transcribed in the momentary activities of the myriad cells of the body (*see* fig. 8). Further, the proteins carry out their functions—that is, act as the vehicles of what we call "life"—by virtue of an unceasing process of what we have spoken of as "publishing" and "interpreting." They are wound into intricate and exact spatial forms which, for example, by mating with corresponding forms throughout the body, selectively block or invoke the processes of respiration, metabolism, or muscular activity. We may conclude that the syntax of this "Book of Life" is at least three-dimensional.

Our task now is to translate these conclusions of the earlier discussion, which had focused on the physiology of metabolic processes, into terms of the activities of the psyche. Our task here is to follow to its culmination the idea of science in our time, and it will best serve that end if we take as hypothesis the assumption that the activities of the psyche—sensing, remembering, feeling, caring—are governed and executed by these molecules, no less than are those of eating, walking, and digesting.

Out of that earlier discussion came the further sense that Aristotle and Leibniz had something to teach us today concerning the unity of living things, and indeed of life itself with the cosmos as a whole. If science is no longer identified with materialism—or "matter" is seen to be intellectual before it is concrete—then it will not be reductive to conclude, as Aristotle did, that the single province of science is "physics" in the old sense of the term, meaning the domain of all of nature—at once that which we call "living" and that which we do not. We may extend this insight now, tentatively, to include the psyche, and not least the works of the mind. It will not be improper to carry to its conclusion a "scientific reading" of the *Theaetetus,* asking, in terms of the still tentative sciences of our time, Plato's ultimate questions concerning knowing and Being, and the meaning of life and death.

It is customary to speak in genetics of the "genotype" and the "phenotype," the underlying genetic plan and its overt, visible expression in the living creature. Traditionally, the phenotype has been thought of primarily in terms of the elements of the visible form—eye color, bodily configuration, blood type. With the maturing of genetic science, however, attention has shifted to the phenotype in a new sense—not merely configurations of bodily forms, but configurations of behavior as well. In the human case it is our ways of speaking and thinking which are our "phenotype" of greatest interest. We will be looking, then, not for bodily structures, but for innate structures of human activity at the level of the mind. In principle, genetic studies coalesce with psychological and even philosophical inquiry into the processes of thought and the nature of human knowledge. Such studies are of course only at their very threshold, but it is important to see that the way is in principle now open. This may well give us pause. Are we prepared to agree that it will not be inappropriate for the scientist to address the questions of the *Theaetetus,* including the overarching questions of knowing and Being?

To entertain such a claim "in principle" is one thing; to figure out how to execute it is another. Having met so many instances already in other contexts of the study of human functions by way of modeling in animal systems, we will not be surprised to find that one way, at least, of approaching the genetics of the human psyche is through a new science of animal behavior, called "ethology," introduced in the years immediately preceding World War I and developed over the period we have been considering. It is the study of animal behavior, not in laboratory situations or under the conditions of artificial experiments, but in nature, in the animal's own domain. [35] In that sense it concerns "ethos"—that is, the natural ways of animals and their societies, as nearly as possible in the environment to which such natural behavior is adapted. It is the ethos, the *way*, which is the object under study; experiments probe its structure and constitution, and evolutionary studies look for its natural history as a product of selection.

At this point, ethology touches upon genetics, for the transmission of such a way is primarily genetic: there is in the DNA's book a text that codes for a phenotype which is a behavior, just as there is a text for eye color. A unit of a behavioral phenotype is an element of the animal psyche, and hence we perceive the psyche as an adaptive product, its ways memories of a past which is as deep as the time scale of the DNA. Animals that behave instinctively are thus acting out relations to ancient environments that may or may not still surround them. (One thinks of the cat in the back alley, the dolphin in the tuna net, the owl contemplating a vanished woodland, the hunter-gatherer at a desk in the financial district.) Natural selection acts to suppress the maladaptive case.

It is important at this point to notice another development of the new sciences, marking a shift in the understanding of the evolutionary process. As we have just characterized the selection process, it seems heavy-handed: adapt, or perish! The methods of population genetics, however, have brought a new perspective to this. It marks a shift to a more global, systematic point of view which rightly suggests other developments we have seen in the direction from earlier focus on the individual case, to attention instead to the larger, inclusive *system* (cf. Theodosius Dobzhansky, *Genetics and the Origin of Species, GBWW* II: 56, 517–688). Here, it means taking into account the diversity within a given population at any given time. Within any population there is a vast diversity of viable mutations (to see this, one has only to look around to note the range of visible phenotypes within a chance human group); the genotype is evidently not a single character but a statistical distribution. Correspondingly, selection operates not on a single genome, to accept or reject it, but on the distribution, favoring certain aspects, disfavoring others, and yielding as a result not simply a different animal in the ordinary sense but, we might say, a different "animal" in the statistical sense. Such plastic favoring and disfavoring under selective pressures and attractors is operating constantly, so that what had been thought of, plausibly, as a very slow timetable of evolutionary change turns out, on the contrary, to be rapidly sensitive to environmental factors of all sorts on a day-by-day basis. The science of ethology has emerged more or less concurrently with that of population genetics, so it is the "ethos" in that more interesting statistical sense which the ethologist will most probably have in mind.

Most animals have no mechanism for teaching and learning; information is passed in subtle detail from generation to generation, but the teaching text is the DNA. If that text is now seen to be statistical, and in this sense subtle and responsive, we see that in a very real way a kind of teaching and learning is going on among creatures of instinct. The gene pool of any local population, though its memory reaches to a deep evolutionary past, will at the same time be indicative of rather current news. If we follow for a moment longer this attractive metaphor of genetic teaching and learning, we may compare the experience of a species, encoded in its DNA and governing the ethos of a particular population at some specific time, to the development of a learning human individual over the span of a lifetime. Adjustment of the DNA behavioral text in sensitive response to its environment we may rightly call "learning" on the part of the species. Let us then speak of *phylogenetic learning*, meaning by the term the behaviors encoded by the processes of evolution in the DNA. We may be looking at the DNA of an individual, but we should keep in mind the genetic composition of any given population—which may "know" more, in its statistical shaping, than the DNA of any individual would reveal.

This notion is of course especially interesting when applied to ourselves. We, it would seem, must bear in our genetic texts a vast library of ancient learning. Much of what I am about to suggest is speculative, for the project of mapping the human genome is immense and is only getting under way. Even for the best-studied animals, understanding of the genetic basis of behavior is still very limited. This is in part because the field is new, the benchmark observations of the phenotype itself—behavior in groups and under natural conditions—having only recently taken definitive form. Further, the "phenotype" itself is harder to recognize and classify with confidence (the eye color of *Drosophila* is a much more empirically convenient entity!). Finally, the DNA text itself seems more complicated in cases of this sort—not a single gene, but sets of genes, may work to produce an observed trait, and as the behavior is emergent during the development of the individual, so the genes in question may be suppressed by regulation at one time and in one context, and expressed only later or earlier in another. Nonetheless, there are good grounds for confidence that we are speaking of a genuine field of scientific study, and if so, surely one of the most important, and most fraught with consequence for science seen as a dialectical endeavor. What is learned in this science must surely bear very directly upon our understanding of ourselves.

We humans of course do depend on the transmission of information culturally, through traditions, verbal teaching and learning, inherited artifacts and the skills to use them, and now, very recently, written language and its transmission through books and an avalanche of other paper. Before the art of writing, memory aided by various informal reminding devices was the carrier of the cultural tradition, running as it does in some way parallel to that of inscription in the DNA. Myth composed to map the human experience, continuously told and retold, was the principal carrier; the use of repetitive poetic forms very much aided the process of recall. Because of the importance of the cultural parallel channel for the successful functioning of even the earliest human societies, it is clear that the ability to support cultural transmission was at least one of the chief selection pressures acting to shape the human brain in its phylogenetic development. Thus the ability to use language is elaborately programmed into our genetic code: in this way, the genetic channel enables the functioning of the cultural channel, while the success of the cultural channel over evolutionary time has through natural selection built its support system into the DNA. The cultural development of language entailed complementary development of the motor system for throat, tongue, lips, and mouth to make this new kind of sound, and of the auditory system to perceive it. As we have seen earlier in this continuing essay, the auditory system for the perception of speech is distinct, both in the cortex and in concept, from that for detecting other sounds. [36]

Mankind learned the value of language incrementally, and our sense for language, the human child's instinctive hunger for language, is the record in an instinctive, behavioral phenotype of this early learning. The "deep structure" of language is, like other "depths" which we will be probing, common to mankind because it is a memory of early speaking-events so distant in our hominid past. We still, in ways which the modern philologists begin to ferret out, talk like prehistoric humans. It seems clear that such genetic factors are shared by other members of our same family. Thus the chimpanzee, who turns out to be very close to us genetically, shares a similar ability and impulse to use language. The infant chimpanzee and the infant human pace one another closely in the first three years of language acquisition, the chimpanzee using a mechanical keyboard to circumvent its lack of voice. [37]

It is interesting to note here a recurrent principle in our efforts to decipher the pasts of living creatures, especially our own. We can look for animal models of our own earlier being: thus the chimpanzee is the animal model for ourselves just before we turned off on the human branch of the evolutionary tree; perhaps the current candidate for "first hominid" is described as "a small (three- to four-foot-tall) bipedal creature with . . . a chimpanzee-sized brain," dated from something more than three million years ago. [38] In this sense, engaging in language exchange with the chimpanzee we are ferreting out the roots of our own speech, or talking to our own prehominid ancestor—one might say, conversing with our prehominid selves. [39] In another way, models of our past selves can be found in the developmental stages of childhood; insofar as the disputed principle of "recapitulation" holds, each of us in infancy has rehearsed the past history of the species. Thus, apart from cultural direction, human children passing universally through developmental stages based on the six reported by Jean Piaget are to some interesting extent revealing innate, genetic programming, and ticking off stages of our human past: children become animal models of human prehistory. [40] One could in principle calibrate childhood by the tens of thousands of years the infant is working through!

In turn, cross correlation of the Piaget stages with primate behavior relates the primate animal model to the human developmental sequence, and even, more hypothetically, relates these stages to their adaptive functions for other species and early humans. [41] They reveal, in effect, instinctive behaviors which spring directly from the long-recording genome; or, we may say, the children are reading to us from the Book of Life. The spontaneously emerging protolanguage of children, which can be shown to have structure and meaning, is thought to be related to functional language used by the earliest humans, related to foraging for and sharing food. [42] Thereafter, language use shifts upward in the brain from subcortical to cortical control—that is, from instinctive utterance to deliberate speech, thus tracking the development of the human neocortical brain.

Finally, of course, the same "depths" which are those of our prehistoric past are probed by analytic psychology, which as it unearths elements from the Unconscious is, too, mining that inheritance which lies at the basis of our civilized behavior. We shall have more to say about this last, in our next section.

With the mechanical reproduction of texts, first—very recently by the time scales of human evolution—through the art of printing on paper, and now suddenly by more powerful and far more promising means of digital recording in more durable and accessible form, the cultural "parallel channel" is threatening to overwhelm the brain itself—to drown us in our own culture, like Alice in the Pool of Tears. The technologies of cultural preservation and transmission are no longer the limiting factor, but rather the ability of the brain to utilize their output. The brain can no longer interpret the information which is captured and made available to it; hence the current new attention to the power of the visual cortex to grasp patterns in multidimensional visual displays of data arrays, through the technology now gaining recognition in the form of "scientific visualization."

If we look at a graph of the evolution of the animal kingdom with the development of brains in view, we sense that the diverging branches of the evolutionary tree point to different brain architectures and functions, corresponding presumably to selective pressures or environing opportunities at the crucial division points. The comparative anatomy of the brain among modern representatives of these alternative paths presents us with a model in which the broadest plan—an underlying topology—is common, while specializations yield very different emphases in the resulting organ.

The old plan is always recognizable in the depths of the modern structure, and at the basis of the modern behavior as well. Thus, for example, it is speculated that the wolf pack may be a suggestive animal model of the pre- or proto-linguistic stage of human development; wolves range over territories a hundred kilometers in extent, marking the terrain by olfactory cues and developing as a group a reliable conceptual navigational map. For australopithecenes, the recognized world (called the *Umwelt* by Jakob von Uexküll) may have been primarily olfactory also, and they may have had the power comparable to that of wolf or dog to recognize a vast number of aromas, which is to say, significantly distinct marker-molecules. The nose reads molecular texts directly and with alacrity, as we recognize when we "smell smoke" or detect a potential gas leak. The rhinencephalon (the "smell brain") which accomplishes this is from the perspective of the modern human a principal element of the "old brain"—though it is new and active enough for a dog or a wolf today. For us, the auditory system took over this marking and recognition of the perceived world construct with the advent of words—markers which were surrogates for smells— in their first level of function as semantic while not yet syntactic. The rhinencephalon became for us the very central and crucial, deep limbic system which we have discussed earlier in connection with our hormonal mode (fig. 4). [43]

To draw the conclusion from the logic of this evolutionary syllogism, we must acknowledge that in some way the governance of our thought and behavior via the limbic system stems from a memory of *Australopithecus,* for which, as we saw, an animal model may be the wolf pack. Is this a distressing thought? Do we not indeed search our world, verbally mark an *Umwelt?* We have seen something of what it does, and does not, mean to say that the limbic system initiates and governs: we are stirred and moved by calls which are deep in our nature. The drumbeat is original and very deep. How we move to it is in part our doing, in part not.

VI. Other brains, other minds: The cetacean intellect

It is quite understandable that we are inclined in discussions of mind, thought, and knowledge to frame the discussion in terms and expectations which are actually very limiting. We suppose, without perhaps sufficient critical examination, that what we know of mind is all that there might be to know, or that knowledge as we understand it is all that knowledge might be. Despite mythic efforts to break out of our mental skins and extend our imaginative boundaries, it seems almost inherently self-contradictory to speak of knowing anything about knowing which was not familiar to us as our own. If there were modes of knowing which were radically different, some logical closure might seem to seal them from us.

We are able to recognize, on the other hand, the fact that evolution has guided our human mental phylogenetic development along one very special course. *Homo sapiens sapiens* is an evolutionary upstart, and we cannot shake off Charles Darwin's dictum that as these plastic forms have been shaped by the exacting disciplines of adaptation, we inevitably look like—map in the forms of our own being—the environment in which our ancestors once triumphed. Competition has been especially sharp and fierce in our particular department: whereas there are many varieties of many species, we are the lone survivors of our branch, having eliminated such alternatives as *Homo neanderthalensis*. One tends to think of evolutionary shaping in terms of bodily forms, but as we have been seeing, the more interesting areas of the genotype involve the forming of the endocrine system and the brain—and in our case especially, the recent explosive development of the human neocortex seems proof inescapable that it is the competitive instrument finely honed for our successful elimination of the competition.

By the evolutionary "environment" we have learned to mean the local biosphere as much as our physical conditions, and while old clichés of "raw nature" are now behind us, the reality of the evolutionary adaptative process is considerably more exacting than it first seemed. The brain of our species is an instrument precisely adapted to a very specific demand powerfully operative upon us many millennia in the past, a demand which no longer exists, except insofar as brains once adapted to an earlier environment perpetually re-create it as that artifact which we substitute for reality: we "think," "know," and act under compulsion of a genotype well-shaped to overcoming Neanderthals. As if compulsively, we invent a world which re-creates the threatening forest. Hence the Judeo-Christian God is half-Neanderthal, and we presuppose forms of social interaction which are in their effects worse than the worst of an archaic past. The notion of "war," organized social aggression, is an oddity which is our special forte and is as inappropriate and counterproductive as it is pervasive in the world of our own construction. Similarly, our intellects, so keen to destroy and by definition so effective in eliminating other forms of life, are now carrying us beyond all limits in the eradication of fellow species on which our future being depends. The terrible inertia of the genome, in the dark side of its projection as our mental misconception of being and truth, locks us to the past and bids fair to sweep us from the face of the Earth we so recently conquered.

Our brains, even more than our fingered and footed bodies, are adapted to peer and run about in a hard, harsh, earth-surface world, keen to kill or fend off and quick to devise and manipulate. Thomas Hobbes, unfortunately, caught us all too well in his characterization of the state of our nature—which is to say, of our genome—when he characterized our ungoverned lives as "solitary, poor, nasty, brutish, and short" (*GBWW* I: 23, 85; II: 21, 85). There is truth enough in such an account, but it is rather a self-portrait of *Homo sapiens sapiens* out of the past than an account of a larger possible truth. Does it, however, make any sense to speak of "larger truths" than those which house comfortably in our sharply tuned brains? With the spaceflights of recent years we have escaped well enough certain of the earthbound limitations of our footed anatomy; could we similarly gain such distance as to think ourselves out of the limitations of our forest-bred minds? We need the ironic perspective of Jonathan Swift, who could spot us as inescapably related to the devising Yahoos yet place us in the conceptual context of nobler natures. Swift was unfair only to the monkeys. [44]

To speak of radical alternatives to our particular notions of mind, truth, or knowledge is not as idle as it might once have seemed, though research is still very preliminary, evidently still groping for terms in which to conduct an investigation. For as is well known, there are other brains on the face of Earth, larger even in proportion to body size than ours, and more developed proportionately in the department of the neocortex, the area of our special pride. Though there may be another candidate, I speak here of the cetaceans, the dolphins and whales. Not only is the ratio of neocortex to the whole higher in their case than in ours, but within the neocortex, it is in the higher "association" areas in which they especially exceed us. [45] While our brains are very recent arrivals on the scale of evolutionary time, theirs are very old, having formed, in approximate terms, a million years ago to our hundred thousand or less (*see* fig. 9). The important point is that they then took a very different path and now swim among us as minds probably a bit more powerful than ours, though of a very different sort. We have not broken through to communicate with their view of the world, which we still can hardly begin to imagine. Not only do we not "speak the same language"; our idea of language is so different from theirs that we have hardly found the first vehicles of a translation. And of course, the deep nastiness of our commercial brains seems very likely to destroy all the evidence before we have a chance to find out what we may have missed. We must know these fellow creatures in their world-ranging free societies if we are to understand them at all. What poor accounts the last survivors will be able to give us, cramped in tanks and cages,

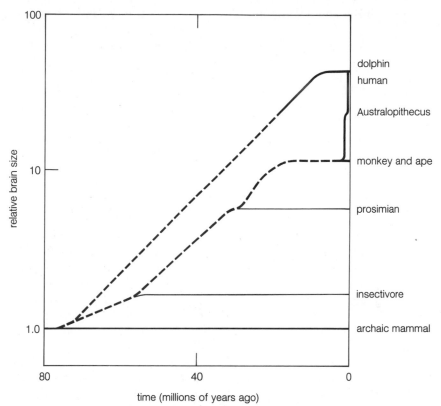

Figure 9. A likely construction of the histories of the cetacean and human brains, in terms of brain size as a fraction of total body size. It is apparent that in evolutionary terms we have made the leap from ape brain to human brain extremely recently, with startling suddenness. Cetaceans, by contrast, have lived with brains of comparable proportions for many millions of years.

in what our limited minds call "experiments." An *experiment,* as Francis Bacon explained in the patent documents he filed with his discovery as the *Advancement of Learning* (*GBWW* I: 30, 1–101; II: 28, 1–101), is an instrument of torture: little likely to serve as gateway to a new understanding of what "knowing" might be!

If as we have been suggesting the mind in its own structure maps the particular world it once grew to know, we may begin a sketch of the cetacean mind by reflecting on the character of the cetacean world. If the oceans of the world, vast as they are, constitute from the point of view of evolutionary theory yet another "niche"—what a "niche" that must be! For the cetaceans, even the lightless depths of the oceans are bright, for the medium of cetacean spatial intuition is not light but their copious sound. Though they have eyes which they use as a secondary mode of perception, they "see" primarily by hearing. Since they

181

thus utter the "light" that they see by, choosing wavelengths astutely to meet varying needs of range or detail (long wavelengths ranging over vast distances, short wavelengths for a high level of local detail), they illumine their world very deftly and fully. Their three-dimensional acoustic maps must be far more thorough and more directed than our visual ones. Since they thus see by hearing, in a system like a better sonar, when they "sing" or speak they are literally and figuratively mapping worlds into speech in complex hieroglyphs which have little in common with our threading of thoughts in our linear, time-bound discourse. We communicate with them better through their reading of our facial gestures than by way of the strictures of trying to "teach" them "language." They might well "teach" us "language," but we are little capable of learning or crediting what does not fit readily into our conception of the world.

If our minds have been crafted to win victories over a harsh environment, it seems that theirs may in fact have always been more benign. They do not on the whole have threatening predators, nor have they lacked for food in the abundant oceans. To swim with exemption from the law of gravity is easier than to walk, run, or climb, and there is no harshness in their seasons. Even the river dolphins, which deal with shallow waters and intricate shores and shallows, have become so equipped with an instant sonar grasp of these details that they, as well, move easily and apparently without major threat. One wonders, then, what forces have indeed acted, in the Darwinian sense, to form their brains? One speculation is that these have been the pressures of selective mating, rather social—in some different sense of the term—than environmental.

They know one another (and our experimenters who enter their environment, as well) very intimately, as their sonar has by nature achieved what our acoustic medical imaging is only beginning to accomplish—clear echographic views of our inner workings. This means, it is thought, that they know one another's physiological and emotional state as a matter of course: they are notably social, erotic, and very playful creatures. Contemplating such creatures, the paradigm of whose world is, it seems, in some ways one of play, where ours is competition and war, it is hard not to fall into romantic conjecture. A literature and a following of that sort have developed among some of our own kind with respect to the cetaceans, and it doubtless requires moderation, but all we can rightly say at this point is, "Who knows?" We have not begun to crack the problem of minds unlike our own. Unless some military use (other than wiring dolphins to blow up ships) shows up for this, it will certainly remain low on the agenda of our "scientific" researches, while so long as economic advantage demands the direct or incidental destruction of cetaceans (or their environments), grim experience teaches that destroyed they will be.

The root meaning of idiocy is to be utterly private in one's interests and awareness. Closure to the possibility of minds and mental realms of altogether other sorts would be systematic idiocy on a species level. One might suppose that there would be no scientifically interesting way to break through a barrier so extreme as the radical separation of alternative language-concepts, but that is not the case. Instrumentation of a kind we now command could intervene, to transduce one physical realm into another in ways which would map in effect from cortex to cortex—to map the acoustic cortex of the cetacean onto the visual cortex of man. As we have seen, the visual cortex is our strong suit; the metaphors which link our knowing to our "seeing" are built very deeply into the roots of our language, and only now we are beginning to advance, as has been mentioned, from primitive "graphing" to more sophisticated and powerful methods of multidimensional visualization of scientific data and relationships. What we do visually, they do, but perhaps more powerfully, in the realm that we call hearing. If we could look at what they are hearing, or see what they are saying, perhaps some significant mental mediation would begin to occur. Recent research has been pressing in that direction. It is perhaps the area of some of the most significant and interesting scientific research that could be imagined today—in ways that have nothing whatever to do with economic interest for any except the longest possible range.

VII. Unconscious process: Instinct and Archetype

We have asserted in an earlier segment of this essay that Freud introduced in effect the quantum theory of the mind: that is, his theory of the Unconscious shook the sciences of the mind in much the way quantum mechanics was transforming physics. Freud holds a curious place among the "scientists of the mind"—at once among the most impressive of pioneers, surely charting the course for a science; yet working with such furious commitment to speculative thought that it is not clear to what extent his work meets the tests of conventional science at all. This curious, prophetic, hermeneutic nature of his work seems to set the stage for a new, more dialectical understanding of the idea of science.

As a reader of Freud quickly senses, he is working at the dialectical edge of a conceptual revolution. Are we sure we know when we are in the presence of "science"? It is hardly necessary to claim that Freud developed a theory which was wholly coherent and regularly supported by empirical data. Challenging our understanding of our own being, he undertook after all a task of an order of magnitude beyond even that of quantum mechanics. The very terms of "investigation" are in flux throughout his work. In another sense, the possibility arises now that the project he always must have intended—namely, that a science of the mind and an art of healing be founded on the ground of neurophysiology—is beginning to seem attainable. Will things at that point become more "scientific"?

The point which is important for present purposes is that, however much he left to be completed or revised by others, Freud placed the disturbing question of the Unconscious squarely before us. We may not yet know how to account for its operations theoretically, or to manage it therapeutically, but an account of the Unconscious must now be central to any contemporary theory of the mind. Again, it does not matter to us if Freud was not the first to treat of the Unconscious: it took Freud to comprehend and articulate its significance.

Perhaps Freud's role here tells us something we need to reconsider about the nature of science and its advances: the most important moves concern the foundations, and one who can so alter a science has accomplished a Copernican transformation. Perhaps persuading the world to abandon the undisputed role of reason in the mind's affairs was not so unlike that earlier persuasion to accept the possibility that the Earth moves about the Sun. Now, it is the ego which must move. There is a telling parallel, here too, to the case of quantum mechanics: each of these strange new sciences—quantum mechanics and Freud's theory of the Unconscious—directs attention to a realm which is of central importance, yet which is radically inconceivable. The transactions of quantum mechanics occur among theoretical entities which we speak of as "particles," but which we know are of such a sort that we could never in principle touch or perceive them: quantum physics is real enough, but it lies on the far side of a horizon radically impassable to us. So it is with the Unconscious. We may see evidences enough, now, of its work; we may interact with it through symbol, allusion, and image; but it must emerge into consciousness only obliquely, by way of mystery, dream, or disguise. This century has told us that in some sense we must learn to do our science with things we cannot think about.

Presumably for all plants and most animals, the question of consciousness does not arise: whatever their life entails, it is unconscious. Somewhere in the recent stretches of evolution, on the other hand, consciousness has arisen; it is hard to look into the eyes of a curious chimpanzee, or one's companion dog, and doubt that there is consciousness present. Broadly, then, we must understand that our consciousness is the most recent part of us, shared to some degree with those creatures we call "higher," that it is in some way an overlay upon an unconscious realm which bears a genetic inheritance from a deeper past and is central to our lives in the way Freud has revealed. How, then, does this older part enter the experience of our daily lives, and what does it bode for us?

The system we have called "chemical"—hormonal and endocrinal—

belongs on the whole to the old domain. In the most general way at least, we can say that consciousness arises with (I do not say it is merely a function of) the electrical neural system, and that beneath this is that chemical system which is a memory of a deeper past—a time when processes were slower and instinct ruled without complication. Clearly, then, the Unconscious is the domain of the drives and instincts we discussed earlier, and as we saw there, this is alike the domain of fear and aggression on the one hand, and of caring, affection, and love on the other. We would fall into a familiar trap if we were to assert that reason is "apart" from these matters. As we have been asserting, reason is never unmoved; always, we reason to an end. Now we must add that the end appears by way of instinct or drive from that Unconscious realm which is its source. We are concluding that reason and our conscious lives would be impossible without unreasoning instinct as its chthonic base.

Are we to grant that our advanced, conscious, and rational realm is built upon and dependent on, even in some most fundamental way *takes its direction from,* the irrational, the Unconscious? We may consider briefly two modes of approach to this question, on the parts of Freud and Jung. They agree on the central role of the Unconscious, but their myths of its function bear different portents for our lives.

Freud seems to have understood the Unconscious first in *quantitative* terms—that is, as that source of undifferentiated energy he called the *id,* essentially the "it" or the nameless, unnameable. Without attempting here even to characterize the various stages of Freud's theories, we can see in the most general terms that the work of the conscious "I" (the *ego*) is to repress the unruly and utterly unacceptable *id* in its shapeless guise, but to give intelligent direction to its forces so as to conform to the demands of reality and to serve conscious aims. These forces are in this way "sublimated," a term which ought to mean that they are elevated to the highest levels. But in their own, unlawful form they are powerful and recur; they find their ways unbidden into our lives, whether in sleep, where they shape the dream work, or in waking, when they lead us to reveal ourselves in rash or errant acts whose significance we do not see. To preserve order in our civilized lives we must forcibly repress the worst incursions of the Unconscious, and this repression itself becomes unconscious to us and may become a pathology—even, Freud comes to think, for civilization as a whole. [46]

For Freud, and quite plausibly for us in this study as well, Sophocles' Oedipus serves as a dark model. Not only in dreams, but in waking life as well, the Unconscious has ways of inserting itself and transforming our purposes to its destructive ends. Rationally Oedipus, as he himself is well aware, is the best of kings; but it is he himself who nonetheless commits the very crimes the Unconscious wished upon him—to take his father as rival and to kill him, and to take his mother as love-object, and to marry her. [47] The rashness by which these unconscious drives thrust aside his reasoned and cautious defenses seems the hallmark of Oedipus himself: he does not and cannot disown that which ultimately manifests itself as his own doing.

Because the Unconscious is at the root of intractable problems of our mental lives, Freud saw the task of the therapist as analytic: psychoanalysis becomes the art of interpreting those conscious events and symbols in which the Unconscious is finding expression so as to reveal the operations of the Unconscious to consciousness, and thereby, if possible, to find rational means to alleviate the problems to which the opacity of our normal unseeing relation to the Unconscious gives rise. Sophocles is in a sense doing the same thing, and we must observe that the theater at its best must have achieved for the Athenians what Freud may never have accomplished among moderns: to reveal the magnificent horror and attraction of the Unconscious—to own it, and to pass beyond. Freud in a sense pits reason against an unruly, purely quantitative energy which, unleashed, will destroy all civilized order; there are no grounds for a working relation between the two. In the case of the Athenian theater, however, we must in every case couple the opening tragedy with its mystic answer. It is not reason, in an ordinary sense of the term, to whose mystic place Oedipus moves inexorably in *Oedipus at Colonus;* rather, a transcendent event is in some way the means by which the gods are to carry him away.

The theater, founded in mystery, has resources—themselves emergent from the Unconscious—which Freud could not command. Aeschylus, in the *Oresteia* trilogy, takes Athens therapeutically by the hand and first reveals the utter horror of the Unconscious which appears in the guise of their deepest past, and then in the third play (the "third cup to Zeus, savior" as we have pointed out before) effects a reconciliation which is the foundation of Athens as the rule of law and reason. [48] Playwrights do not step forward as scientists, yet it would not be an idle remark to suggest that Athens was actually closer to a valid science of psychoanalysis than Freud. That is because Athens was closer to a working relationship with mystery and the Unconscious. The antistrophic dance, an art of interpretation through the rhythms of *logos,* harmony, melody, and bodily motion, provides reason a vehicle which invites mediation, through the Preconscious, with the forces of the Unconscious. The oracular tradition makes dream- and sign-interpretation a social institution. It is this very sense of the operative presence of mystery which I have suggested is the key to an understanding of the *Theaetetus* as well.

"Science" is admittedly on uncomfortable ground in the modern world when its subject is mystery and its aim is therapy. Thus when Freud so rightly placed the Unconscious at the center of scientific attention, he was setting a task with which science could not cope without inner transformation. I am suggesting that science is ready now for this task as it was not in Freud's own time: science having now become overtly dialectical, led by its success, for example, in the easier but transforming case of quantum mechanics, is no longer locked to reductive notions of reason and is able to address a reality as obscure and yet as present for us as the Unconscious. It is possible to begin to reread Aeschylus and Sophocles as counselors of our scientific problem, though it is hardly possible to re-create the therapeutic resources of a vacated tradition. We can very well think about Greek tragedy; but we can only suspect its sustaining effect. Freud's best hope for us is to present the matter, analytically, for the consideration of conscious reason; best to know our problem, and to devise what we can as intelligent beings to hold our civilized world together. But Freud leaves reasoning mankind with a grim prospect, not unlike the one we find depicted in the daily press.

We have spoken earlier of the relation between our human genetic inheritance and the human cultural inheritance which so curiously intertwines with it. Freud goes further in his study of the Unconscious to throw what seems a most promising light on this relationship. In one fundamental aspect, the cultural inheritance runs by his account as much by a subterranean channel as does the genetic. Through the mechanism of the "Oedipus complex," as he describes it, the authority of the father is taken into the psyche of the child not simply as teaching in the ordinary sense but as what we might call the "strong form" of teaching, namely, introjection. What had been the simple figure of the father becomes now an unconscious portion of the ego, the ego-ideal or "superego," an authority-within, which dictates throughout life in modes that express themselves as intimidation and guilt (GBWW I: 54, 703–8; II: 54, 703–8). As this recurs, passing from generation to generation, it becomes a moral or religious tradition in the modality of the Judeo-Christian God, who speaks with the voice of command: "Thou shalt" and "Thou shalt not." [49] Ultimately, Freud concludes, we may almost speak of a superego of the society itself. It is a most persuasive hypothesis, suggesting in effect a second text paralleling the genetic, with its own evolutionary history and selective pressures, and moving through similarly unconscious channels with a comparably formidable inertia. It is utilized and inexorably if innocently perpetuated by those who rule societies, to dominate those who do not. [50]

Perhaps Jung took a fuller measure of our relation to the genetic Unconscious by considering it more fully in what we might call "its own terms"—namely, those of myth and image. Freud's spirit is immense: he writes impressively of Leonardo; he fully recognizes the power of the Oedipus myth and invokes it as central to his own work. Freud is often himself mythmaker: the "Oedipus complex" is not merely an analytic device but an oracular key to powerful forces he finds everywhere at work. Yet Jung makes a very different sort of claim concerning the Unconscious, and I think we may find his approach closer at once to the genetic science and the endocrinal theory we have seen taking shape, and to the Athenian therapy as well.

Jung's claim is, essentially, that the Unconscious is not without shape or structure, merely unruly; that it is strongly configured in forms he calls "Archetypes." We recall that the chemical system contrasted with the neural as being richly qualitative. The molecules begin to look like characters. Since an Archetype is a figure within the Unconscious, we should not expect to find it literally described or depicted. Yet it is not unshaped, or without meaning for us: in myth and image we do give conscious shape to these entities which are always operative within us.

An Archetype is not just an idea but a power, yet power shaped in a form reflecting some elemental aspect of the cosmos or our relation to it. It is the mythic face of instinct. Since it is inscribed in the genetic code, we might call it as well the mythic aspect of the Book of Life, and we see that it must on the whole be common throughout mankind. It is a persuasive insight of Jung's that if the Unconscious is such a figured text written in the genetic material as an inheritance from evolution, then we hold it as a text in common: we must be prepared to speak of a "Collective Unconscious" and expect to find the Archetypes shaping the world's mythologies and art forms in recognizably common themes. We should not even be surprised to find themes reaching beyond the human: the power of the archetypical Serpent is evidenced in a revulsive reaction most of us feel, and which we share with primates.

Jung suggests a principle of homeopathy: terrible and dangerous as unleashed Archetypes may be, we do well to come to know them and to draw upon their power. [51] Christianity does that through the magic and symbol of the Mass. Loss of contact with this inner principle which works within us without our recognition—the split of consciousness from the Unconscious at a crucial phase of evolution—is figured, Jung argues plausibly, in the Fall. We should note the pervasive influence of the motions of the heavens inscribed over the collective experience of evolutionary time in the DNA. The Christian mystery draws upon our deep sense of the death of the year at Christmas, and its resurrection with the spring equinox: but equally, the Platonic metaphysics works constantly with the two apparent motions of the Sun, the daily and the annual, figured as the Same and the Other, and constituting in their interworking the contained flux of the Becoming of our mortal lives.

These metaphors and symbols reference deep sources: the whole experience of the human race operating on our minds and bodies as the subterranean dynamic of our lives. In all this, we now know we are speaking of a molecule: the DNA. That would once have seemed a reductive remark. Now that we have learned to respect a "molecule" as a dynamic, topological text of a kind still almost entirely beyond our power to read, we can only wonder at what may be written on the bottom line of the syllogism which at this moment lies spelled out before us.

Does it make sense that our rational lives are prompted and shaped by such forces, primal and out of a preconscious past? If all affect is from the Unconscious, can we make sense of being passionately moved to ends which spring from that ancient Book of Life? Can we responsibly relate the discussion we have just had to the questions of the *Theaetetus?* I think we might at least attempt a case, borrowing on Jung's terms, for asserting such a connection.

We tend to think of our evolutionary past as bestial, something we are to rise out of—and that of course is in one sense simply true. We are still only at the threshold of the question of what it may one day mean to be fully human. But in another sense there may be wisdom in reflection on those origins. Think in terms of the great origin myths. Timaeus, we know, *derives* the complexity of the present time from an earlier process which began with the One, which was most perfect and good. The accounts of the derivation of the fundamental particles take us back in thought to an unthinkable first time, in which all was together and the particles not yet formed.

Life on this Earth has been formed in a way which derives from the vivifying powers of the Sun and the seas. Is there not wisdom, perhaps, in remembering those principles that are inscribed in our Book of Life? It is almost necessary to revert to terms such as those of Timaeus or the pre-Socratics to speak of things which were once so immediately fundamental to our life on Earth, *and are now still so,* though we have difficulty in recognizing what is fundamental in the midst of distractions. What is the source of desire, of the motion we call that of the psyche, of love? We have seen how it arises in our own limbic system, and we know in turn that all desire for combination arises in ways mirrored by those equations of quantum mechanics which incorporated such a sense of symmetry. The power of what is so inadequately called the "chemical bond," but which we have seen is much more like the syntactic bond which makes *logos,* is, we must admit, the source of all our desiring. Yet its power is just that of number and symmetry. The unity which the completed bond accomplishes derives, as Timaeus said it must, from that One of which Parmenides spoke, and which Aristotle saw as pure act, most figured by the unvarying rotation of the sphere. If our origins *were* such, if at root we *are now* such, then need we longer despair of the "primitive" as unworthy? To see and feel our ways better into these depths of our Being would be wisdom, and elevating beyond most affairs of our daily lives.

The Archetypes are dangerous, and by no means simply benign; they are not at all a set of philosophers. I did not mean to suggest a comic reading of Jung. But if we follow Jung's line of thought, then we must not only see his Archetypes as elemental figurations of the genetic record and what we are calling the "Book of Life," which may be a text as dark as that of Homer; we must see them further in one aspect as the immediate vessels of the Platonic "recollection," a metaphor for the act of knowing. Very simply, as we have seen, unity and Being cannot come *post factum*. Either Being is primary, or there is nothing. We cannot, any more than Theaetetus, make unity out of diversity; unity, if there is any, must preexist. But to say that unity preexists is exactly the case of the quantum-mechanical derivation of the particles which make up our own present being, and it is from such unity that, over the course of evolution, first life and then the diversity of living forms arises. Wisdom for humans consists in finding one's way back to that source of Being which is matter and form, or potentiality and act, together. And that, as we have seen in other contexts, is just the outcome of the *Theaetetus*.

Thus, we may conclude: the genetic view of the human psyche leads to a sense of the DNA text which strongly suggests the likelihood of Jung's account, while in turn Jung is on the right track when he suggests the ultimate identity of his Archetypes with the Platonic forms. [52] They include the extremes that we met in the *Timaeus*: both the One, with the forms which derive from it, and Necessity, which is its unyielding antithesis. The DNA must be the original tragic epic; it is a jumbled affair which it would take Jorge Luis Borges to describe adequately, but it can be read with infinite precision, for we, through our lifetimes, are its readings.

These are, admittedly, no more than suggestions. But they are highly compatible with the idea of a science which on the one hand derives its material world in quantum mechanics from the intellectual concepts of symmetry and form, while on the other it has found that the human mind at work is reading a genetic text inherited from an evolutionary past. I say this is the science at which we have arrived in our time. The idea of this science admits, as we see, consideration of the mystic as object in the form of the Archetypes of the collective Unconscious, and it is not outside its scope to consider that the Book of Life may afford an approach to Theaetetus's most philosophical question. Written there, we find those principles which would make knowledge possible. They are indeed principles of "knowledge," for in the midst of many other factors of every sort, there are those which stem from and refer to that One which is both the source of our comprehension of Being and, at the same time, in some way the source and ultimate object of all love. Can our science speak of such matters? It seems to have arrived at this point, at the gate, we might say, of the temple, and there is in principle no obstacle but refutation itself to stand in the way of a dialectical science as it pursues its ardent course.

VIII. Conclusion: The Republic among us

One single proposition might serve to place before us this emerging picture of the sciences. It appears to me that the claim which has been building throughout the stages of this essay, the principle that science in our time has emerged as "dialectical," comes to this: *The community of scientists today constitutes the counterpart of Plato's* Republic, *founded anew in our time*. That is a very strong claim indeed, certainly most questionable, yet just possibly true. Let us see what it would mean.

The Republic is a polity built in thought in the course of Plato's dialogue of that name (*GBWW* I: 7, 295–441; II: 6, 295–441). It reads two ways: on the one hand, it is a political community which serves as question mark for any existing polity of which we may be members; on the other, it is a metaphor for the human psyche—a mirror to ourselves. I adduce it here because it is the thought of a polity or a citizen whose life is founded on reason as its first principle, which is by no means to claim that it is not the home of passion or imagination. This is just what I have claimed of the sciences, for Plato means by "reason" the dialectical process which holds all principles to examination by the light of whatever we understand to be our highest human insight.

Socrates holds out to the group who have built this image in conversation no hope that it is ever to be seen on Earth: that will happen, he says, only when philosophers become kings. As so often, there is an irony here, for we see well enough that under the astute guidance of Socrates the group itself has constituted the Republic throughout the long night of the dialogue. But it would be astonishing, perhaps simply rash, to claim that the scientists of today have done what Socrates despaired of. Are our scientists, then, such philosophers as to become kings over a realm of working reason in the midst of this troubled world? I propose that in what is now the vast domain of their laboratories, their classrooms, their seminars, their congregations in annual meetings and colloquia, and in the abundant flow of journals they publish—but no less in their appearances before legislative committees and in their assignments on panels of public policy—in short, in all the reaches of their scientific work in its broadest sense in our time, they function ultimately in the service of reason, and I claim finally, reason in its highest sense.

Such a claim must be followed by a quick disclaimer: if the scientists are citizens of a virtual "Republic" in the world's midst, this does not mean that the millennium has arrived. I do not mean to paint a simple picture or to suggest that it is in any simple way a happy prospect. Even as a city built in conversation, the Republic was by no means seen as an image of perfection but rather was pictured as a very human enterprise. It incorporated human failing and tragedy in its bosom. As we have suggested earlier, tragedy is for Plato—as it may be for us—

an inescapable vessel of serious thought. Homer, who had said that the gods told lies and did foul deeds, and that fate rather than the Good ruled events, was banished from the hearing of the children of the Republic; readers rail at Plato's censorship but regularly fail to note that Homer with his tragic message is reinstated for the hearing of those who are prepared to hear him: those for whom the discourse has become mature and dialectical. The Republic was delineated as a city of justice, community, and the health of body and soul; but as the conversation continues and the night grows late, it is acknowledged that there must be a tragic encounter—the city will erode under the influence of a mystic, intractable "number," the signature of necessity, inaccessible to the comprehension of the best of the city's guardians. Births will go wrong, spirits will fail, and the happiness of the city will fall victim to a declining succession: love of honor replacing the love of the good, love of money replacing love of honor, then a chaos of inchoate aims and characters, and finally, descent into the ultimate corruptions of tyranny. It is thus not necessary that the community of our scientists be unfaulted, in order that it qualify as image of the Republic: the essence is not in perfection but principle. So long as it remains that community conceived, we might say, in reason—so long as the intent is not lost— then failure may be wept over, but it can be endured.

To speculate, then, that the scientists of our time have quietly taken over as citizens of a coherent body more interesting than their separate nations is not without ominous implications. Yet it is a serious and important claim, very different from the one almost universally made. For most persons, asked about the sciences at their best, would claim that their integrity consists precisely in their remaining (1) strictly "objective" and removed from politics, which is thought to be as a virus threatening to the very idea of science, and (2) separated from questions of "value," which cannot be addressed by scientific means.

As we have seen, most people—quite possibly, most scientists—think of the white laboratory coat as a kind of symbol of neutrality, a white flag on the battlefields of society: insulation against questions of value, and formal indifference to issues of politics. It is because these "controversial" issues have been ruled out of the discussion, people think, that scientists in their professional capacity belong to a privileged community and are able to maintain rational discourse across lines which would otherwise divide them into warring camps.

We have already given our answer to this. If science is dialectical, these supposedly defining expectations are altogether wrong. Science has by its nature no privilege of separation, no license to ignore politics or set aside questions of the good. Assumptions to this effect are, it is true, great social conveniences. Scientists are enabled to travel, meet, and converse in ways in which others might not—they have almost literally passports to *gather,* and their credentials are honored throughout the world. But if science is dialectical, these claims to immunity are ultimately not well-founded. Quite possibly, that is a secret which we should be careful not to reveal!

If science is thus only *contingently* "objective"—that is, in the context of temporarily unquestioned sets of assumptions—it is also not removed from questions of "value." If our New Pythagoreans follow the lead of their elders in the first and most fundamental things, we will remember that Timaeus asks agreement at the outset with the principle that all will be founded upon what is unchanging, single, and *good*. It would be a strange claim, perhaps, deeply uncomfortable to most practicing scientists and engineers, to insist that their enterprise is suffused with a sense of value and the good. It is supposed, almost universally, that questions of "value" are not to be decided by recourse to "reason" but by other means, private and mysterious or in a deep sense arbitrary; to mix them into rational discussion, it is thought, is to sow confusion, to throw the project off its tracks. Yet if science is indeed genuinely dialectical, that concern is misplaced. Dialectic goes to the deepest questions, probes the ultimate foundations of whatever it governs, and hence is always at least implicitly asking, "Why are we doing this?" And it must mean by its question "why?" not what the world normally assumes to be "rational." The world takes "reason" in a merely instrumental or crafty sense, begging all questions of real purpose, and asking no more than a kind of businessman's or technician's "why?" in the sense of the most efficient means to an assumed end. Dialectic by contrast asks "why?" always in the ultimate sense: to what end are we laboring? What makes it all meaningful, and worth our while? Dialectic is the final solvent, aqua regia to all lesser questions: *really,* it asks, why are we doing this?

A reader who has accepted our distinctions earlier may be ready to agree that there are two very different senses of the word *reason* in use today. One is reason as *logic,* which in principle at least can be spelled out in any desired degree to guarantee consequences once premises have been assigned. That is the most pervasive image of reason, and with it goes the sense that reason is "dispassionate," removed from questions of belief or desire, and inexorably rigid. This sort of talk gives reason its bad name, and devotees of the sciences their reputation for insensitivity.

To claim on the other hand, as this long, many-parted essay does, that science in our time has revealed itself as *dialectical* is to speak of reason in a second, very different way. In its worldwide practice among us today, science is not merely instrumental, mere servant to other concerns, but *final:* it is autonomous, suffused with a sense of purpose which cuts straight through to an illuminating, governing sense of the good. Science in its practice is a working community in which all those who choose to share in it can truly delight. It is a worldwide

Pythagoras (ca. 580 B.C.–ca. 500 B.C.), represented on a medallion from about A.D. 400. His crown suggests the demidivine nature that was attributed to him.

collaboration which derives its dedication and spontaneous friendship from—one almost blushes to put into words in our time anything so simple and seemingly innocent—a common and universal love of truth. One has only to share for a while in a meeting of scientists pursuing their passion together, to see it on their faces, hear it in their words: they deeply want to know what is truly the case with the cosmos. This is what ultimately energizes their labors, their endless hours which become years in their laboratories, their unremitting answerability to one another in the disciplined reports which fill a literature in the global lingua franca of science itself.

Of course, scientists bear all the scars of humanity: they are moved by money, power, fame, and ill will like the rest of us. Current scandals in the ethics of science make this popular knowledge. The very fact that science now knows no convenient boundaries means that it is infected by the ills of the querulous society which misuses and tempts it in a thousand ways, many of which we have traced in the earlier parts of this essay. But that is not my point. The Republic as we have said is, being human, almost inherently corrupted. It fails, we might almost say, by virtue of its own insights. So it is not the perfection of its practice, a hopeless test, but the guiding concept of the enterprise in principle, which is our question. If our claim is one of principle, we must be careful to put it in appropriate terms: as we look at science in our time, we find it governed, however fallibly, by love of truth. Is truth, then, for the scientist, a ruling good? Certainly, for what we in fact love, we love as good. That is what we mean by the term *good*. Are scientists, then, dogmatists? No, certainly not, since what is an object of mind is not a dogma, but a perpetually open question.

It will be a long while before we discover what the New Pythagoreans have in store for us, but we can see that they have made their appearance on the stage of human affairs. Before we startle too abruptly at the thought of unleashing in our midst these battalions in white coats, let us make one more remark, again based on the one perception that science has revealed itself as dialectical: the New Pythagoreans are ourselves. For if science, now recognized for the scope that belongs to it by right of its nature, steps forth as *dialectical* reason itself, then we as reasoners are the scientists of whom we speak. Rest easier: it will be a long while before society discovers that this obligation has devolved upon us. As we remarked earlier, we proceed under some old dispensation, tied to crude notions of science and far cruder notions of human nature and politics, by which it was supposed that education in the sciences was something optional, while literacy in other matters, if not achieved, was at least granted as a matter for concern. Someday it will be seen how wrong this was, and our primitive era will be branded by future historians for its idiocy. Perspective is hard to achieve; it is hard for us to see these things, though any thinking person must have serious qualms. It is hard for us not to think of ourselves as "modern," and engaged in some business of "progress." But it is not so. We live still in darkness, in the grip of a past we are only beginning to shake off: modernity and progress worthy of the names lie far in a future we can barely discern.

To be in such a position, recognizing the alienation of the era in which we live, hardly seeing the outlines of a future to which the present distress cannot but point, is indeed to live in the throes of dialectic. It is an understandable tendency to imagine that the processes of mind take place in quiet backwaters of society, seminar rooms, or over the tea tables of the elders. With dialectic, it is quite the contrary. Ideas are born at the transition points where anguish and anxiety are parents to perceptions which had not been in the world before. Such is the domain of science at its hottest. We do not always note the evidences of these rises in our intellectual temperature.

Perhaps it is some inherent perversity of dialectic which has insured that this truly wondrous result, the inauguration of the Republic of reason among us, be achieved in close conjunction with two of the most archaic of modern society's sins: the practice of warfare, and the systematic domination of the majority of the peoples of the world by a wealthy and hypocritical minority. Science and technology have been instruments of these two linked agencies, and it must be admitted that the sciences would not have flourished, or even perhaps come into existence at all in their modern form—the Republic would not have been forged—had it not been for their incubation in the service of systematic violence and exploitation. My account of this dismal alliance has been given in the first two parts of this series. Nonetheless, if we have at the same time seen what the Republic of the sciences is in principle, and how it has come into being among us, and also see now how it is contradicted, torn, and misled by the lesser societies in which it is housed, the anguish of that rending may be the very vessel of serious second thoughts about the whole. I have said that, no matter who is labeled "scientist" in our society, it is really we who are citizens of the Republic of reason which is the truth behind the idea of science in our time. Its alienation is our own, we bear the distress of the subversion of the sciences in the interests of power and autocracy, and we must make affirmation of the possibilities of the sciences as forum for the world.

---

1. "The New Pythagoreans III: The Scientists of the Mind (Part One)," *GIT* 1990, 174–221.

2. The artificial intelligence debate in the limited form it has tended to take thus far is summarized in a recent pair of articles: John R. Searle, "Is the Brain's Mind a Computer Program?" and Paul M. and Patricia Smith Churchland, "Could a Machine Think?" *Scientific American*, vol. 262, no. 1 (January 1990), pp. 26–31 and 32–37, respectively.

3. René Descartes describes "the object of the geometricians, which I conceived to be a continuous body . . . divisible into various parts, and which might have various figures and sizes, and might be moved or transposed in all sorts of ways . . ." in Part IV of the *Discourse on Method* (*GBWW* I: 31, 52–53; II: 28, 276–77). In Part V, this becomes in effect the "matter" than which, it seems to Descartes, "nothing in the world could be more clear or intelligible" (*GBWW* I: 31, 55; II: 28, 279). But this "object of the geometricians" is just the continuously divisible *magnitude* which is the elusive subject of Book V of Euclid's *Elements,* and which is on its way to becoming the system of the real numbers (*GBWW* I: 11, 81; II: 10, 81). Electricity has properties suggesting such a colorless magnitude, and it is very tempting to describe the operations of the brain as the motions of such an intelligible substance as indeed Descartes himself does, as the *Discourse* proceeds.

4. Alan Turing, "Computing Machinery and Intelligence," *Mind,* October 1950, pp. 40ff., reprinted in part in *The Mind's I,* ed. Douglas R. Hofstadter and Daniel C. Dennett (New York: Bantam Books, 1981), pp. 53ff. Turing's concept and the role of the algorithm are very well discussed in the opening chapters of Roger Penrose, *The Emperor's New Mind* (New York and Oxford: Oxford University Press, 1989).

5. J. W. S. Pringle, "The Mechanism of Knowledge: Limits to Prediction," in John C. Eccles, ed., *Mind and Brain* (Washington: Paragon House, 1982), p. 244; Roger Sperry, "Consciousness, Personal Identity, and the Divided Brain," in Franco Leporé et al., ed., *Two Hemispheres—One Brain* (New York: Alan Liss, Inc., 1986), pp. 16–17. The concept of synchronicity and timing in brain events will come up for further discussion, with additional references, later in this essay.

6. *GIT* 1990, 190. An especially impressive contribution to the contemporary study of the question of "wholeness" is David Bohm, *Wholeness and the Implicate Order* (London: Ark Paperbacks, 1980).

7. Lucretius reflects that his purpose is to present his theory in "sweet-toned Pierian verse and o'erlay it as it were with the pleasant honey of the Muses" as physicians disguise with honey wormwood to be administered to children (*GBWW* I: 12, 44; II: 11, 43).

8. These molecules and their spatial structures were depicted in figures 2–6 and 9 of "The New Pythagoreans II: The Scientists of Life and the World Food Problem" (*GIT* 1989, 203–8, 213.)

9. An impressive overall reference on the chemical approach to the brain and the mind is Richard Bergland, *The Fabric of the Mind* (Victoria, Australia: Viking Books, 1985). Bergland opens with the statement: "There is now little doubt that the brain is a gland . . ." and concludes (p. 139):

> In the past decade, as regulating hormones have been found throughout the body, the soul has lost its home. It is scattered everywhere—in the brain, the gut, the ovary, the pituitary and the adrenal; if paracrinologists are correct, every cell contains the well-chiseled molecules that give life to the soul and guidance to the mind.

10. Without attempting to comment on the conflict of forces or their possible resolution in the course of Goethe's *Faust,* we must recognize from the beginning the working of the principle of the whole, which grips Faust powerfully if briefly as he contemplates the

Sign of the Macrocosm: "Lo, single things inwoven, made to blend, / To work in oneness with the whole, and live . . ." (*GBWW* I: 47, 13; II: 45, 2). As a scientific principle, this was exemplified by Goethe in his theory of color (see *Encyclopædia Britannica*, s.v. "Goethe").

As for Descartes, we have remarked earlier that analysis carries through in the *Discourse on Method* to the elimination of all quality, such as color, and explanation instead in terms of homogeneous, endless divisible and divided magnitude or "extension" (compare note 3, above).

11. Solomon H. Snyder, *Drugs and the Brain* (New York: W. H. Freeman, 1986), pp. 130–33. This is a particularly fine book on all aspects of the mind as a "chemical system." *See also* John Z. Young, *Programs of the Brain* (New York: Oxford University Press, 1978), pp. 156–61; Jeffrey A. Gray, *The Psychology of Fear and Stress* (New York: McGraw-Hill, 1971). On the phenomena of aggression, *see* Konrad Lorenz, *On Aggression* (New York: Harcourt, Brace and World, 1966), pp. 3–56.

12. Snyder, op. cit. *See* chapter 2 on "Opiates" and chapter 5 on "Stimulants." In chapter 2, note the figure on page 58 illustrating the role of natural pain suppressors ("enkephalins") in modulating synaptic function by blocking transmission of pain signals. In chapter 5, note that "norepinephrine" is the formal name of the substance more commonly known as "adrenaline." The figure on page 147 of Snyder's text illustrates the synaptic action of a stimulant, amphetamine.

13. For Aristotle, the question of the priority of the whole becomes that of the priority of form, which is inherently a unity, over matter: ". . . since 'nature' means two things, the matter and the form, of which the latter is the end, and since all the rest is for the sake of the end, the form must be the cause in the sense of 'that for the sake of which'" (*GBWW* I: 8, 276; II: 7, 276). In the *Metaphysics*, this line of reasoning takes us to the god: "There is, then, something which is always moved with an unceasing motion, which is motion in a circle. . . . There is therefore also something which moves it. And since that which moves and is moved is intermediate, there is something which moves without being moved, being eternal, substance, and actuality" (*GBWW* I: 8, 602; II: 7, 602).

From Georg Hegel, it is enough here to cite one governing dictum from the preface to the *Phenomenology of Spirit*: "The true is the whole." Walter Kaufmann, ed., *Hegel: Texts and Commentary* (Garden City, N.Y.: Anchor Books, 1966), p. 32. The complications of the dictum generate Hegel's rich and intricate system.

14. *GIT* 1990, 195.

15. Jean-Pierre Changeux, *Neuronal Man* (New York: Pantheon Books, 1985), p. 108; Young, op. cit., p. 136.

16. Ibid.

17. "The Syzygy: Anima and Animus," in Joseph Campbell, ed., *The Portable Jung* (New York: Viking Press, 1971), pp. 148–162; Emma Jung, *Animus and Anima* (Dallas: Spring Publications, 1957).

18. Snyder points out that from the locus coeruleus in the limbic system, the action of some three thousand nerve cells may reach out to influence several billion, touching as much as one-third to one-half of the cells in the brain (Snyder, op. cit., p. 142). The likeness of time-coherent neural processes to laser action is beginning to appear widely in the literature: J. Röschke and Erol Başar, "The EEG is Not a Simple Noise: Strange Attractors in Intracranial Structures," in Erol Başar, ed., *Chaos in Brain Function* (Berlin: Springer-Verlag, 1990), pp. 49, 61.

19. Karl H. Pribram, "The Neurophysiology of Remembering," in *Progress in Psychobiology* (San Francisco: W. H. Freeman, 1976), pp. 309–20.

20. In the *Physics* (*GBWW* I: 8, 271; II: 7, 271), Aristotle lists four "causes" of physical motions: (1) that out of which [the matter], (2) the form, (3) the primary source [the motive cause], and (4) "in the sense of end (*telos*) or 'that for the sake of which' a thing is done." Our earlier quotation of Aristotle on the question of the primacy of the whole (note 13) can now be extended, for that whole which is first in the cosmos is also the object of desire: "The final cause, then, produces motion as being loved . . ." and "On such a principle, then, depend the heavens and the world of nature" (*GBWW* I: 8, 602; II: 7, 602).

21. This reversal of concept of "cause" has been discussed in earlier parts of the present series, both with respect to quantum mechanics and more generally in terms of a causal priority of a whole system over its parts (*GIT* 1988, 172ff. and 200; *GIT* 1989, 209 and note 41). Isaac Newton above all, his mind heavily charged with theology, has left

with us the concepts of "law" and "force" as the rhetorical forms of scientific knowledge. But the concepts of "principle" and of a system's steering toward an optimal final state are equally valid, and often more convenient and revealing. *See* Cornelius Lanczos, *The Variational Principles of Mechanics* (Toronto: University of Toronto Press, 1949).

22. A general reference on chaos theory is James Gleick, *Chaos: Making a New Science* (New York: Viking, 1987). Further interesting reading: Joseph Ford, "What is Chaos, that We Should Be Mindful of It?" in P. C. Davies, ed., *The New Physics* (Cambridge: Cambridge University Press, 1989), pp. 348ff.; Leo P. Kadanoff, "Chaos: A View of Complexity in the Physical Sciences" (*GIT* 1986, 62–92); Robert M. May, "Simple Mathematical Models with Very Complicated Dynamics," *Nature*, June 10, 1976, pp. 459ff.; and Bruce J. West and Ary L. Goldberger, "Physiology in Fractal Dimensions," *American Scientist*, July–August 1987, p. 355.

23. Başar, op. cit.

24. I estimate, taking a nerve pulse for a "bit," that information is passing over this network as you read this at something in excess of one hundred megabytes/second. I take the number of fibers in the corpus callosum to be on the order of fifty million (Richard M. Restak, *The Brain* [Toronto: Bantam Books, 1984], p. 253).

25. Sperry, op. cit., p. 9.

26. "Organization of the Human Brain," *Science*, vol. 245 (Sept. 1, 1989), p. 951. Gazzaniga has written extensively, and very interestingly; *see*, for example, *The Social Brain* (New York: Basic Books, 1985), and with Joseph E. Ledoux, *The Integrated Mind* (New York: Plenum Press, 1978).

27. Sandra Witelson, "Bumps on the Brain: Right-Left Anatomic Asymmetry," in Sidney J. Segalowitz, ed., *Language Functions and Brain Organization* (New York: Academic Press, 1983), p. 120.

28. Manfred Clynes and Nigel Nettheim, "The Living Quality of Music," in Manfred Clynes, ed., *Music, Mind, and Brain* (New York and London: Plenum Press, 1982), pp. 47–82. This volume explores many aspects of the fundamental entrainment of physiological systems in the experience of music.

29. Eccles, op. cit., and Karl R. Popper and John C. Eccles, ed., *The Self and Its Brain* (London: Routledge and Kegan Paul, 1977). Sir John Eccles has been a leading figure in organizing attention to the inclusion of consciousness in psychological theory and practice. An important representative conference volume is P. A. Buser and A. Rougeul-Buser, eds., *Cerebral Correlates of Conscious Experience* (Amsterdam: North Holland, 1978). There are, however, many other approaches; *see*, for example, Geoffrey Underwood, ed., *Aspects of Consciousness; Awareness and Self-awareness*, vol. 3 (London: Academic Press, 1982).

30. Sperry, op. cit., p. 18.

31. Popper and Eccles, op. cit., pp. 282ff.

32. Changeux, op. cit., pp. 126ff.

33. Ibid., p. 136.

34. *GIT* 1989, 215ff.

35. James L. Gould, *Ethology: the Mechanisms and Evolution of Behavior* (New York: W. W. Norton, 1982). There is a rich literature gathered around this theme, including such classics as Niko Tinbergen, *The Animal in Its World* (Cambridge, Mass.: Harvard University Press, 1972); Lorenz, op. cit.; and a recent collection edited by Martin E. Hahn et al., *Developmental Behavior Genetics: Neural, Biometrical, and Evolutionary Approaches* (New York: Oxford University Press, 1990).

36. *GIT* 1990, 203.

37. Kathleen Rita Gibson, "A Developmental Model for the Evolution of Language and Intelligence in Early Hominids," *The Behavioral and Brain Sciences*, no. 2 (1979), pp. 367ff.

38. Gibson, op. cit., p. 371.

39. It has been found at one experiment station that the young chimpanzee, like its human counterpart, may learn best by walking through an interesting area with human companions, listening to their informal conversation, rather than by more disciplined training methods. E. Sue Savage-Rumbaugh, "From Pan to Man: The Language Link," report at the American Association for the Advancement of Science, Washington, D.C., Feb. 16, 1991.

40. Gibson, op. cit., p. 368. *See* Jean Piaget, "The Mental Development of the Child," in *Six Psychological Studies* (New York: Vintage Books, 1967), pp. 3ff.

41. Gibson, op. cit., p. 368, and Table 3, p. 377.

42. Ibid., p. 373.

43. Harry J. Jerison, "The Evolution of Consciousness," in Eccles, op. cit., p. 216.

44. Gulliver's encounter with the Yahoos and the Houyhnhnms (our nobler alternative) is described in Part IV (*GBWW* I: 36, 133–84; II: 34, 133–84).

45. Sterling Bunnell, "The Evolution of Cetacean Intelligence," in Joan McIntyre, ed., *Mind in the Waters* (New York: Scribner, 1974), pp. 52ff. *See* other articles in this collection as well, especially Myron Jacobs, "The Whale Brain: Input and Output," pp. 78ff., and Peter Warshall, "The Ways of Whales," pp. 110. In the latter, note the discussion of vision and communication on pp. 128ff. As an instance of more recent research, *see* Paul H. Forestell and Louis M. Herman, "Delayed Matching of Visual Materials by a Bottlenosed Dolphin Aided by Auditory Symbols," *Animal Learning and Behavior*, vol. 16, no. 2 (1988), pp. 137ff. Here it was found that the dolphins were solving visual problems (in which they were weak) by translating into auditory codes of their own and then inventing visual clues.

46. In the volume of Freud in the *Great Books of the Western World* series, *see* especially *The Ego and the Id* (I: 54, 697–717; II: 54. 697–717), and *Civilization and Its Discontents* (I: 54, 767–802; II: 54, 767–802). It is in the final chapters of the latter that Freud brings the theory of the introjection of the superego to bear on society itself ("It can be maintained that the community, too, develops a super-ego," p. 800), and that this can take pathological forms (". . . we may expect that one day someone will venture upon this research into the pathology of civilized communities," p. 801). One form of such research was undertaken by Wilhelm Reich in studies of dialectical materialism and psychoanalysis, culminating in *The Mass Psychology of Fascism* (New York: Farrar, Straus and Giroux, 1970).

47. We might say that in Oedipus's words Sophocles balances precisely the relation of the ego to the Unconscious, perhaps in the form of the superego. Wondering at the rage which has moved Oedipus to strike out his own eyesight, Creon asks: "what spirit urged you to it?" Oedipus answers: "It was Apollo, friends, Apollo, that brought this bitter bitterness . . . but the hand that struck me was none but my own . . ." (*GBWW* cf. I: 5, 111; II: 4, 130). If Freud is our Teiresias in revealing to us in the twentieth century the role of the Unconscious in our lives, what is to be our response? With this question in mind, it is a moving experience to read the closing words of *Civilization and Its Discontents* (*GBWW* I: 54, 802; II: 54, 802).

48. Aeschylus's *Oresteia* includes the trilogy: *Agamemnon, The Libation Bearers* (*Choephoroe*), and *The Eumenides* (*GBWW* I: 5, 52–91; II: 4, 54–103). My observations in this series on its relation to our theme appear first in *GIT* 1988, 177.

49. Freud's theory of religion is developed in *The Future of an Illusion* (Garden City, N.Y.: Doubleday, 1957).

50. The concept of a parallel route of evolution, through mechanisms of cultural transmission (sometimes with distinctly Lamarckian characteristics!) is fundamental—*see*, for example, John T. Bonner, *The Evolution of Culture in Animals* (Princeton, N.J.: Princeton University Press, 1980), chap. 8. The disconformity of the two channels troubles Tinbergen: ". . . culturally determined changes in our environment (particularly our social environment) have outpaced adjustments in our behaviour . . . the consequence of our still being adapted to the ancestral environment," op. cit., p. 157. In a very different sense, Freud's suggestion that a deep mechanism of cultural transmission was introjection by way of the superego was taken up and related to Karl Marx's theory of false consciousness by members of the "Frankfurt School"; *see* Herbert Marcuse, *Eros and Civilization* (Boston: Beacon Press, 1955). I have discussed in an earlier essay the way in which Marx's thinking in *Capital* leads him to a dark theory of false consciousness and alienation (*GIT* 1987, 107ff.).

51. Jung, "The Structure of the Psyche," op. cit., pp. 23ff., especially p. 44: ". . . for the archetypes are simply the forms which the instincts assume. From the living fountain of instinct flows everything that is creative. . . ."

52. Jung, "Instinct and the Unconscious," op. cit., p. 55: "In Plato . . . an extraordinarily high value is set on the archetypes as metaphysical ideas, as 'paradigms' or models. . . ."

Great Books and Liberal Arts

Otto Bird

Otto Bird was executive editor of *The Great Ideas Today* from 1964 to 1970 and its consulting editor from 1970 until 1988. He makes frequent suggestions as to articles and reprints, reads faithfully and comments upon each year's manuscripts, and since 1981 has contributed pieces of his own to "Reconsiderations of Great Books and Ideas."

His connection with the *Great Books of the Western World* set goes back to 1947, when he began as associate editor of *The Syntopicon,* a position he held for three years. Trained as a philosopher with particular interest in logic and medieval thought, he subsequently became a member of the faculty at the University of Notre Dame, where he founded and directed the general program of liberal studies from 1950 to 1963. He was university professor at Notre Dame from 1970 until his retirement in 1976.

In addition to essays and reviews, Mr. Bird has written *Syllogistic Logic and Its Extensions* (1964), *The Idea of Justice* (1967), and *Cultures in Conflict: An Essay in the Philosophy of the Humanities* (1976). He was also a major contributor to the *Propædia,* or *Outline of Knowledge,* of the fifteenth edition of the *Encyclopædia Britannica.*

Any good book is a work of liberal art. A great book is a work of that art at its highest reach. As a product of art it is something that has been made. But unlike the work produced by speaking, it transcends both the time and place of its occurrence. The full force of a speech needs the living presence of its hearer, the actual presence of both speaker and hearer such as no secondary recording can ever fully reproduce. Writing establishes a different relation. It is not as direct as that between speaker and hearer. Indeed, nothing would be gained if a reader could look over the shoulder of the writer and understand the writing just as it was being written. Such immediacy is not a requirement, and it is a virtue of writing that it is not. It frees the reader from having to be present at the time and place that the writing occurs.

Writing therefore possesses the great advantage of being able to communicate over time and space. No one now can hear and respond to the funeral oration of Pericles to the Athenians as his living audience did nearly twenty-five centuries ago, but we as readers can overhear it, so to say, ever since Thucydides recorded it almost that long ago (*GBWW* I: 6, 395–99; II: 5, 395–99). Reading it in times and places removed from its occurrence, we can not only appreciate how it could have inspired its original audience but also come to understand the strength and virtue of a free and democratic society.

The liberation that writing can achieve belongs to books and so, of course, to great books; hence the latter should be capable of achieving greater liberation. Such liberation is a feature of a liberal art and provides one reason why some arts are properly called liberal. But there are still other reasons why some arts are liberal as liberating.

Writing, and hence its correlate, reading, serve in the main three different purposes, or some combination of them. One aim is to discover and state the truth about things, so explaining them that they may be understood. A treatise of Aristotle, the *Summa Theologica* of Thomas Aquinas, the *Principia* of Newton, or Dobzhansky's work on genetics— all provide instances of this first function. A second purpose is to provide information and directions needed to accomplish a certain task, or to persuade a person to act in a certain way. Of this, examples can be found in Augustine's advice on how to read the Bible in his book *On Christian Doctrine* and in the arguments that *The Federalist* put forward in urging the adoption of the U.S. Constitution. Still another function is to entertain and even to amaze, as do the comedies of Aristophanes and Shakespeare, Dickens' *Little Dorrit,* and Kafka's *The Metamorphosis.*

Frequently, of course, a book combines several of these different functions. Thus a cookbook, for example, serves the principal purpose of providing recipes for the preparation of food; yet the mere reading of it, apart from any actual cooking, can supply knowledge about food. Or again, a work may serve all three functions, as does the *Georgics* of Virgil. It is a "how-to-do" book in the directions that it offers on the various activities of farming, but in doing so it also has much to say about the human life and the situation in which it is carried on, all of which is expressed in Latin verse of such beauty that Dryden, one of the great English poets, claimed it was the best poem ever written.

To carry out these functions so as to achieve their various purposes and bring about learning, certain skills or arts are needed. All of us possess these arts to a certain degree, since they are rooted in and founded on language, and all human beings, short of an extreme disability, possess the ability to learn a language and to use it. These arts, which are the basic arts of learning, have been known traditionally as the liberal arts and have a long history behind them, not only as they are used, but also in the study and theory of them as arts. The main intent in this essay is to recall that history in order to describe, analyze, and further the knowledge and understanding of the arts. Since great books count as the most masterly use and expression of them, part of our work will involve frequent reference to those books and to use of them. But since these same books can also serve as a means of acquiring and perfecting skill in these arts, we will want also to note how this can be accomplished.

Men may have many arts, of course, not all of them liberal. First, then, we should look to see just where among the many arts the liberal arts stand and how they are distinguished. After some consideration of these arts and their tradition, it will then be possible to identify their main division, namely, those that are linguistic and those that are mathematical. Our discussion will be devoted principally to these two sets of arts. The concluding section will turn directly to the relation between the liberal arts and great books.

Art and its kinds

For the understanding of art and its kinds, the basic distinctions are given by Aristotle. The first of these occurs in the sixth book of his *Nicomachean Ethics,* where he is concerned to identify and distinguish the intellectual virtues (*GBWW* I: 9, 387–94; II: 8, 387–94). These are the habits or activities by which the mind is developed to carry out its various functions. The virtue of any habit is relative to the function it performs. Aristotle distinguishes three intellectual habits or activities, each of which performs a different function. These are knowing, doing, and making.

Knowing, as distinct from the other two, is concerned with what is not of either our doing or making. It is knowing for the sake of knowing. The qualities or habits that give this activity its virtue are understanding or insight (*nous*), speculative or philosophical wisdom (*sophia*), and scientific (not empirical) knowledge (*epistēmē*). *Epistēmē*, which is more relevant to our concern than the other two virtues, is defined as an apodictic habit (my translation of *hexis apodeiktike*, 1139b31; cf. *GBWW* I: 9, 388; II: 8, 388), meaning the ability to demonstrate a conclusion from necessary principles.

Doing (*praxis*) and making (*poiesis*) differ from speculative or theoretical knowing in that they both aim at something more than the knowing itself that is involved: making at the thing to be made, doing at the action to be done, as Aristotle remarks (1140b5; *GBWW* I: 9, 389; II: 8, 389). *Praxis* is the realm of moral and political action—of human behavior—which may be good or evil. Its specific virtue is prudence (*phronēsis*), which is defined as a "practical habit with true reason concerning the goods and evils of human beings" (my translation, 1140b7; ibid.).

Poiesis (from which our word "poetry" comes) is the activity of making something, or producing or performing it. As noted, it aims at something more than either the knowing or action that is involved with it. Its specific virtue is art (*technē*, from which "technology" is derived). It is defined as "a productive habit (*poietike*) with true reason" (my translation, 1140a11; cf. *GBWW* I: 9, 388; II: 8, 388). About it Aristotle notes:

> All art is concerned with coming into being, i.e. with contriving and considering how something may come into being which is capable of either being or not being, and whose origin is in the maker and not in the thing made; for art is concerned neither with things that are, or come into being, by necessity, nor with things that do so in accordance with nature (since these have their origin in themselves). (1140a12–16; *GBWW* I: 9, 388; II: 8, 388.)

One must emphasize how broad this notion of art is, and yet also how distinct. First, art is a disposition or quality of the mind that leads to the intellectual activity of making. Thus it is distinct from science and prudence, which are what we need (i.e., the required capabilities, or virtues) for knowing and doing, respectively. Art or making produces a work that is not natural but artificial, in that were it not for the fact that it is made, the work would not exist in any way. The end of any art is external to its activity. Such an end is a house, hat, pot, chair, lyric, symphony, tragic drama, dance; an automobile, airplane, satellite, computer—or whatever, as long as it is a man-made external object.

Turning back to the definition, we note that some clarification is called for. As a "*productive habit with true reason (logos)*," the fact that it is productive (*poietike*) restricts it to making and the makable, Aristotle says. That it is a habit indicates it is a disposition or quality of mind by which one has developed an ability that others may not have. Thus a carpenter "has" an ability so perfected that he can saw, plane, nail, and put wood together in a way, or a better way, than one who lacks that skill, that being the art that he has.

But why with "true reason"? This qualification indicates two things. First, that an art involves knowledge as reason; and second, that it is one that may fail of its purpose. So an artisan who lacks the skill may fail to saw a straight cut or plane a fine surface just as a beginner may cook a soufflé that falls and tastes bad. The possession of the skill can be seen in the goodness or badness of the product. Hence the adage that art does not fail; the failure lies in the maker who fails to possess it, or to possess it sufficiently. Perhaps a clearer although equally literal translation of the definition is that art is "having the right know-how of things makable."

To include the reference to knowledge and the true, or right, serves to emphasize that art is an intellectual activity, however much it may call also for muscular adaptations and training, such as those needed for playing a musical instrument. The difference between the work that is made and the knowing that contributed to its making makes itself an important point. The work made—a kitchen pot, an automobile, a dramatic or musical production—is in each case a distinct, material individual, regardless of how many times it may be reproduced. However, the knowing involved in art is not individual or singular but universal. The house builder's art is capable of producing not just one but many houses. The thing made, the artwork, may be singular and contingent, and in some cases destined to endure for only a short while, as does a dance, but the knowledge in the art, as skill, contains rules and methods capable of being applied again and again to many diverse singular works.

To narrow in upon the notion of a liberal art, we need a still further distinction. Aristotle provides it in his *Politics* in Book VIII, where he discusses education (*GBWW* I: 9, 542–48; II: 8, 542–48). He notes that one must distinguish between two different sorts of arts according as they are liberal or illiberal. He makes this distinction according to the kinds of activity that befit a freeman or a slave. But that should not be taken as disallowing its ontological sense. Aristotle's language may betray the contingencies of the society in which he lived and wrote. But there is an ontological basis to the distinction that far transcends the sociological contingency of its expression.

Aristotle makes his distinction largely in negative terms, pointing out what is *il*liberal (*aneleutheros*). This is identified as "any occupation, art, or science, which makes the body, soul, or mind of the freeman less fit for the practice or exercise of virtue" (1337b9–11; *GBWW* I: 9, 542; II: 8, 542). But for Aristotle the highest activities of virtue for the freeman consist in fulfilling the duties of civic life or the pursuit of philosophical wisdom. Both of these require the freedom of leisure and the unhampered exercise of the intellect or mind in deliberation and speculation. Hence the great obstacle to both is any activity or occupation that dulls the mind and prevents its full and free operation, and of these the heaviest lies in the concerns of the body tying one down to the needs of the singular here and now. Hence Aristotle's demand is much like the old religious sanction that forbade menial work on the Sabbath. In both instances the need is for freedom of the mind.

The root of such freedom is the ability of the mind to escape from the individualizing constraints of the material singular of the here and now. The mind accomplishes this whenever it deals with ideas and their symbols, which are its natural instruments. An expression may be formulated so as to refer to a singular and call for one definite response, as when a diner says to his companion, "Please, pass me the bread." But no one of the words in this expression is restricted to this one demand, since the meaning of each transcends both time and place.

The liberal arts are those that possess such a liberating capacity. They are the arts of the mind that make it free, hence liberating arts.

Combining the understanding that we have already obtained of art with the additional note of the liberating factor, we are enabled to venture on a definition of a liberal art. If art is having the right know-how of things makable, the note that now has to be added is that the thing made is one that transcends space and time. Thus a liberal art can be defined as having the right know-how of making things that transcend space and time.

As we have already seen from the consideration of art, the know-how contains a rational element in addition to that which produces a singular material object. The carpenter's art is not limited to cutting one board, even though the table or whatever that he makes is one singular material object. The additional note of a liberal art is that it finds in the work produced, as well as in the activity producing it, a rational element. Again, a linguistic statement offers the simplest example. The expression "Please, pass me the bread," as uttered by a diner to his companion, is a singular material utterance of sounds; but it also consists of words with meanings, and these are not singular but universal, applying to and being used in many different places and times.

Aristotle makes still further distinctions that are useful for discriminating among the various arts. His *Poetics* is especially valuable for analyzing those now known as the fine arts. However, our concern here is with the liberal arts, and we may go on to further consideration of these.

The tradition of the liberal arts

The liberal arts have a long history. It extends from the Hellenistic world, Greek as well as Latin, through the Middle Ages in the West, where such arts were greatly treasured, down to the twentieth century. They have, however, at least according to their traditional names and number, received little attention in our time. A liberal arts college as we now know it tends to be more a matter of certain subject matters than of arts. Yet for most of our intellectual history, liberal arts provided the recognized indispensable basis for all higher learning.

Such arts, which by name and number became traditional, were standard by the time of Quintilian (ca. A.D. 35–96). His *Institutio oratoria* on the education of the orator constitutes a great book on the art of rhetoric. His comments on the arts locate many of the crucial questions about them. The first book of the *Institutio* is largely devoted to the elementary teaching of the art of reading and writing known as *grammatica,* or grammar (from the Greek *gramma,* meaning "letter"). But before the pupil leaves the *grammaticus* to go on to the teacher of rhetoric, Quintilian adds "some concise observations on the other departments of study . . . in order that the circle of instruction, which the Greeks call *enkuklios paideia,* may be completed." [1]

Although our word *encyclopaedia* derives from it, this Greek expression has a much simpler and more elementary meaning. Quintilian's phrase "circle of instruction" (*orbis doctrinae*) provides a translation. It comprises a course of study that begins with grammar and, at least for Quintilian, ends with rhetoric. In between, as this same chapter of the *Institutio* points out, are geometry, music, logic, arithmetic, and astronomy. In all there are seven arts listed, and these became the traditional liberal arts. I have listed them in the order that Quintilian mentions them, but except for the first and the last there would seem to be no further significance to this enumeration of them.

The fact that all of the arts except rhetoric are made the responsibility of the *grammaticus,* the pupil's earliest teacher, indicates how elementary they are conceived to be. They constitute the preparatory arts or disciplines that are needed as the basis and means of further learning. The meaning is much the same as that which Plato assigns to mathematics as *propaideia* to the study of philosophy (*The Republic* VII, 536; *GBWW* I: 7, 399; II: 6, 399). The fact that Plato has this *paideia* leading to philosophy whereas Quintilian wants it for rhetoric also indicates that these arts can be ordered to different ends. Indeed, the different ordering of the arts, and which one of them is given primary importance, can serve as indices of what is considered to be the highest knowledge. But more of that later.

It would be misleading to conceive of the arts as together constituting a circle (*kuklios*), despite Quintilian's "circle of instruction." His own practice indicates not a circle but a line that leads from grammar through the other arts to end with rhetoric.

Such a program of studies, even at a very elemental level, must have often been more an ideal than a realized fact. Of this Augustine provides a witness. He was a highly trained rhetorician, and so successful that he was appointed the official orator of the city of Milan, then the seat of government of the Roman Empire in the West. Yet when he became a convert to philosophy as well as Christianity, he resigned from his post and retired to the country with friends to devote himself to philosophy. But he evidently was unsatisfied with his preparation or that of his friends for such a pursuit. For he then started to write manuals on the arts (*disciplinarum libros*). As he reports in the review of his writings he wrote at the end of his life, he completed a book on grammar, which is no longer extant, and most of one on music or prosody, but only a beginning of those on "dialectic, rhetoric, geometry, arithmetic, [and] philosophy." [2] But this work was ended upon his being ordained priest and bishop.

Augustine never lost his conviction of the importance of the liberal arts. But he came to look upon them as being directed to a new end: not to rhetoric or philosophy, but to theology and the worship of God. For this, sacred Scripture was his main source, and his work *On Christian Doctrine* was written to explain how to read the Bible. For this he recommends the various arts as indispensable instruments. Then in the final book he gives a detailed defense of the art of rhetoric with examples from Scripture of its use.

Augustine died in the year 430. Not many years later a work by one Martianus Capella appeared, written perhaps in north Africa like so many of Augustine's books had been, which codified the liberal arts, dressed them in an elaborate allegory, furnished manuals for all seven, and passed them on to the Latin Middle Ages. This was *De nuptiis Philologiae et Mercurii et de septem artibus liberalibus* (*On the Marriage of Mercury and Philology and on the Seven Liberal Arts*). [3]

The historical importance of Martianus' book far outweighs its internal worth. For it proved to be one of the most popular textbooks in the Middle Ages. Its elementary manuals on each of the arts continued in use until the great influx of Greek and Arabic learning in the twelfth century, and the elaborate bombastic allegory of the first two books retained favor into the Renaissance. In fact, the best edition of the text before the nineteenth century was made by Hugo Grotius, in 1599, when he was only sixteen years old and before he had become one of the founders of modern international law.

The allegory that serves as an introduction to the manuals on the arts is fantastic and ridiculous, at least to a modern reader—almost unreadable, partly because it is written in some of the most difficult Latin ever written. It tells of Mercury's efforts to find a wife, of the lady Philology being recommended to him by both Apollo and Virtue, and of the ratification of the marriage by the council of the gods on Mount Olympus. The plot then turns to Philology's preparation for the wedding, of her journey as a mortal to heaven, and of the wedding itself. There she receives, as her dowry gift from Mercury, seven fair handmaids, each of them one of the seven arts. To celebrate the marriage, each of the ladies, dressed with all the accoutrements of her knowledge, proceeds on being presented to deliver a discourse on the elements of her art.

The resulting handbooks are presented in the following order, a separate book being allotted to each one: Grammar, Dialectic, Rhetoric, Geometry, Arithmetic, Astronomy, and Music or Prosody. All are referred to as the *disciplinae cyclicae;* i.e., of *enkuklios paideia.* The first three are termed *artes,* the second four *disciplinae,* thereby distinguishing the linguistic from the mathematical arts, which become respectively the trivium and quadrivium of medieval fame—that is, of the places where three ways and four ways meet.

The longest of the books is devoted to Geometry, but that is due to the fact that most of it is given over to a descriptive geography of the world. The strictly geometric part is very abbreviated, consisting only of a few definitions and propositions, which are given without any of their proofs in the lamentable style of the ancient Roman writers. Best of the quadrivial books, according to historians of science, is that devoted to Astronomy, which receives the praise of Copernicus for making the planets (Venus and Mercury) circle about the Sun rather than the Earth (*GBWW* I: 16, 523; II: 15, 523).

It is significant that the arts are presented as becoming the handmaids of a loftier lady, since this emphasizes that they are not ends in themselves but means in the service of another end.

However, taken all together this work of Martianus shows how popularity and historical importance do not by themselves make a great book. No one except one interested in the history of the liberal arts or in medieval studies would bother to read it.

The linguistic arts

Yet we must consider still another work that is less than a great book, not for its historical importance, but for the light it sheds on the arts, especially that of grammar, and the relations among them. This is a thirteenth-century poem by the French trouvère Henri d'Andeli, entitled *La bataille des sept arts*. The battle that is described is one between Logic and her followers on one side against those led by Grammar on the other. Logic is accused of being the cause of the battle by enticing Grammar's followers away and dominating the whole trivium and quadrivium, including even "a perverse Grammar" as well as a "corrupt Rhetoric," and being so powerful that "every boy runs her course ere he has passed his fifteenth year." [4]

Matters are said to have so far deteriorated that Grammar has no other option than to wage war. She raises her banner outside Orléans, where the university contained more of her followers than that at Paris. Siding with her in opposition to Logic were the ancient grammarians Priscian and Donatus as well as Martianus Capella, and the ancient classical authors—Homer, Virgil, Horace, Ovid, Terence, Martial, Persius, Juvenal, Seneca, Lucan, Statius—and numerous early Christian and medieval poets. Logic gathers her forces outside of Paris. They consist of all the trivium and the quadrivium—Philosophy with Aristotle and all his numerous books, as well as Plato, Socrates, Porphyry, Boethius, Macrobius, and Gilbert de la Porrée. Canon Law and Civil Law are there with their books, as well as Medicine and Surgery, represented by Hippocrates, Galen, and a number of Parisian physicians, and Necromancy and Astrology, too, are in the host.

Battle is joined outside Paris, and though many blows are struck, Grammar is finally defeated and forced to flee while her forces scatter and desert, Logic being victorious. The poet expresses his own regret that the two forces were at odds and notes that Logic, like Astronomy, loves lofty things, whereas Grammar loves fountains. But he criticizes Logic for trying to teach her students to fly before they are able to walk. The poet's own sympathies are clearly with Grammar, and at the end of the poem he prophesies that the victory of Logic will not be a lasting one, and that one day Grammar will return to her place of eminence.

The situation described by the thirteenth-century poet bears similarities to the conflict that the English novelist C. P. Snow described in the 1950s as the conflict of "the two cultures." [5] The forces are the same insofar as literature on one side opposes those of science on the other. However, the forces of science in the twentieth century are led by physics and not by logic. Also, literature no longer consists of the ancient great books. This indicates a significant characteristic of the art of grammar. As Quintilian noted, *grammatica,* which is in origin a Greek word, becomes in Latin *literatura,* [6] and once the fundamentals of a language are acquired, most of the work consists in reading those authors who excel in the use of their language. In thirteenth-century Europe there was but one learned language, Latin, and hence its authors provided the basic texts. After the rise of the national languages, grammar had to accommodate them all, with the result that the literature taught is based on that of the particular language. Thus

Shakespeare has become a source for the learning of English literature, Dante for Italian, Goethe for German, etc.

The "perverse grammar" mentioned in the French poem would provide an alternative to the division of grammar according to the particular languages. In the thirteenth century and later Middle Ages there was considerable speculation about the possibility of discovering and establishing a universal grammar; i.e., one for language itself, whatever particular tongue it might finally be expressed in. In our time the closest parallel is provided by Noam Chomsky in his linguistic theory of generational or transformational grammar; this bases language on a universal innate faculty that human beings possess.

The division between the two forces in the battle just described points to a radical difference between grammar and all the rest of the arts— one that is emphasized and exacerbated by the diversity of our national languages. Mathematics (and with it the sciences) is transcultural in that it has become one and the same, whatever tongue its teachers and students may speak. The same can be said for logic, especially in its mathematical form, and to a lesser extent also for rhetoric. For, as Augustine emphasized, the truths of logic and rhetoric are objectively based on the way things are, and not on the particular culture of its expression (*GBWW* I: 18, 652; II: 16, 652).

Another distinction with respect to the arts appears in the authors mentioned in the account of the battle between Grammar and Logic. Grammar has on her side not only Priscian and Donatus, who were authors of Latin grammars, but also Latin poets such as Virgil and Horace, who wrote not grammars but epic and odes. This distinction serves to indicate that there are two different kinds of books among the arts: books devoted to the analysis of the art itself, its elements, definitions, and rules, such as in Priscian's grammar or Aristotle's *Organon,* on the one hand; and on the other, works written by authors who have mastered the art and put it to work producing poetry or philosophy.

The difference corresponds to the one which Aristotle made, as we have already seen, between science and art. Science seeks to know for the sake of knowing only; hence the attempt to analyze a language, say English, so as to determine what constitutes a meaningful and correct expression in the language amounts to an endeavor of science. But if one possesses that knowledge and puts it to use so as to produce, i.e., to make, such meaningful expressions, that person is engaged in art. Thus among the books devoted to language it is important to distinguish between works that aim at providing a scientific account and those that aim at making an artistic product. A great book in either sense is one that is excellent in its accomplishment.

The justification of logic's high place among the arts that the poet Henri complained of can be found in the introduction that Thomas Aquinas wrote to the *Posterior Analytics* of Aristotle. This is also illuminating in that it provides an analytic description of all the logical works of Aristotle contained in his *Organon,* the first great book on the subject. Logic is well called the *ars artium* (art of arts), Thomas writes, because "it directs us in the operation of reason from which all the arts proceed." [7] Logic is accordingly divided according to the diverse acts of reason.

Of the three acts of reason, the first two achieve a certain understanding. One is the understanding of the indivisible or uncomplex according as it conceives what a thing is; it is this operation that Aristotle treats in the *Categories.*

The second operation of the intellect is the act of judgment in which the true or the false is reached, and this is treated in the book *On Interpretation.*

The third act, which is the one most proper to reason, is that which is discursive from one thing to another, so as to move from the known to the unknown, and to this subject the remaining four books of the *Organon* are devoted.

To distinguish the matter of these books one from another, Thomas appeals to the three degrees of certitude that reason can attain. Although truth is always the aim, it cannot always be grasped with equal certitude. First and strongest is the certitude of science, which is attained by judicative logic. This is the concern of two Aristotelian books: first the theory of the syllogism worked out in the *Prior Analytics* and then the discussion of the demonstrative syllogism or theory of science in the *Posterior Analytics.*

The second process—that of inventive logic, or the logic of discovery—attains to opinion or belief in which there is a high degree of probability. This subject is treated in the *Topics,* devoted to dialectic as Aristotle conceives of it.

When the most that can be achieved is a certain suspicion, we are in the realm where rhetoric rules, to which Aristotle also devoted a book. When the only degree of certitude that can be achieved is a conjecture based on a representation, we have reached the level of poetry, on which Aristotle has left still another book. From this judgment made upon poetry by Logic, it is evident why Grammar had to go to battle.

The final book of the *Organon* is devoted to the failure of reason through fallacy or deceptive argument, which is treated in the work *On Sophistical Refutations.*

Thomas has nothing to say about the mathematical arts in the text just considered. However, since all of these aim at science, they would fall under judicative logic as directive of their work. A much more interesting and serious question about the relation between the two has come about as the result of the development of mathematical or symbolic logic. But that question can be postponed until we come to consider the arts of the quadrivium.

Turning now to the art of rhetoric, we find that Aristotle is the author of the first great book on the subject. His treatment was later systematized and passed on in the form of manuals, of which that of Quintilian is the best. Its material was organized according to the three elements that can be distinguished in any speech or discourse, apart from the speech itself as a linguistic structure: first, the speaker and the impression that he makes as a person, i.e., his character; second, the subject on which he speaks; and third, the audience he addresses and wishes to influence.

With respect to the audience, three kinds of rhetoric or oratory can be identified, based on the way the speaker wishes to influence it. He may look to the future and what is to be done, which is the field of deliberative or political oratory. Or the speaker may regard the past and be concerned about how it is to be judged, which is the concern of forensic or judicial oratory. Or he may look to the present and judge it as praiseworthy or blameworthy, which is the work of epideictic or panegyric oratory.

Rhetoric as an art consists in the knowledge and skill in the use of the means for achieving the three various ends. Its material was divided into five parts:

1. Invention: the discovery of arguments concerning the subject or matter of the speech.
2. Disposition: the arrangement of the arguments to achieve the desired purpose.
3. Elocution: working out the appropriate style for that purpose, including figures of speech.
4. Memory: memorizing the speech.
5. Delivery: how the speech is to be given.

Rhetoric was more responsible than any of the other arts for noting and promoting the idea of great books. Study of the art involved not only learning definitions and rules but also extensive reading and analysis of literature in order to see how they can be applied and used. As Quintilian pointed out, "if there were a single word for every single thing, words would require less care. . . . As some, however, are more appropriate, or more elegant, or more significant, or more euphonious, than others, they ought all, not only be known, but to be kept in readiness. . . . But this object we shall effect by reading and listening to the best language. . . ." [8]

The first part of ancient rhetoric, that concerning invention, has experienced a revival in recent times in the so-called new rhetoric developed by the Belgian professor Chaim Perelman (see *GIT* 1970, 272–312). Invention in rhetoric dealt with the topics or commonplaces of arguments as types that were capable of being adapted to different situations. Thus it was concerned with the ways of thinking and reasoning about moral and practical questions, based on the principle that matters such as these are a proper concern of reason and not merely of taste and emotion. In this, rhetoric provides a defense of practical reason.

Thus far, our concern with the linguistic arts has been mainly historical. However, before leaving them we should note what argument can be put forward for the claim that the three arts of the trivium (grammar, rhetoric, and logic) constitute the fundamental arts of language.

We need to see that at least three different and distinct arts are needed for the use of language, and that all three must work together so as to form a unity. But this will hold only if a linguistic utterance contains at least three distinct aspects or elements, each of which performs a different task and calls for a different art. That such is the case is evident from consideration of a linguistic expression that is sufficiently complex. In the first place it consists, whether spoken or written, of sounds or letters arranged in a pattern that conforms to the rules and practices of the language group to which it belongs. Second, these sounds or letters are something more than singular material entities, whether vibrations of air or ink marks on paper, since as signs they indicate, present, or refer to objects other than themselves. Third, language in use is an expression of a speaker or writer addressed to another in such a way as to cause a certain effect upon its hearer or reader.

As an example of this last, consider the statement of the Pythagorean theorem as Euclid gives it: "In right-angled triangles the square on the side subtending the right angle is equal to the squares on the sides containing the right angle" (*GBWW* I: 11, 28; II: 10, 28). As so stated, this is an expression in the English language that conforms to English usage in such matters as word order, the formation of the plural, and the use of a linking verb whose number is governed by the singular subject. But the sounds or letters so arranged make a statement about something other than themselves, namely, about the areas of squares upon the sides of right-angled triangles and their relation. Further, the statement so made achieves the effect of making known a certain property of right-angled triangles.

Thus it is clear that there are not only three distinct and different aspects to this linguistic expression, but each one makes a different and significant contribution to the utterance as a meaningful structure. The first aspect is the most obvious, since to know and use a language, however simply, one must know a minimum of its vocabulary and syntax. Yet the two other aspects are no less essential. In fact, the extralinguistic object is often the most important of all, since our talk and writing, apart from the present instance, is usually about nonlinguistic objects. The third aspect is no less essential, since no linguistic utterance is without some function or purpose.

But what reason is there for claiming that a distinct art is needed for dealing with each of the three aspects of linguistic use just noted? A certain know-how is necessary for each one. To be able to use a language one must know, in the first place, how to use the vocabulary and syntax of the language; beyond this, to know how to construct a meaningful expression that makes sense with reference to its object; and finally, to know how to achieve the intended purpose, whether that is to communicate a truth, to persuade someone to take a certain course of action, or to please and amuse.

To learn a language consists of acquiring these arts, skills, or know-hows. Since all human beings, with few exceptions, learn how to talk, these three arts are our most common possession and in this sense the most human of all arts. While all of us possess these arts, however, we do not all possess them equally and to the same extent; some may excel in one or the other of them and make more out of them than another can. One person may be able to speak more fluently and gracefully than another; someone else may be better at persuading others to act in a certain way; still another person may excel in the construction and analysis of arguments and explanations. Hence, though the linguistic arts are in origin as natural as language is, the fact that language may be used in better and worse ways indicates that one can have more or less of these arts. This being so, we see how the arts themselves would become the focus of attention, and how there might be, as there have been, formal studies of them in grammar, rhetoric, and logic, with the aim of making art improve upon nature.

The need for grammar, in the sense of skill in arranging words according to the genius of the language, is obvious from the babbling of infants (i.e., nonspeakers) who cannot make themselves understood. The difference between possessing more or less of the art appears in the presence or absence of such qualities as clarity, precision, appropriateness, grace, and beauty. Grammar possessed as an art thus consists not in knowledge of the rules that professional grammarians have stated but rather in the skill of composing with words.

Rhetoric, again in the wide sense that we are considering, is the art of using linguistic means to achieve a nonlinguistic or extralinguistic end. Grammar's aim is strictly verbal—for example, to compose an expression that makes sense in English. Rhetoric looks beyond the act of expressing to the purpose that is to be achieved. Originally, and in the narrow sense, it was limited to the art of using words so as to persuade others to take a certain attitude or course of action. Yet any and every use of language fulfills some purpose, even when it is only that of idling. Hence there is a broader sense of rhetoric in which it can be seen to be at work in a mathematical demonstration, a scientific exposition, as well as in a political speech. In all of these, linguistic materials and means are being organized to achieve a certain end. The changing forms of scientific exposition reveal as much. Galileo presented his scientific discoveries and theories in the form of a dialogue, whereas Newton arranged his in the form of an axiomatic system, while modern scientists write short monographs. These are all rhetorical devices. Science does not do without rhetoric; rhetoric only works differently in science from the way it works in other disciplines.

So much concerning the need for two linguistic arts. But what reason is there for thinking that a third art is necessary for the use of language, and that the art is logic? The Pythagorean theorem, as we have seen, is a linguistic expression, made according to the rules of English, which communicates a truth about triangles. But this truth belongs to the judgment about triangles and not to the language. To see the need for a third art, we have to add another statement to relate to that of the Pythagorean theorem. If that theorem is true, and if it is also true that any two triangles having two sides respectively equal to two sides and equal base lines also have equal angles contained by those equal lines (*GBWW* I: 11, 6; II: 10, 6), then it is true that any triangle having the square on one of its sides equal to the sum of the squares on the other two sides will have a right angle contained by the other two sides (*GBWW* I: 11, 29; II: 10, 29).

The proof of this is given by Euclid as the final proposition of the first book of the *Elements*. It is not the geometry, but the form of the statement that is our concern. This has the form "if p and if q then r." And this final consequent r makes a new statement different from that made in the two antecedents p and q. It also states a property about triangles. It is not about language, and yet it comes about as the result of the relations established by the particles *if, and, then*. Although what results are propositions of the English language, their force is not peculiar to English, nor indeed to any language. It is grounded in the relations that they establish as an objective fact. The connectives join statements, each of which is about a property of triangles, and in so doing they produce a new statement that contains new knowledge about triangles.

The art of using such connectives as "if . . . then," "and," "or," "not" is one that is distinct from both grammar and rhetoric. It concerns neither the arrangement and construction of words to conform to the patterns of a particular language, nor the organizing of them in a particular way so as to achieve a certain effect upon a listener or reader. Instead, it is the function of this art to assure that such connectives do the work they are capable of doing and as they should. This art is that of logic, and logic is particularly interested in consequential truth, to which end it aims to secure the path of inference and keep it from passing wrongly from a true to a false statement. Inferring, reasoning, arguing, and in that manner pushing beyond the immediately evident are its great delight. It is especially important in conceptual and scientific knowledge, but it is by no means limited to these realms. All discourse is studded with "ifs," "ands," "ors," "nots." Hence logic is at work wherever there is language.

The three arts needed for the use of language are distinct in that each has a different function to perform, a different work to make. In actual practice all three work together. Hence "trivium" is an accurate name for them, since the work they produce is a place where three ways meet. That implies that there will not be any conflict between them, either. Yet it is not difficult to see why conflicts should occur. For example, one of the arts may be valued more than another, or a person may have greater talent for one than for another. Also, for some purposes one of the arts may be more important than another. Logic is more important than the others for science in its search for the truth about the way things are. Poetry, from its love for the beauty and music of words, leans more heavily upon the grammatical art. Rhetoric has as its first loyalty the work of persuasion, and this appeals most strongly to the person who is at home in civic and political life.

Each of the arts can also be made an object of study for itself; not for the use of it, but in order to know what it is and how it operates. Hence each provides the subject matter for a distinct science: linguistics, communication, and logic. Yet however important the scientific knowledge so obtained may be, it does not by itself guarantee equal command of the corresponding art. One may be a genius at scientific discovery and yet a veritable dud at explaining it. The arts of the trivium are the skills of using language for any purpose and in any situation. In this sense they are general arts transcending any special subject matter and applicable to all. Their respective sciences, on the other hand, remain special in being restricted to special subject matters and methods of enquiry.

The mathematical arts

The arts of the quadrivium show their age more than those of the trivium do. They are more conditioned by time, and have progressed more in both theory and practice, though logic is something of an exception here, as we will see. For great advances have been made in linguistics and communication theory, but the same is not true of the products they have produced; i.e., as works of art. The epics of Homer, Virgil, Dante, Milton, and Goethe are as good as anything produced since in imaginative literature. On the other hand, the practice as well as the theory of the mathematical arts have far surpassed their early development. As mathematicians are proud of claiming, our age is a golden age of mathematics.

The elements of the quadrivium—their identification, enumeration, and distinction—was the work of the ancient Pythagoreans. As Nicomachus (ca. A.D. 100) noted in his *Introduction to Arithmetic,* distinctions with respect to quantity serve to identify four arts. One is that which distinguishes the discrete from the continuous. The natural or positive whole numbers are discrete, being so many distinct individuals: 1, 2, 3, etc. But a line is continuous in that it does not consist of distinct individual parts, or if it should be considered as consisting of points, there are infinitely many of them. The difference is that between multitude and magnitude. Again, discrete quantity may be considered either as it is in itself or as in relation to another, such considerations constituting respectively the arts of arithmetic and music. Finally, a continuous quantity may be considered either as at rest or in motion, and these considerations give rise accordingly to the arts of geometry and astronomy. Nicomachus then cites with approval the claim of a Pythagorean writer that "in truth lines, numbers, harmonic intervals, and the revolutions of circles bear aid to the learning of the doctrines of wisdom" (GBWW I: 11, 812; II: 10, 600).

The last two items on this list may seem puzzling. The revolution of circles applies to astronomy, since the ancients employed the theory of circles to explain the motions observed in the heavens. The reference to harmonic intervals applies to the art of music and to the Pythagorean discovery that musical intervals depend on the ratio of whole numbers. Thus if lengths of string or tubes of the same substance and tension are vibrated, the harmonic octave will sound when the lengths are as 2:1; the fifth as 3:2; and the fourth as 4:3. Hence the ancient art of music was the study of ratios and could apply to the music of words, i.e., prosody, as well as to that of musical instruments.

Some of these arts created their own great books. In fact, one of the famous books of all time is the *Elements* of Euclid, which provided the basic introduction to the study of mathematics down to the twentieth century. Of its thirteen books, three concern the arithmetic of whole numbers and the rest deal with plane and solid geometry (GBWW I: 11, 127–90; II: 10, 127–90). It is significant that Euclid represents whole numbers by lengths of line. Nicomachus' *Introduction to Arithmetic,* which also achieved the status of a great book, represents numbers graphically by plane figures. Thus the number 4, which is the square of 2, appears as (GBWW I: 11, 834; II: 10, 622):

$$\begin{array}{|cc|} \hline \alpha & \alpha \\ \\ \alpha & \alpha \\ \hline \end{array}$$

Music or harmony failed to inspire a book on its art the equal, at least in fame, to that of the other arts. For astronomy the great book was provided by Ptolemy in his *Mathematical Collection,* which later came to be known as the *Almagest,* meaning "The Greatest."

The quadrivium possesses no account of the battle among its arts corresponding to that of the trivium. Yet in effect such a battle occurred, and it was a much more grievous one in that it resulted in the destruction of the old arts, at least in their old form, and led to logic deserting its former colleagues. This story can be told briefly by considering the following incidents: in arithmetic the introduction of the Arabic notation for numbers and of zero; in geometry the invention of analytic geometry and non-Euclidean geometries; in astronomy the heliocentric theory of our planetary system; the invention of the calculus, and in logic its mathematicization. As a result of these developments the quadrivium was destroyed.

These incidents occur in the story of the arithmetization of mathematics and the overthrow of geometry as the first of the mathematical arts. That this has been a recent development is evident from the fact that Descartes presented his great discovery as a work in geometry and entitled it so, and Newton published his *Principia* in the axiomatized form of geometry, though he performed his calculations by the calculus that he invented.

The first essential step in arithmetization came with the invention of zero and the adoption of the Arabic notation for numbers. The Greek and Roman practice of using letters to represent numbers was highly cumbersome and made calculation difficult without the help of a mechanical aid. The expression of very large numbers was extremely hard. This is shown by Archimedes' little treatise, *The Sand-Reckoner,* in which he claims to discover the number of all the grains of sand in the universe. It is not only the problem that seems incredible, but the fact that he can express it in his cumbersome notations. (Modern translations obscure the latter fact by expressing the solution in Arabic numerals.) In our own day only Eddington has attempted a similar feat by claiming to determine the "cosmical number" of the total number of particles in the Einsteinian universe.

With the adoption of a more satisfactory notation future progress depended upon increasing the possibilities of calculating, or computability. This was achieved by inventing new number systems to overcome obstacles. Ancient arithmetic limited itself to the natural positive whole numbers. Hence certain operations became impossible. Of these, subtraction is the simplest case since it cannot be done unless the subtrahend is smaller than the minuend. Thus 3 cannot be subtracted from 2 if the operation is limited to positive whole numbers. The invention of negative numbers overcomes this obstacle, and $2 - 3 = -1$. Division faces a similar difficulty, since here the dividend must be greater than the divisor. The invention of fractions or rational numbers solves this problem with $1/2$, $1/3$, $1/4$, etc. Sometimes, however, the result does not yield whole-number fractions. Thus the diagonal of a square is a line of a definite length, but if its sides each equal one, the length of the diagonal is $\sqrt{2}$, an irrational number expressible only as an unending decimal. Hence the real numbers are invented, so called because they apply to the real physical world. But even with real numbers added to all the rest there still remains an operation that cannot be performed, namely, the extraction of the square root of negative numbers. Hence the imaginary number "i" is invented so that $i = \sqrt{-1}$. If now real numbers are combined with imaginary numbers, we obtain the complex numbers. Our number system is thus complete, since there is no obstacle to performing any operation we want. The range of our ability to calculate has been enormously extended.

Arithmetic, however, has not yet reached its full development. It still has to overcome the difference separating the discrete from the continuous, which the ancients saw as the radical break between arithmetic and geometry. The victory was slow in coming, but come it eventually did. That the attack was fully under way is evident in the opening paragraph of Descartes's *Geometry*. His very first sentence advances the claim that "any problem in geometry can easily be reduced to such terms that a knowledge of the lengths of certain straight lines is sufficient for its construction." When dealing with many lines, he takes one line as unity "in order to relate it as closely as possible to numbers" (*GBWW* I: 31, 295; II: 28, 523). He then proceeds to show how this claim can be justified and, in doing so, invents analytic or co-ordinate geometry.

A simple example of its operation is one that Whitehead gives in his *Introduction to Mathematics* (cf. *GBWW* II: 56, 151–55). Draw two straight lines at right angles to each other and intersecting, forming the axes x and y. Consider the equation $ax + by = c$. Here a determines a point along the x axis. Say $a = +1$. And b determines a point along the y axis. Say $b = -1$. Let $c = 0$. We then have $1x + -1y = 0$, so that $1x = 1y$ and $-1y = -1x$.

Plotting points accordingly, we have P and P', and connecting them we have the line PP'. In short, the equation $ax + by = c$ defines a straight line. But since all the variable letters in it represent numbers, the geometric line has been defined by arithmetic numbers, and there ceases to be any longer an unbridgeable gulf between geometry and arithmetic. The lines, curves, figures, solids, and their relations can all be determined by equations which ultimately are but variable expressions for numbers. Thus Euclid's Pythagorean theorem, proven as a relation between the sides of a triangle and squares erected on them, can now be stated much more simply as $a^2 + b^2 = c^2$, where at issue is a matter of numbers, even though they may also be taken as the lengths of the sides of a triangle. The arithmetic (or algebraic) expression is admittedly more abstract than the corresponding geometric expression, but it is simpler and easier to work with. Geometry has been arithmetized.

Geometry, at least as understood by Euclid and his followers, suffered still another shock with the discovery of non-Euclidean geometries. This discovery resulted from doubts about Euclid's fifth postulate, which maintains that nonparallel lines must meet (*GBWW* I: 11, 2; II: 10,

2). By relying on this postulate it is eventually proven that the three interior angles of a triangle are equal to two right angles (*GBWW* I: 11, 19–20; II: 10, 19–20). Euclid himself may have had some doubts about this postulate, since he postponed appealing to it as long as possible. The converse of the postulate as stated is proved in Proposition 28 (*GBWW* I: 11, 18; II: 10, 18), and efforts were continually made to prove the postulate itself and so convert it into a theorem. But all such efforts resulted in failure. Finally, attempts were made to abandon the postulate so that the sum of the interior angles of a triangle might be either greater or less than 180°. It then proved possible to develop consistent geometries on either supposition, and non-Euclidean geometry was born, due primarily to the work of Lobachevsky and of Riemann. Euclidean geometry might hold for flat or plane space, but it does not hold for all space, for in a curved space the non-Euclidean geometries and not the Euclidean are true. Such a situation might have remained no more than an abstract mathematical speculation, but that changed with Einstein and his theory of relativity. This called for a non-Euclidean geometry to explain the relation of events occurring in a space that is curved.

While such incidents and developments were shaking the position of arithmetic and geometry as they were understood in the ancient quadrivium, even more serious upsets had happened to astronomy. Whereas geometry as presented by Euclid still remained true as far as it went, the principal basis for ancient astronomy, the *Almagest* of Ptolemy, was replaced. The work of Copernicus, Kepler, Galileo, and Newton based on the heliocentric theory of planetary motions replaced the geocentric theory with its circular orbits of planets traveling around the Earth. At the same time the mathematical and theoretical methods of analysis were tremendously more powerful. Newton, in effect, achieved a marriage of terrestrial and celestial dynamics by producing an explanation of movements in either sphere.

Worst still in its effect upon the traditional understanding of the arts, the mathematicization of logic threatened to breach the gap separating the trivium and the quadrivium. Here, if any one great book were to be singled out for this attempt, it would be the *Principia Mathematica* written by Russell, together with Whitehead.

This huge work, which was ten years in the writing, was published in three large volumes (1910–13) and contains hundreds of propositions. By 1900, when the work was begun, mathematical or symbolic logic (the book uses both names) was already well developed. A notation had been constructed consisting almost entirely of letters and special signs or symbols for the operations to be performed with them, so that the use of English or any other natural language was reduced to a minimum. Efforts were made to reduce to the smallest possible number the undefined notions; rules of inference were stated; and definitions were provided which identified the objects and operations for a given subject matter to be investigated. Putting the system to work resulted in a string of propositions logically following from one another and ultimately depending upon the primitive presuppositions. What made it look still more like a piece of mathematics was that it was presented as an axiomatic system, and up until 1900 the principal examples of this were outright mathematical works, such as Euclid's *Elements* and Newton's *Principia*.

The first part of the *Principia Mathematica*, entitled "Mathematical Logic," opens with an account of the theory of deduction. This is the "theory of how one proposition may be inferred from another," [9] which it can only do if the two propositions are so related that one is a consequence of the other. The development of this theory is needed to accomplish the purpose of the work as a whole. For, as the first sentence of this theory's explication declares, this is nothing less than "the deduction of pure mathematics from its logical foundations." [10] In other words, the aim was to reduce mathematics to logic. For this reason it is the position known in the philosophy of mathematics as Logicism. However, the effort might as readily be known as the arithmetizing of logic, and the great German logician of the time, Frege, held that logic is a branch of arithmetic.

This great and ambitious project ultimately turns out to be a failure. As pointed out in the best account of the development of logic, that of William and Martha Kneale, "although Whitehead and Russell continue to maintain the thesis of Frege, the expedients to which they are driven reveal the peculiarity of their usage of the word 'logic'." [11] Perhaps the most glaring case of this is their introduction of what they call the "axiom of infinity." Arithmetic needs an infinity of natural numbers to make possible some of its operations, notably that of mathematical induction, to assure that any number has a successor. This need is met by postulating the existence of an infinity of such numbers, [12] a need that had not been felt by logic until the advent of mathematical reductionists like Russell and Whitehead.

Hence, as the Kneales claim, it is better to retain the old understanding of logic as the study of the principles that assure the validity of inference and that "its laws are not laws of nature, but laws of the laws of nature." [13] Logic is thus the science of sciences, which recalls the name that Thomas gave to it as the art of arts.

The predominant form that logic has taken in the twentieth century is that of mathematical or symbolic logic. This possesses great advantage for the analysis of argument, making explicit by identifying and distinguishing the different elements that enter into it. It is especially adapted to the clarification of highly technical reasonings as those of mathematics. However, this of itself is no reason for denying that there is a gulf separating mathematics from logic.

What then is the result of the attack of modern mathematics upon the ancient quadrivium of arithmetic, geometry, music, and astronomy? The distinctions on which it was based have been overcome, as we have seen. Considered as the elementary mathematics necessary for continuing on to higher sciences, including those of mathematics, the quadrivium has had to be reformulated, in effect, for the past three centuries. If the choice were to be limited to only four preparatory studies, those four today would consist of arithmetic, geometry, algebra, and the calculus. With grounding in these four, one would possess the mathematical language that is the international learned tongue of the sciences.

The twentieth-century authors added to the Britannica set of great books include several bearing directly upon the mathematical developments that we have been discussing. They tell much of it in greater detail and with much more authority, since they were written by original contributors to that development.

Thus there are books by both Russell and Whitehead. Russell's little handbook, *The Problems of Philosophy,* contains remarks on the contribution that the logic that he had been working on can make to the understanding of those problems. The two works by Whitehead are more directly relevant to our discussion. His *Introduction to Mathematics* in effect tells at some length with many examples the story of arithmetic's coming into power. His *Science and the Modern World* provides a historical account of the rise and conquests of modern science and considers not only "mathematics as an element in the history of thought" (*GBWW* II: 55, 144), the subject of its second chapter, but also and especially the discovery of relativity and quantum theory in physics and the implication for other fields of thought.

Books by the makers of these two revolutionary theories are included in the additions. For example, there is Einstein's popular version of his work, *Relativity: The Special and the General Theory.* Planck's *Scientific Autobiography* is mainly devoted to an account of his discovery that energy has to be conceived as occurring in discrete quanta, with the implication that it opens up "a new era in natural science . . . destined to remodel basically the physical outlook and thinking of man which . . . were founded on the assumption that all causal interactions are continuous" (*GBWW* II: 56, 84). The set also now contains books by two scientists greatly responsible for the impetus given to the development of the quantum theory. Bohr's *Atomic Theory and the Description of Nature* consists of lectures that he delivered in explanation of the theory, and Heisenberg, discoverer of the uncertainty principle in physics, is represented by the book *Physics and Philosophy: The Revolution in Modern Science.* One of the ironies in this revolution is that it has revived the old split between the continuous and the discrete, since it has been discovered that light is sometimes more adequately explained as consisting of discrete quanta of energy and at other times as being a continuous wave. Since both principles are needed to account for the phenomena, Bohr claimed that the result was an instance of what he called the principle of complementarity.

On reading great books

Any book is a work of the liberal arts, a thing made by the use and application of those arts. Some are also books that deal directly with those arts by taking them as the subject for analysis and exposition. Such become textbooks, at least for a time, as manuals or handbooks by which one may acquire the art. If any of these are truly great books, they can still be read for profit and enlightenment. So far it is with the best of them that we have been mainly concerned: those by Aristotle on logic and rhetoric, by Euclid on geometry, and by Nicomachus on arithmetic. No other textbooks on the arts have achieved equal fame or remained so long in use as these.

However, a book, while not concerned with the arts as such, may still be great as an excellent and masterful product of those arts. Hence it is worth considering how such books may be read to improve one's knowledge and understanding of them as well as one's skill in their use. Since reading is an activity which demands the use of the arts, it is by becoming better readers that we can become better liberal artists. But how can this be done?

All of the linguistic arts are needed for reading any book, and all or some of the mathematical arts for reading works of many of the sciences. But some kinds of books call upon one art more than another. For this reason we need a classification of the general kinds of books that can be correlated with the various liberal arts where there is greater emphasis upon particular arts.

To start with, books can be distinguished according to the function or purpose they aim to fulfill. In general they aim either to teach, to move, or to delight. All three results in some cases may be more or less achieved, although one or the other is likely to be predominant. But more needs to be said about each of these three functions.

Teaching in this sense may aim at providing either instruction or understanding. The writing, or talking as the case may be, then takes the form of exposition. The kind of exposition varies accordingly as the matter of its concern is history, science, or philosophy that is theoretic or speculative. The overall end is the truth.

Moving as a function consists in getting one to accept something as good, by having and sharing a certain attitude and emotion, believing that a given course of action should be followed, or showing how a certain action should be performed. In its most elementary form, a book that does this may consist of little more than a set of rules, or it may aim at establishing the principles that govern the rules and setting the norm of what should be done. The latter is particularly the realm of civic and political persuasion and of philosophical and moral theology. In short, we are talking about the realm of practical thinking.

Books whose primary aim is to delight are primarily those of fiction, poetry, and imaginative literature. One reason for this is in the delight that the verbal construct possesses in itself, as well as the delight to be had from experiencing and sharing in the world that it presents.

From even so brief and general a statement of the three functions that books may perform, it becomes clear what their correlative arts are. The expositive form aiming at instructing and understanding, whether in history, science, or philosophy, makes the greatest demand for reasoning. Hence logic is its primary art and, in the case of scientific exposition, that status is assumed by the mathematical arts.

Books that aim at establishing a norm that should be followed call for much persuasion to be successful. Hence their primary art is rhetoric.

The aim of delighting through or by means of words, as exemplified in fiction and poetry, belongs more properly to the art of grammar than either theoretical or practical exposition do. It is more concerned with words: in the music of words as sounding in rhythm and tone; in the imaginary world that is constructed by words which one experiences by understanding them. Both theoretical and practical exposition work through and beyond their words either to the way things are or to the way they should and can become by our practice.

Since some of the liberal arts have more work to do in one kind of book than another, reading accordingly provides a way of strengthening one's hold upon the art each exemplifies. Doing mathematics through rigorous and active reading of scientific works provides an exercise in the use of those arts. The logic of reasoning and argument can be developed following the arguments, i.e., reasoning along with them, as presented in works of philosophy and history as well as those of science. By reading fiction and poetry and paying particular attention to the way words can be used to please ear, imagination, and mind, one can learn better the art of grammar.

Since books are great in large part because of the great art used in formulating and practicing what they in effect teach, they also provide the best means for developing greater skill in how to do that. They demand great art on the reader's part in reading and understanding them. But to see that this is so, there are two mistakes about reading that have to be corrected. Both come from identifying reading almost exclusively with the reading of imaginative literature.

The first mistake lies in the claim that each reader constructs his own text. It is true that in reading a text each reader performs an activity of his own that results in the understanding that he has of the text. But that this is a free construction on the part of the individual reader, having nothing in common with other readers and in no way determined by the text, is simply nonsense. In reading a mathematical text, one is not free to conclude as one likes. One has not understood, has *not read*, the text if he has not followed the steps by which the particular conclusion is reached. The same is true of scientific exposition, while greater differences of interpretation occur in the case of philosophical exposition.

In the reading of imaginative literature there is the greatest possibility of different readings and so also of individual responses. For this there are many reasons. One is that the verbal construction of that imaginary world presents human beings of different character, having a wide range of emotions, engaging in many different activities, and having results good or bad, terrifying or exalting. The reader's response, his reading of the text, will vary accordingly as he views and judges the things presented. One reader may like and admire the character of Little Dorrit while another may dislike, even despise, her.

Another cause of different readings lies in the language itself of fiction and poetry. It employs ambiguity and metaphor much more extensively than other kinds of reading, and this of itself provides ground for multiple interpretations. The fact that poetry and fiction pose more difficulty for translation than other forms of writing indicates their dependence upon the language in which they are originally written. Yet every translator is not free to do as he wishes. One translation is better than another, and it is better just because it is better and more adequately determined by the original text. The texts of mathematics and science raise no such problems for translation. They are transcultural in being readily portable from one culture to another. Whether a text is read correctly or not, especially as it is applied to technological invention, is pragmatically manifested by the success or failure of the invention.

The second mistake about reading derives from the same failure to distinguish between the ways a text is related to the language and culture of its origin. The mistake consists in the claim that all books, and especially great books, are culturally determined by the place and time of their origin. Great books of the Western world are great only in the West, according to this charge. Yet, as we have just seen in considering the theory of individual construction in reading, this is just not true. It is not true of books of science, mathematics, or logic. It is somewhat more true of philosophical works, especially those of moral and political philosophy, where different beliefs and practices affect judgment concerning the good; yet even in such matters the relativity is not complete.

Imaginative literature, especially poetry, is most bound to its culture. This is so mainly because of its close dependence upon the language in which it was written. It is difficult, and almost impossible, to appreciate the greatness of Virgil's *Georgics* when it is read in translation and not in its original Latin. This is less so, say of Shakespeare and Racine, since the characters, situations, and actions in their dramas can evoke more or less comparable responses whether read in translation or not. Yet something of the same difficulty as that with the *Georgics* remains. The English reader who knows no French has more difficulty in seeing the greatness of Racine's theater than does a French reader. The same holds for the French reader of Shakespeare who knows no English.

Yet however much a work of imaginative literature may depend upon the original language of its writing, that dependence is not complete. In any language, one poem or novel may be better than another. The fact that it is so arises from its meeting better the standards of the form it expresses as well as the conventions of that form. The *Iliad, Aeneid, Divine Comedy,* and *Paradise Lost* are each great as achievements of their own languages and cultures; but more than that, and more important, they are supremely great as poetic structures of the epic. Even in religion and theology, where the reading depends still more upon the beliefs of its reader, there remain objective standards of judgment, as Mortimer Adler has just demonstrated in his book entitled *Truth in Religion.* [14] Thus the charge of the cultural dependency and relativity of great books has little more justification than the now fashionable claim that each reader constructs his own text.

In short, the books that have gained a reputation as great have done so by being great achievements of the liberal arts. By exemplifying at the highest the work that these arts are capable of achieving, they can also provide their readers with a superior means of increasing their own command of those arts.

---

1. *Institutes of Oratory,* trans. John S. Watson (London: George Bell and Sons, 1875), I.X.1, p. 77.
2. *Retractationum Libri Duo,* in *Oeuvres de Saint Augustine,* vol. 12 (Paris, 1950), I.vi, p. 298, my translation.
3. *Martianus Capella and the Seven Liberal Arts: The Marriage of Philology and Mercury,* ed. William H. Stahl and Richard C. Johnson (New York: Columbia University Press, 1971).
4. *The Battle of the Seven Arts,* in *Memoirs of the University of California,* vol. 1, no. 4, ed. and trans. Louis J. Paetow (Berkeley: University of California Press, 1914), p. 34.
5. Cf. Otto Bird, *Cultures in Conflict* (Notre Dame, Ind.: University of Notre Dame Press, 1976), pp. 114–16.
6. Quintilian, *Institutes of Oratory,* II.1.4, p. 97.
7. *In Primum Librum Posteriorum Analyticorum Aristotelis Expositio* (Quebec: Laval University, 1944), pp. 1–2.
8. Quintilian, X.1.5–7.
9. Alfred North Whitehead and Bertrand Russell, *Principia Mathematica* (London: Cambridge University Press, 1925), vol. 1, p. 90.
10. Ibid.
11. *Development of Logic* (London: Oxford University Press, 1962), p. 740.
12. Whitehead and Russell, vol. 2, p. 203.
13. Kneale and Kneale, *Development of Logic,* pp. 739, 742.
14. (New York: Macmillan Publishing Company, 1990).

The Transcultural and the Multicultural

Mortimer J. Adler

Mortimer J. Adler, editor of *The Great Ideas Today,* is also chairman of the Board of Editors of Encyclopædia Britannica, Inc., and editor in chief of the 1990 edition of *Great Books of the Western World*. He was associate editor of the 1952 edition of these books, and in that capacity he presided over the staff that created *The Syntopicon,* now revised and expanded.

Dr. Adler is director of the Institute for Philosophical Research in Chicago, founded in 1952 for the study of ideas of Western thought. He is an honorary trustee of the Aspen Institute, where he teaches each summer.

A prolific writer, he has most recently produced *Haves Without Have-Nots* (1991) and the forthcoming *Desires Right and Wrong,* both published by Macmillan Company. His autobiography, *Philosopher at Large,* appeared in 1977, and a sequel is scheduled for publication next year.

What do "transcultural" and "multicultural" mean? Should we expect the domains they characterize to shift their boundaries in the years to come, the one expanding, the other contracting? Should matters that are now regarded as multicultural become transcultural in the future? I will try to answer these questions in the following pages.

In academic circles and in the sphere of public school reform, "multiculturalism" and "cultural diversity" are the buzz words of the '90s. They came into vogue very recently. At the moment they are the slogans or shibboleths which many different groups have emblazoned on their marching banners.

Associated with them are the words used for the foes that the multiculturalist would like to expunge or the demons they seek to exorcise. "Eurocentric" is the name for the traditional values of Western culture, a culture dominated by "dead white males" from Greek antiquity to the first half of the twentieth century in Europe and North America.

Recently my mail contained a half-dozen articles in popular periodicals or reprints from learned journals in which the pros and cons of multiculturalism are debated. My files are overflowing with similar pieces that have appeared since 1988. There may be a few a little earlier than that, but absolutely nothing at all will be found in the '70s or any earlier decade of this century.

The world, certainly, is multicultural, and so we should be taught about its cultural diversity. But this, it seems to me, is the time to ask whether society as a whole or its educational institutions should be multicultural in *all* respects, or only in *some*. If only in some, I propose that the word *transculturalism* should be employed for those respects in which multiculturalism or cultural pluralism should not be safeguarded or promoted. Confronting the antithesis of the multicultural and the transcultural, we should seek to understand what determines the line that divides the one from the other.

Let us begin by considering the cosmopolitan cities of the world, both in the United States and abroad—the cities whose populations are ethnically and culturally heterogeneous. What I am about to say concerning Chicago is true of New York, Dallas, and Los Angeles. It holds also for London, Paris, Toronto, Sydney, and Hong Kong.

For example, Chicago is multicultural in its restaurants but not in its hardware stores. A ruler or tape measure, in centimeters or inches, does not differ from one ethnically special neighborhood to another; nor does the candlepower of a light bulb and the difference between direct and alternating electric current. There is no difference between the tools used in Eurocentric and Afrocentric measurements as there are differences in French, Italian, Japanese, Chinese, and Thai cuisines. Clocks and calendars are the same in all sections of the city. They are the same everywhere in the world.

Chicago is multicultural in its churches but not in its engineering schools. If its educational institutions have courses in geography, in anthropology, or mythology, these are likely to be, or certainly should be, multicultural, but that is not the case with their courses in mathematics or physics.

The mathematics and physics taught in the schools of Japan, China, India, Egypt, and South America have the same scientific content as the mathematics and physics taught in Europe and North America. There are worldwide international journals in these fields, and the leading experts face no obstacles in communicating with one another.

Chicago's international airport is multicultural. The airports of London and Los Angeles are multicultural to an even greater degree. The planes that leave or land represent a large number of the world's diverse cultures in their interior fittings, the dress and the manners of their cabin attendants, but their pilots all communicate with the control towers everywhere in English and the technical jargon of ground-to-air talk is uniformly the same.

With these examples of the multicultural and the transcultural before us, what determines the line that divides the one from the other?

The dividing line is the same line that separates statements which contain such words as "I like" or "I prefer" from statements which contain the words "I know," or "my opinion is."

About likes or preferences there is no point in disputing. One set of likes or preferences does not exclude another.

But when individuals differ in their claims to know, or believe, they are obliged to submit to criteria for judging which of the conflicting claims is correct and which incorrect, or which is more correct than the other.

The line that divides the multicultural from the transcultural is the line that separates all matters of taste or preference from all matters concerned with the truth and falsity of the propositions being entertained or judged.

There are various forms and degrees of skepticism about truth. Complete or extreme skepticism consists in the denial that there is anything true or false. This is tantamount to denying that there is knowledge of anything, either with certainty (or beyond the shadow of a doubt) or with probability (or beyond a reasonable doubt or with some lower degree of doubt).

It follows that such extreme skepticism about truth and falsity entails the denial of anything transcultural. It removes the possibility of putting any restrictions on pluralism or upon the claims of the multiculturalist with regard to the content of education. There are, however, insuperable difficulties about being an extreme skeptic.

In the first place, the extreme skeptic refutes himself. The individual who asserts that there is nothing either true or false must confront the question whether that statement itself is either true or false. If it is true, then it is also false; and if it is false, then skepticism is itself denied. What does one do with a person who answers a question of a verifiable sort by saying both Yes and No? Walk away, for there is no profit in continuing the conversation.

In the second place, if the multiculturalist engages in argument with his opponents, does he not claim a degree of correctness for his views that deserves their predominance over opposing views? If so, then he cannot be a complete or extreme skeptic. If he does not claim that his views have any superiority with respect to truth or correctness, *what* is he arguing or *why* is he arguing? Should he not try to prevail simply by being in the majority and winning the dispute by the force of numbers? Might makes right, he might say.

In the third place, as David Hume pointed out centuries ago in abandoning extreme skepticism, one can be an extreme skeptic in the privacy of one's own closet, but not in one's daily dealings with others— not in conversation with them, not in business transactions with them, not in litigation with them, and so on. In no aspect of one's practical and social life can one honestly espouse extreme skepticism.

However, when David Hume abandoned extreme skepticism as impractical, he did not give up milder or more moderate forms of skepticism. If one or more of these are tenable, as complete skepticism is not, then they constitute challenges to the transcultural, for it is only with respect to that which is either certainly or probably true that anything can be transcultural.

The opponent of the skeptic holds that there are some objective and absolute truths. More moderate forms of skepticism maintain that there may be truths, but they are neither objective nor absolute but instead are subjective and relative.

What is the precise meaning of these words? The objective is that which is the same for you, for me, and for everyone else; the subjective is that which differs from individual to individual. The absolute is that which is the same at all times and places and regardless of changing circumstances; the relative is that which differs from one time to another, or with changing circumstances. Only if there is absolute truth is truth immutable.

One form of moderate skepticism consists in saying that what may be true for you is not true for me, and that's all there is to it. All truth is subjective, differing from individual to individual.

Another form of moderate skepticism consists in saying that what was once true is no longer true, or that what was once false is now true, and that's all there is to it. All truth is relative to changing times and circumstances; no truth is immutable.

The error in these two forms of moderate skepticism lies in the words "and that's all there is to it." What has been ignored is the distinction between propositions entertained and propositions judged, either affirmed or denied. The truth of the proposition as entertained is objective, absolute, and immutable. It is only the judgments we make about propositions that differ from individual to individual and change from time to time.

One example will suffice to make this point clear. Consider the proposition "The atom is divisible." Merely entertain it in your mind. Do not make any judgment or assertion that either affirms or denies it. This is easy to do. The statement "atoms are divisible" is clearly different from the statement "I think that atoms are divisible" or "I think that atoms are indivisible."

The history of atomism in physical theory can be summed up by saying that all physicists who were atomists, from Democritus in Greek antiquity down to the end of the nineteenth century, asserted that atoms were indivisible units of matter. The statement that atoms are divisible—or fissionable—would have been judged false by all of them. It is only in the twentieth century that atomic fission has been produced.

Was it true in all preceding centuries that atoms are divisible, or did it only become true in the twentieth century? The actual fission of atoms occurred only in the twentieth century, but in all preceding centuries atoms were fissionable, although no actual atomic fission had ever occurred before. What, then, should we say about judgments made by physicists before the twentieth century? That they were incorrect, because they affirmed as true that atoms are indivisible, which was then actually false. The truth about the divisibility of atoms has not changed; it is only scientific judgments that have changed.

In short, human judgments about what is factually true or false are both subjective, differing from individual to individual, and also relative, differing with the time of the judgment or with the relevant circumstances. Judgments about what is true or false are mutable, but not what is in fact true or false. If any proposition as entertained is ever true at any time and place, it is true always and everywhere. Only the judgments that human beings make about what is true or false differ from individual to individual and with different times and circumstances.

The error in the two forms of moderate skepticism just pointed out would be avoided if the words *true* and *false* were applied only to propositions as entertained, and the judgments human beings make about them were called "correct" and "incorrect."

What forms of skepticism remain that are tenable? They consist in specifically limited skepticisms. For example, those who deny that there is factual truth in any of the world's religions, or assert that all religions are mythologies misconstrued as being factually instead of poetically true, espouse specifically limited skepticism. Social scientists, and especially cultural anthropologists, who are skeptical about factual truth in religion are not skeptical about factual truth in science.

On the contrary, they are often dogmatic about the truth of scientific conclusions and are opposed by those who, while not being skeptical about truth in the natural sciences, are specifically skeptical about truth in the social sciences and in history.

The latter think, for example, that the knowledge achieved in physical science and in mathematics is transcultural (i.e., that all competent to judge in these fields of knowledge will concur in the same judgments regardless of their ethnic and cultural differences in other respects). They also think that, at the present time at least, there is no similarly transcultural knowledge in the social sciences, especially those with a historical perspective.

In the current controversy about multiculturalism in the courses offered in our educational institutions, it is these specifically limited skepticisms—about religion, philosophy, or one form of science or another—which must be considered. Only the specifically limited skepticisms that are correct indicate the extent to which the claims of the multiculturalist about desirable changes in the curriculum are tenable.

For example, if the specifically limited skepticism with respect to truth in religion is correct, then any instruction in the field of religion should be multicultural. If the specifically limited skepticism with respect to truth in the social sciences and in history is correct, then instruction in these fields should be multicultural.

Two forms of specifically limited skepticism have a crucial bearing on the current controversy.

One is specifically limited to the whole field of philosophy as opposed to the fields of experimental or empirical science; or, perhaps, it would be more accurate to define this skepticism as limited to any mode of philosophy that claims to be knowledge of reality, thus omitting modes of philosophy that restrict themselves to commenting on language as used in ordinary speech or in scientific discourse. To whatever extent logic and mathematics are inseparable, logic must be as transcultural as mathematics.

The other specifically limited skepticism applies to moral and political philosophy insofar as it makes claims to having prescriptive knowledge about what is good and bad, or right and wrong, in human conduct and in human societies. This skepticism is evident in those twentieth-century philosophers who regard ethics as noncognitive. They are philosophers who are themselves specifically skeptical about there being any objectively and universally valid truth in ethics.

Relevant here is the twentieth-century distinction between questions of fact and questions of value, or between factual assertions and value judgments. The skeptical position here consists in holding that there are no correct or incorrect value judgments because there are no entertainable prescriptive statements that are either true or false.

Relevant also is the fourth-century Aristotelian distinction between two kinds of truth—the truth of descriptive propositions (i.e., statements about what is or is not) and the truth of prescriptive propositions (i.e., statements about what ought or ought not to be sought or done).

In the case of descriptive statements, their truth, according to Plato and Aristotle, consists in affirming that that which is, is; and that that which is not, is not. Falsity is found in statements asserting that that which is not, is; or that that which is, is not.

This is the correspondence definition of truth (correspondence between thought and reality) that has prevailed in the Western tradition down to the pragmatic theory of truth, in which William James distinguished between the question of how truth should be defined and the question as to the criteria for telling whether a given statement is correctly judged to be true or false. An exception occurs in modern times with the rise of various forms of idealism and the denial of a reality that is independent of the human mind.

It should be obvious at once that the correspondence theory of truth applies only to descriptive statements about what is or is not the case. It cannot apply to prescriptive statements containing the words *ought* or *ought not*. Aristotle defined prescriptive truth as a different correspondence, not between thought and reality, but between thought and right desire.

It is not necessary here to explain or defend this definition of prescriptive truth. Suffice it to say that only if there is no prescriptive truth are the specifically limited skeptics about moral philosophy correct in thinking that all prescriptive statements are noncognitive—neither true nor false.

They are correct in thinking that they are neither true nor false *in terms of descriptive truth*. That, however, leaves open the possibility that Aristotle may be correct in thinking that there is another mode of truth in accordance with which questions of value—about what is right and wrong, good and bad—can be correctly answered by affirming prescriptive statements that, as entertained, are objectively and universally valid.

If statements about the conduct of a good human life can be objectively and universally valid, then there can be a transcultural ethics. If statements about how society should be organized and governed, in order to be good for human beings to live in, can be objectively and universally valid, then a normative or prescriptive political philosophy can be transcultural. It follows that instruction in these matters should not be multicultural. On the contrary, if there are no objectively and universally valid prescriptions in the field of ethics or politics, then descriptive instruction in these matters should be multicultural.

What are the instructional aims of proponents of multiculturalism in our institutions of learning, first, with respect to basic public schooling (K–12); and second, with respect to college curricula?

The multiculturalists may differ in their aims with respect to public schooling, but they all respond to the same set of facts. In the ethnically diverse and culturally heterogeneous large cities of this country, the school populations include children that come from black (or African-American) homes and from white homes having families of European origin. They also include Hispanics, Chinese, Japanese, and Koreans, and children in families from India, Southeast Asia, and the Arabic and Iranian Near East. For some time now, educators have responded to these facts by making efforts to acquaint this diversified school population with the plurality of ethnic backgrounds and cultural differences that go into the tapestry of American society, in which all the children will participate alike as citizens when they reach the age of consent.

In the summer 1990 issue of *The American Scholar,* Professor Diane Ravitch of Teachers College, Columbia University, published an article entitled "Multiculturalism: E Pluribus Plures." In it she distinguished between two forms of multiculturalism, calling the one "pluralistic" multiculturalism and the other "particularistic" multiculturalism and approving of the first while sharply disapproving of the second.

It is with the teaching of history in the public schools that she is most concerned, but one might have similar concerns about the teaching of social geography. Children should be taught history and geography so that they are made aware of the mixture of ethnic and cultural diversities that have entered into the fabric of American life. They should be made conscious of the contributions of their own forebears to this mixture and take pride in the characteristic traits of the human subgroup that they themselves represent, while at the same time recognizing that those representing other human subgroups among their classmates share the common humanity that makes them all deserving of equal status and treatment.

This applies to subjects that are themselves intrinsically transcultural because they are bodies of objectively valid knowledge, such as mathematics, the natural sciences, and their derivative technologies. The application occurs not in the teaching of these sciences as bodies of knowledge but rather in teaching the history of these sciences.

Here the children should learn that many different cultural groups, especially in antiquity, contributed to the development of mathematics, physics, and astronomy. They should be impressed with the fact that these sciences are not solely of Greek and Roman origin. Contributions to the development of mathematics and astronomy come from ancient Egypt, Mesopotamia, and India, not just Greece. Eurocentrism is thus alleviated, if not cured. Such teaching of the early developments in mathematics and natural science is not inconsistent with the present transcultural character of the disciplines themselves.

What Professor Ravitch calls "particularistic" as opposed to "pluralistic" multiculturalism is, in her view, not multiculturalism at all. It lays stress on one particular human subgroup to the exclusion from consideration of others in the mixture that constitutes our pluralistic American culture.

In educational circles, for example, a group of militant African-Americans are acting as a political lobby for giving the African-American children in our schools a diet of legends about African-American origins of much, if not all, of the treasures that have, in the past, been attributed exclusively to Western European civilization. This is intended to counteract the Eurocentrism of traditional teaching; but at the same time it ignores the fact that whatever truth can now be attributed to mathematics, the natural sciences, technology, moral philosophy, and even religion is now transcultural. It is not the private cultural property of any human subgroup.

Professor Ravitch tells us that such particularism "is unabashedly filiopietistic." It teaches black children that the American pluralistically multicultural society in which they live

> is not their own culture, even though they were born here. That American culture is "Eurocentric," and therefore hostile to anyone whose ancestors are not European. Perhaps the most invidious implication of particularism is that racial and ethnic minorities are not and should not try to be part of American culture; it implies that American culture belongs only to those who are white and European; it implies that those who are neither white nor European are alienated from American culture by virtue of their race or ethnicity; it implies that the only culture they do belong to or can ever belong to is the culture of their ancestors, even if their families have lived in this country for generations.

Professor Ravitch goes on to say that "the war on so-called Eurocentrism is intended to foster self-esteem among those who are not of

European descent," but she questions whether in fact it actually works that way; for, in her view,

> the children of American society today will live their lives in a racially and culturally diverse nation, and their education should prepare them to do so. . . . [The] particularists have no interest in extending or revising American culture; indeed, they deny that a common culture exists . . . [and] reject any accommodation among groups, any interactions that blur the distinct lines between them. The brand of history that they espouse is one in which everyone is either a descendant of victims or oppressors.

We turn now from the controversy at the level of public schools, between the pluralistic multiculturalists and the antipluralistic particularists, to the controversy about multiculturalism at the college level.

This controversy focuses on the books that should be a part of one's general education. It is a dispute about the traditionally recognized canon of the monuments of Western literature in all fields—works of mathematics and science as well as works of poetry, drama, and fiction, and also works of biography, history, philosophy, and theology. Here we are confronted with current attacks upon the canonical list of great books and the responses that those attacks have elicited.

I am involved in this controversy—as associate editor of the first edition of the *Great Books of the Western World,* published in 1952, and as editor in chief of the second, much expanded edition, published in 1990.

The second edition differed from the first in many respects: new translations, a revised *Syntopicon,* and six volumes of twentieth-century authors that did not appear in the first edition, as well as fifteen authors added in the period from Homer to Freud. As in the case of the first edition, so in the case of the second, our Editorial Board and the large group of advisers whom we consulted did not agree unanimously about the authors to be included; but in both cases there was ninety-percent agreement. That, in my judgment, is all one can expect in a matter of this kind.

I would like to call attention to two things about the second edition. In writing an introductory essay, which appeared in a volume that accompanied the set, entitled *The Great Conversation,* I anticipated the controversy that the second edition of the *Great Books of the Western World* would arouse. This did not arise before. In the 1940s, when we were engaged in producing the first edition, "Eurocentric" was not current as a disapprobative term. There was no hue and cry about the absence of female authors; nor had blacks cried out for representation in the canon. In those earlier decades of this century, students and teachers in our colleges and educators in general were not concerned with multiculturalism in our educational offerings.

The second edition contains female authors, some in the nineteenth and some in the twentieth century, but no black authors; and it is still exclusively Western (i.e., European or American authors) with none from the four or five cultural traditions of the Far East.

The controversy over the desirability of multiculturalism having arisen in the late 1980s, I took account of it in my introductory essay, pointing out carefully the criteria in terms of which the authors were selected for inclusion, explaining the difference between the five hundred or so *great* works included in the set and the thousands of *good* books listed in the Recommended Readings at the end of each of the 102 chapters in *The Syntopicon*. These lists included many female and many black authors, but none still from the Far East.

These exclusions were not, and are not, invidious. The difference between *great* and *good* books is one of kind, not of degree. Good books are not "almost great" or "less than great" books. Great books are relevant to human problems in every century, not just germane to current twentieth-century problems. A great book requires to be read over and over, and has many meanings; a good book needs to have no more than one meaning, and it need be read no more than once.

I also explained but did not apologize for the so-called Eurocentrism of the *Great Books of the Western World* by pointing out why no authors or works from the four or five distinct cultural traditions in the Far East were included or should be included. The Western authors are engaged in a great conversation across the centuries about great ideas and issues. In the multicultural traditions of the Far East, there are, perhaps, as many as four or five great conversations about different sets of ideas, but the authors and books in these different cultural traditions do not combine these ideas in one Far Eastern tradition, nor do they participate in the great conversation that has occurred over the last twenty-five centuries in the West. There are undoubtedly great, as distinguished from good, books in all of these Far Eastern traditions.

I did not anticipate that those who responded to the publication of the second edition by challenging its Eurocentrism or complaining about the fact that its authors were still for the most part dead white males, with few females and no blacks, would do so entirely in terms of announcements in the press of the list of included authors, and without reading my introductory essay and without knowing that a large number of female and black authors were included in the 102 lists in *The Syntopicon* of *good* books cited as readings recommended in addition to the great books included in the set, along with many other books by white males, none of them regarded as great.

I should mention one other point that is highly germane to the controversy. Many of those who criticize the traditional canon of great books and call for its rejection incorrectly suppose that its defenders claim that it is a repository of transcultural truth and nothing else. That is not the case. The editors and advisory consultants of the *Great Books of the Western World* know that there is much more error or falsity in the intellectual and cultural tradition of the West than there is truth.

The relation of truth to error is a one–many relation; for every truth, there are many deviations from it that are false. What truth is to be found is, of course, transcultural. The multiple errors, some of them multicultural, that impinge on each truth are of great importance for the understanding of the truth. Without grappling with the errors, one's understanding of the truth that corrects them is shallow. It follows that if the truths to be found in the great books of the West are transcultural, so, too, must be the understanding of the errors, some of which will be discovered in the Far East.

I turn now from the controversy about the second edition of the *Great Books of the Western World* to the controversy that has very recently arisen concerning what books should be required reading in colleges that still have some interest in the general, as opposed to the specialized, education of their students. This controversy started at Stanford University in 1988 and has spread since then to other colleges across the country.

The public prints and the electronic media have given the controversy ample notice, and its pros and cons have been publicly debated. A desirable multiculturalism has been appealed to as the basis not only for including many recent books by female, black, and non-Western authors but also for eliminating from the required readings a large number of authors and books that have long been treasured as Western greats, especially authors and books in classical antiquity, in the Middle Ages, and in modern times up to the nineteenth century.

Unquestionably among the books that have been recommended for addition, some contain recently discovered or restated truths that correct errors to be found in books of earlier centuries. If so, who could reasonably object to such additions? No one. But the same cannot be said for the recommended deletions from the list of required readings— Plato and Aristotle, for example, Herodotus, Thucydides, and Gibbon; Homer, Virgil, Dante, Shakespeare, and Tolstoy; Marcus Aurelius, Rabelais, Montaigne, Hobbes, Locke, Rousseau, and John Stuart Mill. All of these dead white males made important contributions to the pursuit of truth, even if there was much error in their insights, their principles, or their conclusions. Why, then, should many of them, or any of them, be rejected, if their inclusion does not call for the rejection of twentieth-century books written by female or black authors?

If general education is to include not just Western civilization but the other great cultures of the world in the Far East, a question still remains. If Western civilization is included as one of many in the multicultural mélange, why exclude Western authors and books long recognized as truly great for their contribution to the pursuit and understanding of truth?

It may be said, of course, that there is not enough time to include these older authors if twentieth-century authors and Far Eastern authors are also to be added to the required readings. It may be said that general education should be given up and no readings at all should be required for that purpose.

But it should not be said, as some of the proponents of multiculturalism seem to think, that truth is merely what some people assert. And that they would like to be the ones to assert what is true, or elect those who are to assert it. Or, if objective truth is held to exist somewhere, it is in natural science, but not in speculative philosophy, theology, or religion, and especially not in moral philosophy, which is concerned with questions of value—good and evil, right and wrong, what ought to be sought and done.

For such multiculturalists, these are all held to be matters of subjective personal predilection. They are not matters of public knowledge, not even knowledge with residual doubt, but only private or individual opinion, unsupported by the weight of evidence or reasons. What is or is not desirable is, therefore, entirely a matter of taste (about which there should be no disputing), not a matter of truth which can be disputed in terms of empirical evidence and reasons.

That being the case, we are left with a question that should be embarrassing to the multiculturalists, though they are not likely to feel its pinch. When they proclaim the desirability of the multicultural, they dispute about matters that should not be disputed. What, then, can possibly be their grounds of preference? Since in their terms it cannot appeal to any relevant body of truth, what they demand in the name of multiculturalism must arise from a wish for power or a belief that their self-esteem will be somehow served.

When dispute on a basis of empirical evidence or by appeal to rational grounds is ruled out, conflicting claims can only be resolved by power politics, either by force or by dominance of a majority. In either case, it comes down to might makes right. That is exactly what is happening today in the efforts of the multiculturalists to change the curriculum in the public schools and in our colleges.

Multiculturalism is cultural pluralism. In the twentieth century, pluralism has become part of the democratic ideal, opposed to the monolithic totalitarianism that is now being challenged in the Soviet Union, and also to the equally monolithic rigidity of Islamic, Jewish, or Christian fundamentalism.

While democracy and socialism, and with them pluralism, are ideal in the social and economic dimensions of society, cultural pluralism is not wholly desirable in other dimensions of our life. What is desirable is a *restricted* cultural pluralism; that is, the promotion and preservation of pluralism in all matters of taste, but not in any matters that are concerned with objectively valid truth, either descriptive factual truth or prescriptive normative truth.

In this century, mathematics, the hard-core natural sciences, and their attendant technologies have become transcultural. What truth they have so far attained is at present acknowledged everywhere on earth. Whether or not, in the next century or in a more distant future, transcultural truth will be attained in philosophy, in the social sciences, in institutional history, and even in religion is an open question that should not be dogmatically answered by the present breed of multiculturalists whose unrestricted pluralism substitutes power or might for truth and right in the effort to control what should be taught or thought.

PART THREE

Special Features

The State of Christian Theology in North America

William J. Abraham

William J. Abraham was educated at Portora Royal School in Enniskillen, Northern Ireland. After studying psychology, philosophy, and theology, he received his doctorate in philosophical theology from the University of Oxford. Prior to coming to Perkins School of Theology at Southern Methodist University in Dallas, he taught at Culham College, Oxford, and Seattle Pacific University, Seattle. He now teaches philosophy of religion, systematic theology, and evangelism at Perkins.

Professor Abraham has written five books, including *Divine Revelation and the Limits of Historical Criticism* (1982), *An Introduction to the Philosophy of Religion* (1985), and *The Logic of Evangelism* (1989). He is currently engaged in research on the logic of ecclesial and spiritual renewal, divine agency and divine action, and canon and norm in Christian theology.

A shrewd friend from Ireland who is currently attempting to revitalize an old, dying Methodist church in North Carolina remarked caustically to me recently that we were due for another bout from the theologians any day now. Undoubtedly his mind was flooded with memories of the sixties when theologians had declared with enthusiasm that we needed a new Reformation, or that the church was destined to disappear off the face of the planet, or that God had recently died. I was a little embarrassed by his comment. I make my living in part by teaching theology, and I could not in the least assure him that my colleagues would necessarily disappoint his implied predictions.

Current assessments

Summaries of the trade tend to confirm this assessment. We have been told that the spectrum has been shattered, [1] and that we have come to the end of the line. [2] One leading American philosopher entitled his devastating review of a \recently acclaimed book on theology as "Sheehan's Shenanigans: How Theology Becomes Tomfoolery." [3]

Another perceptive commentator, Van A. Harvey, who was once a leading insider in theology, and who wrote one of the best books to be produced in his generation on the relation between faith and history, [4] began a recent review of the state of contemporary theology with this unflattering comment:

> There are few Protestant Christian theologians in the United States who would not concede that the intellectual enterprise called theology has fallen on evil days in their own country. It is not merely that the basic themes, categories, and types of argumentation of theology are regarded as irrelevant by most intellectuals, but that theological argumentation has virtually become a forgotten and lost mode of discourse. [5]

Yet another leading insider, John B. Cobb, Jr., who has made a distinguished contribution to theology over the last generation, has recently concluded that the great promise of the postwar generation was not fulfilled.

My generation received from its predecessors a great heritage. The
generation of Barth and Bultmann, of Tillich and the Niebuhrs in
theology, and of Heidegger and Sartre, Wittgenstein and Whitehead
in philosophy, will long appear as a special and remarkable one. We
saw ourselves as critical heirs of a great tradition of theological work—
progressive and open-minded, yet deeply rooted in our heritage. We
saw our responsibility as appropriating this tradition critically and
constructively and passing it on to future generations. But now, forty
years later, we see that we have not succeeded. Today the situation is
polarizing in a way that leaves this theological project on the sidelines in
both church and academy. The churches and many of their theologians
are swinging to the right, largely ignoring the more critical challenges to
faith. On the other side, most of those truly sensitive to these challenges
have largely repudiated the task of constructing a theology for the
church. Whereas we once saw ourselves as in the mainstream of religious
reflection in this country, those who now follow in our basic program
are clearly but one small embattled element in the wider scene of
religious studies and reflection. [6]

As Cobb suggests here, many theologians see themselves as deeply
alienated from the church, and some are very uneasy with the present
direction of the whole theological enterprise. Some have taken refuge
in ancillary disciplines like religious studies or literary criticism. I wonder if this is not jumping out of the frying pan and into the fire. I
know of one theologian whose commitment to serious work in theology
initially led him to flee to a department of religious studies. In time
he fled from there and escaped to the philosophy department. He felt
that there, at least, he could still be committed to the life of the mind,
and he would avoid what he judged to be the intellectual corruption of
relativism which he saw as widespread in the field of religion. Even that
may now be a vain solution to his initial problem.

Certainly, there is a sense in the culture at large that theology is
mostly an ailing enterprise. This has little or nothing to do with the
scandals associated with television religion. The latter do not even make
a pretense of theological inquiry, serious or otherwise. Everyone knows
that the meager cognitive resources they have are really a public relations exercise designed to create an aura of respectability and help roll
in the dollars. Rather, the disillusionment about theology stems in part
from the obvious fact that there are no theological giants abroad in the
land anymore. There is nowhere the equivalent of a Jonathan Edwards
in the eighteenth century, or a Horace Bushnell in the nineteenth
century, or a Reinhold Niebuhr in the earlier half of the twentieth
century.

Many felt this keenly even in the seventies. When I was a graduate
student at Oxford in the mid-seventies, we used to play an informal
game of trying to identify a modern theological text to which we
would unreservedly refer inquiring laypersons if they asked for a really

good book on theology. We never came up with anything. This may have been a matter of intellectual arrogance or ignorance on our part, yet I am not at all sure that the situation has really changed since then. [7] As one leading English sociologist, a scholar with no commitment to theism or Christianity, once graphically expressed it to me after a lecture: "Modern theologians are so worried about being kicked in the ditch by the modern world that they hastily jump into it to avoid this fate." [8] By this I took him to mean that theologians are so keen to be up-to-date and so afraid of being caught appearing out of step with current academic orthodoxies that they do not cultivate their own independent convictions in a thorough way.

To be sure, this judgment is overdrawn. It needs to be tempered by a variety of considerations. First, splendid work is being done in the vast array of disciplines which are cultivated within theology. Intellectually invigorating work is being executed in biblical studies, in church history, in theological ethics, and the like.

Second, any evaluation of modern theology will inevitably reflect the prepossessions and prejudices of the judge offering it. Part of the predicament of the modern theologian and his or her critic is precisely that there is no agreement on the data and warrants to be deployed in assessing the state of modern theology. Prima facie it looks as if one is expressing one's sense of taste rather than offering a genuinely intellectual analysis. To entertain this line is, of course, a counsel of despair which we need not take very seriously. Theology clearly belongs in the humanities, and it is a commonplace judgment that in this area it is extremely difficult to separate the criteria used in competing proposals from one's own personal proposals. This only becomes otiose, however, if one is not prepared to subject one's own convictions to intellectual scrutiny and challenge.

Third, complaining of the absence of theological giants betrays in itself a certain view of the theological enterprise. It assumes that theology is an individualistic affair which is best executed by the autonomous theologian alone in the ivory tower minting new theological materials. Yet it is precisely this which has been called into question of late. It is becoming increasingly common to have courses offered on theological movements rather than on particular theologians. This is a fascinating development, and we will need to dig below the surface to see what it entails for our understanding of the theological task.

Despite all these disclaimers, what is remarkable is the extraordinary consensus in many quarters about the low estate of modern theology. Even with a substantial catalog of qualifications, it would take a sturdy optimist to argue that modern theology is in satisfactory shape. When it comes to a coherent, comprehensive vision of the great themes which have been the marrow of theology in the past—say, revelation, creation, and redemption—it is extremely difficult to overturn the analysis offered above. In short, good systematic renderings of the Christian faith are extremely hard to find.

Presupposed here is a certain minimal understanding of the nature of systematic theology. The task is not to provide a theology of this or that area of life, say, a theology of work, or justice, or play. The task is to lay out an orderly account of what the Christian community is to teach as constituting its basic, normative vision of God, creation, salvation, the church, and the like. Theologians have been doing this from at least the time of the catechetical lectures given in the early church. This enterprise has generally been seen as the crown of the intellectual life of the church, for the challenge is to lay out a vision which will be at once Christian and credible. The task is to gather up the relevant data and evidence and forge a presentation of the Christian faith which will stand alongside those of Thomas, Calvin, Friedrich Schleiermacher, or Karl Barth. At critical turning points, say, in the battle against Gnosticism in the early centuries, or in the crisis precipitated by the Reformers, the church has found it indispensable to provide such a vision. It is from within such a vision that the church expresses and orders its life and mission before God and in the world.

Mapping the current terrain

In what follows I shall seek to attempt to identify and assess the state of play in this arena. For the most part I shall limit the field to current work in North America. [9] The exception to this involves a group of Anglo-American scholars who are a genuinely transatlantic coalition. I make no claim to be comprehensive. Indeed one of the intriguing features of the current scene is the fact that North American theology has come into its own, and it is well-nigh impossible to cover the territory in all its length and breadth. The tendency heretofore was to look to Europe for inspiration and then put a North American spin to the chosen hero. Efforts along these lines nowadays are probably doomed to fail. For example, a major attempt in the late sixties to absorb the theology of Jürgen Moltmann, one of the leading theologians in Germany at the moment, did not materialize. A current foray into the North American scene by one of Moltmann's key rivals, Wolfhart Pannenberg, is likely to suffer the same fate. One of the genuine novelties of the present situation is that some European theologians now actually look to North America for fresh light and inspiration.

As we proceed it is worth pausing to identify a crucial assumption which has governed the conventions of academic theology for at least two centuries in the West. The assumption is that the primary task of theology is to take the essentials of the Christian tradition and express those essentials in the language and thought forms of the culture or environment of the time. The fundamental goal is to be faithful to the tradition and relevant to the culture. This accounts for an obvious feature of the present situation, namely, radical pluralism. Theologians differ in very deep ways on how to satisfy the two conditions of faithfulness to tradition and credibility in the modern world.

Process theology

The tendency a generation ago was to worry more about credibility than about the tradition. In a splendid review of a half-century of theology written in the mid-sixties, the perceptive Carl Michalson astutely observed that theology in North America was a pluralistic affair in search of a new identity. [10] He identified four major schools or movements. Process theology, represented by Schubert M. Ogden and Cobb, attempted to develop a metaphysical naturalism inspired by the brilliant English philosopher and mathematician Alfred N. Whitehead. The goal was to express the Christian faith in the categories of a mature philosophy which would spell out an intimate connection between the world and God and which would offer a redemption that related positively to the tragedy and suffering of the world. Hermeneutical theology, represented by James M. Robinson, took a very different line. It construed faith as itself a mode of understanding. The truth of faith is not brought to light by expressing it in terms of some theory of reality; the truth is what is brought to light in the events which are constitutive of faith. Theology is more like poetry in that the events of faith, the life of Christ, for example, evoke or bring to birth their own unique light. A third school, which Michalson identified as secularizing theology and which was represented by Paul Van Buren and Harvey Cox, focused intentionally on the meaning of the faith for "secular man." This could mean finding a rendering of the faith which would be empirically verifiable, or one which would make sense to those who revel in the reality of the modern city and feel they no longer need God. Finally, there was the "death of God" theology, represented by William Hamilton and Thomas J. Altizer. Here one experiences the complete collapse of the tradition in which the cry of dereliction, "My God, my God, why hast thou forsaken me?" is taken as the end of God's presence in the world. We now simply have to come to terms with the absence of God even from faith.

The only one to survive into the new generation in a substantial way has been process theology. The others are now historical curiosities. The process tradition is diverse enough to house a coalition of themes and interests, but in terms of sheer intellectual horsepower it is best represented by Ogden, who for a time was Paul Tillich's successor at the University of Chicago. [11]

Christian theology, for Ogden, is an essentially critical enterprise which evaluates putative efforts at explicit Christian witness in terms of two criteria: its adequacy to re-present the earliest witness to Christ as reconstructed by rigorous historical investigation, and its truthfulness as determined by universal norms of truth given with human existence itself. [12] The former can be seen as a radicalization of the Lutheran account of canonicity, in that it makes what preaches Christian salvation the ultimate norm of the Christianness of any theological proposal. The latter expresses the Enlightenment goal of universal reason; in Ogden's constructive philosophical proposals it leads him to embrace the metaphysical position staked out by Whitehead and Charles Hartshorne.

Over a lifetime of teaching Ogden has established a loyal band of disciples which stretches all the way from Texas to Korea. Yet his theology has had limited impact on the church. In part this is because his style is austere to the point of being impenetrable. More generally it stems from the extent to which Ogden's revisions of the Christian message leave it so minimalist and reduced that one has difficulty seeing how it could begin to nourish the life and ministry of the church in a really deep fashion. It is difficult for Christian ministers, for example, to officiate at a funeral and maintain any deep continuity with the past when eternal life is reduced to the possibility that one will be remembered to all eternity in the mind of God. Eternal life must surely be more than ending up on God's floppy disk forever. The full canonical claims of the faith cannot be so readily set aside as incredible or redundant.

Yet the reason for this reductionism is clear. Where in the past such claims were logically related to the promises of God in revelation, Ogden has eliminated revelation as an epistemological category from the language of theology. Christian canons such as scripture or creed can in principle now only function as criteria of religious identity, and even then they are reduced from their rich variety to the "original" apostolic witness to Christ. They are not grounded in any unique source of insight or information. Strictly speaking, theological truth can only be grounded in universal criteria of rationality. Once these are applied to the vast body of Christian tradition, not much remains as true, although Ogden would quickly insist that this and only this is the ultimate issue worth pressing. Nor is it clear that we will ever know what remains of the Christian tradition, for Ogden is still so preoccupied with questions of method and with the establishing of a rational, theistic metaphysics that we may never see the full flowering of his position. If this is true, it is a matter of regret for Ogden is undoubtedly one of the most conscientious theologians one is likely to meet.

Another problem with Ogden's position is that it appears to be tied to the fortunes of what is generally known as foundationalism in the field of epistemology. According to this view, it is essential that all claims to knowledge be grounded in evidence. Nothing is allowed to stand unless it can be shown to be true by the canons of reason or experience. The last decade of philosophy has seen a major attack on this whole enterprise, so Ogden's obsession with getting the foundations straight looks to many like shoveling melting snow. Moreover, it prevents a really deep hearing of the tradition in its own terms before it is run through the tightly drawn nets of an outdated theory of knowledge. Foundationalism in its modern guises invariably sets unfounded and unnecessarily restricted limits to what we can know, so that theological material which does not fit the mold is re-presented to echo a position which has already been determined in advance.

Critical orthodoxy

The response of many ordinary believers to both Ogden and those whom he has intellectually outlived is not very enthusiastic. Some are simply angry that the faith of the church can be set aside in order to make room for the findings of the latest esoteric philosopher. Some of the anger stems from the general plight of the modern believer. Ordinary Christians are only partially aware of the existence of systematic theology. Even when they are aware of it they are not likely to know what it is. Most Christians adopt their faith either through absorbing the faith in the family or through conversion. They are not initially privy to the labors of academic teachers. Most of them do not have the first clue about the internal life of seminaries or schools of theology. They often harbor the friendly illusion that schools of theology are oases of deep piety and of enthusiastic commitment. Indeed, if they come to a seminary, they may nurture this illusion for several years, constantly confused and baffled.

Their theological position might be generally described as the common sense of Christendom. They have picked up various bits and pieces of Christianity from the Bible, church feasts, hymns, the classical creeds of the church, sermons, television, and a limited amount of reading. Rarely have they put this together into a coherent vision. What they believe is a basic story of creation and redemption, of incarnation and salvation, of love, forgiveness, and a vague immortality. They cannot articulate this very well, but they know it when they see it. They are very quickly captivated by the writings of C. S. Lewis, for example, whose concept of mere Christianity has helped many to get a hold on their basic beliefs for the first time. [13]

Beyond that, modern Western Christians are restless souls who are constantly on the search for something deeper and more authentic. They are insecurely grounded in the faith, and they are distrustful of professional theologians. Their commonsense version of Christianity has taken a beating over the last generation, and they know it. They

Seminary students in a relaxed moment at their refectory, after breakfast.

are astonished to find a theologian who can preach the gospel with conviction or can speak in accessible discourse. One suspects that the gap between academic lectern and the pew is much wider than it was a generation ago, when many ordinary Christians after a superficial boon in religion felt good about the world and were hungry for relevance. Thus they were more ready to seek out those who could express the content of the faith in predominantly modern categories.

It would be very unwise to underestimate the strength and tenacity of the faith of the ordinary believer. I suspect that it constitutes a fragile bridge of continuity across the years. So long as the church has a canon of scripture and a relatively stable liturgical life, then the common sense of the Christian tradition is unlikely to disappear. Moreover, in every generation there is usually a group of theologians who happily give themselves to handing on the general faith of the church. This is often seen as a reactionary operation, but it clearly has a vital part to play in the transmission of the Christian heritage across the generations. In the present scene several theologians have taken this route and together have produced a solid body of ecumenical theology. Especially noteworthy is the work of Geoffrey Wainwright, [14] Thomas C. Oden, [15] Carl E. Braaten and Robert W. Jenson, [16] Gabriel Fackre, [17] and James W. McClendon. [18] In their own way these writers have continued the agenda of the mid-century. Taking on board the critical aspirations and studies of the mediating theologians of the last century, they have sought to retrieve and express the theology of the early Fathers, the Reformers, and the lesser known figures of the Evangelical Awakenings, like John Wesley and Edwards. They are suspicious of modernist tactics in theology, they are uneasy with alliances with philosophical systems, they eschew the narrowness of fundamentalism, and they still entertain hopes that the Christian churches may yet unite under the auspices of the apostolic consensus which emerged in the patristic era. The support for this within the higher echelons of the World Council of Churches is not inconsiderable. [19]

It is worthwhile to pause and look for a moment at the work of Oden. [20] Oden currently teaches at Drew University (Madison, N.J.) and has been a prolific writer, opening up new vistas, for example, in pastoral theology. [21] For years he appeared to mirror the current fashion, so that his return to a traditional orthodoxy could easily have been read as his embracing one more popular fad. His conversion, however, is a deep one, and he is currently embarked on a three-volume work which is the prelude to a major study of the theological legacy of Wesley. The last volume of his systematic theology has not yet been published, but the whole thrust of his work is very clear. Oden's strategy is to summarize the ecumenical consensus of the church on the key topics which have been the marrow of theology for centuries. He provides a crisp overview of the terrain, identifies clearly his rendering of the central claims of the classical Christian tradition, and lards the text with a wealth of references and quotations from the great theologians of the past.

The great value of this exercise is that it gives the reader a useful review of what the church has formally decided and what major theologians of the past have believed. This is a great service to have rendered, especially to those who need a guide through the maze of what has been said in the past. However, there are at least three difficulties to be faced. First, there is a tendency to gloss over the divisions which exist within what is said by those who are identified as classical or ecumenical teachers of the church. To be sure, it is clearly the case that the schism in the church brought about in the West by the Enlightenment may well be the most crucial schism of all. Compared to this, the division between East and West, and within the West the division between Protestant and Roman Catholic, may well be inconsequential divisions. However, this does not dispel the doubt that Oden is shaping the traditions of the past to make them look much more in agreement than they really are.

Second, there is a tendency to ignore the deep challenges to the tradition which have been in place for two centuries, and which deserve an answer. Oden is familiar with, say, the objections to any traditional conception of special revelation, or, say, the impact of the inner logic of historical study on claims about God's action in the world, but more is required to satisfy such concerns than he has been able to provide.

Third, Oden needs to provide a much more rigorous account of the nature, method, and task of theology as a whole. More particularly, he needs to provide a deeper account of those issues that cluster around the topic of biblical authority and the justification of religious belief. In the absence of these, students will gravitate toward theologians who have raised deep questions about the viability of the tradition as a whole and have worked out a thorough set of answers to the methodological questions that inevitably arise within theology. Those who want to return to a traditional orthodoxy will appear to be merely repeating past answers to outdated questions unless they can turn a corner at this point in the discussion. Not unnaturally, they will be dismissed as irrelevant and reactionary.

The quest for liberation

Process theology and critical orthodoxy represent significant minority reports in the contemporary conversation. We will turn later on to other minority reports. It is time now, however, to take up what we can identify as the most favored option on the modern scene. In what initially follows I will attempt to paint a composite picture of what we might call the predominant academic orthodoxy in modern theology in

North America. Insofar as there is a modern orthodoxy, there is no doubt but that it is some version of liberation theology. We are not speaking here of an exotic import from Latin America, although the inspiration for much liberation theology clearly lies there. It lies also to some extent in the political theologies of modern Europe. We have in mind a distinctive voice from within North America which deserves to be heard on its own terms. [22]

It is fair and fitting to speak of there being such an orthodoxy, even though it would be difficult to establish this conclusively. Clues to its existence show up in a variety of places. They are manifest in the jargon which new students feel they have to adopt to be acceptable, in the code words of the policies which currently govern conventions for hiring new faculty, in the scrutiny currently extended to reading lists for new courses, in the topics most likely to occasion defense or attack, and in the extent to which other options cast themselves as a version of liberation theology, as has happened, for example, in the case of Ogden. [23]

The predominant orthodoxy begins with the rejection of the classical Christian tradition as that is generally known in Western culture. Here there is much affinity with the major movements of theology of the last generation. Traditional Christianity is, strictly, incredible. It is committed to a patriarchal deity who is supposed to have intervened in the world in Israel and in Christ for its redemption here and hereafter. Such a theology is otiose. Invented by the patriarchal leadership of a patriarchal community, its fundamental claims have been shattered by the canons of science and critical history. The history of science and humankind has taught us that God does not act in the gaps of nature or experience. If we want to know what has really happened in either domain we turn to the relevant disciplines of science and history. Neither can allow for the direct activity of God. This is ruled out either because critical history cannot allow for such categories, or because such categories are intimately connected with a perspective of the past which is culturally relative and now out-of-date.

Any theology we build must therefore be constructed after we have carried out the prerequisite work in these areas, according to this view. In doing so we cannot make allowances for any kind of divine revelation as traditionally conceived. The classical theologies of both Roman Catholicism and Protestantism depended at this juncture on a doctrine of divine revelation. It was generally held that God had acted decisively in word and deed to reveal His intentions and purposes for the creation and the salvation of the world. There was disagreement, of course, on the scope and locus of this revelation. Protestants limited it to scripture; Roman Catholics extended it further into the life of the church through councils and the pope. There was also disagreement on how this revelation was to be related to reason. Catholics tended to look for harmony between faith and reason and the perfection of nature by grace. Protestants were more ambivalent, swinging from one extreme to the other. At times they made common cause with reason when they constructed various kinds of natural theology, or when they looked to miracles and prophecy as proofs that a revelation had actually occurred. At other times they rejected any positive relation between faith and reason.

All this has been swept aside. It is simply no longer possible, according to much American liberation theology, to believe in a patriarchal deity who sent his son into the world to save us from the original sin and guilt of Adam, and who will intervene again in some climactic act to inaugurate a new heaven and a new earth. Any kind of traditional theology as enshrined, say, in the classical creeds of the church is therefore impossible. To cling to it is to be a theological fundamentalist, and every schoolchild now knows, or is supposed to know, that fundamentalism is the Western version of theological escapism and ignorance. In many circles this is not even taken seriously as a legitimate option. Moreover, the whole theological enterprise can no longer rest on a doctrine of revelation. Insofar as there can be intellectual foundations for theology, the only legitimate options are those which can be located in some account of experience, construed as sociopolitical practice, and reason, construed as political and philosophical reflection. If we are to speak of revelation at all, it can only be in terms of an emerging new awareness or consciousness of the divine which develops in the actual course of history itself.

If one rejects the common faith of Christendom, however, what then is the theologian to do? Certainly one can look the other way and ignore the mediating theologies of past and present; but one cannot reject the tradition completely. To go that far would be to abandon theology entirely. So the task is to reinterpret the tradition in terms which will speak meaningfully to the oppressed. After all, it will be said, that is how the scriptures and the creeds originally functioned. Together they embody the experience, insights, intuitions, provocative suggestions, metaphors, half-truths, myths, and symbols of earlier generations. In their own way they may have once been liberating and transforming for those who invented and used them. The more likely possibility is that they were deeply oppressive of various groups which they kept hidden from view. The traditional doctrines of the church, on this view, were really tools used to serve the interests of various hierarchies of power.

The task now is to take the creeds and rework them, or carefully screen them, so that they can act as agents of liberation in the modern world. They need to be cleansed of their hierarchical and oppressive content and used creatively to help the church cope with the new situation in which it finds itself. Thus the call has gone out to develop themes of liberation which will set free the poor, the oppressed, the handicapped, those trapped in society as racial minorities, those sexually discriminated against, and the like. More broadly, the hope is expressed that a new synthesis in theology will enable the modern world to cope with the prospects of nuclear annihilation, and it will re-create its social and political order to accommodate the radical religious pluralism which is sweeping the world. This synthesis will be built on and deliberately geared to action; theology must now be intimately related to the social and political realities which are transparently oppressive to those who think seriously about the matter.

This account of the general character of liberation theologies can only serve as a heuristic device to map out some of the landscape occupied. It is difficult to find a representative liberation theologian who would accept all or even most of the above as an acceptable summary of his or her position. Differences within liberation surface on a wide variety of factors. Proponents differ on the extent to which they still want to take the Christian heritage or the institutional church seriously; they differ on the extent to which they want to pursue epistemological and methodological issues; they differ on the designated oppressed group; and they differ on the use they make of Marxist categories and convictions. This naturally results in a great variety of positions possible. Yet we should not exaggerate the differences. There clearly is a set of themes and proposals that forms an identifiable family of positions, and it is relatively clear that such theologians live within the neighborhood of the territory we have sketched.

The case for liberation

At the popular level, ordinary Christians represented, say, by the evangelicals, dismiss all this as Marxism or communism in disguise. Given that evangelical churches have been growing steadily over the last twenty years or so, and given that they have much greater social and political clout than they used to have, such criticism tends to be dismissed, in turn, with scorn as an expression of bourgeois, capitalist faith. There is some truth to this countercharge, for it is certainly the case that conservative religion and conservative politics are intimately joined in modern North America. Presidential elections make the fact only too clear. Perhaps that is one reason why conservatives themselves have failed to provide any serious alternative to the theologies of liberation which currently make the rounds. Their political orientation often breeds a defensiveness and a timidity that fails to nourish a really penetrating approach to the deep issues with which the theologian has to wrestle. Alternatively, it encourages them to fasten on recent events in the October revolution of 1989 in Eastern Europe in order to discredit both the political and particular claims of liberation theology.

For now, it is enough to note that critics often fail to grapple with the intention behind the quest for liberation in modern theology. The latter is driven by a variety of concerns which the theologian must face with robust determination. In fact, some evangelical theologians have astutely recognized that they may well need the pluralism and inclusivism which liberation theology has ignited, if they are to overcome the discrimination they have suffered in the academy and in the church for over two generations.

Primarily, the impetus behind much liberation theology is moral in character. It is a sincere attempt to cope with the ravages of oppression, poverty, discrimination, and political cruelty. It seeks to explore the inner dynamics of politics and culture in order to find clues to the etiology of suffering and oppression. In a deep sense it is gripped with the problem of theodicy. How can we speak of God in a world of political and social oppression? But it is not interested in the traditional theodicies so beloved of philosophers like Hume, his critics, and his admirers. Hume focused on how one could hold to the triad of belief in divine benevolence, belief in divine omnipotence, and belief in the reality of evil. This was construed as an intellectual issue of consistency; to perceive it as a viable problem, all one needed was the least amount of evil imaginable.

Liberation theologians dismiss this issue as a snare and a distraction. The real issue for them is not intellectual but practical and sociopolitical. Western theology went astray because it took as its partner in discussion the likes of the well-fed and cosseted Hume; it became obsessed with an intellectual apologetic which neglected the plight of the poor and the marginalized. What is imperative now is how to speak of God in the midst of barbaric cruelty and suffering. To play the intellectual games of the past is an insult to the poor and an abomination to God. The task of theology is to facilitate the actual liberation of the poor and the oppressed from their misery. This is clearly a moral agenda with very specific social and political content. It is very difficult to see how Christians can ignore the concerns expressed both within and around it. Primarily, then, liberation theologies are seeking to understand some deep problems in the modern world and to make a genuine effort at their resolution. It is cheap and inadequate to dismiss this as Marxism in disguise.

Secondarily, liberation theologies are an effort to break loose from the canons of rationality adopted in the West from the time of the Enlightenment as these have been deployed in much systematic theology. Thus, African-American theologians have wanted to draw on sources like the hymns and spirituals of their tradition, which have been ignored by mainline scholars; and women have wanted to develop revisionist accounts of their own place in the history of the church which call for a radical change of perspective elsewhere in theology. At yet another level, the quest for liberation is an attempt to find space for the laity and the ordinary clergy in the thinking of the church, especially for those laity and clergy who come from parts of the world where the standard educational equipment of the scholar is impaired or quite impossible to attain. All these concerns deserve to be taken with the utmost seriousness.

A sociological query

At the sociological level, there is a strong tendency to adopt some kind of qualified Marxism as the way ahead. There is little sense of the complexity of the relation between, say, class and religious commitment. One meets a kind of naive social realism, as if the real forces at work in society could be discerned with ease. Within this, notions like "the poor" or "the third world" become code words laden with ideological freight which cannot be dislodged with contrary evidence. "The poor" are redefined to designate those who have had the approved consciousness-raising into the preferred vision of the world, and "the third world" is evoked as a category that conveniently ignores the millions who are currently flocking into Pentecostalism. [24] Moreover, for the sake of inclusion a whole new hierarchy of leaders emerges. As a result, those giving papers to learned audiences find themselves compelled to make the appropriate apologies about their place in the social order before they begin, or they deftly display their sympathy with the values of the new hierarchy by an introductory anecdote. Contrary voices are screened out of serious dialogue as threats to the new consensus and as inimical to the ensuing politics of liberation. Alternative positions are dismissed because of the persons who present them rather than because of the data or warrants that support them.

Ironically, one of the more aggressive critics of liberation theology is a sociologist who through his writings taught many theologians to take sociology seriously, namely, Peter L. Berger. Berger has proposed that we view the current scene as shaped by a new class whose members share a common ideology which is in part designed to protect their vested interests in the social order. The essential characteristic of this new class is that it is engaged in the production and distribution of symbolic knowledge. It includes such professions as educators, communicators, therapists, and bureaucrats. As a rising class, it finds itself in conflict with the old middle class located in the business community and the traditional professions. Generally it is left-of-center in its political philosophy, a fact which is neatly explained by the further fact that it has a vested interest in domestic policies which expand the welfare state and in foreign policies which de-emphasize military power. Liberation theology, in this analysis, is to be expected. It is the natural expression of cultural and ideological propensities, one more phase of *Kulturprotestantismus.*

Berger does not hide his moral and theological assessment of this development. On the moral plane, he considers the agenda of the new class reprehensible for its commitment to unilateral disarmament, a vague socialism, and an assault on the family. Theologically he is even more emphatic. He is not just irritated by the analytic inadequacies of those who espouse liberation theology; he considers their doctrine to be a clear form of apostasy. It involves the substituting of a left-of-center political agenda for the good news of the gospel. Far from liberating us, it "restores us to the yoke of slavery that is imprisonment in history and imprisonment in the typically tragic web of our own projects in history." [25] The politicalization of the gospel leads in fact to an act of implicit excommunication, not just of those who disagree with the politics advocated, but of the church itself. The church ceases to be the church because it rejects the gospel under the banner of its political agenda.

What is most interesting and significant about this analysis is not that it may be right or wrong as a piece of sociological theorizing but that no one who professes liberation theology is in the least interested in it. Berger is simply dismissed on the grounds that his own articulation of the gospel is an expression of his political commitments, and everyone knows that Berger is a neoconservative who cannot any longer be taken seriously. It is not even considered essential to argue this; it is enough to identify the group to which he belongs.

A philosophical query

Liberation theology is not without its philosophical corollaries. Among the latter, some are epistemological. Especially favored is a version of relativism developed from Thomas S. Kuhn's work in the philosophy of science, namely, his notion of paradigm shifts. According to this, intellectual revolutions in science involve radical shifts in perspective which make it impossible to adjudicate rationally between competing theories. It is not clear that Kuhn himself maintained as much, for it has been cogently argued that he was in fact attempting to broaden the rather narrow conception of rationality that natural scientists have tended to canonize. [26]

All this, and the intense debate about it in the philosophy of science, has been conveniently ignored. It is much easier for the theologian to dispose of the opposition by claiming that the notion of data, warrants, evidence, and the like, is already theory laden, so there is no point in continuing the conversation as equals. Neutrality, disinterestedness, the quest for the truth for its own sake—all these are dismissed with a pleasing sense of victory as part of the old paradigm which is now to be displaced. The issue then becomes one of politics, and at that stage one returns to talk about classism, sexism, racism, and oppression, as controlling the debate. Not all want to embrace this kind of historicism or relativism, of course, but it is difficult to find a good old-fashioned objectivist who is prepared to hold out against it. One, at least, is Rosemary Ruether, who skillfully redefines the objectivism or universalism she subscribes to in a thoroughly self-serving fashion.

What it all means is that the theologian has become intellectually lazy. This is initially expressed in a lamentable failure to deal with the sociological and philosophical issues related to the fundamental claims which are being advanced. Philosophy and sociology are disciplines omitted from the basic training of many theologians. Sociology of religion hardly exists as a subject within contemporary theological studies, and philosophy of religion is not taken very seriously. Even at the graduate level the introduction to these disciplines is perfunctory. Insufficient time is given for the budding theologian to find his or her bearings in the relevant material. Where philosophy is taken seriously, the approach tends to be in the tradition of Hegel and Heidegger, with disparaging glances directed here and there at the debate on the nature of religious language in recent Anglo-American philosophy.

The crucial underlying problem is that the deeply contested canon of literature related to these matters is not transmitted. One is reminded of Locke's famous remarks about the relation between theology and reason. Theologians hail the taxi of reason and then conveniently dismiss it when they have reached their destination. One must object to this practice as arbitrary in character and point out the consequences of its application elsewhere in theology. It would have been impossible for a theologian trained in the last generation to tolerate a discussion of the historical meaning of the Bible that ignored the lessons of historical research. Yet it appears that many contemporary theologians are prepared to tolerate that kind of intellectual sloppiness when they make what in fact are philosophical and sociological claims.

As a result, the most astonishing assertions as to the nature of society, or about the relation between interests and truth, or about the character and meaning of religious discourse, or about the fundamental character of all knowledge, or about the rationality of religious belief, can be advanced without any sense of internal self-criticism and with unchallenged dogmatism. [27] It is well-nigh impossible to get a foothold in the conversation. Moral passion displaces intellectual rigor; righteous indignation and thinly veiled anger do service for analytic skill; primary sources in the field, including that of approved authorities like Marx, are treated as already read; where one needs carefully conducted empirical research, one is offered flimsy anecdotal evidence; worse still, opponents are dismissed because they do not belong to the favored group or class. By wielding a set of code words and by stitching together a diverse set of elusive sociological and philosophical concepts, the theologian is able to give the impression that we are confronted by a passionate and enduring vision of reality. In truth, what we have for the most part is the dubious reworking and expansion of one wing of the Western political Enlightenment.

It is also small wonder, moreover, that much modern theology is sometimes scarred by bigotry. The symptoms of this judgment are no less real for being impressionistic in origin. Indeed it would not be difficult to use large tracts of modern theology to illustrate John Henry Newman's penetrating analysis of bigotry in the thirteenth of his *University Sermons* (1843). Supposedly new views are presented as the truth which will unlock all mystery.

> They think that their own views are exactly fitted to solve all the facts which are to be accounted for, to satisfy all objections, and to moderate and arbitrate between all parties. They conceive that they profess just the truth which makes all things easy. They have their one idea or their favourite notion, which occurs to them on every occasion. They have their one or two topics, which they are continually obtruding, with a sort of pedantry, being unable to discuss, in a natural unconstrained way, or to let their thoughts take their course, in the confidence that they will come home safe at last. [28]

Partisan proposals are offered as the sum and summary of the gospel, or of Christian doctrine. Even though the whole edifice requires a repudiation of the biblical traditions as patriarchal and oppressive, elements of the tradition will be marshaled as rhetorical devices.

> They are ready with the very places of Scripture—one, two or three— where it is to be found; they profess to say what each passage and each verse means, what it cannot mean, and what it must mean. [29]

Neologisms and code words become indispensable to conversation and dialogue.

> They have their own terms and names for everything; and these must not be touched any more than the things which they stand for. Words of party or politics, of recent date and unsatisfactory origin, are as much a portion of the Truth in their eyes, as if they were the voice of Scripture or Holy Church. [30]

Consequently, it is difficult to find those who can enter into contrary points of view with real and prolonged sympathy. There is a vexation with alternative principles of arrangement. Wide tracts of inquiry, such as the emergence of Pentecostalism or the rationality of religious belief, are treated as forbidden territory which only the pious or the ignorant or the egghead would enter. Underneath there is an alarmism and even, at times, a secret misgiving about the truth of the principles canvased. The outcome is predictable: stubborn material will break the tools being used, a state of uncertainty and distress will follow, and the prevailing bigotry will be replaced either by another bigotry or by skepticism. "They who thought their own ideas could measure all things, end in thinking that even a Divine oracle is unequal to the task." [31]

Although the final outcome of this kind of thinking is not difficult to guess, there is no end actually in sight. There are signs that critical voices are on the horizon, which is understandable simply on the grounds of intergenerational development. Already a second line of research is appearing, and some of these voices are bound to challenge various aspects of the prevailing opinion. [32] However, we have only begun to see what the next round of arguments will be as to God, Christ, sin, salvation, spirituality, and the like. [33] The full implications of the prevailing consensus remain as yet unarticulated. We can be sure that they will be pursued by the initiated with characteristic enthusiasm. We can be equally sure that the fragile unity that currently exists will disintegrate as the consensus becomes more widely known.

The new Yale school

The most significant alternative voice to the one I have described is undoubtedly provided by a group of scholars who teach or were trained at Yale University over the last generation. Some of these would readily identify with the concerns of liberation theology and would be happy to incorporate the theme of liberation into their material proposals; but the whole thrust and ethos of their work is entirely different. Two features stand out: a concern to transmit the full logic of the Christian heritage and a sense of indebtedness to the insights of linguistic analysis. The aim is to develop a postliberal theology that will extricate itself from the strictures of the Enlightenment and yet be fully critical in character. The most succinct account of the tradition has been supplied by George A. Lindbeck, whose short book *The Nature of Doctrine: Religion and Theology in a Postliberal Age* has become a landmark document. [34]

One way into the postliberal school is to compare and contrast it with the minority reports we mentioned earlier. On the one side this school is uneasy with the traditional claim that in theology one can objectively describe God in ordinary declarative sentences. Christian doctrines are said not to be assertions, as many of the mediating theologians who stand for a critical orthodoxy would maintain. Nor, however, are they regarded as the nondiscursive symbols of existential orientations, inner feelings, and attitudes, as was maintained by the liberal, existential, secular, and radical theologies which were common in the sixties. Most importantly, they are not put forth as attempts to bring to expression in Christian form the metaphysical or philosophical conclusions arrived at by means of metaphysical analysis, as is partially argued by the process theologians. The latter view, in fact, is a carryover from the liberal Protestant theology of the last century. It involves an implicit acceptance of the quest for rational foundations of knowledge which has been a marked feature of Enlightenment philosophy since Descartes. The new Yale theology has abandoned this quest; there are no such universal foundations, in its view. Our experience is not looked upon as something we know independently of the concepts we employ to identify, describe, and explain it. We are thought of as born into a world of language, culture, and tradition, which we bring to our experience of the world and God, and which cannot be justified by any universal criteria of truth.

This immediately opens a door to a fresh reading and appropriation of the Christian tradition, in the view of the Yale school. The Christian faith is not to be reduced to some speculative historical reconstruction of the earliest witness to Jesus; it is to be taken in all its biblical, creedal, and liturgical fullness. Taken together, these are seen to constitute a narrative which has its own internal logic. This is regarded not as a bloodless, rational abstraction, but as a way of thinking and being which is rooted in the particularities of the Christian community of faith. Such logic is thought to need no external justification. It is held to offer its own distinctive grammar for parsing theological discourse across the centuries of cultural change. What is essential in theology in these terms is merely to be true to the rationality and grammar of Christian discourse so construed. That in no way precludes thorough examination of various theological claims, these theologians hold. Nor does it inhibit conversation with those of all faiths and of none. On the contrary, it is thought to permit precisely the kind of frank exchange which is essential in the emergence of the radically pluralistic, postmodern world that is seen as now upon us after the collapse of the Enlightenment ideal of knowledge. More positively, this radical reorientation in theology is seen as allowing the Christian tradition to bring to birth its own distinctive voice in debates about God, the human situation, the good life, and the like. This is not the creation of some imagined theological ghetto; it is professed as the sober consequence of facing up to the new intellectual landscape which is thought to be now in place.

The jury is still very much in session on the fortunes of the new Yale theology. Part of the problem is that at times it borders on the obscurantist. It is very difficult to know what its proponents really want to say materially about God, creation, redemption, and the like. Indeed they seem to make it their business not to say very much along these lines. Theology is seen not as first-order talk about God but as "the scholarly activity of second-order reflection on the data of religion . . . and of formulating arguments for or against material positions." [35] However, there is no gainsaying the erudition, grace, and intellectual felicity of the school. Its adherents have a lively agenda to work on, and they will be around a long time working out the details.

Equally, there is no denying the deep problems that lie at the heart of this operation. Two stand out. First, there is a profound ambivalence if not outright obscurantism concerning what is to be said materially about creation, salvation, the church, and the like. Nowhere is this more evident than in the handling of the classical creeds of the church. These are not remotely akin to the grammar of a language. They are a body of brief but substantial claims about the reality of God, Jesus Christ, the future life, and so on. Yet Lindbeck and his allies treat them merely as essential patterns of Christian discourse. This is simply a category mistake.

What is especially interesting is Lindbeck's claim that theological discourse cannot depict reality. Ironically, the veto on this possibility rests with Kant's strictures about the inability of language to go beyond mundane reality. Certain of Kant's writings maintain that our language can only deal with phenomena; it cannot deal with anything beyond the world of everyday experience (GBWW I: 42, 1–252; II: 39, 1–252). (In other writings Kant argues, however, that such ideas as God and immortality are essential postulates of the moral life [GBWW I: 42, 291–364; II: 39, 291–364].) If this stricture is accepted, then the claim to have escaped the regulative ideals of the Enlightenment paradigm of knowledge is unfounded. In fact, the legacy of the Enlightenment is visible in another area of postliberal theology. Postliberal theologians are as much obsessed with their method as are their opponents in the revisionist tradition, represented, say, by Ogden. It is all very well to call, for example, for the cultivation of vision and discernment as essential to good theology, [36] but to stake out this arena as the heart of the matter is to remain stranded on the territory one has professed to vacate.

This leads naturally to the second issue. Consider the following summary of the Christian message as expressed by a second-generation postliberal theologian.

> To summarize: (1) Christians believe that no subsequent experience will refute the essential pattern we as Christians now see in things. (2) We believe that the pattern of which Christians now catch a glimpse will ultimately be perspicuous to all. (3) Mysterious as all talk of God is, we believe that our actions in faith respond to prior acts of God, and therefore talk of God cannot be interpreted without remainder as a way of talking about human thoughts or practices. [37]

The rejection of reductionism here is most welcome. One is left, however, with severe misgivings. On the one hand, what is offered is more talk about talk; theology has become a set of quasi-epistemological comments on talk about God. On the other hand, the actual claims advanced are thin and emaciated compared to the rich fare offered in the classical traditions of the church over the centuries. An explanation of this lies in the neighborhood. While postliberal theologians have challenged the legacy of the Enlightenment at a formal level, at a basic level they have taken on board the material results of the Enlightenment project as that has been applied to the whole sweep of the Christian tradition. The old premises are rejected, but the conclusions derived from them remain intact. If there was a new Babylonian captivity of the church, there appears to be limited liberation from its strictures here.

In the search for a positive and constructive presentation of the great themes of the Christian faith one turns instead to those who stand for some kind of orthodoxy. Unfortunately, one cannot report that the yield in such quarters is at all promising. On the Roman Catholic side, the impression one gets is that modern Roman Catholic theologians are for the most part echoing the proposals already well developed in the Protestant traditions. Among evangelicals we have the development of a defensive scholasticism.

A Roman Catholic voice

The most significant voice among Roman Catholics is undoubtedly that of David Tracy. [38] Tracy currently teaches at the University of Chicago. The most important thing to say about him is that he is as liberal as the most stouthearted liberal Protestant. The term he uses to describe his theology is *revisionism*. The fundamental task of theology, in his view of it, is to correlate common human experience and language with the Christian tradition as expressed in Christian texts. When examined with care they turn out to be expressing the same fundamental insights. Using the hermeneutical perspective developed by Heidegger and supplemented by Hans-Georg Gadamer, Tracy reads the Christian texts in such a way as to bring out what he perceives as "the-way-of-being-in-the-world" portrayed therein.

Common experience of the world requires, however, a different approach. One analyzes phenomenologically the religious dimension that appears to be present in scientific, moral, and everyday experience. One attends to sacred aspects of experience not captured in our conventional forms of analysis and reflection. This brings to light a horizon which, however named, is the uncontrollable limit of the very meaning of existence itself. In Christian texts this limit is identified in a particular way. In the-way-of-being-in-the-world manifest in Tracy's analysis of Christian texts, it is characterized as the unbounded love of God represented in Jesus Christ.

Given that these are the same, that is, the deliverances of both phenomenology and Christianity, the task now is to deal with the question of truth. Here Tracy turns to a transcendental or metaphysical mode of reflection and, drawing on process philosophy, he argues that the limit at issue here is not just a coherent notion of God but a God whose existence we must necessarily affirm if we are to avoid self-contradiction. So Christian faith re-presents that basic trust in the worth of existence which itself is regarded as in some sense constitutive of existence and which necessarily entails, Tracy thinks, the existence of God. In other words, existence itself involves a form of trust which in turn involves affirming that God exists.

The affinities with Ogden here are obvious and numerous. What makes Tracy distinctive is the sources he blends together in the vision he articulates. It takes enormous intellectual dexterity to bring together under one roof the work of Heidegger, Hartshorne, Gadamer, Ian Ramsey, and Bernard Lonergan. Kierkegaard, however, is turning in his grave as he watches Jesus Christ being fitted into this grand philosophical scheme. In any case, to forge these into a bold apologetic that will convince the reader of the intellectual necessity of Christian doctrine is a very demanding enterprise. Tracy simply does not bring it off. His philosophical claims are as rickety as the natural theology whose place they take in the tradition as a whole. Even if they were correct, they do not begin to speak to the great masses of humankind, oppressed or otherwise. Above all, Tracy's reading of the Christian tradition is an unconvincing tour de force. He manages to sustain the Christian character of his claims only by engaging in the kind of revisionist discourse which really redefines the Christian heritage to suit his philosophical purposes, but does not effectively articulate its content. Once again, a favored philosophical synthesis is wearing the trousers, while the faith is left suspended by buttons held down by tattered and fragile threads. The single redeeming factor in this is that, despite Tracy's claim to having offered a hard rather than a soft apologetic, there is a note of uncertainty in his work which leaves space for the revision of his own revisionism.

The evangelical alternative

The yield from evangelical Protestantism is equally unpromising. Evangelical theologians are a diverse group of Christians loosely held together by a formal intention to preserve the content of the historic Christian tradition against the threat from a hostile environment. The environment is indeed hostile at times, although many evangelicals have themselves assiduously courted hostility by their defensiveness, by their pugnacious spirit, by their obsession with the trappings and externals of scholarship, and by their love of power, which is paradoxically connected to a spirit of isolation. It is common knowledge that thoroughly competent evangelicals were excluded from key jobs in the academy merely because of their particular concerns and commitments. Even yet, mainline Christianity has enormous difficulty opening the ecumenical door to let what it perceives as the riffraff in. [39] "Inclusiveness" is the new code word that permits various establishments to appear open, while acting in a thoroughly exclusive mode. This needs mention, because evangelicals do have some excuse for their failings.

In fact the evangelicals have made extraordinary progress in at least two areas. In the work of Alvin Plantinga and Nicholas Wolterstorff they have produced philosophers of the first rank who are part of a wider development which we shall discuss shortly. Moreover, in historical studies evangelism has reached a degree of sophistication which is equally if not more impressive. Historians like George Marsden, Nathan Hatch, and Mark Noll have produced work of the highest order. In systematic theology, however, the situation is less promising.

There has been a rush of volumes produced of late by evangelicals, and there are more on the way. [40] Most of them come close in form and content to the mediating theologies which we have already discussed. They repeat the traditional evangelical theologies of the past intending to deal with the critical problems which have arisen over the last century or so. They share, therefore, in the strengths and weaknesses of the mediating theologians. If anything, they exhibit those weaknesses more conspicuously. For example, they find it difficult to enter into the modern alternatives. There is a tendency to be on the defensive, and this inhibits creativity. [41]

Looking more closely, it is clear that the benchmark of evangelical theology in the last generation is the multivolume work of Carl F. H. Henry. [42] Henry was one of the key architects of the neo-evangelical movement that has been represented in the public eye in an exceptional way by Billy Graham. The hope was that a reworking of fundamentalism would provide the context for the emergence of a profoundly fresh and relevant expression of the gospel in both a popular and an intellectually informed manner. As a result, a network of institutions was created to foster and mediate the aspirations of a new generation of evangelicals who wanted to leave the backwater of fundamentalism and engage in mainstream debate and discussion. That desire has not been realized.

One looks in vain for a fresh, invigorating expression of the gospel in Henry's work. There is no deeply illuminating account of the human predicament, no penetrating analysis of the possibilities of grace, no compelling account of the work of Christ, no fresh insight into the work of the Holy Spirit, no alluring presentation of the possibility of Christian community, and the like. Instead we have three thousand pages of turgid scholasticism, where readers swirl around in a sea of names who are called as witnesses for the defense or worked over as inconsistent heretics. A dead and barren orthodoxy invented out of the philosophical and theological debris of the late nineteenth century is presented as the riches of the Christian faith.

There is a deep imbalance in the presentation. Four of the volumes are devoted to epistemological issues and develop fifteen theses on revelation. We see in this devotion to the cause of epistemology the impact of the Enlightenment obsession with getting the foundations straight. The Enlightenment tradition has taken its revenge on its opponents in the evangelical tradition by determining the field on which the battles are to be lost and won. Henry stakes everything on getting the foundations right; as a consequence, he only has time to deal with the doctrine of God. There is no room left to deal with such great themes as redemption, ecclesiology, or eschatology. Throughout, he is locked into a doctrine of the inerrancy of scripture which rests on a profound confusion of the canons of the church with norms in epistemology. The whole edifice is a narrow and rationalistic presentation of the Christian intellectual heritage; it is the scholastic summary of a tradition which deserves a better articulation of its peculiar insights and diversity. Even its friends are wont to be embarrassed at this attempt to provide a massive counterblast to Barth. Ironically, the second generation of evangelicals schooled in the tradition created by Henry and his allies have taken to Barth like the proverbial duck takes to water. [43] Others, watching with fear such a development, have regressed into an old-fashioned, aggressive fundamentalism. [44]

An offer of salvation from philosophers

Thus far we have sought to provide an overview of the main alternatives available within the ranks of those officially and professionally responsible for work in theology. Theologians, however, are not the only folk who are paid to write and think about God. Over the years other groups of academics have lent a hand or two. Nowhere is this more true than in the field of philosophy. Sometimes this has happened out of a keen sense of dissatisfaction with what is offered in theology. This is undoubtedly the case in the contemporary scene. Failing to receive help from the theologians, those in other disciplines have taken to doing theology themselves. One of the most astonishing features of the current theological scene is the spectacle of accomplished philosophers turning to articulate, discuss, and even at times uphold the kind of basic theological doctrines that theologians have dismissed as antediluvian and incredible. [45]

In the last decade or so, several highly respected philosophers have either been converted to Christianity or have come back to the faith after dismissing it as nonsense in the early part of their careers. These have been joined by Christians who have been trained as philosophers and who have earned a solid reputation by their work in the classical disciplines of the trade. Together they constitute a remarkable group from diverse Christian traditions. They form a loose Anglo-American coalition, have founded their own society with over eight hundred members, and meet regularly at places like the University of Notre Dame to share their ruminations.

Outside philosophy they are scarcely known. Inside, they add up to a formidable intellectual horsepower. Michael Dummett, Basil Mitchell, Peter Geach, David Brown, John Lucas, Keith Ward, Brian Hebblethwaite, Grace Jantzen, Richard Swinburne, Janet Martin Soskice, and Caroline Franks Davis represent a core in England; William Alston, Thomas Morris, George Mavrodes, Peter Van Inwagen, Marilyn Adams, Keith Yandell, Eleonore Stump, Alan Donagan, Nancey Murphy, and Alasdair MacIntyre, as well as Plantinga and Wolterstorff, work in North America. Underneath and around these, a large number of younger scholars are eagerly attending to themes which were once thought essential to serious theology but have somehow been lost in recent years.

This development has taken most theologians by surprise. They were used to an adversarial relationship with philosophers trained in the Anglo-American analytic tradition inspired by Ludwig Wittgenstein and the positivists of an earlier generation. Hence they were not expecting such friendly overtures. Where theologians had made their peace with philosophy—say, with the later Wittgenstein—it had created a sense of relative ease in Zion. In fact, as we noted in the case of the new Yale theology, a particular interpretation of Wittgenstein is a crucial ingredient in the ambivalence about the objectivity of theological claims which has long prevailed. In the new wave of the philosophy of religion, Wittgenstein is a thoroughly marginal figure. This should not surprise us, for Wittgenstein's own writings in the philosophy of religion are meager in the extreme. One suspects that they would not have got the attention they received but for the name to which they were attached. Generally speaking, theologians understood Wittgenstein as underwriting a unique grammar or logic of theological discourse, a claim which indirectly called into question the cognitive status of theology.

The first wave of new work in the philosophy of religion took up this question and very quickly reached the point where the debate was no longer about whether theological claims *could* be true or false, but whether they actually were true or false. It focused, that is, on the justification of religious belief. A surprisingly large number of philosophers are prepared to argue that traditional theistic and even Christian belief is thoroughly credible. This is an amazing turnabout. When I trained in philosophy in the late sixties, it was taken as a canon of philosophical orthodoxy that the truth of religious belief was not even worthy of rational consideration, much less refutation. Courses in the philosophy of religion were often not available, so that one had to become self-taught or look around for special tutoring in the subject from lukewarm lecturers in neighboring fields. There are still deep pockets of resistance in many philosophy departments, but the landscape as a whole is utterly changed.

On the justification of religious belief, two alternatives currently hold center stage. One has been developed by Plantinga. On the one hand, Plantinga has attempted a major demolition job on the canons of Enlightenment rationality. Plantinga rejects the Enlightenment requirement that our beliefs must be supported by evidence if they are to be considered rational. [46] The enemy here is Descartes, together with the rationalist and empiricist traditions he initiated. A combination of historical and technical arguments are marshaled to show that many of our perfectly respectable beliefs, like belief in other minds or belief in the external world, neither have nor need rational support. They are properly basic beliefs. Moreover, it is perfectly coherent to construe belief in God as such a properly basic belief. It is like belief in the external world or belief in the past; one can rationally hold all of these without evidence. On the other hand, Plantinga has attempted to draw on new developments in modal logic to produce a fresh rendering of the ontological argument for the existence of God. [47] For Plantinga, such an exercise is not essential for the defense of belief in God; hence he is not contradicting the principal thrust of his position. Yet the effect is to throw down a gauntlet to the prevailing orthodoxy in both philosophy and theology, which has taken it as a given that Hume and Kant had settled this issue for all time.

The other main alternative as to the justification of religious belief has been developed in a quartet of volumes by Swinburne. [48] Picking up a tradition which has a distinguished pedigree in English philosophy and which was subtly and brilliantly articulated in the early seventies by Mitchell, [49] Swinburne has attempted to develop a rigorous cumulative case argument for the rationality of belief in God. The key to this is the claim that it is perfectly in order to support a proposal by assembling a battery of arguments which taken together underwrite the conclusion. On this view an argument can be like the strands of a rope as much as it can be like the steps in a ladder. When this is applied to claims about God, then a good case can be assembled for positions which have been too hastily dismissed as incredible.

There is a deep division of the house on whether or not Swinburne's proposals represent an improvement on the position staked out by Mitchell, but there is no denying the intellectual depth and rigor which the discussion has sparked. [50] Nor do these two alternatives exhaust the possibilities available. Alston, a professional of professionals in the last generation, is currently bringing to completion a decade of study exploring the positive analogies that exist between ordinary perception and perception of the divine. As a consequence, the modern theist has now a range of options to turn to on questions about the rationality of religious belief which were unthinkable a generation ago. One is no longer obliged to lean on the remains of the Idealist tradition as mediated by philosophers like Whitehead and Hartshorne. In fact, Christian philosophers have even taken to seeking their own solutions to deep metaphysical issues which are as yet unresolved. [51]

The matter has not stopped there. Having gained a new confidence in the intelligibility, coherence, and content of the tradition, Christian philosophers have turned to specific Christian doctrines to see how they might articulate and defend them in the light of the profoundly changed philosophical situation. Swinburne is currently engaged in the writing of another quartet of books which tackle such subjects as atonement and incarnation. [52] This represents a second wave of activity which is now gaining enormous momentum. In this wave the focus is on the articulation of specific Christian doctrines. At one recent conference, scholars tackled such themes as original sin, the Christian scheme of salvation, the Trinity, weakness of will, the indwelling of the Holy Spirit, the nature of Christian liberty, and the suffering of God. [53] Other scholars have tackled such central topics as inspiration, revelation, and incarnation. [54] Still others have joined together to bring about an extraordinary resurrection of debate about the relation between religion and morality. Until recently it was common, following Plato's arguments in the *Euthyphro,* to claim that theology had nothing to contribute to the status and content of morality. There is now, however, a lively discussion as to whether modern moral philosophy and the crisis it faces is intelligible outside the history of the Christian faith. Moreover, it is now possible to inquire if the sources for its intellectual renewal do not lie in part in a fresh encounter with Christian material which was cast aside in the Enlightenment. [55]

The response of the theologians

At one level the new school of philosophers is seen as a group of quintessential patriarchs whose male logic and hard-nosed emphasis on rigor are rejected out of hand. I heard one critic castigate the concern for rationality as a form of "methodicide," a neologism clearly meant to suggest genocide. This is wide of the mark, of course, not least because women have been a part of the new wave from the outset, just as they have become established figures within philosophy for a generation. However, that rejoinder is easily dispatched by some of its antagonists: the relevant women are viewed as too formed by patriarchal modes of thought to be taken seriously.

A graver criticism is that the new philosophers of religion are thoroughly conservative thinkers in their theology, whatever may be the case as regards their philosophical sophistication and dexterity. They are out of touch with the new developments in hermeneutics, a source of great value for those who are the guardians of sacred texts. They are also unacquainted with the conversation which is emerging out of the dialogue between the world religions; they have only a superficial knowledge of the highways and byways of the history of Christian doctrine; they approach the whole development of modern Christian theology from Schleiermacher onward in a gladiatorial and patronizing manner; and they are almost completely ignorant of the most recent findings of historical criticism as applied to the Bible. Not surprisingly, feelings can run high on those few occasions when theologians and philosophers have sought to talk to each other. In one recent encounter, a leading New Testament scholar ended a scorching response to a paper by one of the leading philosophers of the present generation with the remark that Jesus would surely turn in his grave if he knew what some modern philosophers were saying in his name.

Some of these criticisms have merit, but it is important to weigh them sensibly. The philosophers involved are themselves Christians, so they have a right to speak for the tradition in their own terms. Many of them are well acquainted with other religious traditions, and they are not uninformed about the methods and results of biblical criticism. Indeed they are sufficiently informed to be aware of the acute philosophical issues raised, say, by inter-religious dialogue and by the application of the canons of historical judgment to claims about divine action.

What makes them wary is the philosophical dogmatism which is often the mark of theological writings on these topics. Theologians appear at times to be naive about the philosophical dimensions of such work, or they too hastily invoke the authority of a contested philosophical tradition. [56] As to their attitude to modern theology generally, the aversion of Christian philosophers is not unrelated to the disappointing talk that appears in the sermons which they have to endure regularly when they go to church; more positively, it is intimately connected to their dissatisfaction with the earlier philosophical proposals that served as part of the raw material for schools of theology over the last two centuries.

A crucial methodological assumption

As we noted earlier, a deeply entrenched methodological assumption in modern theology is that the primary task of the theologian is to take the inner depths of the Christian tradition and make it intelligible to the modern or postmodern world. Opinions differ, of course, on what constitutes the inner depth of the tradition. The Barthian strand identifies it with an encounter with the Word of God through the apostolic witness to Christ. The more classical Protestant liberalism stemming from the nineteenth century, which has outlived and outwitted the fierce Barthian attack launched against it two generations ago, tends to identify the essence of the tradition with some kind of deep, ineffable experience of the divine, mediated through the traditions emanating in one way or another from Jesus. In both cases, however, the basic theological task is identical. The goal is to find that modern conceptuality which will best express, preserve, and render intelligible the underlying depths of the tradition.

The early theologians of the church are conceived as having had two and really only two options to follow. Either they could bury their heads in the sand and have nothing to do with the conceptualities available in the culture; or, adopting one or another of the conceptualities of the ancient world, they could express the faith in ways which would be intelligible to their neighbors. On this analysis, figures like Augustine, Clement of Alexandria, Origen, and the great Cappadocians (Gregory of Nyssa, Gregory of Nazianzus, and Basil the Great) clearly took the second route. They adopted the categories and thought forms of Platonism and gave birth to theology proper. Thomas made a similar move when in his times he appealed to Aristotle. It will be said, therefore, that contemporary theology is the same enterprise which it has been from the start. Philosophers who object to it are either ignoring the culturally relative character of the enterprise, or they are surreptitiously smuggling their own philosophical terms into theology without acknowledgment. Revisionism is therefore not a contingent feature of some theology; it is constitutive of the very definition of theology. It is the first lesson which the neophyte has to learn, and the sooner he learns it and gets on with his work, the better.

I venture that some such assumption is at the heart of the modern theological academy. It is so much a part of the fabric of thought that anyone who challenges it is likely to be shown the door and invited to leave. Yet this is a thoroughly debatable question, and there will be no way out of the current predicament until it is faced and resolved. For one thing, the assumption represents what Mitchell has wittily described as a case of playing theological Ping-Pong. [57] In such a game, one is first presented with a problem. In this instance the problem is how to construe the relation between formative or canonical Christian tradition and the philosophies of the age. Then a principle is expounded: there are two and only two solutions to this problem, namely, either ping or pong. On this occasion the alternatives are: either bury your head in the sand, or relate positively to the thought forms of the age. We know, however, that ping is wrong: only traditionalists would favor burying their heads in the sand; therefore, the only alternative is pong:

we must express the tradition in a chosen conceptuality or cluster of conceptualities of our age.

The obvious objection to the whole procedure is that it rests on the unfounded assumption that there are two and only two solutions to the problem of the relation between faith and cultural conceptuality. Logically, this assumption is completely groundless. That there are actually more than two options is provided by a more thorough and careful reading of the patristic period. [58] In fact, the option canvased above was precisely the position championed by one crucial group of early Christians, namely, the Gnostic Christians. This wing of the church sincerely and assiduously sought to find a contemporary conceptuality which would best express their Christian experience of the divine. Read in their own terms and categories, they were profoundly modern in their outlook, and modern revisionists who disdain their conclusions are their next of kin.

This was not the position which was adopted by the Cappadocians, for example. Formally schooled though they were in philosophy, they were deeply aware that what they borrowed from philosophy needed to be cleansed and transformed when it was put to use in theology. Success in this venture was a high prize which was far from easy to attain, as was witnessed in the late and retrospective judgment on the work of Origen. Moreover, the church in its judgments was at once lenient and firm. It did not forbid careful and even highly speculative attempts to resolve a variety of intellectual puzzles, but it was adamant about safeguarding those mysteries and intellectual treasures related to the gift of revelation and salvation which had come in the person of Christ through the agency of the Holy Spirit.

In later centuries, as the legacy of the church was transmitted through the rubble and ruins of the Byzantine empire, the matter was succinctly summed up by a namesake of two of the Cappadocians, Gregory Palamas. The summary is all the more compelling when we recall that it was in part a direct response to the challenge thrown down by a follower of Thomas who had insisted that philosophy was essential to the foundations of theology.

> What then should be the work and the goal of those who seek the wisdom of God in creatures? Is it not the acquisition of the truth, and the glorification of the Creator? This is clear to all. But the knowledge of the pagan philosophers has fallen away from both these aims.
>
> Is there anything of any use to us in this philosophy? Certainly. For just as there is much therapeutic value even in substances obtained from the flesh of serpents, and the doctors consider there is no better and more useful medicine than that derived from this source, so there is something of benefit to be had even from the profane philosophers—but somewhat as in a mixture of honey and hemlock. So it is most needful that those who wish to separate out the honey from the mixture should

beware that they do not take the deadly residue by mistake. And if you were to examine the problem, you would see that all or most of the most harmful heresies derive their origin from this source. [59]

This displays a radically different approach to the thought forms of the age than that current in contemporary academic theology. Not surprisingly, it is related to a very different nest of proposals about the purpose, the nature, and the content of Christian theology.

Good news from the East

Theology needs to be deeply rooted in revelation and tradition in history, in worship and prayer in the Christian community, in compassion and service in the world, in fear and trembling before the wonder of the Christian gospel, and in humble dependence on the grace and agency of the Holy Spirit. It requires an immersion in the life of God, so that one can identify and begin to grasp the tenderness and subtlety of the divine mind. It is impossible without a teachable spirit and without a profound sense of the inadequacies of one's cognitive capacities in the presence of the richness and mystery of the action of God. So, being a theologian will require not just stamina, brains, courage, access to libraries, appropriate intellectual formation in the relevant disciplines, and the like. It will crucially depend on the daily inspiration of the Holy Spirit graciously given in the liturgy of the church and in the devotional life of the individual. The latter are for the most part set aside as peripheral by the modern theologian, who places himself or herself primarily either within a secularized university or out on the streets of protest and perceives the church as an impoverished institution badly in need of a good course of lectures.

Without these experiences, and the dispositions and insights they evoke and foster, it is hard to see how theology will avoid being the echo of the populist ideologies, the crude common sense, or the technical philosophies of the day. Yet with such experiences one hopes that one might be on the outskirts of the company of the saints and martyrs, or even of the apostle Paul. This radically alters the whole theological landscape.

> Anyone who follows the Apostle advances with him into the inexpressible and unspeakable mysteries of life and incorruption. Whoever does not, asks questions and makes comments bearing no relation to life, to the mystery which draws creation together, making it incorruptible and transfiguring it, but only to the isolated, created world of cerebral knowledge and of the fragmentation which causes weariness and disintegration, and collects like a deposit in the veins of life so that the circulation of the blood finally stops. [60]

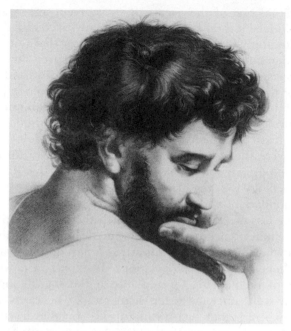

The apostle Paul, engraving after a drawing of a detail from
Raphael's painting "St. Cecilia."

It is precisely these notes that are missing from the prevailing canons of
theological discourse.

Interestingly, they are sounded in a version of the Christian tradition
long ignored or summarily dismissed by the West, namely, in the heart
of the Eastern Orthodox tradition. Few theological schools take this
tradition seriously. Eastern Orthodox Christians are commonly seen as
Catholics who kiss icons, or as nominal Christians in league with the
secret police forces of their states. Moreover, Eastern Orthodox theology is understood to have been summarized and frozen forever in the
eighth century in the work of John of Damascus. That is a historical
travesty which is now being slowly corrected, but the suspicion that the
whole tradition is at best a network of pious traditionalists out of touch
with modernity dies hard.

The Eastern Orthodox tradition recognizes at most about five great
theologians. By Western standards, where everyone can become a theologian after suitable training, this appears nonsensical. To some extent,
it can be attributed to the insensitivity, presumption, arrogance, and
hubris which are the besetting sins of all academics. There is something
exhilarating in seeing oneself as saving the church from intellectual
disaster by being one of the theologians of one's generation; even receiving honorable mention in the ranks of theology or being recognized

275

as the disciple of one of the greats of the current age is an attractive temptation. Indeed it is taken as a given in many circles that anyone who is prepared to apply himself can be a theologian; that one may belong to the Christian church is merely a contingent matter. In some circles, that one is a deeply committed person of faith is construed as a serious handicap, for it prevents the exercise of genuine objective judgment.

These positions can be cogently argued, and we shall not try to overturn them formally here. But what if the Eastern Orthodox tradition is closer to the truth and the Western traditions are wide of the mark on this? If that were the case, then the present malaise in theology might well be something we should expect. In terms of this diagnosis, contemporary theology is in the grim state in which it finds itself because it is built on foundations which were faulty from the outset, and because it involves the loss of factors without which theology is deprived of the resources essential to making it a viable intellectual operation.

On that analysis, much of the quest for a new and relevant theology stems from hopelessly high expectations. It expects a new theologian, or a cluster of theologians formed into a theological movement, to appear on the scene once every ten years or so, whereas what we might legitimately expect is that such would appear once every five hundred years. When they do appear, they are a charismatic gift to the church, arising out of the providential activity of God in history. They may well have a lay vocation in the church. Standing in deep continuity with the tradition, they deliver a word which is inescapably contemporary and relevant. In doing so they may completely fail to satisfy the Enlightenment requirement that one first specify one's theological method, and then proceed to put it to work to produce a new vision of God, Christ, salvation, and the like. This does not even happen in the natural sciences, as the history of science makes abundantly clear. [61] Nor need the primary task of truly original theologians be that of offering a new summa for his or her generation; they may achieve the more modest goal, say, of expanding our grasp of some particular doctrine or of exploring a major aspect of how to enrich our way of thinking about God in the first place.

This does not mean that there is nothing for the more common intellectuals in the church to do. Those who in the West count as theologians should really be seen in much more modest terms as students and teachers of Christian doctrine. They clearly have plenty to occupy them. Their task is to make manifest as best they can the mystery, profundity, and clarity of the gospel, to spell out its implications for the various contexts in which the church must minister and serve, to clear away obstacles from the path to understanding, to renew the life of worship, mission, and faithfulness from within, and to relate the faith of the church to the profound questions and challenges which crop up from time to time. That will keep a genius or two occupied for three score years and ten in any generation. Georges Florovsky and Alexander Schmemann come to mind as examples of this kind of activity in the last generation of the Eastern Orthodox tradition in North America. [62]

Whether the Eastern Orthodox tradition will make any impact on the Western traditions of theology is an open question. The political revolution currently under way in Eastern Europe and the Soviet Union could pave the way for a profound encounter between the East and West which could well provide the catalyst for fresh theological reflection. Florovsky's fascinating interpretation of the ways of Russian theology provides the starting point for discussion at this juncture. [63] Its latter part traces an encounter between the gospel and the Enlightenment which evoked eventually a very different response than what became the paradigm in the West. Florovsky's interpretation is by no means uncontested, but it is deeply suggestive and provocative. New material documenting the ferment in Russian theology at the end of the nineteenth century and the beginning of the twentieth badly needs to be made available in the West to complete the picture and provide fresh analysis of the issues.

Unfortunately, the Eastern Orthodox churches in the West currently live in a diaspora that tends to foster a fortress mentality; this conceals the vast riches they have to offer. Its converts from Western forms of Christianity tend to be wounded Christians limping toward Moscow or Constantinople in search of healing. Some are dissatisfied conservatives who are vehemently opposed to the ordination of women and who would therefore find it impossible to enter into a serious consideration of Western theological issues. If they fail here, they are unlikely to be able to enter into the tortured mind of the West, and the rich legacy of Florovsky will be betrayed.

A deeper analysis of the Western predicament

The reference to the Eastern Orthodox tradition prompts us to take a deeper look at the predicament of Western theology. The crucial problem with almost all the Western options available is that they are seeking to do theology without a full deck of cards. The full panoply of materials which was available and central in the early church and which was housed firmly within a spiritual and liturgical framework has been whittled away to such an extent that theologians are constantly attempting to reconstruct a deep theological vision from the dregs of their own disintegrating activity. The results are predictably meager.

We can chart this by taking fresh stock of the two great premodern schisms in the church. When the church split between East and West, this was not merely a verbal squabble about the procession of the Holy

Spirit from the Father. On it there may well have hinged two competing conceptions of knowing God which took centuries to play themselves out. The West, as represented by Augustine, had already incorporated into its ethos an appeal to philosophy as fundamental. [64] Yet within this scheme the crucial elements of one's theology were given by divine revelation. When the West changed the Nicene Creed and incorporated into it the famous *filioque* clause, there clearly was a deep question of authority at stake in this decision. If it could not be grounded on reason, then the only alternative was to claim that the Western church, represented by its center in Rome, had special access to the mind of God. This is eventually what happened in the West. Consequently, the pope became the first protestant; indeed he became an infallible protestant.

This constituted a deep breach in the fabric of the Christian tradition. The sensitive, corporate, nonjuridical conception of ecclesiastical authority which had been worked out in the early centuries was disrupted. In time, as we see in Thomas, the twin elements of appeal to philosophy and of appeal to revelation became a two-tiered synthesis where philosophy was given a position of prominence and even priority. Furthermore, the new status accorded to Rome became increasingly hierarchical and demanding in its orientation. Matters which were originally accorded a subtle and carefully balanced place in the economy of divine action, like the role of Mary, or the communion of the saints, were distorted and exaggerated. In turn, the defense of these changes only enhanced and made more juridical the place of the pope in the adjudication of theological matters.

The result was a suffocation of the life of the mind and spirit which led inevitably to revolt and rebellion. A second schism broke the back of the church in the West. It erupted into deep disputes about the canons of theology which eventually led to death and destruction. Initially the intention of the Reformers was simply to return to the mind of the early church. The crucial weapon used to bring this about was the appeal to *sola scriptura*. For the Reformers this was a de jure decision; de facto they made lavish use of the work of the early Fathers. Thus Calvin, when he came to compose his magnificent systematic theology, borrowed the very ordering of his material from the early creeds of the church.

The deeper issue, however, was the de jure decision to work with scripture as the sole canon of theological discourse. Once this was asserted, the creeds of the church become secondary and dispensable, and the race was on to find material which would perform the crucial role played by the creeds in the assembly of rich canonical material developed to express and mediate the treasures of revelation and salvation. Protestantism became constituted by a wild goose chase to find a replacement for the modest vision summarized and transmitted in the creedal and other non-scriptural canons of the early church.

By the time the Reformation spread to England its adherents were backpedaling to incorporate selective elements of patristic tradition, like creeds and bishops, into the canons of the church. They also desired to appeal to reason. This was an extraordinary move whose origins and significance have barely begun to be unraveled. At one level it can be seen as a return to the logic of patristic theology, for clearly the Fathers believed in the use of reason in theology. What is less clear, however, is whether it was a return to the restraint and caution of the Fathers in their use of reason. Gregory of Nyssa, for example, is very restrained in his use of reason, as his avowals on this subject make manifest. [65] Moreover, the debate about how exactly one uses reason is not over and done with in patristic theology—as if one can appeal to the tradition of the early centuries and ignore the extended conversations which take place after the eighth century. The work of Gregory Palamas in the fourteenth century, for example, is a crucial contribution to the unfolding insights and development of the fourth century. [66] Hence, merely to appeal to a static patristic theology does not begin to do justice to the complex logic of patristic thinking. In fact, what happens in the West is that the appeal to reason is worked out in a very different way from that common in the East. In the West it takes the form of an independent natural theology of the sort championed by Thomas. In the East this is generally and rightly treated with great caution.

There is another side to the issue which deserves mention. It is insufficiently recognized that the Reformation had extraordinary consequences for the intellectual life of the West. It is not at all implausible to argue that the Cartesian revolution in philosophy is the transposition of the Reformation disputes about canon in Christian theology into a dispute about the norms of epistemology.

Descartes found that the debate between Protestants and Roman Catholics about canon could not be resolved in the terms in which it was posed. Both traced their justifications for their chosen canons of theology back to the internal witness of the Holy Spirit. This was obviously unsatisfactory, for the same fundamental warrant was supporting competing accounts of canon which in turn were supporting contradictory visions of the Christian faith. In a move which prompts one to suggest that Descartes was the first really deep thinker to demythologize vital elements of the Christian faith, Descartes posited the inner light of reason as the true foundation of knowledge. By degrees he restored experience as a crucial secondary source of truth about the world. In time, these became the watchwords of the European Enlightenment. Two trajectories of thought—the rationalist represented by Descartes, Spinoza, and Leibniz, and the empiricist represented by Locke, Berkeley, and Hume—played themselves out in dazzling displays of intellectual virtuosity which are rightly seen as the jewels of

Western intellectual history. Where one originally looked for the sanctifying enlightenment of the Holy Spirit, one now looked for the plain enlightenment of reason and experience.

The most obvious expression of this takes place in the new move to put reason and experience alongside scripture and tradition as the canons of Christian theology. Anglican theologians began this process when they appealed to scripture, tradition, and reason. The followers of John Wesley in time completed the process by insisting that theological disputes be settled by an appeal to scripture, tradition, reason, and experience. The latter are especially significant, for it was the enthusiastic followers of Wesley who spread their Methodist version of Christianity to every nook and cranny of the New World.

The results of this for theology were devastating. Having broken the subtle harmonies and having restructured the rich canonical material developed in the formative period of Christian theology, Western theologians in their search for new theological visions became locked in endless battles about theological foundations and method. Their vast schemes of articles of religion, confessions of faith, and contradictory proposals, which were founded on these endless battles about method, bred in the end only skepticism and relativism. Theology became a barren slave to the prevailing philosophies of the day, or it regressed into forms of fundamentalism which tried to reject reason altogether by erecting its theology on scripture alone. Even the so-called biblical theology of a generation ago, which was thought to be such a secure way forward in the aftermath of Barth's appeal to the strange new world of the Bible, turned out to be one more short-lived experiment to find the functional equivalent of the creeds of the early church.

The explanation I have offered here is a quasi-historical one. It is historical in that it involves a summary narrative of the whole sweep of Western theology. Yet it is not merely historical, for it incorporates a normative judgment about the inevitable outcome of the fundamental moves that lie buried in the complexity of the Western traditions. The conclusion to which it tends is that we are at the kind of impasse which cannot be resolved by one more turn of the Western wheel. There needs to be a radical transcending of the options which have been played out, not just in the last generation but in the preceding generations which stretch back into the deep wells of the past. Disputes within modern Western theology about which philosophical dancing partner to take on the floor are as futile. Discussions about which sociopolitical positions to use in place of the philosophical positions of Plato and Aristotle are as irrelevant as spirited conversations about whether to appeal to *sola scriptura* or to scripture and tradition. The whole nest of issues centering on such themes needs to be cast in a radically different framework if we are to make progress.

Toward the future

Clearly these final comments call for extensive elaboration and defense. More importantly, they will evoke in the reader a request for some indication as to where they might positively lead in the field of systematic theology. The latter is clearly the more pressing concern, so let us ponder briefly some implications of the journey we have essayed. En route, let us dispose of some obvious misunderstandings which may arise.

First, nothing I have argued here should be taken as an expression of disrespect for the various North American experiments in theology. North Americans have their own unique relation to the Christian tradition, and they have their own unique rendering of the Christian heritage. It is abundantly clear that they have cast off the apron strings of attachment to the Old World which have so often led them to disparage their particular gifts and graces. Moreover, the Christian world as a whole gains nothing from a weak theological tradition in North America. So theological weeping and gnashing of teeth is not to be encouraged or applauded.

Second, whatever our final assessment of the current scene, it must be said that there is a vitality about theological discussion in North America which is interesting and exhilarating. Despite the continuation of polarities which have a long history in the culture, and despite the protracted fight over the control of ecclesiastical institutions, there is a combination of conviction and civility in the discussion which is a welcome change from the theological apathy one still finds in parts of Europe. There are vast constituencies of Christians, albeit ill-informed about the riches of the Christian tradition, who have a reservoir of talent and resources which is relevant to the fostering of commendable theological reflection. Moreover, there is a yearning for spiritual reality, which, if properly directed, may yet find expression in a deep reappropriation of the Christian gospel. [67]

Third, my diagnosis does not call for some kind of retreat into the past as the way ahead. We need neither a reawakening of pietism nor a return to some kind of patristic fundamentalism. We live at the end of the second millennium, so we cannot sweep aside the discoveries of the modern world, however difficult it may be to map what these are and how they relate to theology. Nor should we look to the addition of a new wing to theology—say, practical or applied theology—as the way ahead. These are mere gimmicks which do not reckon with the gravity of the situation.

What is called for is this. First, we must acknowledge that in theology our first task is to speak of God. Insofar as the theologian does not offer a set of proposals about God, Christ, salvation and the like, the primary task has not been executed. Critical conversation in theology must proceed far beyond reflection on theological method, and second-order discourse, to actual claims about the divine order. Without this, systematic theology is empty.

Second, systematic theology must find a more modest place for itself in the economy of the intellectual life of the Christian tradition. It cannot see itself any longer as providing an endless array of alternatives to replace the ecumenical creeds of the church. These are as much a part of the canonical heritage of the church as the scriptures, so the task of systematic theology must be radically reconceived. Its task is to provide a critically systematic articulation of the Christian faith as a whole that lays out its internal logic and makes manifest its inner connectedness. This may follow the topics laid out in the creeds of the early church, as is generally the case, but it need not do so, for its role is different from that of the creeds. The function of systematic theology is to provide a rounded account of the Christian faith that summarizes sharply and succinctly its fundamental content in ways which relate that content to the issues and problems of the day. Within this, there is ample space for the consideration of unresolved issues, for the identification of new problems in the tradition which come to light, for the examination of competing accounts of how to address fundamental issues of the day, and for the exploration of the ethical and political significance of Christian doctrine. [68]

Third, it is clear that in order to carry out these tasks, there is need of great intellectual skills and materials to be deployed and consulted. Theologians must continue to foster work in the relevant languages, in the study of scripture, in the historical investigation of doctrine, and in all the other disciplines which have a bearing on the content of the Christian heritage. Moreover, attention must be given to critical analyses of the life, ministry, and service of the church in the world and to the tangled problems which emerge in the interaction between faith and culture. Especially important in this regard is the revitalization of the philosophical conversation about the nature and merits of theological materials. This is not a call to make philosophy the foundation of systematic theology; even philosophically this is a thoroughly contested proposal. It is merely to recognize that theology involves claims which cannot be identified, clarified, and in some cases resolved without a deep exposure to the literature which deals with general questions about truth, meaning, justification, agency, explanation, causality, and a host of other topics which crop up again and again in both philosophy and theology.

Finally, there can be no theology without a substantial exposure to the divine revelation enshrined in the canonical traditions of the church. This is initially an epistemological point. God is made known through what God has done for the salvation of the world in creation, in history, in Jesus Christ, in the sacramental and liturgical life of the church, and in the work of the Holy Spirit in the life of the individual. It is these,

not the latest philosophy from Harvard, or Yale, or some populist movement dressed up in the language of French deconstructionism, which
are the foundations of all Christian discourse about God. However,
in the case of Christian theology, argument cannot be divorced from
spirituality. It is the pure in heart who see God. Knowledge about God
cannot be divorced from knowledge of God, and knowledge of God is
intimately related to repentance, to radical immersion in the life of the
Holy Spirit, to trusting obedience to the commands of God, to the fear
of the Lord, and to a deep humility before the ineffable mystery of
the divine reality.

> For the Law was a guide and a custodian leading us by the hand,
> teaching us righteousness and telling us, "You must do such and such,"
> and on the contrary, "You must not do such and such." But grace and
> truth (Jn. 1:17) are different. In what way? "You are to do and say all
> things in accordance with the grace given to you" (Rom. 12:3) "and
> speaking through you" (Mt. 10:20; Mk. 13:11). As it is written, "They
> shall all be taught by God" (Jn. 6:45), learning goodness not by writings
> and letters (cf. 2 Cor. 3:3, 6), but by being taught by the Holy Ghost.
> Not by word alone, but in the light of the word and in the word of the
> light are they mystically initiated into things divine. For He says, "Then
> will you become teachers both for yourselves and for your neighbors;
> more than that, you will be the light of the world and the salt of the
> earth" (cf. Mt. 5:13f.). [69]

---

1. Lonnie D. Kliever, *The Shattered Spectrum: A Survey of Contemporary Theology* (Atlanta:
John Knox Press, 1981).
2. John H. S. Kent, *The End of the Line? The Development of Christian Theology in the
Last Two Centuries* (Philadelphia: Fortress Press, 1982).
3. Alvin Plantinga, *Reformed Journal* 37 (1987), pp. 19–25.
4. *The Historian and the Believer* (Toronto: Macmillan, 1969).
5. "On the Intellectual Marginality of American Theology," in Michael J. Lacey, ed.,
Religion and Twentieth-Century American Intellectual Life (New York: Cambridge University
Press, 1989), p. 172.
6. "Theology in the USA: Whence and Whither," a paper presented at the American
Academy of Religion Annual Meeting, 1989, pp. 1–2.
7. The most elegantly written systematic theology of the last generation is, in my view,
the much used text of John Macquarrie, who taught at Union Seminary, New York,
before migrating to Oxford. *See* his *Principles of Christian Theology* (New York: Scribner,
1977). For a review of theology in the seventies, *see* Wallace M. Alston, Jr., et al.,
"Whatever Happened to Theology?," *Christianity and Crisis* 35 (1975), pp. 106–20.
8. The sociologist in question was Bryan Wilson of All Souls College, Oxford.
9. For a review of the English scene, *see* Dennis Nineham, "The Last Half-Century of
Theology: A Personal Impression," *Epworth Review* 16 (1989), pp. 47–57.
10. "History and the Question of Faith—Fifty Years of Theology in Retrospect," in
his *Worldly Theology* (New York: Scribner, 1967).
11. Ogden is currently University Distinguished Professor of Theology at Southern
Methodist University.
12. Ogden has explored this theme in his characteristically rigorous set of essays, *On
Theology* (San Francisco: Harper & Row, 1986).
13. There is an amazing industry devoted to the legacy of this Northern Irish lay

theologian. For a useful placing of Lewis in his intellectual context, *see* James Patrick, *The Magdalen Metaphysicals: Idealism and Orthodoxy at Oxford 1901–1945* (Macon, Ga.: Mercer University Press, 1985). For an account of his theology, *see* John Randolph Willis, *Pleasures Forevermore: The Theology of C. S. Lewis* (Chicago: Loyola University Press, 1983).

14. *Doxology: The Praise of God in Worship, Doctrine, and Life* (New York: Oxford University Press, 1980).

15. *The Living God* (San Francisco: Harper & Row, 1987); *The Word of Life* (San Francisco: Harper & Row, 1989).

16. *See* the separate contributions of Braaten and Jenson in their jointly edited two-volume work, *Christian Dogmatics* (Philadelphia: Fortress Press, 1984). This is an attempt by a team of theologians to provide a systematic theology in the American context from a Lutheran perspective.

17. *The Christian Story* (Grand Rapids, Mich.: W. B. Eerdmans Publishing Company, 1984).

18. *Ethics: Systematic Theology* (Nashville: Abingdon Press, 1986).

19. Member churches of the WCC are currently giving extended attention to the Nicene Creed.

20. See *After Modernity . . . What? Agenda for Theology* (Grand Rapids, Mich.: Academie Books, 1990).

21. *Pastoral Theology: Essentials of Ministry* (San Francisco: Harper & Row, 1982).

22. There is a wealth of material to consult. *See*, especially, James H. Cone, *A Black Theology of Liberation* (Maryknoll, N.Y.: Orbis Books, 1990); Rosemary Radford Ruether, *Sexism and God-Talk: Toward a Feminist Theology* (Boston: Beacon Press, 1983); Sallie McFague, *Models of God: Theology for an Ecological Nuclear Age* (Philadelphia: Fortress Press, 1987); Elisabeth Schüssler Fiorenza, ed., *In Memory of Her: A Feminist Theological Reconstruction of Christian Origins* (New York: Crossroad, 1983); Jacquelyn Grant, *White Women's Christ and Black Women's Jesus* (Atlanta: Scholars Press, 1989); and Justo L. González, *Mañana: Christian Theology From a Hispanic Perspective* (Nashville: Abingdon Press, 1990).

23. *Faith and Freedom: Toward a Theology of Liberation* (Nashville: Abingdon Press, 1989).

24. *See* David Martin, *Tongues of Fire: The Explosion of Protestantism in Latin America* (Oxford: B. Blackwell, 1990); and David Stoll, *Is Latin America Turning Protestant? The Politics of Evangelical Growth* (Berkeley: University of California Press, 1990).

25. "Different Gospels: The Social Sources of Apostasy," *This World* 17 (1987), p. 14.

26. *See*, e.g., Richard J. Bernstein, *Beyond Objectivism and Relativism* (Philadelphia: University of Pennsylvania Press, 1983); and W. H. Newton-Smith, *The Rationality of Science* (Boston: Routledge and Kegan Paul, 1981).

27. An excellent exception which proves the rule is undoubtedly the work of Cornel West, *The American Evasion of Philosophy, A Genealogy of Pragmatism* (Madison: University of Wisconsin Press, 1989).

28. *Sermons, Chiefly on the Theory of Religious Belief, Preached before the University of Oxford* (London: F. and J. Rivington, 1844), p. 304.

29. Ibid., p. 305.

30. Ibid., p. 306.

31. Ibid., p. 310.

32. *See*, e.g., the highly critical work of the Austrian feminist Susanne Heine, *Matriarchs, Goddesses, and Images of God* (Minneapolis: Augsburg, 1989).

33. *See*, e.g., Mark Kline Taylor, *Remembering Esperanza* (Maryknoll, N.Y.: Orbis Books, 1990). Taylor sees postmodern theology as faced with dealing with the trilemma of acknowledging the demands of tradition, of plurality, and of domination. Skillfully drawing on philosophical debates in hermeneutics and on nineteenth-century German debates about the relation between Christ and Jesus, he eventually makes the third element primary and overriding. Thereby he hopes to affirm the priority of the privilege of the oppressed.

34. (Philadelphia: Westminster Press, 1984).

35. Ibid., p. 10.

36. *See* Charles Monroe Wood, *Vision and Discernment* (Decatur, Ga.: Scholars Press, 1985).

37. William C. Placher, *Unapologetic Theology* (Louisville: Westminster/John Knox, 1989), p. 166.

38. *See* David Tracy, *Blessed Rage for Order: The New Pluralism in Theology* (New York: Seabury Press, 1975).

39. *See* Donald W. Dayton, "Yet Another Layer of the Onion: Or Opening the Ecumenical Door to Let the Riffraff in," *The Ecumenical Review*, vol. 40 (1988), pp. 87–110.

40. *See* Donald G. Bloesch, *Essentials of Evangelical Theology* (San Francisco: Harper & Row, 1978); H. Ray Dunning, *Grace, Faith and Holiness: A Wesleyan Systematic Theology* (Kansas City: Beacon Hill Press, 1988); Millard J. Erickson, *Christian Theology* (Grand Rapids, Mich.: Baker Book House, 1983); Gordon R. Lewis and Bruce A. Demarest, *Integrative Theology* (Grand Rapids, Mich.: Academie Books, 1987, 1990); Thomas N. Finger, *Christian Theology: An Eschatological Approach* (Nashville: Thomas Nelson, 1985); Dale Moody, *The Word of Truth* (Grand Rapids, Mich.: W. B. Eerdmans Publishing Company, 1981); J. Rodman Williams, *Renewal Theology: Salvation, the Holy Spirit and Christian Living* (Grand Rapids, Mich.: Academie Books, 1988, 1990); and James Leo Garrett, Jr., *Systematic Theology* (Grand Rapids, Mich.: W. B. Eerdmans Publishing Company, 1990).

41. For an evangelical review of modern theology, *see* Clark H. Pinnock, *Tracking the Maze* (San Francisco: Harper & Row, 1990).

42. *God, Revelation, and Authority* (Waco, Texas: Word Books, 1976).

43. *See*, e.g., Bernard Ramm, *After Fundamentalism: The Future of Evangelical Theology* (San Francisco: Harper & Row, 1983); and Gregory G. Bolich, *Karl Barth and Evangelicalism* (Downers Grove, Ill.: Intervarsity Press, 1980).

44. Harold Lindsell, *The Battle for the Bible* (Grand Rapids, Mich.: Zondervan Publishing House, 1976).

45. For an overoptimistic analysis of the situation in Britain, *see* Keith Ward, *The Turn of the Tide* (London: BBC Publications, 1986).

46. "Reason and Belief in God," in Alvin Plantinga and Nicholas Wolterstorff, eds., *Faith and Rationality: Reason and Belief in God* (Notre Dame, Ind.: University of Notre Dame, 1983), pp. 16–93.

47. *God, Freedom, and Evil* (New York: Harper & Row, 1974) and *The Nature of Necessity* (Oxford: Oxford University Press, 1974).

48. *The Coherence of Theism* (Oxford: Clarendon Press, 1977), *The Existence of God* (Oxford: Clarendon Press, 1979), *Faith and Reason* (Oxford: Clarendon Press, 1981), and *The Evolution of the Soul* (Oxford: Clarendon Press, 1986).

49. *The Justification of Religious Belief* (New York: Seabury Press, 1974).

50. For a review, *see* William J. Abraham, *An Introduction to the Philosophy of Religion* (Englewood Cliffs, N.J.: Prentice-Hall, 1985), ch. 9 and 10.

51. *See* Thomas V. Morris, ed., *Divine and Human Action: Essays in the Metaphysics of Theism* (Ithaca, N.Y.: Cornell University Press, 1988); and Alfred J. Freddoso, ed., *The Existence and Nature of God* (Notre Dame, Ind.: University of Notre Dame Press, 1983).

52. *Responsibility and Atonement* (Oxford: Clarendon Press, 1989).

53. Thomas V. Morris, *Philosophy and the Christian Faith* (Notre Dame, Ind.: University of Notre Dame Press, 1988).

54. *See*, e.g., George I. Mavrodes, *Revelation in Religious Belief* (Philadelphia: Temple University Press, 1988); Thomas V. Morris, *The Logic of God Incarnate* (Ithaca, N.Y.: Cornell University Press, 1986); William J. Abraham, *The Divine Inspiration of the Holy Scripture* (Oxford: Oxford University Press, 1981), and *Divine Revelation and the Limits of Historical Criticism* (Oxford: Oxford University Press, 1982).

55. *See* Alasdair C. MacIntyre, *After Virtue* (Notre Dame, Ind.: University of Notre Dame Press, 1981), *Whose Justice? Which Rationality?* (Notre Dame, Ind.: University of Notre Dame Press, 1988), and *Three Rival Versions of Moral Enquiry* (Notre Dame, Ind.: University of Notre Dame Press, 1990); Basil Mitchell, *Morality, Religious and Secular* (Oxford: Clarendon Press, 1980); and Jean Porter, *The Recovery of Virtue* (Louisville: Westminster/John Knox Press, 1990).

56. This should not be pressed too far. There is here a common problem of what to do when confronted with deep differences of opinion among experts. For a discussion of this, *see* Basil Mitchell, "The Layman's Predicament," in his *On How to Play Theological Ping-Pong*, ed. William J. Abraham and Robert Prevost (Grand Rapids, Mich.: W. B. Eerdmans Publishing Company, 1990).

57. *See* "On How to Play Theological Ping-Pong," in the volume of essays with this title cited above.

58. This is beautifully laid out in an older classic in the field. *See* Henry Chadwick, *Early Christian Thought and the Classical Tradition* (Oxford: Clarendon Press, 1966).

59. *The Triads* (New York: Paulist Press, 1983), p. 28.

60. Archimandrite Vasileios of Stavronikíta, *Hymn of Entry* (Crestwood, N.Y.: St. Vladimir's Seminary Press, 1984), p. 28.

61. *See*, e.g., Peter Medawar, *Memoir of a Thinking Radish* (New York: Oxford University Press, 1986), p. 77.

62. *See* Georges Florovsky, *The Collected Works* (Büchervertriebsanstalt, 1987), and also Alexander Schmemann, *Introduction to Liturgical Theology* (Crestwood, N.Y.: St. Vladimir's Seminary Press, 1986), and *The Eucharist—Sacrament of the Kingdom* (Crestwood, N.Y.: St. Vladimir's Seminary Press, 1988).

63. *Ways of Russian Theology*, vols. 5 and 6 of *The Collected Works*.

64. This claim should be received with great caution. It is unlikely that any of the theologians of the patristic period had a governing theory of the relation between faith and philosophy. One suspects that particular hints made quite tentatively are picked up and formalized at a later point in the West.

65. Gregory of Nyssa, *The Life of Moses* (New York: Paulist Press, 1978), pp. 56–57.

66. *See* John Meyendorff, *A Study of Gregory Palamas* (Crestwood, N.Y.: St. Vladimir's Seminary Press, 1964).

67. Much will depend on the spiritual and ecclesial renewal of the Christian faith in North America. For a useful discussion of this, *see* John H. Leith, *From Generation to Generation* (Louisville: Westminster/John Knox Press, 1990).

68. It is in this last domain that we need to speak to the issues raised by liberation theologians. For a significant analysis, *see* Glenn E. Tinder, *The Political Meaning of Christianity* (Baton Rouge: Louisiana State University, 1989).

69. Symeon the New Theologian, *The Discourses*, trans. C. J. deCatanzaro (New York: Paulist Press, 1980), p. 297.

Music as a Liberal Art

Bruce Venable

Bruce Venable was born in Portland, Oregon, where he was educated in public and parochial schools. He attended St. Mary's College of California, from which he received a B.A. (philosophy), and in 1976 he got a doctorate in classics at the University of Washington, Seattle. His professional career has been spent at St. John's College, Santa Fe, New Mexico, where he has been a tutor—the only rank recognized by the faculty there—since 1973.

Although the limited writing that his rigorous teaching program allows time for has been devoted to Plotinus, whose *Six Enneads* appear in the *Great Books of the Western World* (I: 17, 1–360; II: 11, 301–678), and to a certain St. Symeon, of whom he has published a discussion in *Orthodox Outlook* (U.K.), 6, no. 1 (1989), his chief interest is in liturgical music. He often leads choral groups at St. John's and enjoys choir singing himself at the Russian Cathedral in London. His other interests are cycling and hiking, gardening, and concertgoing. A second article by him on music will appear in next year's *The Great Ideas Today*.

The question to which I shall address myself here concerning the significance of music is relevant in a variety of contexts. We can ask, and indeed it has been asked, whether music is essentially an emotional, a moral, a cosmological, or a purely formal thing. The question is especially relevant with respect to teaching and learning, where there is a certain obscurity in our inherited scheme of the liberal arts. These have a traditional order, namely: grammar, rhetoric, logic (the trivium), arithmetic, geometry, music, astronomy (the quadrivium). The position of music in that scheme appears anomalous because, although music stands next to astronomy in the quadrivium as a science of some real objects or phenomena—related to arithmetic, as number in motion, in the same way as astronomy is related to geometry, as figure in motion—music nonetheless has rhetorical functions as well, appealing as it seems to do to the emotions, that would ally it rather with the arts of the trivium. Like rhetoric also, music is both a theory and a practice.

That music seems to occupy a position between the two divisions of the liberal arts may possibly indicate not only the amphibious nature of music but also some fundamental incoherence in the system itself. There is nothing sacred after all in the traditional classification of the liberal arts, itself a scholastic convention of late antiquity, [1] but most theorists of music have continued to think within the framework of the system, preferring to rearrange it rather than question or abandon it. The history of these rearrangements forms the framework of this essay, giving, I hope, new meaning to the tired argument about whether music is essentially a language of the emotions, like rhetoric, or a construction of significant forms, like astronomy.

The broader tradition contains some doubts whether music is intellectually or even humanly significant at all. Immanuel Kant, for example, says that music, although it is agreeable to the senses and speaks eloquently about the emotions, is nonetheless incoherent and almost completely lacking in intellectual content (*GBWW* I: 42, 534–39; II: 39, 534–39). Even William James, who as a psychologist might be supposed to have been more sensitive to the value of human emotions, felt compelled to conclude that a love of music was, like fear of high places and a liability to seasickness, "a mere incidental peculiarity of the nervous system . . . with no teleological significance" (chap. 24;

GBWW I: 53, 723; II: 53, 723). That is, it does not contribute to the success of the species or to the fulfillment of the individual. But neither Kant nor James seems to have been close to the traditional understanding of music.

Within the traditional context of the liberal arts, several questions may be profitably asked. Why does music seem to share the character of the trivial arts as a kind of language of the emotions, and like them not completely rational, as well as that of the arts of the quadrivium? Also, what would the traditional definition of music as "number in motion" mean at all? Can numbers move? Finally, if music is a liberal art, from what does it liberate us?

Returning briefly to James, one may note that he had studied the theories that had multiplied in the nineteenth century concerning the emotional content of music but found them imprecise and impressionistic, demonstrating only that there are, in certain cultures, certain habitual responses to various recognizable kinds of music, as waltzes, hymns, marches, love songs, and the like.

Twentieth-century theorists remain similarly perplexed about the alleged emotional significance of music; many seem to reject it with a certain regret, but also with wonderment that a theory so obviously inadequate should be so deeply rooted in the common sense of things in our culture. It may be important that much twentieth-century art music appears to many listeners to be without obvious emotional content and is in fact often offered by its composers as having a purely formal, even mathematical, beauty. Many people who love music are disappointed in modern music because it does not give them the sort of emotional satisfaction that they seek and find in older music (e.g., that of Brahms or Bach or even Monteverdi), whereas contemporary theorists find themselves unable to explain how this desired emotional satisfaction can be felt at all, in any music, except because of conventional associations that have nothing to do with the musical structure itself. There appears then to be a certain impasse in the contemporary understanding of music. It will, I hope, be useful to return to a much earlier stage in the discussion and to consider in this matter the curious and apparently eccentric view of Proclus, the fifth-century commentator on Plato and Euclid, that not only music but the soul itself is a mathematical construction.

Ancient views of music

Everyone is familiar with the fundamental "Pythagorean" discovery that all the tones of the ordinary diatonic scale are derived from a single root tone by a series of simple ratios: one to two, two to three, three to four, and so forth, where the numbers refer to the lengths of vibrating strings, as on the lyre, or to the heights of vibrating columns of air, as in the flute. The Pythagoreans, we are told, thought that the diatonic order was fundamental not only to music but to the inner structure and form of the universe. We are told in Plato's *Phaedo,* moreover, that they regarded the human soul as a harmony or attunement of its parts, and that a disease or neurosis of the soul was a false tuning or cacophony of these parts.

Later literature about the Pythagoreans—for example, the lives of Pythagoras by Porphyry and by Iamblichus, who were not, however, themselves Pythagoreans but Neoplatonists of the third and fourth centuries of our era, a thousand years after the time of Pythagoras—tells us that the Pythagoreans believed in the therapeutic value of music. Thus in their communities they played a certain melodic mode in the morning to induce a cheerful attitude to the day's work, another in the afternoon to refresh the soul after the day's labors, yet another in the evening to promote peaceful slumber and harmless dreams, and had still other melodies that answered to specific disorders: fear, anxiety, or hypertension. These Pythagorean beliefs in the moral and therapeutic value of music are already implied by Homer's story that the gods sent epic poets to guard the virtue of Clytemnestra and Penelope and by the old genealogy that made Asclepius, the god of healing, the son of Apollo, the god of music. What is significant in this discussion is that the Pythagoreans seem to have combined an appreciation of the emotional value of music with a deep conviction of its fundamentally mathematical character.

We are often told that Pythagorean ideas are present in the *Timaeus* of Plato. It is not then surprising to find that the soul of the universe is there described as mathematical: it is ordered by numerical ratios, laid out along a straight line, then divided into perfect circles, and the whole system set in regular motion. Timaeus declares that this mathematical formation of the world soul is the *arche,* the beginning and principle, of its eternal life, self-contained, blessed, happy, and serene. Here again is an intimate connection between order and contentment.

Individual souls are formed after this pattern, but from inferior materials, so it is not so easy for them—that is, for us—to be happy. Such happiness as we are able to possess we may attain if we strive to assimilate the usually disordered movements of our souls to the harmonious pattern of the movements of the world soul. Because the world soul is not confined to a single place but is present at every point in the universe, its influence is felt everywhere and can be perceived even by the senses: the unvarying procession of the stars and planets, the sun, the moon, and the seasons, are seen by the eyes, while the ears perceive no less clearly the harmonies of sound.

> God invented and gave us sight so that, perceiving the cycles of the
> intellect (*nous*) in the heavens, we might apply them to the cycles of our

reasoning (*dianoēsis*) which are akin to them, applying their ordered motion to our perturbed motion, and that we, learning from them and participating in the correctness of natural calculation (*logismas*), imitating the unerring paths of God, might so regulate our own wanderings. The same can be said of . . . hearing. . . . Harmony, which has motions that are related by birth to the revolutions of our souls, seems to have been given by the Muses not for the sake of an irrational pleasure, as people now think, but to be our ally in bringing the discordant motion of our souls into concord and symphony with itself. Rhythm too was given as our helper against our irregular and graceless habits. [2] (Cf. *GBWW* I: 7, 455; II: 6, 455.)

The exhortation to rediscover and to actualize the likeness of the soul to its divine archetype, and so to bring the soul into harmony both with itself and with the universe, is a common theme in Plato. One especially memorable passage is the famous digression in the *Theaetetus* describing the vocation of the philosopher as attaining likeness to God, but the idea is clearly presupposed also by the doctrine of knowledge as recollection.

What is especially relevant here is the suggestion that the soul's perfection is somehow mathematical, at least in the not entirely metaphorical sense that this perfection consists in an ordered succession of clearly articulated moments, like the seasons of the orbits of the planets, all subordinated to the single idea of the whole. The individual soul finds its perfection and happiness in contemplating itself transparently contained and grounded in this universal whole as a part of it and yet self-sufficient as an image of the perfect whole. Happiness consists in the simultaneous apprehension of its partial yet complete life and the life of the world soul which includes and perfects it.

Something characterized as mere pleasurable satisfaction is disparaged in the *Theaetetus* (176a–177a; *GBWW* I: 7, 530; II: 6, 530). In fact, this idea of perfection and human happiness seems to leave no room for anything so transitory as an emotion, except for the final assurance and stillness of soul that accompany self-knowledge. Nevertheless, such perfection is truly musical insofar as music too has its foundation in mathematical relations. I shall, however, delay to consider the emerging contradiction concerning the alleged emotional character of music until I have explored the consequences of supposing, as Plato does in this dialogue, that the nature of the soul is mathematical and that it satisfies itself in the perception and enjoyment of its inherent, relatively autonomous, perfection rather than in the pathos of an emotion, where it rather surrenders itself to an external object of desire or, it may be, of aversion.

The *Timaeus* began to be studied again during the early years of the Roman Empire, after what seems to have been a period of comparative neglect during the Hellenistic Age; its popularity continued right through the Middle Ages in western Europe, when it was the only work of Plato commonly known, and into the Renaissance. During these 1,500 years the dialogue, especially the passage about the construction of the world soul, was much admired and studied. It will be pertinent, therefore, to see how this passage was interpreted, what beliefs it inspired, and to what hopes it seemed to promise fulfillment.

Many of these interpretations were clearly religious: they sought to arouse in the soul a lively sentiment of its kinship with the divine world and a desire to purify itself of earthly involvements and return to its heavenly home. Religious impulses can also be strongly felt in a vaguely defined group of ideas that scholars have agreed to call Gnosticism. The historical origins of this remain obscure, but it is clear enough that some Gnostic writers known to us were influenced by the *Timaeus,* especially its tendency to see the fate of the individual soul in the context of the whole universe. Moreover, Plotinus, the founder of a revival of interest in Plato called Neoplatonism, a school of thought to which Proclus also belonged, was personally acquainted with some Gnostics at Rome and in his fervent attack on their teaching accuses them of having stupidly or maliciously distorted the ideas of Plato about the nature of the soul. The Neoplatonists, in fact, struggled continuously with Gnosticism, precisely because of the disturbing similarities between the two doctrines, until both were supplanted by their common rival, orthodox Christianity.

The struggle with Gnosticism can profitably be seen in terms of the question posed by the *Timaeus:* how is the soul related to the universe? Neoplatonists shared with Gnostics a belief in the immortality of the soul. For both of them this meant that the soul was divine in nature or, mythologically speaking, celestial in origin. The soul was originally born from or created by the divine intellect, and remains essentially related to the divine world despite the soul's descent into earthly life. The challenge to the incarnate soul is to realize its unearthly nature, to purify itself from the incrustations of its temporary life in the body, and to ascend to the happiness that it enjoyed in the company of the gods before it became entangled with earth. (All this is purely Platonic as well. Although individual emphases vary, one may say in general that Gnostics preferred a literal or mythological representation but Neoplatonists a metaphorical or intellectualized interpretation of these common ideas.) [3]

What makes the difference between Neoplatonists and Gnostics is that the latter refused to identify the divine intellect with the demiurge of the *Timaeus* because they insisted that this visible world—not just the human body, but the entire cosmos as well—was not in any sense the creation of God. They asserted that the cosmos was artfully fashioned by the demiurge as a prison for incarnate souls who had somehow fallen into it from their true supercelestial home with the divine intellect. The very beauty of the cosmos was seen by them as a seduction, and the perfect regularity of its seasonal movements struck them as an inescapable machine devised by a malicious genius to entrap and detain souls in subjection to his evil will. The souls were not originally and are not naturally subject to the laws of destiny, because these only enslave them within the universe. Souls are rather essentially free of the world order and superior to it, having been born in the immaterial realm of the divine intellect. The Gnostic felt that his soul had been cast out of its luminous home into this gloomy, murky morass of sensuality and decay where it wandered about, a stranger and alone, searching for a passage of escape up through the celestial spheres, a narrow way that it could scarcely find, since its vision was blinded and its mind intoxicated by the vain delights of this deceitful world.

Neoplatonists responded to this "melodrama of terrors" [4] with an unconcealed hostility that is a bit hard to understand at first. Indeed, much of the Gnostic mythology sounds familiar. Neoplatonists too had read the *Phaedo* and received eagerly its urgent call for renunciation, purification, and escape, but even so, when they heard Gnostics say that the world was simply evil, that its creator was malicious, that its beauty, frail and brief though it is, was simply a lie and a trap, and that the benighted Gnostic believer, confident of his kinship with a God who reigned beyond the whole universe, imagined himself superior even to the blessed sun and moon, they lost their tempers. Indeed, they accused the Gnostics, even those who had once been their friends (Plotinus, 2nd Ennead, IX.10; *GBWW* I: 17, 72; II: 11, 375), of preaching sentimental, paranoid fantasies, megalomaniacal delusions of self-importance, grotesque, operatic exaggerations of both the misery and grandeur of human life, and, in general, of misinterpreting the teachings of Plato.

Despite their deeply-held belief that the world is a confusing place in which to work out one's eternal salvation, Neoplatonists believed that our destiny cannot be understood outside of it. We are an integral part of the world order, not mere victims or wayfarers; we belong to the cosmos essentially and cannot project ourselves beyond it by any gesture of renunciation, transcendence, or disgust.

The place of mathematics

It is in the context of the spiritual struggle with Gnosticism that we may approach Proclus's interpretation of the *Timaeus*. I shall confine myself to a few of his very abundant comments on the construction of the world soul.

The construction, according to Proclus, has three phases. In the first, the demiurge, or creator, takes a huge mixing bowl. He pours into it some indivisible existence and an equal quantity of divisible existence—

that is, equal amounts of ideal and material existence—and mixes them well together. He makes, in other bowls, similar mixtures of indivisible and divisible sameness and of indivisible otherness and adds them to the first mixture, blending the whole until he forms a workable dough which he then rolls out into a long strip. [5] In the second phase, he marks off this strip into divisions corresponding to the intervals of a musical scale—what the Greeks called a "harmony." The details are fairly intricate, but it works out that he forms a continuous diatonic scale, down to the whole tones and semitones, using arithmetic, geometric, and harmonic proportions to fill in the intervals, and extending the whole series to the number 27. The strip is then (the third phase) cut in half lengthwise and the halves bent around to form two circles which are joined to one another at an acute angle, like the Greek letter X (*chi*). The circles, although fastened together, move independently of one another with the motion of the same and the motion of the other creating the celestial equator and the oblique motion of the ecliptic.

The two basic ideas Proclus extracts from this complex construction is that the soul is intermediate between the ideal and the material worlds, and that this intermediacy consists in the fact that the soul is composed of every sort of mathematical proportion, not just some kinds. [6]

Proclus means that the soul is neither simply divine, as the Gnostics held, nor simply material, as various other philosophical schools and innumerable ordinary people held and do hold, but rather intermediate between the completely divine world of the archetypes of the universe and the merely corporeal world we seem to experience.

The intermediacy of the world is also mathematical. Proclus explains that real, ideal being is completely indivisible, while the pseudo being of bodies is infinitely divisible. The ideas, as stated in Plato's *Sophist,* form a unified system with each other, whereas bodies have no unity of their own, and form an indefinite plurality. The soul, however, is mathematical, that is, it is an ordered and unified plurality. Thus the soul is indeed divisible, like the objects of perception, but is properly so only in regular patterns. It thus shares somewhat in the confused life of divided things and somewhat also in the coherence and unity of divine things.

Moreover, Proclus insists that these mathematical ratios and objects already existed when the soul was made—the demiurge already knew about them—and that they are not caused by the mixture of divisible and indivisible being. Thus if, like Proclus and almost everyone else in antiquity except Aristotle, we interpret the *Timaeus* not mythologically, as describing the primeval activities of a real creator, but rather analytically, as describing the eternal state of the universe, [7] it results that the soul is not in fact composed from divisible and indivisible being as elements but is itself a third kind of being, eternally intermediate between them and binding them together; this can only be mathematical being. Further, if the soul is eternal and the mathematicals are eternal, then music too is eternal.

Proclus on Euclid

The nature and divisions of mathematics are discussed more completely in Proclus's commentary on Euclid, to which we now turn. The sequence of subjects in the prologue is most significant.

Proclus begins by stating the triple division of being, with mathematics lying between ideal or indivisible being and material or composite being, and sharing the qualities of the extreme terms. The fact that mathematical propositions are incontrovertible—that they possess demonstrable certainty—indicates that mathematical objects are superior to the things that move in matter and cannot, in a strict sense, be known at all, but can only be guessed at by opinion. But the fact that the procedure of mathematics is discursive and uses imagination to consider its objects as extended in space indicates that its objects are inferior in purity and simplicity to the indivisible being of the forms. This has no cause or foundation but itself, and can therefore be grasped purely in itself, without reference to any possible representation.

One sees here that Proclus argues, as modern philosophers put it, "transcendentally." He moves from the various acts of human knowledge to the corresponding objects that their diverse characters imply. From the fact that our knowledge of the forms is unmixed with sensation or imagery, that it is immediate, precise, and certain, he concludes that the forms themselves are completely independent of matter and any imaginable shape, and that they are always what they are and never anything else. In short, he concludes that the forms have exactly those characteristics which alone would make them the objects of the kind of knowledge we actually have of them. Similarly, Proclus concludes from the fact that mathematics demonstrates its theorems with perfect clarity and certitude, but must use for these demonstrations a discursive, argumentative process and must conceive its objects as extended in space, where they are divisible and multiple—that these objects themselves are more coherent and self-consistent than the objects of sensation, but more diffuse and less unified with themselves than the forms.

To summarize, because mathematical knowledge is intermediate in character between intuitive certainty and sense perception or opinion, Proclus concludes that its objects, the mathematicals, are intermediate in character between the ideal forms and material things.

Proclus is explicit about this conclusion, but states it in reverse: he says that because there are three degrees of being, there are three degrees of knowledge that refer to them. Of course the same correlation of degrees of being and degrees of knowledge results, but it is significant that Proclus presents his argument, which is in fact from knowledge to being, as if it had been from being to knowledge. The argument gains in clarity because it begins from what is closest to ourselves, from our own experience of knowledge and ignorance. But, because it relates these experiences to objective degrees of being, it gives them an irrefutable foundation in reality. Our experience of ourselves becomes self-knowledge only when it is thus transparently grounded in reality. We know ourselves, clearly and certainly, when we relate ourselves, in knowledge, to being itself. I shall consider later in greater detail the significance of this tendency to find the true nature of the self in relation to what is not self.

Proclus next considers the first principles of mathematical being and finds them to be the same as the first principles of all being: namely, the limit (*to peras*) and the unlimited (*apeiron*). These are discussed as first principles in the *Philebus* of Plato (*GBWW* I: 7, 612, 615ff.; II: 6, 612, 615ff.) and are assumed, under the names "the one" and "the indefinite dyad," in Aristotle's various accounts of Platonism. [8]

From the limit and the unlimited are caused or derived, in an ordered procession, all other beings. The forms are the first to be derived, and then, *from them,* the mathematicals, while from the mathematicals we get living nature, and finally material things. The limit and the unlimited are themselves derived from a single superior cause, but it, or He, does not come into this story; Proclus does not, in the narrowest sense, present a *theo*logy of music.

Everything caused by the limit and the unlimited share their opposed characters. Even the forms have these two kinds of character. They derive their simplicity, self-identity, and stability from the limit; but their variety and diversity, their fertility as generators of everything that lies below them in the order of procession, and the fact that they have themselves proceeded from unity into manyness, are all derived from the power of the unlimited. Still, the power of the limit prevails, in that the forms are finite in number. Mathematicals show a greater dominance of the power of the unlimited; because, for example, the numbers are infinitely many, ratios can be indefinitely extended, and magnitudes are continuously divisible. But mathematical operations are ordered sequences and remain therefore under the control of the limit. In the realities that appear in matter, both original causes still make themselves felt: the limit as the vestiges of rational ordering, the unlimited as the restless power that tends always to obscure, blur, and in general to undo the designs of reason.

Proclus then asks himself what are the most fundamental theorems of mathematics? He answers that they are those concerning equality and inequality and those concerning proportion, this last being a universal power that reduces even inequality to order and makes all things beautiful. [9]

He then inquires after the origin of these fundamental theorems. They prove to be absolutely prior to their many separate instances and are not derived from them by some abstractive effort of human thought. This is what people mean when they say that Proclus teaches the self-subsistence of the mathematicals.

However, as we remember he has said, mathematical principles are not completely independent. Just as higher sciences lend their principles to inferior sciences (e.g., as geometry provides axioms for astronomy), so mathematical principles, precisely because they are discursive or dianoetic, are derived from the more concentrated power of *nous* and from *nous* derive their validity. This fact is called the relative self-subsistence of mathematicals.

Consequently, it is possible to proceed from the lower sciences to the higher and from lower degrees of reality to higher degrees, because the lower degrees imply their causes. Therefore the order of discovery is the reverse of the order of causation. This is a principle of great generality.

The reverse movement of inference is called "regression" and corresponds in all details to procession. Proclus had already referred to these symmetrical movements at the beginning of the commentary in a passage that now becomes clear. "Mathematical reasoning unfolds the content of *nous* by making articulate its concentrated intellectual insight and then gathers together the things it has distinguished and refers them back to *nous*." [10] *Dianoia* [reasoning] takes its principles from *nous* [intellect] but cannot understand them unless it expresses their simple truth in more or less complicated arguments and diffuse representations. But *dianoia* strives also, by gathering together again its many diagrams and theorems, to approximate the simple insight of *nous*. Proclus always speaks in this way of intellectual operations as if they were alive.

Proclus asks again where the mathematicals come from, again denies that they are abstracted from sensations, because in that case their precision would be unexplained, and asserts, not that the *nous* contains them, but that the soul itself generates the mathematicals, both the *eide* and the *logoi*. [11] The *eide* are the *onta*, the real things that are the natural objects of knowing; the *logoi* are the acts by which the *eide* are actually known. Here again is the close correlation of kinds of being with kinds of knowledge. The mathematicals belong to the soul essentially (*kat'ousian*) so that when the soul labors at mathematics it is not bringing knowledge into itself, as if the soul were poor and hungry and lacking in content, but is striving to bring to light the eternal forms that abide always within it.

But how can the soul generate the mathematicals if, as already stated, the mathematicals are derived from *nous*? Does the soul obtain the mathematicals from itself alone or from *nous* alone or from both? If from itself alone, the mathematicals will not be images or expressions of the intelligible forms contained in *nous* and the soul will be cut off from its cause, without, as it were, any way back. Yet if the mathematicals come from *nous* alone, how can the soul be moving and discovering itself when it knows them? Because he has already denied these undesirable consequences, Proclus now chooses the third alternative: the mathematicals come from *nous* and the soul. The soul is the fullness or *pleroma* of the mathematicals, which in turn depend for their existence upon the more universal *eide* (e.g., sameness and difference) that belong to *nous*. "The soul therefore was never a writing tablet empty of writing, but was always written upon, writing itself, and being written by *nous*." [12] This fact is called the relative self-subsistence of the soul.

The soul thus is a life, not merely a substance, that expresses itself in acts of thinking its own objects of thought. But this life is itself derived from *nous,* a higher, more powerful, and concentrated center and source of life. Although relatively independent, certainly, of the body that seems to confine it, the life of the soul points beyond itself to this source of its life. In fact, there is only one life, not just one source of life, but a single, universal life that from itself creates and within itself contains the various forms of life. The procession of these forms is an eternal order, although manifested in time, so that the various forms of life are simultaneous and their interrelations more like logical implications than a line of causality. When the soul "returns" to *nous* it does not really go anywhere, it simply lives a different act of life. Thus Proclus says that soul *is nous* when it shares in the life and activity of *nous.* [13] In fact, he says elsewhere that everything is everything else, but lest everything mush together into a monotonous sameness like the primeval oatmeal from which the demiurge made the world, he adds: "Everything is in everything, but in each thing after its own fashion [*panta en pasin, all'oikeiōs en ekastō*]." [14]

When he says here that the soul is *nous,* he means that all the contents of *nous* are given by it to the soul so that the soul is rich and need desire no alien thing to know or love. But soul and *nous* are distinct because the soul possesses the contents of *nous* in its own fashion. *Nous* concentrates these contents in a single unifying act of intuition; in the soul they are diffused and expanded after the fashion of an ordered sequence. The modes of existence are different but the content of their being is the same. Thus, nothing changes in the universe but the modes of existence or, to put it otherwise, the motions of procession and regression are real only for the individual. Individual souls, for example, have histories: they tend to wander off in search of external satisfactions because they forget that their happiness lies within themselves and their own power. The soul needs only to realize, that is, to understand and so make real for itself, the perfection inherent in its existence, a perfection that is always near to it, always available to it, and which is obscured by ignorance alone. The fact that the soul has proceeded from *nous* does not mean that it has fallen away from its perfection, that it has lost its happiness, nor does regression mean that the soul needs to escape from its life to find happiness elsewhere. Procession and regression rather express the fact that the soul essentially participates in a universal life that gives it a life of its own without abandoning it to itself.

Therefore, Proclus concludes, Plato is correct when he constructs the soul from mathematical forms and makes its vital motions intelligent. Only mathematics can bind together the disordered world of random physical motion with the stable, but aloof, world of pure reason; only mathematics, likewise, can link the confused sense experience of the soul with ideas of pure order; only mathematics, finally, can lead the erratic emotions of the soul into paths of grace and decorum. In Proclus's own terms, the mathematical order of the soul is a second world order (*diakosmos*) that is an image but also a participation in the purely intelligible or eidetic world order that belongs to *nous*. The eternal, regular movements of the world soul contain unmistakable reference to the intellectual order, altogether outside of time or any change, upon which they depend.

After inquiring into a variety of interesting questions about mathematics, Proclus concludes his prologue by dedicating the commentary to Hermes, the awakener and guide of souls. [15]

How mathematics is like the soul

Now then, returning to the *Timaeus* commentary, what is centrally important is the way in which Proclus has described the intermediacy of mathematicals and the soul.

The intermediacy of mathematics is formal: if mathematics did not provide the logical connection between real being and corporeal being, the universe would fall apart into two unrelated halves and cease to be a universe at all.

The intermediacy of the soul is vital because the soul gives an ordered motion to the chaos of matter, makes natural things sympathetic to each other, and illuminates the darkness of passion with the contented radiance of its own inner life.

The coincidence of the soul and the mathematicals must be understood as reciprocal: not only does the soul move in mathematical proportion but, conversely, these proportions are motive and living. Life and movement are not added to the mathematicals from without— from the disordered motions of physical things, for example. Rather, these live and move, organizing the entire world of natural forms as a part of the perfection of their own nature, permeating all things with their eternal blessed life, binding all things into a unique and perfect whole. There are no dead forms in nature: even a crystal *grows*. The harmonious movement of the world soul, impregnating nature with number and measure, is the eternal melody of its inner life, knowing and loving itself and its creator and making all natural things aware of one another as joined in a single being. Human music, too, simply because it is number in harmonious motion, sound arranged in shapes and lines, is an image and participation of this life moving peacefully within itself, simple and self-contained.

In short, if the mathematicals were not alive, order would be dead, cold, and foreign to the soul. If the soul were not mathematical, life would be aimless and out of sympathy with itself. Therefore the soul and the mathematicals form a single, eternal, ordered, but living motion, bursting with diversity, but whole and serene.

This serenity is not, perhaps, all that we desire of a happy life, but it is an ideal that we might profitably reconsider when we are able to withdraw ourselves a bit, as we are now, from the excitements, passions, and disappointments of our usual loves, reminding ourselves, under the guidance of Hermes, of what usually happens to us when we surrender to them.

Individual souls, although eternal beings and images of the world soul, must choose their personal character. They sometimes choose to forget themselves and their own happiness, becoming fascinated by the superficial beauties of the disordered world and entangled in the disordered responses to them that they call their emotions. The soul falls in love because of a despairing belief that it has nothing of its own, that it is poor and empty and must try to fill itself with experiences that are in fact temporary, external, and accidental. Thus the soul wanders helpless and forlorn through the squalid quarters of sensuality and the splendid palaces of art, seeking, yet ever in vain, for some experience or passion, something that merely happens to it, to satisfy its restless desire to mean something, not realizing, in its drunkenness and ignorance, that it is beautiful and noble in itself and is only seeking to be filled by worthless things that can never make it content.

The soul is always related, in the unchangeable center of its being, to the realm of ideal being which is truly beautiful and which alone can satisfy it. This world truly belongs to the soul because it is the power and presence of its cause and the source of its inner life. The soul must turn toward the ideal world, as to the fountain of its happiness, by its innate power of converging upon itself in self-knowledge, understanding itself to be strong, vivid, and alive with a life that is truly its own but whose inner movement is directed upward or, more accurately, yet more deeply within itself, to the power of intellect that orders and fulfills all things. The soul enters into itself and there discovers the harmonious rational order that is the real meaning of the violent movements of the material world and the clamorous emotions of the soul's own material life. This order is also the soul's private access to the immutable world of real being that is the only finally peaceful and satisfying object of desire, because it alone can be known and had as an everlasting possession.

Here is the meaning of the intermediacy of the soul: that the soul, precisely because of its mathematical nature, possesses the power to order the appearances of the material world as well as its own disordered passions. This power is the impress and presence in the soul of the providential power of divine intellect, of which it is the manifestation and living energy. The power of the soul to ordain is at once a power of perfecting itself according to its own inherent law and also the power of transcending itself by relating itself to the inner source of this very power. The way by which it affirms itself is the way in which it surpasses itself. This is precisely the double power of mathematics: a self-sufficient system that orders the world of the senses but also refers upward to the all-encompassing power of the intellect.

Music is, for Proclus, not only an image of this reaching for happiness but also a door that stands open within ourselves to this happiness. Let us explore the image first. During the Middle Ages and Renaissance, as long as the tradition of the *Timaeus* endured, hundreds of passages were written describing the world order as an immense symphony that weaves diverse forces and elements into a complex but unitary texture ruled by the friendship of harmony. A familiar literary version is the music of the spheres—the sweet but, alas, inaudible harmony produced by the revolutions of the stars and planets.

Kepler, writing at the beginning of a new age that found this idea a mere poetic fancy and had little use for the intermediate world of the imagination, offers an elaborate account of the celestial harmony; he compares the apparent irregularities of the planetary motions to passing discords in polyphonic music that are resolved again into perfect consonances (*GBWW* I: 16, 1040–48; II: 15, 1040–48). For him and for the long tradition that he summarizes, the human art of music is the image of the universal mathematical art by which God governs the universe.

According to this ancient conception, the primary power of music is to create coherent systems of sound and not to express or excite any emotion whatever. It is exactly these momentary passions that are shown, like passing dissonances, to be inessential when they are included in a rational pattern. The writers of the Renaissance were quite conscious of the emotional power of music; they frequently refer to the exploits of Amphion, constructing the walls of Thebes by leading even the stones into place with the sound of his lyre, and Orpheus, taming savage beasts with his lute. They emphasized also the pleasure that the soul takes when its transitory emotions are resolved and sublimated in repose. When the soul listens to music, it hears, at least subliminally, its formal structure and rejoices, perceiving an order akin to itself but

Orpheus, who was a half-god of the ancient Greeks in having for his mother Calliope, the Muse of epic—that is, narrative—poetry, is represented here playing a lyre to tame the animals. Roman mosaic from Palermo, Italy.

deeper than its passions, those momentary and superficial disturbances of its enduring tranquillity. The soul accepts the beautiful order it perceives and so brings its own inner motions into sympathy with those regular motions. But because the principles of mathematical order in music—symmetry, balance, and proportion—are present universally as the principles of all cosmic order, the soul is brought by its experience of music into a closer sympathy with the cosmos itself; that is to say, its attention is directed in contemplation toward the principles of the universal harmony that pervades the visible and audible world order.

This entire development of cosmology, ontology, and psychology—what I have been talking about to this point—hangs on the Pythagorean discovery of the natural laws of tones: the fact, which could never have been predicted, that the tones of the octave and of its most serene division into a perfect fourth and fifth were related by the ratios of the first four integers 1:2, 2:3, and 3:4. That discovery revealed a natural law inherent in these acoustic events, not governing them from above, nor yet the products of human abstraction. The discovery suggested a grand insight into the nature of the universe: that matter and form are not contraries. The octave comprises the coincidence of numbers and their material embodiments, the coincidence of the silent world of numbers and the world of sound. The existence of the octave, the fact that two tones an octave apart sound as if in unison, is a fact of music independent of any possible art but also the foundation of all musical art. Without this purely natural phenomenon no tonal scale would make any sense to us. Even the twelve-tone compositional technique of Arnold Schoenberg treats tones of the same name sounded in any octave as identical.

Two further insights arise: that nature and art are not contraries and that the one and the dyad, from which all number and all diversity proceed, are not contraries either, since they are sounded in the octave as one. These facts alone confirm music as the primary image of the cosmos, for music alone rejoices in the perfect conjunction of its perceptible form, the attunement of the octave, fourth, and fifth, and within these, its mathematical essence. Only music sees this mathematical essence as essence and not as a subsidiary or abstract description.

Our ancestors of ancient and medieval times, wishing to regard the universe as truly a universe, that is, as a whole turning upon unity—a unity in no way external to its extended matter, a unity in no way imposed upon matter but rather connaturally inherent—seized upon music as the supreme manifestation of an all-pervasive cosmic conjunction of matter and order. The idea of universal harmony expressed the universe as unific, never departing from its unity, content with itself, a happy place for rational creatures to live, perceive, and think.

One would of course like to observe this serene understanding exemplified in the human art of music as practiced by the Greeks—

to hear the therapeutic modes of the Pythagoreans, Proclus's disciples singing his hymns to the ineffable gods, and the awesome chant of the Eleusinian Mysteries. But here music is revealed as the most fragile of arts, for its ancient remnants are few and difficult to interpret.

We do know, nonetheless, that the proper name for the art of music was *harmonikē*, a word derived from a verb meaning "join, adapt, bind." (The term *music* was of far wider application.) A *harmonia* was originally a fitting together of planks in a ship, any kind of framework or structure, the stringing of a bow or lyre, and finally a row of tones, a scale or mode. The idea that musical composition is a carpentry of sound is a favorite one with Pindar, who addresses his boy-choristers as "craftsmen of the honey-voiced hymns." [16] The *sophia* of the hymn-singer is both his perilous vocation to celebrate the coincidence of human virtue and divine favor in any victorious achievement and his laborious mastery of an exacting craft. No other Greek poet grasps with such fervent tenacity the union of divine and human power in the working of art, as in any exploit of splendor, ardor, strength, and finesse. His poise is difficult for us to imagine, and unfortunately we have no record of the music and dance that accompanied the gorgeous convolutions of Pindar's verse.

The realization and failure of Proclus's vision

The idea of music as the art of joining remains useful nonetheless. A kind of review of the history of the Western music of the last millennium, music that we can decipher and can perform, may provide some ideas of how the musical ideal of Proclus can be realized and yet how difficult it may be to realize in the world of artificial sounds.

Music cannot be the joining of the perfect consonances alone, because these are eternally and inalterably joined. We have certainly never had any music whose whole artistic purpose was the manifestation of just these perfect consonances, although every music must manifest them that does not abandon tone for noise.

One might think of early medieval organum, with its sequence of cadences all on the perfect consonances, as such a pure Pythagorean music, but if we imagine that this organum is all a marmoreal sculpture of sonorous perfection, we shall be quite unprepared for what we actually hear in it, where between the static consonances occurs every variety of movement. In order to grasp this variegated movement in its succession we need a different idea of joining.

The human art of music imitates the natural law of music by striving for the joining of a perfect form, one in which the continuous texture of the music from moment to moment is conjoined with the shape of the musical design as a whole.

304

The joining of texture and shape in music takes the place of the joining, the fitting together, of content and form in the literary arts. Content in literature always derives from the meaning of the words; it can have no place in the art of music, because the simple tones, even consonances and chords, unlike words, have no content in isolation. Music can therefore have no meaning analogous to the meaning of a work of literature.

Can we imagine music in which texture and shape are not conjoined? We might consider American eight-bar blues, especially its degenerate big-city variety, in which there is no music but the bare structure of the eight-bar phrase, the succession of four chords, endlessly repeated, the melody being insignificant (most blues singers, especially in the big-city style, do not actually sing in the usual sense of art singing, they rather declaim the words), the whole being tolerable only because of the poetry of the words themselves.

At the other extreme we find the contemporary rock number in which the harmony is likewise rudimentary, the rhythm and tempo invariable, the words unintelligible, and the whole having no overall shape whatever; one number never actually ends but merely fades into the next number. Musical interest is concentrated in the invention of new textures, through the layering of instrumental and vocal colors, rough or sweet, dense or thin, and so forth. Their ideal visual representation is the rock video with its parallel succession of quirky, bizarre, and discontinuous images. When there is no video the people dance, producing a collective image of discontinuous movement.

We can therefore have music that is, musically speaking, all shape or all texture.

We find medieval organum as well almost completely devoted to texture. In accordance with Pythagorean law, the beginning, end, and all intermediate points of repose are on perfect consonances, but in the long intervals the ear is flattered by a variegated iridescence of sonic effects: overlapping or intertwined rhythmic patterns, bits of melodic imitation, a sonority enriched with luscious major thirds, and an indulgence in sheer vocal virtuosity. Its last great master, Pérotin, does make an effort to prepare for the points of repose by sequences of even more rapid rhythms and some shockingly harsh dissonances, contriving what no one could refuse to call a cadence. The cadences refresh the ear, otherwise saturated and wearied by a too relentless vitality, with a moment of calm, and serve moreover to articulate the overall shape; this dispels the fear that the music might literally last forever, drowning the ear in a measureless ocean of sweetness. The important thing to notice is that although the music has a coherent overall shape and an elaborate repertory of textures, the two formal elements are contrasted rather than complementary: the principles of cadence and of contrapuntal texture are utterly different.

After the time of Pérotin we may observe one of those instructive events that punctuate the history of Western music. People more or less abruptly stop writing organum. It continues to be performed for a while, especially in less progressive regions, and is occasionally regretted, but professional musicians begin to compose in an altogether new idiom that was and is called the "new art." Not a new style, but a whole new art.

In any case, after about 1300, music begins to sound completely different. The difference is largely rhythmic. In the new art, the *ars nova,* the cadences or points of articulation are all the same as in the *ars antiqua,* but what happens in between is even more original and weird. The texture in the old art was dominated by the rhythmic modes, as expounded by Franco of Cologne, that we call poetic feet: iambs, trochees, dactyls, spondees, and tribrachs. The old art would organize a scintillating texture from short phrases all formed on the same metrical unit, but overlapped to fashion an undulating surface. The new art favors longer, rhythmically freer phrases, more supple and asymmetrical, overlaid and underlaid with other phrases equally irregular and unexpected, colliding in inessential dissonances, but coordinated with a delicacy and spontaneity that compel our admiration and even wonder. Rhythmic variety dominates everything. Accordingly the great treatise of Philippe de Vitry, entitled *Ars nova (The New Art),* is almost entirely taken up with a new kind of notation adequate to record the new irregularities and subtleties. (The predilection of composers to discuss technique should not be overlooked.) By the end of the fourteenth century the surface texture became so intricate with cross-rhythms, extended syncopations, written-out *rubati,* and fussy French refinements of every kind that almost nobody was able to understand it, claiming that it was mannered, extravagant, and over-refined.

We find it, I daresay, more *interesting* than expressive. The texture seems to disintegrate into a mass of restless figurations, brilliant but unintelligible. We feel the lack of a unifying meter and a discernible *tune.* It is not that composers did not know what tunes were. The troubadors, not to mention ordinary folks, had been singing lovely tunes for centuries, but contemporary theorists ignored them because these songs were not polyphonic and did not therefore require art, that is, the knowledge of how to join one melody with another.

About the beginning of the fifteenth century the tune invades art music in Italy, and the musical problem becomes how to reconcile the new Italian lyricism with fussy French polyphony. Either the tune usurps the center stage, reducing everything else to accompaniment, or the tune is submerged in the restless flow of artful counterpoint.

A reconciliation was eventually found in the canonic art of the Renaissance. If we want the unifying power, not to mention the expressive power, of the tune, but we love polyphony as well, let us then combine the tune polyphonically with itself, letting every voice sing the tune but not all at the same time. A well-defined tune, moreover, will preserve an audible rhythmic contour and, when artfully overlaid and underlaid with itself, will engender a pleasantly and continually varied but still intelligible overall rhythmic texture. The tunes themselves may be long or brief, wide-ranging or narrow, lyrical or austere, so as to provide every desired character. The texture may be made as crowded or diaphanous, as tense or as calm, as urgently declamatory or as diffused and contemplative, just as one desires, by an accumulation or relaxation of the canonic combinations of the component tunes. Lastly, the final cadences and intermediate points of repose are also evolved polyphonically so that the overall shape is articulated in a fashion consistent with the texture. Thus all the problems of music are solved. Polyphonic music generates its entire self, its overall shape and its texture of inner life and movement, entirely from itself, just like the soul. The contrapuntal style was developed by church composers but was found in the sixteenth century to be the ideal vehicle, in the form of the madrigal, of sentiments more frivolous, flirtatious, and amatory.

In about 1580 certain people in Italy came forward to attack the polyphonic art of the great Renaissance masters, for example, Josquin des Prez, Orlando di Lasso, and Palestrina, and the theorists of this art, especially Gioseffo Zarlino. They introduced in its place a new musical ideal, although they presented this new ideal as a revival of the music of the ancients. One of the most vigorous defenders of the new music was Vincenzo Galilei, the father of Galileo. He asserted that the sole purpose of music was to express emotions—especially heightened, exaggerated, or violent ones—and to excite these passions in the souls of the listeners. He asserted that for this purpose the learned contrapuntal art of the previous several hundred years was manifestly unsuited, that it ought therefore to be replaced by that new musical art that we now name the Baroque style. He says:

> If the practice of music . . . arose primarily to express the passions with
> greater effectiveness . . . and secondarily to communicate these with
> equal force to the minds of mortals . . . , then it will be clear that the
> rules observed by the modern contrapuntists as inviolable laws . . . will
> be directly opposed to the perfection of the true and best harmonies and
> melodies. . . . They [the contrapuntists of the Renaissance] have not a
> book . . . that speaks of how to express the conceptions of the mind and
> of how to impress them with the greatest possible effectiveness on the
> minds of the listeners. . . . In truth the last thing the moderns think of is
> the expression of the words with the passion that these require. . . . [17]

He states elsewhere that the purpose of the polyphonic art was to create beautiful forms of sound that only *refer* to the emotions without expressing them directly, and it is perfectly clear that such was indeed

L'ORFEO

FAVOLA IN MVSICA

DA CLAVDIO MONTEVERDI

RAPPRESENTATA IN MANTOVA

l'Anno 1607. & nouamente data in luce.

AL SERENISSIMO SIGNOR

D. FRANCESCO GONZAGA

Prencipe di Mantoua, & di Monferato, &c.

In Venetia Appresso Ricciardo Amadino.

M D C IX.

(Facing page) Portrait (assumed) of Claudio Monteverdi (1567–1643), composer of dances, madrigals, operas, and church music. (Above) The title page of his opera *Orfeo* (1607), from the text published (1609) in Venice.

the purpose of those composers. He states that those composers sought to ravish the minds of their listeners by the sweetness of the harmonies and the elaborate symmetries of the composition. [18] This is exactly the ideal as stated by Zarlino.

Like other musical revolutions, this one was accompanied by a great deal of journalistic brouhaha, containing a spirited attack, as always, upon the technical restrictions of the art hitherto in vogue. The journalists claimed that the old art was too occupied with formal perfection to encompass the immediate expression of violent passions, mostly grief actually, together with surprise, anger, and fear. The lyric monody was its characteristic initial form: a solo voice declaims its feelings to the accompaniment of an instrument that plays chords to support and punctuate the tragic recital. Polyphony was discarded, nor was there any real melody. Such music took little talent to compose (the role of amateurs was very large at first) and no learning at all to appreciate, and was in consequence an instant popular success.

It was not only Galilei and the other journalists who rejected the polyphonic style and its Neoplatonizing theory; the new style was adopted by everyone, and the old art relegated to a self-consciously archaizing style of church music, the so-called first practice.

The new art form of opera was invented to provide a plausible context for the newly-beloved dramatic declamation. A highly characteristic piece of it is the recitative "Tu sei morta" from Monteverdi's *Orfeo* of 1607. There is little to say, from the spiritual point of view adopted by this essay, about something so obviously and immediately affecting, except perhaps that it is obvious and immediate.

The reasons why the new style was so quickly and generally accepted are part of a great episode in cultural history that I am unqualified to discuss. It is apparent, however, that the new musical style, because of its emphasis on expressive power over against perfection of form, is somehow related to the similar separation of emotion and intellect in the new philosophy of reason that begins with René Descartes, himself an advocate of the new style of music and impatient of all Neoplatonizing, and also related somehow to the new sentimental religiosity of Protestantism and the Roman Catholic Counter-Reformation.

It was not, therefore, a question of a change in musical taste alone, because what was rejected was not only a style but the explicit theoretical basis of that style, and its perceived and articulated connection with the rest of human concern. [19] The notion that music reflects the natural order is simply abandoned, derided, and disgraced, and replaced by a notion that music's task is to express and transmit human passions, events, as Proclus would say, that merely happen and never are, transitory reactions of the soul to events that are external to it and which cannot ever become a part of it. The emotions contained in the old style were rather expressions of the *ecstasis,* the advance from within, of the human soul toward the luminous order of its eternal causes and were therefore the essential expression of the inner nature of the soul.

The movement that culminated in the invention of opera was strongly literary and in fact philosophical. In the interest of an unlimited display of passion, all musical limitations were cast off. Passions succeeded in displacing even consciousness, because consciousness is always a form of self-limitation, of control and reserve, the eternal characteristics of the mathematical world order. Music for the first time masqueraded as a rhetorical sign language in which fixed musical gestures signified the passions that were held to be represented thereby. The result was a parody not only of music but of language as well. The passions were not represented because they were not in fact present at all, but only suggested by certain conventional reflexes. No one actually felt the passions, neither the performers nor the audience; the passions were only the subject matter, a content external to the music itself. Music as the exquisite art of adjusting shape and texture simply ceased to exist, except in the works of those composers, including the resourceful Monteverdi, who recognized that musical meaning must be sought in immanent musical means and not in the supposititious passions. Even Monteverdi, however, was able to attain coherence and sustain interest only in smaller secular forms like the madrigal or in sophisticated imitations of popular dances, previously beneath serious artistic notice. In his magnificent church music, Monteverdi wrote not the new style but a decadent form of the old style. Decadence is always interesting. Just as capitalists, Adam Smith informs us, make their largest profits when the economic system of a country is lapsing into anarchy, so artists can produce the most interesting works when an old compositional technique is being subverted by a hostile one.

In this church music of Monteverdi we hear an echo of the pompous, illusionistic grandeur of Baroque architecture, a style that represents all the pathos of the modern world, the passionate longing to lose oneself in the gratuitous experience of a profound emotion. Whereas some of the typical moods of the polyphonic style are tranquil reflection, austere melancholy, and lyrical joy, the typical moods of the Baroque style are intoxicated rapture, hysterical sorrow, loud agony, and sumptuous immensity. It is all larger, more spacious, but more exterior as well. One feels disturbed by overwhelming magnificence, insupportable grief, or uncontainable and insatiable desire. The finite and comprehensible is everywhere refused, while the imagination demands to be overpowered by heaviness or exalted in preternatural lightness, soaring aloft like Saint Teresa in ecstasy. Helpless to grasp anything earthly, the soul yields itself erotically to the infinite, having no longer any desire for restraint, simplicity, or repose in its own nature, no calm, no sense of completeness, but instead a resistless tension, being drawn forward and upward and utterly lost to itself.

What begins as a desire to enrich the soul and intensify its life through experience of ever more unimaginable emotions is finally carried away beyond itself into an endless vertical abyss from which the soul cannot return again to itself. When its very emotions become fantastic, the soul is volatilized and its feelings dissolve into an abstract, inhuman sentimentality, the counterfeited idea of an emotion that cannot move the soul any longer because the soul has given up its power to move itself. This exhaustion of the soul is why, it seems to me, so much of this music that tries so hard to impress and carry us away—and the trying only becomes more insistent as time goes on—is in fact so tedious and lifeless, so bombastic and insipid. In striving for the sublime and the infinite, music loses all human measure and deprives us of our own way, proportionate to our natural powers, to an experience of the divine, even if it is not God itself.

The effect on the art of music was also disastrous because music lost its very dignity as an art. By condescending to imitate the passions, to become their handmaiden, slave, and minion, music resigned its high, Pindaric vocation as an art, indeed the freest and most autarkic of all the arts, because its material medium is the least impeded by content of its own. (The colors and forms of the material world lend to the plastic arts so much inherent content that many people still believe that the role of painting is to render the appearances of nature.) Music had been able, before the irruption of all this meretricious Baroque excitement, to propose to itself musical goals, musical problems, and musical solutions, without regard to external forces or constraints. Its artifacts, because self-subsistent and autonomous, could be compared with the autonomous constructions of the other arts, of architecture, theology, and the universe itself, not as expressing them, since they do not need expression in another medium, but manifesting them in a human analogy.

Proclus revived in Bach's counterpoint

The primary end of the contrapuntal art of the Renaissance was to create in sound an image of perfection at rest within itself, a self-subsistent being like the Platonic world soul, developed and involved in itself, a whole of free and articulated parts. A piece of music is a unitive state of being, not a description of anything or any emotion, but a performance of the emotion itself, not the way that emotion seems from the narrow time frame of the ego, but the way it takes its place within the whole of psychic life.

To realize this ideal in sound, the older masters invented a polyphonic art by whose intricacies a single theme can be combined with itself in ever-new melodic evolutions to form a continuously developing and various whole, unified by its single melodic source. All the voices, being derived from the same theme, are of equal melodic value and harmonic importance, while each voice moves freely through the whole, following its own rhythmic impulse, not coinciding with the others but complementing them. One has the impression that the voices move from within while the whole remains in serene repose. The beauty of the whole lies in the full apprehensible clarity of its complex structure. Each voice reveals itself as a part transparently contained within the whole, which, although composite and extended in time, is a single existence, everywhere present to itself and satisfied with itself. The energy of the individual voices is not to escape from the whole in search of some unique self-expression, some emotional statement of its own, but rather to form a living whole through their free interactions and complementary oppositions, their dissonances and concords. Thus a polyphonic composition includes the maximum of textural diversity that is compatible with the integrity of the complete design.

To use philosophical language, one might say that the old art was monist, that is, homogeneous, because it developed closely woven textures from a single melodic idea and deduced, as it were, the harmony directly from a formal pattern of melodic relations. The new style might be called dualistic because in it the melody is opposed to the harmony.

Baroque composers, perceiving the incoherence and monotony of their first efforts, sought to invent new harmonic forms that would provide a context for the new harmonic gestures. In so doing, music again followed its innate desire to unify texture and overall shape. If the texture is to be harmonic, that is, composed of chords felt as solid blocks of sound and not as the free conjunction of polyphonic motions, then the overall shape ought to be determined by harmony as well. When the texture, in the form of accompanied melody, can be treated not as a succession of gestures but as the vehicle and embodiment of the overall design, the result is that incomparable artistic invention, the system of tonality, of the definition, interrelation, and extension of keys.

When this system became flexible enough, after a few generations, to be extended over a period of any desired length, music recovered its true character as an independent constructive art and could no longer be considered an adjunct or ornamentation of literary rhetoric. The new music then showed itself as an addition to, not a substitute for, the old music. Musicians learned how to incorporate counterpoint, once derided as stiff and learned, as the inner texture of the new large harmonic shapes, with a corresponding gain in rhythmic finesse. Thus arrived after one hundred years of incessant experimentation another climax in the history of Western music: the works of Johann Sebastian Bach, in which once again music attained the effortless mastery of the golden age of vocal polyphony.

Music then recovered, at least for a time, its high calling as anagogic and therefore redemptive, lifting the soul above the sordid and accidental, leading it back into itself, and again into the timeless realm beyond suffering and pity. The ruinous project of imitating the passions makes trivial both emotion and art by separating them from the higher integrating power of intellect. Musical art becomes then a specialized business concerned with the passions, a private and unstable department of human life, and one increasingly detached from the grander concerns, leaving the emotions passionately felt perhaps but not very deeply rooted in the soul, as music becomes in modern times, like religion, a sentimental if harmless indulgence.

The finished works of such an art of music tolerate moments, episodes, and asides no more than does a Chippendale armchair or a Doric temple. There are no decorations or ornaments, no digressions or special pleadings for sympathy. All is form, substance, and function, all the unfolding of a single law.

Such music is an image of the world order as Proclus understood

Johann Sebastian Bach (1685–1750) composed many organ works and chorales, the most elaborate scores before the day of the symphony orchestra. (Facing page) An autograph page of *Es ist das Heil uns kommen her* (*Salvation Has Come to Us*), undated.

it: a luminous unity of freely coordinated and clearly articulated parts, each part an image of the whole. This music is also an ideal of human blessedness, a state of peace and self-knowledge serene in its participation in and reflection of the divine order where there is no separation or loneliness, no poverty, no sorrow, no struggle, no striving except to belong more nearly to oneself, because each soul hears within itself, present to itself, the glory of the divine law. To realize that law in oneself is the highest form of life.

> Let man's soul be a sphere, and then, in this,
> The intelligence that moves, devotion is,
> And as the other spheres, by being grown
> Subject to foreign motions, lose their own,
> And being by others hurried every day,
> Scarce in a year their natural form obey:
> Pleasures or business, so, our souls admit
> For their first mover and are whirled by it. [20]

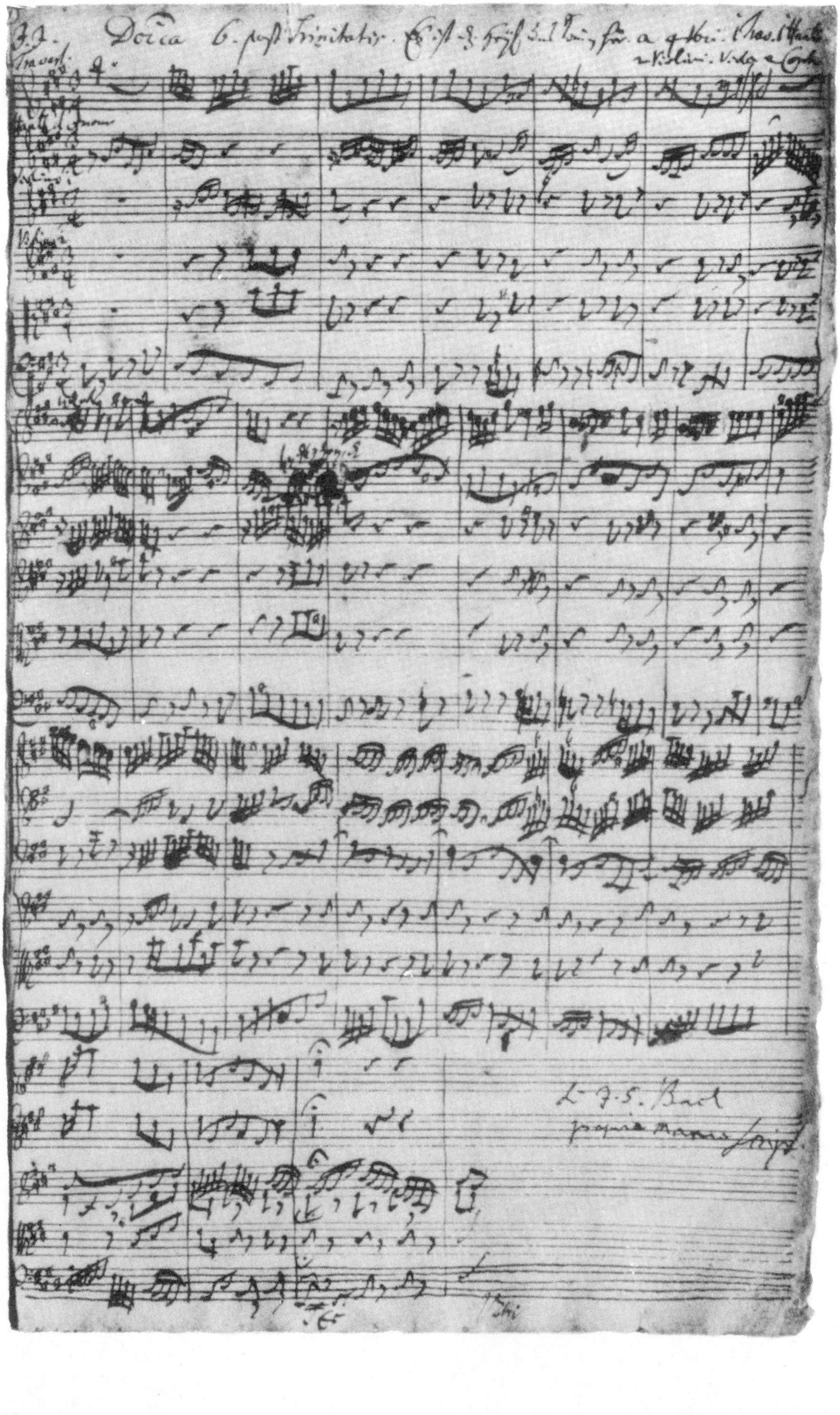
Dorica 6. post Trinitatis
J. S. Bach

If music is a servant or instrument of the passions, it only betrays and more inextricably entangles the soul in the delusions that it contrives to mislead itself. But if it is rather a liberal art, akin, in its desire for self-perfection, to mathematics, it frees the soul from those delusions, giving it a confirmed conviction of its spirituality, its richness, its integrity, and the validity of that desire for eternal life that is the enduring legacy of Plato.

1. Philip Merlan, *From Platonism to Neoplatonism* (The Hague: Martinus Nijhoff, 1968), 3rd ed., chap. 4, "The Origin of the Quadrivium," pp. 88–95. Cf. also, for the difficulties of including music in the quadrivium, Hermann Abert, *Die Musikanschauung des Mittelalters in ihre Grundlagen* (1905; Nachdruck: Tutzing, 1964), pp. 14–15, 29–43.

2. Plato, *Timaeus,* 47b–d, my translation.

3. Hans Jonas speaks of the philosophical "demythologization" (*Entmythologisierung*) and "conceptualization" (*Verbegrifflichung*) of Gnostic mythological images in *Gnosis und spätantiker Geist* [*Gnosis and the Spirit of Late Antiquity*] (Göttingen: Vandenhoeck and Ruprecht, 1964), II.1, p. 169.

4. Plotinus uses the expression *tragodia ton phoberon* in the *Enneads* (2nd Ennead, IX.13; *GBWW* I: 17, 73; II: 11, 377). For similar expressions in Proclus, *see* his *Platonic Theology,* I.4 (*Théologie platonicienne,* ed. H. D. Saffrey and L. G. Westerink [Paris: Société d'édition "Les Belles Lettres," 1968], tome 1, 21.3–4 and 26.20–21).

5. This interpretation, now enshrined as standard in Francis Cornford's commentary, *Plato's Cosmology* (London: Kegan Paul, Trench, Trubner, & Co., 1937), is in fact due to Proclus, as Cornford himself states, pp. 59–66. The text of Proclus is in his *Commentaria in Platonis Timaeum,* ed. E. Diehl (Leipzig: Teubner, 1903), II.119ff. The excellent French translation by A. J. Festugière (*Commentaire sur le Timée* [Paris: Libraire philosophique J. Vrin, 1966]) is a great help.

6. Plutarch tells us in his *de animae procreatione in Timaeo* [*On the generation of the soul in the Timaeus*] (Leipzig: Teubner, 1959) that the soul was identified by some scholars with only a part of the mathematicals *de an proc* (1–2, 22).

7. A. E. Taylor in his *A Commentary on Plato's Timaeus* (Oxford: Clarendon Press, 1928), pp. 66–69, gives the lineup of the opposing sides.

8. An immense controversy has arisen about what Plato meant and about whether Aristotle understood Plato's meaning. I ignore this breathtaking controversy because Proclus had none of the hesitations of modern scholars on these points.

9. Proclus, *Procli Diadochi in primum Euclidis Elementorum librum Commentaria,* ed. G. Friedlein (Leipzig: Teubner, 1873), 7.13–8.12. There is an English translation by Glen R. Morrow (Princeton, N.J.: Princeton University Press, 1970).

10. Ibid., 4.11–14.

11. Ibid., 13.6–8.

12. Ibid., 16.8–10.

13. Ibid., 16.10–13.

14. *Elements of Theology,* ed. and trans. E. R. Dodds (Oxford: Clarendon Press, 1963), 2nd ed., theorem 103.

15. Proclus, 46.25–47.8.

16. *Nemean Odes,* 3.4. (Leipzig: Teubner, 1987).

17. *Source Readings in Music History,* ed. Oliver Strunk (New York: W. W. Norton and Company Inc., 1950), pp. 306–7, 312–13.

18. Ibid., p. 314.

19. Cf. ibid., pp. 393–415, where the wider significance of the change of style is already brought out in the lively controversy between Monteverdi and Giovanni Artusi, the disciple of Zarlino.

20. John Donne, "Good Friday, 1613. Riding Westward," *The Divine Poems,* ed. Helen Gardner (Oxford: Clarendon Press, 1978), pp. 30–31.

PART FOUR

Additions
to the
Great Books Library

The Making of the Bill of Rights, 1791

arranged by George Anastaplo

Facsimile of the original Bill of Rights, or amendments to the Constitution, of 1791. Although reproduced too small to be read with certainty here, the text, including the first two proposed amendments (Articles the First and Second) that were rejected, may be found in the following pages.

Introduction

The last two articles of the American Bill of Rights, the Ninth and the Tenth Amendments, remind us that the rights and powers provided for by the Constitution and its amendments had long been claimed by the people and remain within their ultimate control. These two amendments are:

> The enumeration in the Constitution, of certain rights, shall not be construed to deny or disparage others retained by the people.
> The powers not delegated to the United States by the Constitution, nor prohibited by it to the States, are reserved to the States respectively, or to the people.

It is evident from the Ninth Amendment that there are rights in addition to those set forth in the Constitution and its Bill of Rights. The continued validity of those unenumerated rights is insisted upon in the Ninth Amendment, which indicates in effect that the rights enumerated in the Bill of Rights would have been available to the American people even without these amendments. Various of these rights had been invoked in, for instance, the Declaration of Independence, even though they may never have been incorporated in formal guarantees.

The drafters of the Bill of Rights in the First Congress did not create the diverse rights that they listed, however much they may have refined some of them. Rather, they had to select in 1789, from the many rights under consideration, those that they wanted to incorporate in a bill of rights. Hundreds of suggestions had come from the state conventions which had ratified the Constitution the year before. Many of these suggestions referred to rights which were already widely understood to be among the rights of the American people. Those conventions had drawn on considerable experience and discussion in both North America and Great Britain throughout the eighteenth century and before.

The collection of documents set forth below suggests where some of the rights both in the Bill of Rights and, earlier, in the Constitution came from. Many other documents could have been included here, such as the Habeas Corpus Act of 1679. Three particularly important documents are omitted here because they are already available in *Great*

Books of the Western World: the Declaration of Independence, the Articles of Confederation, and the Constitution of 1787 (*GBWW* I: 43, 1–20; II: 40, 1–21). Also influential were other well-known texts in the *Great Books,* which helped educate the developers of the Anglo-American legal tradition, such as Plato's *Apology* (*GBWW* I: 7, 200–72; II: 6, 200–12), Shakespeare's history plays (*GBWW* I: 26–27; II: 24–25), and Milton's *Areopagitica* (*GBWW* I: 32, 381–412; II: 29, 381–412).

This collection of documents begins with a few of the underlying constitutional documents in the Anglo-American tradition: Magna Carta, the Petition of Right, and the English Bill of Rights. These are supplemented by a request made of the English King (Henry VIII) by Sir Thomas More (as Speaker of the House of Commons). The Speaker sought the traditional assurance of that freedom of speech which is necessary if there is to be meaningful and productive discussion of the public business in Parliament. This parliamentary privilege can be considered an instructive prototype of the guarantee of freedom of speech and of the press included in the First Amendment. Chapter 39 of Magna Carta was important to the development of the common law in England. Then there are key statements by pre-Revolutionary American congresses leading up to the Declaration of Independence, statements which include invocations of various rights of the American people.

These rights are developed further in documents that were issued in 1776 and thereafter. The Virginian efforts here are particularly significant in light of the vital part that James Madison (of Virginia) played in shaping the Bill of Rights in the First Congress. The North Carolina Constitution displays an early development of a bill of rights in a state constitution, while the Northwest Ordinance is the first national constitutional document with a bill of rights of its own. Among the provisions in the Northwest Ordinance, which was enacted by the Confederation Congress in 1787 and reenacted by the First Congress in 1789, is a prohibition of slavery in the Northwest Territory. This prohibition anticipates by four score years the Thirteenth Amendment which came out of the Civil War. The Thirteenth Amendment, ratified in 1865, provides, "Neither slavery nor involuntary servitude, except as a punishment for crime whereof the party shall have been duly convicted, shall exist within the United States, or any place subject to their jurisdiction."

The subsequent documents collected here show how the Bill of Rights took the form it now has. These begin with excerpts from Madison's *Notes of Debates in the Federal Convention,* displaying the futile attempts, especially in the closing days of that convention, to have a bill of rights prepared for the Constitution that was being drafted. Thereafter samples are provided of the proposed amendments that were sent to Congress by the state conventions that ratified the Constitution. These samples are taken from the last two state conventions that ratified the

Constitution before its implementation began. (These 1788 conventions, one in the South and the other in the North, could draw upon similar statements that had come out of the other state conventions. It should be noticed that Congress did *not* adopt any of the proposed amendments that would have cut down the substantive powers of the new national government.) There are then taken from the 1789 congressional debates the principal stages of the Bill of Rights as prepared in the First Congress, beginning with the Madison proposals and culminating in the roster of twelve proposed amendments finally sent to the state legislatures for their ratification. Those congressional deliberations began with the assumption that any amendments agreed upon should be placed at appropriate places within the original Constitution; they ended with the agreement that amendments should be *appended* to the Constitution, which is what has been done ever since.

All but the first two of the twelve proposed amendments finally sent by Congress to the states were ratified. The first of these rejected amendments, regulating the size of the House of Representatives, was soon overtaken by population growth in the United States; the second, with respect to the compensation of members of Congress, is adhered to in practice by Congress. State ratifications of amendments proposed by Congress have usually moved faster than one might expect. The Twenty-second Amendment, limiting the President to two full terms in office, required the longest time, forty-seven and one-half months. (It was ratified in 1951.) The Twenty-sixth Amendment, assuring eighteen-year-olds the right to vote in both national and state elections, required the shortest period, four months. (It was ratified in 1971.) The average time for ratification of a constitutional amendment has been eighteen months. This reflects the fact that amendments are likely to be proposed by Congress only when there is widespread support for a change. Often an amendment does little more than formally confirm what has already been generally accepted, as in the case of the Bill of Rights. There have been only thirty-three amendments proposed by Congress since 1789. Of these thirty-three proposed amendments, seven have failed to be ratified. Two of these seven are the first two of the twelve amendments proposed by Congress for the Bill of Rights in 1789, the texts of which are provided in the collection below. The principal provisions in the other five proposed amendments that failed to secure enough state assents for ratification are the following:

> *Proposal of 1810:* If any citizen of the United States shall accept, claim, receive or retain any title of nobility or honour, or shall, without the consent of Congress, accept and retain any present, pension, office or emolument of any kind whatever, from any emperor, king, prince or foreign power, such person shall cease to be a citizen of the United States, and shall be incapable of holding any office of trust or profit under them, or either of them.

Proposal of 1861: No amendment shall be made to the Constitution which will authorize or give to Congress the power to abolish or interfere, within any State, with the domestic institutions thereof, including that of persons held to labour or service by the laws of said State.

Proposal of 1924: The Congress shall have power to limit, regulate, and prohibit the labour of persons under 18 years of age.

Proposal of 1972: Equality of rights under the law shall not be abridged by the United States or by any State on account of sex.

Proposal of 1978: For purposes of representation in the Congress, election of the President and Vice President, and article V of this Constitution, the District constituting the seat of government of the United States shall be treated as though it were a state.

The concern of the 1810 proposal is no longer a lively one; the concern of the 1861 proposal was rendered moot by the Civil War; the concerns of the 1924 and 1972 proposals have been largely dealt with by constitutional interpretations and congressional statutes; and the concern of the 1978 proposal may eventually be dealt with by a congressional grant of statehood to the District of Columbia.

Fittingly enough, it was the consent of the Virginia legislature, on Dec. 15, 1791, that completed the ratification of those ten of the twelve proposed amendments to the Constitution that we now know as the Bill of Rights. We celebrate this year, therefore, the Bicentennial of the Ratification of the Bill of Rights. A proper celebration depends on an informed awareness of how deeply rooted these rights were, and still are, in centuries of experience and reflection, providing thereby a salutary discipline in interpreting and applying the Constitution and its amendments. These documents should contribute to the required awareness.

The Making of the Bill of Rights, 1791

Table of Contents

Magna Carta, 1215

John, by the grace of God, king of England, lord of Ireland, duke of Normandy and Aquitaine, count of Anjou, to the archbishops, bishops, abbots, earls, barons, justiciars, foresters, sheriffs, reeves, servants, and all bailiffs and his faithful people greeting. Know that by the inspiration of God and for the good of our soul and those of all our predecessors and of our heirs, to the honour of God and the exaltation of holy church, and the improvement of our kingdom, by the advice of our venerable fathers Stephen, archbishop of Canterbury, primate of all England and cardinal of the holy Roman church, Henry, archbishop of Dublin, William of London, Peter of Winchester, Jocelyn of Bath and Glastonbury, Hugh of Lincoln, Walter of Worcester, William of Coventry, and Benedict of Rochester, bishops; of Master Pandulf, sub-deacon and member of the household of the lord Pope, of Brother Aymeric, master of the Knights of the Temple in England; and of the noblemen William Marshall, earl of Pembroke, William, earl of Salisbury, William, earl of Warren, William, earl of Arundel, Alan of Galloway, constable of Scotland, Warren Fitz-Gerald, Peter Fitz-Herbert, Hubert de Burgh, steward of Poitou, Hugh de Nevil, Matthew Fitz-Herbert, Thomas Bassett, Alan Bassett, Philip d'Albini, Robert de Roppelay, John Marshall, John Fitz-Hugh, and others of our faithful.

1. In the first place, we have granted to God, and by this our present charter confirmed, for us and for our heirs forever, that the English church shall be free, and shall hold its rights entire and its liberties uninjured; and we will that it be thus observed; which is shown by this, that the freedom of elections, which is considered to be most important and especially necessary to the English church, we, of our pure and spontaneous will, granted, and by our charter confirmed, before the contest between us and our barons had arisen; and obtained a confirmation of it by the lord Pope Innocent III; which we shall observe and which we will shall be observed in good faith by our heirs forever.

We have granted moreover to all free men of our kingdom for us and our heirs forever all the liberties written below, to be had and holden by themselves and their heirs from us and our heirs.

2. If any of our earls or barons, or others holding from us in chief by military service shall have died, and when he has died his heir shall be of full age and owe relief,* he shall have his inheritance by the ancient relief; that is to say, the heir or heirs of an earl for the whole barony of an earl a hundred pounds; the heir or heirs of a baron for a whole barony a hundred pounds; the heir or heirs of a knight for a whole knight's fee a hundred shillings at most; and who owes less let him give less according to the ancient custom of fiefs.

3. If moreover the heir of any one of such shall be under age, and shall be in wardship, when he comes of age he shall have his inheritance without relief and without a fine.†

4. The custodian of the land of such a minor heir shall not take from the land of the heir any except reasonable products, reasonable customary payments, and reasonable services, and this without destruction or waste of men or of property; and if we shall have committed the custody of the land of any such a one to the sheriff or to any other who is to be responsible to us for its proceeds, and that man shall have caused destruction or waste from his

*Payment owed by the heir to the king for obtaining the estate of his ancestor.

†An agreement or composition involving payment by the heir.

custody we will recover damages from him, and the land shall be committed to two legal and discreet men of that fief, who shall be responsible for its proceeds to us or to him to whom we have assigned them; and if we shall have given or sold to any one the custody of any such land, and he has caused destruction or waste there, he shall lose that custody, and it shall be handed over to two legal and discreet men of that fief who shall be in like manner responsible to us as is said above.

5. The custodian moreover, so long as he shall have the custody of the land, must keep up the houses, parks, warrens, fish ponds, mills, and other things pertaining to the land, from the proceeds of the land itself; and he must return to the heir, when he has come to full age, all his land, furnished with ploughs and implements of husbandry according as the time of wainage* requires and as the proceeds of the land are able reasonably to sustain.

6. Heirs shall be married without disparity, so nevertheless that before the marriage is contracted, it shall be announced to the relatives by blood of the heir himself.

7. A widow, after the death of her husband, shall have her marriage portion and her inheritance immediately and without obstruction, nor shall she give anything for her dowry or for her marriage portion, or for her inheritance, which inheritance her husband and she held on the day of the death of her husband; and she may remain in the house of her husband for forty days after his death, within which time her dowry shall be assigned to her.

8. No widow shall be compelled to marry so long as she prefers to live without a husband, provided she gives security that she will not marry without our consent, if she holds from us, or without the consent of her lord from whom she holds, if she holds from another.

9. Neither we nor our bailiffs will seize any land or rent for any debt, so long as the chattels of the debtor are sufficient for the payment of the debt; nor shall the pledges of a debtor be distrained so long as the principal debtor himself has enough for the payment of the debt; and if the principal debtor fails in the payment of the debt, not having the wherewithal to pay it, the pledges shall be responsible for the debt; and if they wish, they shall have the lands and the rents of the debtor until they shall have been satisfied for the debt which they have before paid for him, unless the principal debtor shall have shown himself to be quit in that respect towards those pledges.

[10. If any one has taken anything from the Jews, by way of a loan, more or less, and dies before that debt is paid, the debt shall not draw interest so long as the heir is under age, from whomsoever he holds; and if that debt falls into our hands, we will take nothing except the chattel contained in the agreement.]†

[11. And if any one dies leaving a debt owing to the Jews, his wife shall have her dowry, and shall pay nothing of that debt; and if there remain minor children of the dead man, necessaries shall be provided for them corresponding to the holding of the dead man; and from the remainder shall be paid the debt, the service of the lords being retained. In the same way debts are to be treated which are owed to others than the Jews.]

[12. No scutage or aid‡ shall be imposed in our kingdom except by the common council of our kingdom, except for the ransoming of our body, for the making of our oldest son a knight, and for once marrying our oldest daughter, and for these purposes it shall be only a reasonable aid; in the same way it shall be done concerning the aids of the city of London.]

13. And the city of London shall have

---

*Agricultural instruments.

†Brackets indicate articles omitted from the reissues of 1216, 1217, and 1225.

‡A "scutage" was a money payment in lieu of knight's service. An "aid" was a grant by the tenant to his lord in times of distress.

all its ancient liberties and free customs, as well by land as by water. Moreover, we will and grant that all other cities and boroughs and villages and ports shall have all their liberties and free customs.

[14. And for holding a common council of the kingdom concerning the assessment of an aid otherwise than in the three cases mentioned above, or concerning the assessment of a scutage, we shall cause to be summoned the archbishops, bishops, abbots, earls, and greater barons by our letters under seal; and besides we shall cause to be summoned generally, by our sheriffs and bailiffs all those who hold from us in chief, for a certain day, that is at the end of forty days at least, and for a certain place; and in all the letters of that summons, we will express the cause of the summons, and when the summons has thus been given the business shall proceed on the appointed day, on the advice of those who shall be present, even if not all of those who were summoned have come.]

[15. We will not grant to any one, moreover, that he shall take an aid from his free men, except for ransoming his body, for making his oldest son a knight, and for once marrying his oldest daughter; and for these purposes only a reasonable aid shall be taken.]

16. No one shall be compelled to perform any greater service for a knight's fee, or for any other free tenement than is owed from it.

17. The common pleas shall not follow our court, but shall be held in some certain place.

18. The recognitions* of *novel disseisin,*† *mort d'ancestor,*‡ and *darrein presentment*§ shall be held only in their own counties and in this manner: we, or if we are outside of the kingdom our principal justiciar, will send two justiciars through each county four times a year, who with four knights of each county, elected by the county, shall hold in the county and on the day and in the place of the county court the aforesaid assizes ‖ of the county.

[19. And if the aforesaid assizes cannot be held within the day of the county court, a sufficient number of knights and freeholders shall remain from those who were present at the county court on that day to give the judgments, according as the business is more or less.]

20. A free man shall not be fined for a small offence, except in proportion to the measure of the offence; and for a great offence he shall be fined in proportion to the magnitude of the offence, saving his freehold; and a merchant in the same way, saving his merchandise; and the villain shall be fined in the same way, saving his wainage, if he shall be at our mercy; and none of the above fines shall be imposed except by the oaths of honest men of the neighbourhood.

21. Earls and barons shall be fined only by their peers, and only in proportion to their offence.

22. A clergyman shall be fined, like those before mentioned, only in proportion to his lay holding, and not according to the extent of his ecclesiastical benefice.#

23. No manor or man shall be compelled to make bridges over the rivers except those which ought to do it of old and rightfully.

24. No sheriff, constable, coroners, or other bailiffs of ours shall hold pleas of our crown.

[25. All counties, hundreds, wapentakes, and trithings** shall be at the ancient rents and without any increase, excepting our demesne manors.††]

---

*Trials.

†An action to recover land following dispossession.

‡An action involving a disputed right to inherit land.

§An action involving the right to ecclesiastical benefit.

‖ Trials.

#Office and dignities.

**"Hundreds, wapentakes, and trithings" were subdivisions of counties.

††The lands reserved by a lord for his private use.

26. If any person holding a lay fief from us shall die, and our sheriff or bailiff shall show our letters-patent of our summons concerning a debt which the deceased owed to us, it shall be lawful for our sheriff or bailiff to attach and levy on the chattels of the deceased found on his lay fief, to the value of that debt, in the view of legal men, so nevertheless that nothing be removed thence until the clear debt to us shall be paid; and the remainder shall be left to the executors for the fulfilment of the will of the deceased; and if nothing is owed to us by him, all the chattels shall go to the deceased, saving to his wife and children their reasonable shares.

27. If any free man dies intestate,* his chattels shall be distributed by the hands of his near relatives and friends, under the oversight of the church, saving to each one the debts which the deceased owed to him.

28. No constable or other bailiff of ours shall take anyone's grain or other chattels, without immediately paying for them in money, unless he is able to obtain a postponement at the good will of the seller.

29. No constable shall require any knight to give money in place of his ward of a castle† if he is willing to furnish that ward in his own person or through another honest man, if he himself is not able to do it for a reasonable cause; and if we shall lead or send him into the army he shall be free from ward in proportion to the amount of time by which he has been in the army through us.

30. No sheriff or bailiff of ours or any one else shall take horses or wagons of any free man for carrying purposes except on the permission of that free man.

31. Neither we nor our bailiffs will take the wood of another man for castles, or for anything else which we are doing, except by the permission of him to whom the wood belongs.

32. We will not hold the lands of those convicted of a felony for more than a year and a day, after which the lands shall be returned to the lords of the fiefs.

33. All the fish-weirs‡ in the Thames and the Medway, and throughout all England shall be done away with, except those on the coast.

34. The writ which is called *praecipe* shall not be given for the future to any one concerning any tenement by which a free man can lose his court.§

35. There shall be one measure of wine throughout our whole kingdom, and one measure of ale, and one measure of grain, that is the London quarter, and one width of dyed cloth and of russets and of halbergets, that is two ells within the selvages; of weights, moreover, it shall be as of measures.

36. Nothing shall henceforth be given or taken for a writ of inquisition concerning life or limbs, but it shall be given freely and not denied.

37. If any one holds from us by fee farm ‖ or by soccage# or by burgage,** and from another he holds land by military service, we will not have the guardianship of the heir or of his land which is of the fief of another, on account of that fee farm, or soccage, or burgage, nor will we have the custody of that fee farm, or soccage, or burgage, unless that fee farm itself owes military service. We will not have the guardianship of the heir or of the land of any one, which he holds from another by military service on account of

---

*Without a will.

†"Ward of a castle" refers to the duty of a knight to guard the castle near which he lived.

‡Bulky contrivances which interfered with navigation on the rivers.

§"Free man" here means a lord. By the writ of *praecipe* the king could deprive the lord's court of jurisdiction.

‖ Tenure whereby land was held of another at a yearly rent.

#Tenure whereby land was held of another in consideration of certain inferior services of husbandry.

**Tenure whereby houses and lands which were formerly the site of houses in an ancient borough were held of some lord by a certain rent.

any petty serjeanty* which he holds from us by the service of paying to us knives or arrows, or things of that kind.

38. No bailiff for the future shall place any one to his law on his simple affirmation, without credible witnesses brought for this purpose.

39. No free man shall be taken or imprisoned or dispossessed, or outlawed, or banished, or in any way destroyed, nor will we go upon him, nor send upon him, except by the legal judgment of his peers or by the law of the land.†

40. To no one will we sell, to no one will we deny, or delay right or justice.

41. All merchants shall be safe and secure in going out from England and coming into England and in remaining and going through England, as well by land as by water, for buying and selling, free from all evil tolls, by the ancient and rightful customs, except in time of war, and if they are of a land at war with us; and if such are found in our land at the beginning of war, they shall be attached without injury to their bodies or goods, until it shall be known from us or from our principal justiciar in what way the merchants of our land are treated who shall then be found in the country which is at war with us; and if ours are safe there, the others shall be safe in our land.

[42. It is allowed henceforth to any one to go out from our kingdom, and to return, safely and securely, by land and by water, saving their fidelity to us, except in time of war for some short time, for the common good of the kingdom; excepting persons imprisoned and outlawed according to the law of the realm, and people of a land at war with us, and merchants, of whom it shall be done as is before said.]

43. If any one holds from an escheat, as from the honour of Wallingford, or Nottingham, or Boulogne, or Lancaster, or from other escheats which are in our hands and are baronies, and he dies, his heir shall not give any other relief, nor do to us any other service than he would

do to the baron, if that barony was in the hands of the baron; and we will hold it in the same way as the baron held it.

[44. Men who dwell outside the forest shall not henceforth come before our justiciars of the forest, on common summons, unless they are in a plea of, or pledges for any person or persons who are arrested on account of the forest.]

[45. We will not make justiciars, constables, sheriffs or bailiffs except of such as know the law of the realm and are well inclined to observe it.]

46. All barons who have founded abbeys for which they have charters of kings of England, or ancient tenure, shall have their custody when they have become vacant, as they ought to have.

47. All forests which have been afforested in our time shall be disafforested immediately; and so it shall be concerning river banks which in our time have been fenced in.

[48. All the bad customs concerning forests and warrens and concerning foresters and warreners, sheriffs and their servants, river banks and their guardians shall be inquired into immediately in each county by twelve sworn knights of the same county, who shall be elected by the honest men of the same county, and within forty days after the inquisition has been made, they shall be entirely destroyed by them, never to be restored, provided that we be first informed of it, or our justiciar, if we are not in England.]

[49. We will give back immediately all hostages and charters which have been liberated to us by Englishmen as security for peace or for faithful service.]

---

*Tenure whereby land was held of the king in consideration of rendering him some small implement of war such as a sword, arrow, or lance.

†In Latin, "Nullus liber homo capiatur, vel imprisonetur, aut dissaisiatur, aut utlagetur, aut exuletur, aut aliquo modo destruatur, nec super eum ibimus, nec super eum mittemus, nisi per legale judicium parium suorum vel per legem terrae."

"To no one will we sell, to no one will we deny, or delay right or justice."
King John (1167–1216) signs Magna Carta on June 15, 1215, in a meadow
called Runnymede, not far from Windsor, England.

[50. We will remove absolutely from their bailiwicks the relatives of Gerard de Athyes, so that for the future they shall have no bailiwick in England; Engelard de Cygony, Andrew, Peter and Gyon de Chancelles, Gyon de Cygony, Geoffrey de Martin and his brothers, Philip Mark and his brothers, and Geoffrey his nephew and their whole retinue.]

[51. And immediately after the re-establishment of peace we will remove from the kingdom all foreign-born soldiers, cross-bow men, servants, and mercenaries who have come with horses and arms for the injury of the realm.]

[52. If any one shall have been dispossessed or removed by us without legal judgment of his peers, from his lands, castles, franchises, or his right, we will restore them to him immediately; and if contention arises about this, then it shall be done according to the judgment of the twenty-five barons, of whom mention is made below concerning the security of the peace. Concerning all those things, however, from which any one has been removed or of which he has been deprived without legal judgment of his peers by King Henry our father, or by King Richard our brother, which we have in our land, or which others hold, and which it is our duty to guarantee, we shall have respite till the usual term of crusaders; excepting those things about which the suit has been begun or the inquisition made by our writ before our assumption of the cross; when, however, we shall return from our journey or if by chance we desist from the journey, we will immediately show full justice in regard to them.]

[53. We shall, moreover, have the same respite and in the same manner about showing justice in regard to the forests which are to be disafforested or to remain forests, which Henry our father or Richard our brother made into forests; and concerning the custody of lands which are in the fief of another, custody of which we have until now had on account of a fief which any one has held from us by military service; and concerning the abbeys which have been founded in fiefs of others than ourselves, in which the lord of the fee has asserted for himself a right; and when we return or if we should desist from our journey we will immediately show full justice to those complaining in regard to them.]

54. No one shall be seized nor imprisoned on the appeal of a woman concerning the death of any one except her husband.

[55. All fines which have been imposed unjustly and against the law of the land, and all penalties imposed unjustly and against the law of the land are altogether excused, or will be on the judgment of the twenty-five barons of whom mention is made below in connection with the security of the peace, or on the judgment of the majority of them, along with the aforesaid Stephen, archbishop of Canterbury, if he is able to be present, and others whom he may wish to call for this purpose along with him. And if he should not be able to be present, nevertheless the business shall go on without him, provided that if any one or more of the aforesaid twenty-five barons are in a similar suit they should be removed as far as this particular judgment goes, and others who shall be chosen and put upon oath, by the remainder of the twenty-five shall be substituted for them for this purpose.]

[56. If we have dispossessed or removed any Welshmen from their lands, or franchises, or other things, without legal judgment of their peers, in England, or in Wales, they shall be immediately returned to them; and if a dispute shall have arisen over this, then it shall be settled in the borderland by judgment of their peers, concerning holdings of England according to the law of England, concerning holdings of Wales according to the law of Wales, and concerning holdings of the borderland according to the law of the borderland. The Welsh shall do the same to us and ours.]

[57. Concerning all those things, however, from which any one of the Welsh shall have been removed or dispossessed without legal judgment of his peers, by King Henry our father, or King Richard our brother, which we hold in our hands, or which others hold, and we are bound to warrant to them, we shall have respite till the usual period of crusaders, those being excepted about which suit was begun or inquisition made by our command before our assumption of the cross. When, however, we shall return or if by chance we shall desist from our journey, we will show full justice to them immediately, according to the laws of the Welsh and the aforesaid parts.]

[58. We will give back the son of Lewellyn immediately, and all the hostages from Wales and the charters which had been liberated to us as a security for peace.]

[59. We will act toward Alexander, king of the Scots, concerning the return of his sisters and his hostages, and concerning his franchises and his right, according to the manner in which we shall act toward our other barons of England, unless it ought to be otherwise by the charters which we hold from William his father, formerly king of the Scots, and this shall be by the judgment of his peers in our court.]

60. Moreover, all those customs and franchises mentioned above which we have conceded in our kingdom, and which are to be fulfilled, as far as pertains to us, in respect to our men; all men of our kingdom as well clergy as laymen, shall observe as far as pertains to them, in respect to their men.

[61. Since, moreover, for the sake of God, and for the improvement of our kingdom, and for the better quieting of the hostility sprung up lately between us and our barons, we have made all these concessions; wishing them to enjoy these in a complete and firm stability forever, we make and concede to them the security described below; that is to say, that they shall elect twenty-five barons of the kingdom, whom they will, who ought with all their power to observe, hold, and cause to be observed, the peace and liberties which

we have conceded to them, and by this our present charter confirmed to them; in this manner, that if we or our justiciar, or our bailiffs, or any of our servants shall have done wrong in any way toward any one, or shall have transgressed any of the articles of peace or security; and the wrong shall have been shown to four barons of the aforesaid twenty-five barons, let those four barons come to us or to our justiciar, if we are out of the kingdom, laying before us the transgression, and let them ask that we cause that transgression to be corrected without delay. And if we shall not have corrected the transgression or, if we shall be out of the kingdom, if our justiciar shall not have corrected it within a period of forty days, counting from the time in which it has been shown to us or to our justiciar, if we are out of the kingdom; the aforesaid four barons shall refer the matter to the remainder of the twenty-five barons, and let these twenty-five barons with the whole community of the country distress and injure us in every way they can; that is to say by the seizure of our castles, lands, possessions, and in such other ways as they can until it shall have been corrected according to their judgment, saving our person and that of our queen, and those of our children; and when the correction has been made, let them devote themselves to us as they did before. And let whoever in the country wishes take an oath that in all the above-mentioned measures he will obey the orders of the aforesaid twenty-five barons, and that he will injure us as far as he is able with them, and we give permission to swear publicly and freely to each one who wishes to swear, and no one will we ever forbid to swear. All those, moreover, in the country who of themselves and their own will are unwilling to take an oath to the twenty-five barons as to distressing and injuring us along with them, we will compel to take the oath by our mandate, as before said. And if any one of the twenty-five barons shall have died or departed from the land or shall in any other way be prevented from taking the above mentioned action, let the remainder of the aforesaid twenty-five barons choose another in his place, according to their judgment, who shall take an oath in the same way as the others. In all those things, moreover, which are committed to those five and twenty barons to carry out, if perhaps the twenty-five are present, and some disagreement arises among them about something, or if any of them when they have been summoned are not willing or are not able to be present, let that be considered valid and firm which the greater part of those who are present arrange or command, just as if the whole twenty-five had agreed in this; and let the aforesaid twenty-five swear that they will observe faithfully all the things which are said above, and with all their ability cause them to be observed. And we will obtain nothing from any one, either by ourselves or by another by which any of these concessions and liberties shall be revoked or diminished; and if any such thing shall have been obtained, let it be invalid and void, and we will never use it by ourselves or by another.]

[62. And all ill-will, grudges, and anger sprung up between us and our men, clergy and laymen, from the time of the dispute, we have fully renounced and pardoned to all. Moreover, all transgressions committed on account of this dispute, from Easter in the sixteenth year of our reign till the restoration of peace, we have fully remitted to all, clergy and laymen, and as far as pertains to us, fully pardoned. And moreover we have caused to be made for them testimonial letters-patent of lord Stephen, archbishop of Canterbury, lord Henry, archbishop of Dublin, and of the aforesaid bishops and of master Pandulf, in respect to that security and the concessions named above.]

[63. Wherefore we will and firmly command that the Church of England shall be free, and that the men in our kingdom shall have and hold all the aforesaid liberties, rights and concessions, well and peacefully, freely and quietly, fully and completely, for themselves and their heirs, from us and our heirs, in all things and places, forever, as before said. It has been sworn, moreover, as well on our part as on the part of the barons, that all these things spoken of above shall be observed in good faith and without any evil intent. Witness the above named and many others. Given by our hand in the meadow which is called Runnymede, between Windsor and Staines, on the fifteenth day of June, in the seventeenth year of our reign.] [1]

Thomas More's Petition to the King
on Parliamentary Freedom of Speech, 1521*

... **M**yne other humble requeste, most excellent prince, is this: Forasmuche as there be of the Commons here by your high commandment assembled for your Parliament, a greate nomber which are, after the accustomed manner, appoynted in the Common House to treate and advise of the common affayres amongst themselves aparte; and albeit, most deere leige lord, that accordinge to your prudente advise, by your honourable writtes everye where declared, there hath beene as due dilligence used in sendinge up to your highnes courte of parliament the most discreete persons out of everye quarter that menne could esteeme meete thereto; whereby yt is not to be doubted but that ther is a substanciall assemblye of right wise, and politicke persons; yet, moste victorious prince, sithe amonge soe many wise menne, neither is every man wise alike, nor among soe many men like well witted is every man like well spoken, and it often happenethe that likewise as muche follye is uttered with paynted polished speeche, soe many, boysterious and rude in language, see deepe indeede, and give righte substanciall councell; and sithe also in matters of great importance, the mynde is often soe occupyed in this matter, that a man rather studiethe what to saye, then howe; by reason whereof the wisest man and best spoken in a whole countrye fortunethe, while his mynde is fervent in the matter, somewhat

---

*Addressed to King Henry VIII.

Sir Thomas More (1477–1535), drawing by Hans Holbein the Younger.

to speake in such wise as he would after-wardes wishe to have beene uttered other-wise, and yet noe worse will had when he spoke it, then he hathe when he would soe gladly change it. Therfore, most gratious Soveraygne, consideringe that in your high courte of Parliament is nothing intreated but matter of weyghte and importance concerning your Realme and your owne Royall Estate, yt could not faile to lett and put to silence from the givinge of their advise and councell many of your discreete Commons, to the greate hinder-ance of the common affayres, excepte that everye one of your Commons were utterly dischardged of all doubtes and feare howe any thinge that it should happen them to speake, should happen of your highnes to be taken. . . . Yt may therfore like your most aboundante grace, our most be-nigne and godly Kinge, to give all your Commons here assembled your most gra-tious lycence and pardon, freely witheout doubte of your dredfull displeasure, ev-erye man to dischardge his conscience, and boldly in every thinge incidente amongst us, to declare his advise; and what soever happen any man to say, that yt maye like your majestie of your inestimable goodnes to take all in good parte, interpreting everye mans wordes, howe unconningly* soever they be couched, to proceede yet of good zeals towards the profitt of your realme, and honour of your Royall per-sonne, the prosperous estate and preserva-cion whereof, most excellent sovereygne, is the thing which we all, your most hum-ble loving subjects, according to the most bounden dewtye of our naturall allegeance, moste highly desire and praye for. [2]

Petition of Right, 1628

To the King's most excellent majesty

Humbly shew unto our sovereign lord the King, the lords spiritual and tempo-ral, and commons in parliament assembled, That whereas it is declared and enacted by a statute made in the time of the reign of King Edward the First commonly called *Statutum de tallagio non concedendo*,† That no tallage or aid‡ shall be laid or levied by the King or his heirs in this realm, without the good will and assent of the archbishops, bishops, earls, barons, knights, burgesses, and other the freemen of the commonalty of this realm; (2) and by authority of parlia-ment holden in the five and twentieth year of the reign of King Edward the Third, it is declared and enacted, That from thence-forth no person should be compelled to make any loans to the King against his will, because such loans were against reason and the franchise of the land; (3) and by other laws of this realm it is provided, That none should be charged by any charge or im-position called a benevolence, nor by such like charge: (4) by which the statutes before mentioned, and other the good laws and statutes of this realm, your subjects have inherited this freedom, That they should not be compelled to contribute to any tax, tallage, aid or other like charge not set by common consent in parliament.

II. Yet nevertheless, of late divers com-missions directed to sundry commissioners in several counties, with instructions, have issued; by means whereof your people have been in divers places assembled, and re-quired to lend certain sums of money unto your Majesty, and many of them, upon their refusal so to do, have had an oath administred unto them not warrantable by the laws or statutes of this realm, and have been constrained to become bound to make appearance and give attendance be-fore your privy council and in other places, and others of them have been therefore im-

---

*Unlearnedly, ignorantly.

†A statute concerning taxes not to be levied.

‡"Tallage" is a tax; "aid" is a tribute or contribution.

prisoned, confined, and sundry other ways molested and disquieted; (2) and divers other charges have been laid and levied upon your people in several counties by lord lieutenants, deputy lieutenants, commissioners for musters, justices of peace and others, by command or direction from your Majesty, or your privy council, against the laws and free customs of the realm.

III. And where also by the statute called *The great charter of the liberties of England,* it is declared and enacted, That no freeman may be taken or imprisoned, or be disseised of his freehold or liberties, or his free customs, or be outlawed or exiled or in manner destroyed, but by the lawful judgment of his peers, or by the law of the land.

IV. And in the eight and twentieth year of the reign of King Edward the Third, it was declared and enacted by authority of parliament, That no man of what estate or condition that he be, should be put out of his land or tenements, nor taken, nor imprisoned, nor disherited, nor put to death without being brought to answer by due process of law:

V. Nevertheless against the tenor of the said statutes, and other the good laws and statutes of your realm to that end provided, divers of your subjects have of late been imprisoned without any cause shewed; (2) and when for their deliverance they were brought before your justices by your Majesty's writs of *habeas corpus,* there to undergo and receive as the court should order, and their keepers commanded to certify the causes of their detainer, no cause was certified, but that they were detained by your Majesty's special command, signified by the lords of your privy council, and yet were returned back to several prisons, without being charged with any thing to which they might make answer according to the law:

VI. And whereas of late great companies of soldiers and mariners have been dispersed into divers counties of the realm, and the inhabitants against their wills have been compelled to receive them into their houses, and there to suffer them to sojourn, against the laws and customs of this realm, and to the great grievance and vexation of the people:

VII. And whereas also by authority of parliament, in the five and twentieth year of the reign of King Edward the Third, it is declared and enacted, That no man should be forejudged of life or limb against the form of the great charter and the law of the land; (2) and by the said great charter and other the laws and statutes of this your realm, no man ought to be adjudged to death but by the laws established in this your realm, either by the customs of the same realm, or by acts of parliament: (3) and whereas no offender of what kind soever is exempted from the proceedings to be used, and punishments to be inflicted by the laws and statutes of this your realm: nevertheless of late time divers commissions under your Majesty's great seal have issued forth, by which certain persons have been assigned and appointed commissioners with power and authority to proceed within the land, according to the justice of martial law, against such soldiers or mariners, or other dissolute persons joining with them, as should commit any murder, robbery, felony, mutiny or other outrage or misdemeanor whatsoever, and by such summary course and order as is agreeable to martial law, and as is used in armies in time of war, to proceed to the trial and condemnation of such offenders, and them to cause to be executed and put to death according to the law martial:

VIII. By pretext whereof some of your Majesty's subjects have been by some of the said commissioners put to death, when and where, if by the laws and statutes of the land they had deserved death, by the same laws and statutes also they might, and by no other ought to have been judged and executed:

IX. And also sundry grievous offenders, by colour thereof claiming an exemption, have escaped the punishments due to them by the laws and statutes of this your realm, by reason that divers of your officers and ministers of justice have unjustly refused or forborn to proceed against such offenders according to the same laws and statutes, upon pretence that the said offenders were punishable only by martial law, and by authority of such commissions as aforesaid: (2) which commissions, and all other of like nature, are wholly and directly contrary to the said laws and statutes of this your realm:

X. They do therefore humbly pray your most excellent Majesty, That no man hereafter be compelled to make or yield any gift, loan, benevolence, tax, or such-like charge, without common consent by act of parliament; (2) and that none be called to make answer, or take such oath, or to give attendance, or be confined, or otherwise molested or disquieted concerning the same, or for refusal thereof; (3) and that no freeman, in any such manner as is before-mentioned, be imprisoned or detained; (4) and that your Majesty would be pleased to remove the said soldiers and mariners, and that your people may not be so burthened in time to come; (5) and that the aforesaid commissions, for proceeding by martial law, may be revoked and annulled; and that hereafter no commissions of like nature may issue forth to any person or persons whatsoever to be executed as aforesaid, lest by colour of them any of your Majesty's subjects be destroyed, or put to death contrary to the laws and franchise of the land.

XI. All which they most humbly pray of your most excellent Majesty as their rights and liberties, according to the laws and statutes of this realm; and that your Majesty would also vouchsafe to declare, That the awards, doings and proceedings, to the prejudice of your people in any of the premisses, shall not be drawn hereafter into consequence or example; (2) and that your Majesty would be also graciously pleased, for the further comfort and safety of your people, to declare your royal will and pleasure, That in the things aforesaid all your officers and ministers shall serve you according to the laws and statutes of this realm, as they tender the honour of your Majesty, and the prosperity of this kingdom. *Qua quidem petitione lecta et plenius intellecta per dictum dominum regem taliter est responsum in pleno parliamento,* viz. *Soit droit fait come est desire.** [3]

English Bill of Rights, 1689

An act for declaring the rights and liberties of the subject, and settling the succession of the crown

Whereas the lords spiritual and temporal, and commons assembled at Westminster, lawfully, fully, and freely representing all the estates of the people of this realm, did upon the thirteenth day of February, in the year of our Lord one thousand six hundred eighty eight, present unto their Majesties, then called and known by the names and stile of William and Mary, prince and princess of Orange, being present in their proper persons, a certain declaration in writing, made by the said lords and commons, in the words following; viz.

Whereas the late King James the Second, by the assistance of divers evil counsellors, judges, and ministers employed by him, did endeavour to subvert and extirpate the protestant religion, and the laws and liberties of this kingdom.

1. By assuming and exercising a power of dispensing with and suspending of laws, and the execution of laws, without consent of parliament.

---

*"Which petition having been read and fully understood, the answer by word of the Lord king in full parliament was 'Let it be made law as is desired.'"

2. By committing and prosecuting divers worthy prelates, for humbly petitioning to be excused from concurring to the said assumed power.

3. By issuing and causing to be executed a commission under the great seal for erecting a court called, The court of commissioners for ecclesiastical causes.

4. By levying money for and to the use of the crown, by pretence of prerogative, for other time, and in other manner, than the same was granted by parliament.

5. By raising and keeping a standing army within this kingdom in time of peace, without consent of parliament, and quartering soldiers contrary to law.

6. By causing several good subjects, being protestants, to be disarmed, at the same time when papists were both armed and employed, contrary to law.

7. By violating the freedom of election of members to serve in parliament.

8. By prosecutions in the court of King's bench, for matters and causes cognizable only in parliament; and by divers other arbitrary and illegal courses.

9. And whereas of late years, partial, corrupt, and unqualified persons have been returned and served on juries in trials, and particularly divers jurors in trials for high treason, which were not freeholders.

10. And excessive bail hath been required of persons committed in criminal cases, to elude the benefit of the laws made for the liberty of the subjects.

11. And excessive fines have been imposed; and illegal and cruel punishments inflicted.

12. And several grants and promises made of fines and forfeitures, before any conviction or judgment against the persons, upon whom the same were to be levied.

All which are utterly and directly contrary to the known laws and statutes, and freedom of this realm.

And whereas the said late King James the Second having abdicated the government, and the throne being thereby vacant, his highness the prince of Orange (whom it hath pleased Almighty God to make the glorious instrument of delivering this kingdom from popery and arbitrary power) did (by the advice of the lords spiritual and temporal, and divers principal persons of the commons) cause letters to be written to the lords spiritual and temporal, being protestants; and other letters to the several counties, cities, universities, boroughs, and cinque-ports, for the choosing of such persons to represent them, as were of right to be sent to parliament, to meet and sit at Westminster upon the two and twentieth day of January, in this year one thousand six hundred eighty and eight, in order to such an establishment, as that their religion, laws, and liberties might not again be in danger of being subverted: upon which letters, elections have been accordingly made.

And thereupon the said lords spiritual and temporal, and commons, pursuant to their respective letters and elections, being now assembled in a full and free representative of this nation, taking into their most serious consideration the best means for attaining the ends aforesaid; do in the first place (as their ancestors in like case have usually done) for the vindicating and asserting their ancient rights and liberties, declare;

1. That the pretended power of suspending of laws, or the execution of laws, by regal authority, without consent of parliament, is illegal.

2. That the pretended power of dispensing with laws, or the execution of laws, by regal authority, as it hath been assumed and exercised of late, is illegal.

3. That the commission for erecting the late court of commissioners for ecclesiastical causes, and other commissions and courts of like nature are illegal and pernicious.

4. That levying money for or to the use of the crown, by pretence of prerogative, without grant of parliament, for longer time, or in other manner than the same is or shall be granted, is illegal.

5. That it is the right of the subjects to petition the King, and all committments and prosecutions for such petitioning are illegal.

6. That the raising or keeping a standing army within the kingdom in time of peace, unless it be with consent of parliament, is against law.

7. That the subjects which are protestants, may have arms for their defence suitable to their conditions, and as allowed by law.

8. That election of members of parliament ought to be free.

9. That the freedom of speech, and debates or proceedings in parliament, ought not to be impeached or questioned in any court or place out of parliament.

10. That excessive bail ought not to be required, nor excessive fines imposed; nor cruel and unusual punishments inflicted.

11. That jurors ought to be duly impanelled and returned, and jurors which pass upon men in trials for high treason ought to be freeholders.

12. That all grants and promises of fines and forfeitures of particular persons before conviction, are illegal and void.

13. And that for redress of all grievances, and for the amending, strengthening, and preserving of the laws, parliaments ought to be held frequently.

And they do claim, demand, and insist upon all and singular the premises, as their undoubted rights and liberties; and that no declarations, judgments, doings or proceedings, to the prejudice of the people in any of the said premisses, ought in any wise to be drawn hereafter into consequence or example.

To which demand of their rights they are particularly encouraged by the declaration of his highness the prince of Orange, as being the only means for obtaining a full redress and remedy therein.

Having therefore an entire confidence, That his said highness the prince of Orange will perfect the deliverance so far advanced by him, and will still preserve them from the violation of their rights, which they have here asserted, and from all other attempts upon their religion, rights, and liberties.

II. The said lords spiritual and temporal, and commons, assembled at Westminster, do resolve, that William and Mary prince and princess of Orange be, and be declared, King and Queen of England, France, and Ireland, and the dominions thereunto belonging, to hold the crown and royal dignity of the said kingdoms and dominions to them the said prince and princess during their lives, and the life of the survivor of them; and that the sole and full exercise of the regal power be only in, and executed by the said prince of Orange, in the names of the said prince and princess, during their joint lives; and after their deceases, the said crown and royal dignity of the said kingdoms and dominions to be to the heirs of the body of the said princess; and for default of such issue to the princess Anne of Denmark, and the heirs of her body; and for default of such issue to the heirs of the body of the said prince of Orange. And the lords spiritual and temporal, and commons, do pray the said prince and princess to accept the same accordingly.

III. And that the oaths hereafter mentioned be taken by all persons of whom the oaths of allegiance and supremacy might be required by law, instead of them; and that the said oaths of allegiance and supremacy be abrogated.

I *A. B.* do sincerely promise and swear, That I will be faithful, and bear true allegiance, to their Majesties King William and Queen Mary: *So help me God.*

I *A. B.* do swear, That I do from my heart abhor, detest, and abjure as impious and heretical, that damnable doctrine and position, *That princes excommunicated or deprived by the pope, or any authority of the see of* Rome, *may be deposed or murdered by their subjects, or any other whatsoever.*

And I do declare, That no foreign prince, person, prelate, state, or potentate hath, or ought to have any jurisdiction, power, superiority, pre-eminence, or authority ecclesiastical or spiritual, within this realm: *So help me God.*

IV. Upon which their said Majesties did accept the crown and royal dignity of the kingdoms of England, France, and Ireland, and the dominions thereunto belonging, according to the resolution and desire of the said lords and commons contained in the said declaration.

V. And thereupon their Majesties were pleased, That the said lords spiritual and temporal, and commons, being the two houses of parliament, should continue to sit, and with their Majesties royal concurrence make effectual provision for the settlement of the religion, laws, and liberties of this kingdom, so that the same for the future might not be in danger again of being subverted; to which the said lords

spiritual and temporal, and commons, did agree and proceed to act accordingly.

VI. Now in pursuance of the premises, the said lords spiritual and temporal, and commons, in parliament assembled, for the ratifying, confirming and establishing the said declaration, and the articles, clauses, matters, and things therein contained, by the force of a law made in due form by authority of parliament, do pray that it may be declared and enacted, That all and singular the rights and liberties asserted and claimed in the said declaration, are the true, ancient, and indubitable rights and liberties of the people of this kingdom, and so shall be esteemed, allowed, adjudged, deemed, and taken to be, and that all and every the particulars aforesaid shall be firmly and strictly holden and observed, as they are expressed in the said declaration; and all officers and ministers whatsoever shall serve their Majesties and their successors according to the same in all times to come. [4]

Resolutions of the Stamp Act Congress, 1765

Declaration of Rights

The members of this congress, sincerely devoted, with the warmest sentiments of affection and duty to his majesty's person and government, inviolably attached to the present happy establishment of the protestant succession, and with minds deeply impressed by a sense of the present and impending misfortunes of the British colonies on this continent; having considered as maturely as time would permit, the circumstances of said colonies, esteem it our indispensable duty to make the following declarations, of our humble opinions, respecting the most essential rights and liberties of the colonists, and of the grievances under which they labour, by reason of several late acts of parliament.

1st. That his majesty's subjects in these colonies, owe the same allegiance to the

crown of Great Britain, that is owing from his subjects born within the realm, and all due subordination to that august body, the parliament of Great Britain.

2d. That his majesty's liege subjects in these colonies are entitled to all the inherent rights and privileges of his natural born subjects within the kingdom of Great Britain.

3d. That it is inseparably essential to the freedom of a people, and the undoubted rights of Englishmen, that no taxes should be imposed on them, but with their own consent, given personally, or by their representatives.

4th. That the people of these colonies are not, and from their local circumstances, cannot be represented in the house of commons in Great Britain.

5th. That the only representatives of the people of these colonies, are persons chosen therein by themselves; and that no taxes ever have been, or can be constitutionally imposed on them, but by their respective legislatures.

6th. That all supplies to the crown, being free gifts of the people, it is unreasonable and inconsistent with the principles and spirit of the British constitution, for the people of Great Britain to grant to his majesty the property of the colonists.

7th. That trial by jury is the inherent and invaluable right of every British subject in these colonies.

8th. That the late act of parliament entitled, an act for granting and applying certain stamp duties, and other duties in the British colonies and plantations in America, etc., by imposing taxes on the inhabitants of these colonies, and the said act, and several other acts, by extending the jurisdiction of the courts of admiralty beyond its ancient limits, have a manifest tendency to subvert the rights and liberties of the colonists.

9th. That the duties imposed by several late acts of parliament, from the peculiar circumstances of these colonies, will be extremely burthensome and grievous, and from the scarcity of specie, the payment of them absolutely impracticable.

10th. That as the profits of the trade of these colonies ultimately centre in Great Britain, to pay for the manufactures which they are obliged to take from thence, they eventually contribute very largely to all supplies granted there to the crown.

11th. That the restrictions imposed by several late acts of parliament, on the trade of these colonies, will render them unable to purchase the manufactures of Great Britain.

12th. That the increase, prosperity, and happiness of these colonies, depend on the full and free enjoyment of their rights and liberties, and an intercourse, with Great Britain, mutually affectionate and advantageous.

13th. That it is the right of the British subjects in these colonies, to petition the king or either house of parliament.

Lastly, That it is the indispensable duty of these colonies to the best of sovereigns, to the mother country, and to themselves, to endeavour, by a loyal and dutiful address to his majesty, and humble application to both houses of parliament, to procure the repeal of the act for granting and applying certain stamp duties, of all clauses of any other acts of parliament, whereby the jurisdiction of the admiralty is extended as aforesaid, and of the other late acts for the restriction of the American commerce. [5]

Declaration and Resolves of the First Continental Congress, 1774

Whereas, since the close of the last war, the British parliament, claiming a power, of right, to bind the people of America by statutes in all cases whatsoever, hath, in some acts, expressly imposed taxes on them, and in others, under various pretences, but in fact for the purpose of raising a revenue, hath imposed rates and duties payable in these colonies, established a board of commissioners, with unconstitutional powers, and extended the jurisdiction of courts of admiralty, not only for collecting the said duties, but for the trial of causes merely arising within the body of a county.

And whereas, in consequence of other statutes, judges, who before held only estates at will in their offices, have been made dependant on the crown alone for their salaries, and standing armies kept in times of peace: And whereas it has lately been resolved in parliament, that by force of a statute, made in the thirty-fifth year of the reign of King Henry the Eighth, colonists may be transported to England, and tried there upon accusations for treasons and misprisions, or concealments of treasons committed in the colonies, and by a late statute, such trials have been directed in cases therein mentioned:

And whereas, in the last session of parliament, three statutes were made; one entitled, "An act to discontinue, in such manner and for such time as are therein mentioned, the landing and discharging, lading, or shipping of goods, wares and merchandise, at the town, and within the harbour of Boston, in the province of Massachusetts Bay in North America;" another entitled, "An act for the better regulating the government of the province of Massachusetts Bay in New England;" and another entitled, "An act for the impartial administration of justice, in the cases of persons questioned for any act done by them in the execution of the law, or for the suppression of riots and tumults, in the province of the Massachusetts Bay in New England;" and another statute was then made, "for making more effectual provision for the government of the province of Quebec, etc." All which statutes are impolitic, unjust, and cruel, as well as unconstitutional, and most dangerous and destructive of American rights:

And whereas, assemblies have been frequently dissolved, contrary to the rights of the people, when they attempted to deliberate on grievances; and their dutiful, humble, loyal, and reasonable petitions to the crown for redress, have been repeatedly treated with contempt, by his Majesty's ministers of state:

The good people of the several colonies of New Hampshire, Massachusetts Bay, Rhode Island and Providence Plantations, Connecticut, New York, New Jersey, Pennsylvania, Newcastle, Kent, and Sussex on Delaware, Maryland, Virginia, North Carolina, and South Carolina, justly alarmed at these arbitrary proceedings of parliament and administration, have severally elected, constituted, and appointed deputies to meet, and sit in general Congress, in the city of Philadelphia, in order to obtain such establishment, as that their religion, laws, and liberties, may not be subverted: Whereupon the deputies so appointed being now assembled, in a full and free representation of these colonies, taking into their most serious consideration, the best means of attaining the ends aforesaid, do, in the first place, as Englishmen, their ancestors in like cases have usually done, for asserting and vindicating their rights and liberties, DECLARE,

That the inhabitants of the English colonies in North America, by the immutable laws of nature, the principles of the English constitution, and the several charters or compacts, have the following RIGHTS:

Resolved, N. C. D. * 1. That they are entitled to life, liberty and property: and they have never ceded to any foreign power whatever, a right to dispose of either without their consent.

Resolved, N. C. D. 2. That our ancestors, who first settled these colonies, were at the time of their emigration from the mother country, entitled to all the rights, liberties, and immunities of free and natural-born subjects, within the realm of England.

Resolved, N. C. D. 3. That by such emigration they by no means forfeited, surrendered, or lost any of those rights, but that they were, and their descendants now are, entitled to the exercise and enjoyment of all such of them, as their local and other circumstances enable them to exercise and enjoy.

Resolved, 4. That the foundation of English liberty, and of all free government, is a right in the people to participate in their legislative council: and as the English colonists are not represented, and from their local and other circumstances, cannot properly be represented in the British parliament, they are entitled to a free and exclusive power of legislation in

_____

* No one dissenting.

their several provincial legislatures, where their right of representation can alone be preserved, in all cases of taxation and internal polity, subject only to the negative of their sovereign, in such manner as has been heretofore used and accustomed: But, from the necessity of the case, and a regard to the mutual interest of both countries, we cheerfully consent to the operation of such acts of the British parliament, as are bona fide, restrained to the regulation of our external commerce, for the purpose of securing the commercial advantages of the whole empire to the mother country, and the commercial benefits of its respective members; excluding every idea of taxation internal or external, for raising a revenue on the subjects, in America, without their consent.

Resolved, N. C. D. 5. That the respective colonies are entitled to the common law of England, and more especially to the great and inestimable privilege of being tried by their peers of the vicinage, according to the course of that law.

Resolved, 6. That they are entitled to the benefit of such of the English statutes, as existed at the time of their colonization; and which they have, by experience, respectively found to be applicable to their several local and other circumstances.

Resolved, N. C. D. 7. That these, his majesty's colonies, are likewise entitled to all the immunities and privileges granted and confirmed to them by royal charters, or secured by their several codes of provincial laws.

Resolved, N. C. D. 8. That they have a right peaceably to assemble, consider of their grievances, and petition the king; and that all prosecutions, prohibitory proclamations, and commitments for the same, are illegal.

Resolved, N. C. D. 9. That the keeping a standing army in these colonies, in times of peace, without the consent of the legislature of that colony, in which such army is kept, is against law.

Resolved, N. C. D. 10. It is indispensably necessary to good government, and rendered essential by the English constitution, that the constituent branches of the legislature be independent of each other; that, therefore, the exercise of legislative power in several colonies, by a council appointed, during pleasure, by the crown, is unconstitutional, dangerous and destructive to the freedom of American legislation.

All and each of which the aforesaid deputies, in behalf of themselves, and their constituents, do claim, demand, and insist on, as their indubitable rights and liberties; which cannot be legally taken from them, altered or abridged by any power whatever, without their own consent, by their representatives in their several provincial legislatures.

In the course of our inquiry, we find many infringements and violations of the foregoing rights, which, from an ardent desire, that harmony and mutual intercourse of affection and interest may be restored, we pass over for the present, and proceed to state such acts and measures as have been adopted since the last war, which demonstrate a system formed to enslave America.

Resolved, N. C. D. That the following acts of parliament are infringements and violations of the rights of the colonists; and that the repeal of them is essentially necessary, in order to restore harmony between Great Britain and the American colonies, viz.

The several acts of 4 Geo. III. ch. 15, and ch. 34.—5 Geo. III. ch. 25.—6 Geo. III. ch. 52.—7 Geo. III. ch. 41 and ch. 46.—8 Geo. III. ch. 22, which impose duties for the purpose of raising a revenue in America, extend the power of the admiralty courts beyond their ancient limits, deprive the American subject of trial by jury, authorise the judges certificate to indemnify the prosecutor from damages, that he might otherwise be liable to, requiring oppressive security from a claimant of ships and goods seized, before he shall be allowed to defend his property, and are subversive of American rights.

Also 12 Geo. III. ch. 24, entitled, "An act for the better securing his majesty's dockyards, magazines, ships, ammunition, and stores," which declares a new offence in America, and deprives the American subject of a constitutional trial by jury of the vicinage, by authorising the trial of any person, charged with the committing any offence described in the said act, out of the realm, to be indicted and tried for the same in any shire or county within the realm.

Also the three acts passed in the last session of parliament, for stopping the port and blocking up the harbour of Boston, for altering the charter and government of Massachusetts Bay, and that which is entitled, "An act for the better administration of justice, etc."

Also the act passed in the same session for establishing the Roman Catholic religion, in the province of Quebec, abolishing the equitable system of English laws, and erecting a tyranny there, to the great danger (from so total a dissimilarity of religion, law and government) of the neighbouring

British colonies, by the assistance of whose blood and treasure the said country was conquered from France.

Also the act passed in the same session, for the better providing suitable quarters for officers and soldiers in his majesty's service, in North America.

Also, that the keeping a standing army in several of these colonies, in time of peace, without the consent of the legislature of that colony, in which such army is kept, is against law.

To these grievous acts and measures, Americans cannot submit, but in hopes their fellow subjects in Great Britain will, on a revision of them, restore us to that state, in which both countries found happiness and prosperity, we have for the present, only resolved to pursue the following peaceable measures: 1. To enter into a non-importation, non-consumption, and non-exportation agreement or association. 2. To prepare an address to the people of Great Britain, and a memorial to the inhabitants of British America: and 3. To prepare a loyal address to his majesty, agreeable to resolutions already entered into. [6]

Constitution of North Carolina, 1776

A Declaration of Rights

I. That all political power is vested in and derived from the people only.

II. That the people of this State ought to have the sole and exclusive right of regulating the internal government and police thereof.

III. That no man or set of men are entitled to exclusive or separate emoluments or privileges from the community, but in consideration of public services.

IV. That the legislative, executive, and supreme judicial powers of government, ought to be forever separate and distinct from each other.

V. That all powers of suspending laws, or the execution of laws, by any authority, without consent of the Representatives of the people, is injurious to their rights, and ought not to be exercised.

VI. That elections of members, to serve as Representatives in General Assembly, ought to be free.

VII. That, in all criminal prosecutions, every man has a right to be informed of the accusation against him, and to confront the accusers and witnesses with other testimony, and shall not be compelled to give evidence against himself.

VIII. That no freeman shall be put to answer any criminal charge, but by indictment, presentment, or impeachment.

IX. That no freeman shall be convicted of any crime, but by the unanimous verdict of a jury of good and lawful men, in open court, as heretofore used.

X. That excessive bail should not be required, nor excessive fines imposed, nor cruel or unusual punishments inflicted.

XI. That general warrants—whereby an officer or messenger may be commanded to search suspected places, without evidence of the fact committed, or to seize any person or persons, not named, whose offences are not particularly described, and supported by evidence—are dangerous to liberty, and ought not to be granted.

XII. That no freeman ought to be taken, imprisoned, or disseized of his freehold, liberties or privileges, or outlawed, or exiled, or in any manner destroyed, or deprived of his life, liberty, or property, but by the law of the land.

XIII. That every freeman, restrained of his liberty, is entitled to a remedy, to inquire into the lawfulness thereof, and to remove the same, if unlawful; and that such remedy ought not to be denied or delayed.

XIV. That in all controversies at law, respecting property, the ancient mode of trial, by jury, is one of the best securities of the rights of the people, and ought to remain sacred and inviolable.

XV. That the freedom of the press is one of the great bulwarks of liberty, and therefore ought never to be restrained.

XVI. That the people of this State ought not to be taxed, or made subject to the payment of any impost or duty, without the consent of themselves, or their Representatives in General Assembly, freely given.

XVII. That the people have a right to bear arms, for the defence of the State; and, as standing armies, in time of peace, are dangerous to liberty, they ought not to be kept up; and that the military should be kept under strict subordination to, and governed by, the civil power.

XVIII. That the people have a right to assemble together, to consult for their common good, to instruct their Representatives, and to apply to the Legislature, for redress of grievances.

XIX. That all men have a natural and unalienable right to worship Almighty God according to the dictates of their own consciences.

XX. That, for redress of grievances, and for amending and strengthening the laws, elections ought to be often held.

XXI. That a frequent recurrence to fundamental principles is absolutely necessary, to preserve the blessings of liberty.

XXII. That no hereditary emoluments, privileges or honours ought to be granted or conferred in this State.

XXIII. That perpetuities and monopolies are contrary to the genius of a free State, and ought not to be allowed.

XXIV. That retrospective laws, punishing facts committed before the existence of such laws, and by them only declared criminal, are oppressive, unjust, and incompatible with liberty; wherefore no *ex post facto* law ought to be made.

XXV. The property of the soil, in a free government, being one of the essential rights of the collective body of the people, it is necessary, in order to avoid future disputes, that the limits of the State should be ascertained with precision; and as the former temporary line between North and South Carolina, was confirmed, and extended by Commissioners, appointed by the Legislatures of the two States, agreeable to the order of the late King George the Second, in Council, that line, and that only, should be esteemed the southern boundary of this State as follows: that is to say, beginning on the sea side, at a cedar stake, at or near the mouth of Little River (being the southern extremity of Brunswick county), and running from thence a northwest course, through the boundary house, which stands in thirty-three degrees fifty-six minutes, to thirty-five degrees north latitude; and from thence a west course so far as is mentioned in the Charter of King Charles the Second, to the late Proprietors of Carolina. Therefore all the territories, seas, waters, and harbours, with their appurtenances, lying between the line above described, and the southern line of the State of Virginia, which begins on the sea shore, in thirty-six degrees thirty minutes, north latitude, and from thence runs west, agreeable to the said Charter of King Charles, are the right and property of the people of this State, to be held by them in sovereignty; any partial line, without the consent of the Legislature of this State, at any time thereafter directed, or laid out, in anywise notwithstanding: *Provided always,* That this Declaration of Rights shall not prejudice any nation or nations of Indi-

ans, from enjoying such hunting-grounds as may have been, or hereafter shall be, secured to them by any former or future Legislature of this State: *And provided also,* That it shall not be construed so as to prevent the establishment of one or more governments westward of this State, by consent of the Legislature: *And provided further,* That nothing herein contained shall affect the titles or possessions of individuals holding or claiming under the laws heretofore in force, or grants heretofore made by the late King George the Second, or his predecessors, or the late lords proprietors, or any of them. [7]

Virginia on Rights and Liberties

1. Virginia Declaration of Rights, 1776

A declaration of rights made by the Representatives of the good people of Virginia, assembled in full and free Convention; which rights do pertain to them and their posterity, as the basis and foundation of Government.

1. That all men are by nature equally free and independent, and have certain inherent rights, of which, when they enter into a state of society, they cannot, by any compact, deprive or divest their posterity; namely, the enjoyment of life and liberty, with the means of acquiring and possessing property, and pursuing and obtaining happiness and safety.

2. That all power is vested in, and consequently derived from, the People; that magistrates are their trustees and servants, and at all times amenable to them.

3. That Government is, or ought to be, instituted for the common benefit, protection, and security of the people, nation, or community; of all the various modes and forms of Government that is best which is capable of producing the greatest degree of happiness and safety, and is most effectually secured against the danger of mal-

administration; and that, whenever any Government shall be found inadequate or contrary to these purposes, a majority of the community hath an indubitable, unalienable, and indefeasible right, to reform, alter, or abolish it, in such manner as shall be judged most conducive to the publick weal.

4. That no man, or set of men, are entitled to exclusive or separate emoluments and privileges from the community, but in consideration of publick services; which, not being descendible, neither ought the offices of Magistrate, Legislator, or Judge, to be hereditary.

5. That the Legislative and Executive powers of the State should be separate and distinct from the Judicative; and, that the members of the two first may be restrained from oppression, by feeling and participating the burdens of the people, they should, at fixed periods, be reduced to a private station, return into that body from which they were originally taken, and the vacancies be supplied by frequent, certain, and regular elections, in which all, or any part of the former members, to be again eligible, or ineligible, as the law shall direct.

6. That elections of members to serve as

*". . . all power is vested in, and consequently derived from, the People; . . .
magistrates are their trustees and servants, and at all times amenable to them."*
George Mason (1725–92), etching by H. B. Hall, 1872.

Representatives of the people, in Assembly, ought to be free; and that all men, having sufficient evidence of permanent common interest with, and attachment to, the community, have the right of suffrage, and cannot be taxed or deprived of their property for publick uses without their own consent or that of their Representative so elected, nor bound by any law to which they have not, in like manner, assented, for the publick good.

7. That all power of suspending laws, or the execution of laws, by any authority, without consent of the Representatives of the people, is injurious to their rights, and ought not to be exercised.

8. That in all capital or criminal prosecutions a man hath a right to demand the cause and nature of his accusation, to be confronted with the accusers and witnesses, to call for evidence in his favour, and to a speedy trial by an impartial jury of his vicinage, without whose unanimous consent he cannot be found guilty, nor can

he be compelled to give evidence against himself; that no man be deprived of his liberty except by the law of the land, or the judgment of his peers.

9. That excessive bail ought not to be required, nor excessive fines imposed, nor cruel and unusual punishments inflicted.

10. That general warrants, whereby any officer or messenger may be commanded to search suspected places without evidence of a fact committed, or to seize any person or persons not named, or whose offence is not particularly described and supported by evidence, are grievous and oppressive, and ought not to be granted.

11. That in controversies respecting property, and in suits between man and man, the ancient trial by Jury is preferable to any other, and ought to be held sacred.

12. That the freedom of the Press is one of the greatest bulwarks of liberty, and can never be restrained but by despotick Governments.

13. That a well-regulated Militia, composed of the body of the people, trained to arms, is the proper, natural, and safe defence of a free State; that Standing Armies, in time of peace, should be avoided as dangerous to liberty; and that, in all cases, the military should be under strict subordination to, and governed by, the civil power.

14. That the people have a right to uniform Government; and, therefore, that no Government separate from, or independent of, the Government of Virginia, ought to be erected or established within the limits thereof.

15. That no free Government, or the blessing of liberty, can be preserved to any people but by a firm adherence to justice, moderation, temperance, frugality, and virtue, and by frequent recurrence to fundamental principles.

16. That Religion, or the duty which we owe to our Creator, and the manner of discharging it, can be directed only by reason and conviction, not by force or violence; and, therefore, all men are equally entitled to the free exercise of religion, according to the dictates of conscience; and that it is the mutual duty of all to practise Christian forbearance, love, and charity, towards each other. [8]

2. Virginia Statute of Religious Liberty, 1785

An Act for establishing Religious Freedom

I. Whereas Almighty God hath created the mind free; that all attempts to influence it by temporal punishments or burthens, or by civil incapacitations, tend only to beget habits of hypocrisy and meanness, and are a departure from the plan of the Holy author of our religion, who being Lord both of body and mind, yet chose not to propagate it by coercions on either, as was in his Almighty power to do; that the impious presumption of legislators and rulers, civil as well as ecclesiastical, who being themselves but fallible and uninspired men, have assumed dominion over the faith of others, setting up their own opinions and modes of thinking as the only true and infallible, and as such endeavouring to impose them on others, hath established and maintained false religions over the greatest part of the world, and through all time; that to compel a man to furnish contributions of money for the propagation of opinions which he disbelieves, is sinful and tyrannical; that even the forcing him to support this or that teacher of his own religious persuasion, is depriving him of the comfortable liberty of giving his contributions to the particular pastor whose morals he would make his pattern, and whose powers he feels most persuasive to righteousness, and is withdrawing from the ministry those temporary rewards, which proceeding from an approbation of their personal conduct, are an additional incitement to earnest and unremitting labours for the instruction of mankind; that our civil rights have no dependence on our religious opinions, any more than our opinions in physics or geometry; that therefore the proscribing any citizen as unworthy the public confidence by laying upon him an incapacity of being called to offices of trust and emolument, unless he profess or renounce this or that religious opinion, is depriving him injuriously of those privileges and advantages to which in common with his fellow-citizens he has a natural right; that it tends only to corrupt the principles of that religion it is meant to encourage, by bribing with a monopoly of worldly honours and emoluments, those who will externally profess and conform to it; that though indeed these are criminal who do not withstand such temptation, yet neither are those innocent who lay the bait in their way; that to suffer the civil magistrate to intrude his powers into the field of opinion, and to restrain the profession or propagation of principles on supposition of their ill tendency, is a dangerous fallacy, which at once destroys all religious liberty, because he being of course judge of that tendency will make his opinions the rule of judgment, and approve or condemn the sentiments of others only as they shall square with or differ from his own; that it is time enough for the rightful purposes of civil government, for its officers to interfere when principles break out into overt acts against peace and good order; and finally, that truth is great and will prevail if left to herself, that

she is the proper and sufficient antagonist to error, and has nothing to fear from the conflict, unless by human interposition disarmed of her natural weapons, free argument and debate, errors ceasing to be dangerous when it is permitted freely to contradict them.

II. Be it enacted by the General Assembly, that no man shall be compelled to frequent or support any religious worship, place or ministry whatsoever, nor shall be enforced, restrained, molested, or burthened in his body or goods, nor shall otherwise suffer on account of his religious opinions or belief; but that all men shall be free to profess, and by argument to maintain their opinion in matters of religion, and that the same shall in no wise diminish, enlarge or affect their civil capacities.

III. And though we well know that this Assembly, elected by the people for the ordinary purposes of legislation only, have no power to restrain the acts of succeeding Assemblies, constituted with powers equal to our own, and that therefore to declare this Act to be irrevocable would be of no effect in law; yet as we are free to declare, and do declare, that the rights hereby asserted are of the natural rights of mankind, and that if any Act shall hereafter be passed to repeal the present, or to narrow its operation, such Act will be an infringement of natural right. [9]

The Northwest Ordinance, 1787

An Ordinance for the Government of the Territory of the United States North-West of the River Ohio

[Section 1.] BE IT ORDAINED by the United States in Congress assembled, That the said territory, for the purposes of temporary government, be one district; subject, however, to be divided into two districts, as future circumstances may, in the opinion of Congress, make it expedient.

[Section 2.] Be it ordained by the au-

thority aforesaid, That the estates both of resident and non-resident proprietors in the said territory, dying intestate, shall descend to, and be distributed among their children, and the descendants of a deceased child in equal parts; the descendants of a deceased child or grand-child, to take the share of their deceased parent in equal parts among them: And where there shall be no children or descendants, then in equal parts to the next of kin, in equal degree; and among collaterals, the children of a deceased brother or sister of the intestate, shall have in equal parts among them their deceased parents share; and there shall in no case be a distinction between kindred of the whole and half blood; saving in all cases to the widow of the intestate, her third part of the real estate for life, and one third part of the personal estate; and this law relative to descents and dower, shall remain in full force until altered by the legislature of the district. And until the governor and judges shall adopt laws as herein after mentioned, estates in the said territory may be devised or bequeathed by wills in writing, signed and sealed by him or her in whom the estate may be (being of full age), and attested by three witnesses; and real estates may be conveyed by lease and release, or bargain and sale, signed, sealed, and delivered by the person being of full age, in whom the estate may be, and attested by two witnesses, provided such wills be duly proved, and such conveyances be acknowledged, or the execution thereof duly proved, and be recorded within one year after proper magistrates, courts, and registers shall be appointed for that purpose; and personal property may be transferred by delivery, saving, however, to the French and Canadian inhabitants, and other settlers of the Kaskaskies, Saint Vincent's, and the neighbouring villages, who have heretofore professed themselves citizens of Virginia, their laws and customs now in force among them, relative to the descent and conveyance of property.

[Section 3.] Be it ordained by the authority aforesaid, That there shall be appointed from time to time, by Congress, a governor, whose commission shall continue in force for the term of three years, unless sooner revoked by Congress; he shall reside in the district, and have a freehold estate therein, in one thousand acres of land, while in the exercise of his office.

[Section 4.] There shall be appointed from time to time, by Congress, a secretary, whose commission shall continue in force for four years, unless sooner revoked, he shall reside in the district, and have a freehold estate therein, in five hundred acres of land, while in the exercise of his office; it shall be his duty to keep and preserve the acts and laws passed by the legislature, and the public records of the district, and the proceedings of the governor in his executive department; and transmit authentic copies of such acts and proceedings, every six months, to the secretary of Congress: There shall also be appointed a court to consist of three judges, any two of whom to form a court, who shall have a common law jurisdiction, and reside in the district, and have each therein a freehold estate in five hundred acres of land, while in the exercise of their offices; and their commissions shall continue in force during good behaviour.

[Section 5.] The governor and judges, or a majority of them, shall adopt and publish in the district, such laws of the original states, criminal and civil, as may be necessary, and best suited to the circumstances of the district, and report them to Congress, from time to time, which laws shall be in force in the district until the organization of the general assembly therein, unless disapproved of by Congress; but afterwards the legislature shall have authority to alter them as they shall think fit.

[Section 6.] The governor for the time being, shall be commander in chief of the militia, appoint and commission all officers in the same, below the rank of general officers; all general officers shall be appointed and commissioned by Congress.

[Section 7.] Previous to the organization of the general assembly, the governor shall appoint such magistrates and other civil officers, in each county or township, as he shall find necessary for the preservation of the peace and good order in the same: After the general assembly shall be organized, the powers and duties of magistrates and other civil officers shall be regulated and defined by the said assembly; but all magistrates and other civil officers, not herein otherwise directed, shall, during the continuance of this temporary government, be appointed by the governor.

[Section 8.] For the prevention of crimes and injuries, the laws to be adopted or made shall have force in all parts of the district, and for the execution of process, criminal and civil, the governor shall make proper divisions thereof—and he shall proceed from time to time, as circumstances may require, to lay out the parts of the district in which the Indian titles shall have been extinguished, into counties and townships, subject, however, to such alterations as may thereafter be made by the legislature.

[Section 9.] So soon as there shall be five thousand free male inhabitants, of full age, in the district, upon giving proof thereof to the governor, they shall receive authority, with time and place, to elect representatives from their counties or townships, to represent them in the general assembly; provided that for every five hundred free male inhabitants there shall be one representative, and so on progressively with the number of free male inhabitants, shall the right of representation increase, until the number of representatives shall amount to twenty-five, after which the number and proportion of representatives shall be regulated by the legislature; provided that no person be eligible or qualified to act as a representative, unless he shall have been a citizen of one of the United States three years and be a resident in the district. or unless he shall have resided in the district three years, and in either case shall likewise hold in his own right, in fee simple, two hundred acres of land within the same: Provided also, that a freehold in fifty acres of land in the district, having been a citizen of one of the states, and being resident in the district; or the like freehold and two years residence in the district shall be necessary to qualify a man as an elector of a representative.

[Section 10.] The representatives thus elected, shall serve for the term of two years, and in case of the death of a rep-

resentative, or removal from office, the governor shall issue a writ to the county or township for which he was a member, to elect another in his stead, to serve for the residue of the term.

[Section 11.] The general assembly, or legislature, shall consist of the governor, legislative council, and a house of representatives. The legislative council shall consist of five members, to continue in office five years, unless sooner removed by Congress, any three of whom to be a quorum, and the members of the council shall be nominated and appointed in the following manner, to wit: As soon as representatives shall be elected, the governor shall appoint a time and place for them to meet together, and, when met, they shall nominate ten persons, resident in the district, and each possessed of a freehold in five hundred acres of land, and return their names to Congress; five of whom Congress shall appoint and commission to serve as aforesaid; and whenever a vacancy shall happen in the council, by death or removal from office, the house of representatives shall nominate two persons, qualified as aforesaid, for each vacancy, and return their names to Congress; one of whom Congress shall appoint and commission for the residue of the term; and every five years, four months at least before the expiration of the time of service of the members of council, the said house shall nominate ten persons, qualified as aforesaid, and return their names to Congress, five of whom Congress shall appoint and commission to serve as members of the council five years, unless sooner removed. And the governor, legislative council, and house of representatives, shall have authority to make laws in all cases for the good government of the district, not repugnant to the principles and articles in this ordinance established and declared. And all bills having passed by a majority in the house, and by a majority in the council, shall be referred to the governor for his assent; but no bill or legislative act whatever, shall be of any force without his assent. The governor shall have power to convene, prorogue and dissolve the general assembly, when in his opinion it shall be expedient.

[Section 12.] The governor, judges, legislative council, secretary, and such other officers as Congress shall appoint in the district, shall take an oath or affirmation of fidelity, and of office, the governor before the president of Congress, and all other officers before the governor. As soon as a legislature shall be formed in the district, the council and house, assembled in one room, shall have authority by joint ballot to elect a delegate to Congress, who shall have a seat in Congress, with a right of debating, but not of voting, during this temporary government.

[Section 13.] And for extending the fundamental principles of civil and religious liberty, which form the basis whereon these republics, their laws and constitutions are erected; to fix and establish those principles as the basis of all laws, constitutions and governments, which for ever hereafter shall be formed in the said territory; to provide also for the establishment of states, and permanent government therein, and for their admission to a share in the federal councils on an equal footing with the original states, at as early periods as may be consistent with the general interest:

[Section 14.] It is hereby ordained and declared by the authority aforesaid, That the following articles shall be considered as articles of compact between the original states and the people and states in the said territory, and forever remain unalterable, unless by common consent, to wit:

Article the First. No person, demeaning himself in a peaceable and orderly manner, shall ever be molested on account of his mode of worship or religious sentiments in the said territory.

Article the Second. The inhabitants of the said territory shall always be entitled to the benefits of the writ of habeas corpus, and of the trial by jury; of a proportionate representation of the people in the legislature, and of judicial proceedings according to the course of the common law; all persons shall be bailable unless for capital offenses, where the proof shall be evident, or the presumption great; all fines shall be moderate, and no cruel or unusual punishments shall be inflicted; no man shall be deprived of his liberty or property but by the judgment of his peers, or the law of the land; and should the public exigencies make it necessary for the common preservation to take any person's property, or to demand his particular services, full compensation shall be made for the same; and in the just preservation of rights and property it is understood and declared, that no law ought ever to be made, or have force in the said territory, that shall in any manner whatever interfere with, or affect private contracts or engagements, bona fide and without fraud previously formed.

Article the Third. Religion, morality and knowledge, being necessary to good government and the happiness of mankind, schools and the means of education shall forever be encouraged. The utmost good faith shall always be observed towards the Indians; their lands and property shall never be taken from them without their consent; and in their property, rights and liberty, they never shall be invaded or disturbed, unless in just and lawful wars authorized by Congress; but laws founded in justice and humanity shall from time to time be made, for preventing wrongs being done to them; and for preserving peace and friendship with them.

Article the Fourth. The said territory, and the states which may be formed therein, shall forever remain a part of this confederacy of the United States of America, subject to the articles of confederation, and to such alterations therein as shall be constitutionally made; and to all the acts and ordinances of the United States in Congress assembled, conformable thereto. The inhabitants and settlers in the said territory, shall be subject to pay a part of the federal debts contracted or to be contracted, and a proportional part of the expences of government, to be apportioned on them by Congress, according to the same common rule and measure by which apportionments thereof shall be made on the other states; and the taxes for paying their proportion, shall be laid and levied by the authority and direction of the legislatures of the district or districts or new states, as in the original states, within the time agreed upon by the United States in Congress assembled. The legislatures of those districts, or new states, shall never interfere with the primary disposal of the soil by the United States in Congress assembled, nor with any regulations Congress may find necessary for securing the title in such soil to the bona fide purchasers. No tax shall be imposed on lands the property of the United States; and in no case shall non-resident proprietors be taxed higher than residents. The navigable waters leading into the Mississippi and St. Lawrence, and the carrying places between the same shall be common highways, and forever free, as well to the inhabitants of the said territory, as to the citizens of the United States, and those of any other states that may be admitted into the confederacy, without any tax, impost or duty therefor.

Article the Fifth. There shall be formed in the said territory, not less than three nor more than five states; and the boundaries of the states, as soon as Virginia shall alter her act of cession and consent to the same, shall become fixed and established as follows, to wit: The western state in the said territory, shall be bounded by the Mississippi, the Ohio and Wabash rivers; a direct line drawn from the Wabash and Post Vincent's due north to the territorial line between the United States and Canada, and by the said territorial line to the lake of the Woods and Mississippi. The middle state shall be bounded by the said direct line, the Wabash from Post Vincent's to the Ohio; by the Ohio, by a direct line drawn due north from the mouth of the Great Miami to the said territorial line, and by the said territorial line. The eastern state shall be bounded by the last mentioned direct line, the Ohio, Pennsylvania, and the said territorial line; Provided however, and it is further understood and declared, that the boundaries of these three states, shall be subject so far to be altered, that if Congress shall hereafter find it expedient, they shall have authority to form one or two states in that part of the said territory which lies north of an east and west line drawn through the southerly bend or extreme of lake Michigan: and whenever any of the said states shall have sixty thousand free inhabitants therein, such state shall be admitted by its delegates into the Congress of the United States, on an equal footing with the original states in all respects whatever; and shall be at liberty to form a permanent constitution and state government: Provided the constitution and government so to be formed, shall be republican, and in conformity to the principles contained in these articles, and so far as it can be consistent with the general interest of the confederacy, such admission shall be allowed at an earlier period, and when there may be a less number of free inhabitants in the state than sixty thousand.

Article the Sixth. There shall be neither slavery nor involuntary servitude in the said territory, otherwise than in punishment of crimes whereof the party shall have been duly convicted: Provided always, that any person escaping into the same, from whom labour or service is lawfully claimed in any one of the original states, such fugitive may be lawfully reclaimed and conveyed to the person claiming his or her labour or service as aforesaid.

Be it ordained by the authority aforesaid, That the resolutions of the 23d of April, 1784, relative to the subject of this ordinance, be, and the same are hereby repealed and declared null and void.

DONE by the UNITED STATES in CONGRESS assembled, the 13th day of July, in the year of our Lord 1787, and of their sovereignty and independence the 12th. [10]

James Madison's Notes of Debates in the Federal Convention, 1787

August 20, 1787

Mr. Pinkney submitted to the House, in order to be referred to the Committee of detail, the following propositions—

"Each House shall be the Judge of its own privileges, and shall have authority to punish by imprisonment every person violating the same; or who, in the place where the Legislature may be sitting and during the time of its Session, shall threaten any of its members for any thing said or done on the House—or who shall assault any of them therefor—or who shall assault or arrest any witness or other person ordered to attend either of the Houses in his way going or returning; or who shall rescue any person arrested by their order."

"Each branch of the Legislature, as well as the supreme Executive shall have authority to require the opinions of the supreme Judicial Court upon important questions of law, and upon solemn occasions."

"The privileges and benefit of the Writ of Habeas Corpus shall be enjoyed in this Government in the most expeditious and ample manner; and shall not be suspended by the Legislature except upon the most urgent and pressing occasions, and for a limited time not exceeding _____ months."

"The liberty of the Press shall be inviolably preserved."

"No troops shall be kept up in time of peace, but by consent of the Legislature."

"The military shall always be subordinate to the Civil power, and no grants of money shall be made by the Legislature for supporting military Land forces, for more than one year at a time."

"No soldier shall be quartered in any House in time of peace without consent of the owner."

"No person holding the office of President of the U.S., a Judge of their supreme Court, Secretary for the department of Foreign Affairs, of Finance, of Marine, of War, or of _____, shall be capable of holding at the same time any other office of Trust or Emolument under the U.S. or an individual State."

"No religious test or qualification shall ever be annexed to any oath of office under the authority of the U.S."

"The U.S. shall be for ever considered as one Body corporate and politic in law, and entitled to all the rights, privileges and immunities, which to Bodies corporate do or ought to appertain."

"The Legislature of the U.S. shall have the power of making the great seal which shall be kept by the President of the U.S. or in his absence by the President of the Senate, to be used by them as the occasion may require. It shall be called the great Seal of the U.S. and shall be affixed to all laws."

"All Commissions and writs shall run in the name of the U.S."

"The Jurisdiction of the supreme Court shall be extended to all controversies between the U.S. and an individual State, or the U.S. and the Citizens of an individual State."

These propositions were referred to the Committee of detail without debate or consideration of them, by the House. . . .

September 12, 1787

. . . Mr. Williamson, observed to the House that no provision was yet made for juries in Civil cases and suggested the necessity of it.

Mr. Gorham. It is not possible to discriminate equity cases from those in which juries are proper. The Representatives of

James Madison (1751–1836), often called the father of the Constitution, engraving after Gilbert Stuart. Madison's day-by-day notes of debates at the Federal Convention in 1787 furnish the only detailed record of the proceedings.

the people may be safely trusted in this matter.

Mr. Gerry urged the necessity of Juries to guard against corrupt Judges. He proposed that the Committee last appointed should be directed to provide a clause for securing the trial by Juries.

Col. Mason perceived the difficulty mentioned by Mr. Gorham. The jury cases can not be specified. A general principle laid down on this and some other points would be sufficient. He wished the plan*

had been prefaced with a Bill of Rights, and would second a Motion if made for the purpose. It would give great quiet to the people; and with the aid of the State declarations, a bill might be prepared in a few hours.

Mr. Gerry concurred in the idea and moved for a Committee to prepare a Bill of Rights. Col. Mason seconded the motion.

Mr. Sherman, was for securing the rights

_____

*The Constitution.

354

of the people where requisite. The State Declarations of Rights are not repealed by this Constitution; and being in force are sufficient. There are many cases where juries are proper which can not be discriminated. The Legislature may be safely trusted.

Col. Mason. The Laws of the U.S. are to be paramount to State Bills of Rights.

On the question for a Committee to prepare a Bill of Rights.

New Hampshire no. Massachusetts absent. Connecticut no. New Jersey no. Pennsylvania no. Delaware no. Maryland no. Virginia no. North Carolina no. South Carolina no. Georgia no. . . .

September 15, 1787

Art. III. Sect. 2. parag. 3. Mr. Pinkney and Mr. Gerry moved to annex to the end, "And a trial by jury shall be preserved as usual in civil cases."

Mr. Gorham. The constitution of Juries is different in different States and the trial itself is *usual* in different cases in different States.

Mr. King urged the same objections.

Gen. Pinkney also. He thought such a clause in the Constitution would be pregnant with embarrassments.

The motion was disagreed to nem. con.*

Art. IV. Sect. 2. parag. 3. the term "legally" was struck out, and "under the laws thereof" inserted after the word "State," in compliance with the wish of some who thought the term legal equivocal, and favouring the idea that slavery was legal in a moral view. . . .

Mr. Randolph animadverting on the indefinite and dangerous power given by the Constitution to Congress, expressing the pain he felt at differing from the body of the Convention, on the close of the great and awful subject of their labours, and anxiously wishing for some accommodating expedient which would relieve him from his embarrassments, made a motion importing "that amendments to the plan might be offered by the State Conventions, which should be submitted to and finally decided on by another general Convention." Should this proposition be disregarded, it would he said be impossible for him to put his name to the instrument. Whether he should oppose it afterwards he would not then decide but he would not deprive himself of the freedom to do so in his own State, if that course should be prescribed by his final judgment.

Col. Mason seconded and followed Mr. Randolph in animadversions on the dangerous power and structure of the Government, concluding that it would end either in monarchy, or a tyrannical aristocracy; which, he was in doubt, but one or other, he was sure. This Constitution had been formed without the knowledge or idea of the people. A second Convention will know more of the sense of the people, and be able to provide a system more consonant to it. It was improper to say to the people, take this or nothing. As the Constitution now stands, he could neither give it his support or vote in Virginia; and he could not sign here what he could not support there. With the expedient of another Convention as proposed, he could sign.

Mr. Pinkney. These declarations from members so respectable at the close of this important scene, give a peculiar solemnity to the present moment. He descanted on the consequences of calling forth the deliberations and amendments of the different States on the subject of Government at large. Nothing but confusion and contrariety could spring from the experiment. The States will never agree in their plans, and the Deputies to a second Convention coming together under the discordant impressions of their Constituents, will never agree. Conventions are serious things, and ought not to be repeated. He was not without objections as well as others to the plan. He objected to the contemptible weakness and dependence of the Executive. He ob-

---

*No one contradicting.

jected to the power of a majority only of Congress over Commerce. But apprehending the danger of a general confusion, and an ultimate decision by the sword, he should give the plan his support.

Mr. Gerry, stated the objections which determined him to withhold his name from the Constitution. 1. the duration and re-eligibility of the Senate. 2. the power of the House of Representatives to conceal their journals. 3. the power of Congress over the places of election. 4. the unlimited power of Congress over their own compensations. 5. Massachusetts has not a due share of Representatives allotted to her. 6. three-fifths of the Blacks are to be represented as if they were freemen. 7. under the power over commerce, monopolies may be established. 8. the vice president being made head of the Senate. He could however he said get over all these, if the rights of the Citizens were not rendered insecure 1. by the general power of the Legislature to make what laws they may please to call necessary and proper. 2. raise armies and money without limit. 3. to establish a tribunal without juries, which will be a Star-chamber as to Civil cases. Under such a view of the Constitution, the best that could be done he conceived was to provide for a second general Convention.

On the question on the proposition of Mr. Randolph. All the States answered—no.

On the question to agree to the Constitution, as amended. All the States ay.

The Constitution was then ordered to be engrossed.

And the House adjourned. [11]

Selected Amendment Proposals by States' Ratifying Conventions, 1788

1. Virginia Convention, June 27

Mr. Wythe reported, from the committee appointed, such amendments to the proposed Constitution of government for the United States as were by them deemed necessary to be recommended to the consideration of the Congress which shall first assemble under the said Constitution, to be acted upon according to the mode prescribed in the 5th article thereof; and he read the same in his place, and afterwards delivered them in at the clerk's table, where the same were again read, and are as follows:

"That there be a declaration or bill of rights asserting, and securing from encroachment, the essential and unalienable rights of the people, in some such manner as the following:

"1st. That there are certain natural rights, of which men, when they form a social compact, cannot deprive or divest their posterity; among which are the enjoyment of life and liberty, with the means of acquiring, possessing, and protecting property, and pursuing and obtaining happiness and safety.

"2d. That all power is naturally invested in, and consequently derived from, the people; that magistrates therefore are their trustees and agents, at all times amenable to them.

"3d. That government ought to be instituted for the common benefit, protection, and security of the people; and that the doctrine of non-resistance against arbitrary power and oppression is absurd, slavish, and destructive to the good and happiness of mankind.

"4th. That no man or set of men are entitled to separate or exclusive public emoluments or privileges from the community, but in consideration of public services, which not being descendible, neither ought the offices of magistrate, legislator, or judge, or any other public office, to be hereditary.

"5th. That the legislative, executive, and judicial powers of government should be separate and distinct; and, that the members of the two first may be restrained from oppression by feeling and participating the public burdens, they should, at fixed periods, be reduced to a private station, return into the mass of the people, and the vacancies be supplied by certain and regular elections, in which all or any part of the former members to be eligible or ineligible, as the rules of the Constitution of government, and the laws, shall direct.

"6th. That the elections of representatives in the legislature ought to be free and frequent, and all men having sufficient evidence of permanent common interest with, and attachment to, the community, ought to have the right of suffrage; and no aid, charge, tax, or fee, can be set, rated, or levied, upon the people without their own consent, or that of their representatives, so elected; nor can they be bound by any law to which they have not, in like manner, assented, for the public good.

"7th. That all power of suspending laws, or the execution of laws, by any authority, without the consent of the representatives of the people in the legislature, is injurious to their rights, and ought not to be exercised.

"8th. That, in all criminal and capital prosecutions, a man hath a right to demand the cause and nature of his accusation, to be confronted with the accusers and witnesses, to call for evidence, and be allowed counsel in his favour, and to a fair and speedy trial by an impartial jury of his vicinage, without whose unanimous consent he cannot be found guilty (except in the government of the land and naval forces) nor can he be compelled to give evidence against himself.

"9th. That no freeman ought to be taken, imprisoned, or disseized of his freehold, liberties, privileges, or franchises, or outlawed, or exiled, or in any manner destroyed, or deprived of his life, liberty, or property, but by the law of the land.

"10th. That every freeman restrained of his liberty is entitled to a remedy, to inquire into the lawfulness thereof, and to remove the same, if unlawful, and that such remedy ought not to be denied nor delayed.

"11th. That, in controversies respecting property, and in suits between man and man, the ancient trial by jury is one of the greatest securities to the rights of the people, and to remain sacred and inviolable.

"12th. That every freeman ought to find a certain remedy, by recourse to the laws, for all injuries and wrongs he may receive in his person, property, or character. He ought to obtain right and justice freely, without sale, completely and without denial, promptly and without delay; and that all establishments or regulations contravening these rights are oppressive and unjust.

"13th. That excessive bail ought not to be required, nor excessive fines imposed, nor cruel and unusual punishments inflicted.

"14th. That every freeman has a right to be secure from all unreasonable searches and seizures of his person, his papers, and property; all warrants, therefore, to search suspected places, or seize any freeman, his papers, or property, without information on oath (or affirmation of a person religiously scrupulous of taking an oath) of legal and sufficient cause, are grievous and oppressive; and all general warrants to search suspected places, or to apprehend any suspected person, without specially naming or describing the place or person, are dangerous, and ought not to be granted.

"15th. That the people have a right peaceably to assemble together to consult for the common good, or to instruct their representatives; and that every freeman has a right to petition or apply to the legislature for redress of grievances.

"16th. That the people have a right to

357

freedom of speech, and of writing and publishing their sentiments; that the freedom of the press is one of the greatest bulwarks of liberty, and ought not to be violated.

"17th. That the people have a right to keep and bear arms; that a well-regulated militia, composed of the body of the people trained to arms, is the proper, natural, and safe defence of a free state; that standing armies, in time of peace, are dangerous to liberty, and therefore ought to be avoided, as far as the circumstances and protection of the community will admit; and that, in all cases, the military should be under strict subordination to, and governed by, the civil power.

"18th. That no soldier in time of peace ought to be quartered in any house without the consent of the owner, and in time of war in such manner only as the law directs.

"19th. That any person religiously scrupulous of bearing arms ought to be exempted, upon payment of an equivalent to employ another to bear arms in his stead.

"20th. That religion, or the duty which we owe to our Creator, and the manner of discharging it, can be directed only by reason and conviction, not by force or violence; and therefore all men have an equal, natural, and unalienable right to the free exercise of religion, according to the dictates of conscience, and that no particular religious sect or society ought to be favoured or established, by law, in preference to others."

Amendments to the Constitution

"1st. That each state in the Union shall respectively retain every power, jurisdiction, and right, which is not by this Constitution delegated to the Congress of the United States, or to the departments of the federal government.

"2d. That there shall be one representative for every thirty thousand, according to the enumeration or census mentioned in the Constitution, until the whole number of representatives amounts to two hundred; after which, that number shall be continued or increased, as Congress shall direct, upon the principles fixed in the Constitution, by apportioning the representatives of each state to some greater number of people, from time to time, as population increases.

"3d. When the Congress shall lay direct taxes or excises, they shall immediately inform the executive power of each state, of the quota of such state, according to the census herein directed, which is proposed to be thereby raised; and if the legislature of any state shall pass a law which shall be effectual for raising such quota at the time required by Congress, the taxes and excises laid by Congress shall not be collected in such state.

"4th. That the members of the Senate and House of Representatives shall be ineligible to, and incapable of holding, any civil office under the authority of the United States, during the time for which they shall respectively be elected.

"5th. That the journals of the proceedings of the Senate and House of Representatives shall be published at least once in every year, except such parts thereof, relating to treaties, alliances, or military operations, as, in their judgment, require secrecy.

"6th. That a regular statement and account of the receipts and expenditures of public money shall be published at least once a year.

"7th. That no commercial treaty shall be ratified without the concurrence of two thirds of the whole number of the members of the Senate; and no treaty ceding, contracting, restraining, or suspending, the territorial rights or claims of the United States, or any of them, or any of their rights or claims to fishing in the American seas, or navigating the American rivers, shall be made, but in cases of the most urgent and extreme necessity; nor shall any such treaty be ratified without the concurrence of three fourths of the whole number of the members of both houses respectively.

"8th. That no navigation law, or law regulating commerce, shall be passed without the consent of two thirds of the members present, in both houses.

"9th. That no standing army, or regular troops, shall be raised, or kept up, in time of peace, without the consent of two thirds of the members present, in both houses.

"10th. That no soldier shall be enlisted for any longer term than four years, except in time of war, and then for no longer term than the continuance of the war.

"11th. That each state respectively shall have the power to provide for organizing, arming, and disciplining its own militia, whensoever Congress shall omit or neglect to provide for the same. That the militia shall not be subject to martial law, except when in actual service, in time of war, invasion, or rebellion; and when not in the actual service of the United States, shall be subject only to such fines, penalties, and punishments, as shall be directed or inflicted by the laws of its own state.

"12th. That the exclusive power of legislation given to Congress over the federal town and its adjacent district, and other places, purchased or to be purchased by Congress of any of the states, shall extend only to such regulations as respect the police and good government thereof.

"13th. That no person shall be capable of being President of the United States for more than eight years in any term of sixteen years.

"14th. That the judicial power of the United States shall be vested in one Supreme Court, and in such courts of admiralty as Congress may from time to time ordain and establish in any of the different states. The judicial power shall extend to all cases in law and equity arising under treaties made, or which shall be made, under the authority of the United States; to all cases affecting ambassadors, other foreign ministers, and consuls; to all cases of admiralty and maritime jurisdiction; to controversies to which the United States shall be a party; to controversies

between two or more states, and between parties claiming lands under the grants of different states. In all cases affecting ambassadors, other foreign ministers, and consuls, and those in which a state shall be a party, the Supreme Court shall have original jurisdiction; in all other cases before mentioned, the Supreme Court shall have appellate jurisdiction, as to matters of law only, except in cases of equity, and of admiralty, and maritime jurisdiction, in which the Supreme Court shall have appellate jurisdiction both as to law and fact, with such exceptions and under such regulations as the Congress shall make: but the judicial power of the United States shall extend to no case where the cause of action shall have originated before the ratification of the Constitution, except in disputes between states about their territory, disputes between persons claiming lands under the grants of different states, and suits for debts due to the United States.

"15th. That, in criminal prosecutions, no man shall be restrained in the exercise of the usual and accustomed right of challenging or excepting to the jury.

"16th. That Congress shall not alter, modify, or interfere in the times, places, or manner of holding elections for senators and representatives, or either of them, except when the legislature of any state shall neglect, refuse, or be disabled, by invasion or rebellion, to prescribe the same.

"17th. That those clauses which declare that Congress shall not exercise certain powers, be not interpreted, in any manner whatsoever, to extend the powers of Congress; but that they be construed either as making exceptions to the specified powers where this shall be the case, or otherwise, as inserted merely for greater caution.

"18th. That the laws ascertaining the compensation of senators and representatives for their services, be postponed, in their operation, until after the election of representatives immediately succeeding the passing thereof; that excepted which shall first be passed on the subject.

"19th. That some tribunal other than the Senate be provided for trying impeachments of senators.

"20th. That the salary of a judge shall not be increased or diminished during his continuance in office, otherwise than by general regulations of salary, which may take place on a revision of the subject at stated periods of not less than seven years, to commence from the time such salaries shall be first ascertained by Congress." [12]

2. New York Convention, July 26

We, the delegates of the people of the state of New York, duly elected and met in Convention, having maturely considered the Constitution for the United States of America, agreed to on the 17th day of September, in the year 1787, by the Convention then assembled at Philadelphia, in the commonwealth of Pennsylvania (a copy whereof precedes these presents) and having also seriously and deliberately considered the present situation of the United States, Do declare and make known,

That all power is originally vested in, and consequently derived from, the people, and that government is instituted by them for their common interest, protection, and security.

That the enjoyment of life, liberty, and the pursuit of happiness, are essential rights, which every government ought to respect and preserve.

That the powers of government may be reassumed by the people whensoever it shall become necessary to their happiness; that every power, jurisdiction, and right, which is not by the said Constitution clearly delegated to the Congress of the United States, or the departments of the government thereof, remains to the people of the several states, or to their respective state governments, to whom they may have granted the same; and that those clauses in the said Constitution, which declare that Congress shall not have or exercise certain powers, do not imply that Congress is en-

titled to any powers not given by the said Constitution; but such clauses are to be construed either as exceptions to certain specified powers, or as inserted merely for greater caution.

That the people have an equal, natural, and unalienable right freely and peaceably to exercise their religion, according to the dictates of conscience; and that no religious sect or society ought to be favoured or established by law in preference to others.

That the people have a right to keep and bear arms; that a well-regulated militia, including the body of the people capable of bearing arms, is the proper, natural, and safe defence of a free state.

That the militia should not be subject to martial law, except in time of war, rebellion, or insurrection.

That standing armies, in time of peace, are dangerous to liberty, and ought not to be kept up, except in cases of necessity; and that at all times the military should be under strict subordination to the civil power.

That, in time of peace, no soldier ought to be quartered in any house without the consent of the owner, and in time of war only by the civil magistrate, in such manner as the laws may direct.

That no person ought to be taken, imprisoned, or disseized of his freehold, or be exiled, or deprived of his privileges, franchises, life, liberty, or property, but by due process of law.

That no person ought to be put twice in jeopardy of life or limb, for one and the same offence; nor, unless in case of impeachment, be punished more than once for the same offence.

That every person restrained of his liberty is entitled to an inquiry into the lawfulness of such restraint, and to a removal thereof if unlawful; and that such inquiry or removal ought not to be denied or delayed, except when, on account of public danger, the Congress shall suspend the privilege of the writ of *habeas corpus*.

That excessive bail ought not to be required, nor excessive fines imposed, nor cruel or unusual punishments inflicted.

That (except in the government of the land and naval forces, and of the militia when in actual service, and in cases of impeachment) a presentment or indictment by a grand jury ought to be observed as a necessary preliminary to the trial of all crimes cognizable by the judiciary of the United States; and such trial should be speedy, public, and by an impartial jury of the county where the crime was committed; and that no person can be found guilty without the unanimous consent of such jury. But in cases of crimes not committed within any county of any of the United States, and in cases of crimes committed within any county in which a general insurrection may prevail, or which may be in the possession of a foreign enemy, the inquiry and trial may be in such county as the Congress shall by law direct; which county, in the two cases last mentioned, should be as near as conveniently may be to that county in which the crime may have been committed; and that, in all criminal prosecutions, the accused ought to be informed of the cause and nature of his accusation, to be confronted with his accusers and the witnesses against him, to have the means of producing his witnesses, and the assistance of counsel for his defence; and should not be compelled to give evidence against himself.

That the trial by jury, in the extent that it obtains by the common law of England, is one of the greatest securities to the rights of a free people, and ought to remain inviolate.

That every freeman has a right to be secure from all unreasonable searches and seizures of his person, his papers, or his property; and therefore, that all warrants to search suspected places, or seize any freeman, his papers, or property, without information, upon oath or affirmation, of sufficient cause, are grievous and oppressive; and that all general warrants (or such in which the place or person suspected are not particularly designated) are dangerous, and ought not to be granted.

That the people have a right peaceably to assemble together to consult for their common good, or to instruct their representatives, and that every person has a right to petition or apply to the legislature for redress of grievances.

That the freedom of the press ought not to be violated or restrained.

That there should be, once in four years, an election of the President and Vice-President, so that no officer, who may be appointed by the Congress to act as President, in case of the removal, death, resignation, or inability, of the President and Vice-President, can in any case continue to act beyond the termination of the period for which the last President and Vice-President were elected.

That nothing contained in the said Constitution is to be construed to prevent the legislature of any state from passing laws at its discretion, from time to time, to divide such state into convenient districts, and to apportion its representatives to and amongst such districts.

That the prohibition contained in the said Constitution, against *ex post facto* laws, extends only to laws concerning crimes.

That all appeals in causes determinable according to the course of the common law, ought to be by writ of error, and not otherwise.

That the judicial power of the United States, in cases in which a state may be a party, does not extend to criminal prosecutions, or to authorize any suit by any person against a state.

That the judicial power of the United States, as to controversies between citizens of the same state, claiming lands under grants from different states, is not to be construed to extend to any other controversies between them, except those which relate to such lands, so claimed, under grants of different states.

That the jurisdiction of the Supreme Court of the United States, or of any other court to be instituted by the Congress, is not in any case to be increased, enlarged, or extended, by any faction, collusion, or mere suggestion; and that no treaty is to be construed so to operate as to alter the Constitution of any state.

Under these impressions, and declaring that the rights aforesaid cannot be abridged or violated, and that the explanations aforesaid are consistent with the said Constitution, and in confidence that the amendments which shall have been proposed to the said Constitution will receive an early and mature consideration, We, the said delegates, in the name and in the behalf of the people of the state of New York, do, by these presents, assent to and ratify the said Constitution. In full confidence, nevertheless, that, until a convention shall be called and convened for proposing amendments to the said Constitution, the militia of this state will not be continued in service out of this state for a longer term than six weeks, without the consent of the legislature thereof; that the Congress will not make or alter any regulation in this state, respecting the times, places, and manner, of holding elections for senators or representatives, unless the legislature of this state shall neglect or refuse to make laws or regulations for the purpose, or from any circumstance be incapable of making the same; and that, in those cases, such power will only be exercised until the legislature of this state shall make provision in the premises; that no excise will be imposed on any article of the growth, production, or manufacture of the United States, or any of them, within this state, ardent spirits excepted; and the Congress will not lay direct taxes within this state, but when the moneys arising from the impost and excise shall be insufficient for the public exigencies, nor then, until Congress shall first have made a requisition upon this state to assess, levy, and pay, the amount of such requisition, made agreeably to the census fixed in the said Constitution, in such way and manner as the legislature of this state

shall judge best; but that in such case, if the state shall neglect or refuse to pay its proportion, pursuant to such requisition, then the Congress may assess and levy this state's proportion, together with interest, at the rate of six per centum per annum, from the time at which the same was required to be paid.

Done in Convention, at Poughkeepsie, in the county of Duchess, in the state of New York, the 26th day of July, in the year of our Lord 1788.

By order of the Convention. George Clinton, *President.*

Attested. John M'Kesson, A. B. Banker, *Secretaries.*

And the Convention do, in the name and behalf of the people of the state of New York, enjoin it upon their representatives in Congress to exert all their influence, and use all reasonable means, to obtain a ratification of the following amendments to the said Constitution, in the manner prescribed therein; and in all laws to be passed by the Congress, in the mean time, to conform to the spirit of the said amendments, as far as the Constitution will admit.

That there shall be one representative for every thirty thousand inhabitants, according to the enumeration or census mentioned in the Constitution, until the whole number of representatives amounts to two hundred, after which that number shall be continued or increased, but not diminished, as the Congress shall direct, and according to such ratio as the Congress shall fix, in conformity to the rule prescribed for the apportionment of representatives and direct taxes.

That the Congress do not impose any excise on any article (ardent spirits excepted) of the growth, production, or manufacture of the United States, or any of them.

That Congress do not lay direct taxes but when the moneys arising from the impost and excise shall be insufficient for the public exigencies, nor then, until Congress shall first have made a requisition upon the states to assess, levy, and pay, their respective proportions of such requisition, agreeably to the census fixed in the said Constitution, in such way and manner as the legislatures of the respective states shall judge best; and in such case, if any state shall neglect or refuse to pay its proportion, pursuant to such requisition, then Congress may assess and levy such state's proportion, together with interest at the rate of six per centum per annum, from the time of payment prescribed in such requisition.

That the Congress shall not make or alter any regulation, in any state, respecting the times, places, and manner, of holding elections for senators and representatives, unless the legislature of such state shall neglect or refuse to make laws or regulations for the purpose, or from any circumstance be incapable of making the same, and then only until the legislature of such state shall make provision in the premises; provided, that Congress may prescribe the time for the election of representatives.

That no persons, except natural-born citizens, or such as were citizens on or before the 4th day of July, 1776, or such as held commissions under the United States during the war, and have at any time since the 4th day of July, 1776, become citizens of one or other of the United States, and who shall be freeholders, shall be eligible to the places of President, Vice-President, or members of either house of the Congress of the United States.

That the Congress do not grant monopolies, or erect any company with exclusive advantages of commerce.

That no standing army or regular troops shall be raised, or kept up, in time of peace, without the consent of two thirds of the senators and representatives present in each house.

That no money be borrowed on the credit of the United States without the assent of two thirds of the senators and representatives present in each house.

That the Congress shall not declare war without the concurrence of two thirds of the senators and representatives present in each house.

That the privilege of the *habeas corpus* shall not, by any law, be suspended for a longer term than six months, or until twenty days after the meeting of the Congress next following the passing the act for such suspension.

That the right of Congress to exercise exclusive legislation over such district, not exceeding ten miles square, as may, by cession of a particular state, and the acceptance of Congress, become the seat of government of the United States, shall not be so exercised as to exempt the inhabitants of such district from paying the like taxes, imposts, duties, and excises, as shall be imposed on the other inhabitants of the state in which such district may be; and that no person shall be privileged within the said district from arrest for crimes committed, or debts contracted, out of the said district.

That the right of exclusive legislation, with respect to such places as may be purchased for the erection of forts, magazines, arsenals, dock-yards, and other needful buildings, shall not authorize the Congress to make any law to prevent the laws of the states, respectively, in which they may be, from extending to such places in all civil and criminal matters, except as to such persons as shall be in the service of the United States; nor to them with respect to crimes committed without such places.

That the compensation for the senators and representatives be ascertained by standing laws; and that no alteration of the existing rate of compensation shall operate for the benefit of the representatives until after a subsequent election shall have been had.

That the Journals of the Congress shall be published at least once a year, with the exception of such parts, relating to treaties or military operations, as, in the judgment of either house, shall require secrecy; and that both houses of Congress shall always keep their doors open during their sessions, unless the business may, in their opinion, require secrecy. That the yeas and nays shall be entered on the Journals whenever two members in either house may require it.

That no capitation tax* shall ever be laid by Congress.

That no person be eligible as a senator for more than six years in any term of twelve years; and that the legislatures of the respective states may recall their senators, or either of them, and elect others in their stead, to serve the remainder of the time for which the senators so recalled were appointed.

That no senator or representative shall, during the time for which he was elected, be appointed to any office under the authority of the United States.

That the authority given to the executives of the states to fill up the vacancies of senators be abolished, and that such vacancies be filled by the respective legislatures.

That the power of Congress to pass uniform laws concerning bankruptcy shall only extend to merchants and other traders; and the states, respectively, may pass laws for the relief of other insolvent debtors.

That no person shall be eligible to the office of President of the United States a third time.

That the executive shall not grant pardons for treason, unless with the consent of the Congress; but may, at his discretion, grant reprieves to persons convicted of treason, until their cases can be laid before the Congress.

That the President, or person exercising his powers for the time being, shall not command an army in the field in person, without the previous desire of the Congress.

That all letters patent, commissions, pardons, writs, and processes of the United States, shall run in the name of *the people of the United States,* and be tested in the name of the President of the United States, or the person exercising his powers for the

time being, or the first judge of the court out of which the same shall issue, as the case may be.

That the Congress shall not constitute, ordain, or establish, any tribunals of inferior courts, with any other than appellate jurisdiction, except such as may be necessary for the trial of cases of admiralty and maritime jurisdiction, and for the trial of piracies and felonies committed on the high seas; and in all other cases to which the judicial power of the United States extends, and in which the Supreme Court of the United States has not original jurisdiction, the causes shall be heard, tried, and determined, in some one of the state courts, with the right of appeal to the Supreme Court of the United States, or other proper tribunal, to be established for that purpose by the Congress, with such exceptions, and under such regulations, as the Congress shall make.

That the court for the trial of impeachments shall consist of the Senate, the judges of the Supreme Court of the United States, and the first or senior judge, for the time being, of the highest court of general and ordinary common-law jurisdiction in each state; that the Congress shall, by standing laws, designate the courts in the respective states answering this description, and, in states having no courts exactly answering this description, shall designate some other court, preferring such, if any there be, whose judge or judges may hold their places during good behavior; provided, that no more than one judge, other than judges of the Supreme Court of the United States, shall come from one state.

That the Congress be authorized to pass laws for compensating the judges for such services, and for compelling their attendance; and that a majority, at least, of the said judges shall be requisite to constitute the said court. That no person impeached shall sit as a member thereof; that each member shall, previous to the entering

---

*Tax laid on individuals as such.

upon any trial, take an oath or affirmation honestly and impartially to hear and determine the cause; and that a majority of the members present shall be necessary to a conviction.

That persons aggrieved by any judgment, sentence, or decree, of the Supreme Court of the United States, in any cause in which that court has original jurisdiction, with such exceptions, and under such regulations, as the Congress shall make concerning the same, shall, upon application, have a commission, to be issued by the President of the United States to such men learned in the law as he shall nominate, and by and with the advice and consent of the Senate appoint, not less than seven, authorizing such commissioners, or any seven or more of them, to correct the errors in such judgment, or to review such sentence and decree, as the case may be, and to do justice to the parties in the premises.

That no judge of the Supreme Court of the United States shall hold any other office under the United States, or any of them.

That the judicial power of the United States shall extend to no controversies respecting land, unless it relate to claims of territory or jurisdiction between states, and individuals under the grants of different states.

That the militia of any state shall not be compelled to serve without the limits of the state, for a longer term than six weeks, without the consent of the legislature thereof.

That the words *without the consent of the Congress,* in the seventh clause of the ninth section of the first article of the Constitution, be expunged.

That the senators and representatives, and all executive and judicial officers of the United States, shall be bound by oath or affirmation not to infringe or violate the constitutions or rights of the respective states.

That the legislatures of the respective states may make provision, by law, that the electors of the election districts, to be by them appointed, shall choose a citizen of the United States, who shall have been an inhabitant of such district for the term of one year immediately preceding the time of his election, for one of the representatives of such state. [13]

Stages of the Bill of Rights in Congress, 1789

1. James Madison's Proposals to the House of Representatives, June 8

I believe that the great mass of the people who opposed it [the Constitution in 1787–89], disliked it because it did not contain effectual provisions against encroachments on particular rights, and those safeguards which they have been long accustomed to have interposed between them and the magistrate who exercises the sovereign power; nor ought we to consider them safe, while a great number of our fellow-citizens think these securities necessary.

It is a fortunate thing that the objection to the Government has been made on the ground I stated; because it will be practi-cable, on that ground, to obviate the objection, so far as to satisfy the public mind that their liberties will be perpetual, and this without endangering any part of the Constitution, which is considered as essential to the existence of the Government by those who promoted its adoption.

The amendments which have occurred to me, proper to be recommended by Congress to the State Legislatures, are these:

First, That there be prefixed to the Constitution a declaration, that all power is originally vested in, and consequently derived from, the people.

That Government is instituted and ought to be exercised for the benefit of the people; which consists in the enjoyment of life and liberty, with the right of acquiring and using property, and generally of pursuing and obtaining happiness and safety.

That the people have an indubitable, unalienable, and indefeasible right to reform or change their Government, whenever it be found adverse or inadequate to the purposes of its institution.

Secondly. That in article 1st, section 2, clause 3, these words be struck out, to wit: "The number of Representatives shall not exceed one for every thirty thousand, but each State shall have at least one Representative, and until such enumeration shall be made;" and that in place thereof be inserted these words, to wit: "After the first actual enumeration, there shall be one Representative for every thirty thousand, until the number amounts to _____, after which the proportion shall be so regulated by Congress, that the number shall never be less than _____, nor more than _____, but each State shall, after the first enumeration, have at least two Representatives; and prior thereto."

Thirdly. That in article 1st, section 6, clause 1, there be added to the end of the first sentence, these words, to wit: "But no law varying the compensation last ascertained shall operate before the next ensuing election of Representatives."

Fourthly. That in article 1st, section 9, between clauses 3 and 4, be inserted these clauses, to wit: The civil rights of none shall be abridged on account of religious belief or worship, nor shall any national religion be established, nor shall the full and equal rights of conscience be in any manner, or on any pretext, infringed.

The people shall not be deprived or abridged of their right to speak, to write, or to publish their sentiments; and the freedom of the press, as one of the great bulwarks of liberty, shall be inviolable.

The people shall not be restrained from peaceably assembling and consulting for their common good; nor from applying to the Legislature by petitions, or remonstrances, for redress of their grievances.

The right of the people to keep and bear arms shall not be infringed; a well armed and well regulated militia being the best security of a free country: but no person religiously scrupulous of bearing arms shall be compelled to render military service in person.

No soldier shall in time of peace be quartered in any house without the consent of the owner; nor at any time, but in a manner warranted by law.

No person shall be subject, except in cases of impeachment, to more than one punishment or one trial for the same offence; nor shall be compelled to be a witness against himself; nor be deprived of life, liberty, or property, without due process of law; nor be obliged to relinquish his property, where it may be necessary for public use, without a just compensation.

Excessive bail shall not be required, nor excessive fines imposed, nor cruel and unusual punishments inflicted.

The rights of the people to be secured in their persons; their houses, their papers, and their other property, from all unreasonable searches and seizures, shall not be violated by warrants issued without probable cause, supported by oath or affirmation, or not particularly describing the places to be searched, or the persons or things to be seized.

In all criminal prosecutions, the accused shall enjoy the right to a speedy and public trial, to be informed of the cause and nature of the accusation, to be confronted with his accusers, and the witnesses against him; to have a compulsory process for obtaining witnesses in his favour; and to have the assistance of counsel for his defence.

The exceptions here or elsewhere in the Constitution, made in favour of particular rights, shall not be so construed as to diminish the just importance of other rights retained by the people, or as to enlarge the powers delegated by the Constitution; but either as actual limitations of such powers, or as inserted merely for greater caution.

Fifthly. That in article 1st, section 10, between clauses 1 and 2, be inserted this clause, to wit:

No State shall violate the equal rights of conscience, or the freedom of the press, or the trial by jury in criminal cases.

Sixthly. That, in article 3d, section 2, be annexed to the end of clause 2d, these words, to wit:

But no appeal to such court shall be allowed where the value in controversy shall not amount to _____ dollars: nor shall any fact triable by jury, according to the course of common law, be otherwise re-examinable than may consist with the principles of common law.

Seventhly. That in article 3d, section 2, the third clause be struck out, and in its place be inserted the clauses following, to wit:

The trial of all crimes (except in cases of impeachments, and cases arising in the land or naval forces, or the militia when on actual service, in time of war or public danger) shall be by an impartial jury of freeholders of the vicinage, with the requisite of unanimity for conviction, of the right of challenge, and other accustomed requisites; and in all crimes punishable with loss of life or member, presentment or indictment by a grand jury shall be an essential preliminary, provided that in cases of crimes committed within any county which may be in possession of an enemy, or in which a general insurrection may prevail, the trial may by law be authorized in some other county of the same State, as near as may be to the seat of the offence.

In cases of crimes committed not within any county, the trial may by law be in such county as the laws shall have prescribed. In suits at common law, between man and man, the trial by jury, as one of the best securities to the rights of the people, ought to remain inviolate.

Eighthly. That immediately after article

6th, be inserted, as article 7th, the clauses following, to wit:

The powers delegated by this Constitution are appropriated to the departments to which they are respectively distributed: so that the Legislative Department shall never exercise the powers vested in the Executive or Judicial nor the Executive exercise the powers vested in the Legislative or Judicial, nor the Judicial exercise the powers vested in the Legislative or Executive Departments.

The powers not delegated by this Constitution, nor prohibited by it to the States, are reserved to the States respectively.

Ninthly. That article 7th be numbered as article 8th.

The first of these amendments relates to what may be called a bill of rights. I will own that I never considered this provision so essential to the Federal Constitution, as to make it improper to ratify it, until such an amendment was added; at the same time, I always conceived, that in a certain form, and to a certain extent, such a provision was neither improper nor altogether useless. I am aware, that a great number of the most respectable friends to the Government, and champions for republican liberty, have thought such a provision, not only unnecessary, but even improper; nay, I believe some have gone so far as to think it even dangerous. Some policy has been made use of, perhaps, by gentlemen on both sides of the question: I acknowledge the ingenuity of those arguments which were drawn against the Constitution, by a comparison with the policy of Great Britain, in establishing a declaration of rights; but there is too great a difference in the case to warrant the comparison: therefore, the arguments drawn from that source were in a great measure inapplicable. In the declaration of rights which that country has established, the truth is, they have gone no farther than to raise a barrier against the power of the Crown; the power of the Legislature is left altogether indefinite. Although I know whenever the great rights, the trial by jury, freedom of the press, or liberty of conscience, come in question in that body, the invasion of them is resisted by able advocates, yet their Magna Charta does not contain any one provision for the security of those rights, respecting which the people of America are most alarmed. The freedom of the press and rights of conscience, those choicest privileges of the people, are unguarded in the British Constitution.

But although the case may be widely different, and it may not be thought necessary to provide limits for the legislative power in that country, yet a different opinion prevails in the United States. The people of many States have thought it necessary to raise barriers against power in all forms and departments of Government, and I am inclined to believe, if once bills of rights are established in all the States as well as the Federal Constitution, we shall find that although some of them are rather unimportant, yet, upon the whole, they will have a salutary tendency.

It may be said, in some instances, they do no more than state the perfect equality of mankind. This, to be sure, is an absolute truth, yet it is not absolutely necessary to be inserted at the head of a Constitution.

In some instances they assert those rights which are exercised by the people in forming and establishing a plan of Government. In other instances, they specify those rights which are retained when particular powers are given up to be exercised by the Legislature. In other instances, they specify positive rights, which may seem to result from the nature of the compact. Trial by jury cannot be considered as a natural right, but a right resulting from a social compact which regulates the action of the community, but is as essential to secure the liberty of the people as any one of the pre-existent rights of nature. In other instances, they lay down dogmatic maxims with respect to the construction of the Government; declaring that the Legislative, Executive,

and Judicial branches shall be kept separate and distinct. Perhaps the best way of securing this in practice is, to provide such checks as will prevent the encroachment of the one upon the other.

But whatever may be the form which the several States have adopted in making declarations in favour of particular rights, the great object in view is to limit and qualify the powers of Government, by excepting out of the grant of power those cases in which the Government ought not to act, or to act only in a particular mode. They point these exceptions sometimes against the abuse of the Executive power, sometimes against the Legislative, and, in some cases, against the community itself; or, in other words, against the majority in favour of the minority. . . . [14]

2. Amendments Reported by the House of Representatives' Select Committee, July 28

In the introductory paragraph before the words, "*We the people*," add, "Government being intended for the benefit of the people, and the rightful establishment thereof being derived from their authority alone."

Art. 1, Sec. 2, Par. 3—Strike out all between the words, "*direct*" and "*and until such*," and instead thereof insert, "After the first enumeration there shall be one representative for every thirty thousand until the number shall amount to one hundred; after which the proportion shall be so regulated by Congress that the number of Representatives shall never be less than one hundred, nor more than one hundred and seventy-five, but each State shall always have at least one Representative."

Art. 1, Sec. 6—Between the words "*United States*," and "*shall in all cases*," strike out "*they*," and insert, "But no law varying the compensation shall take effect until an election of Representatives shall have intervened. The members."

Art. 1, Sec. 9—Between Paragraphs 2 and 3 insert, "No religion shall be established by law, nor shall the equal rights of conscience be infringed."

"The freedom of speech, and of the press, and the right of the people peaceably to assemble and consult for their common good, and to apply to the government for redress of grievances, shall not be infringed."

"A well regulated militia, composed of the body of the people, being the best security of a free State, the right of the people to keep and bear arms shall not be infringed, but no person religiously scrupulous shall be compelled to bear arms."

"No soldier shall in time of peace be quartered in any house without the consent of the owner, nor in time of war but in a manner to be prescribed by law."

"No person shall be subject, except in case of impeachment, to more than one trial or one punishment for the same offence, nor shall be compelled to be a witness against himself, nor be deprived of life, liberty, or property without due process of law; nor shall private property be taken for public use without just compensation."

"Excessive bail shall not be required, nor excessive fines imposed, nor cruel and unusual punishments inflicted."

"The right of the people to be secure in their person, houses, papers and effects, shall not be violated by warrants issuing, without probable cause supported by oath or affirmation, and not particularly describing the places to be searched, and the persons or things to be seized."

"The enumeration in this Constitution of certain rights shall not be construed to deny or disparage others retained by the people."

Art. 1, Sec. 10, between the 1st and 2d Paragraphs insert, "No State shall infringe the equal rights of conscience, nor the freedom of speech, or of the press, nor of the right of trial by jury in criminal cases."

Art. 3, Sec. 2, add to the 2d Paragraph "But no appeal to such court shall be allowed, where the value in controversy shall not amount to one thousand dollars; nor

shall any fact, triable by a Jury according to the course of the common law, be otherwise re-examinable than according to the rules of common law."

Art. 3, Sec. 2—Strike out the whole of the 3d paragraph, and insert—"In all criminal prosecutions the accused shall enjoy the right to a speedy and public trial, to be informed of the nature and cause of the accusation, to be confronted with the witnesses against him, to have compulsory process for obtaining witnesses in his favour, and to have the assistance of counsel for his defence."

"The trial of all crimes (except in cases of impeachment, and in cases arising in the land or naval forces, or in the militia, when in actual service in time of war or public danger) shall be by an impartial jury of freeholders of the vicinage, with the requisite of unanimity for conviction, the right of challenge and other accustomed requisites; and no person shall be held to answer for a capital, or otherwise infamous crime, unless on a presentment or indictment by a Grand Jury; but if a crime be committed in a place in the possession of an enemy, or in which an insurrection may prevail, the indictment and trial may by law be authorized in some other place within the same State; and if it be committed in a place not within a State, the indictment and trial may be at such place or places as the law may have directed."

"In suits at common law the right of trial by jury shall be preserved."

Immediately after Art. 6, the following to be inserted as Art. 7.

"The powers delegated by this Constitution to the government of the United States, shall be exercised as therein appropriated, so that the Legislative shall never exercise the powers vested in the Executive or the Judicial; nor the Executive the powers vested in the Legislative or Judicial; nor the Judicial the powers vested in the Legislative or Executive."

"The powers not delegated by this Constitution, nor prohibited by it to the States,

are reserved to the States respectively."
Art. 7 to be made Art. 8. [15]

3. Amendments Passed by the House of Representatives, August 24

Article the First

After the first enumeration, required by the first Article of the Constitution, there shall be one Representative for every thirty thousand, until the number shall amount to one hundred, after which the proportion shall be so regulated by Congress, that there shall be not less than one hundred Representatives, nor less than one Representative for every forty thousand persons, until the number of Representatives shall amount to two hundred, after which the proportion shall be so regulated by Congress, that there shall not be less than two hundred Representatives, nor less than one Representative for every fifty thousand persons.

Article the Second

No law varying the compensation to the members of Congress, shall take effect, until an election of Representatives shall have intervened.

Article the Third

Congress shall make no law establishing religion or prohibiting the free exercise thereof, nor shall the rights of Conscience be infringed.

Article the Fourth

The Freedom of Speech, and of the Press, and the right of the People peaceably to assemble, and consult for their common good, and to apply to the Government for a redress of grievances, shall not be infringed.

Article the Fifth

A well regulated militia, composed of the body of the People, being the best security of a free State, the right of the People to keep and bear arms, shall not be infringed, but no one religiously scrupulous of bearing arms, shall be compelled to render military service in person.

Article the Sixth

No soldier shall, in time of peace, be quartered in any house without the consent of the owner, nor in time of war, but in a manner to be prescribed by law.

Article the Seventh

The right of the People to be secure in their persons, houses, papers and effects, against unreasonable searches and seizures, shall not be violated, and no warrants shall issue, but upon probable cause supported by oath or affirmation, and particularly describing the place to be searched, and the persons or things to be seized.

Article the Eighth

No person shall be subject, except in case of impeachment, to more than one trial, or one punishment for the same offence, nor shall be compelled in any criminal case, to be a witness against himself, nor be deprived of life, liberty or property, without due process of law; nor shall private property be taken for public use without just compensation.

Article the Ninth

In all criminal prosecutions, the accused shall enjoy the right to a speedy and public trial, to be informed of the nature and cause of the accusation, to be confronted with the witnesses against him, to have compulsory process for obtaining witnesses in his favour, and to have the assistance of counsel for his defence.

Article the Tenth

The trial of all crimes (except in cases of impeachment, and in cases arising in the land or naval forces, or in the militia when in actual service in time of War or public danger) shall be by an Impartial Jury of the Vicinage, with the requisite of unanimity for conviction, the right of challenge, and other accostomed [*sic*] requisites; and no person shall be held to answer for a capital, or otherways [*sic*] infamous crime, unless on a presentment or indictment by a Grand Jury; but if a crime be committed in a place in the possession of an enemy, or in which an insurrection may prevail, the indictment and trial may by law be authorised in some other place within the same State.

Article the Eleventh

No appeal to the Supreme Court of the United States, shall be allowed, where the value in controversy shall not amount to one thousand dollars, nor shall any fact, triable by a Jury according to the course of the common law, be otherwise re-examinable, than according to the rules of common law.

Article the Twelfth

In suits at common law, the right of trial by Jury shall be preserved.

Article the Thirteenth

Excessive bail shall not be required, nor excessive fines imposed, nor cruel and unusual punishments inflicted.

Article the Fourteenth

No State shall infringe the right of trial by Jury in criminal cases, nor the rights of conscience, nor the freedom of speech, or of the press.

Article the Fifteenth

The enumeration in the Constitution of certain rights, shall not be construed to deny or disparage others retained by the people.

Article the Sixteenth

The powers delegated by the Constitution to the government of the United States, shall be exercised as therein appropriated, so that the Legislative shall never exercise the powers vested in the Executive or Judicial; nor the Executive the powers vested in the Legislative or Judicial; nor the Judicial the powers vested in the Legislative or Executive.

Article the Seventeenth

The powers not delegated by the Constitution, nor prohibited by it, to the States, are reserved to the States respectively. [16]

4. Amendments Passed by the Senate, September 9

Article the First

After the first enumeration, required by the first article of the Constitution, there shall be one Representative for every thirty thousand, until the number shall amount to one hundred; to which number one Representative shall be added for every subsequent increase of forty thousand, until the Representatives shall amount to two hundred, to which number one Representative shall be added for every subsequent increase of sixty thousand persons.

Article the Second

No law, varying the compensation for the services of the Senators and Representatives, shall take effect, until an election of Representatives shall have intervened.

Article the Third

Congress shall make no law establishing articles of faith, or a mode of worship, or prohibiting the free exercise of religion, or abridging the freedom of speech, or of the press, or the right of the people peaceably to assemble, and to petition to the government for a redress of grievances.

Article the Fourth

A well regulated militia, being necessary to the security of a free State, the right of the people to keep and bear arms, shall not be infringed.

Article the Fifth

No soldier shall, in time of peace, be quartered in any house, without the consent of the owner, nor in time of war, but in a manner to be prescribed by law.

Article the Sixth

The right of the people to be secure in their persons, houses, papers, and effects, against unreasonable searches and seizures, shall not be violated, and no warrants shall issue, but upon probable cause, supported by oath or affirmation, and particularly describing the place to be searched, and the persons or things to be seized.

Article the Seventh

No person shall be held to answer for a capital, or otherwise infamous crime, unless on a presentment or indictment of a Grand Jury, except in cases arising in the land or naval forces, or in the militia, when in actual service in time of war or public danger; nor shall any person be subject for the same offence to be twice put in jeopardy of life or limb; nor shall be compelled in any criminal case, to be a witness against himself, nor be deprived of life, liberty or property, without due process of law; nor shall private property be taken for public use without just compensation.

Article the Eighth

In all criminal prosecutions, the accused shall enjoy the right to a speedy and public trial, to be informed of the nature and cause of the accusation, to be confronted with the witnesses against him, to have compulsory process for obtaining witnesses in his favour, and to have the assistance of counsel for his defence.

Article the Ninth

In suits at common law, where the value in controversy shall exceed twenty dollars, the right of trial by Jury shall be preserved, and no fact, tried by a Jury, shall be otherwise re-examined in any court of the United States, than according to the rules of the common law.

Article the Tenth

Excessive bail shall not be required, nor excessive fines imposed, nor cruel and unusual punishments inflicted.

Article the Eleventh

The enumeration in the Constitution, of certain rights, shall not be construed to deny or disparage others retained by the people.

Article the Twelfth

The powers not delegated to the United States by the Constitution, nor prohibited by it to the States, are reserved to the States respectively, or to the people. [17]

5. Amendments Proposed by Congress for Ratification by the States, September 25

Congress of the United States

Begun and held at the City of New York, on Wednesday, the 4th of March, 1789.

The conventions of a number of the states having, at the time of their adopting the Constitution, expressed a desire, in order to prevent misconstruction or abuse of its powers, that further declaratory and restrictive clauses should be added; and as extending the ground of public confidence in the government will best insure the beneficent ends of its institution;

Resolved, by the Senate and House of Representatives of the United States of America, in Congress assembled, two thirds of both houses concurring, that the following articles be proposed to the legislatures of the several states, as amendments to the Constitution of the United States, all or any of which articles, when ratified by three fourths of the said legislatures, to be valid, to all intents and purposes, as part of the said Constitution, namely,

Articles in Addition to, and Amendment of, the Constitution of the United States of America, proposed by Congress, and ratified by the Legislatures of the several States, pursuant to the Fifth Article of the original Constitution.

Art. I. After the first enumeration required by the first article of the Constitution, there shall be one representative for every thirty thousand, until the number shall amount to one hundred, after which the proportion shall be so regulated by Congress, that there shall not be less than one hundred representatives, nor less than one representative for every forty thousand persons, until the number of representatives shall amount to two hundred, after which the proportion shall be so regulated by Congress, that there shall not be less than two hundred representatives, nor more than one representative for every fifty thousand persons.

Art. II. No law varying the compensation for services of the senators and representatives shall take effect, until an election of representatives shall have intervened.

Art. III. Congress shall make no law respecting an establishment of religion, or prohibiting the free exercise thereof, or abridging the freedom of speech, or of the press, or the right of the people peaceably to assemble, and to petition the government for a redress of grievances.

Art. IV. A well-regulated militia being necessary to the security of a free state, the right of the people to keep and bear arms shall not be infringed.

Art. V. No soldier shall, in time of peace, be quartered in any house without the consent of the owner, nor in time of war, but in a manner prescribed by law.

Art. VI. The right of the people to be secure in their persons, houses, papers, and effects, against unreasonable searches and seizures, shall not be violated; and no warrants shall issue, but upon probable cause, supported by oath or affirmation, and particularly describing the place to be searched, and the persons or things to be seized.

Art. VII. No person shall be held to answer for a capital or otherwise infamous crime, unless on a presentment or indictment of a grand jury, except in cases arising in the land or naval forces, or in the militia when in actual service, in time of war or public danger; nor shall any person be subject, for the same offence, to be twice put in jeopardy of life or limb; nor shall be compelled, in any criminal case, to be a witness against himself; nor be deprived of life, liberty, or property, without due process of law; nor shall private property be taken for public use without just compensation.

Art. VIII. In all criminal prosecutions, the accused shall enjoy the right of a speedy and public trial, by an impartial jury of the state and district wherein the crime shall have been committed, which district shall have been previously ascertained by law; and to be informed of the nature and cause of the accusation; to be confronted with the witnesses against him; to have compulsory process for obtaining witnesses in his favour; and to have the assistance of counsel for his defence.

Art. IX. In suits at common law, where the value in controversy shall exceed twenty dollars, the right of trial by jury shall be preserved, and no fact tried by a jury shall be otherwise reëxamined, in any court of the United States, than according to the rules in common law.

Art. X. Excessive bail shall not be required, nor excessive fines imposed, nor cruel and unusual punishments inflicted.

Art. XI. The enumeration, in the Constitution, of certain rights, shall not be construed to deny or disparage others retained by the people.

Art. XII. The powers not delegated to the United States by the Constitution, nor prohibited by it to the states, are reserved to the states, respectively, or to the people.

Frederick Augustus Muhlenberg, *Speaker of the House of Representatives.*

John Adams, *Vice-President of the United States, and President of the Senate.*

Attest. John Beckley, *Clerk of the House of Representatives.*

Samuel A. Otis, *Secretary of the Senate.*

Which, being transmitted to the several state legislatures, were decided upon by them, according to the following returns:

By the State of New Hampshire. Agreed to the whole of the said amendments, except the 2d article.

By the State of New York. Agreed to the whole of the said amendments, except the 2d article.

By the State of Pennsylvania. Agreed to the 3d, 4th, 5th, 6th, 7th, 8th, 9th, 10th, 11th, and 12th articles of the said amendments.

By the State of Delaware. Agreed to the whole of the said amendments, except the 1st article.

By the State of Maryland. Agreed to the whole of the said twelve amendments.

By the State of South Carolina. Agreed to the whole [of the] said twelve amendments.

By the State of North Carolina. Agreed to the whole of the said twelve amendments.

By the State of Rhode Island and Providence Plantations. Agreed to the whole of the said twelve articles.

By the State of New Jersey. Agreed to the whole of the said amendments, except the second article.

By the State of Virginia. Agreed to the whole of the said twelve articles.

No returns were made by the states of Massachusetts, Connecticut, Georgia, and Kentucky.

The amendments thus proposed became a part of the Constitution, the first and second of them excepted, which were not ratified by a sufficient number of the state legislatures. [18]

Amendments Ratified by the States, 1791

Article I

Congress shall make no law respecting an establishment of religion, or prohibiting the free exercise thereof; or abridging the freedom of speech, or of the press; or the right of the people peaceably to assemble, and to petition the Government for a redress of grievances.

Article II

A well regulated militia, being necessary to the security of a free State, the right of the people to keep and bear arms, shall not be infringed.

Article III

No soldier shall, in time of peace be quartered in any house, without the consent of the owner, nor in time of war, but in a manner to be prescribed by law.

Article IV

The right of the people to be secure in their persons, houses, papers, and effects, against unreasonable searches and seizures, shall not be violated, and no warrants shall issue, but upon probable cause, supported by oath or affirmation, and particularly describing the place to be searched, and the persons or things to be seized.

Article V

No person shall be held to answer for a capital, or otherwise infamous crime, unless on a presentment or indictment of a Grand Jury, except in cases arising in the land or naval forces, or in the militia, when in actual service in time of war or public danger; nor shall any person be subject for the same offence to be twice put in jeopardy of life or limb; nor shall be compelled in any criminal case to be a witness against himself, nor be deprived of life, liberty, or property, without due process of law; nor shall private property be taken for public use, without just compensation.

Article VI

In all criminal prosecutions, the accused shall enjoy the right to a speedy and public trial, by an impartial jury of the State and district wherein the crime shall have been committed, which district shall have been previously ascertained by law, and to be informed of the nature and cause of the accusation; to be confronted with the witnesses against him; to have compulsory process for obtaining witnesses in his favour, and to have the assistance of counsel for his defence.

Article VII

In suits at common law, where the value in controversy shall exceed twenty dollars,

the right of trial by jury shall be preserved, and no fact tried by a jury, shall be otherwise reexamined in any court of the United States, than according to the rules of the common law.

Article VIII

Excessive bail shall not be required, nor excessive fines imposed, nor cruel and unusual punishments inflicted.

Article IX

The enumeration in the Constitution, of certain rights, shall not be construed to deny or disparage others retained by the people.

Article X

The powers not delegated to the United States by the Constitution, nor prohibited by it to the States, are reserved to the States respectively, or to the people. [19]

1. *Sources of Our Liberties,* ed. Richard L. Perry (Chicago: American Bar Foundation, 1978), pp. 11–22.

2. George Anastaplo, *The Constitutionalist: Notes on the First Amendment* (Dallas: Southern Methodist University Press, 1971), pp. 538–39.

3. *Sources of Our Liberties,* pp. 73–75.

4. *The Founders' Constitution,* ed. Philip B. Kurland and Ralph Lerner (Chicago: University of Chicago Press, 1987), V, pp. 1–3.

5. *Sources of Our Liberties,* pp. 270–71.

6. Ibid., pp. 286–89.

7. Ibid., pp. 355–57.

8. *The Founders' Constitution,* V, pp. 3–4.

9. *Sources and Documents Illustrating the American Revolution 1764–1788 and the Federal Constitution,* ed. S. E. Morison (Oxford: Clarendon Press, 1929), pp. 206–8.

10. Anastaplo, *The Constitution of 1787: A Commentary* (Baltimore, Md.: Johns Hopkins University Press, 1989), pp. 258–65.

11. *Notes of Debates in the Federal Convention of 1787 Reported by James Madison,* ed. Adrienne Koch (Athens, Ohio: Ohio University Press, 1966), pp. 485–87, 630, 647–48, 650–52.

12. *The Founders' Constitution,* V, pp. 15–17.

13. Ibid., pp. 11–15.

14. Ibid., pp. 25–26.

15. Edward Dumbauld, *The Bill of Rights and What It Means Today* (Westport, Conn.: Greenwood Press, 1963), pp. 210–12.

16. Ibid., pp. 213–16.

17. Ibid., pp. 217–19.

18. *The Founders' Constitution,* V, pp. 40–41.

19. *The Constitution of 1787,* pp. 288–90.

Concerning Liberal Education

William Whewell

Editor's Introduction

The Great Books movement has had many fathers. Among them have been Mortimer J. Adler, editor of *The Great Ideas Today* and chief architect of *Great Books of the Western World;* Robert M. Hutchins, former president of the University of Chicago; the several founders, especially Scott Buchanan, of St. John's College; John Erskine, of Columbia University; and before them all, Matthew Arnold, whose insistence upon reading "the best that has been said and thought in the world" prefigured later formulations.

One who is not so well remembered nowadays, but who greatly influenced some of these later figures, was William Whewell (1794–1866), the master of Trinity College, Cambridge, from 1841 until his death. Whewell (whose name is pronounced with the first letter silent) was himself a broadly educated man—proficient in Latin and Greek, learned in moral theology, a writer of works both on mineralogy and the history of the inductive sciences, and at least well-read in serious mathematics, of which indeed he seems to have known the entire literature, most of it in languages other than English, so far as it had developed in his time. It was thus with authority that he could argue, as from his influential position he consistently did, for the necessity of a broad range of university studies in a liberal education, and the reading of what he called "capital texts," by which he meant pretty much what we mean by great books. His argument cannot be said really to have established the curriculum he wished to have at Cambridge, where the opposition was as strong as it would have been in our own day, though of a different kind. But what he said was remembered later in the United States, where it was to some extent realized in certain institutions of higher learning.

Whewell's position was set forth in a work (1845) devoted to liberal education in general, with special reference to the curriculum at Cambridge—of which the first, very long chapter containing the thrust of the argument is reprinted here. As this has the address of a series of lectures, which it probably was, it is repetitious in the manner of one trying to persuade an audience as to the merits of the point at issue. But there is no mistaking what the issue was. It was whether both classical and mathematical studies would be required for an undergraduate degree with honors at Cambridge. Whewell thought they should be. "No education can be considered as liberal which does not cultivate both the

377

faculty of reason and the faculty of language, one of which is cultivated by the study of mathematics, and the other by the study of classics," he wrote. "To allow the student to omit one of these is to leave him half educated. If a person cannot receive such culture, he remains, in the one case, irrational, in the other, illiterate." Whewell realized, however, that this requirement would be difficult to establish—for the reason, mainly, that it would be thought "hard upon a particular class of men, especially classical students, for example, to require them to read mathematics, which they dislike." Such a step could be defended, he said, only if mathematics and science were seen as at bottom classical also—as having the same importance that the literary and historical classics of Greece and Rome were believed to have in higher education. Accordingly, he undertook to show how in his judgment that view of the matter was correct.

In the process he made his famous distinction between what he called "permanent" and "progressive" studies—meaning, not that between the humanities and the sciences, as he is sometimes thought to have done, but the portion of both which could be called permanent, as against the portion that had to be regarded as progressive. He allowed that an undergraduate education should be limited for the most part to permanent studies, but he thought these went well beyond Greek and Latin literature, extending to a good part of mathematics and empirical science—even what we now call the social sciences, at least so far as its "capital texts" might serve.

This was quite different from C. P. Snow's later distinction between "the two cultures" of science and humanities. Whewell's was a division within each of these. And while the immediate obstacle to his reform was the predominance at Cambridge of students and faculty who had come from the English public (in our terms, private) schools of that day, where the curriculum was heavily weighted toward Greek and Latin studies, and where these meant nothing more than an endless drill in writing and translation—yet, in the long run, his idea of the right sort of curriculum was defeated by academic specialization. Within a few decades the progressive studies, as Whewell regarded them, had taken over the universities, so that in Cambridge now, and at Oxford too, the undergraduate has even less of a requirement in "general" (or permanent) studies than does his counterpart at Harvard or Princeton. The resulting undergraduate curriculum at these institutions, so far as they have any, is notoriously hard to explain or defend, however, except as the supermarket is held to be a good source of nourishment, in that everything can be got there somehow. And despite some datedness in Whewell's prose, he remains interesting and valuable as perhaps the last college president who not only believed in education by the liberal arts, but who also had mastered them and understood why they were necessary.

Concerning Liberal Education

Education in general

The education of the youth of any community in general is one of the most important concerns about which members of the community can have to deliberate; for upon this education depend the preservation, the order, the prosperity of the community, its moral and its intellectual condition. The education of the upper classes of the community is still more especially important; both because the characters of members of those classes have a greater influence upon the conduct and fortunes of the general body, and because the education of the lower classes will in a great measure depend upon that of the upper. The education of the upper classes is termed *liberal education,* and *higher education;* the education of the middle classes will commonly be, in its highest parts, an imitation of higher education, more or less incomplete; and the education of the people, when they are educated, must generally be an elementary education including little more than the first elements of higher education. A liberal education then—the higher education in every community—is important, both as being the education of those who must direct the course of the community, and as alone exhibiting, in any completeness, the idea of education.

In proportion to the great importance of our deliberations on the subject, is the difficulty of deciding what the higher education ought to be, in our own nation. Such a decision requires a deep insight into the circumstances, character, and tendencies of the nation, and a comprehensive and correct knowledge of the past history and future prospects of all branches of education: that is, of the studies, employments, and influences by which the minds and characters of young men in past times have been, and hereafter may be formed. The consideration of the greatness of this difficulty ought, perhaps, to operate in making men less ready than they often are to deliver their opinions of the modes in which education may be improved. Perhaps, also, the same consideration may tend to procure a more favourable reception for remarks on this subject, which do not arise from mere transient, general, speculative views, but which are suggested and directed by a long continued careful attention to the subject, growing out of official position, and applied with a view to practical results.

The remarks now offered to the reader, however, though based upon the general conditions to which a liberal education must necessarily be subject, solicit attention in the first place with reference to their practical application to the present state of the University of Cambridge. On this subject the writer has various grounds for venturing to offer his opinion. He has during a long course of years occupied a series of active educational offices in the University, and has been engaged along with others in shaping most of the changes which have during that time taken place in the educational system of the University; and he has so far attended to the general principles of education as to have repeatedly published upon them. This latter circumstance makes him hesitate the less to offer himself again to the notice of the University and the public with such remarks—inasmuch as, looking back to what he has previously published on this subject, he finds nothing which subsequent thought and experience do not appear to him to have confirmed.

It may be a matter of interest to some persons out of our University to know something of the principles on which we conduct, or attempt to conduct, education within it. And even within the University, a publication of such principles by one who has necessarily to take a share in what is done may not be without its use, since the constitution of the University makes it very important that, in administering the educational system, various classes of persons should cooperate and sympathize; while the habits of the University do not provide any common channel through which a person in one class makes known to persons belonging to other classes the principles on which he acts, and the views which he entertains. It may tend to make the continuation of our system more steady, and changes in it, when any have to be made, less abrupt, if those who necessarily must take a part in producing or resisting change explain to each other their objects and their reasons. I trust, therefore, that the publication of such remarks as I have to make will be found to be a step naturally connected with the official position to which I have already referred.

If my leisure allowed me, I should be desirous of discussing the subject of a liberal English education in its general aspect— of examining what is involved in the idea of such an education, and in what measure the actual education of England may be brought nearer to this idea. But for the present, I must confine myself within much narrower limits. Omitting the consideration of moral and religious education, I shall now treat of intellectual education only; and even with regard to that subject, I shall direct my remarks so as to make them applicable in an especial manner to the present condition of the University of Cambridge. On questions connected with this point, I shall perhaps go into details

which may appear to a general reader uninteresting or obscure. Such readers can, of course, cease to follow my remarks, when they become too local or technical. But in order that they may excuse me for this mode of treating the subject, they will perhaps recollect, not only that our local questions are important to ourselves, but also that general doctrines, on this as on other subjects, are saved from the danger of being loose, impracticable, and extravagant by being treated with a view to their actual practical application in a special instance; and further, that the general doctrines respecting intellectual education which are true with regard to one institution, must be true with regard to others also. If I can succeed in bringing into view solid and comprehensive principles applicable to education at Cambridge, such principles cannot well fail to have some value for those who are concerned in administering other existing institutions of higher education, or in establishing new institutions of the same kind.

I hope, also, that the special purpose aimed at in the remarks here made will be accepted as an excuse for any want of symmetry or comprehensiveness in the course of intellectual culture here recommended. It would not be difficult to draw up a much more complete scheme of literature and science, and to require that our plans of a liberal education should be based upon this scheme. I do not think it would be found easy, under any circumstances, to carry into effect an education so planned; but at any rate, it is not likely that the discussion of such a plan would be the best way of pointing out what steps are advisable in the present condition of our University. I state this, hoping that the view here given of the proper elements of our liberal education will not be regarded as if it were intended for a complete scheme of human knowledge. I am well aware how much it falls short of the latter idea.

In order to indicate the relation be-

Trinity College, where Whewell was master, is the largest college of Cambridge University. Although Trinity was founded in the Renaissance by Henry VIII, the architecture of the courtyard reflects monastic influences, while affording protection from the English weather. Academic gowns are occasionally still worn, though often cut down to the minimum.

tween the subject of liberal education in general, and that portion of it which I shall at present examine, I may remark that I have already distinguished moral and religious education, which I here pass by, from intellectual education, which I here consider. Further—of this branch of the subject, there is a subdivision which I shall employ in my discussion. The studies by which the intellectual education of young men is carried on include two kinds; which, with reference to their subjects, we may describe as *permanent,* and *progressive* studies. To the former class belong those portions of knowledge which have long taken their permanent shape—ancient languages with their literature, and long-established demonstrated sciences. To the latter class belong the results of the mental activity of our own times; the literature of our own age, and the sciences in which men are making progress from day to day. The former class of subjects connects us with the past; the latter, with the present and the future. By the former class of studies, each rising generation, in its turn, learns how former generations thought, and felt, and reasoned, and expressed their thoughts, and feelings, and reasonings. By the latter class of studies, each generation learns that thought and feeling and reasoning are still active, and is prepared to take a share in the continuation and expression of this activity. Both these kinds of studies give man a conscious connection with his race. By the former he becomes conscious of a past, by the latter, of a present, humanity.

Since the studies which are employed as means of education thus have it for their office to connect a man's mind with the general mind of the human race, the subjects of these studies cannot be mere casual and arbitrary trains of thought and feeling, either of past or of present times. It is not merely because some men in former times have had certain thoughts, and have expressed them in certain books, that their books are proper means of education for us. In order to render books fit for

such a use, they must contain thoughts and expressions of thought which are sympathized in by men in general, by successive generations, by distant nations, by the human race. And hence it is that we describe the books which discharge this office in education as *permanent* subjects of study. Such books form the educational studies, not of one generation or one country only, but of all generations and all countries, so far as they are educated. Such books have supplied the subject of sympathy among civilized nations ever since civilization began—at least the civilization with which the European world is concerned. Such books express thoughts which belong to humanity in its general and permanent character; and express them in words on which the human mind delights to dwell. And again, with regard to the progressive studies which are to form a portion of a liberal education, it is not enough that we take for this purpose any expression of the present activity of men's minds. Progressive studies, too, must be a part of the development of humanity in its general form. They must express an activity which belongs to man as man. They must be, though not permanent in their form, universal in their principles. They must be the results, not of individual caprice, or fancy, but of human reason. They must aim, not at mere change or novelty, but at truth. And since the progress of the human mind is from truth to truth, the new truths must be founded upon the old ones: the progressive studies which education embraces must rest upon the permanent studies which it necessarily includes. The former must be its superstructure, the latter, its foundation.

The term *education* especially implies, by its etymology, that character in the studies of the rising generation which I have attempted to describe: namely, that these studies draw forth and unfold a portion of our common human nature. They *educe* the elements of the humanity which we have within us. The studies and occupations of the young are not properly called education, merely because they draw out something, without considering whether it is an attribute of the race, or an accident of the individual. Young persons may be so employed and so treated that their caprice, their self-will, their individual tastes and propensities, are educed and developed; but this is not education. It is not the education of a man; for what is educed is not that which belongs to man as man, and connects man with man. It is not the education of a man's humanity, but the indulgence of his individuality.

Permanent educational studies

Turning our attention first to the permanent educational studies, we may further remark that they are mainly such as are fitted to educe two principal faculties of man considered as an intellectual being: namely, language and reason.

Language and reason are attributes of humanity intimately connected with each other. Without the use of language we could not express general propositions or derive them from each other in virtue of their forms of expression, in the manner which also we call reasoning. Without the use of reason we could not conceive objects and their connections in a general and abstract manner, and therefore could not apply to them names and use language. Reason cannot express itself without language; language cannot be employed without reason. The books in which we read the thoughts of former generations of men do not exhibit to us, in any part, language alone, or reason alone; but necessarily everywhere, language and reason combined—language expressing rational thought, or at least expressing human feelings modified and molded by rational thought.

But though language and rational thought must thus be always combined in books, at least in books which are permanently studied by men, our attention may be especially directed to the one or to the other of these two elements. Language may be considered as the outward vesture of thought; thought, as a body which is contained within this clothing; and we may attend especially to the one or to the other, to the body or to the garment. But further, language includes within its folds, not merely thought, the result of reason operating purely and simply, but as we have already intimated, thought excited, unfolded, and swayed by the various feelings which belong to man. Language is a necessary help of the mind, when engaged in reasoning; but language is far more commonly and generally used in expressing the sentiments which arise out of the desires, affections, emotions, and occupations of men, in their habitual intercourse, than in obtaining and enunciating the propositions which pure reason contemplates. It is much more familiar, as an implement in our daily outward life, than as an instrument in our occasional internal ratiocinations. The body of which language is the clothing is not reason merely but the whole nature of man; and hence, this vesture of our humanity draws to it men's attention far more generally and more strongly than it could do if it were merely connected with the most recondite and central portions of man's being, his reason.

Language, then, naturally draws men's attention as the clothing or vehicle of emotion, as well as of thought. But yet language is so far properly the clothing or the vehicle of thought only, that it can express emotion only so far as it is molded or informed by thought. The expression of mere emotion, unshaped by the operation of thought, is not language; it gives rise to interjections, which are language only so far as they bear the traces of previous thought, or have meaning given them by accompanying words. And hence, when we turn our attention upon language, we have to think of our thoughts; we have to turn the mind's operation back upon itself; we have to perform a reflex act of thought.

Reflex acts of thought imply a clearness and flexibility of mind, of which, perhaps, all men are in a great degree capable, but for which some nations, in some stages of their progress, appear to have had a peculiar aptitude. The attention to the lines of connection and shades of difference in the modes of expressing thought and emotion, which arises out of this clearness and flexibility of mind, enabled the nations so gifted to choose expressions which they, and other men since them, have dwelt upon with unfading pleasure and interest. The books of these nations, expressing the thoughts and emotions of humanity in its general and permanent character, and thus expressing them in forms on which men's minds can dwell with satisfaction and delight, are, according to what we have said, fitted to supply the permanent subjects of educational study for succeeding ages. These books contain the means of the higher education of civilized nations, so far as the faculty of language is the basis of education.

The nations of which I speak, as having thus left us, in their books, expressions of the thoughts of man, in a form fitted for permanent educational study, are, as the reader will already have understood, ancient Greece and Rome. Those nations, at certain periods of their history, produced books which men accepted as fit subjects of permanent attention and abiding admiration; and these books have, in consequence, ever since occupied a prominent place in the education of civilized Europe. They have connected one generation and one nation with another. They have influenced the course of men's thoughts and the mode in which thoughts have been expressed; they have affected the language of each nation, and have thus operated upon men's minds through all the innumerable channels through which language modifies thought. I need not attempt to enumerate all the modes in which ancient Greece and Rome thus exercise an influence upon modern England; but I may mention two ways in which this influence familiarly appears: the study of classical authors and the study of philology.

The classical authors of Greece and Rome are, by that very designation, understood to be accepted both as models of literary excellence and as general and familiar subjects of the study of liberally educated men. By the existence of such familiar models, and by their place in a liberal education, the ideas of literary beauty of thought and expression are embodied and exemplified; and these ideas, thus becoming familiar to men in the course of their education, mold the taste and awaken the discernment of those who, without such direction, would not have assigned to the highest literary excellence its proper place. Moreover classical authors, adopted as subjects of study on the ground of their literary merits, become a bond of mental union among all liberally educated men, by supplying to their memories a common store of thoughts, images, turns of expression, histories, arguments, and modes of treating all subjects of human thought and interest, from the most trivial to the most solemn. These common intellectual possessions of educated men make them feel themselves members of a common human family, not bound together by ties of origin, or territorial abode, or material desires, but by a common mind; a family which has a community of thought and expression, not the result of extraneous accidents, but of the very internal constitution of human nature.

Again, besides the effect thus produced upon educated men, by their acquaintance with the matter of the classical writings, there is a further effect, which is produced by the attempts which have been made to analyze the form of literary works. Language, and the expressions by which thought, feeling, and imagination are conveyed, have been made themselves the subject of attention, classification, and rule. The discussions connected with these points have been conducted with especial reference to the writings of the classical authors; and the methods and doctrines thus produced have been generally accepted and studied by the students of the classical authors themselves. Thus the grammar and rhetoric and criticism of Greece and Rome, as well as the great original authors of those countries, have always been included in a liberal education. And these common studies of liberally educated men have given them a common phraseology in which they can discuss questions of grammar and rhetoric; and have furnished them with known examples of criticism such as call out the powers of literary analysis which belong to the human mind. The Latin and Greek grammar supply to the educated man a type, or at least a starting point, for universal grammar; and the series of labours of critics and commentators from the time of the original authors to our own time, exhibit to him the mind of man in a constant habit of self-examination and self-analysis, by means of which the classical forms of language and expression are not merely unconsciously used and admired, but consciously accepted and recognized, as truly exemplifying the genuine utterance of humanity.

But while the classical literature of Greece and Rome thus supplies us with studies by means of which the powers and properties belonging to one of our principal human faculties, language, may be exhibited in their most complete form, and each man's share in them realized by their influence in his education; we have, in other writings, both of ancient and of comparatively modern times, works by the study of which, as a part of education, the other principal human faculty lately mentioned, the reason, may also be exemplified in its most complete form, and educed in each person's mind. I speak now of mathematical works, in which truths respecting measurable quantities are demonstrated by chains of the most rigorous reasoning, proceeding from principles self-evident, or at least certain. The geometry which took

a distinct form in Greece in the time of Plato, has been commonly used ever since for this purpose, both by the Greeks themselves and by other nations; and such studies derived, from this employment of them, their name of *mathematics* or disciplinal studies. In such works we have the pure operation of reason exhibited to our consideration. In them, the external clothing of language is no longer the object of our regard; we fix our attention upon the internal connection of the ideas thus presented to us. We regard the matter, not the form, of the thought; and here, the matter almost completely determines the form; for the matter depends upon the universal and necessary processes of human reason, and is not modified by those differences of individual taste, disposition, and mental habit, from which arise the differences of style in different authors. Accordingly, it has been remarked by critics that, in the Greek geometers, there is no difference of style; and while an argument of Plato is at once recognized as different in its expression from an argument of Aristotle, in a geometric demonstration we cannot distinguish, by internal evidence, whether it be of Euclid, or Apollonius, or Archimedes. This severe necessity of form, arising from the inflexible connection of the matter, belongs to geometry eminently, and almost alone. But other portions of mathematics, though perhaps never yet put in a form so rigorously rational as geometry assumed in the *Elements* of Euclid, may still be employed in cultivating and unfolding reason in the course of education. Arithmetic exhibits to us a series of truths and processes leading to truth, of which the demonstrative evidence is not inferior to that of geometry. Mechanics and hydrostatics were reduced by Archimedes to a shape in which they contained propositions deduced by the severest processes of demonstration from manifest fundamental principles; and these studies might have been used, as geometry was used, as a discipline of reason.

At first, however, this was not done. The speculative powers of men in general did not take firm hold of these demonstrated truths when they were first brought to light. After the time of Archimedes they were again let slip as speculative truths, and were not recovered and ranged among the results of demonstrated mathematical reasoning, until comparatively modern times. Having, however, now taken this place, they may be used, along with geometry, as a means of educating reason. And besides the direct effect of the study of the mathematical sciences of mechanics as an intellectual discipline, the introduction of this study into a liberal education opens the way to the student's possessing a clear and steady comprehension of the greatest of the achievements of man in the domain of material knowledge, the Newtonian system of the universe. At the present day no education can be called good, which leaves the pupil in ignorance, or with a loose and merely verbal knowledge, of these discoveries. Mechanics then, as teaching the principles, both of machines, and of the mechanism of the heavens, should be one of the permanent studies which belongs to our higher education.

Other branches of mathematics have grown up in modern times, which may also be used with advantage as parts of a liberal education; but these, for the most part, have the character of the progressive rather than the permanent educational studies.

But before I proceed to speak of those progressive studies I may remark, with regard to the mode of educating reason, that there has been in this case, as in the education of the faculty of language, not only a direct study of the great models of excellence, but an attempt to analyze the means of success. The Greeks employed themselves in discovering and stating in a technical form the conditions under which reasoning is rigorously demonstrative. They had, here also, a *critical* as well as an *exemplary* branch of study: logic, as well as mathematics. In the work of reasoning, as

in the work of literary composition, the reflex tendencies of their minds came into play. As they laid down rules excluding solecisms in grammar, they laid down also rules excluding fallacies in logic. And logic has, from their times, held its place in a liberal education, along with grammar and rhetoric.

Progressive educational studies

Besides the permanent results of human thought, which, once brought into being, remain ever after as subjects of human study, there are other works of the intellect which from time to time change their form. There are progressive portions of literature and knowledge—new sciences, or new methods of science, new forms of criticism and philosophy. And as the permanent subjects of educational study educe in men those human faculties and those ideas by which they are connected with the past condition of humanity, so these progressive subjects of study connect men with the condition of humanity in their own time, and give them their share in the future intellectual prospects of the race. Even among the ancient Greeks, these progressive subjects of study were already cultivated. Astronomy had been brought into being as a mathematical science at the time of Plato; and the subject made some remarkable advances soon afterward. Optics and harmonics were also cultivated as mathematical sciences among the Greeks. And these sciences, especially astronomy, were employed as portions of higher education. Such sciences derive their fundamental principles from observation of the material world and deduce results from these principles by mathematical processes. Besides these portions of knowledge, thus obtained in various ways, the Greeks employed themselves in speculating concerning the nature of knowledge in general, and the mode in which man may and must acquire it. Such speculations formed a large portion of their philosophy; and such philosophy has occupied every succeeding generation up to the present time; and most, the generations of greatest intellectual activity.

In this portion of human knowledge, which has thus been progressive, it naturally follows that the subjects are expanded, transformed, and multiplied by the successive steps of progress. The science and philosophy of modern times differ from, or at least extend beyond, those of the ancient world. Even those sciences which had begun to exist among them have so changed their aspect and enlarged their boundaries that the ancient portion is the smallest part of them. Our mechanics and our hydrostatics are much more extensive and profound than those of the Greeks. Our astronomy has undergone revolutions which have made it belong eminently to modern times, although the ancient foundations laid by the Greek geometers have not even at this day lost their validity or importance. But in addition to these ancient sciences, others have sprung up which did not exist at all, or at least in any scientific form, among the Greeks and Romans. Such are the classificatory sciences, botany and zoology. Such are those sciences which I have elsewhere termed palaetiological, and which explore the past history of the world by studying the causes of change, among which we may especially notice geology, the history of the material earth, and ethnography, or glossology, the history of languages. Such, again, are the sciences which consider bodies according to the elements of which they are composed: chemistry, which analyzes them, and mineralogy, which classifies them with a view to their analysis. Such sciences, finally, are those which attend to the structure, the symmetry, and the functions of living beings: anatomy, comparative anatomy, morphology, biology. On these subjects, whatever sparks and gleams of intelligence we may discover in ancient authors, the broad light of science was not shed, until the human mind, in the course of its movements, arrived at its modern period of activity. These are the subjects with which a person must acquaint himself who wishes fully to appreciate the progress which man has made and is making in the pursuit of truth. And though it may not be possible for anyone to give his attention to the whole of these; and though it is not necessary for educational purposes that a man should attempt to acquaint himself with any large portion of them; yet it is requisite, as a part of a liberal education, that a person should so far become acquainted with some portion of this body of accumulated and imperishable knowledge, as to know of what nature it is, what is the evidence of its reality, by what means additions to it are made from time to time, and what are the prospects which it opens to the present generation of mankind. The progressive sciences, to this extent, ought to enter into the scheme of a liberal education.

The sciences just mentioned derive their new truths in part from experiment and observation, and are progressive in virtue of new facts as well as new reasonings which they incorporate into their texture. But even those sciences which consist altogether of reasonings are progressive, and require to be noticed under this aspect. Mathematics must be studied in the character of a progressive, as well as of a permanent science. For the mathematics of modern times involves processes unknown to the ancients. Results are now deduced from principles by combinations of symbols of number and quantity, rather than by reasoning upon the relations of space. And thus, in addition to the elementary geometry and conic sections of the Greeks, and the calculation of numerical questions directly, we have the calculation of such questions by symbols (algebra), and the calculation of the properties of curves by the symbols of their coordinates (the algebra of curves), and by the symbols of the changes of such quantities (the differential calculus); and these modes of calculation form additions to the body of mathematics which may overlay and almost put out of sight the original form of mathematical sciences.

Again, as the study of the exact reasoning of the ancients pointed to logic, which defines the methods of strict reasoning; so the sciences which are, as we have said, derived from facts, direct us to the study of those processes which determine the methods of obtaining truth from facts. To obtain consequences from principles is deduction; to obtain general truths from particular facts is induction. The logic of induction, or at least a philosophy which includes induction within its scope, is a necessary accompaniment of the progressive sciences; and such a philosophy ought also to make a part of our liberal education.

I have said that a portion of the sciences which have come into existence in modern times, and which are still in progress, should be introduced into a liberal education to such an extent as to acquaint the student with their nature and principles. It is an important inquiry, in determining the proper scheme of a liberal education, what portion of science is best fitted for this purpose. I have already remarked elsewhere* that among the sciences, natural history affords very valuable lessons which may beneficially be made a portion of education: the more so, inasmuch as this study may serve to correct prejudices and mental habits which have often been cherished by making pure mathematics the main instrument of intellectual education. The study of natural history teaches the student that there may be an exact use of names, and an accumulated store of indisputable truths, in a subject to which names are not appropriated by definitions, but by the condition that they shall serve for the expression of truth. These sciences show also that there may exist a system of descriptive terms which shall convey a conception of objects almost as distinct as the senses themselves can acquire for us, at least when the senses have been edu-

cated to respond to such a terminology.† Botany, in particular, is a beautiful and almost perfect example of these scientific merits; and an acquaintance with the philosophy of botany will supply the student with a portion of the philosophy of the progressive sciences, highly important, but for the most part hitherto omitted in the usual plans of a liberal education. But the philosophy of botany cannot be really understood without an acquaintance with a considerable portion, at least, of the details of systematic botany. On these grounds, I should much desire to see botany, or some other branch of natural history, or natural history in general, introduced as a common element into our higher education, and recommended to the study of those who desire to have any clear view of the nature of the progressive sciences; since it is, in fact, the key and groundwork of a large portion of those sciences.

I have ventured to give reasons‡ why the chemical sciences (chemistry, mineralogy, electrochemistry) are not at the present time in a condition which makes them important general elements of a liberal education. But there is another class of sciences, the palaetiological sciences, which from the largeness of their views and the exactness of the best portions of their reasonings are well fitted to form part of that philosophical

---

*Philosophy of the Inductive Sciences, Book XIII. Chap. 3. Intellectual Education.

†Philosophy of the Inductive Sciences, Book XIII. Chap. 2. The Education of the Senses.

‡Philosophy of the Inductive Sciences, Book XIII. Chap. 3. Intellectual Education. Of course it is not here intended to imply that chemistry and the sciences connected with it are not studies highly philosophical and important, and very suitable and instructive parts of a liberal education; but only, that if we select some of the progressive sciences as necessary portions of our educational scheme, there are much stronger reasons in favour of taking natural history than chemistry, for this purpose. It is further to be recollected, that a knowledge of chemistry is quite essential as a part of the professional education in medicine.

discipline which a liberal education ought to include. Of these sciences, I have mentioned two, one depending mainly upon the study of language and the other upon the sciences which deal with the material world. These two sciences, ethnography, or comparative philology, and geology, are among those progressive sciences which may be most properly taken into a liberal education as instructive instances of the wide and rich field of facts and reasonings with which modern science deals, still retaining, in many of its steps, great rigour of proof; and as an animating display also of the large and grand vistas of time, succession, and causation, which are open to the speculative powers of man. Moreover these sciences have the further recommendation of giving occasion to pointed and striking applications of some of the more limited sciences which we have noticed as fit elements of our higher education. Geology uses as her instruments, among others, the sciences of mechanics and hydrostatics, and the various branches of natural history. And ethnography, or comparative philology, though it cannot be pursued at all without a knowledge of several other languages besides Greek and Latin, may very conveniently and naturally begin from those relations between Greek, Latin, and English which a classical education forces upon our notice, and from that ready perception of the relations of language which a classical education cultivates.

Of the two classes of studies above mentioned, the permanent and the progressive studies, the former are the most essential as part of education and must be mastered before the others are entered on, in order to secure such an intellectual culture as we aim at. A full apprehension of the force of reason and the beauty of language are necessary to connect men with the most gifted and most cultivated portions of their species which have hitherto existed. When they have arrived at such an apprehension, but not until then, they may go on to sympathize with the most gifted and cultured minds of their own time in the activity of their progressive tendencies. But the former step must necessarily precede the latter. An acquaintance with the past must be a portion of education in order that there may be an intelligence as to the present. Intellectual progress cannot be a part of the occupation of life if intellectual discipline be not included in education. Attempts at progressive knowledge can have no value or real result in the minds of those who have not been prepared to understand what is still to do, by understanding what has already been done. It is very possible to introduce a large portion of progressive studies into education; but they can never properly constitute the whole of it; nor can the education of the youth include the whole intellectual progress of the man, if he is really to share in the progress of his times. A man who really participates in the progress of the sciences must do so by following their course when the time of education is past. The progressive sciences are to be begun toward the end of a liberal education. On the other hand, the permanent studies, classical literature and solid reasoning, are fundamental parts of a liberal education, and cannot be dispensed with. Modern science and philosophy ought to be introduced into education so far as to show their nature and principles; but they do not necessarily make any considerable or definite part of it. The intellectual culture, though it will be incomplete if these are excluded, may still be a culture which connects a man with the past, and prepares him for the present; but an education from which classical literature or mathematical reasoning is omitted, however familiar it may make a man with the terms of modern literature and philosophy, must leave him unprepared to understand the real purport of literature and philosophy, because he has not the intellectual culture which the greatest authors in literature and philosophy have always had.

English education

The above views are drawn from the idea of a liberal education considered in the most general manner. They have been to a great extent realized in the education given in this country as higher education to those who pass through the usual course of English schools and universities—at least so far as the permanent studies are concerned. Grammar and arithmetic at the schools; classical authors and logic, or classical authors and mathematics, at the universities, have represented the two classes of permanent studies by which the two faculties of language and reason are to be educed and unfolded, as the completeness of man's intellectual constitution requires them to be educed and unfolded. In the University of Cambridge, the classical authors have always formed a leading part of the subjects of study. The other portion of higher education by which reason is especially cultivated may be considered as having been logic in former times, [when] disputations in set logical forms, both in the colleges and in the public schools of the University, constituted a large part of the business of a university student; and as being mathematics in recent and present times, the disputations being now in a great measure done away, and a proficiency in mathematics forming a large portion of the knowledge required by the University as the condition of conferring her degrees and awarding her honours.

In this general scheme of the subjects with which the intellectual education of the University of Cambridge is concerned, we find nothing but what is right and conformable to the necessary general idea of the higher education of youth, as we have attempted to show on general principles. But the same principles, if they are applied to the detail of such a scheme, will point out some more special rules with regard to the subjects thus employed in a liberal education and the mode of employing them; and we may be thus led to make, respecting the present modes of teaching among us, and respecting possible changes, some remarks which may not be without a more especial bearing and interest.

In the first place, I remark that, since the two kinds of studies I have spoken of, classical and mathematical, have their value primarily as permanent subjects of thought, connecting us with past generations and fixing in our minds the stable and universal principles of language and of reason, these studies must be pursued in such a way as to imply a regard for this, their permanent character. For instance, with respect to the classical authors, the reason why we make *them,* especially, the subjects of our educational studies is, that having been selected at first as objects of especial admiration on account of the truth of their thoughts and the felicity of their expressions, they have continued to be studied by the successive generations of well-educated men; and thus they connect all such men with one another, by their common familiarity with these subjects of study. Hence we cannot, consistently with the meaning of a liberal education, substitute for the classical authors of Greece and Rome any other authors; for instance, eminent modern writers of our own or other countries. Even if the genius and skill shown in modern poems and orations were as great as that which appear in Homer or Virgil, Demosthenes or Cicero, the modern works could not supply the place of the ancient ones in education. No modern works can, in men's minds, take their station in the place of the familiar models of poetry and eloquence which have been recognized as models for two thousand years—which have, for so many generations, called forth and unfolded the ideas of poetry and eloquence, and furnished standard examples and ready illustrations of human powers of thought and expression. The most remarkable examples of poetry and eloquence in modern times have been the works of educated men, and have themselves shared in the influence of the ancient models. We cannot rightly admire the greatest modern poets and orators—we cannot admire them as they sought to be admired—if we read them in ignorance of the works of their great predecessors in the ancient world. If we attempt to elevate modern authors into *classics* by deposing the ancient classics, we break the classical tradition of thought which alone gives meaning to the term; and which alone gives classical authors their value in education.

Again: the acquaintance with classical authors which a good education requires is an acquaintance with the works themselves, and not merely with any speculations to which they may have given rise. The educated man must read and understand the great writers of antiquity in their original languages. He must not merely know, in a general manner, the views which they present, of the progress of history, and philosophy, and art, and knowledge: he must know the sentences and expressions in which these views are conveyed, or from which they are deduced. So far as the Greek and Roman writers form part of a liberal education, the study of the *text* of those writers is the permanent element of education, whatever interest or merit may belong to antiquarian, or critical, or philosophical speculations, of which those writings furnish the materials. Antiquity and ancient history, ancient philology and criticism, ancient philosophy and metaphysics, may be the subjects of progressive sciences among ourselves at the present day: for new writers may present, on such subjects, views very different from their predecessors; may even assume the character of discoverers; and may, by their sagacity and gift of generalization, draw to them the admiration of classical scholars. But such progressive studies cannot answer the purpose of the permanent studies. An acquaintance, however exact, with these new antiquarian, or philological, or philosophical views, cannot supply the want of a familiarity with the classical authors. To be able to translate Homer and Thucydi-

des, Virgil and Livy, is a necessary part of a good education. Such a power must be acquired in youth. To learn the current theories concerning the Greek and Latin languages, or Greek and Roman early history, however ingenious and plausible the theories be, cannot make an education good, in which such a knowledge of the original authors is wanting. Indeed, such theories are not necessarily any parts at all of a good education. They may be very fitly attended to as the studies of the man, when the education of the youth is completed; and to be able through life to follow, with an intelligent interest and sound criticism, contemporary discussion on such theories, is one of the beneficial results of a good education.

Thus, to be able to understand and translate the ancient classical authors is the primary and indispensable part of the classical branch of a good education. This acquirement implies, of course, an intimate acquaintance with the system of Greek and Latin grammar, and such a knowledge of the customs and institutions of the Greeks and Romans, as may explain expressions in which these are referred to. Moreover, as I have already said, an acquaintance with Greek and Latin grammar supplies a type of universal grammar, and has always answered this purpose in the minds of educated men. It is true, that grammar also may be dealt with as a progressive science, and that, in proportion as philosophical grammarians have had to treat of languages very different in their structure from the Greek and Latin, or as they have included a larger range of languages in their generalizations, they have molded their science into forms different from the traditional forms of Greek and Latin grammar. But still those familiar forms answer as a starting point for the widest generalizations, and have furnished the technical phraseology in which grammatical and philological questions have been discussed among cultivated persons in all ages. And thus a knowledge of the traditional forms of Greek and Latin grammar is itself one of the permanent studies of a liberal education. The necessity of such knowledge cannot be superseded by any new modes of learning languages which may, perhaps, be applied to the Greek and the Latin with apparent success. Supposing a boy were to learn one or both these languages by the habit of hearing and speaking, as children learn languages, this knowledge could not stand in the place of that grammatical study which is an essential point in education. Even if a person who had so learned were to read the classical authors, he might still know nothing of Greek and Latin grammar. He might read Homer and Virgil as many Englishmen read Shakespeare or Milton, without thinking of the grammar, and without being able to give any account of it. And if it be said that such a person has no need for Greek and Latin grammar, since without these he can do that to which they are merely instruments, namely, understand the best authors, we should reply by denying this doctrine. We should say that such a person, if he is to be a well-educated person, *has* a need of grammar. A knowledge of English grammar is essential to a good education; a person familiar with the Greek and Latin grammar, even if he be not taught English grammar directly, frames such a grammar for himself by applying to English construction the analysis and analogies of Greek and Latin. And if a person cannot do this, but, though understanding what he reads, is unable to analyze the construction of an ungrammatical sentence, so as to point out in what the fault consists, we do not look upon him as a well-educated man. He may be a lover and reader of poetry, or of eloquence, and may have a good practical knowledge of the language; but he has not the spirit of analysis and the perception of rule which are among the habits of all well-educated men. Faults in grammar are the most palpable and universally recognized indications of the want of a good education. Solecisms and barbarisms in language are inconsistent with a good education, because the well-educated man is saved from such errors by principle as well as by habit; by a clear insight into the rules and relations of language, as well as by the imitation of other men. And thus, not only to know and understand the text of classical authors, but to understand the grammar of their sentences, is included in the permanent studies which belong to a liberal education.

As in classical, so also in mathematical studies, we must, for the purposes of a good education, attend to the distinction of the permanent and the progressive parts of such studies. It will easily be conceived that there are, in mathematics, progressive as well as permanent portions. The sciences which are founded upon a knowledge of the phenomena of the world, as astronomy, optics, and the like, make repeated steps of progress by new observations of phenomena, or new combinations of old observations. It may be that in such sciences some progress is making in our own time; and if this be so, such progress naturally draws men's notice in an especial manner. And moreover, mathematical science has changed its aspect, not only by the observation of new facts, but also by the invention of new methods of calculation. As we have already said, calculation by means of symbols of number and quantity has in many instances taken the place of reasoning by means of the properties of space: and thus, in addition to the ancient geometry, we have in modern times new branches of pure mathematics, algebra, the algebra of curves, and the differential calculus. In these branches, new steps and modes of calculation, new advances in generalization and abstraction, new modes of dealing with symbols, such as may each be termed a new calculus, have been constantly, in modern times, invented and published by mathematical writers. And these novelties, because they are novelties, and often because they render easy what before was difficult, are received with pleasure, and followed with interest by mathematical readers. And it is very fit that this should be so. But still, these progressive portions of mathematics cannot take the place of the permanent portions in our higher education without destroying the value of our system. Wherever mathematics has formed a part of a liberal education, as a discipline of the reason, geometry has been the branch of mathematics principally employed for this purpose. And for this purpose geometry is especially fitted. For geometry really consists entirely of manifest examples of perfect reasoning, the reasoning being expressed in words which convince the mind in virtue of the special forms and relations to which they directly refer. But in algebra, on the contrary, and in all the branches of mathematics which have been derived from algebra, we have, not so much examples of reasoning, as of application of rules; for the rules being at first proved by reasoning once for all, the application of them no longer comes before us as an example of reasoning. And in the reasoning itself, quantities and their relations are not expressed in words and brought before the mind as objects of intuition, but are denoted by symbols and rules of symbolic combination. This mode of denoting the relations of space and number, and of obtaining their results, is in the highest degree ingenious and beautiful; but it can be an intellectual discipline to those only who fully master the higher steps of generalization and abstraction by a firm and connected mental progress from the lower of such steps upward; and this requires rather a professional mathematical education, than such a study of mathematics as must properly form part of a liberal education. Moreover, supposing these higher forms of algebra to be thus completely mastered, the intellectual discipline which they afford is not a discipline in reasoning, but in the generalization of symbolic expression, and this appears to be a mental process of which a very small exercise is all that a liberal education requires. For instance, the general student may, es-

pecially if his mind has an aptitude for such studies, derive intellectual profit from learning how the forms and properties of given curves are determined by symbolic expressions of coordinates, and of the relative rate of change of these coordinates, as in the differential calculus: but it can hardly be worth the while of such a student to bestow much time in ascending to that higher generalization in which these changes of the coordinate of a given curve are mixed with other changes, by which any one curve may be transformed into any other, as in the calculus of variations. Such steps of wide symbolic abstraction, however beautiful as subjects of contemplation to persons of congenial minds, are out of the range of any general system of liberal education.

All these branches of algebra of which we have spoken may, as I have intimated, be considered rather as progressive than as permanent studies; and therefore, not necessarily parts even of a higher education, since in order to the full cultivation of reason they need not be possessed at all. They are fit matters of the study of the professed mathematician, when his general education is terminated. But of geometry, on the other hand, it is not too much to say that it is a necessary part of a good education. There is no other study by which reason can be so exactly and rigorously exercised. In learning geometry the student is rendered familiar with the most perfect examples of strict inference; he is compelled habitually to fix his attention on those conditions on which the cogency of the demonstration depends; and in the mistakes and imperfect attempts at demonstration made by himself and others, he is presented with examples of the more natural fallacies, which he sees exposed and corrected. He is accustomed to a chain of deduction in which each link hangs from the preceding, yet without any insecurity in the whole; to an ascent, beginning from solid ground, in which each step, as soon as it is made, is a foundation for a further ascent, no less solid than the first self-evident truths. Hence he learns continuity of attention, coherency of thought, and confidence in the power of human reason to arrive at the truth. These great advantages, resulting from the study of geometry, have justly made it a part of every good system of liberal education from the time of the Greeks to our own.

Arithmetic has usually been a portion of education on somewhat different grounds: namely, not so much on account of its being an example of reasoning, as on account of its practical use in the business of life. To know and to be able familiarly to apply the rules of arithmetic is requisite on innumerable occasions of private and public business; and since this ability can never be so easily or completely acquired as in early youth, it ought to be a part of the business of the boy at school. For the like reasons, mensuration ought to be learned at an early period: that is, the rules for determining the magnitude in numbers of lines, spaces, and solids, under given conditions, a branch of knowledge which differs from geometry as the practical from the speculative, and which, like other practical habits, may be most easily learned in boyhood, leaving the theoretical aspect of the subject for the business of higher education which comes at a later period. There is another reason for making arithmetic a part of the school-learning of all who are to have a liberal education: namely, that without a very complete familiarity with actual arithmetic processes, none of the branches of algebra can be at all understood. Algebra was, at first, a generalization and abstraction of arithmetic; and whatever other shape it may take by successive steps in the minds of mathematicians, it will never be really understood by those students who do not go through this step. And, as we have already said, there is, in a general education, little or nothing gained by going beyond this. The successive generalizations of one or another new calculus may form subjects of progressive study for those whose edu-

cation is completed, but cannot enter into a general education without destroying the proportion of its parts.

I have spoken of geometry as a necessary part of a liberal education. It may be asked how far this geometry extends? The *Elements* of Euclid, especially the first six books, are generally accepted as the essential portion of geometry for this purpose. This portion of mathematics is, however, insufficient fully to exercise the activity of reason, and to balance the influence of classical studies. If we consider what portions of mathematics may most properly be added to elementary geometry, the parts that offer themselves are solid geometry, conic sections, mechanics, hydrostatics, optics, and astronomy. Of solid geometry, we have an elementary portion in the eleventh and twelfth books of Euclid, and which has often and very suitably been used for purposes of education. Conic sections are a very beautiful extension of elementary geometry, and would probably have been made a part of a general education more commonly than it has been, if we had inherited from the Greeks any treatise on the subject, as perfect as the *Elements* of Euclid are on their subjects. The properties of conic sections are not merely so many propositions added to those of elementary geometry; there are introduced, in this branch of geometry, new geometric conceptions: for instance, that of the curvature of a curve at any point. The proofs of the properties of conic sections, discovered by the Greek geometers, have come down to us only in a fragmentary manner, and although there have appeared several modern treatises which are very good examples of geometry, no one of them has acquired a permanent and general place as a part of a liberal education. This has arisen in part, at least in England, from the prevalence of a disposition among mathematical students in modern times to adopt the algebraic mode of treating these as well as other curves. But we may observe that the subject of conic sections, so treated, is of small comparative value as a portion of education. If we make conic sections merely examples of the application of algebra to curves, they are of no more importance than cissoids, conchoids, or any other curves, and have little claim to be considered as a distinct part of our educational studies; while a geometric system of conic sections is both a striking example of geometric reasoning, a distinct member of an enlarged system of geometry, and a necessary introduction to other mathematical studies which may very fitly be brought before the student when he has mastered these.

Mechanics and hydrostatics are subjects in some respects in the same condition as conic sections. The Greeks, especially Archimedes, established with full evidence some of the fundamental propositions of these mathematical sciences; but they did not transmit the sciences to us in a form in which they have retained a place in educational study; and no particular modern treatises have permanently and generally acquired such a place. Yet these sciences, as a mathematical portion of our higher education, are eminently fitted to promote the development of reason, since they not only offer examples of reasoning as solid and evident as that of geometry, but also show to the student that such reasoning is not confined, in its power, to space and number only, but may be extended to the ideas of force and motion. And there is another reason why mechanics and hydrostatics are valuable educational studies. The truths which they teach are perpetually exemplified in the external world and serve to explain the practical properties of machines, structures, and fluids. If the sciences of mechanics and hydrostatics be introduced into education in a proper form, the habits thence acquired, of coherent and conclusive thought on such subjects, will be continually confirmed and extended by the consideration of the mechanical problems which come before men in a practical form.

There is a further reason, as we have already remarked, why mechanics and hydrostatics are studies which may be introduced into a liberal education. These sciences are the key to the understanding of all the great discoveries of modern times with regard to the constitution of the universe, and especially the discoveries of Newton. By these discoveries, the motions of the earth, planets, moons, and other cosmic bodies are explained upon mechanical principles, and their apparent irregularities deduced from their mutual forces by mathematical reasoning. These discoveries also offer the best example which the world has yet seen of *induction,* the inference of a true theory from phenomena by philosophical sagacity, as well as of the *deduction* of consequences from hypotheses by direct reasoning. These discoveries of Newton are still so recent, and have been followed by so continuous a train of similar discoveries with regard to other parts of the system of the universe, that they may be considered as belonging to the progressive sciences—as exemplifying a mental activity which is still going on, and as a portion of the subjects of intellectual research and promise which at present interest men. But yet Newton's exposition of his system has been so long before the world, is so complete in its reasonings, and is so familiar to all who have shared in the intellectual culture of recent times, that it may now be very properly used also as a portion of our permanent educational studies—a specimen of what such reasoning ought to be, and a groundwork on which all must build in doing more than is there done. The propositions contained in the *Principia* of Newton are beautiful examples of mathematical combination and invention, following the course of ancient geometry; and for the purpose of general education, a portion might be selected from this work without difficulty which should be not too long or complex for the student, and which should come in a natural order after conic sections and mechanics.

Isaac Newton, author of the *Principia Mathematica* (1687), was a student at Trinity College and taught there for nearly thirty years, beginning in 1669. He made mathematics the preeminent subject of study at Cambridge, which it still is. Not until 1824 was an honors examination offered in classics as well. Whewell wanted students to be qualified in both.

Astronomy is a subject in which the Greeks made some of the steps which form the foundation of the mathematical science, especially the doctrine of the sphere and the doctrine of the relative motions of the sun, moon, and planets. These portions of knowledge, ever since they were brought to light, have been taught as a necessary part of the instruction of well-educated men. The geocentric theory of the solar system held by the ancients has, in modern times, been superseded by the heliocentric or Copernican theory; and astronomy in this form is, for additional reasons, a necessary part of a liberal education; namely, not only as a beautiful example of the mode in which common phenomena are made the subject of mathematical demonstration and calculation, but also as a most conspicuous instance of the progress of science and the full establishment of truths which at first sight seem opposed to the evidence of the senses. It is highly desirable that astronomy should form a part of a liberal education to the extent just stated, the doctrine of the sphere and the doctrine of the solar system; to which may be added dialing, as an application of the doctrine of the sphere in a special and familiar case.

In optics, as a mathematical science, the Greeks made little progress, though even in this they made a beginning. The science had its rise for the most part in the sixteenth century. Its main problems, the determination of the foci and images which spherical surfaces produce by reflection and refraction, deserve to be introduced into a liberal education on the ground already assigned in the case of astronomy— namely, their being beautiful and simple examples of common phenomena, made the subject of mathematical demonstration, and a portion of knowledge commonly diffused among educated men. Perspective, which may be considered as a branch of optics, may be made part of education on more general grounds. It was cultivated by the ancients as well as the moderns, and a knowledge of it is necessarily assumed in judging of paintings, a subject in which all educated persons feel a lively interest.

I have now completed the enumeration of the branches of mathematics which belong to a liberal education in general. The mathematical part of such an education may, of course, be carried further if the mathematical aptitude of the student make such an exercise of it easy and satisfactory to his teachers and to him. The *Principia* of Newton, indeed, is so extensive a work that the student may find an abundant store of employment in the extension of his studies from one part of that book to another; and he will everywhere find in it what is admirable in its mathematical character, philosophically important, and historically interesting. He may also pursue the differential calculus and the other portions of algebra to an unlimited extent, and especially the solutions which more modern analysts, by means of that calculus, have given of problems such as those which Newton solved by his geometric method. These solutions must not be allowed to supersede those of Newton as permanent studies; for they have neither the mathematical instructiveness nor the permanent interest of the Newtonian propositions. They are mere examples of a method of symbolic calculation. But they are proper and necessary objects of attention to a person who wishes to share in the progressive mathematical studies of his time: and the speculations which belong to this kind of mathematics are so beautiful an exercise of abstraction, generalization, and ingenuity that we cannot wonder at their being pursued with an exclusive enthusiasm by many of those who attend to mathematical science for its own sake. With us, who have here to regard mathematical science only as an instrument of education, the case is, of course, different. We take parts of the geometry of Newton as a standard portion of our educational course; but we cannot consider, as containing anything essential to our ob-

ject, the beautiful symbolic reasonings of the *Mécanique Analytique* of Lagrange, or the *Mécanique Céleste* of Laplace; nor can we accept, as substitutes for our simpler forms of the science of mechanics, any of the elementary treatises in which the like symbolic generalizations are presented in a more elementary manner. As we have already said, the main purpose of mathematical studies in a liberal education is not to familiarize the student with symbolic abstraction and generalization, but with rigorous demonstrations, which exercise the reason, and which have long been accepted and referred to by educated men, as examples of solid reasoning.

Analytic mathematics as an educational study

The question of the kind of mathematics which is to be used in the course of education has not been exempt from difference of opinion in modern times. According to what we have said, the mathematical studies which belong generally to a liberal education must be portions of mathematics which are established among mathematicians in a permanent form, and in which the reasoning is intelligible without learning a new mathematical language. But the beauty of the symbolic reasonings of modern times, and the interest which belongs to them as a part of the progressive science of our own day, have, as we have intimated, excited an enthusiasm in many persons; and these persons have often been disposed to substitute such symbolic forms of mathematics in the place of the geometric modes of treating the subject which we have represented as essential to the object of our higher education. Thus, proofs of the properties of conic sections, by means of symbolic combinations of coordinates, have been proposed as substitutes for the geometric demonstrations of the like properties; and the relations between the curves described by moving bodies and the forces which act upon them have been investigated by applying the differential calculus to the coordinates of the curves, instead of establishing those relations in the way in which Newton did. Such branches of mathematical science are often called analytic, and analysis is often opposed to geometry. This opposition is not very exact; for geometry has also its analysis. We demonstrate a theorem, or solve a problem, by means of geometric analysis, when we suppose the theorem proved, or the problem solved, and trace the consequences of this supposition into a known theorem, or a problem obviously soluble. In solving a question by means of algebra we, in like manner, express the given supposition in algebraic language, using symbols of unknown as well as of known quantities and by tracing the consequences of this expression, we can often find the value of the unknown quantities. And this analytic process is so much more common in algebra than in geometry that processes conducted by means of algebraic symbols are commonly called analytic. I will adopt this phraseology, though, as I have said, it is not very exact, while I make a few remarks on the use of analytic mathematics as an instrument of education.*

The recommendation of the geometric branches of mathematics, as parts of education, is, as we have seen, that they are an effectual discipline of the reason, and have always been familiar as such among educated men. On the other hand, the recommendations of analytic forms of mathematics are such as these; their supplying easier solutions of the problems with which the mathematician has to deal; the symmetry and generality of their processes; and their having, in consequence of these qualities, superseded geometric methods in the mathematical literature of modern times. These merits of analytic processes have been shown, in a most striking manner, in the works of many great mathematicians of modern times who have given to such processes great completeness and beauty, and have solved, by means of them, prob-

lems which had foiled the attempts of previous calculators. And these great works have been accompanied by many elementary works which expound the like methods in a more limited form, accessible to common students and applicable to simpler problems. We have to consider the advantages and disadvantages of employing in our higher education such analytic elementary treatises, to the exclusion of geometric modes of treating the same subjects.

The first reason which we have mentioned, why mathematics, in the shape of geometry, holds its place as an element of great and incomparable value among the permanent studies of a liberal education, is this: that it offers to us examples of solid and certain reasoning, by which the reasoning powers, and the apprehension of demonstrative proof, may be exercised, unfolded, and confirmed. This is eminently true of the geometric forms of elementary geometry, trigonometry, conic sections, statics, and dynamics. It is not true to the same extent, and hardly at all, of the analytic methods of treating the same subjects. For, in the geometric form of these sciences, we reason concerning subjects in virtue of the manner in which the subjects are conceived in the mind. In the analytic methods, on the other hand, we reason by means of symbols, by which symbols, quantities, and the relations of quantity, are represented; and by means of the general rules of combining and operating upon such symbols, without thinking of anything but these rules. When the supposed fundamental conditions are once translated into the language of analysis, we

---

*The reader may observe that the reasons here given for adopting geometric rather than analytic modes of reasoning in our elementary university course of mathematics, apply rather against analytic generalities and special calculus, than against the introduction of simple algebraic processes. For example, these reasons would not exclude from mechanics the method of finding the space fallen through in a given time, by means of assuming an arithmetic series and taking its limit: and the like processes.

dismiss from our minds altogether the conceptions of the things which the symbols represent; whether lines, angles, velocities, forces, or whatever else they may be. The mode of proceeding is the same, whichever of these be the matters in question; and the steps of the process are not acts of thought in any other way than as the application of an assumed general rule to a particular case is an act of thought. We arrive at our conclusion, not by a necessary progress, in which we see the necessity at every step, but by a compulsory process, in which we accept the conclusion as necessary in virtue of the necessary truth of our rules of procedure, previously proved or supposed to be proved. In the one case, that of geometric reasoning, we tread the ground ourselves, at every step feeling ourselves firm, and directing our steps to the end aimed at. In the other case, that of analytic calculation, we are carried along as in a railroad carriage, entering it at one station and coming out of it at another, without having any choice in our progress in the intermediate space.

It is plain that the latter is not a mode of exercising our own locomotive powers; and in the same manner analytic processes are not a mode of exercising our reasoning powers. It may be said that much thought and skill are required in the analyst, in order that he may choose the best scheme of symbols, the best mode of combining them, the best analytic artifices for arriving at his result, and shortening the way to it. And in like manner, in traveling by a railroad, thought and skill are requisite in order to select the line and the train, or the combination of lines and trains, which will lead us to the intended place. We must know the stations and times of the system in order to use it. But still, this is not any exercise or discipline of the bodily frame. It may be the best way for men of business to travel, but it cannot fitly be made a part of the gymnastics of education. And just as little is mere analysis a discipline of the intellectual frame. It may be the best way

for the professed mathematician to deal with the problems which he has to solve, but it cannot answer the purpose of that gymnastic of the reason, without which a liberal education cannot subsist.

Thus mere analysis is not a suitable discipline of the reasoning powers, because analytic processes do not exhibit reasoning, in the common sense of the term, and in a form which resembles the common reasonings with which men are concerned; whereas geometry does exhibit reasoning in a form which resembles such common reasonings, except insofar as geometric reasoning is more perfect and certain than most such reasonings. Geometry sets out from certain first principles, namely, axioms and definitions, and at every step uses formulae which, if they are really applicable, lead necessarily to the next step by an evidence which the like forms of language express and convey on all subjects as well as geometry. Its *because* and *whereas,* its *but* and *for,* its *wherefore* and *therefore,* are its connecting links, in the same sense in which they are the connecting links of all reasoning. If in other subjects we have first principles equally certain, and definitions equally precise, we can reason in the same manner as in geometry; and to reason conclusively, we must do so. All geometric reasoning may be resolved into a series of syllogisms, and in its proper form consists of a chain of enthymemes, or implied syllogisms; and in like manner, all other sound reasoning on all subjects consists of a like chain of enthymemes. In geometric reasoning, each proposition when once established is used in establishing ulterior propositions with as much confidence and promptitude as if it were itself a self-evident axiom. And in like manner, in all sound connected reasoning, a proposition once established is to be used with confidence and promptitude in establishing ulterior propositions. And the habit of thus advancing, with clear conviction and active thought, from step to step of certain truth, is an intellectual habit of the greatest value which a good education ought to form and render familiar, and which nothing but geometric study can impart. In analytic reasoning we have no such chains of syllogisms present to the mind. It may be said, indeed, that every step in analysis is a syllogism in which the major is the axiom, *things which are equal to the same are equal to one another;* and the minor is a proposition that *two certain forms of symbols* have been proved to be *equal to the same.* But to this we shall reply that the perpetual repetition of this elementary kind of syllogism, even if the process were so conceived, is no sufficient discipline in reasoning: and further, that the algebraic equality of two symbols does not exemplify a member of a syllogism in any way which can make such reasoning an intellectual exercise. I repeat, therefore, that mere analytic processes are no proper discipline of the reason, on account of the difference of form between such reasoning and the reasoning with which men are mainly and commonly concerned.

But again: analytic reasoning is no sufficient discipline of the reason, on account of the way in which it puts out of sight the subject matter of the reasoning. In geometric reasoning we reason concerning things as they are: in the first place, in virtue of certain axioms concerning them, which are self-evident from our conceptions of the things; and then, in virtue of propositions deduced from those axioms, which propositions are considered as properties of the things. We reason concerning straight lines, angles, spaces, curves, forces, inert masses, conceiving them as straight lines, angles, spaces, curves, forces, inert masses. We are thus led to see that such reasoning as we employ in one case is not applicable to such case only, but also to other classes of cases in which the things reasoned of are of altogether a different kind. We pass from geometry to mechanics, not by identifying forces with lines, but by taking axioms concerning force, evident by its nature as force, and by applying these axioms, one after another; bearing in mind, at every step, the peculiar nature of force. In this way, we are prepared to pass on, and to apply reasoning of the like rigour to other subjects, as different from these as force is from space. In this way, geometry and geometric mechanics are a discipline for every kind of sound reasoning. We are prepared to bring the mental power to act by its syllogistic chain upon all classes of conception. In analysis, the contrary is the case. The analyst does not retain in his mind, in virtue of his peculiar processes, any apprehension of the differences of the things about which he is supposed to be reasoning. All things alike, lines, angles, forces, masses, are represented by the letters of the alphabet. All curves, conic sections, transcendental curves, curve surfaces, are alike represented by the relations of coordinates; and for the sake of uniformity, straight lines are represented in the same manner. All relations of motion and force are, in like manner, represented by the equations of coordinates of the points moving and acted on. When he has once placed before him these equations of coordinates, he no longer thinks at all about the special nature of the things originally spoken of. His reasonings are operations upon symbols; his results are equations. His final equation may give him an angle, or a radius of curvature, or an angular velocity, or a central force; but he has no separate processes of thought for these different cases. He obtains his result equally well if he has forgotten, or does not know, which of these things his x represents. I am quite willing to allow that this peculiarity arises from the perfection of analysis; from the entire generality of its symbols and its rules. What I am here saying is, that this is a kind of perfection which makes analysis of little value as a discipline of the reason for general purposes. For in reasoning for general purposes it is quite necessary to bear in mind, at every step, the peculiar nature and attributes of things about which we reason. We cannot, in any subject except analytic mathematics, express things by symbols once for all, and then go on with our reasoning, forgetting all their peculiarities. Any attempt to do this (for such attempts have not been wanting) leads to the most extravagant and inapplicable conclusions. Anything in common reasoning resembling such an attempt, as when men start with the definition of certain technical terms and build systems by the combinations and supposed consequences of these, belongs to a class of intellectual habits which it is the business of a good education to counteract, correct, and eradicate, not to confirm, aggravate, and extend. And therefore I say, that mere analytic reasoning is a bad discipline of the intellect, on account of the way in which it puts out of sight the subject matter of the reasoning; on the right apprehension of which, with its peculiar character and attributes, all good reasoning, on all other subjects, must depend.

It is easy to show by examples taken from the branches of mathematics which I have mentioned, that analytic modes of treating those subjects have, in fact, put out of sight the peculiarities of the conceptions which belong to each subject, and have merged all their special trains of reasoning in undistinguishing symbolic generalizations.

In the elements of geometry, *ratio* and *proportion* are among the peculiar conceptions which belong to the subject, and of which the properties, as treated by Euclid, rest upon an especial axiom (Book v. Axiom v.). The mode in which, by means of this axiom, the case of incommensurable quantities is reasoned upon, without any introduction of arbitrary assumptions or ungeometric notions, has always been admired by the cultivators of geometry as a beautiful and instructive example of mathematical subtlety and exactness of thought. In the analytic mode of treating the subject, a ratio is identified with an algebraic fraction, and the reasonings about ratios become operations upon algebraic fractions; in which operations, everything dependent upon the peculiar character of the

conception disappears; and all the propositions of geometry, in which proportion is involved, are on this scheme made to depend upon algebra.

Trigonometry was a science invented for the purpose of measuring angles by means of lines drawn in a certain manner, in a circle whose centre is the angular point; and of using these measures for the solution of triangles. This subject has recently been modified so that angles are measured by certain algebraic fractions, the original conception of the circle being rejected. And in this manner, all the propositions of trigonometry have been superseded by certain analytic formulae involving those algebraic fractions.

Conic sections were, until lately, treated as a geometric subject; the curves being defined, in some treatises, by the sections of a cone by a plane; in others, by certain simple relations of lines drawn in their own plane. But in either method, various conceptions were introduced, extensions of those of elementary geometry: as the conceptions of *tangents* to such curves; of properties *analogous* to those of the circle; of properties of *conjugate diameters;* of properties of the *circle of curvature;* and the like. These properties were proved by geometric reasonings, built upon some simple fundamental properties, exhibiting at every step the evidence of the relation of the properties of the conic sections to those of the circle; and supplying a transition to the properties of curves in general. Of late, conic sections has been treated as a mere branch of analysis; the definitions of tangents and circles of curvature have become algebraic or differential formulae; the analogies with the circle have also appeared only as interpretations of algebraic formulae; and the subject of conic sections has ceased to be of any meaning as an introduction to the subject of curves in general, because the conic sections are treated only as curves in general; and any other class of curves might with equal propriety be made a separate branch; or rather, there is no propriety in so treating any class of curves, for all their mathematical interest, so treated, consists in their being examples of general methods.

Statics, the mechanics of equilibrium, depends upon certain fundamental truths which were established by Archimedes, among the ancients, and by Stevinus [Simon Stevin, 1548–1620, Flemish mathematician], Galileo, and others, among the moderns. From these fundamental truths, by keeping steadily in view the conception of statical force, all ordinary problems may be solved by geometric methods. But in modern times the subject has been differently treated. The fundamental proposition, the composition of forces, or some equivalent one, has been proved (sometimes, even this, by analytic reasoning from assumed axioms); and then, all problems alike have been made to depend upon the equations which apply the fundamental properties, in the most general form, to every possible system of matter. In this manner, the conception of force has been dismissed from the mind as soon as the first steps of the science had been made.

The doctrine of bodies in motion acted upon by forces was created by Galileo and his successors, and was applied by Newton to the system of the universe in such a manner as to draw to this doctrine the universal attention of the educated portion of mankind. Independently of the immense importance in the history of inductive astronomy which belongs to the propositions of Newton's *Principia,* the work is a very beautiful series of examples of the application of the principles of mechanics, combined with the properties of the conic sections and other known geometric propositions. In virtue of its combined merit and interest, this work is eminently fitted to be a part of the permanent mathematical studies of a liberal education, and specially of a liberal English education. But this subject also has been treated analytically. The forces by which bodies describe conic sections or any other orbits, the orbits

which bodies will describe under the influence of any forces, the attraction of masses of attractive particles, and the like problems have been investigated symbolically by means of the differential calculus and other analytic processes; and hence the peculiar mechanical conceptions with which the speculators of Newton's time had to struggle, and which he followed out until they led to his remarkable discoveries, have been obliterated from the minds of most of our modern analytic mathematicians.

Even in astronomy, though so much a science of observed phenomena, explanations of observed phenomena, and reasonings from them, mathematicians of analytic propensities have had a tendency to pass as briefly as possible over such observations, explanations, and reasonings, and to dwell mainly upon parts of the subject where principles, once established, gave a hold for their analytic instrument, the calculus. They have thus assimilated this to other parts of their body of mathematics; and though astronomy is an inductive science, explaining phenomena by its theories they have omitted out of it all that is inductive, explanatory, or especially astronomical.

Remarks of the same kind might be made respecting other branches of mathematics, but the subject has been pursued far enough, I trust, to justify the general opinion which I have delivered.

I assert, therefore, that these branches of mathematics, thus analytically treated, do not possess that value as instruments of an exact and extensive discipline of the reason which the geometric branches of mathematics do possess. Indeed it must appear, I think, from what has been said, not only that mere analytic mathematics does not possess so much value as geometric mathematics for such purposes, but that, in truth, it possesses none at all, or at least very little. Analytic operations in mathematics do not discipline the reason; they do not familiarize the student with a chain of syllogisms connected by a manifest necessity at every link; they do not show that many kinds of subjects may be held by such chains: and at the same time, that the possibility of so reasoning on any subject must depend upon our conceiving the subject so distinctly as to be able to lay down axiomatic principles as the basis of our reasoning.

With reference to analytic mathematics, the argument in favour of the use of mathematics as a permanent educational study loses all its force. If we can only have analytic mathematics in our system of education, we have little reason to wish to have in it any mathematics at all. Our education will be very imperfect without mathematics, or some substitute for that element; but mere analytic mathematics does not remedy the imperfection. If we can only have analytic mathematics, it is well worth considering whether we may not find a much better educational study to supply its place in logic, or jurisprudence. The general belief, for undoubtedly it is a general belief, that mathematics is a valuable element in education, has arisen through the use of geometric mathematics. If mathematics had only been presented to men in an analytic form, such a belief could not have arisen. If in any place of education mathematics is studied only in an analytic form, such a belief must soon fade away.

I must request the reader to observe that the consequences which I have spoken of are spoken of as resulting from the use of *mere* analysis, as the mathematical element of education. If the geometric modes of treating mechanics, conic sections, and the dynamics of the universe, are carefully preserved and steadily employed as permanent educational studies, such analytic methods as I have mentioned may be brought before the student with advantage, as further illustrations of the standard mathematical truths to which he is introduced; as examples of the various modes of arriving at mathematical truth; and as manifestations of the extent to which the solutions of problems may be simplified and extended. But this pursuit of simplic-

ity and generality must not be allowed to interfere with the attention which is to be given to the standard modes of establishing such truths. Such a pursuit of mathematical variety, simplicity, and generality, if it take the place of the study of standard reasonings, can only end in destroying all the benefit of a mathematical training of the mind. When the student has before him a standard proof of a proposition, he has to make it his business completely to understand this proof; and if there be in it any difficulties or obscurities, to understand completely the solutions of such difficulties and the explanations of such obscurities. This struggle is the very condition and essential point of intellectual discipline. And since all the standard proofs are (in a right scheme) really demonstrations, the student's not fully seeing their evidence can arise only from the imperfection of his intellectual culture, which imperfection ought to be remedied, not acquiesced in. If the proof be long and complex, the discipline is none the worse on that account; and the standard course being well selected, the proofs will have a connection and coherence which is a beauty of a higher kind than mere brevity and facility. But if, instead of adhering to such a standard train of mathematical demonstrations, the student be allowed or encouraged to substitute, for its steps, brief and easy methods of arriving at each result, there is for him no exercise of intellectual vigour and power. Instead of overcoming difficulties, he tries to evade them, or is unaware of their existence. He has no conception of the relation of the subject, in that point of view in which alone it is worthy of being selected as a subject of educational study. He does not give his attention to understand any one proof, but employs all his mental activity in casting about for short and easy proofs, of which he does not see the meaning or connection, and which he very likely accepts as proofs on the credit of teachers who admire and recommend such a line of mathematical acquirement. Mathematics, so studied, tends to fill the mind not with chains of reasoning, of which the evidence is seen and felt, but with detached conventional operations upon symbols, which are supposed to supply the place of such evidence, and with a craving curiosity as to where such proofs are to be found. Such a course of study tends to unsettle and dissipate the mind and to busy it with the recollection of ill-understood symbols, just as much as a true mathematical culture tends to give to the intellect stability, concentration, and clear insight.

It may be said that if we have a series of standard demonstrations with which the student is required to acquaint himself, he may acquire these by rote, through the mere exercise of memory, without any really intellectual process going on in his mind. But, this objection is as valid against any one set of proofs as another—as valid against the new analytic processes as the old geometric demonstrations. If we accept the novelty of a proof as evidence of the student who produces it really understanding it, we are quite as liable to be deceived, as if we accept the accuracy with which he gives an old proof, as evidence of his understanding *that*—indeed, much more so; for it is more likely that men will understand what they have long had the opportunity and the motive to study carefully and thoroughly. Besides which, by such a preference of novelty, we drive the active student to seek, not for a way of showing that he understands a proof, but for a new proof, or a new form of an old one.

But in truth, with moderate care on the part of the teacher, there is no danger of the student being undetected, when he gives a proof by memory alone, without understanding it. The smallest question proposed to him with regard to any part of the proof will show whether his understanding has gone along with the steps of the demonstration. Everyone must know this who has examined a student in the propositions of Euclid's *Elements,* and ex-

actly the same is the case with every other geometric subject.

But further: it is easy to annex to the examination of the student in the standard propositions, applications and examples of them, or easy problems founded upon them; and the student who understands the propositions will be able to solve such examples and problems; and he who has learned by rote will not be able to do this. Such examples and problems ought to form part of all examinations of students in a standard course: and if this is done, there is no danger of the study of such a course degenerating into a mere act of memory.

A standard course of geometric demonstrations being retained and upheld, analytic processes which run parallel to these proofs may be usefully taught to the student as a preparation for progressive mathematical studies; for these must mainly consist of analytic methods. I will add further, that if the study of analysis is not thus begun in connection with geometry and arithmetic, in which the evidence of the truth is simple and evident, analysis itself will never be rightly understood by the student. Algebra was originally a generalization of arithmetic, and by common students is never understood, except when it is so taught; although accomplished mathematicians may delight the lovers of symbolic generality by presenting it as an independent science. The analytic doctrine of curves must be built upon geometric foundations; and common students will never understand its language, or be able to use it with intelligence, except they are, for a considerable period of their progress, practiced in translating its conclusions, when obtained, into the language of geometry. Analytic mechanics, in like manner, must begin from mechanical truths expressed in words, not in symbols; and the student will never understand mechanical truths, expressed in symbols, except he has been well disciplined in the study of them expressed in their own proper form.

Hence, for the sake of having analysis itself understood by our students, we must retain our geometric studies (along with arithmetic) as standard and fundamental elements of our education. If we do not do this, our students may indeed learn to write down the symbols which analysis uses, and the combinations of them which are contained in books, even the most general and complex of such combinations. But they will do so without any intelligence of the truths which such combinations express, or of the real import of the language. It is very possible for a student to write down the proof of the formula for drawing a tangent to a curve of double curvature in terms of its three coordinates, and yet not be able to find where the tangent to the parabola cuts the axis—to give the investigation for finding the path of a body acted on by any forces in space, and yet not to be able to find where a projectile acted upon by gravity hits a given plane, the velocity and direction being given. Such consequences flow very naturally, and with regard to the greater part of students, inevitably, from a study of analysis which has not been begun, and supported, by geometric reasonings and exemplifications. But such consequences, when they occur, are evidences of a very worthless system of mathematical education.

And there is a further evil in such a system, in its effect upon the dispositions of the students toward mathematical studies. Clear demonstrative proofs, and chains of such proofs, have a great charm for all well-constituted intellects. The human mind loves light and coherence: it delights to see a few evident principles solidly built up into a large system of unexpected but undeniable truth. Geometry, rightly studied, is admired and dwelt upon with complacency by most students. The same is the case with other geometric studies, more or less, according to the capacity of the student. But analysis, pursued without a proper geometric and arithmetic foundation, has in it no clearness or light. The

student who is led on in such a course, is immersed in a mist of symbols, in which he only here and there sees a dim twilight of meaning. When this is presented to him as an exercise of his intellect, he is naturally perplexed, repelled, and disgusted. He cannot fail to perceive that this is, for him, no intellectual exercise. He finds in such a course no advantage or satisfaction, and gives to it a reluctant and unsympathetic labour. He considers it as an arbitrary and useless imposition, tries to evade the task, and casts it from his thoughts as soon as his purpose is answered.

Or if he have a taste for the symmetry and generality of expressions at which analysts aim, he attends only to those fundamental relations of symbols on which the processes of analysis depend. He is curious to see how far these conventions, without any other principles being added, may be made to lead to analytic operations and results. He dwells upon the new forms that can be given to the fundamental contentions of analytic language, the subtle distinctions which such new forms bring into view, the further generalization of that which seemed most general, the characters of analytic language by which it is most removed from common language. So far as his mind is occupied in such speculation, it may have some of its powers exercised and unfolded, but these are not the powers which it is the object of a liberal education to unfold. The qualities thus educated are rather the subtlety and technicality of the schoolmen of the middle ages than the clear apprehension of demonstrated truth in which the intellectual culture of man has consisted during all the progressive periods of man's intellectual history.

On all these accounts, then, I venture to assert that while we hold mathematics to be of inestimable value as the permanent study by which the reason of man is to be educated, we must hold also that the geometric forms of mathematics must be especially preserved and maintained, as essentially requisite for this office; that analytic mathematics can in no way answer this purpose; and if the attempt be made so to employ it, will not only be worthless, but highly prejudicial to men's minds.

But besides the value of mathematical studies in education as a perfect example and complete exercise of demonstrative reasoning, mathematical truths have this additional recommendation, that they have always been referred to, by each successive generation of thoughtful and cultivated men, as examples of truth and of demonstration; and have thus become standard points of reference among cultivated men whenever they speak of truth, knowledge, or proof. Thus mathematics has not only a disciplinal but a historical interest. This is peculiarly the case with those portions of mathematics which we have mentioned. We find geometric proof adduced in illustration of the nature of reasoning, in the earliest speculations on the subject, the Dialogues of Plato; we find geometric proof one of the main subjects of discussion in some of the most recent of such speculations, those of Dugald Stewart [1753–1828] and his contemporaries. The recollection of the truths of elementary geometry has in all ages given a meaning and a reality to the best attempts to explain man's power of arriving at truth. Other branches of mathematics have in like manner become recognized examples, among educated men, of man's powers of attaining truth. Thus when trigonometry was invented, mathematicians had the means of calculating in numbers the lines of diagrams, by means of a canon, or table, of sines, cosines, tangents, secants, and the like, already calculated to a given radius. Here was a striking example, and one which has ever since produced an effect to men's views of intellectual labour, how calculation might be abridged by the accumulated results of previous calculation. This was still more completely exemplified by the additional invention of logarithms. No one can use trigonometric and logarithmic tables without seeing that they give

man a new power of numerical calculation. Conic sections, again, containing a remarkable extension of geometry beyond its elementary limits, introduced also a number of new geometric notions and terms, as parabola, ellipse, hyperbola, directrix, focus, normals, diameters, conjugate and transverse diameters, circles of curvature, asymptotes, infinite branches. These terms, and the like, when they become familiar, offer many means of referring to the properties and analogies brought into view in this higher geometry, and enable the man who is instructed in such studies to follow many of the applications of mathematics to matters of general interest. Mechanics, again, is another branch of mathematics, quite distinct, but possessing an interest of the same kind. The properties of the center of gravity, and of the mechanical powers, the lever, wheel and axle, pulley, inclined plane, wedge and screw, have been long familiar to the minds of mathematicians, and may be made to serve as images of all statical action, and as modes of conceiving and solving all statical problems. These, and a few other terms, form a mechanical language by means of which all men of education understand each other in discussing mechanical questions. In the mechanics of motion, we find no truths permanently established until we come to modern times; but the propositions proved by Galileo concerning falling bodies and projectiles have ever since been standard portions of mathematical knowledge. And the truths mathematically demonstrated by Newton, respecting the forces by which the universe is regulated, have been regarded with admiration as the triumphs of man's reasoning powers. By the attention bestowed by men in general upon these investigations, many terms referring to mechanical action have become generally current: as attractive and repulsive forces, centers of attraction, centripetal and centrifugal forces, inertia, and the like. These terms may often be loosely and improperly applied by half-educated persons. It is the business of a good education to enable the student to understand and apply them rightly and clearly. To these subjects, belonging to the mechanics of the universe, we may add, as also familiar among men of mathematical culture, the cycloidal pendulum, as simplified by Newton's pupil, Cotes; and the center of oscillation, investigated by several mathematicians of that period. The doctrines of astronomy have been familiar among educated men from the earliest period, and the terms and theories of that science must be known by anyone who would share in the historical influence of intellectual culture.

Now these branches of mathematics, in order to be possessed as a portion of the intellectual culture which has been historically transmitted from one generation to another, must be studied in that geometric form in which they were originally produced and have generally been exhibited, not in some new analytic form, which supersedes the old, however elegant or compendious the new form may be. These mathematical studies connect successive generations of educated men by an intellectual sympathy, not merely in virtue of their subjects, but of the mode of treating them. If we have a science concerning lines and angles, analytically or however otherwise treated, quite different from the geometry of Euclid, such a science cannot supersede Euclid as an element of education. It cannot make the philosophical speculations of ancient and modern times intelligible to us, as a knowledge of the ancient geometry does. And the same is the case with regard to the other subjects. If our trigonometry differs entirely from the trigonometry which appears in the history of mathematics; if our conic sections is a different science from the conic sections with which all ancient and most modern mathematicians are familiar, our new mathematics cannot connect us with the ancient thinkers, as educational mathematics ought to do. If our mechanics is a new science reducing all special cases, as

the mechanical powers, to one universal case of equilibrium, and obliterating their peculiar characters, it cannot enable us to understand the familiar discussions of those whose mechanics is of a more historical complexion. If our knowledge of the mechanics of the universe, though it implicitly includes the Newtonian truths, do not explicitly exhibit the Newtonian proofs and methods, it will not enable us to share in the interest with which those who know the history of science dwell upon the philosophical events and revolutions of the great Newtonian epoch. And even with regard to smaller problems, such as the motion of projectiles or the oscillations of pendulums, a person, in order to understand the principles which have been applied to their solution, must have them brought before him in the distinct and elementary form in which they were at first treated, and not merely as cases included in wide symbolic expressions of mechanical principles.

Thus the geometric form of the mathematics subjects which have been mentioned are valuable parts of a liberal education, not only as being the best examples of rigorous reasoning, but as having been always regarded as the standard achievements of human reason; and thus possessing a historical as well as a disciplinal character. This historical character of the branches of mathematics may be much obscured, and the consequent value of a mathematical education much impaired, by treating the subjects in a merely analytic manner. Analysis presents each subject under its symbolic general forms, obtained by symbolic operations from fundamental principles, and thus puts out of sight, entirely or nearly, all the peculiar conceptions and terms which the original mathematical explorers of these subjects, proceeding in the geometric way, had employed. A person may possess great knowledge of the analytic forms of geometry, trigonometry, conic sections, mechanics, dynamics, and yet know nothing at all of their history, or even of the principal terms in which

407

their history is told. A person may be well acquainted with the formulae of analytic trigonometry, and even able to combine them with skill, and may yet be ignorant of the meaning which the words *sine, cosine, tangent, secant, versed sine,* have had in all mathematical books until within these few years. With the same knowledge, he may be unable to solve a triangle in numbers, or to use a table of logarithms. A person may be well taught in analytic conic sections and may not know a single proposition of those which constituted the study of conic sections from the time of Apollonius to that of Newton, and which alone gave it its interest. A person who is thus ignorant of the propositions which belonged to conic sections in Newton's time, and of their demonstrations, will necessarily be unable to understand Newton's reasonings in the *Principia;* for these reasonings assume the ancient propositions, and follow a like mode of proof. And he may be entirely ignorant of every line of the *Principia,* and of every step of Newton's train of discovery and demonstration, and even unable to follow Newton's reasoning as presented by himself, though he is intimately acquainted with the modes in which the mechanics of the universe has been analytically treated.

Now if the analytic modes of treating the various branches of mathematics produce this effect, they destroy one of the main reasons why mathematical studies are accepted as parts of education. For undoubtedly it has always been supposed, by those who have approved of such education, that the mathematics so taught was to make men acquainted with those mental triumphs of past generations which have always occupied a conspicuous place in man's intellectual history. If our educational mathematics does not do this, men in general, when they learn that the case is so, will be far less ready to assent to the value which we set upon the study. If our educational mathematics give us no acquaintance with the works of Euclid and Archimedes, Galileo and Newton, men in general will

look upon our mathematical education as illusory and worthless. If anyone moderately acquainted with the general literature of the country knows more than our best mathematical students do, of the history of mathematical and physical discoveries, a praiser of our system will find, in general, averse and incredulous auditors. To know accurately those events in scientific history which other men know vaguely, is a most proper and characteristic superiority of a well-educated man; but to know certain general symbolic results, which are supposed to render all scientific history superfluous, is an accomplishment which can only be of little value in education; for a good education must connect us with the past as well as with the future, even if such mere generalities did supply the best mode of dealing with all future problems, which in fact they are very far from doing.

For (to add one more to the points of advantage of geometric over analytic forms of mathematics for common educational purposes), it will generally be found that a person who has studied the branches of mathematics in the more special and detached forms in which they were treated geometrically, before analytic generalities became so common, will be able to apply his knowledge to the calculation of practical results and the solution of problems, better than a person who has acquired his mathematical learning under general analytic forms. The geometric student has a firmer hold of his principles than the analytic student has. The former holds his fundamental truths by means of his conceptions; the latter, by means of his symbols. In applying doctrines to particular cases, or in solving new problems, the former sees his way at every step and shapes his course accordingly; the latter must commit himself to his equations; which, except he be a consummate analyst, he will not readily understand and interpret in their particular application. I have no doubt that in any application of geometric, mechanical, or hydrostatic principles to a problem of moderate difficulty, supposing the problem new to both of two students; one, a geometer of the English school of forty or fifty years back, the other, a modern analyst, instructed in equal degrees; the former would much more accurately and certainly obtain a definite and correct solution. In the application of mathematics to problems of engineering and the like, the generalities in which the analyst delights are a source of embarrassment and confusion, rather than of convenience and advantage. When particular problems are solved by particular considerations or particular artifices, the ingenuity thus exercised is a talent really more generally available than a knowledge of the general methods which express all problems alike, but actually solve none.

From the considerations which have thus been stated, I am led to the conclusion that the geometric modes of treating the various branches of mathematics are those which are to be employed as educational studies. The geometric forms of trigonometry, conic sections, statics, and dynamics, and not any analytic substitutes for them, must be parts of a liberal education. This must be so, because thus alone can mathematics be an intellectual discipline, strengthening the reasoning powers for other nonmathematical occupations; thus alone can the mathematical sciences be known in that historical shape with which a liberally educated person ought to be acquainted; and thus best is a person of moderate mathematical attainments able to apply to practical cases the knowledge which he possesses.

I have hitherto spoken of that part of education which consists of permanent mathematical studies. But progressive mathematics may also advantageously enter into our higher education; and I proceed to speak of this portion of educational studies.

Progressive mathematics as an educational study

As I have already said, a liberal education ought to include both permanent studies which connect men with the culture of past generations, and progressive studies which make them feel their community with the present generation, its businesses, interests, and prospects. The permanent studies must necessarily precede, in order to form a foundation for the progressive; for the present progress has grown out of the past activity of men's minds, and cannot be intelligible except to the student of past literature and established opinions. But the progressive studies must be added to the permanent; for without this step, the meaning and tendencies of the past activity of men cannot be seen, nor our own business understood. And though progressive studies may form the business of life, as well as of the specially educational period of it, they may with advantage be begun in that period, before each man's course of study is, as in after life it generally is, disturbed and perplexed by the constant necessity of action.

This necessity of progressive, as well as permanent studies, may be applied to mathematical studies in particular. For mathematics, for the last three centuries, has been, and still is, a science in which a rapid progress is taking place. Old problems have been solved by new and simpler methods: new problems, formerly insoluble, have been successfully attacked; and the methods by which these successes have been attained have excited a strong admiration in men, on account of their ingenuity, generality, and symmetry. On these accounts, it is to be expected that those persons who cultivate mathematics will be drawn to give some of their attention to these modern and progressive portions of mathematics; and those who have to teach mathematics as a part of education may naturally be led to introduce into their teaching a large share of this kind of mathematics.

Almost all these modern portions of mathematics are of the analytic kind. It may be useful to mention some of the most conspicuous of these newer mathematical trophies. The expression of the form and properties of curves by means of their co-ordinates was introduced by Descartes; and the like methods have since been extended to curve surfaces, giving rise to an extensive subject, the application of algebra to geometry. The rates of change of variable quantities related in a given manner became the subject of the differential calculus, invented by Newton (under the form of fluxions) and by Leibniz. The inverse process connected with this is the integral calculus (the method of quadratures of the Newtonians). Then come, as additional branches, differential equations, finite differences (originally termed the method of increments); definite integrals, and finally, the calculus of variations, which treats of the change in the forms of relation of related variable quantities. Moreover we have the application of all these modes of calculation to mechanics (including hydrostatics) and to the mechanics of the universe, cultivated to a wide extent by Euler, and carried to the highest pitch of generality and symmetry by Lagrange. To this may be added the application of analytic methods to other subjects, as optics. All these portions of mathematics lie open to us as parts of progressive science, and it is our business to select from them such a portion as may suit the purposes of a liberal education.

I have argued against the exclusive, or even the copious use of analytic mathematics among permanent educational studies. It may be asked, whether the same objections apply to the study of such subjects as I have recommended, most of which are analytic in their form. To this we may reply, that the objections by no means apply in this case. When, by the pursuit of permanent mathematical studies, the reasoning faculties have been educed and confirmed, the student's powers of symbolic calculation, and his pleasure in symbolic symmetry and generality, need no longer be repressed or limited. He may go on following the reasonings and processes of the beautiful portions of mathematics above

mentioned, as far as his taste and talents prompt him, or as the demands of other studies will allow. When the student is once well disciplined in geometric mathematics, he may pursue analysis safely and surely to any extent.

But though modern mathematics may thus be very fitly studied as a sequel to the older forms of mathematical science which must enter into a liberal education, these modern methods cannot supply the place of the ancient subjects as the permanent studies in our educational course. This is sufficiently shown already by what we have said of the unfitness of mere analysis either to exercise the reasoning powers, or to render intelligible the history of human knowledge. Yet perhaps it may sometimes appear, both to teachers and to students, that it is a waste of time and a perverseness of judgment to adhere to the ancient kinds of mathematics, when we have, in the modern analysis, an instrument of greater power and range for the solution of problems, giving us the old results by more compendious methods: an instrument, too, in itself admirable for its beauty and generality. But to this we reply, that we require our permanent mathematical studies, not as an instrument, but as an exercise of the intellectual powers: that it is not for their results, but for the intellectual habits which they generate, that such studies are pursued. To this we may add, as we have already stated, that in most minds, the significance of analytic methods is never fully understood, except when a foundation has been laid in geometric studies. There is no more a waste of time in studying geometry before we proceed to solve questions by the differential calculus, than there is a waste of time making ourselves acquainted with the grammar of a language before we try to read its philosophical or poetic literature. And a knowledge of the sciences, as they have historically existed, is the best mode of enabling ourselves to understand their ultimate and most recent generalizations, as a knowledge of the etymology of words, and their transitions from one shade of meaning to another, is the best mode of learning to perceive all that is implied by words in their later use. There is therefore no waste of time, or perverseness of taste, when the mathematician retains and upholds, as an essential part of a general education, mathematical reasonings different from those which he would himself study or employ, if he had to deal with difficult and extensive problems. He does this, just as the most accomplished scholar requires the student to study his grammar, though he himself has outgrown such study. Nor does the most careful regard to the maintenance of our geometric studies, on this ground, imply any want of the intellectual taste which can perceive the beauty, and the intellectual power which can follow and continue the processes, of the most refined modern analysis.

As I have already said, we have to select out of the whole range of modern mathematical literature those portions which are best suited to be admitted, as progressive studies, into a liberal education. In order to discuss this selection more conveniently, I will divide mathematical writings into three classes, which I will call respectively capital works, original investigations, and systematic treatises.

By capital works in mathematics, I mean works which hold a conspicuous place, both in mathematical history and in mathematical literature, this distinction being secured to them by their containing comprehensive and important truths connected by solid reasoning, and in them first presented as a connected whole. Such are the *Principia* of Newton, the *Mechanics* of Euler, the *Théorie des Fonctions* of Lagrange, the *Mécanique Analytique* of the same author, the *Application de l'Algebre à la Géométrie* of Monge, the *Mécanique Céleste* of Laplace.

By original investigations, I mean such publications as memoirs in the transactions of scientific bodies, and the like, in which mathematical investigations of detached problems are presented. Such investigations may afterward be included in more complete treatises, as many of Euler's and Laplace's investigations and original memoirs were afterward included in those capital works of the same authors which have just been mentioned; or they may as yet not have taken this place in mathematical literature, as is the case with many highly important memoirs of modern mathematicians; for instance, Poisson and Gauss among foreigners, and several of our own countrymen.

By systematic treatises I mean treatises compiled out of the two preceding classes of works, of elementary treatises, intended as introductions to such works. Such are Lacroix's larger *Traité des Calcul Differential et Integral,* and his smaller *Traité Elémentaire* on the same subject. Such are the innumerable elementary treatises on the differential calculus, on mechanics, and on other subjects, which have been published in recent times in France, Germany, and England.

I do not pretend that this division of modern mathematical literature can always be applied without difficulty; but, without attempting any rigour in the separation, the distinction will enable me, I hope, to speak intelligibly.

I remark, then, in the first place, that candidates for our highest mathematical honours ought to be encouraged to acquaint themselves with capital works, rather than with systematic treatises in which the same results are presented, more symmetrically and simply perhaps, but by mathematicians of inferior eminence. The historical interest belonging to every great work, added to its intellectual value, makes it fit that a man of liberal education, whose studies extend to the subject of the work, should be acquainted with the work itself, and not with any transcript of it. Moreover, it is always instructive and animating to study the works of men of genius. The mind appears to be elevated and ennobled by direct intercourse with the highest minds. On this account I recommend, for the highest students, Newton's *Principia,* rather than Maclaurin's account of Newton's discoveries; Euler's *Mechanica,* rather than any modern collection of mechanical problems; Lagrange's *Mécanique Analytique,* rather than Poisson's or Francoeur's *Mechanics;* Laplace's *Mechanics of the Universe,* rather than Pontecoulant's. The derivative works which I have mentioned are excellent for their proper purposes, but the great original works are the proper study of a man who would pursue mathematics for the highest purposes of intellectual culture.

The works which I have enumerated as capital works appear to me to suffice for the purposes of the highest education; although others of equal, or almost equal, eminence might be added to the list, and will, of course, be read by a person who would be an accomplished mathematician. I think there are no works which have claims upon our notice superior to those above enumerated. Euler's other works, as for instance, the treatise *De Motu Corporum Rigidorum,* and the solutions of *Isoperimetrical Problems,* have been so far superseded by more general methods that they are not capital works in the same degree as the *Mechanica.* The *Calculus Integralis* of Euler is truly a capital work, but does not make so great a figure in mathematical history as the others which we have mentioned, and in which its substance, so far as most purposes are concerned, is included. Clairaut's *Théorie de la Lune,* d'Alembert's *Dynamique,* and various other works, on the other hand, are of capital importance in mathematical history, but are included, as to their import, in the great works of Laplace and Lagrange. And since it is not possible to require or suppose, even in our highest students, an acquaintance with *all* the great works of mathematicians, I think it will be found that the list which I have given is ample, without being overwhelming as to its extent.

Whether any given mathematical work can properly be distinguished as one of the capital works of the subject is a matter to be decided by the general and permanent judgment of the mathematical world, and it must therefore be difficult to decide this question with regard to any new work. It is desirable, for the purposes of education at least, that we should not be hasty in elevating the works of our contemporaries into this rank, and directing the attention of men to them as part of their educational studies. For the list of capital works which we already possess is sufficiently ample to occupy the time and thought even of the most gifted student, and to encourage a too ready pursuit of novelties, tends to promote the neglect or superficial study of the older works. For the same reason it is not desirable, in general, to require or suppose in our students a knowledge of original investigations which have not yet found their way into capital works or systematic treatises. To urge young men, even of the greatest talents and industry, to rush into the vast field of mathematical memoirs which exists in the transactions of societies, and in detached opuscules, would be to bewilder and overwhelm them. Such a course of reading is fit only for those who make mathematics a main business of life. And such a study could lead to no advantage comparable with the study of the great works of the best authors. I do not say that active-minded and industrious students should be prevented from pursuing such a line of reading, as far as their taste and their time will allow, but this is not the course of reading which we ought to encourage by the turn which we give to the mathematical instructions and requirements which our education includes.

Perhaps we may be a little more facile in encouraging the study of new investigations with regard to practical problems, than in recondite and speculative subjects. Problems of engineering and practical mechanics naturally receive new solutions, as, in the progress of art, they take new forms; and it is desirable that our mathematical education should make our students acquainted with the best and most recent solutions of such problems, because by this means their mathematical knowledge has solidity and permanence given it, by its verification in facts, and its coincidence with the experience of practical men. Hence, I would advise that we should introduce among the books of which we encourage the study among our best mathematical students, three excellent works of recent date: namely, Poncelet's *Mécanique Industrielle,* in which he has given modes of calculating the amount and expenditure of labouring force; Professor Willis's *Principles of Mechanism,* in which he has classified all modes of communicating motion by machinery, and investigated their properties; and Count de Pambour's *Theory of the Steam Engine,* in which a sound mathematical theory is confirmed by judicious experiments. The study of these works would put our students in possession of the largest and most philosophical doctrines which apply to engineering, and would thus give a tangible reality and practical value to their mathematical acquirements; while, at the same time they would find, in the works thus brought before them, excellent examples of mathematical rigour, ingenuity, and beauty.

Besides the great works of mathematical inventors, there have been produced many systematic treatises in which the original inventions have been collected, methodized, and often simplified. I have said that our best mathematical students are to be directed to the great original works, rather than to these compilations. But in some measure, it will be necessary for all students to have recourse to such works. It is, for instance, more convenient for all students to acquire their knowledge of the differential and integral calculus in a systematic work like Lacroix's *Traité,* rather than to gather up the various artifices of the calculus out of the successive works of their inventors. And for the like reason, the *Collection of Examples of the Applications of the Differential and Integral Calcu-*

lus, by Dr. Peacock, and the *Collection of Examples of the Application of the Calculus of Finite Differences,* by Sir John Herschel (both originally intended as a supplement to the translation of Lacroix's smaller treatise) may be recommended as containing, within a convenient space, the substance of many investigations very instructive, but too numerous and extensive to be studied in their original form. To these works on pure mathematics, we may add Mr. Airy's *Tracts* on certain subjects of applied mathematics, namely, the lunar and planetary theories, the figure of the earth, precession and nutation, and the undulatory theory of optics. These works are proper subjects of the labours of our best mathematical students.

With regard to students who have inferior ability and diligence, but who still are candidates for distinction in their mathematical studies, their course of reading must necessarily be different from that which I have described. Their acquaintance with analytic processes, and their habits of general reasoning will, in most cases, not allow them to go far in the reading of such capital works as we have spoken of; and they must, for the most part, acquire their knowledge from systematic treatises, and principally from elementary treatises. The selection of the elementary treatises which are thus to be used is an important point in a scheme of education; and on this subject I shall venture to make one or two remarks.

In the first place, I remark that the elementary treatises which we use in our course of education ought not to be too rapidly changed. For the change itself is an evil, inasmuch as it turns the student's attention to new proofs, instead of the application of known truths; and excites a craving for fresh novelties, in the place of a desire to overcome known difficulties. And moreover the new elementary treatises which are produced in modern times, for the most part, treat their subjects more entirely in an analytic manner than their predecessors had done, and are therefore more unfit for general educational purposes for the reasons already given. If new elementary treatises of an analytic cast are easily introduced into our educational system, the result will be very pernicious. If this be the case, the new parts of our course will naturally attract the most notice, and the greater part or the whole of the student's attention will be employed upon such novelties, without any real profit. For this change in the elementary treatises which are commonly read is not attended with any real progress of the sciences treated of. In every subject, treated analytically, the earliest steps of generalization admit of being variously presented; and every writer, and almost every teacher, thinks he can make some new advance in generality and symmetry. And all those devices, while new, please some readers, though they leave the science where they found it. Mere novelty appears like improvement, because it implies activity of mind in him who produces it. And thus, if new elementary treatises be readily admitted, the student will be perpetually carried by his teachers or his fellow students from one elementary form of the subject to another. Instead of employing his mental labour in mastering the difficulties of any one connected course of study, his thoughts are occupied in pursuing these detached novelties, and in considering which of them is most worthy of admiration, or in conjecturing which is most likely to receive honour. The result of such an occupation will probably be that he will know nothing well. He will ascribe an exaggerated value to those parts of his studies in which the new methods differ from the old. The conceit of a supposed knowledge of something which his predecessors did not know will take the place of the satisfaction which he might feel from understanding what generations of thoughtful men before him have understood, or from following the intellectual processes by which real difficulties are overcome.

A too facile admission of new elementary works, and new forms of old truths, into our educational scheme, is likely to occasion a multiplication of such works, to the detriment rather than the advantage of our mathematical literature. For such works, produced on the first suggestion of some slight advance, fancied or real, in simplicity or generality or ingenuity, would not be likely to obtain any wide or permanent notice among the general mathematical public. Works so produced at a place of education might form a perpetual stream of transient local literature, and the students, in bestowing their attention upon such works, might be toiling on in paths held in no value in the rest of the mathematical world; and might be bestowing much labour on mathematical subjects, without approaching to any community of thought with the good mathematicians of their own and preceding times. In order to avoid such evils, I conceive that no book should be adopted into a course of education except by proper authority, and after mature deliberation. I shall afterward venture to suggest the grounds on which such a choice should turn, and the nature of the authority by which the decision might be carried into effect.

It will of course be understood from what has been said that even when elementary analytic treatises upon the various branches of mathematics have been selected and adopted in our educational course, they are not to supersede the permanent studies of which we have already spoken. Conic sections, mechanics, hydrostatics, optics, and explanatory astronomy, in their hitherto common form, should be mastered by every mathematical student, however he may afterward study these subjects in the shape in which they have been presented by modern analysts. He will travel all the more securely in his analytic course in each subject, from having already gone over a part of the same ground with the clear intuition which belongs to geometric reasoning.

It may be remarked that the works which I have mentioned as "capital works," except Newton's *Principia,* are all by foreigners, and with the exception of Euler, by French writers of modern times. No English mathematician will be surprised at this, for the French mathematicians have undoubtedly of late been our masters and teachers. The pertinacity with which the English mathematicians clung to Newton's methods, and the mathematical controversies which soon after his time arose between Englishmen and foreigners, for a long time prevented his countrymen from adopting and following out the analytic generalizations introduced by his continental contemporaries. Yet it is not because we have no English works worthy of the mathematician's study that I have mentioned none in my list, but because it appeared to me necessary to limit the list to a few works of which the eminent place in mathematical literature is clear and undeniable. I might have recommended the beautiful geometric investigations of Maclaurin; many ingenious solutions of problems by Emerson and Simpson; many labours of Ivory, not inferior in analytic elegance to any works of continental analysts. But this would have made the mass of subjects too large for a course of education. The English mathematician will hardly fail to acquaint himself with these works, when he is out of the hands of his teachers. For the same reason I have not spoken of the mathematical labours of the Bernoullis, which form such remarkable points in mathematical history, or of those of many other great mathematicians. I speak only of mathematical education: and I am convinced that I have provided sufficiently for the mathematical progress of our best students, by placing before them the works already enumerated as the highest subjects of their educational study.

If it be objected that since I have allowed that the tenacious adherence to Newton's methods checked the progress of mathematics in England, I shall discourage such progress by obstinately retaining his works as our permanent studies, I reply that I do not require our mathematicians to stop with those works, but to begin with them, or at least to make them a part of their studies. Let our mathematical students by all means go on with their analytic teachers as far as they will and can, but they will not do this the better for being ignorant of Newton; and as I have said, the works of their analytic teachers cannot discharge the educational office which our permanent studies, and Newton among them, are required to discharge. We have around us many instances that those who are most fully acquainted with Newton's works are most likely to go on as successful rivals of the foreign analysts in the solution of difficult problems. Indeed, no persons in our own time appear to have studied Newton's works more carefully than Lagrange and Laplace themselves.

If it be said, that by beginning with geometry we shall lose all chance of having a school of English mathematicians able to compete with the mathematicians of other countries, I reply that I do not believe this to be the case, because I believe such a mathematical education as I have described to be the one best fitted to give the student a complete understanding of mathematical processes, and therefore, the most likely to lead to a solid and extensive progress. I do not believe that men will make better analysts because they are ignorant of geometric mathematics, but the contrary. And I do not think it has been found that those who have exclusively studied analysis have been the persons to make the greatest advances in mathematical science in our own times.

But I reply further that the use of mathematical study, with which we have to do, is not to produce a school of eminent mathematicians, but to contribute to a liberal education of the highest kind. I am, indeed, fully persuaded that the mathematical education which I have described is that most adapted to evoke the mathematical talent of the nation, and that among students so taught we shall have a better chance of giving to great mathematical genius its full scope than by involving them in discussion about elementary symbolic novelties. But even if I thought otherwise—if I thought that a course beginning with analytic generalities was the most likely to give us a celebrated school of English analysts—I should still think that while such permanent mathematical studies as I have recommended are most likely to impart the intellectual culture which belongs to a liberal education, they should be steadily retained in the seats of English education.

Having thus considered the nature of the permanent and of the progressive mathematical studies which belong to a liberal education, I proceed to make some remarks on classical studies, as belonging to such an education; and therefore under the same aspects of permanent and progressive studies.

Classical educational studies, permanent and progressive

Classical studies necessarily occupy an important place in education, both as permanent studies which connect men with the culture of past generations and as progressive studies which engage them in the speculations, discussions, and mental movements still going on among men. The former office more especially belongs to the literature of Greece and Rome. An acquaintance with that literature has been a leading character of all literary educated men in all ages. This study has educed men's apprehension of the powers of language in their highest form, as we have already said, and has connected man with man, giving them a common acquaintance with standard books of history, poetry, philosophy, and morality. There has also, as we have said, been diffused among classical students a knowledge of philology by means of the grammatical and critical comments to which the study of standard authors has led. These effects have been more generally produced by Latin literature, for Latin has been more generally read than Greek. The study of the Latin authors has never been interrupted among cultivated men. The language has always been known to such persons. For many centuries it was the language of a great part of the civilized globe, first as the language of the Roman Empire, then as the language of the Western Church and, until within a short time, of the whole literary world. Through this long prevalence, this language contains in its literature the works which have most influenced every age up to modern times. The languages of many nations in modern Europe are mainly derived from the Latin, and those which are not so derived are still much tinged by the mixture of Latin words and modes of speech. In English, in particular, this mixture is very large, and the connection of our language with the Latin is so intimate, that the reader who has no knowledge of that language will inevitably miss some part of the meaning of our best writers. In general the study of Latin, as a portion of a liberal education, is directed mainly to the principal writers of the best times: for example, Livy, Caesar, Sallust, Tacitus, Lucretius, Virgil, Horace, Ovid, Cicero. And a sound knowledge of these authors is, in truth, a sufficient educational basis for a knowledge of the Latin literature of all ages, and for a due apprehension of the influence which these great models of composition have exercised upon the vernacular literature of each country, and especially upon its poetry and criticism.

But a knowledge of the Greek language and literature is also necessary to complete this classical culture, both on account of the manner in which the greatest Roman writers were stimulated and formed by the example and teaching of their Grecian predecessors, and also, on account of the direct operation of the Greek writers upon modern thinkers and writers, ever since the revival of the study of Greek literature in the fifteenth century. In philosophy the

Roman works do little more than transmit to us the influence of Greek speculations: in history, Herodotus and Thucydides occupy a greater place in the thoughts of cultivated men than any Roman historians; and even in poetry, although the tradition of the Latin forms and style of composition has been more extensive and continual than of the Greek, the Greek classical writers have, in later times, been more diligently studied and more warmly admired than the Roman poets. No one can be considered as furnished with the knowledge, tastes, and sympathies which connect the successive generations of liberally educated men, who is not familiar with Homer and the Greek tragedians, as well as with Virgil, Horace, and Ovid. These two great families of writers, the Greek and the Roman classics, form the intellectual ancestors of all the cultivated minds of modern times, and we must be well acquainted with their language, their thoughts, their forms of composition, their beauties, in order that we may have our share in that inheritance by which men belong to the intellectual aristocracy of mankind. The study of these title-deeds and archives of the culture of our race must be a permanent portion of the best education of men, so long as the tradition of such culture is preserved upon the face of the earth.

But though the classical writers are to be looked upon mainly as permanent studies, in their educational office, they are also the subjects of progressive studies in every age, and especially in ages of great intellectual activity. The full understanding of these writers implies views of the structure and relations of language, of the principles and significance of philosophy, of the origin and progress of states, which views each age, borrowing much from its predecessors, molds in some degree for itself. Ancient philology, philosophy, and history are the subjects of progressive speculations. Those persons in our own time, for instance, who have most diligently studied these subjects, have been led to views

which have in them a considerable share of novelty, and men's minds are still employed in eager endeavours to obtain a more complete and profound insight into the causes on which philological and philosophical and historical progress depend. The origin, growth, revolutions, and decline of languages, systems, and states, are now, as they have almost always been, matters full of interest for the classical student. A classical education would not be the highest education if it did not impart to the student a share in this interest—if it did not give him some acquaintance with such speculations as they are carried on in his own time, and enable his mind to go along with them. To carry on such speculations is, for classical scholars, the business of life: but in this, for the same reason as in other departments of knowledge, this business ought to be begun in the educational period of life. Our education is limited and incomplete if it does not lead our students into the portal at least of this great edifice, on which thoughtful and learned men are constantly labouring. Classical learning, in order to be a worthy part of a liberal education, must include progressive as well as permanent studies.

Having thus shown that classical, as well as mathematical educational studies are partly of a permanent and partly of a progressive kind, I may make some remarks on classical, of a similar tendency to some of those which I have made respecting mathematical, studies.

In the first place, it is important to keep the two kinds, the permanent and the progressive studies, distinct; and especially, not to allow the latter to supersede the former, or to impair the attention given to them. The permanent classical studies, which give a thorough acquaintance with the Greek and Latin languages, and a familiarity with the best classical writers, are indispensable, both as cardinal parts of a liberal education and as necessary to any intelligent participation in the progress of speculations concerning the language, philosophy, or history of the Greeks and Romans. No secondhand knowledge of the philological criticism, philosophical doctrines, and political events of these nations, can at all compensate, as a branch of education, for the lack of a knowledge of the original authors in the original languages. If a person does not read and understand the Greek and Latin poets, historians, and philosophers, he cannot be deemed to have received a liberal education, though he may be ever so well acquainted with the discussions which have taken place in modern times respecting the antiquities and histories of those nations, or the peculiarities and merits of their writers. To be liberally educated, a man must have acquired knowledge of the languages so that it is a solid and permanent possession, as the actual knowledge of a language is: and he must have familiarized himself with the classical writings so that they have imbued and molded his mind, as the literature with which we are familiar in youth does. If he has not done this, it is to no purpose, as constituting a really good education, that he reads translations and criticisms and dissertations. By such kinds of study he may know as much about the Greek and Roman writers as a man, by the study of peerage books, may know much about the aristocracy of his own country; but he cannot by such a study imbibe that spirit of classical literature which is, as we have said, the inheritance of the intellectual aristocracy of the world.

I remark, in the next place, that it is not enough for our purpose to study the literature of one of the two languages. I have already given reasons why the cultivation of the Latin language and literature is not sufficient, except the study of Greek be added to it. Still less is the study of Greek sufficient for the classical part of a good education, if the Latin language and literature be neglected, or slightly attended to. For however admirable may be the Greek models, and however superior in many respects to the Latin writers, Latin literature has, after all, exercised a far larger sway

over the civilized and literary world than Greek. Greek may be the finer study, but Latin is the more necessary accomplishment. For many centuries, in modern times, Greek was comparatively little known; and during those centuries the Latin writers operated powerfully in the literary and intellectual culture of men's minds. Nor has this tradition of Roman influence ever ceased or been interrupted. Latin models, trains of thought as expressed by Latin writers; Latin as a language with which all educated persons are familiar, are far more generally and promptly operative among cultivated men than Greek literature is. To neglect Latin, and to concentrate our classical study upon the Greek writers, would be to put ourselves out of sympathy with the literary world of all past ages, and, in a great degree, of our own also. And if this were done out of an ardent admiration for the Greek language and nation, as compared with the Latin, it would not the less be a mistake in education; for education has it for its business, not merely to find something which we can admire, and to dwell upon that, but to place before us objects which cultivated men in all ages have admired and dwelt upon, and thus to connect our minds with theirs. To turn from Latin and to confine our studies to Greek, on such grounds, would be to confound progressive with permanent classical study; it would be to let the assumed progress of literary taste in the present day break off the tradition of literary sympathy with past generations. It would be, in classical studies, the same kind of error as the substitution of analytic for geometric methods in mathematics, of which we have already explained the ruinous effect upon education.

It may perhaps be said by some that a knowledge of the Latin and Greek languages is not necessary in order that we may share in the influences which the thoughts and writings of the classical authors have exercised upon succeeding ages, since we may become acquainted with these authors by means of translations. So far as such authors are intelligible, it may be said, their meaning may be expressed in our own language; and in fact, all the principal classical authors have been translated into modern languages, and may thus be studied without the labour of mastering the original tongues. This may be said; nor do I deny that a certain portion of classical culture may be thus received; but such culture must be very imperfect. For all translations must be very defective in conveying the impression of the original, as everyone who has read an original work, and a translation of it, must be aware. In poetry, the defect is immense. We have in our literature nothing closely resembling or equivalent to the Greek and Roman forms of composition, and the finest beauties of poetry consist in expressions and touches which cannot be transferred from one language to another. Our possession of a foreign language—and that language one so different in its structure from our own, and from modern languages in general, as Greek and Latin are—gives a peculiar aspect and colour to all that we apprehend through such a medium. The criticism which is applicable to the original work must bear quite as much upon the language as upon the matter, and must necessarily lose its significance if we have before us only a translation. In short, knowledge acquired by translations can hardly be considered as education, in any proper sense of the word. It evokes none of those peculiar powers by which the mind deals with language. When, however, we possess the Greek and Latin languages, and are already familiar with the best classical authors, it is by no means clear that we may not usefully extend our acquaintance with Greek and Latin literature by means of translations; for most students will read English with more facility and rapidity than Greek or Latin; and he who possesses the languages will constantly be led to compare the translation with the original, and thus will become

acquainted with the spirit and form of the work as well as with its substance and meaning. Translations of Greek and Latin authors have undoubtedly been very effective in extending a knowledge of classical literature, even among classically educated men. The discussions and comparisons to which the translations have given rise have made the originals better known; and by means of such translations, the classical authors have promoted the culture of many persons who could not read the originals. Thus such translations have extended the range of the sympathies by which classical studies bind men together.

It might at first appear as if the existence of translations of classical authors would make it difficult to ascertain whether the student who is required, as a part of his education, to translate or *construe,* as it is called, such authors, does so from his knowledge of the language, or from his acquaintance with the translation. But all classical teachers are aware that this is, in reality, no difficulty at all. As we said before, with regard to examinations in geometry, a question or two with reference to the grammatical construction of a passage is quite sufficient to enable the teacher to decide whether the learner performs his task by rote or with intelligence. Moreover the student may be required himself to write or speak in the language, and will then make it evident whether he possesses the language or not. With regard to the Latin language, such exercises have always been part of the usual classical discipline, and are a requisite part of the education which is to connect a man with the literary community of past and present times.

With regard to the fidelity and accuracy with which translations convey the meaning of the original, each translation will of course have the tinge of its own period in the national literature to which it belongs, but it is not likely that much progress will be made from age to age in better understanding the sense of the ancient authors. Scholars in all periods, at least since the

419

revival of literature, have well understood the Greek and Latin languages, and what the best authors have written in those languages. It is not likely that we have, in modern times, anyone who knows Latin better than Erasmus did, or Greek better than Bentley. Still, new translations of ancient authors may be made useful works, as parts of progressive classical studies. They may convey the sense in phrases suited to our modern apprehension, and they may have appended to them notes and comments by which the newest views of philologers, antiquaries, and historians may be exhibited to the modern reader. This advantage of new translations belongs especially to works relating to philosophy; for the language of philosophy, to be generally intelligible, must be modified from age to age, more than that of poetry or history, as new philosophical views succeed each other in our own nation. And the continued study of the ancient philosophers by modern philosophical scholars may really bring to view much more clearly their meaning and import than to other readers, however well versed in the general significations of words, it has before appeared. And thus translations of the philosophical works of Plato, and of Aristotle, especially if philosophical and critical comments be annexed, may be a most effective and instructive mode of showing to the world the progress that our classical scholars have recently made in the study of the Greek philosophy. Such translations have accordingly appeared in recent times by eminent philosophers and scholars in Germany and in France. I am not aware that anything of the same kind has been attempted by our English scholars. And yet I cannot imagine any boon which they could confer upon the world, at the present time, which would be more interesting and instructive than one of this kind: a translation, for instance, with illustrative comments, of the *Republic* of Plato, or the *Ethics* of Aristotle. Such translations, so executed as to convey the meaning and force of the philosophi-

cal reasoning to the English reader, would be a worthy evidence of the philosophical scholarship of our times and a means of extending its beneficial influence to a wider circle than that of mere scholars, or even of the present generation.

Translations or editions of classical authors, accompanied with commentaries of a philological, philosophical, antiquarian, or historical character, are natural and obvious means of laying before the literary world the progressive speculations of classical scholars. But such speculations appear in other forms also, as dissertations, controversial writings, and the like; and in works of a more independent form, as histories of ancient states and races, customs and opinions. Among such works, whether commentatorial or independent, we may reckon many as capital works; such as the works of Sigonius on Roman, and Meursius on Greek antiquities; of Scaliger on chronology, and Cluverius on geography. And a fully-instructed classical scholar will be acquainted with the works of such authors, as a fully-instructed mathematician will be acquainted with the works of Archimedes and Euler. In classics, however, still more than in mathematics, there is a tendency to study the elementary books of recent writers, founded, it may be, at second or third hand, upon the labours of great men, rather than the works of the great men themselves. But yet in classics, as in mathematics, for the most part, the capital works—those which have made each its epoch in the study of ancient literature—are the most instructive and striking books which can be read; and compilations, which are supposed to include all that great scholars have established with regard to antiquity, do really impart only a vague, dim, and incomplete knowledge, compared with that which arises from the habit of consulting the great original works of celebrated philologers, antiquaries, and historians. These capital works bearing upon classical literature belong to various periods, and are of various extent: Bentley's *Dissertation on the Epistles of Phalaris;* Potter's *Greek Antiquities;* Porson's Preface to his edition of the Hecuba; Wolf's Preface to Homer; and the like. Several have been produced in our own time: thus, Müller's *History of the Dorians,* Boeckh's *Public Economy of Athens,* Niebuhr's *History of Rome,* have recently been main subjects of attention of the classical students of this country; and these may be taken as exhibiting the leading points in the progressive classical studies of the modern world.

We may say with regard to classical, as we have said with regard to mathematical studies, that a system which, consisting in private teaching, substitutes some unpublished views of the teachers respecting the subjects taught, for the study of the capital published works on those subjects, is likely to deprave our education by bringing before the student knowledge which has only a conventional value, acknowledged in a certain circle, in the place of the works which the whole literary world admires; and by substituting for a participation, in the general recognition of excellence, a complacency in some supposed peculiar superiority of criticism.

The knowledge of the Latin language which belongs to a liberal education when complete, includes not only the power of translating Latin into English, but also the power of writing Latin. The latter faculty is not, indeed, so essential a part of a good education as the former; for a student may feel the force of the language, and admire the beauties of the classical writers, without being himself able to write correct Latin with facility, or to write good Latin at all. Writing Latin, as well as translating Latin, must be practiced in order that the student may write the language correctly and well. The faculty, if formed, must be formed by exercise especially directed to that end and such exercise is not at present an indispensable part of a liberal education. Some generations back, the faculty of writing and speaking Latin was indispensable to a liberally educated man; for Latin was

the universal vehicle of intercourse, both written and oral, among liberally educated men of different nations.

And this brings to view another way, in addition to those already mentioned, in which the study of the Latin language connects us with the general course of European civilization. For Latin was, for all literary purposes, as much the language of all Europe during the middle ages as it was of Rome at the time of Augustus. Divines, jurists, philosophers, historians, statesmen, critics, commentators, used no other language until modern times: and though the style of the writers of the middle ages is so inferior to that of the classical times that it can no longer supply us with models, the train of thought is often full of interest and value. The study of the writers of the middle ages is not to be spoken of as a part of our permanent classical studies. But these writers offer very important subjects of study to those who in various ways pursue their researches beyond the boundary of our permanent studies.

The general practice of writing Latin, which gave rise to such works as I have just referred to, no longer prevails. Nor is the Latin language now the means of intercourse between strangers. So far as Englishmen are concerned, the wide difference which has been established between their pronunciation of Latin and that of all other nations, has made it difficult to use the language for such purposes, even in cases of necessity. The means at present employed for social and literary communication among persons of different nations are modern languages; and these are learned with a view of speaking and writing them so as to answer the purposes of such intercourse; but Latin is no longer learned with a view of its answering such purposes. To write Latin is now no longer an art of social intercourse, but a literary exercise. It is an accomplishment, however, which very naturally grows out of and follows upon an intimate acquaintance with the best Latin authors. A student who is familiar with the most elegant and expressive phrases which the Roman writers have employed upon various subjects, will probably be able to find combinations of them by which he may express his own meaning, or that of English authors, passages of whom he may wish to clothe in a Latin dress. In this way, writing in Latin or translating into Latin, is both a test and a discipline of Latin scholarship. And the art has held this place during every age of the civilized European world. To appreciate and sympathize with the difficulties and triumphs of such a task is one of the characters of a person who has imbibed the traditional spirit of European education; and the practice of writing Latin, extended so far as is requisite for this purpose, is one of the permanent portions of a liberal English education.

The writing of Latin verse has long been one of the usual portions of a classical education in England, especially as conducted at the great classical schools which have flourished among us for so many generations. This practice is in some measure recommended by the same reasons as the writing of prose Latin. A student will have his attention sharpened, with regard to the turns of poetical expression and the rules of versification of the Latin poets, when he makes it his habitual business to imitate them; and he will thus become more familiar with their beauties, at least with those which he especially makes his model. It has often happened among Englishmen that the habit of writing Latin verse has been retained through all the distractions and occupations of a life of active business and elevated office, and has thus kept alive the sympathy in classical literature which belongs to a liberal English education. Where the student's other pursuits allow sufficient time for the cultivation of this accomplishment, it adds much to the completeness and elegance of his Latin scholarship, especially if his mind have an aptitude for such poetical exercises. But on the other hand, it is to be recollected that the accomplishment of writing Latin verse with

a considerable degree of elegance does not necessarily or universally imply the faculty of writing correct Latin prose, or even of translating Latin into English correctly. A facility and skill in writing Latin verse are acquired by a special practice in that employment, and this practice does not discipline the student effectually in a general knowledge of the language. In short, a person may write Latin verses well and yet be a very indifferent Latin scholar— unacquainted with Latin literature in general, and liable to gross mistakes in translating Latin authors. This being the case, it is evident that the writing of Latin verse ought to come after the interpretation of Latin authors and the writing of Latin prose, in the order of classical study. After a due degree of proficiency in the latter two branches of scholarship has been secured, the first may be very fitly cultivated as a supplementary grace. But to make the writing of Latin verse a primary part of classical culture, and to exercise the student abundantly in this, while the writing of Latin prose, and even the intelligence of the Latin language itself, are comparatively neglected, is to pervert this part of education. So cultivated, the Latin language no longer answers those purposes which we have assigned to it, as an element of a liberal education. So cultivated, the Latin language is far from holding its proper place as a part of the education of Englishmen.

Some of the same reasons which exist for practicing the writing of Latin prose exist also for writing Greek prose, or for translating passages of English or Latin into Greek. Such a practice fixes the attention upon the forms of expression used by Greek authors and makes students familiar with those passages which they make their models. But, on the other hand, there is not the same reason for acquiring a familiar use of Greek as there is of Latin, for Greek is not, and never has been, a language of familiar use among scholars and men of letters. The writing of Greek is, in a far greater degree than the writing of Latin, a mere literary exercise, a trial of skill like the imitation of the style of a standard author in our own language. As writing Latin verse ought not much to occupy the student's time, until a skill in writing Latin prose is secured, still less ought the writing of Greek prose to hold a leading place in the classical student's employments. This exercise may perhaps come with advantage at an advanced period of the progress of a scholar of eminent aptitude, but it cannot be considered as at all essential to the character, even of a good Greek scholar. Many, perhaps most, of the more distinguished Greek scholars who have existed, would probably have failed in an attempt to write Greek well. It is possible that practice directed to this special point may enable young students at the present day to perform such tasks with surprising correctness and ingenuity; but such practice can hardly form a large part of the general course of classical teaching, without leading to losses which far over-balance this gain. It is almost inevitable that in such a course of instruction the far more valuable object of attaining a real and complete acquaintance with all the best classical authors must be abandoned, as well as the possession of an easy and correct Latin style; for if the possession of a Greek style be aimed at, it must almost inevitably become the student's main object, in consequence of the great attention which it will require.

We may make nearly the same remarks with regard to composition in Greek verse, which we have made respecting composition in Greek prose. It is very likely that an accomplished Greek scholar may, by practice, pursued through a love of the language, and of its best models of excellence, acquire a habit of successfully imitating those models, and especially, some one particular author, or class of authors. He may, for instance, succeed in expressing the thoughts of modern dramatic writers in an imitation of the language of the Greek tragedians. The performances of some modern scholars have shown that an extraordinary degree of success is attainable in such exercises. But it does not appear judicious to make such performances an essential part of Greek scholarship, or even a necessary test of an accomplished Greek scholar. If they are so treated, they are likely to draw to them a disproportioned amount of the student's time and attention, and however completely such an accomplishment may be acquired, it does not imply any profound or extensive acquaintance with Greek authors in general. We may even add that this accomplishment may be pursued in such a manner as to direct the student's labours from good Greek authors—when, for instance, the faculty is cultivated by studying rules and collections of phrases made for this purpose, or by imitating previous imitations which we conceive to be remarkably successful. Such modes of classical study are very unworthy of being parts of a liberal education.

Without pretending to define with any exactness the amount of attention which may advantageously be given by the classical student to those higher classical accomplishments—Greek prose and Latin and Greek verse composition—we may say, in general, that they are the higher accomplishments, and not the essential instruction of the scholar. A person may be educated in the highest degree without possessing these, for no man can possess all accomplishments. And to sacrifice to these that which is essential to a good education—an exact and extensive acquaintance with the classical authors in their original languages—is to deprive our education of real meaning and value. It is to sacrifice the substances of a good classical education to a very shallow semblance of superiority; for though a scholar who has been practiced in these accomplishments may seem, to an ignorant spectator, to be superior to the great scholars of former times who did not possess them, anyone really acquainted with the study of languages knows that this seeming is altogether illusory. The performance of such exercises may show that the modern scholars can do what the good scholars of former times could not do; but it does not show that he can do what they could do; or that he knows what they knew. The substitution of such exercises for general scholarship is the corruption of classical education; as it would be the corruption of gymnastics to substitute some practiced feat of agility for a general discipline of wind and limb.

I have stated Latin to be a more important element of a liberal education than Greek. To this it may be objected that the Greek literature is of a higher character of excellence than the Roman—that the minds of the Greeks were more thoughtful, more acute, more refined, more poetical; and that the Romans, in their literature, were little more than imitators of the Greeks. To this we should reply, that the peculiar power and character of the Grecian intellect and genius were, indeed, among the principal reasons which made the literary productions of the Greeks the standards of excellence, and the subjects of study for all succeeding ages; and that Latin literature very probably owes much of the notice it has drawn, and the influence it has exercised, to the merits which the Romans derived from their Greek masters. And this superior beauty and originality of the Greek writers is a very sufficient reason why any scholar may prefer them as the subjects of his own private study, and give more attention to them than he would otherwise have done. But this relative superiority does not deprive the Latin literature of its positive place in a liberal education; nor destroy the force of the reasons which render a sound knowledge of the Latin language, and a familiarity with the best Latin authors, necessary attainments of a well-educated man. The extended and more profound study of the Greek writers which their greater beauty and originality may very naturally procure

them is something beyond the common course of education. It is rather a result of individual taste than a rule for general culture; rather a part of the studies of the man, than of the business of education. It is absolutely necessary in education to give so much time and attention to the Latin language that we cannot give to Greek a greater amount of these, in proportion to its greater merits as estimated by its admirers. And to preserve this proportion by diminishing the amount of time and attention given to the Latin is to do homage to Grecian genius by making the most important part of our classical education worthless.

The value of permanent studies

Perhaps some persons may object in general to our assigning so prominent a place in a liberal education to what we have called permanent studies: that is, to certain fixed specimens of solid reasoning and models of literary excellence. They may say that the mind thus bound to certain predetermined subjects will become narrow and servile—that study, thus bestowed by successive generations on subjects authoritatively fixed, leads to a stationary and commentatorial literature, like that of the commentators on Aristotle in the middle ages—that the essence of mental activity consists in advancing from point to point, and not in clinging blindly to established points—that the study of fixed subjects pursued in a prescribed manner can do no more than fill the mind with certain conventional forms, and can produce no real education.

This, and much more of the same kind, may be said; and the reply to such remarks is so important in its bearing upon the subject of education, that in stating it, I would beg the reader's especial attention. I reply then, that by the importance which we assign to permanent studies, we do not make our education stationary and unprogressive, because, along with these studies, we recommend also progressive studies, in which the subjects taught are brought up to their most recent condition; and the books on which our students are employed, are the capital works which mark the most recent epoch in each branch of literature and science. But in order to prepare the student for the reading and understanding of such works, there is a necessity for permanent studies, by which the habits of following scientific reasonings and interpreting classical writings, may be formed and fixed. The progress of the human mind is, undoubtedly, one of the main objects of education; and the progress of the individual mind, as a participator in the faculties and fortunes of the mind of man in general: but in order to present and future progress, an acquaintance with the past is requisite. In order that we may share in what men are doing in the world of intellect, we must share in what they have done. In order that we may walk onward, we must feel the ground solid under our feet. Considered with reference to mental progress, a large portion of education is preparatory only; but it is an indispensable preparation. Any attempt to put aside this permanent preparatory portion of education would make our education worthless. It would make our real progress impossible. The past alone can make the present and the future intelligible. If we reject the discipline of our permanent studies, we may indeed still learn to use the phrases in which men express the recent progress of science or literature, and may flatter ourselves that we share in the superiority which such a progress bestows; but, in reality, such phrases have for us no real meaning. They are mere empty forms of language. The charge of filling the mind with conventional forms, void of real value and efficacy, lies far more truly against those who pretend to teach new truths to persons incapable of understanding them through their want of ordinary culture than to those who dwell long upon those parts of human science and literature which have, in all ages, been found to be the most effective means of cultivating the intellect and the taste.

For in fact (and this brings us to some of the other forms in which the objection is put), the mind is not narrowed or made servile by dwelling long upon models of real excellence, whether literary or intellectual. Works which have acquired a sway over men's minds and retained it for ages by their truth, by their fidelity to the deepest and most universal parts of men's nature—such works may continue to occupy the time and thoughts of our students without giving ground for any fear that their minds will thereby become inert, or frivolous, or formal. We are to recollect that, when we insist upon permanent studies, we do not mean by such studies any merely conventional selection of books or subjects. We take our selection from the universal voice of civilized man. The objects on which we permanently dwell are Homer, Aeschylus, Sophocles, Herodotus, Thucydides, Demosthenes, Terence, Virgil, Horace, Cicero, Livy, Tacitus. We shall hardly be told that men's minds will become servile and narrow by dwelling upon the works of these writers until they fully understand them.

Even when such authors are studied and pondered over with the help of commentators and notators, it does not appear likely that any intellectual harm will arise from such a commentatorial literature, if the commentator be really read in subordination to the author, which we require and assume. And in the same manner with regard to mathematical subjects: we need not be afraid that men's minds should become inert or narrow by dwelling upon the books of Euclid, or Archimedes, or Newton, until they full understand them; and if, for this purpose, they find some comments and explanations necessary, it would be very foolish to take alarm at the sound of the word "commentator." We know that in these authors there is an irresistible reasoning, leading to solid truth, which may be understood by reasoning men, and which, being understood, must be valued as truth. If the commentator helps us then to understand the reasoning and to perceive the truth, he renders us a good service. He puts us in possession of some of the indestructible intellectual possessions of our race, and thus aids us in our purpose of feeling our participation in the universal reason of mankind, and in its results. If in doing this we dwell long upon the subject, it is not that we are thus acquiring stationary habits of mind; it is that we are learning that without which we must be forever stationary. It may be that in those abstruse studies we advance slowly to the full apprehension of the cardinal truths there exhibited; but until we have apprehended them, we cannot really understand anything which lies beyond them. If we are so slow as to need a long time, or the aid of commentators, in order to understand the ancient reasonings, we cannot make ourselves quick by passing them by, not understood. If we cannot understand that which wise and thoughtful men have written and have understood in the ages which have preceded us, we have not unfolded in us that intellectual element, in virtue of which men so reasoned. Our reason is not educed; we are, in that respect, uneducated.

And when the study of works of reasoning by the aid of commentators is likened to the study of Aristotle in the middle ages, we are to recollect that, in those periods, the works of Aristotle were studied not as reasoning, but as authority. The commentators were employed in interpreting his dogmas, not in explaining his arguments. Aristotle himself is remarkable for the want of real mathematical insight in the mathematical illustrations which he has introduced; and when the sway of that which passed for his philosophy was overthrown, the main instrument in the reform was that mathematical education of man which we are here recommending, and which can only be carried on by the study of mathematical works occupying a perma-

nent place in education on account of their real truth and excellence.

We have already mentioned the fear which, in speaking of education, men sometimes express: that fixed subjects of educational study should become an exercise for the memory, rather than for the intellect—the forms of speech, which seem to contain the knowledge required, being, in fact, retained by rote, and uttered with no real intelligence. We have stated that this fear is one with very little foundation, since one or two very simple questions will at once ascertain whether the student really understands the language which he pretends to translate, or the reasoning which he pretends to give. We may add that if in such employments, especially with slow intellects, memory and repeated attention come in for a share of the student's success in performing his task, we are not on that account to suppose that reason is left uncultivated. The truth is, that in most persons it is only by exertions of memory and attention that reason can be cultivated. To overcome the difficulties of a long train of mathematical reasoning is one of the best ways of cultivating reason; but to do this is, with most persons, a matter of time and thought, and of memory also; for while the student is attending to one part of the chain, he loses, for the moment, his clear apprehension of the other, and only bears it in mind as what he had before proved. But by successive efforts of this kind, the whole becomes clear, and reason acquires the power of grasping the whole at once. And thus reason is educated by means of the memory. And the same is the case, not infrequently, with the interpretation of difficult passages in ancient authors. Such interpretations, accepted at first upon authority, and retained in the memory, are afterward made more fully intelligible by similar examples, until at last they are seen to belong to the genius of the language. Such exercises of memory and attention are the necessary means of intellectual culture. It is, no doubt, possible that the comment or the interpretation may be lodged in the memory without producing any effect upon reason; and in this case, it is an acquisition of small value. But then in this case it is also possible that the mind may be one to which it is difficult to impart anything much more valuable. Reason may be so inert and obscure in its operations that the education of that faculty cannot proceed very prosperously by any process. The exercise of the memory may lead to the best development of the mental faculties which their native constitution will permit. The case in which it is most likely that the employment of the memory will lead to no real education of the mental faculties is when the memory is employed principally not upon old, but upon new points of literature and science: for, in such a case, the traditional knowledge which alone can make the new advances fully intelligible being wanting, the phrases which express the novel views, and the processes which are supposed to replace the ancient demonstrations, will really be mere formalities—extraneous matters contained in the memory as a repository, but not assimilated by mental operations and converted into intellectual nutriment.

The opposition between information merely accumulated in the memory by labour, on the one side; and acts of understanding and reasoning on the other, is often dwelt upon as very important in directing the conduct of education; and no doubt is so. But as we have seen, the relation of these operations is misconceived if it is conceived as a mere contrast, for the labour of attention and the exercise of memory are the means by which we form active habits of reasoning and expressing reasons. Juvenile views of education are especially apt to fasten upon and to exaggerate this contrast. Schoolboys and very young students, and those of them especially who are most impatient of steady thought and continued labour, find an easy gratification of their self-complacency in identifying all intellectual labour with the want of originality and vivacity of mind. It is their practice to affix terms of grotesque contempt to the mental habits which they thus wish to depreciate: and some of these terms are sometimes used indiscriminately for all exercise of the memory, whether in its necessary educational functions, or in that forced preparation for examinations which is, as we shall see, a pernicious vice in educational systems. For instance, the former as well as the latter is sometimes, by thoughtless people, called *cramming*. Such terms, once put in circulation, exercise an almost unbounded sway over the young men's minds, and deprive them of the use of reason on these subjects. The contemptuous phrases so used seem to remove at once all intellectual dignity and value from the subject of such satire, in the eyes of the young satirist. We may pass by this schoolboy trick as too shallow to cause any confusion. But that it can succeed even with boys shows how necessary it is to estimate duly the office of labour, industry, and attention, in the business of education.

Even with men, as well as with schoolboys, contempt and ridicule, directed toward one or another part of the methods of education, may interfere with a sound judgment on the subject. The methods of education which have been in use through all ages have had their technical terms, rules, and customs. All methods which are to be applied to great numbers of learners by ordinary teachers, must have such technicalities. But all technicalities, detached from their use and meaning, are easily made objects of ridicule and contempt. The technicalities of education, which are rendered familiar to the boy before he can understand their purpose, may easily provoke a smile in the man, especially if in a more advanced season of life he finds that his understanding retains its hold of the subject in other ways than by means of these technicalities. Hence one man speaks with ridicule of the rules of arithmetic as commonly given: for instance, the rule of three inverse, the rule of five, alligation, barter, and the like. Another laughs at the technicalities of the common grammars: gerunds in *di, do,* and *dum;* supines in *um,* and *u;* deponent and impersonal verbs; and so on. We are not at all concerned to maintain that these are essential or important parts of education; but that which it is necessary for us to recollect is, that some *such* technicalities as these are essential parts of every general method of education—that such technicalities are not at all necessarily useless because they do not explain themselves, or because they depend upon views which are fanciful, or even false—and that in the course of education, boys must often learn and apply technical phrases and technical rules, before they can understand them. It usually happens that boys who are made to learn and apply rules begin to see the meaning of the rules, when their habits of thought are further unfolded; and though this may lead their friends or themselves to suppose that the rules at first were of no value to them, this supposition would be a great mistake. Boys can easily learn to apply rules before they can easily learn to understand them, and are likely to understand them the better from being already familiar with the mode in which they are applied. The memory may be brought into extensive action before the understanding can, and may be made to assist powerfully in unfolding the understanding by supplying it with materials to operate upon. If no boy was allowed to learn anything of which he did not, at the time, understand the reason, no general system of teaching could be applied; the progress of learners must be slow and irregular; and after all, there is no ground to believe that boys so taught would understand their rules better than those who begin by applying, and end by understanding the reasons of them. For it can admit of no doubt that to understand the rules and their reasons *at a subsequent period* is a necessary portion of the system of education to which they belong. To make the student understand fully both the

rules of arithmetic and grammar, and their reasons, is an important step in that higher education which succeeds the education of the schoolboy. But on this ground, no valid argument against any particular form of such rules can be drawn from the ridicule to which they are subject, as being unintelligible to the boys who use them.

Nor is it, as we have said, any sufficient condemnation of such rules and technical expressions, that they are founded on fanciful or even false opinions. It may be true that supines are mere nouns, that deponents are really passive verbs, and the like; yet no disadvantage arises from the use of such terms as *supines* and *deponents* to mark those cases. Or rather, it would be a great disadvantage that the learner should not know the meaning of such terms so as to be able to understand those grammatical discussions in which they are employed. It may be that many of the rules given in the common books of arithmetic are arbitrary and superfluous, and that they might all be reduced, with advantage, to a smaller number. As they are given they serve at least to classify and multiply examples of numerical operations, and are themselves multiplied examples of the simpler and more comprehensive principles to which the student is afterward to be led, when his mind is matured and prepared for dealing with such principles. The boy learns rules as rules, which he can do easily and well; and the youth learns reasons and principles all the more easily, because the process of learning rules has preceded. But these considerations belong rather to the mode of teaching. . . .

It may be said that, by thus defending and commending the use of the rules and technicalities belonging to the old methods of teaching, we do not adequately appreciate the great recent improvements in education: the new views of grammar and of the relations of language, and of the foundations and reasons of arithmetic, algebra, and geometry—and the simplicity and clearness which have been introduced into the teaching of these subjects. To this I reply that the new views of the fundamental principles, both of philology and of mathematics which have recently been published, have been, as I believe, very efficacious in promoting a better understanding of those subjects; but that they have not produced this effect merely in virtue of their being better views, superseding worse, but in virtue of their being the results of the activity of thought and research of the teachers. For though technical phrases and rules and maxims may be very useful instruments of education before they are fully understood by the learners, they cannot be used with any great efficacy for such purposes, except they are understood by the *teachers:* and the new views of recent speculators, regarding language and antiquities, geometry and algebra, have been the results of their endeavours to ascertain fully the significance, truth, and foundations of the doctrines which the traditional forms of classical and mathematical literature take for granted. Precisely because the new doctrines are expressions of advances toward clear insight and full conviction in the minds of the teachers, they are better doctrines *for them,* and enable them to teach better, than without such an intellectual movement going on among them they could have done. Such a mental advance will make their instructions both more rationally sound and more zealous and persevering than they would otherwise be. I believe it will be found that this is the source of any greater effectiveness of modern systems of teaching classics and mathematics which may have occurred, rather than any virtue inherent in the new methods themselves. When the expressions which convey the new views have come, in their turn, to be familiar technicalities, dimly understood; and when the new methods are applied by a number of teachers, of ordinary zeal and intelligence, to learners of all variable degrees of capacity, it is probable that the average success of the new methods will not be much greater than that of the old ones; and certainly it does not appear likely that the new methods will produce better scholars and better mathematicians, either in the most eminent cases or on the average, than the old methods produced. There appears to be no disadvantage, but rather a considerable means of instruction, in having our education consist of ancient methods, which though sound and good, may be simplified, extended, and clothed in a deeper significance by newer methods which the teacher himself suggests. The new method comes as a commentary upon the old, and gives to the education so conducted the combined advantages of the stability of a fixed system and the vivacity of a present reform.

It is, therefore, with no want of admiration for the subtlety and comprehensiveness of intellect which has been shown in many recent views of algebra and geometry, that I recommend our adhering to the ancient methods of treating such subjects, so far as the general purposes of a liberal education are concerned. Such views are truly admirable as corrections and extensions, or it may be as the antithesis of the established and traditional modes of treating the subjects; but if they were to become themselves established and traditional, they would be (as I have already endeavoured to show) far less effective in the discipline of the reason than the older methods, besides depriving us of the continuity of that intellectual tradition which I have already spoken of as one of the great ends of mathematical teaching in the course of a liberal education. I recommend the rejection, in our ordinary educational system, of the many novelties in notation and expression which have recently appeared in our Cambridge mathematical works; but I admire the mathematical talents of those who have produced these works; and I think that such speculations are both very remarkable manifestations of mathematical skill and thought and very fit subjects of attention for our mathematical students, where they reach the higher stages of their progress.

There is one leading question, in such an education as we are contemplating, on which I have already spoken, but on which it may not be useless to add a few words— I mean, the question whether both mathematical and classical instruction should be considered necessary in the case of every student. It is sometimes said that we shall educate men better, by encouraging in each that study for which he has talent and inclination—not tormenting the man of classical taste with fruitless lessons of algebra, or the man of mathematical intellect with obscure passages of Greek. It is said, sometimes, that by such a genial education alone, do we really *educate* the man or *bring out* his genius—that the seeming of mathematical prowess, or of classical learning which we wring by force from ungenial and unwilling minds is of no value, and is no real culture. But to this we reply, that if men come really to understand Greek or geometry, there is then, in each study, a real intellectual culture, however unwillingly it may have been entered upon. There can be no culture without some labour and effort; to some persons, all labour and effort are unwelcome; and such persons cannot be educated at all without putting some constraint upon their inclinations. No education can be considered as liberal which does not cultivate both the faculty of reason and the faculty of language, one of which is cultivated by the study of mathematics, and the other by the study of classics. To allow the student to omit one of these is to leave him half educated. If a person cannot receive such culture, he remains, in the one case, irrational, in the other illiterate, and cannot be held up as a liberally educated person. To allow a person to follow one of these lines of study, to the entire neglect of the

other, is not to educate him. It may draw out his special personal propensities, but it does not draw out his general human faculties of reason and language. The object of a liberal education is not to make men eminently learned or profound in some one department, but to educe all the faculties by which man shares in the highest thoughts and feelings of his species. It is to make men truly men, rather than to make them men of genius, which no education can make them.

But even with regard to men of genius, it is not true that they have generally been men of one kind of cultivation only, or capable only of one kind of intellectual excellence. The case has been quite the reverse. During the middle ages, and down to the last century, the greatest mathematicians were almost invariably good classical scholars; and good scholars were almost invariably well acquainted with mathematical literature, and often very fond of it. And this connection, in the main, has continued to our own day, so far as the mathematics and classics belonging to a liberal education are concerned. Not to speak of living persons whose career at Cambridge might be adduced to prove this, the greatest Greek scholar of the last generation, Porson, was fond of algebra and was a proficient in it— and if we run over the highest wranglers of the last sixty years, we find at every period, men known to be well versed in classical literature, as Otter, Brinkley, Outram, Raincock, Wrangham, Palmer, T. Jackson, R. Grant, and many others.

Indeed, there can be no doubt but that the clearness of mind and vigour of character which make a man eminent in one line of study will also enable him to master the elementary difficulties of another subject, if it is fairly brought before him as something which must be done; although, if it be presented to him as a matter of choice whether he will make the attempt, caprice, fastidiousness, and the pleasure of doing what he can already do easily and well may make him turn with repugnance from a subject in which he has not learned to feel any interest.

To which we may add, that to be able to command the attention and direct the mental powers so as to master a subject which is not particularly attractive to us, is a very valuable result of mental discipline. Whatever acuteness or sagacity a man may have on a special subject, if he be so helpless or so fastidious that he cannot employ his thoughts to any purpose or any other subject, we cannot consider him as a well-cultured person; nor ought we to frame our education so as to give to men such an intellectual character.

We come back therefore to the doctrine stated sometime ago, that mathematical and classical studies, both permanent and progressive, are the leading and essential parts of a liberal education for Englishmen. We have already, in some measure, pointed out the kind of mathematics and of classics which are to form the matter of such teaching as we contemplate; but we must now speak more at length of the methods according to which this teaching is to be conducted. . . .

Ward Number Six

Anton Chekhov

Editor's Introduction

Sooner or later, everyone who gets interested in reading short stories comes to Anton Chekhov, and the common estimate of his work in this field is that it is supreme--matched only, perhaps, by that of Guy de Maupassant, his near contemporary, who had an equally short life. But it is not easy to say what the quality is in Chekhov that makes him so good. His tales have always seemed perfectly transparent, revealing nothing but what goes on, or is said, in them—with such apt and impartial comment as this appears to require. Otherwise Chekhov himself, as an author, never seems to be there, nor have readers been able to decide what point of view, if any, he takes with respect to the people whose lives and feelings he perfectly conveys. This may suggest that he is easy to imitate, but in fact he has been impossible; no one else has ever written "like" Chekhov in any important way. The student can only be referred to him for a model of what to do, as distinct from how to do it. Thus Tolstoy, when he was visited by the young Maksim Gorky, read only the beginnings of several stories Gorky showed him before putting them aside and, when Gorky protested that he was making up his mind about them after he had read only a sentence or two, replied by asking the young writer if he had read the beginnings of Chekhov's stories— the clear message being that if you were really good, you should write a very good beginning, as Chekhov always does, and if you could not do that, you should regard yourself as in need of improvement.

Chekhov seems not at first to have realized that he was a writer at all, or that he wished to be one. Born at Tagenrog, Russia, near the Black Sea, in 1860, he moved to join his family in Moscow in 1879 to study medicine and became indeed a physician, though he never practiced. While studying he made a little money, which his family needed, by writing humorous sketches under a pseudonym for a magazine in St. Petersburg. The space allowed him was too short for anything but "thoughtless and frivolous tales," as he said, but he wrote hundreds of such pieces over the next few years and acquired, perhaps, the economy—the absence of unnecessary or wasted words—that eventually showed in his best stories. These he began to write about 1885, publishing them in monthly periodicals.

What may have made Chekhov serious enough to write them was a one-man journey he made in 1890, for obscure reasons, to Sakhalin, a remote island on the other side of Siberia that could only be reached by coach and riverboat (the Trans-Siberian railway not having been constructed yet), and where the Russian tsar maintained a notorious penal colony. A book Chekhov eventually wrote about this prison is still honored in the literature of Russian penology. The experience seems, moreover, to have distanced him from Tolstoy, whose spell he had fallen under while a young man, but whose doctrine of nonresistance to evil he could no longer accept after what he saw at Sakhalin. That is what appears to have been on his mind when he wrote "Ward Number Six" in 1892, though even there, he is anything but judgmental as to the unfortunate protagonist of his story, and it is gratuitous in us to imagine Doctor Ragin as constituting Chekhov himself in disguise. It was certainly after the Sakhalin expedition that he wrote the series of tales called "Peasants" (1897), whose characters are depicted in anything but the sentimental and kindly terms that Russian writers up to then had tended to use.

In the last decade of his life, Chekhov wrote the plays that made him famous. Of these the best-known were *The Seagull* (1896), *Uncle Vanya* (1896), *Three Sisters* (1901), and *The Cherry Orchard* (1904). Chekhov was never happy with the way in which these works were produced. In vain he protested to Konstantin Stanislavsky of the Moscow Art Theatre that melancholy was not the note he intended to sound, and that to take his characters as spokesmen for a dying order, or even a coming one, was to take them without the comedy he thought they contained. Perhaps Chekhov was only being hard-boiled, in the best comic tradition, about that. Most people are not able to sit through *The Cherry Orchard* without sadness, and he must have recognized that this would be the case, however he thought such a response might in turn be overtaken by a richer and more profound insight.

The last two of these plays were written while Chekhov was living by medical decree variously at Yalta or the French Riviera, in an effort to control the tuberculosis which he had recognized in himself, but which he had chosen to ignore. He was thus not able to oversee Stanislavsky's productions as he would like to have done and could not prevent what became a tradition of acting the plays in what he thought the wrong, melancholy way. He was able to attend the opening performance of *The Cherry Orchard* at Moscow in January 1904, six months before he died, but he did not like it and was in any case by then a dying man. His last years were at least made happy by his marriage (in 1901) to Olga Knipper, a young actress in Stanislavsky's company. Perhaps it was she who commissioned the charming memorial, surrounded by more pretentious stones, under which he now lies among his countrymen in Moscow's most celebrated cemetery.

Ward Number Six

I

At the side of the hospital yard stands a large wing, nearly surrounded by a forest of burdocks, nettles, and wild hemp. The roof is red, the chimney is on the point of tumbling, the steps are rotten and overgrown with grass, and of the plaster only traces remain. The front gazes at the hospital, the back looks into the fields, from which it is separated only by a gray, spiked fence. The spikes with their sharp points sticking upward, the fence, the wing itself, have that melancholy, Godforsaken air which is seen only in hospitals and prisons.

If you are not afraid of being stung by nettles, come along the narrow path, and see what is going on inside. Open the hall door and enter the hall. Here, against the walls and around the stove, are heaped whole mountains of rubbish. Mattresses, old tattered dressing gowns, trousers, blue-striped shirts, worn-out footgear, all good-for-nothing, lie in tangled and crushed heaps, rot, and exhale a suffocating smell.

On the top of this rubbish heap, pipe eternally in mouth, lies the watchman Nikita, an old soldier. His face is coarse and drink-sodden, his hanging eyebrows give him the appearance of a sheepdog, he is small and sinewy, but his carriage is impressive and his fists are strong. He belongs to that class of simple, expeditious, positive, and dull persons, who above all things in the world worship order, and find in this a justification of their existence. He beats his charges in the face, in the chest, in the back, in short, wherever his fists get

chance to strike; and he is convinced that without this beating there would be no order in the universe.

After you pass through Nikita's hall, you enter the large, roomy dormitory which takes up the rest of the wing. In this room the walls are painted a dirty blue, the ceiling is black with soot like the ceiling of a chimneyless hut; it is plain that in winter the stove smokes, and the air is suffocating. The windows are disfigured with iron bars, the floor is damp and splintered, there is a smell of sour cabbage, a smell of unsnuffed wicks, a smell of bugs and ammonia. And at the moment of entry all these smells produce upon you the impression that you have entered a cage of wild beasts.

Around the room stand beds, screwed to the floor. Sitting or lying on them, dressed in blue dressing gowns, and wearing nightcaps after the manner of our forefathers, are men. It is the lunatic asylum, and these are the lunatics.

There are only five patients. One is of noble birth, the others are men of lower origin. The nearest to the door, a tall, thin man of the petty trading class, looks fixedly at one point. He has a red mustache and tear-stained eyes, and supports his head on one hand. In the books of the asylum his complaint is described as hypochondria; in reality, he is suffering from progressive paralysis. Day and night he mourns, shakes his head, sighs, and smiles bitterly. In conversation he seldom joins, and usually refuses to answer questions. He eats and drinks mechanically. Judged by his emaciation, his flushed cheeks, and his painful, hacking cough, he is wasting away from consumption.

435

Beside him is a little, active old man with a pointed beard, and the black, fuzzy hair of a Negro. He spends all day in walking from window to window, or sitting on his bed, with legs doubled underneath him as if he were a Turk. He is as tireless as a bullfinch, and all day chirrups, titters, and sings in a low voice. His childish gaiety and lively character are shown also at night, when he rises to "pray to God," that is, to beat his breast with his clenched fists, and pick at the doors. This is Moseika, a Jew and an idiot. He went out of his mind twenty years ago when his cap factory was destroyed by fire.

Of all the captives in Ward Number Six, he alone has permission to leave the asylum, and he is even allowed to wander about the yard and the streets. This privilege, which he has enjoyed for many years, was probably accorded to him as the oldest inmate of the asylum, and as a quiet, harmless fool, the jester of the town, who may be seen in the streets surrounded by dogs and little boys. Wrapped in his old dressing gown, with a ridiculous nightcap and slippers, sometimes barefooted, and generally without his trousers, he walks the streets, stopping at doorways and entering small shops to beg for kopecks. Sometimes he is given *kvas,* sometimes bread, sometimes a kopeck, so that he returns to the ward wealthy and sated. But all that he brings home is taken by Nikita for his own particular benefit. The old soldier does this roughly and angrily, turning out the Jew's pockets, calling God to witness that he will never allow him outside the asylum again, and swearing that to him disorder is the most detestable thing in the world.

Moseika loves to make himself useful to others. He fetches water for his companions, tucks them in when they go to bed, promises to bring each a kopeck when he next returns from the town, and to make them new caps. He feeds with a spoon his paralytic neighbor on the left; and all this he does, not out of sympathy for others or for considerations of humanity, but from a love of imitation, and in a sort of involuntary subjection to his neighbor on the right, Ivan Gromof.

Ivan Dmitritch Gromof is a man of thirty-three years of age. He is a noble by birth, and has been an usher in the law courts, and a government secretary; but now he suffers from the mania of persecution. He lies upon his bed twisted into a lump resembling a roll of bread, or marches from corner to corner for the sake of motion. He is always in a state of excitement and agitation; and seems strained by some dull, indefinable expectation. It needs but the slightest rustle in the hall, the slightest noise in the yard, to make him raise his head and listen intently. Is it for him they are coming? Are they searching for him? And his face immediately takes on an expression of restlessness and repulsion.

There is something attractive about his broad, high cheek-boned face, which reflects, as a mirror, the tortured wrestlings and eternal terror of his mind. His grimaces are strange and sickly; but the delicate lines engraven on his face by sincere suffering express reason and intelligence, and his eyes burn with a healthy and passionate glow. There is something attractive also in his character, in his politeness, his attentiveness, and in the singular delicacy of his bearing toward everyone except Nikita. If his neighbor drops a spoon or a button he jumps immediately out of bed and picks it up. When he wakes he invariably says, "Good morning!" to his companions; and every evening on going to bed wishes them "good night!"

But madness shows itself in other things besides his grimaces and continual mental tension. In the evening he wraps himself in his dressing gown, and, trembling all over, and chattering his teeth, he walks from corner to corner, and in between the beds. He seems to be in a state of fever. From his sudden stoppages and strange looks at his fellow prisoners, it is plain that he has something very serious to say; but, no doubt, remembering that they will neither listen nor understand, he says nothing, shakes his head impatiently, and continues his walk. But at last the desire to speak conquers all other considerations, and he gives way, and speaks passionately. His words are incoherent, gusty, and delirious; he cannot always be understood; but the sound of his voice expresses some exceptional goodness. In every word you hear the madman and the man. He speaks of human baseness, of violence trampling over truth, of the beautiful life on earth that is to come, and of the barred windows which remind him every moment of the folly and cruelty of the strong. And he hums medleys of old but forgotten songs.

II

Fifteen years before, in his own house, in the best street in the town, lived an official named Gromof—a solid and prosperous man. Gromof had two sons, Sergei and Ivan. Sergei, when a student in the fourth class, was seized with consumption and died; and his death was the first of a series of misfortunes which overtook the Gromofs. A week after Sergei's death his old father was tried for forgery and misappropriation of public moneys, and soon afterward died of typhus in the prison infirmary. His house and all his belongings were sold by auction, and Ivan Dmitritch and his mother remained without a penny.

When his father was alive, Ivan Dmitritch studied at St. Petersburg University, received an allowance of sixty or seventy rubles a month, and had no idea of the meaning of poverty. Now he had to change his whole life. From early morning till late at night he gave cheap lessons to students and copied documents, yet starved, for all his earnings went to support his mother. The life was impossible, and Ivan Dmitritch ruined his health and spirits, thew up his university studies, and returned home. Through interest he obtained an appointment as clerk in the district school; but he was disliked by his colleagues, failed to get on with the pupils, and gave up the post. His mother died. For six months he lived without resources, eating black bread and drinking water, until at last he obtained an appointment as Clerk of the Court. This duty he fulfilled until he was discharged owing to illness.

Never, even in his student days, had he had the appearance of strong man. He was pale, thin, and sensitive to cold; he ate little and slept badly. A single glass of wine made him giddy and sent him into hysterics. His disposition impelled him to seek companionship, but thanks to his irritable and suspicious character he never became intimate with anyone, and had no friends. Of his fellow citizens he always spoke with contempt, condemning as disgusting and repulsive their gross ignorance and torpid, animal life. He spoke in a tenor voice, loudly and passionately, and always seemed to be in a sincere state of indignation, excitement, or rapture. However he began a conversation, it ended always in one way—in a lament that the town was stifling and tiresome, that its people had no high interests, but led a dull, unmeaning life, varied only by violence, coarse debauchery, and hypocrisy; that scoundrels were fed and clothed while honest men ate crusts; that the town was crying out for schools, honest newspapers, a theater, public lectures, a union of intellectual forces; and that the time had come for the townspeople to awaken to, and be shocked at, the state of affairs. In his judgments of men he laid on his colors thickly, using only white and black, and recognizing no gradations; for him humanity was divided into two sections, honest men and rogues—there was nothing between. Of woman and woman's love he spoke passionately and with rapture. But he had never been in love.

In the town, notwithstanding his nervous character and censorious temper, he was loved, and called caressingly "Vanya." His innate delicacy, his attentiveness, his neatness, his moral purity, his worn coat, his sickly appearance, the misfortunes of his

family, inspired in all feelings of warmth and compassion. Besides, he was educated and well-read; in the opinion of the towns-men he knew everything; and occupied among them the place of a walking refer-ence book. He read much. He would sit for hours at the club, pluck nervously at his beard, and turn over the pages of books and magazines—by his face it might be seen that he was not reading but devour-ing. Yet reading was apparently merely one of his nervous habits, for with equal avidity he read everything that fell into his hands, even old newspapers and calendars. At home he always read, lying down.

III

One autumn morning, Ivan Dmitritch, with the collar of his coat turned up, trudged through the mud to the house of a certain tradesman to receive money due on a writ of execution. As always in the morning, he was in a gloomy mood. Pass-ing through a lane, he met two convicts in chains and with them four warders armed with rifles. Ivan Dmitritch had often met convicts before, and they had awakened in him a feeling of sympathy and confusion. But this meeting produced upon him an unusual impression. It suddenly occurred to him that he too might be shackled and driven through the mud to prison. Having finished his work, he was returning home when he met a police inspector, an ac-quaintance, who greeted him and walked with him a few yards down the street. This seemed to him for some reason suspicious. At home visions of convicts and of soldiers armed with rifles haunted him all day, and an inexplicable spiritual dread prevented him from reading or concentrating his mind. In the evening he sat without a fire, and lay awake all night thinking how he also might be arrested, manacled, and flung into prison. He knew that he had commit-ted no crime, and was quite confident that he would never commit murder, arson, or robbery; but then, he remembered, how easy it was to commit a crime by accident or involuntarily, and how common were convictions on false evidence and owing to judicial errors! And in the present state of human affairs how probable, how little to be wondered at, were judicial errors! Men who witness the sufferings of others only from a professional standpoint; for in-stance, judges, policemen, doctors, became hardened to such a degree that even if they wished otherwise they could not resist the habit of treating accused persons for-mally; they got to resemble those peasants who kill sheep and calves in their back-yards without even noticing the blood. In view of the soulless relationship to human personality which everywhere obtains, all that a judge thinks of is the observance of certain formalities, and then all is over, and an innocent man perhaps deprived of his civil rights or sent to the galleys. Who indeed would expect justice or interces-sion in this dirty, sleepy little town, two hundred versts [around 130 miles] from the nearest railway? And indeed was it not ridiculous to expect justice when society regards every form of violence as rational, expedient, and necessary; and when an act of common mercy such as the acquittal of an accused man calls forth an explosion of unsatisfied vindictiveness!

Next morning Ivan Dmitritch awoke in terror with drops of cold sweat on his fore-head. He felt convinced that he might be arrested at any moment. That the evening's gloomy thoughts had haunted him so per-sistently, he concluded, must mean that there was some ground for his apprehen-sions. Could such thoughts come into his head without cause?

A policeman walked slowly past the win-dow; that must mean something. Two men in plain clothes stopped outside the gate, and stood without saying a word. Why were they silent?

For a time, Ivan Dmitritch spent his days and nights in torture. Every man who passed the window or entered the yard was a spy or detective. Every day at twelve

o'clock the Chief Constable drove through the street on his way from his suburban house to the Department of Police, and every day it seemed to Ivan Dmitritch that the Constable was driving with unaccustomed haste, and that there was a peculiar expression on his face; he was going, in short, to announce that a great criminal had appeared in the town. Ivan Dmitritch shuddered at every sound, trembled at every knock at the yard gate, and was in torment when any strange man visited his landlady. When he met a gendarme in the street, he smiled, whistled, and tried to assume an indifferent air. For whole nights, expecting arrest, he never closed his eyes, but snored carefully so that his landlady might think he was asleep; for if a man did not sleep at night it meant that he was tormented by the gnawings of conscience, and that might be taken as a clue. Reality and healthy reasoning convinced him that his fears were absurd and psychopathic, and that, regarded from a broad standpoint, there was nothing very terrible in arrest and imprisonment for a man whose conscience was clean. But the more consistently and logically he reasoned the stronger grew his spiritual torture; his efforts reminded him of the efforts of a pioneer to hack a path through virgin forest, the harder he worked with the hatchet the thicker and stronger became the undergrowth. So in the end, seeing that his efforts were useless, he ceased to struggle, and gave himself up to terror and despair.

He avoided others and became more and more solitary in his habits. His duties had always been detestable, now they became intolerable. He imagined that someone would hide money in his pockets and then denounce him for taking bribes, that he would make mistakes in official documents which were equivalent to forgery, or that he would lose the money entrusted to him. Never was his mind so supple and ingenious as when he was engaged in inventing various reasons for fearing for his freedom and honor. On the other hand,

his interest in the outside world decreased correspondingly, he lost his passion for books, and his memory daily betrayed him.

Next spring when the snow had melted, the semidecomposed corpses of an old woman and a boy, marked with indications of violence, were found in a ravine beside the graveyard. The townspeople talked of nothing but the discovery and the problem: who were the unknown murderers? In order to avert suspicion, Ivan Dmitritch walked about the streets and smiled; and when he met his acquaintances, first grew pale and then blushed, and declared vehemently that there was no more detestable crime than the killing of the weak and defenseless. But this pretense soon exhausted him, and after consideration he decided that the best thing he could do was to hide in his landlady's cellar. In the cellar therefore, chilled to the bone, he remained all day, all next night, and yet another day, after which, waiting until it was dark, he crept secretly back to his room. Till daylight he stood motionless in the middle of the room, and listened. At sunrise a number of artisans rang at the gate. Ivan Dmitritch knew very well that they had come to put up a new stove in the kitchen; but his terror suggested that they were constables in disguise. He crept quietly out of his room, and overcome by panic, without cap or coat, fled down the street. Behind him ran barking dogs, a woman called after him, in his ears the wind whistled, and it seemed to him that the scattered violences of the whole world had united and were chasing him through the town.

He was captured and brought home. His landlady sent for a doctor. Doctor Andrei Yefimitch Ragin, of whom we shall hear again, prescribed cold compresses for his head, ordered him to take drops of bay rum, and went away saying that he would come no more, as it was not right to prevent people going out of their minds. So, as there were no means of treating him at home, Ivan Dmitritch was sent to hospital, and put into the ward for sick men. He did not sleep at night, was unruly, and disturbed his neighbors, so that soon, by arrangement with Doctor Andrei Yefimitch, he was transferred to Ward Number Six.

Before a year had passed, the townspeople had quite forgotten Ivan Dmitritch; and his books, piled up in a sledge by his landlady and covered with a curtain, were torn to pieces by children.

IV

Ivan Dmitritch's neighbor on the left, I have already said, was the Jew Moseika; his neighbor on the right was a fat, almost globular muzhik with a dull, meaningless face. This torpid, gluttonous, and uncleanly animal had long lost all capacity for thought and feeling. He exhaled a sharp, suffocating smell. When Nikita was obliged to attend on him he used to beat him terribly, beat him with all his strength and without regard for his own fists; and it was not this violence which was so frightful—the terror of that was mitigated by custom—but the fact that the stupefied animal made no answer to the blows either by sound or movement or even by expression in his eyes, but merely rocked from side to side like a heavy cask.

The fifth and last occupant of Ward Number Six was a townsman who had served once as a sorter in the Post Office. He was a little, thin, fair-headed man, with a kindly, but somewhat cunning face. Judged by his clever, tranquil eyes, which looked out on the world frankly and merrily, he was the possessor of some valuable and pleasant secret. Under his pillow and mattress he had something hidden which he refused to show to anyone, not out of fear of losing it, but out of shame. Occasionally he walked to the window, and turning his back upon his fellow prisoners, held something to his breast, and looked earnestly at it; but if anyone approached he became confused and hid it away. But it was not hard to guess his secret.

"Congratulate me!" he used to say to Ivan Dmitritch. "I have been decorated with the Stanislas of the second degree with a star. As a rule the second degree with a star is given only to foreigners, but for some reason they have made an exception in my case." And then, shrugging his shoulders as if in doubt, he would add: "That is something you never expected, you must admit."

"I understand nothing about it," answered Ivan Dmitritch, gloomily.

"Do you know what I shall get sooner or later?" continued the ex-sorter, winking slyly. "I shall certainly receive the Swedish Pole Star. An order of that kind is worth trying for. A white cross and a black ribbon. It is very handsome."

In no other place in the world, probably, is life so monotonous as in the wing. In the morning the patients, with the exception of the paralytic and the fat muzhik, wash themselves in a great bucket which is placed in the hall, and dry themselves in the skirts of their dressing gowns. After this they drink tea out of tin mugs brought by Nikita from the hospital. At midday they dine on *shtchi* made with sour cabbage, and porridge, and in the evening they sup on the porridge left over from dinner. Between meals they lie down, sleep, look out of the windows, and walk from corner to corner.

And so on every day. Even the ex-sorter talks always of the same decorations.

Fresh faces are seldom seen in Ward Number Six. Years ago the doctor gave orders that no fresh patients should be admitted, and in this world people rarely visit lunatic asylums for pleasure.

But once every two months comes Semion Lazaritch the barber. With Nikita's assistance, he cuts the patients' hair; and on the consternation of the victims every time they see his drunken, grinning face, there is no need to dwell.

With this exception no one ever enters the ward. From day to day the patients are condemned to see only Nikita. But at last a strange rumor obtained circulation in the hospital. It was rumored the doctor had begun to pay visits to Ward Number Six.

V

It was indeed a strange rumor!

Doctor Andrei Yefimitch Ragin was a remarkable man in his way. In early youth, so they said, he was very pious, and intended to make a career in the Church. But when in the year 1863 he finished his studies in the gymnasium and prepared to enter the Ecclesiastical Academy, his father, a surgeon and a doctor of medicine, poured ridicule on these intentions, and declared categorically that if Andrei became a priest he would disown him forever. Whether this story is true or not it is impossible to say, but it is certain that Andrei Yefimitch more than once admitted that he had never felt any vocation for medicine or, indeed, for specialized sciences at all.

Certain it is, also, that he never became a priest, but completed a course of study in the medical faculty of his university. He showed no particular trace of godliness, and at the beginning of his medical career was as little like a priest as at the end.

In appearance he was as heavy and rudely built as a peasant. His bearded face, his straight hair, and his strong, awkward build recalled some innkeeper on a main road—incontinent and stubborn. He was tall and broad-shouldered, and had enormous feet, and hands with which, it seemed, he could easily crush the life out of a man's body. Yet his walk was noiseless, cautious, and insinuating; and when he met anyone in a narrow passage he was always the first to step aside, and to say—not as might be expected in a bass voice—in a soft, piping tenor: "Excuse me!"

On his neck Andrei Yefimitch had a small tumor which forbade his wearing starched collars; he always wore a soft linen or print shirt. Indeed, in no respect did he dress like a doctor; he wore the same suit for ten years, and when he did buy new clothing—at a Jew's store—it always looked as worn and crumpled as his old clothes. In one and the same frock coat he received his patients, dined, and attended entertainments; and this not from penuriousness but from a genuine contempt for appearances.

When Andrei Yefimitch first came to the town to take up his duties as physician to the hospital, that "charitable institution" was in a state of inconceivable disorder. In the wards, in the corridors, and even in the open air of the yard it was impossible to breathe owing to the stench. The male attendants, the nurses and their children, slept in the dormitories together with the patients. It was complained that the hospital was becoming uninhabitable owing to the invasion of beetles, bugs, and mice. In the surgical department there were only two scalpels, nowhere was there a thermometer, and the baths were used for storing potatoes in. The superintendent, the housekeeper, and the feldsher robbed the sick, and of the former doctor, Andrei Yefimitch's predecessor, it was said that he sold the hospital spirits secretly, and kept up a whole harem recruited from among the nurses and female patients. In the town these scandals were well-known and even exaggerated; but the townspeople were indifferent, and even excused the abuses on the ground that the patients were all either petty tradespeople or peasants who lived at home among conditions so much worse that they had no right to complain; such gentry, they added, must not expect to be fed on grouse! Others argued that as no small town had sufficient resources to support a good hospital without subsidies from the zemstvo, they might thank God they had a bad one; and the zemstvo refused to open a hospital in the town on the ground that there was already one.

When he inspected the hospital for the first time Andrei Yefimitch saw at once that the whole institution was hopelessly bad, and in the highest degree dangerous to the health of the inmates. He concluded that the best thing to do was to discharge the patients and to close the hospital. But he knew that to effect this his wish alone was not enough; and he reasoned that if the physical and moral uncleanliness were driven from one place it would merely be transplanted to another; it was necessary, in fact, to wait until it cleaned itself out. To these considerations he added that if people opened a hospital and tolerated its abuses they must have need of it; and, no doubt, such abominations were necessary, and in the course of time would evolve something useful, as good soil results from manuring. And, indeed, on this earth there is nothing good that has not had evil germs in its beginnings.

Having taken up his duties, therefore, Andrei Yefimitch looked upon the abuses with apparent indifference. He merely asked the servants and nurses not to sleep in the wards, and bought two cases of instruments; but he allowed the superintendent, the housekeeper, and the feldsher to remain in their positions.

Andrei Yefimitch was passionately enamored of intellect and honesty, but he had neither the character nor the confidence in his own powers necessary to establish around himself an intelligent and honest life. To command, to prohibit, to insist, he had never learned. It seemed almost that he had sworn an oath never to raise his voice or to use the imperative mood. . . . Even to use the words "give" or "bring" was difficult for him. When he felt hungry, he coughed irresolutely and said to his cook, "Suppose I were to have a cup of tea," or "I was thinking about dining." To tell the superintendent that he must cease his robberies, to dismiss him, or to abolish altogether his parasitical office he had not the strength. When he was deceived or flattered, or handed accounts for signature which he knew to have been falsified, he would redden all over and feel guilty, yet sign the accounts; and when the patients complained that they were hungry or had been ill-treated by the nurses, he mere-ly got confused, and stammered guiltily:

"Very well, very well, I will investigate the matter. . . . No doubt there is some misunderstanding. . . ."

At first Andrei Yefimitch worked very zealously. He attended to patients from morning until dinnertime, performed operations, and even occupied himself with obstetrics. He gained a reputation for exceptional skill in the treatment of women and children. But he soon began visibly to weary of the monotony and uselessness of his work. One day he would receive thirty patients, the next day the number had grown to thirty-five, the next day to forty, and so on from day to day, from year to year. Yet the death rate in the town did not decrease, and the number of patients never grew less. To give any real assistance to forty patients in the few hours between morning and dinnertime was physically impossible; in other words, he became an involuntary deceiver. The twelve thousand persons received every year, he reasoned, were therefore twelve thousand dupes. To place the serious cases in the wards and treat them according to the rules of medical science was impossible, because there were no rules and no science; whereas if he left philosophy and followed the regulations pedantically as other doctors did, he would still be in difficulty, for in the first place were needed cleanliness and fresh air, and not filth; wholesome food, and not *shtchi* made of stinking sour cabbage; and honest assistants, not thieves.

And, indeed, why hinder people dying, if death is the normal and lawful end of us all? What does it matter whether some tradesman or petty official lives, or does not live, an extra five years? We pretend to see the object of medical science in its mitigation of suffering, but we cannot but ask ourselves the question: Why should suffering be mitigated? In the first place, we are told that suffering leads men to perfection; and in the second, it is plain that if men were really able to alleviate their sufferings with pills and potions, they would abandon that religion and philosophy in which until now they had found not only consolation, but even happiness. Pushkin suffered agonizing torment before his death; Heine lay for years in a state of paralysis. Why, then, interfere with the sufferings of some mere Andrei Yefimitch or Matrena Savishin, whose lives are meaningless, and would be as vacuous as the life of the amoeba if it were not for suffering?

Defeated by such arguments, Andrei Yefimitch dropped his hands upon his knees, and ceased his daily attendances at the hospital.

VI

His life passed thus. At eight in the morning he rose and took his breakfast. After that he either sat in his study and read, or visited the hospital. In the hospital in a narrow, dark corridor waited the outpatients. With heavy boots clattering on the brick floor, servants and nurses ran past them; emaciated patients in dressing gowns staggered by; and vessels of filth, and corpses were carried out. And among them children cried and drafts blew. Andrei Yefimitch knew well that to the fevered, the consumptive, and the impressionable such surroundings were torment; but what could he do? In the reception room he was met by the feldsher, Sergei Sergeyitch, a little fat man, with a beardless, well-washed, puffy face, and easy manners. Sergei Sergeyitch always wore clothes which resembled a senator's more than a surgeon's; in the town he had a large practice, and believed that he knew more than the doctor, who had no practice at all. In the corner of the room hung a case of icons with a heavy lamp in front; on the walls were portraits of bishops, a view of Sviatogorsk Monastery, and garlands of withered cornflowers. Sergei Sergeyitch was religious, and the images had been placed in the room at his expense; every Sunday by his command one of the patients read the acathistus, and when the

reading was concluded, Sergei Sergeyitch went around the wards with a censer and sprinkled them piously.

There were many patients and little time. The examination was therefore limited to a few short questions, and to the distribution of such simple remedies as castor oil and ointments. Andrei Yefimitch sat with his head resting on his hands, lost in thought, and asked questions mechanically; and Sergei Sergeyitch sat beside him, and sometimes interjected a word.

"We become ill and suffer deprivation," he would sometimes say, "only because we pray too little to God."

In these hours Andrei Yefimitch performed no operations; he had got out of practice, and the sight of blood affected him unpleasantly. When he had to open a child's mouth, to examine its throat for instance, if the child cried and defended itself with its hands, the doctor's head went round and tears came into his eyes. He made haste to prescribe a remedy, and motioned to the mother to take it away as quickly as possible.

He quickly wearied of the timidity of the patients, of their shiftless ways, of the proximity of the pompous Sergei Sergeyitch, of the portraits on the walls, and of his own questions—questions which he had asked without change for more than twenty years. And he would sometimes leave the hospital after having examined five or six patients, the remainder in his absence being treated by the feldsher.

With the pleasant reflection that thank God he had no private practice and no one to interfere with him, Andrei Yefimitch on returning home would sit at his study table and begin to read. He read much, and always with pleasure. Half his salary went on the purchase of books, and of the six rooms in his flat three were crowded with books and old newspapers. Above all things he loved history and philosophy; but of medical publications he subscribed only to *The Doctor,* which he always began to read at the end. Every day he read uninterruptedly for several hours, and it never wearied him. He read, not quickly and eagerly as Ivan Dmitritch had read, but slowly, often stopping at passages which pleased him or which he did not understand. Beside his books stood a decanter of vodka, and a salted cucumber or soaked apple; and every half hour he poured himself out a glass of vodka, and drank it without lifting his eyes from his book, and then—again without lifting his eyes—took the cucumber and bit a piece off.

At three o'clock he would walk cautiously to the kitchen door, cough, and say:

"Daryushka, I was thinking of dining...."

After a bad and ill-served dinner, Andrei Yefimitch walked about his rooms, with his arms crossed on his chest, and thought. Sometimes the kitchen door creaked, and the red, sleepy face of Daryushka appeared.

"Andrei Yefimitch, is it time for your beer?" she would ask solicitously.

"No, not yet," he would answer. "I'll wait a little longer...."

In the evening came the postmaster, Mikhail Averyanitch, the only man in the town whose society did not weary Andrei Yefimitch. Mikhail Averyanitch had once been a rich country gentleman and had served in a cavalry regiment, but having ruined himself he took a position in the Post Office to save himself from beggary in his old age. He had a brisk, wholesome appearance, magnificent gray whiskers, well-bred manners, and a loud but pleasant voice. When visitors at the Post Office protested, refused to agree with him, or began to argue, Mikhail Averyanitch became purple, shook all over, and roared at the top of his voice: "Silence!" so that the Post Office had the reputation of a place of terror. Mikhail Averyanitch was fond of Andrei Yefimitch and respected his attainments and the nobility of his heart. But the other townspeople he treated haughtily as inferiors.

"Well, here I am!" he would begin. "How are you, my dear? . . . But perhaps I bore you? Eh?"

"On the contrary. I am delighted," answered the doctor. "I am always glad to see you."

The friends would sit on the study sofa and smoke for a time silently.

"Daryushka, suppose I were to have a little beer . . ." said Andrei Yefimitch.

The first bottle was drunk in silence. The doctor was lost in thought, while Mikhail Averyanitch had the gay and active expression of a man who has something very interesting to relate. The conversation was always begun by the doctor.

"What a pity!" he would say, slowly and quietly, looking away from his friend—he never looked anyone in the face. "What a pity, my dear Mikhail Averyanitch, what a pity it is that there is not a soul in this town who cares to engage in an intellectual or interesting conversation! It is a great deprivation for us. Even the so-called intelligent classes never rise above commonplaces; the level of their development, I assure you, is no higher than that of the lower order."

"Entirely true. I agree with you."

"As you yourself know very well," continued the doctor, pausing intermittently, "as you know, everything in this world is insignificant and uninteresting except the higher phenomena of the human intellect. Intellect creates a sharp distinction between the animal and the man, it reminds the latter of his divinity, and to a certain extent compensates him for the immortality which he has not. As the result of this, intellect serves as the only fountain of enjoyment. When we say we see and hear around us no evidence of intellect, we mean thereby that we are deprived of true happiness. True, we have our books, but that is a very different thing from living converse and communication. If I may use a not very apt simile, books are the accompaniment, but conversation is the singing."

"That is entirely true."

A silence followed. From the kitchen came Daryushka, and, with her head resting on her hands and an expression of stupid vexation on her face, stood at the door and listened.

"Akh!" sighed Mikhail Averyanitch, "Why seek intellect among the men of the present day?"

And he began to relate how in the old days life was wholesome, gay, and interesting, how the intellect of Russia was really enlightened, and how high a place was given to the ideas of honor and friendship. Money was lent without IOUs, and it was regarded as shameful not to stretch out the hand of aid to a needy friend. What marches there were, what adventures, what fights, what companions-in-arms, what women! The Caucasus, what a marvelous country! And the wife of a commander of his battalion—what a strange woman!—who put on an officer's uniform and drove into the mountains at night without an escort. They said she had a romance with a prince in one of the villages.

"Heavenly mother! Lord preserve us!" sighed Daryushka.

"And how we drank! How we used to eat! What desperate Liberals we were!"

Andrei Yefimitch listened, but heard nothing; he was thinking of something else and drinking his beer.

"I often dream of clever people and have imaginary conversations with them," he said, suddenly, interrupting Mikhail Averyanitch. "My father gave me a splendid education, but, under the influence of the ideas current in the sixties, forced me to become a doctor. It seems to me that if I had disobeyed him I might now be living in the very center of the intellectual movement—probably a member of some faculty. Of course intellect itself is not eternal but transitory—but you already know why I worship it so. Life is a vexatious snare. When a reflecting man attains manhood and ripe consciousness, he cannot but feel himself in a trap from which there is no escape. . . . By an accident, without consulting his own will, he is called from nonexistence into life. . . . Why? He wishes to know the aim and significance of his existence; he is answered with silence or absurdities; he knocks but it is not opened to him; and death itself comes against his will. And so, as prisoners united by common misfortune are relieved when they meet, men inclined to analysis and generalization do not notice the snare in which they live when they spend their days in the exchange of free ideas. In this sense intellect is an irreplaceable enjoyment."

"Entirely true!"

And still with his face averted from his companion, Andrei Yefimitch, in a soft voice, with constant pauses, continues to speak of clever men and of the joy of communion with them, and Mikhail Averyanitch listens attentively and says: "It is entirely true."

"Then you do not believe in the immortality of the soul?" asks the postmaster.

"No, my dear Mikhail Averyanitch. I do not believe, and I have no reason for believing."

"I admit that I also doubt it. Still I have a feeling that I can never die. 'Come,' I say to myself, 'Come, old man, it's time for you to die.' But in my heart a voice answers: 'Don't believe it, you will never die.'"

At nine o'clock Mikhail Averyanitch takes leave. As he puts on his overcoat in the hall, he says with a sigh:

"Yes, what a desert fate has planted us in! And what is worst of all, we shall have to die here. *Akh!*"

VII

When he has parted from his friend, Andrei Yefimitch sits at his table and again begins to read. The stillness of evening, the stillness of night is unbroken by a single sound; time, it seems, stands still and perishes, and the doctor perishes also, till it seems that nothing exists but a book and a green lampshade. Then the rude, peasant face of the doctor, as he thinks of the achievements of the human intellect, becomes gradually illumined by a smile of emotion and rapture. Oh, why is man not immortal? he asks. For what end exist brain-centers and convolutions, to what end vision, speech, consciousness, genius, if all are condemned to pass into the earth, to grow cold with it, and for countless millions of years, without aim or object, to be borne with it around the sun? In order that the human frame may decay and be whirled around the sun, is it necessary to drag man with his high, his divine mind, out of nonexistence, as if in mockery, and to turn him again into earth?

Immortality of matter! What cowardice to console ourselves with this fictitious immortality! Unconscious processes working themselves out in Nature—processes lower even than folly, for in folly there is at least consciousness and volition, while in these processes there is neither! Yet they say to men, "Be at rest, thy substance, rotting in the earth, will give life to other organisms"—in other words, thou wilt be more foolish than folly! Only the coward, who has more fear of death than sense of dignity, can console himself with the knowledge that his body in the course of time will live again in grass, in stones, in the toad. To seek immortality in the indestructibility of matter is, indeed, as strange as to prophesy a brilliant future for the case when the costly violin is broken and worthless.

When the clock strikes, Andrei Yefimitch leans back in his chair, shuts his eyes, and thinks. Under the influence of the lofty thoughts which he has just been reading, he throws a glance over the present and the past. The past is repellent, better not think of it! And the present is but as the past. He knows that in this very moment, while his thoughts are sweeping round the sun with the cooling earth, in the hospital building in a line with his lodgings, lie men tortured by pain and tormented by uncleanliness; one cannot sleep owing to the insects, and howls in his pain; another

is catching erysipelas, and groaning at the tightness of his bandages; others are playing cards with the nurses, and drinking vodka. In this very year no less than twelve thousand persons were duped; the whole work of the hospital, as twenty years before, is based on robbery, scandal, intrigue, nepotism, and gross charlatanry; altogether, the hospital is an immoral institution, and a source of danger to the health of its inmates. And Andrei Yefimitch knows that inside the iron bars of Ward Number Six, Nikita beats the patients with his fists, and that, outside, Moseika wanders about the streets begging for kopecks.

Yet he knows very well that in the last twenty-five years a fabulous revolution has taken place in the doctor's art. When he studied at the university it had seemed to him that medicine would soon be overtaken by the lot of alchemy and metaphysics, but now the records of its feats which he reads at night touch him, astonish him, and even send him into raptures. What a revolution! what unexpected brilliance! Thanks to antiseptics, operations are every day performed which the great Pigorof regarded as impossible. Ordinary zemstvo doctors perform such operations as the resection of the knee articulations, of a hundred operations on the stomach only one results in death, and the stone is now such a trifle that it has ceased to be written about. Complaints which were once only alleviated are now entirely cured. And hypnotism, the theory of heredity, the discoveries of Pasteur and Koch, statistics of hygiene, even Russian zemstvo medicine! Psychiatry, with its classification of diseases, its methods of diagnosis, its method of cure—what a transformation of the methods of the past! No longer are lunatics drenched with cold water and confined in straight waistcoats; they are treated as human beings, and even—as Andrei Yefimitch read in the newspapers—have their own special dramatic entertainments and dances. Andrei Yefimitch is well aware that in the modern world such an abomination as Ward Number Six is possible only in a town situated two hundred versts from a railway, where the Mayor and Councillors are half-educated tradesmen, who regard a doctor as a priest to whom everything must be entrusted without criticism, even though he were to dose his patients with molten tin. In any other town the public and the press would long ago have torn this little Bastille to pieces.

"But in the end?" asks Andrei Yefimitch, opening his eyes. "What is the difference? In spite of antiseptics and Koch and Pasteur, the essence of the matter has no way changed. Disease and death still exist. Lunatics are amused with dances and theatricals, but they are still kept prisoners. . . . In other words, all these things are vanity and folly, and between the best hospital in Vienna and the hospital here there is in reality no difference at all."

But vexation and a feeling akin to envy forbid indifference. It all arises out of weariness. Andrei Yefimitch's head falls upon his book, he rests his head comfortably on his hands and thinks:

"I am engaged in a bad work, and I receive a salary from the men whom I deceive. I am not an honest man. . . . But then by myself I am nothing; I am only part of a necessary social evil; all the officials in the district are bad, and draw their salaries without doing their work. . . . In other words, it is not I who am guilty of dishonesty, but Time. . . . If I were born two hundred years hence I should be a different man."

When the clock strikes three, he puts out his lamp and goes up to his bedroom. But he has no wish to sleep.

VIII

Two years ago, in a fit of liberality, the zemstvo determined to appropriate three hundred rubles a year to the increase of the personnel of the hospital, until such time as they should open one of their own. They sent, therefore, as assistant to Andrei Yefimitch, the district physician Yevgenii Feodoritch Khobotov. Khobotov was a very young man, under thirty, tall and dark, with small eyes and high cheekbones; evidently of Asiatic origin. He arrived in the town without a kopeck, with a small portmanteau as his only luggage, and was accompanied by a young, unattractive woman, whom he called his cook. This woman's child completed the party. Khobotov wore a peaked cap and high boots, and—in winter—a short fur coat. He was soon on intimate terms with the feldsher, Sergei Sergeyitch, and with the bursar, but the rest of the officials he avoided and denounced as aristocrats. He possessed only one book, *Prescriptions of the Vienna Hospital in 1881,* and when he visited the hospital he always brought it with him. He did not care for cards, and in the evenings spent his time playing billiards at the club.

Khobotov visited the hospital twice a week, inspected the wards, and received outpatients. The strange absence of antiseptics, cupping glasses, and other necessaries seemed to trouble him, but he made no attempt to introduce a new order, fearing to offend Andrei Yefimitch, whom he regarded as an old rogue, suspected of having large means, and secretly envied. He would willingly have occupied his position.

IX

One spring evening toward the end of March, when the snow had disappeared and starlings sang in the hospital garden, the doctor was standing at his gate saying good-bye to his friend the postmaster. At that moment the Jew Moseika, returning with his booty, entered the yard. He was capless, wore a pair of galoshes on his stockingless feet, and held in his hand a small bag of coins.

"Give me a kopeck?" he said to the doctor, shuddering from the cold and grinning.

Andrei Yefimitch, who could refuse no one, gave him a ten-kopeck piece.

"How wrong this is!" he thought, as he looked at the Jew's bare legs and thin ankles. "Wet, I suppose?"

And impelled by a feeling of pity and squeamishness he entered the wing after Moseika, looking all the time now at the Jew's bald head, now at his ankles. When the doctor entered, Nikita jumped off his rubbish heap and stretched himself.

"Good evening, Nikita!" said the doctor softly. "Suppose you give this man a pair of boots . . . that is . . . he might catch cold."

"Yes, your Honor. I will ask the superintendent."

"Please. Ask him in my name. Say that I spoke about it."

The door of the ward was open. Ivan Dmitritch, who was lying on his bed, and listening with alarm to the unknown voice, suddenly recognized the doctor. He shook with anger, jumped off his bed, and with a flushed, malicious face, and staring eyeballs, ran into the middle of the room.

"It is the doctor!" he cried, with a loud laugh. "At last! Lord, I congratulate you, the doctor honors us with a visit! Accursed monster!" he squealed, and in an ecstasy of rage never before seen in the hospital, stamped his feet. "Kill this monster! No, killing is not enough for him! Drown him in the closet!"

Andrei Yefimitch heard him. He looked into the ward and asked mildly:

"For what?"

"For what!" screamed Ivan Dmitritch, approaching with a threatening face, and convulsively clutching his dressing gown. "For what! Thief!" He spoke in a tone of disgust, and twisted his lips as if about to spit.

"Charlatan! Hangman!"

"Be quiet!" said Andrei Yefimitch, smiling guiltily. "I assure you I have never stolen anything. . . . I see that you are angry with me. Be calm, I implore you,

if you can, and tell me why you want to kill me."

"For keeping me here."

"I do that because you are ill."

"Yes! Ill! But surely tens, hundreds, thousands of madmen live unmolested merely because you in your ignorance cannot distinguish them from the sane. You, the feldsher, the superintendent, all the rascals employed in the hospital are immeasurably lower in morals than the worst of us; why, then, are we here instead of you? Where is the logic?"

"It is not a question of morality or logic. It depends on circumstances. The man who is put here, here he stays, and the man who is not here lives in freedom, that is all. For the fact that I am a doctor and you a lunatic neither morals nor logic is responsible, but only empty circumstance."

"This nonsense I do not understand!" answered Ivan Dmitritch, sitting down on his bed.

Moseika, whom Nikita was afraid to search in the doctor's presence, spread out on his bed his booty—pieces of bread, papers, and bones; and trembling with the cold, talked Yiddish in a singsong voice. Apparently he imagined that he was opening a shop.

"Release me!" said Ivan Dmitritch. His voice trembled.

"I cannot."

"Why not?"

"Because it is not in my power. Judge for yourself! What good would it do you if I released you? Suppose I do! The townspeople or the police will capture you and send you back."

"Yes, that is true, it is true . . ." said Ivan Dmitritch, rubbing his forehead. "It is terrible! But what can I do? What?"

His voice, his intelligent, youthful face pleased Andrei Yefimitch. He wished to caress him and quiet him. He sat beside him on the bed, thought for a moment, and said:

"You ask what is to be done. The best thing in your position would be to run away. But unfortunately that is useless. You would be captured. When society resolves to protect itself from criminals, lunatics, and inconvenient people, it is irresistible. One thing alone remains to you, to console yourself with the thought that your stay here is necessary."

"It is necessary to no one."

"Once prisons and asylums exist, someone must inhabit them. If it is not you it will be I, if not I then someone else. But wait! In the far future there will be neither prisons nor madhouses, nor barred windows, nor dressing gowns. . . . Such a time will come sooner or later."

Ivan Dmitritch smiled contemptuously.

"You are laughing at me," he said, winking. "Such gentry as you and your assistant Nikita have no business with the future. But you may be assured, sir, that better times are in store for us. What if I do express myself vulgarly—laugh at me!—but the dawn of a new life will shine, and truth will triumph . . . and it will be on our side the holiday will be. I shall not see it, but our posterity shall. . . . I congratulate them with my whole soul, and rejoice—rejoice for them! Forward! God help you, friends!"

Ivan Dmitritch's eyes glittered; he rose, stretched out his eyes to the window, and said in an agitated voice:

"For these barred windows I bless you. Hail to the truth! I rejoice!"

"I see no cause for rejoicing," said Andrei Yefimitch, whom Ivan Dmitritch's movements, though they seemed theatrical, pleased. "Prisons and asylums will no longer be, and justice, as you put it, will triumph. But the essence of things will never change, the laws of Nature will remain the same. Men will be diseased, grow old, and die, just as now. However glorious the dawn which enlightens your life, in the end of ends you will be nailed down in a coffin and flung into a pit."

"But immortality?"

"Nonsense!"

"You do not believe, but I believe. Dostoevsky or Voltaire or someone said that if there were no God men would have invented one. And I am deeply convinced that if there were no immortality it would sooner or later have been invented by the great human intellect."

"You speak well," said Andrei Yefimitch, smiling with pleasure. "It is well that you believe. With such faith as yours you would live happily though entombed in a wall. May I ask where you were educated?"

"I was at college, but never graduated."

"You are a thoughtful and penetrating man. You would find tranquillity in any environment. The free and profound thought which aspires to the comprehension of life; and high contempt for the vanity of the world—these are two blessings higher than which no man can know. And these you will enjoy though you live behind a dozen barred windows. Diogenes lived in a tub, yet he was happier than all the kings of the earth."

"Your Diogenes was a blockhead!" cried Ivan Dmitritch gloomily. "What do you tell me about Diogenes and the understanding of life?" He spoke angrily, and sprang up. "I love life, love it passionately. I have the mania of persecution, a ceaseless, tormenting terror, but there are moments when I am seized by the thirst of life, and in those moments I fear to go out of my mind. I long to live . . . terribly!"

He walked up and down the ward in agitation, and continued in a lower voice:

"When I meditate I am visited by visions. Men come to me, I hear voices and music, and it seems to me that I am walking through woods, on the shores of the sea; and I long passionately for the vanities and worries of life. . . . Tell me! What is the news?"

"You ask about the town, or generally?"

"First tell me about the town, and then generally?"

"What is there? The town is tiresome to the point of torment. There is no one to talk to, no one to listen to. There are no new people. But lately we got a new doctor, Khobotov, a young man."

"He has been here. A fool?"

"Yes, an uneducated man. It is strange, do you know. If you judge by metropolitan life there is no intellectual stagnation in Russia, but genuine activity; in other words, there are real men. But for some reason or other they always send such fellows here. It is an unfortunate town."

"An unfortunate town," sighed Ivan Dmitritch. "And what news is there generally? What have you in the newspapers and reviews?"

In the ward it was already dark. The doctor rose, and told his patient what was being written in Russia and abroad, and what were the current tendencies of the world. Ivan Dmitritch listened attentively, and asked questions. But suddenly, as if he had just remembered something terrible, he seized his head and threw himself on the bed, with his back turned to the doctor.

"What is the matter?" asked Andrei Yefimitch.

"You will not hear another word from me," said Ivan Dmitritch rudely. "Go away!"

"Why?"

"I tell you, go away! Go to the devil!"

Andrei Yefimitch shrugged his shoulders, sighed, and left the ward. As he passed through the hall, he said:

"Suppose you were to clear some of this away, Nikita. . . . The smell is frightful."

"Yes, your Honor!"

"What a delightful young man!" thought Andrei Yefimitch, as he walked home. "He is the first man worth talking to whom I have met all the time I have lived in this town. He can reason and interests himself only with what is essential."

As he read in his study, as he went to bed, all the time, he thought of Ivan Dmitritch. When he awoke next morning, he remembered that he had made the acquaintance of a clever and interesting man. And he decided to pay him another visit at the first opportunity.

X

Ivan Dmitritch lay in the same position as on the day before, holding his head in his hands, his legs being doubled up underneath him.

"Good morning, my friend," said Andrei Yefimitch. "You are not asleep?"

"In the first place I am not your friend," said Ivan Dmitritch, keeping his face turned toward the pillow, "and in the second, you are troubling yourself in vain; you will not get from me a single word."

"That is strange," said Andrei Yefimitch. "Yesterday we were speaking as friends, but suddenly you took offense and stopped short. . . . Perhaps I spoke awkwardly, or expressed opinions differing widely from your own."

"You won't catch me!" said Ivan Dmitritch, rising from the bed and looking at the doctor ironically and suspiciously. "You may go and spy and cross-examine somewhere else; here there is nothing for you to do. I know very well why you came yesterday."

"That is a strange idea," laughed the doctor. "But why do you assume that I am spying?"

"I assume it. . . . Whether spy or doctor it is all the same."

"Yes, but . . . excuse me. . . ." The doctor sat on a stool beside the bed, and shook his head reproachfully. "Even suppose you are right, suppose I am following your words only in order to betray you to the police, what would happen? They would arrest you and try you. But then, in the dock or in prison would you be worse off than here? In exile or penal servitude you would not suffer any more than now. . . . What, then, do you fear?"

Apparently these words affected Ivan Dmitritch. He sat down quietly.

It was five o'clock, the hour when Andrei Yefimitch usually walked up and down his room and Daryushka asked him whether it was time for his beer. The weather was calm and clear.

"After dinner I went out for a walk, and you see where I've come," said the doctor. "It is almost spring."

"What month is it?" asked Ivan Dmitritch. "March?"

"Yes, we are at the end of March."

"Is it very muddy?"

"Not very. The paths in the garden are clear."

"How glorious it would be to drive somewhere outside the town!" said Ivan Dmitritch, rubbing his red eyes as if he were sleepy, "and then to return to a warm comfortable study . . . and to be cured of headache by a decent doctor. . . . For years past I have not lived like a human being. . . . Things are abominable here— intolerable, disgusting!"

After last evening's excitement he was tired and weak, and he spoke unwillingly. His fingers twitched, and from his face it was plain that his head ached badly.

"Between a warm, comfortable study and this ward there is no difference," said Andrei Yefimitch. "The rest and tranquillity of a man are not outside but within him."

"What do you mean by that?"

"Ordinary men find good and evil outside, that is, in their carriages and comfortable rooms; but the thinking man finds them within himself."

"Go and preach that philosophy in Greece, where it is warm and smells of oranges—it doesn't suit this climate. With whom was it I spoke of Diogenes? With you?"

"Yes, yesterday with me."

"Diogenes had no need of a study and a warm house, he was comfortable without them. . . . Lie in a tub and eat oranges and olives! Set him down in Russia—not in December, but even in May. He would freeze even in May with the cold."

"No. Cold, like every other feeling, may be disregarded. As Marcus Aurelius said, pain is the living conception of pain; make an effort of the will to change this conception, cease to complain, and the pain disappears. The wise man, the man of thought and penetration, is distinguished by his contempt for suffering; he is always content and he is surprised by nothing."

"That means that I am an idiot because I suffer, because I am discontented, and marvel at the baseness of men."

"Your discontent is in vain. Think more, and you will realize how trifling are all the things which now excite you. . . . Try to understand life—in this is true beatitude."

"Understand!" frowned Ivan Dmitritch. "External, internal. . . . Excuse me, but I cannot understand you. I know only one thing," he continued, rising and looking angrily at the doctor. "I know only that God created me of warm blood and nerves; yes! and organic tissue, if it be capable of life, must respond to irritation. And I respond to it! Pain I answer with tears and cries, baseness with indignation, meanness with repulsion. In my mind, that is right, and it is that which is called life. The lower the organism the less susceptible is it, and the more feebly it responds to irritation; the higher it is the more sensitively it responds. How is it you do not know that? A doctor—yet you do not know such truisms! If you would despise suffering, be always contented, and marvel at nothing, you must lower yourself to the condition of that . . ." Ivan Dmitritch pointed to the fat, greasy muzhik, "or inure yourself to suffering until you lose all susceptibility—in other words, cease to live. Excuse me, but I am not a wise man and not a philosopher," continued Ivan Dmitritch irritably, "and I do not understand these things. I am not in a condition to reason."

"But you reason admirably."

"The Stoics whom you travesty were remarkable men, but their teaching died two thousand years ago, and since then it has not advanced, nor will it advance, an inch, for it is not a practical or a living creed. It was successful only with a minority who spent their lives in study and trifled with gospels of all sorts; the majority never understood it. . . . A creed which teaches indifference to wealth, indifference to the conveniences of life, and contempt for suffering, is quite incomprehensible to the great majority who never knew either wealth or the conveniences of life, and to whom contempt for suffering would mean contempt for their own lives, which are made up of feelings of hunger, cold, loss, insult, and a Hamlet-like terror of death. All life lies in these feelings, and life may be hated or wearied of, but never despised. Yes, I repeat it, the teaching of the Stoics can never have a future; from the beginning of time, life has consisted in sensibility to pain and response to irritation."

Ivan Dmitritch suddenly lost the thread of his thoughts, ceased speaking, and rubbed his forehead irritably.

"I had something important to say, but have gone off the track," he continued. "What was I saying? Yes, this is it. One of these Stoics sold himself into slavery to redeem a friend. Now what does that mean but that even a Stoic responded to irritation, for to perform such a magnanimous deed as the ruin of one's self for the sake of a friend demands a disturbed and sympathetic heart. I have forgotten here in prison all that I learned, otherwise I should have other illustrations. But think of Christ! Christ rebelled against actuality by weeping, by smiling, by grieving, by anger, even by weariness. Not with a smile did He go forth to meet suffering, nor did He despise death, but prayed in the garden of Gethsemane that this cup might pass from Him."

Ivan Dmitritch laughed and sat down.

"Suppose that contentment and tranquillity are not outside but within a man," he continued. "Suppose that we must despise suffering and marvel at nothing. But you do not say on what foundation you base this theory. You are a wise man? A philosopher?"

"I am not a philosopher, but everyone must preach this because it is rational."

"But I wish to know why in this matter of understanding life, despising suffering, and the rest of it, you consider yourself competent to judge? Have you ever suffered? What is your idea of suffering? Were you ever flogged when you were a child?"

"No my parents were averse to corporal punishment."

"But my father flogged me cruelly. He was a stern hemorrhoidal official with a long nose and a yellow neck. But what of you? In your whole life no one has ever laid a finger on you, and you are as healthy as a bull. You grew up under your father's wing, studied at his expense, and then dropped at once into a fat sinecure. More than twenty years you have lived in free lodgings, with free fire and free lights, with servants, with the right to work how, and as much as, you like, or to do nothing. By character you were an idle and a feeble man, and you strove to build up your life so as to avoid trouble. You left your work to feldshers and other scoundrels, and sat at home in warmth and quiet, heaped up money, read books, and enjoyed your own reflections about all kinds of exalted nonsense, and"—Ivan Dmitritch looked at the doctor's nose—"drank beer. In one word, you have not seen life, you know nothing about it, and of realities you have only a theoretical knowledge. Yes, you despise suffering and marvel at nothing for very good reasons; because your theory of the vanity of things, external and internal happiness, contempt for life, for suffering and for death, and so on—this is the philosophy best suited to a Russian lie-abed. You see, for instance, a muzhik beating his wife. Why interfere? let him beat her! It is all the same, both will be dead sooner or later, and then, does not the wife-beater injure himself and not his victim? To get drunk is stupid and wrong, but the man who drinks dies, and the woman who drinks dies also!

A woman comes to you with a toothache. Well, what of that? Pain is the conception of pain, without sickness you cannot live, all must die, and therefore take yourself off, my good woman, and don't interfere with my thoughts and my vodka! A young man comes to you for advice: what should he do, how ought he to live? Before answering, most men would think, but your answer is always ready: Aspire to understand life and to real goodness! And what is this fantastic real goodness? No answer! We are imprisoned behind iron bars, we rot and we are tortured, but this, in reality, is reasonable and beautiful because between this ward and a comfortable warm study there is no real difference! A convenient philosophy; your conscience is clean, and you feel yourself to be a wise man. No, sir, this is not philosophy, not breadth of view, but idleness, charlatanism, somnolent folly. . . . Yes," repeated Ivan Dmitritch angrily. "You despise suffering, but squeeze your finger in the door and you will howl for your life!"

"But suppose I do not howl," said Andrei Yefimitch, smiling indulgently.

"What! Well, if you had a stroke of paralysis, or if some impudent fellow, taking advantage of his position in the world, insulted you publicly, and you had no redress—then you would know what is meant to tell others to understand life and aspire to real good."

"This is original," said Andrei Yefimitch, beaming with satisfaction and rubbing his hands. "I am delighted with your love of generalization; and the character which you have just drawn is simply brilliant. I confess that conversation with you gives me great pleasure. But now, as I have heard you out, will you listen to me. . . ."

XI

This conversation, which lasted for an hour longer, apparently made a great impression on Andrei Yefimitch. He took to visiting the ward every day. He went there in the morning, and again after dinner, and often darkness found him in conversation with Ivan Dmitritch. At first Ivan Dmitritch was shy with him, suspected him of some evil intention, and openly expressed his suspicions. But at last he got used to him; and his rude bearing softened into indulgent irony.

A report soon spread through the hospital that Doctor Andrei Yefimitch paid daily visits to Ward Number Six. Neither the feldsher, nor Nikita, nor the nurses could understand his object; why he spent whole hours in the ward, what he was talking about, or why he did not write prescriptions. His conduct appeared strange to everyone. Mikhail Averyanitch sometimes failed to find him at home, and Daryushka was very alarmed, for the doctor no longer drank his beer at the usual hour, and sometimes even came home late for dinner.

One day—it was at the end of June—Doctor Khobotov went to Andrei Yefimitch's house to see him on a business matter. Not finding him at home, he looked for him in the yard, where he was told that the old doctor was in the asylum. Khobotov entered the hall of the ward, and standing there listened to the following conversation:

"We will never agree, and you will never succeed in converting me to your faith," said Ivan Dmitritch irritably. "You are altogether ignorant of realities, you have never suffered, but only, like a leech, fed on the sufferings of others. But I have suffered without cease from the day of my birth until now. Therefore I tell you frankly I consider myself much higher than you, and more competent in all respects. It is not for you to teach me."

"I certainly have no wish to convert you to my faith," said Andrei Yefimitch softly, and evidently with regret that he was misunderstood. "That is not the question, my friend. Suffering and joy are transitory—leave them, God be with them! The essence of the matter is that you and I recognize in one another men of thought, and this makes us solid however different our views. If you knew, my friend, how I am weary of the general idiocy around me, the lack of talent, the dullness—if you knew the joy with which I speak to you! You are a clever man, and it is a pleasure to be with you."

Khobotov opened the door and looked into the room. Ivan Dmitritch with a nightcap on his head and Doctor Andrei Yefimitch sat side by side on the bed. The lunatic shuddered, made strange faces, and convulsively clutched his dressing gown; and the doctor sat motionless, inclining his head, and his face was red and helpless and sad. Khobotov shrugged his shoulders, laughed, and looked at Nikita. Nikita also shrugged his shoulders.

Next day Khobotov again came to the wing, this time together with the feldsher. They stood in the hall and listened:

"Our grandfather, it seems, is quite gone," said Khobotov going out of the wing.

"Lord, have mercy upon us—sinners!" sighed the pompous Sergei Sergeyitch, going round the pools in order to keep his shiny boots clear of the mud. "I confess, my dear Yevgenii Feodoritch, I have long expected this."

XII

After this incident, Andrei Yefimitch began to notice that he was surrounded by a strange atmosphere of mystery. . . . The servants, the nurses, and the patients whom he met looked questioningly at one another, and whispered among themselves. When he met little Masha, the superintendent's daughter, in the hospital garden, and smilingly went over to her, as usual, to stroke her hair, for some inexplicable reason she ran away. When the postmaster, Mikhail Averyanitch, sat listening to him he no longer said: "Entirely true!" but got red in the face and stammered, "Yes, yes . . . yes . . ." and sometimes, looking at his friend thoughtfully and sorrowfully, advised him to give up vodka and beer.

But when doing this, as became a man of delicacy, he did not speak openly, but dropped gentle hints, telling stories, now of a certain battalion commander, an excellent man, now of the regimental chaplain, a first-rate little fellow, who drank a good deal and was taken ill, yet having given up drink got quite well. Twice or thrice Andrei Yefimitch was visited by his colleague Khobotov, who also asked him to give up spirits, and, without giving him any reason, advised him to try bromide of potassium.

In August Andrei Yefimitch received a letter from the Mayor asking him to come and see him on very important business. On arriving at the Town Hall at the appointed time he found awaiting him the head of the recruiting department, the superintendent of the district school, a member of the Town Council, Khobotov, and a stout, fair-haired man, who was introduced as a doctor. This doctor, who bore an unpronounceable Polish name, lived on a stud farm some thirty versts away, and was passing through the town on his way home.

"Here is a communication about your department," said the Town Councillor, turning to Andrei Yefimitch. "You see, Yevgenii Feodoritch says that there is no room for the dispensing room in the main building, and that it must be transferred to one of the wings. That, of course, is easy, it can be transferred any day, but the chief thing is that the wing is in want of repair."

"Yes, we can hardly get on without that," answered Andrei Yefimitch after a moment's thought. "But if the corner wing is to be fitted up as a dispensary you will have to spend at least five hundred rubles on it. It is unproductive expenditure."

For a few minutes all were silent.

"I had the honor to announce to you, ten years ago," continued Andrei Yefimitch in a soft voice, "that this hospital, under present conditions, is a luxury altogether beyond the means of the town. It was built in the forties, when the means for its support were greater. The town wastes too much money on unnecessary buildings and sinecure offices. I think that with the money we spend we could keep up two model hospitals; that is, of course, with a different order of things."

"Well, then, let us reform the present order," said the Town Councillor.

"I have already had the honor to advise you to transfer the medical department to the zemstvo."

"Yes, and hand over to the zemstvo funds which it will pocket," laughed the fair-haired doctor.

"That is just what happens," said the Town Councillor, laughing also.

Andrei Yefimitch looked feebly at the fair-haired doctor, and said:

"We must be just in our judgments."

Again all were silent. Tea was brought in. The chief of the recruiting department, apparently in a state of confusion, touched Andrei Yefimitch's hand across the table, and said:

"You have quite forgotten us, doctor. But then you were always a monk; you don't play cards, and you don't care for women. We bore you, I'm afraid."

And all agreed that it was tiresome for any decent man to live in such a town. Neither theaters, nor concerts, and at the last club dance about twenty women present and only two men. Young men no longer danced, but crowded round the supper table or played cards together. And Andrei Yefimitch, in a slow and soft voice, without looking at those around him, began to lament that the citizens wasted their vital energy, their intellects, and their feelings over cards and scandal, and neither cared nor knew how to pass the time in interesting conversation, in reading, or in taking advantage of the pleasures which intellect alone yields. Intellect is the only interesting and distinguished thing in the world; all the rest is petty and base. Khobotov listened attentively to his colleague, and suddenly asked:

"Andrei Yefimitch, what is the day of the month?"

Having received an answer, he and the fair-haired doctor, both in the tone of examiners convinced of their own incapacity, asked Andrei Yefimitch a number of other questions: what was the day of the week, how many days were there in the year, and was it true that in Ward Number Six there was a remarkable prophet?

In answer to this last question Andrei Yefimitch got red in the face, and said:

"Yes, he is insane. . . . But he is a most interesting young man."

No other questions were asked.

As Andrei Yefimitch put on his coat, the chief of the recruiting department put his hand on his shoulder and said, with a sigh:

"For us—old men—it is time to take a rest."

As he left the Town Hall, Andrei Yefimitch understood that he had been before a commission appointed to test his mental sanity. He remembered the questions put to him, reddened, and for the first time in his life felt pity for the medical art.

"My God!" he thought. "These men have only just been studying psychiatry and passing examinations! Where does their monstrous ignorance come from? They have no ideas about psychiatry."

For the first time in his life he felt insulted and angry.

Toward evening Mikhail Averyanitch came to see him. Without a word of greeting, the postmaster went up to him, took him by both hands, and said in an agitated voice:

"My dear friend, my dear friend, let me see that you believe in my sincere affection for you. Regard me as your friend!" And preventing Andrei Yefimitch saying a word, he continued in extreme agitation: "You know that I love you for the culture and nobility of your mind. Listen to me, like a good man! The rules of their profession compel the doctors to hide the truth from you, but I, in soldier style, will tell it to you flatly. You are unwell! Excuse me, old friend, but that is the plain truth, and it has been noticed by everyone around you. Only this moment Doctor Yevgenii

Feodoritch said that for the benefit of your health you needed rest and recreation. It is entirely true! And things fit in admirably. In a few days I will take my leave, and go off for change of air. Prove to me that you are my friend, and come with me. Come!"

"I feel very well," said Andrei Yefimitch, after a moment's thought; "and I cannot go. Allow me to prove my friendship in some other way."

To go away without any good reason, without his books, without Daryushka, without beer—suddenly to destroy the order of life observed for twenty years—when he first thought of it, the project seemed wild and fantastic. But he remembered the talk in the Town Hall, and the torments which he had suffered on the way home; and the idea of leaving for a short time a town where stupid men considered him mad, delighted him.

"But where do you intend to go?" he asked.

"To Moscow, to Petersburg, to Warsaw. . . . In Warsaw I spent some of the happiest days of my life. An astonishing city! Come!"

XIII

A week after this conversation, Andrei Yefimitch received a formal proposal to take a rest, that is, to retire from his post, and he received the proposal with indifference. Still a week later, he and Mikhail Averyanitch were sitting in the post tarantass and driving to the railway station. The weather was cool and clear, the sky blue and transparent. The two hundred versts were traversed in two days and two nights. When they stopped at the posthouses and were given dirty glasses for tea, or were delayed over the horses, Mikhail Averyanitch grew purple, shook all over, and roared "Silence! Don't argue!" . . . And as they sat in the tarantass he talked incessantly of his travels in the Caucasus and in Poland. What adventures he had, what meetings!

He spoke in a loud voice, and all the time made such astonished eyes that it might have been thought he was lying. As he told his stories he breathed in the doctor's face and laughed in his ear. All this incommoded the doctor and hindered his thinking and concentrating his mind.

For reasons of economy they traveled third-class, in a nonsmoking carriage. Half of the passengers were clean. Mikhail Averyanitch struck up acquaintance with all, and as he shifted from seat to seat, announced in a loud voice that it was a mistake to travel on these tormenting railways. Nothing but rascals around! What a different thing to ride on horseback; in a single day you cover a hundred versts, and at the end feel wholesome and fresh. Yes, and we had been cursed with famines as the result of the draining of the Pinsky marshes! Everywhere nothing but disorder! Mikhail Averyanitch lost his temper, spoke loudly, and allowed no one else to say a word. His incessant chatter, broken only by loud laughter and expressive gesticulations, bored Andrei Yefimitch.

"Which of us is the more mad?" he asked himself. "I who do my best not to disturb my fellow travelers, or this egoist who thinks he is cleverer and more interesting that anyone else, and gives no one a moment's rest?"

In Moscow, Mikhail Averyanitch donned his military tunic without shoulder straps, and trousers with red piping. Out of doors he wore an army forage cap and cloak, and was saluted by the soldiers. To Andrei Yefimitch he began to seem a man who had lost all the good points of the upper classes and retained only the bad. He loved people to dance attendance on him even when it was quite unnecessary. Matches lay before him on the table and he saw them, yet he roared to the waiter to hand them to him; he marched about in his underclothing before the chambermaid; he addressed the waitresses—even the elderly ones—indiscriminately as "thou," and when he was irritated called them blockheads and fools. This, thought Andrei Yefimitch, is no doubt gentlemanly, but it is detestable.

First of all, Mikhail Averyanitch brought his friend to the Iverskaya.* He prayed piously, bowed to the ground, shed tears, and when he had finished, sighed deeply and said:

"Even an unbeliever feels himself at peace after he has prayed. Kiss the image, dear!"

Andrei Yefimitch got red in the face and kissed the image; and Mikhail Averyanitch puffed out his lips, shook his head, prayed in a whisper; and again into his eyes came tears. After this they visited the Kremlin and inspected the Tsar Cannon and the Tsar Bell, touched them with their fingers, admired the view across the Moscow River, and spent some time in the Temple of the Savior and afterward in the Rumyantsev Museum.

They dined at Testov's.† Mikhail Averyanitch stroked his whiskers, gazed long at the menu, and said to the waiter in the tone of a gourmet who feels at home in restaurants:

"We'll see what you'll feed us with to-day, angel!"

XIV

The doctor walked and drank and ate and inspected, but his feelings remained unchanged; he was vexed with Mikhail Averyanitch. He longed to get a rest from his companion, to escape from him, but the postmaster considered it his duty not to let him out of his sight, and to see that he tasted every possible form of recreation. For two days Andrei Yefimitch endured it, but on the third declared that he was unwell, and would remain all day at home. Mikhail Averyanitch said that in that case he also would remain at home. And indeed, he added, a rest was necessary, otherwise they would have no strength left. Andrei Yefimitch lay on the sofa with his face to the wall, and with clenched teeth listened to his friend, who assured him that France would sooner or later inevitably destroy Germany, that in Moscow there are a great many swindlers, and that you cannot judge of the merits of a horse by its appearance. The doctor's heart throbbed, his ears hummed, but from motives of delicacy he could not ask his friend to leave him alone or be silent. But happily Mikhail Averyanitch grew tired of sitting in the room, and after dinner went for a walk.

Left alone, Andrei Yefimitch surrendered himself to the feeling of rest. How delightful it was to lie motionless on the sofa and know that he was alone in the room! Without solitude true happiness was impossible. The fallen angel was faithless to God probably only because he longed for solitude, which angels knew not. Andrei Yefimitch wished to reflect upon what he had seen and heard in the last few days. But he could not drive Mikhail Averyanitch out of his mind.

"But then he obtained leave and came with me purely out of friendship and generosity," he thought with vexation. "Yet there is nothing more detestable than his maternal care. He is good and generous and a gay companion—but tiresome! Intolerably tiresome! He is one of those men who say only clever things, yet you cannot help feeling that they are stupid at bottom."

Next day Andrei Yefimitch said he was still ill, and remained in his room. He lay with his face to the back of the sofa, was bored when he was listening to conversation, and happy only when he was left alone. He was angry with himself for leaving home, he was angry with Mikhail Averyanitch, who every day became more garrulous and free-making; to concentrate his thoughts on a serious, elevated plane he failed utterly.

---

*A celebrated icon kept in a small chapel near the Moscow Town Hall. It is supposed to possess miraculous healing virtues.

†A Moscow restaurant noted for genuine Russian cookery.

"I am now being tested by the realities of which Ivan Dmitritch spoke," he thought, angered at his own pettiness. "But this is nothing. . . . I will go home, and things will be as before."

In St. Petersburg the incidents of Moscow were repeated; whole days he never left his room, but lay on the sofa, and rose only when he wanted to drink beer.

All the time, Mikhail Averyanitch was in a great hurry to get to Warsaw.

"My dear friend, why must I go there?" asked Andrei Yefimitch imploringly. "Go yourself, and let me go home. I beg you!"

"Not for a million!" protested Mikhail Averyanitch. "It is an astonishing city! In Warsaw I spent the happiest days of my life."

Andrei Yefimitch had not the character to persist, and with a twinge of pain accompanied his friend to Warsaw. When he got there he stayed all day in the hotel, lay on the sofa, and was angry with himself, and with the waiters who stubbornly refused to understand Russian. Mikhail Averyanitch, healthy, gay, and active as ever, drove from morning to night about the city and sought out his old acquaintances. Several nights he stayed out altogether. After one of these nights, spent it is uncertain where, he returned early in the morning, disheveled and excited. For a long time he walked up and down the room, and at last stopped and exclaimed:

"Honor before everything!"

Again he walked up and down the room, seized his head in his hands, and declaimed tragically:

"Yes! Honor before everything! Cursed be the hour when it entered my head to come near this Babylon! . . . My dear friend," he turned to Andrei Yefimitch, "I have lost heavily at cards. Lend me five hundred rubles!"

Andrei Yefimitch counted the money, and gave it silently to his friend. Mikhail Averyanitch, purple from shame and indignation, cursed incoherently and needlessly, put on his cap, and went out. After two hours' absence he returned, threw himself into an armchair, sighed loudly, and said:

"Honor is saved! Let us go away, my friend! Not another minute will I rest in this accursed city! They are all scoundrels! . . . Austrian spies!"

When the travelers returned it was the beginning of November, and the streets were covered with snow. Doctor Khobotov occupied Andrei Yefimitch's position at the hospital, but lived at his own rooms, waiting until Andrei Yefimitch returned and gave up the official quarters. They ugly woman whom he called his cook already lived in one of the wings.

Fresh scandals in connection with the hospital were being circulated in the town. It was said that the ugly woman had quarreled with the superintendent, who had gone down before her on his knees and begged forgiveness. On the day of his return Andrei Yefimitch had to look for new lodgings.

"My friend," began the postmaster timidly, "forgive the indelicate question, what money have you got?"

Andrei Yefimitch silently counted his money, and said:

"Eighty-six rubles."

"You don't understand me," said Mikhail Averyanitch in confusion. "I ask what means have you—generally?"

"I have told you already—eighty-six rubles. . . . Beyond that I have nothing."

Mikhail Averyanitch was well aware that the doctor was an honest and straightforward man. But he believed that he had at least twenty thousand rubles in capital. Now learning that his friend was a beggar and had nothing to live on, he began to cry, and embraced him.

XV

Andrei Yefimitch migrated to the three-windowed house of Madame Byelof, a woman belonging to the petty trading class. In this house were only three rooms and a kitchen. Of these rooms two, with windows opening on the street, were occupied by the doctor, while in the third and in the kitchen lived Daryushka, the landlady, and three children. Occasionally the number was added to by a drunken workman, Madame Byelof's lover, who made scenes at night and terrified Daryushka and the children. When he came, sat in the kitchen, and demanded vodka, the others were crowded out, and the doctor in compassion took the crying children to his own room, and put them to sleep on the floor. This always gave him great satisfaction.

As before, he rose at eight o'clock, took his breakfast, and sat down and read his old books and reviews. For new books he had no money. But whether it was because the books were old or because the surroundings were changed, reading no longer interested him, and even tired him. So to pass the time he compiled a detailed catalog of his books, and pasted labels on the backs; and this mechanical work seemed to him much more interesting than reading. The more monotonous and trifling the occupation the more it calmed his mind, he thought of nothing, and time passed quickly. Even to sit in the kitchen and peel potatoes with Daryushka or to pick the dirt out of buckwheat meal interested him. On Saturdays and Sundays he went to church. Standing at the wall, he blinked his eyes, listened to the singing, and thought of his father, his mother, the university, religion; he felt calm and melancholy, and when leaving the church, regretted that the service had not lasted longer.

Twice he visited the hospital for the purpose of seeing Ivan Dmitritch. But on both occasions Gromof was unusually angry and excited; he asked to be left in peace, declared that he had long ago wearied of empty chatter, and that he would regard solitary confinement as a deliverance from these accursed, base people. Was it possible they would refuse him that? When Andrei Yefimitch took leave of him and wished him good night, he snapped and said:

"Take yourself to the devil!"

And Andrei Yefimitch felt undecided as to whether he should go a third time or not. But he wished to go.

In the old times Andrei Yefimitch had been in the habit of spending the time after dinner in walking about his rooms and thinking. But now from dinner to teatime he lay on the sofa with his face to the wall and surrendered himself to trivial thoughts, which he found himself unable to conquer. He considered himself injured by the fact that after twenty years' service he had been given neither a pension nor a grant. True he had not done his duties honestly, but then were not pensions given to all old servants indiscriminately, without regard to their honesty or otherwise? Modern ideas did not regard rank, orders, and pensions as the reward of moral perfection or capacity, and why must he alone be the exception? He was absolutely penniless. He was ashamed to pass the shop where he dealt or to meet the proprietor. For beer alone he was in debt thirty-two rubles. He was in debt also to his landlady. Daryushka secretly sold old clothing and books, and lied to the landlady, declaring that her master was about to come into a lot of money.

Andrei Yefimitch was angry with himself for having wasted on his journey the thousand rubles which he had saved. What could he not do with a thousand rubles now? He was annoyed, also, because others would not leave him alone. Khobotov considered it his duty to pay periodic visits to his sick colleague; and everything about him was repulsive to Andrei Yefimitch—his sated face, his condescending bad manners, the word "colleague," and the high boots. But the greatest annoyance of all was that he considered it his duty to cure Andrei Yefimitch, and even imagined he was curing him. On every occasion he brought a vial of bromide of potassium and a rhubarb pill.

Mikhail Averyanitch also considered it his duty to visit his sick friend and amuse him. He entered the room with affected freeness, laughed unnaturally, and assured Andrei Yefimitch that today he looked splendid, and that, glory be to God! he was getting all right. From this alone it might be concluded that he regarded the case as hopeless. He had not yet paid off the Warsaw debt, and being ashamed of himself and constrained, he laughed all the louder, and told ridiculous anecdotes. His stories now seemed endless, and were a source of torment both to Andrei Yefimitch and to himself.

When the postmaster was present, Andrei Yefimitch usually lay on the sofa, his face turned to the wall, with clenched teeth, listening. It seemed to him that a crust was forming about his heart, and after every visit he felt the crust becoming thicker, and threatening to extend to his throat. To exorcise these trivial afflictions he reflected that he, and Khobotov, and Mikhail Averyanitch would, sooner or later, perish, leaving behind themselves not a trace. When a million years had passed by, a spirit flying through space would see only a frozen globe and naked stones. All—culture and morals—everything would pass away; even the burdock would not grow. Why, then, should he trouble himself with feelings of shame on account of a shopkeeper, of insignificant Khobotov, of the terrible friendship of Mikhail Averyanitch. It was all folly and vanity.

But such reasoning did not console him. He had hardly succeeded in painting a vivid picture of the frozen globe after a million years of decay, when from behind a naked rock appeared Khobotov in his top boots, and beside him stood Mikhail Averyanitch, with an affected laugh, and a shamefaced whisper on his lips: "And the Warsaw debt, old man, I will repay in a few days . . . without fail!"

XVI

Mikhail Averyanitch arrived after dinner one evening when Andrei Yefimitch was lying on the sofa. At the same time came Khobotov with his bromide of potassium. Andrei Yefimitch rose slowly, sat down again, and supported himself by resting his hands upon the sofa edge.

"Today, my dear," began Mikhail Averyanitch, "today your complexion is much healthier than yesterday. You are a hero! I swear to God, a hero!"

"It's time, indeed it's time for you to recover, colleague," said Khobotov, yawning. "You must be tired of the delay yourself."

"Never mind, we'll soon be all right," said Mikhail Averyanitch gaily. "Why, we'll live for another hundred years! Eh?"

"Perhaps not a hundred, but a safe twenty," said Khobotov consolingly. "Don't worry, colleague, don't worry!"

"We'll let them see!" laughed Mikhail Averyanitch, slapping his friend on the knee. "We'll show how the trick is done! Next summer, with God's will, we'll fly away to the Caucasus, and gallop all over the country—trot, trot, trot! And when we come back from the Caucasus we'll dance at your wedding!" Mikhail Averyanitch winked slyly. "We'll marry you, my friend, we'll find the bride!"

Andrei Yefimitch felt that the crust had risen to his throat. His heart beat painfully.

"This is absurd," he said, rising suddenly and going over to the window. "Is it possible you don't understand that you are talking nonsense?"

He wished to speak to his visitors softly and politely, but could not restrain himself, and, against his own will, clenched his fists, and raised them threateningly above his head.

"Leave me!" he cried, in a voice which was not his own. His face was purple and he trembled all over. "Begone! Both of you! Go!"

Mikhail Averyanitch and Khobotov rose, and looked at him, at first in astonishment, then in terror.

"Begone both of you!" continued Andrei Yefimitch. "Stupid idiots! Fools! I want neither your friendship nor your medicines, idiots! This is base, it is abominable!"

Khobotov and the postmaster exchanged confused glances, staggered to the door, and went into the hall. Andrei Yefimitch seized the vial of bromide of potassium, and flung it after them, breaking it upon the threshold.

"Take yourselves to the devil!" he cried, running after them into the hall. "To the devil!"

After his visitors had gone he lay on the sofa, trembling as if in fever, and repeated—

"Stupid idiots! Dull fools!"

When he calmed down, the first thought that entered his head was that poor Mikhail Averyanitch must now be terribly ashamed and wretched, and that the scene that had passed was something very terrible. Nothing of the kind had ever happened before. What had become of his intellect and tact? Where were now his understanding of the world and his philosophical indifference?

All night the doctor was kept awake by feelings of shame and vexation. At nine o'clock next morning, he went to the post office and apologized to the postmaster.

"Do not refer to what happened!" said the postmaster, with a sigh. Touched by Andrei Yefimitch's conduct, he pressed his hands warmly. "No man should trouble over such trifles. . . . Lubiakin!" he roared so loudly that the clerks and visitors trembled. "Bring a chair! . . . And you just wait!" he cried to a peasant woman, who held a registered letter through the grating. "Don't you see that I am engaged? . . . We will forget all that," he continued tenderly, turning to Andrei Yefimitch. "Sit down, my old friend!"

He stroked his eyebrows silently for a minute, and continued:

"It never entered my head to take offense. Illness is a very strange thing, I understand that. Yesterday your fit frightened both the doctor and myself, and we talked of you for a long time. My dear friend, why will you not pay more attention to your complaint? Do you think you can go on living in this way? Forgive the plain speaking of a friend." He dropped his voice to a whisper. "But you live among hopeless surroundings—closeness, uncleanliness, no one to look after you, nothing to take for your ailment. . . . My dear friend, both I and the doctor implore you with all our hearts—listen to our advice—go into the hospital. There you will get wholesome food, care and treatment. Yevgenii Feodoritch—although, between ourselves, *de mauvais ton*—is a capable man, and you can fully rely upon him. He gave me his word that he would take care of you."

Andrei Yefimitch was touched by the sincere concern of his friend, and the tears that trickled down the postmaster's cheeks.

"My dear friend, don't believe them!" he whispered, laying his hand upon his heart. "It is all a delusion. My complaint lies merely in this, that in twenty years I found in this town only one intelligent man, and he was a lunatic. I suffer from no disease whatever; my misfortune is that I have fallen into a magic circle from which there is no escape. It is all the same to me—I am ready for anything."

"Then you will go into the hospital?"

"It is all the same—even into the pit."

"Give me your word, friend, that you will obey Yevgenii Feodoritch in everything."

"I give you my word. But I repeat that I have fallen into a magic circle. Everything now, even the sincere concern of my friends, tends only to the same thing—to my destruction. I am perishing, and I have the courage to acknowledge it."

"Nonsense, you will get all right!"

"What is the use of talking like that?" said Andrei Yefimitch irritably. "There are very few men who at the close of their lives do not experience what I am experiencing now. When people tell you that you have disease of the kidneys or a dilated heart, and set about to cure you; when they tell you that you are a madman or a criminal—in one word, when they begin to turn their attention on to you—you may recognize that you are in a magic circle from which there is no escape. You may try to escape, but that makes things worse. Give in, for no human efforts will save you. So it seems to me."

All this time, people were gathering at the grating. Andrei Yefimitch disliked interrupting the postmaster's work, and took his leave. Mikhail Averyanitch once more made him give his word of honor, and escorted him to the door.

The same day toward evening Khobotov, in his short fur coat and high boots, arrived unexpectedly, and, as if nothing had happened the day before, said:

"I have come to you on a matter of business, colleague. I want you to come with me to a consultation. Eh?"

Thinking that Khobotov wanted to amuse him with a walk, or give him some opportunity of earning money, Andrei Yefimitch dressed, and went with him into the street. He was glad of the chance to redeem his rudeness of the day before, thankful for the apparent reconciliation, and grateful to Khobotov for not hinting at the incident. From this uncultured man who would have expected such delicacy?

"And where is your patient?" asked Andrei Yefimitch.

"At the hospital. For a long time past I have wanted you to see him. . . . A most interesting case."

They entered the hospital yard, and passing through the main building, went to the wing where the lunatics were confined. When they entered the hall, Nikita as usual jumped up and stretched himself.

"One of them has such strange complications in the lungs," whispered Khobotov as he entered the yard with Andrei Yefimitch. "But wait here. I shall be back immediately. I must get my stethoscope."

And he left the room.

XVII

It was already twilight. Ivan Dmitritch lay on his bed with his face buried in the pillow; the paralytic sat motionless, and wept softly and twitched his lips; the fat muzhik and the ex-sorter slept. It was very quiet.

Andrei Yefimitch sat on Ivan Dmitritch's bed and listened. Half an hour passed by, but Khobotov did not come. Instead of Khobotov came Nikita carrying in his arm a dressing gown, some linen, and a pair of slippers.

"Please to put on these, your Honor," he said calmly. "There is your bed, this way, please," he added, pointing at a vacant bed, evidently only just set up. "And don't take on; with God's will you will soon be well!"

Andrei Yefimitch understood. Without a word he walked over to the bed indicated by Nikita and sat upon it. Then, seeing that Nikita was waiting, he stripped himself and felt ashamed. He put on the hospital clothing; the flannels were too small, the shirt was too long, and the dressing gown smelt of smoked fish.

"You will soon be all right, God grant it!" repeated Nikita.

He took up Andrei Yefimitch's clothes, went out, and locked the door.

"It is all the same," thought Andrei Yefimitch, shamefacedly gathering the dressing gown around him, and feeling like a convict in his new garments. "It is all the same. In dress clothes, in uniform . . . or in this dressing gown."

But his watch? And the memorandum book in his side pocket? And the cigarettes? Where had Nikita taken his clothes? To the day of his death he would never again wear trousers, a waistcoat, or boots. It was strange and incredible at first. Andrei Yefimitch was firmly convinced that there was no difference whatever between Madame Byelof's house and Ward Number Six, and that all in this world is folly and vanity; but he could not prevent his hands trembling, and his feet were cold. He was hurt, too, by the thought that Ivan Dmitritch would rise and see him in the dressing gown. He rose, walked up and down the room, and again sat down.

He remained sitting for half an hour, weary to the point of grief. Would it be possible to live here a day, a week, even years, as these others had done? He must sit down, and walk about and again sit down; and then he might look out of the window, and again walk from end to end of the room. And afterward? Just to sit all day still as an idol, and think! No, it was impossible.

Andrei Yefimitch lay down on his bed, but almost immediately rose, rubbed with his cuff the cold sweat from his forehead, and felt that his whole face smelt of dried fish. He walked up and down the ward.

"This is some misunderstanding . . ." he said, opening his arms. "It only needs an explanation, it is a misunderstanding. . . ."

At this moment Ivan Dmitritch awoke. He sat up in bed, rested his head on his hands, and spat. Then he looked idly at the doctor, apparently at first understanding nothing. But soon his sleepy face grew contemptuous and malicious.

"So they have brought you here, my friend," he began in a voice hoarse from sleep. He blinked one eye. "I am very glad! You drank other men's blood, and now they will drink yours! Admirable!"

"It is some misunderstanding . . ." begged Andrei Yefimitch, frightened by the lunatic's words. He shrugged his shoulders and repeated. "It is a misunderstanding . . . of some kind."

Ivan Dmitritch again spat, and lay down on his bed.

"Accursed life!" he growled. "But what is most bitter, most abominable of all, is that this life ends not with rewards for suffering, not with apotheoses as in operas, but in death; men come and drag the corpse by its arms and legs into the cellar. Brrrrr! . . . Well, never mind! . . . For all that we have suffered in this, in the other world we will be repaid with a holiday! From the other world I shall return hither

as a shadow, and terrify these monsters! . . . I will turn their heads gray!"

Moseika entered the ward, and seeing the doctor, stretched out his hand, and said:

"Give me a kopeck!"

XVIII

Andrei Yefimitch went across to the window, and looked out into the fields. It was getting dark, and on the horizon rose a cold, livid moon. Near the hospital railings, a hundred fathoms away, not more, rose a lofty, white building, surrounded by a stone wall. It was the prison.

"That is actuality," thought Andrei Yefimitch, and he felt terrified.

Everything was terrible: the moon, the prison, the spikes in the fence, and the blaze in the distant bone mill. Andrei Yefimitch turned away from the window, and saw before him a man with glittering stars and orders upon his breast. The man smiled and winked cunningly. And this, too, seemed terrible.

He tried to assure himself that in the moon and in the prison there was nothing peculiar at all, that even sane men wear orders, and that the best of things in their turn rot and turn into dust. But despair suddenly seized him, he took hold of the grating with both hands, and jerked it with all his strength. But the bars stood firm.

That it might be less terrible, he went to Ivan Dmitritch's bed, and sat upon it.

"I have lost my spirits, friend," he said, stammering, trembling, and rubbing the cold sweat from his face. "My spirits have fallen."

"But why don't you philosophize?" asked Ivan Dmitritch ironically.

"My God, my god! . . . Yes, yes! . . . Once you said that in Russia there is no philosophy; but all philosophize, even triflers. But the philosophizing of triflers does no harm to anyone," said Andrei Yefimitch as if he wanted to cry. "But why, my dear

friend, why this malicious laughter? Why should not triflers philosophize if they are not satisfied? For a clever, cultivated, proud, freedom-loving man, built in the image of God, there is no course left but to come as doctor to a dirty, stupid town, and lead a life of jars, leeches, and gallipots. Charlatanry, narrowness, baseness! Oh, my God!"

"You chatter nonsense! If you didn't want to be a doctor, why weren't you a minister of state?"

"I could not. We are weak, my friend. I was indifferent to things, I reasoned actively and wholesomely, but it needed but the first touch of actuality to make me lose heart, and surrender. . . . We are weak, we are worthless! . . . And you also, my friend. You are able, you are noble, with your mother's milk you drank in draughts of happiness, yet hardly had you entered upon life when you wearied of it. . . . We are weak, weak!"

In addition to terror and the feeling of insult, Andrei Yefimitch had been tortured by some importunate craving ever since the approach of evening. Finally he came to the conclusion that he wanted to smoke and drink beer.

"I am going out, my friend," he said. "I will tell them to bring lights. . . . I cannot in this way. . . . I am not in a state. . . ."

He went to the door and opened it, but immediately Nikita jumped up and barred the way.

"Where are you going to? You can't, you can't!" he cried. "It's time for bed!"

"But only for a minute. . . . I want to go into the yard. . . . I want to have a walk in the yard," said Andrei Yefimitch.

"You can't. I have orders against it. . . . You know yourself."

Nikita banged the door and set his back against it.

"But if I go out what harm will it do?" asked Andrei Yefimitch. "I don't understand! Nikita, I must go out!" he cried in a trembling voice. "I must go!"

"Don't create disorder; it is not right!" said Nikita in an edifying tone.

"The devil knows what is the meaning of this!" suddenly screamed Ivan Dmitritch, jumping from his bed. "What right has he to refuse to let us go? How dare they keep us here? The law allows no man to be deprived of freedom without a trial! This is violence . . . tyranny!"

"Of course it is tyranny," said Andrei Yefimitch, encouraging Gromof. "I must go! I have to go out! He has no right! Let me out, I tell you!"

"Do you hear, stupid dog!" screamed Ivan Dmitritch, thumping the door with his fists. "Open, or I will smash the door! Bloodsucker!"

"Open!" cried Andrei Yefimitch, trembling all over. "I demand it!"

"Talk away!" answered Nikita through the door. "Talk away!"

"Go, then, for Yevgenii Feodoritch! Say that I ask him to come. . . . For a minute!"

"Tomorrow he will come all right."

"They will never let us go!" cried Ivan Dmitritch. "We will all die here! Oh, God, is it possible that in the other world there is no hell, that these villains will be forgiven? Where is there justice? Open, scoundrel, I am choking!" Gromof cried out in a hoarse voice, and flung himself against the door. "I will dash my brains out! Assassins!"

Nikita flung open the door, and with both hands and his knees roughly pushed Andrei Yefimitch back into the room, and struck him with his clenched fist full in the face. It seemed to Andrei Yefimitch that a great salt wave had suddenly dashed upon his head and flung him upon his bed; in his mouth was a taste of salt, and the blood seemed to burst from his gums. As if trying to swim away from the wave, he flourished his arms and seized the bedstead. But at this moment Nikita struck him again and again in the back.

Ivan Dmitritch screamed loudly. He also had evidently been beaten.

Then all was quiet. Liquid moonlight

poured through between the iron bars, and on the floor lay a network shadow. All were terrified. Andrei Yefimitch lay on the bed and held his breath in terror, awaiting another blow.

It seemed as if someone had taken a sickle, thrust it into his chest and turned it around. In his agony he bit his pillow and ground his teeth, and suddenly into his head amid the chaos flashed the intolerable thought that such misery had been borne year after year by these helpless men who now lay in the moonlight like black shadows about him. In twenty years he had never known of it, and never wanted to know. He did not know, he had no idea of their wretchedness, therefore he was not guilty; but conscience, as rude and unaccommodating as Nikita's fists, sent an icy thrill through him from head to foot. He jumped from his bed and tried to scream with all his might, to fly from the ward and kill Nikita, and Khobotov, and the superintendent, and the feldsher, and himself. But not a sound came from his throat, his feet rebelled against him, he panted, he tore his gown and shirt, and fell insensible on the bed.

XIX

Next morning his head ached, his ears hummed, and he was weak. The memory of his weakness on the day before made him feel ashamed. Yesterday he had shown a petty spirit, he had feared even the moon, and honestly expressed feelings and thoughts which he had never suspected could exist in himself. For instance, the thought about the discontent of philosophic triflers. But now he was quite indifferent.

He neither ate nor drank, but lay motionless and silent.

"It is all the same to me," he thought when he was questioned. "I shall not answer. . . . It is all the same. . . ."

After dinner Mikhail Averyanitch brought him a quarter of a pound of tea and a pound of marmalade. Daryushka also came, and for a whole hour stood beside the bed with a dull expression of uncomprehending affliction. Doctor Khobotov also paid him a visit. He brought a vial of bromide of potassium, and ordered Nikita to fumigate the ward.

Toward evening Andrei Yefimitch died from an apoplectic stroke. At first he felt chill, and sickness; something loathsome like rotting sour cabbage or bad eggs seemed to permeate his whole body even to his fingers, to extend from his stomach to his head, and to flow in his eyes and ears. A green film appeared before his eyes. Andrei Yefimitch realized that his hour had come; and remembered that Ivan Dmitritch, Mikhail Averyanitch, and millions of others believed in immortality. But immortality he did not desire, and thought of it only for a moment. A herd of antelopes, extraordinarily beautiful and graceful, of which he had been reading the day before, rushed past him; then a woman stretched out to him a hand holding a registered letter. . . . Mikhail Averyanitch said something. Then all vanished and Andrei Yefimitch died.

The servants came in, took him by the shoulders and legs, and carried him to the chapel. There he lay on a table with open eyes, and at night the moon shone down upon him. In the morning came Sergei Sergeyitch, piously prayed before a crucifix, and closed the eyes of his former chief.

Next day Andrei Yefimitch was buried. Only Mikhail Averyanitch and Daryushka were present at the funeral.

PICTURE CREDITS

Authors

in Great Books of the Western World

Homer	Nicomachus
Aeschylus	Ptolemy
Sophocles	Marcus Aurelius
Herodotus	Galen
Euripides	Plotinus
Thucydides	Augustine
Hippocrates	Thomas Aquinas
Aristophanes	Dante
Plato	Chaucer
Aristotle	Machiavelli
Euclid	Copernicus
Archimedes	Rabelais
Apollonius	Montaigne
Lucretius	Gilbert
Virgil	Cervantes
Plutarch	Francis Bacon
Tacitus	Galileo
Epictetus	Shakespeare
	Kepler